CONSUMER BEHAVIOUR

SAGE was founded in 1965 by Sara Miller McCune to support the dissemination of usable knowledge by publishing innovative and high-quality research and teaching content. Today, we publish over 900 journals, including those of more than 400 learned societies, more than 800 new books per year, and a growing range of library products including archives, data, case studies, reports, and video. SAGE remains majority-owned by our founder, and after Sara's lifetime will become owned by a charitable trust that secures our continued independence.

Los Angeles | London | New Delhi | Singapore | Washington DC | Melbourne

3rd EDITION

ZUBIN SETHNA & JIM BLYTHE

CONSUMER BEHAVIOUR

SAGE

Los Angeles | London | New Delhi
Singapore | Washington DC | Melbourne

Los Angeles | London | New Delhi
Singapore | Washington DC | Melbourne

SAGE Publications Ltd
1 Oliver's Yard
55 City Road
London EC1Y 1SP

SAGE Publications Inc.
2455 Teller Road
Thousand Oaks, California 91320

SAGE Publications India Pvt Ltd
B 1/I 1 Mohan Cooperative Industrial Area
Mathura Road
New Delhi 110 044

SAGE Publications Asia-Pacific Pte Ltd
3 Church Street
#10-04 Samsung Hub
Singapore 049483

Editor: Matthew Waters
Development editor: Gemma Shields
Editorial assistant: Lyndsay Aitken
Production editor: Nicola Marshall
Copyeditor: Gemma Marren
Proofreader: Sharon Cawood
Indexer: Silvia Benvenuto
Marketing manager: Alison Borg
Design: Francis Kenney
Typeset by: C&M Digitals (P) Ltd, Chennai, India
Printed and bound in Great Britain by Bell and Bain Ltd,
Glasgow

Library of Congress Control Number: 2016940913

British Library Cataloguing in Publication data

A catalogue record for this book is available from the British Library

ISBN 9781473919129
ISBN 9781473919136 (pbk)

At SAGE we take sustainability seriously. Most of our products are printed in the UK using FSC papers and boards. When
we print overseas we ensure sustainable papers are used as measured by the PREPS grading system. We undertake an
annual audit to monitor our sustainability.

This book may contain links to both internal and external websites. All links included were active at the time the book was
published. SAGE does not operate these external websites and does not necessarily endorse the views expressed within
them. SAGE cannot take responsibility for the changing content or nature of linked sites, as these sites are outside of our
control and subject to change without our knowledge. If you do find an inactive link to an external website, please try to
locate that website by using a search engine. SAGE will endeavour to update inactive or broken links when possible.

BRIEF CONTENTS

CONTENTS

PART ONE CONSUMER BEHAVIOUR IN CONTEXT

1

UNDERSTANDING CONSUMER BEHAVIOUR

2

CONSUMER BEHAVIOUR AND THE MARKETING MIX

3

THE DECISION-MAKING PROCESS, BUYER BEHAVIOUR AND BRAND INTERACTION

4

INNOVATION AND DIGITAL TECHNOLOGIES

5

CONSUMPTION IN B2C VS. B2B

PART TWO
PSYCHOLOGICAL ISSUES IN CONSUMER BEHAVIOUR

6

DRIVE, MOTIVATION AND HEDONISM

7

THE SELF AND PERSONALITY

8

PERCEPTION

9

LEARNING AND KNOWLEDGE

10

ATTITUDE FORMATION AND CHANGE

PART THREE SOCIOLOGICAL ISSUES IN CONSUMER BEHAVIOUR

11

REFERENCE GROUPS

13

CULTURE AND CLASS

14

ETHICAL CONSUMPTION

12

AGE, GENDER AND FAMILIAL ROLES

PART FOUR CONSUMER BEHAVIOUR IN CONCLUSION

15

POST-PURCHASE BEHAVIOUR

LIST OF FIGURES

LIST OF TABLES

ABOUT THE AUTHORS

ZUBIN SETHNA

Zubin Sethna was born and bred in Wimbledon and this is from where he remembers his earliest lesson in consumer behaviour. Year after year he would watch the crowds gather in neat queues to buy tickets to watch the tennis; all in the heat of summer. So one year, as an 11 year old, he decided to sell ice-cold cans of a famous cola drink to the waiting crowds. And whilst John McEnroe was shouting the now infamous words "*you cannot be serious*" on Centre Court, Zubin was thinking the very same thing when, much to his surprise, captive individuals in the crowd were willing to spend £3 a can to quench their thirst!

As an avid proponent of 'practice what you preach', Zubin has successfully launched five businesses (one of which won a National Award). As Managing Consultant at Baresman Consulting (www.baresman.com), he has integrated marketing/consumer behavioural strategy with management consultancy and training for numerous organisations both in the UK and internationally, and across a variety of industry sectors (including Health Care, Professional Services, Music, Travel, Manufacturing, Retail, IT, Education and 'cottage' industries).

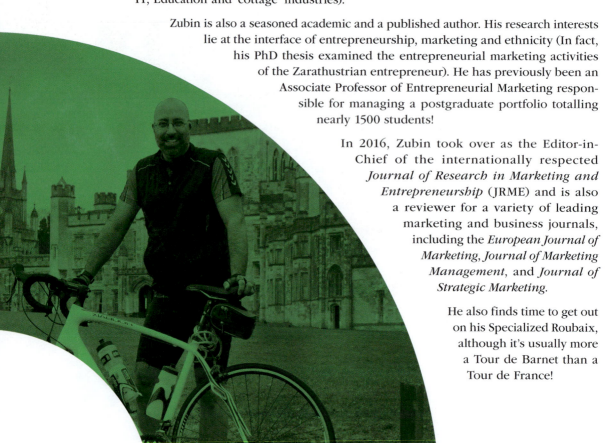

Zubin is also a seasoned academic and a published author. His research interests lie at the interface of entrepreneurship, marketing and ethnicity (In fact, his PhD thesis examined the entrepreneurial marketing activities of the Zarathustrian entrepreneur). He has previously been an Associate Professor of Entrepreneurial Marketing responsible for managing a postgraduate portfolio totalling nearly 1500 students!

In 2016, Zubin took over as the Editor-in-Chief of the internationally respected *Journal of Research in Marketing and Entrepreneurship* (JRME) and is also a reviewer for a variety of leading marketing and business journals, including the *European Journal of Marketing, Journal of Marketing Management,* and *Journal of Strategic Marketing.*

He also finds time to get out on his Specialized Roubaix, although it's usually more a Tour de Barnet than a Tour de France!

Photo credit: Emma Edes

JIM BLYTHE

Jim Blythe has been a Merchant Navy officer, a ladies' hairdresser, a business consultant, a rock musician, a truck driver, a company director, and an award-winning playwright before becoming an academic – he always planned on having a varied life, and likes learning new skills. Currently he is trying to learn to grow vegetables, with limited success, but he has a pilot's licence and has learned to play drums in a samba band, so the beat goes on. His next venture is to study for a degree in modern languages – having left school at 16 he thinks it's time to get the education he missed out on.

Jim has written 18 books and over 50 journal articles and has contributed chapters to eight other books. He has also written open-learning packs for international training organisations, has been a senior examiner for the Chartered Institute of Marketing, holds four real degrees and one fake one, and therefore feels somewhat irritated that he is mainly known for winning the Cardiff heat of Come Dine With Me. Perhaps this latest edition of *Consumer Behaviour* will redress the balance a bit.

Jim is recipient of the Life Contribution Award from the Academy of Marketing 2016 in recognition of extraordinary and distinguished services to Marketing.

PREFACE TO THE THIRD EDITION

We live in a world in which consumers are greatly influenced by the 'haves' and 'have-nots'; by those who have the ability to spend (and *oh boy* do they spend!) and those who are just starting to gear-up to demand products and services in the near future. Thus, all of us consume, even those who lead a relatively monastic existence: this is what makes the study of consumer behaviour so interesting and delves into the heart of the marketing concept. From the earliest utterings of religious Prophets such as Zarathustra, who lived in the 6th Century BC, to political Prophets in the 21st Century AD, we know that without customers, there is no business, and since everything is ultimately driven by the consumers, their needs and wants become paramount. However, over the past 10 years we have seen many changes in *consumer behaviour* which have been driven, predominantly, by changes in geo-demographics and technology. Innovation has been followed by disruptive innovation, and many products and brands have swiftly found themselves being launched into globalised consumer markets. We've seen these changes (both macro- and micro-environmental) highlighted in academic research as well as commercial research, and we've taken the opportunity to talk about the effects of these on consumer behaviour. The newcomers in this space are undoubtedly technology-driven: the increasing dominance of all-things mobile related (not least of all mobile-marketing), social media platforms, etc and on the flip-side we have cyber-attackers, who are also continuously finding ways to illegally and unknowingly engage the consumer through a variety of media. Changes of this nature are likely to continue as we hurtle towards 2020. This raises many questions: are we prepared and able to face all the challenges that may come our way? Do we continue to understand who the customers are, and why they behave in the way that they do? Do we know where they are and where they are heading? Do we understand what they are saying?!

The success of the first two editions of *Consumer Behaviour* is largely due, not just to the contemporary nature of the material, but to a relaxed yet informative writing style; a style that has Jim Blythe written all over it! With the third edition, Jim and I (Zubin) have ensured that the text, theoretical depth and the practical examples of consumer behaviour in action all remain very accessible to the reader. Our approach with this edition of *Consumer Behaviour* has been to take a truly international perspective on the subject. Our case studies incorporate examples from a variety of geographic locations (United Kingdom, Europe, and the United States of America) as well as from a number of different industry sectors (fashion, technology, start-ups, politics, education, travel and leisure, and social enterprise). This has also meant that academic disciplines other than marketing have also made tremendous contributions – psychology, sociology, anthropology, economics and neuroscience form the scientific base on which consumer behaviour stands as an academic subject. We have tried, in this book, to provide a concise and fairly comprehensive overview of the main aspects of consumer behaviour, but inevitably there are omissions, so at the end of each chapter we have offered some further reading on aspects which you may find particularly insightful.

Core textbooks like this one cannot just be the creation of a couple of people. In particular we would like to thank Matt Waters, Amy Jarrold and Gemma Shields at SAGE. This edition would not have seen the light of day without their dedication, support and understanding. Our families, the communities within which we live and our life experiences have all provided a consistently rich source of examples – many of which have been used here. Perhaps most importantly, our students should be thanked for making us think: some by asking us awkward questions, some by submitting thought-provoking coursework, some by making us laugh, and some by needing a deeper explanation than we were really ready to provide. Any errors, omissions and misconceptions are of course our own.

Zubin Sethna

North London

Jim Blythe

The Alpujarras

LEARNING FEATURES

LEARNING OBJECTIVES

After reading this chapter you should be able to:

- Explain how the study of consumer behaviour has evolved.
- Show how consumer behaviour relates to marketing decision-making.
- Explain why relationships are harder to establish in business-to-consumer situations than in business-to-business situations.
- Describe the scope and nature of psychology and sociology.
- Describe the scope and nature of anthropology
- Describe the relationship of economics study of consumer behaviour.
- ...lain the role of exchange in im...

LEARNING OBJECTIVES

Highlight everything you should know or understand by the end of each chapter.

GLOSSARY TERMS

To help you spot the important terms you will need for revision purposes, each new concept appears in coloured text and is defined in the margin.

Mass marketing

A situation in which a standardised product is purchased by a very large number of people

Niche marketing

Targeting a small group of customers

Micro marketing

Those elements of the environment that affect the individual firm

To
and
large
low. Th
to carry
product t
marketing
embedde

Tradition

1. Se
s

...enanism...
...ve identified a dedicate
...ior 2008). Work on neuro-econ
...he irrationality of the voter during po...

SUMMARY

Consumer decision-making is therefore n
People try to behave in ways that enable
friends and families, and to contribute t
behaviour is likely to involve consumpt
other people: this is the province of con

Consumer behaviour studies derive from
from direct studies by marketing acade
...us because it is, after all, about
...ys in which people make
...tance in pl...

SUMMARY

Covers all the essential information from each chapter and puts in context of consumer behaviour as a whole.

CHALLENGING THE STATUS QUO

Designed to develop your critical thinking and employability skills. They are short challenges from the workplace.

CONSUMER BEHAVIOUR IN ACTION

Additional examples to highlight what actually goes on in the real world.

KEY POINTS

Recaps the key topics for review at the end of each chapter.

HOW TO IMPRESS YOUR EXAMINER

The authors' own advice for standing out from the crowd and proving you know your stuff!

CHAPTER QUESTIONS

Help test your understanding of what you have just read.

CASE STUDY AND QUESTIONS

Offer a detailed look at real life examples and help you apply your knowledge by working through the questions.

FURTHER READING

Suggested titles for further reading to enhance your background knowledge.

THANKS FROM THE PUBLISHER

The Publisher would like to thank the following individuals for their valuable feedback and suggestions to help shape this new edition:

Dr. Lien Le Monkhouse, Sheffield University Management School

Rebecca Biggins, York St John University Business School

Dr. Declan Scully, University of Roehampton

Dr. Lara Spiteri Cornish, Coventry Business School

Dr. Anita Lifen Zhao, Swansea University

Jenny Bratherton, Regent's University London

Keith Brighty, York St John University

Dr. Bruno Schivinski, Nottingham Business School

Burak Tunca, University of Agder, Norway

Dr. Jan Breitsohl, Aberystwyth University

Dr. Clay Gransden, Liverpool Hope University

Professor Victoria Wells, Sheffield University Management School

We are grateful to everyone who granted us permission to reproduce copyrighted material in this book.

COMPANION WEBSITE

The 3rd edition of *Consumer Behaviour* is supported by a wealth of online resources for students to aid study, which are available at https://study.sagepub.com/sethnaandblythe

For students:

- Multiple choice questions
- Website exercises
- Useful video links
- Flashcards
- Multimedia links

For instructors:

- Instructors manual
- PowerPoint slides
- Further online case studies

PART ONE

CONSUMER BEHAVIOUR IN CONTEXT

The environment within which business is conducted may have changed since the start of the *global financial crisis* in 2008 but, ultimately, all business still depends on someone buying something. We buy things in order to meet our physical and emotional needs: business exists to create wealth, and to distribute it in ways that enable people to create relatively worthwhile lives for themselves.

If businesses are to succeed in this, they need to understand what it is that people need and want, and to ensure that it is available in the right place, at the right time and at a price consumers are willing to pay. This is the very foundation of all marketing – even businesses that sell only to other businesses rely, ultimately, on consumers buying products.

Apart from the obvious importance of understanding how people buy and consume, consumer behaviour is inherently interesting because it is about people (and we are *all* consumers, of course). Part One of this book looks at the basics of understanding consumer behaviour (Chapter 1) and its relationship to the 'marketing mix' (Chapter 2). Chapter 3 then examines the processes that people go through when making decisions and, of course, this would not be complete without investigating the interaction that consumers have with brands. Chapter 4 then takes a look at one of the most important areas for marketers – innovation and digital technologies. Companies must always have new products coming to market if they are to stay ahead of the competition, but at the same time innovation means taking a risk. Understanding how people relate to new products is an essential component of any company's new product strategy. Finally, in Chapter 5, we'll take a look at the differences between consumption patterns exhibited by individuals in B2C (business-to-consumer) and B2B (business-to-business) markets. These introductory chapters set the scene for the more detailed chapters that follow.

CHAPTER 1

UNDERSTANDING CONSUMER BEHAVIOUR

LEARNING OBJECTIVES

After reading this chapter you should be able to:

- Explain how the study of consumer behaviour has evolved.
- Show how consumer behaviour relates to marketing decision-making.
- Explain why relationships are harder to establish in business-to-consumer situations than in business-to-business situations.
- Describe the scope and nature of psychology and sociology.
- Describe the scope and nature of anthropology.
- Describe the relationship of economics with the study of consumer behaviour.
- Explain the role of exchange in improving people's welfare.
- Explain how the terms 'luxury' and 'necessity' relate to consumer behaviour.

INTRODUCTION

Every day we buy things. We exchange our money for goods and services, for our own use and for the use of our families: we choose things we think will meet our needs on a day-to-day basis, and we occasionally make buying decisions which will affect our lives for years to come. At the same time, we make decisions about disposing of worn-out or used-up possessions. All these decisions and exchanges have implications for ourselves, our families, our friends, the environment, the businesses we buy from, the employees of those businesses, and so on.

Customer

Someone who makes the decision to buy a product

The key concept of marketing is customer centrality: we cannot ignore customer decision-making. Understanding the processes involved in making those decisions is central to establishing policy.

Consumer behaviour and industrial buyer behaviour have been studied by marketers since long before marketing became an academic subject. The academic subjects that preceded marketing include economics (the study of supply and demand), sociology (the study of group behaviour), psychology (the study of thought processes), neurology (the study of brain function) and anthropology (the study of what makes us human). Each of these disciplines has looked at the problem from a different angle, and each will be discussed in greater detail throughout the book.

DEFINING CONSUMER BEHAVIOUR

Consumer

Someone who uses, consumes and/or enjoys the benefit of a product/service

Products

A bundle of benefits

App

Software designed to fulfil a particular purpose; an application, usually downloaded by a user onto a mobile device

All of us are consumers: all of us behave in a particular way. This does not mean that all of our behaviour can be defined as consumer behaviour, of course. Specific consumer behaviour has been defined as follows:

Consumer behaviour is the activities people undertake when obtaining, consuming and disposing of products and services. (Blackwell et al. 2001)

This definition is widely used, but it still leaves some questions to answer. First, what do we mean by 'obtaining'? This presumably includes all the activities that lead up to making a purchase, including searching for information about products and services, and evaluating the alternatives. 'Obtaining' may not involve an actual purchase, but most consumer behaviour researchers and writers ignore this angle: a child who promises to keep his room tidy in exchange for payment towards a new gaming app is clearly obtaining a product, but this is not usually regarded as part of a study of consumer behaviour. Likewise, presumably for ethical reasons, theft is usually ignored as an aspect of consumer behaviour.

CHALLENGING THE STATUS QUO

Where does the ethical/moral line lie when grocery shopping? For instance, is it acceptable to pick and eat a grape, while walking around the supermarket, in the name of 'sampling'? Or would you deem it acceptable to keep quiet if the checkout person charged you a lower price for an item which you knew to have a much higher one? And in these times of austerity, when a lot of people face severe financial hardship, would you turn a blind eye to someone stealing a carton of milk? Of course these questions are not new to us; in the 6th century, a philosopher in Ancient Greece called Anacharsis said, 'the market is a place set apart where men may deceive one and other'. Thus, *trust* becomes of paramount importance. Individuals who trust themselves to 'do the right thing', trust between people and in organisations is the key. Let's take, for example, the self-checkout in grocery stores. In 2014, British supermarkets reported that stealing amounted to £1.6 billion worth of items. Research from the National Association for Shoplifting Prevention in the USA showed that there are approximately 27 million shoplifters (or 1 in 11 people) in the USA. And all of this is in spite of various measures being taken to deter the would-be thief – including more visible security guards, anti-theft packaging and CCTV surveillance cameras with video analytical software to monitor customer behaviour. This enables the retailer to make assumptions about, for instance, why someone lingers in a particular area for longer than is 'normal' in a supermarket!

Is the overall environment easier to steal? The retailers have certainly made it easier to steal their products, but from a manufacturer's viewpoint, shoplifting can only be a good thing. If the product is attractive to shoplifters, more of it will leave the retailer's premises, and since the retailer has already paid the manufacturer for the goods, the

©iStock.com/stnazkul

manufacturer doesn't care whether the goods are bought or stolen from the retailer! Of course that's not to say that manufacturers are actively encouraging pilfering; it's just that retailers are partly trusting us to 'do the right thing'. What is for sure is that technology has a big part to play. Social media and the various platforms and forums that exist make it easier to dispose of stolen items. Websites such as YouTube have numerous videos showing people how to steal; some from seemingly experienced criminals divulging the 'tricks of the trade'. Other forums provide a platform for unhappy employees to expose organisational secrets. You could assume that a sure way of dealing with such behaviour is to toughen up on aspects of punishment. But with resources being stretched every which way, some interesting decisions are being made on how to tackle this situation; the police department in Dallas, Texas are questioning the cost benefit of operations which try and capture a teenager who has stolen something worth $20 and will actually refuse to prosecute anyone who steals something for less than $50. We'll let you decide what message this sends out to the public ...

Other issues in the 'obtaining' category might include where people buy the product (offline or online), the ways in which people pay for the products (cash, credit card, bank loan, payday loan, hire purchase, interest-free credit, and so forth), whether the product is for themselves or is a gift, how the new owner gets the purchases home, and how all of these decisions are affected by branding, and by social elements such as influence and peer-pressure.

Consuming refers to the ways in which people use the products they have, whether bought or acquired. This includes where the product is consumed, when (in terms of on what occasions the product might be used) and how the product is used. In some cases people use products in ways that were not intended by the manufacturer: this is called re-invention. For example, a biologist might buy a turkey-basting syringe to use for taking water samples from a river, a gardener might buy a china serving dish to use as a plant pot, and a cleaner may use vinegar in a spray-bottle to remove lime scale. Consumption is necessary for our health and well-being: obviously some consumption is not good for us (over-consumption of alcohol, drug abuse, or even using a mobile device while driving) but most of our consumption is essential for living and relating to other people (Richins 2001).

Disposal

Divestment of a product when it is worn out or used up

Disposal of products when they are worn out or no longer needed has become a 'hot topic' in recent years due to environmentalism. Disposal includes the disposal of packaging – whether it is recycled, burned or goes into landfill, packaging represents a major problem for the 21st century. Given that landfill sites around the world are filling up fast, turning non-recyclable material into recyclable is something that many consumers are thinking about and something which a company called TerraCycle (www.terracycle.com) has excelled at. Knowing how people dispose of products can be crucial to marketing them. For example, in many developing countries empty metal cans are used to make oil lamps, ashtrays, drinking vessels, and so forth. Changing the design or size of the can may well affect sales. Likewise, a system for trading in used or worn-out items can be a major boost for sales of new items: second-hand car trading is based entirely on this principle.

CONSUMER BEHAVIOUR IN ACTION: TRADE-IN

Trading in old cars for new ones was reputedly invented by General Motors dealers in the 1930s as a way of stimulating the market for new cars. Trade-in also solved the problem of what to do with a car once it was a few years old and perhaps not looking as new as it once had. The second-hand cars that were traded in could be sold to people who could not afford a new car, and so the number of people who were driving could be increased dramatically.

In 1995 Mrs Katherine Freund of Portland, Oregon, had an idea for extending the trade-in concept and at the same time improving road safety. Her son was run over by an elderly driver in 1988 (the son recovered fully) and it occurred to Katherine that there were many elderly people on the road who really shouldn't be driving, but who felt that they had little choice in a world (and especially in a country) dominated by cars. So Katherine instituted a scheme whereby senior-citizen drivers could trade in their cars in exchange for rides. The elderly people are credited with rides, but the cars are operated by volunteers supplemented by a few paid drivers, and the scheme is self-financing. The rides are very much cheaper than using taxis so the credit in the scheme lasts a long time, and the service runs 24 hours a day, seven days a week. One of the main advantages of the scheme is that it allows elderly people to remain part of the community and continue to do everything they used to do when they were still driving. The other advantage is that the roads are much safer – the over-75 age group has more accidents than any other group except teenagers.

This novel approach to trade-in has created an entirely new opportunity for older drivers: at the same time, it maintains their mobility and makes life safer for others. As a way of disposing of no-longer-needed cars it is second to none!

Although the traditional model of using buses and trains is one of the best ways of moving people in high density areas, the digital environment (technology

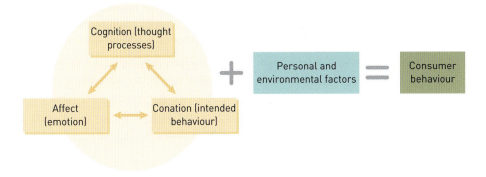

FIGURE 1.1 Consumer behaviour dynamics

and the Internet) plays a strong part in such examples of transportation. IT and global positioning systems, together with data from online networks, provide us with information on when and where vehicles (public and private) and people are located and therefore create efficient transportation opportunities. Private for-profit organisations such as Uber and Zipcar are taking full advantage of such revolutions in transportation by offering an alternative model to the traditional shared community mobility model of mass transportation using buses and trains.

Another definition of consumer behaviour runs as follows:

> *The dynamic interaction of affect and cognition, behaviour, and environmental events by which human beings conduct the exchange aspects of their lives.* (Bennett 1995)

This definition, while 20 years old, still has the advantage that it regards consumer behaviour as dynamic, and emphasises the interaction of many different elements in determining consumer behaviour. This is the main reason why strategy needs constant review: a strategy that worked well in the past may not work nearly as well in the future, because the forces that shape behaviour may have changed out of all recognition.

The general model of consumer behaviour shown in Figure 1.1 shows that basic attitudes (formed of thought, emotion and intended behaviour) together with personal and environmental factors result in the creation of actual behaviour. Marketers are able to influence this process at several points – they can influence thought processes by providing relevant information at the right time, they can influence emotion by using appealing communication and imagery, and they can provide suitable environmental stimuli (for example, user-friendly websites or inviting shops) to stimulate purchase. Marketers can even encourage greater consumption of the product – good marketing does not stop at the point of sale.

From the viewpoint of academic researchers, consumer behaviour might be considered as the field of study that concentrates on consumption activities. In the past the study of consumer behaviour has mainly focused on why people buy. More recently, the focus has moved to include looking at consumption behaviour – in other words, how and why people consume.

Studying consumer behaviour is an interesting study not just for marketers, but even for non-marketers, because we are all consumers. Ultimately, consumers hold all the power in the business world – as Sam Walton, founder of WalMart, famously said:

> There is only one boss – the customer. And he can fire everyone in the company, from the chairman on down, simply by spending his money somewhere else.

Walton always regarded himself as an agent for his customers, finding them the best value for money: this simple philosophy moved WalMart from one small store in Arkansas to being the world's largest retailer within Walton's lifetime.

CONSUMER BEHAVIOUR IN CONTEXT

The fundamental basis for marketing thinking is that the customer (or consumer) should be at the centre of everything the firm does. While there may be some dissent about whether the marketing concept always applies, for marketers, customers are the key concern. This means that an understanding of how and why people make purchasing decisions is crucial to formulating a marketing plan.

Segmentation

The act of dividing up a market into groups of people with similar needs

In the first instance, purchasing behaviour relates strongly to how the market is segmented. The whole purpose of **segmentation** is to determine which potential buyers are most likely to behave favourably towards our organisation and its products and services: most segmentation methods bear at least some relationship to consumer behaviour issues.

Geographic segmentation

Dividing a market into smaller groups based on location

Geographic segmentation breaks the market down according to the location in which the potential customers live. Where someone chooses to live, or is forced to live, is either an example of decision-making or dictates decision-making. Someone living in a cold climate is compelled to buy warm clothing, heating equipment, insulation products for the home, and so forth.

Psychographic segmentation

Dividing a market according to the psychological profiles of potential customers

Psychographic segmentation and behavioural segmentation clearly relate very directly to consumer characteristics and behaviour. Psychographic segmentation is based on people's thought processes and attitudes – clearly the starting-points for behaviour.

Behavioural segmentation

Dividing up a potential market according to the behaviour of its members

Behavioural segmentation is based on what people do – what hobbies they have, what foods they eat, how they travel, work and spend their spare time.

Demographic segmentation

Dividing up a market according to people's age, income and social standing

Demographic segmentation is based on consumers' wealth, age, gender and education levels (among other things), each of which relate directly to purchasing decisions. There is more on psychological factors in Chapters 6 to 9, and more on attitude in Chapter 10.

Service-dominant logic

The view that all value is co-created by the consumer and the supplier, and thus that all value can be considered as a service

Over a decade ago an idea was proposed that consumers are not simply users of value (and, by extension, destroyers of value as they use up products) but should instead be considered as co-creators of value (Vargo and Lusch 2004). The thinking is that goods and services only have value when they are used – an electric drill has no value if it simply stays on the retailer's shelf, but it does create value when someone buys it and uses it. This perspective, known as **service-dominant logic** (S-DL), supposes that in fact all products are service products, since consumers are not buying a drill, nor are they buying holes, but are in fact buying a hole-drilling service for which they will provide some of the effort and therefore create some of the value. S-DL has a strong appeal – after all, someone who needs to drill a hole could (presumably) hire someone to come and drill the hole for them, or could buy (or hire) a drill and do it themselves. The value created is much the same in each case, but the relative contribution by the consumer and the supplier is very different.

There are a great many conceptual implications involved in service-dominant logic, and academics continue to debate the practical implications for organisations. However, there is certainly research supporting the idea that modern consumers are not prepared simply to accept what manufacturers provide for them, but instead seek to re-invent, add value and communicate new ideas to each other entirely independently of producers (Hewer and Brownlie 2010).

CONSUMER BEHAVIOUR AND THE MARKETING MIX

Marketing management is usually considered to consist of controlling the marketing mix. Table 1.1 shows how consumer behaviour relates to the seven Ps (7P) model of the marketing mix developed by Booms and Bitner (1981).

Marketing mix

The combination of activities which creates an overall approach to the market

Although the marketing mix has been widely criticised by academics because it tends to imply things being done *to* consumers rather than things being done *for* consumers, it is still widely taught and accepted because it offers a relatively simply way to understand what marketers do. Putting each element of the mix into a separate 'silo' is one way of simplifying the real world, but looked at from the consumer's viewpoint the distinctions between the elements may not be valid at all. For example, price is regarded as a cost from the consumer's viewpoint, but might also be regarded as a promotion – a money-off special offer could be regarded as a major incentive to buy now rather than postpone the purchase. In other words, the 7P model may be fine for the marketers to understand, but may not be appropriate from the consumer's viewpoint.

TABLE 1.1 Consumer behaviour and the seven Ps

Product	The bundle of benefits consumers acquire is the basis of their decision-making. Deciding which benefits are essential, which are desirable, which do not matter and which are actually not benefits at all but drawbacks is the starting point for all rational decisions
Price	The cost of a product goes beyond the price tag in most cases. If the product is complex, there will be a learning cost attached to figuring out how to use it: if the product is dangerous, there may be a cost attached to consequent injury. If the product is visible to others, there may be an embarrassment cost. Some products require more effort to use – an electric can opener is easier to use than a hand-operated one, but costs more money. In some cases, these extra costs may exceed the price tag – consumers will take account of them, and will weigh them in the decision, but producers will only be able to obtain the price on the tag
Place	Convenient locations for making purchases are essential; in fact it would not be too much to say that the easier marketers make it for consumers to find the product, the more product will be sold – this is partly why some brands pay a lot of money for their products to be displayed prominently in numerous retail outlets. Like price, the location can affect the decision in ways which do not benefit the producer – equally, producers can sometimes charge a premium for delivering location benefits. Corner shops (convenience stores) used to be a good example: although they are invariably more expensive than supermarkets, being within easy reach of home offers a clear advantage that is worth paying for. However, this level of advantage has not gone unnoticed by the big retailers who have, over the past few years, utilised their price advantage and muscled in on this turf by opening their smaller, local stores, for example – 'Sainsbury's Local', 'Tesco Express', 'Little Waitrose'

(Continued)

TABLE 1.1 (Continued)

Promotion	Promotion is not something that is done to consumers, it is something they consume. People surf the web, buy magazines, watch TV shows, go to the cinema and ride on public transport. Although they do not usually do these things in order to be exposed to advertisements, when bombarded with advertising, they usually pay at least some attention to them and frequently they enjoy the experience. Furthermore, people often use media such as classified advertisements and directories (offline and online) in an active search for information about goods they might like to buy
People	Business is not about money, it is about people. The people who run businesses and deal with the public need to understand how other people react in purchasing situations. In some cases, the product is the person: people consumers become loyal to the same hairdresser, the same doctor, the same restaurant chef. Unsurprisingly, the people who work with the customers – who are customer facing – tend to be the most customer-orientated. Proximity to the customer is a more important factor in this than is the attitude and behaviour of senior management (Hui and Subramony 2008). In other words, senior management may or may not be customer-orientated, but the very nature of working with customers will in itself tend to focus people on customer need
Process	The way in which services are delivered affects the context within which people buy as well as their propensity to buy. For example, a meal out might be a ten-minute lunch stop at a fast-food outlet, or it might be a prolonged, eight-course dinner for two in a Michelin starred restaurant. The process is completely different in each case, and so is the price: in the first case, the consumer may only go through a limited problem-solving process; in the second case, the process may well be longer because the need to get it right is greater. This is called involvement
Physical evidence	Physical aspects of the service encounter often relate to the pleasure one feels from receiving the service rather than the practical aspects. The surroundings and ambience of a restaurant, the food itself and the quality of the menus, all affect people's perception of the 'whole' service

Chapter 2 further explores the practical issues around consumer behaviour within the marketing mix.

CONSUMERS, RELATIONSHIP MARKETING AND MARKETING PLANNING

Relationship marketing seeks to establish long-term relationships with customers rather than focusing on the single transaction. The differences between relationship marketing and transactional marketing are shown in Table 1.2.

Establishing a relationship in a business-to-business (B2B) context turns out to be a great deal easier than establishing a relationship in a business-to-consumer (B2C) context (see Chapter 5 for more on organisational buyer behaviour). The reasons for this are currently obscure, but may include the following:

1. Businesses change their needs less often than do consumers.

2. There are fewer suppliers and customers in B2B markets.

3. B2B transactions almost always involve the personal relationships which seek engagement from the organisation, its salespeople and the buyers; whereas B2C relationships are often impersonal, since people often buy goods online or in self-service stores.

4. The possibilities for mutual advantage in establishing relationships are often much greater in a B2B context.

TABLE 1.2 Transactional marketing vs. relationship marketing

Transactional marketing	Relationship marketing
Focus on single sale	Focus on customer retention
Orientation on product features	Orientation on product benefits
Short timescale	Long timescale
Little emphasis on customer service	High emphasis on customer service
Limited customer commitment	High customer commitment
Moderate customer contact	High customer contact
Quality is the concern of the production department	Quality is the concern of all

Source: Christopher et al. (1991)

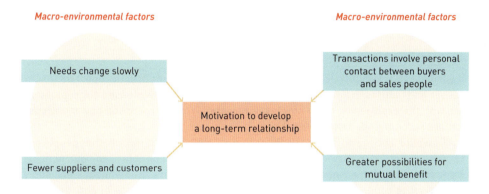

FIGURE 1.2 Businesses and relationship marketing

Relationship marketing is firmly rooted in the basic idea that it is cheaper to retain an existing customer than to recruit a new one. There is a certain appeal to this idea: acquiring new customers is a difficult business, whereas keeping someone on-board should only be a matter of making sure their needs are continuously met and perhaps occasionally exceeded. In consumer markets, this is a great deal harder than it sounds. As shown in Figure 1.2, consumer needs change relatively rapidly: the needs of someone aged 18 are likely to change dramatically by the time he or she is 25, and again by age 40. Likewise, a couple who have just had a baby together will find that their needs are perhaps not as urgent as their baby's, quite apart from the probable change in their spending pattern which will bring its own financial needs and requirements. Second, there is a great deal more choice as regards suppliers in consumer markets, leading to a great many more ways to spend one's money. People can easily be tempted away from their existing supplier and towards a new supplier. Third, with greater choice provided by the Internet and so many tempting offers around, suppliers need to ask themselves the crucial question – 'what is the incentive for my consumers to remain loyal to me?' Providing an extra-nice service is just not enough.

People generally have become much more aware of marketing and marketers. There is now a much greater understanding of the marketing techniques used to influence the buyer's decision-making process, and consequently a greater distrust of marketers. There is evidence that this alienation of consumers is linked to the use of new technology – the Internet allows consumers to take control of the exchange process in a way that has been impossible in the past, and thus they are able to take over some of the role of marketers in managing exchange (Mady 2011).

Relationship marketing has become closely associated with direct marketing, simply because the best way to establish a relationship with a customer is to have direct dealings. Unfortunately, direct marketing has also become associated with other forms of marketing communication – unsolicited direct mail and direct telephone marketing, both of which are extremely unpopular with the public in general; this is probably another reason why relationship marketing is less successful with consumers than with industrial buyers.

Understanding how people create and maintain relationships in their personal lives is obviously useful when considering how people create and maintain business relationships. Businesses are not about profits: they are about people.

CHALLENGING THE STATUS QUO

If businesses are about people, why is it that companies consistently report their successes and failures in financial terms? Why not report on how pleased our customers are with the experience, or on how loyal they are? Why not report on how many customers recommended us to their friends?

Or would it be too difficult to do these things? How do we know whether people are recommending us anyway? The market researchers should be able to find out. Actually it's just a different perspective on 'reporting' the numbers. But while it's obviously easier just to count up the money coming in, just a little more use of data analytics could help us to identify how the numbers translate into customers. For example, the National Customer Satisfaction Index in the UK helps organisations to 'benchmark customer satisfaction results with industry peers and best-in-class companies' (http://ncsiuk.com/). What this means for marketers is that they can link their company's market strength and financial performance with the various drivers of satisfaction and loyalty, and report on what businesses are actually about – people!

Marketing planning has often been considered in terms of managing the product/service portfolio, developing new offerings, launching products, managing the product life cycle, and so forth. This involves planning communications that explain the features and benefits of an organisation's offerings, and seek to persuade consumers to buy from them. It involves deciding which channels of distribution should be used and what price will provide the organisation with a good return on its investment.

This way of looking at marketing suffers from a serious flaw in that it is not customer-centric; it is very firm-centric. Suppose we were to act in a completely customer-centred manner. We would then be seeking to manage the customer portfolio, considering which customers (or groups of customers) we can serve profitably and which we cannot. We would consider which marketing communications would appeal most to the groups we want to keep, and which would be off-putting to the groups we want to lose. We might consider the customer's life cycle rather than the product's life cycle, and consider price in terms of what consumers will think is fair. For example, Denmark's largest bank, Danske Bank, has an interesting way of being customer-centric. They have really understood what appeals to today's banking customers and have developed a variety of product and service offerings to meet their needs. Danske Bank has used innovative digital solutions to ensure that their marketing planning takes account of the things that matter to their customers. They provide a graphic, real time overview of their customers spend using a variety of formats – eBanking, tablet and mobile banking. The importance of the smartphone is taken into account with apps such as MobilePay, which enable business customers to receive payments from their customers via smartphone. One of the biggest gripes that banking customers have today, especially business customers, is that their bank managers are inaccessible and therefore it's difficult to develop a relationship. So Danske Bank's 'online meeting' tools enable customers to 'meet' their bank representatives at a time and place that suits both the customer and the bank.

CHALLENGING THE STATUS QUO

Can we really let consumers run the business? After all, if we ask people what they are willing to pay for a product, they are likely to pitch the price as low as they think they can get away with. The same applies to service – everybody wants a lot, but is only prepared to pay a little!

Not to mention the competitive nature of the race. As one organisation offers one level of service, everyone else has to, at the very least, match it, if not exceed it. Does this mean that before long we get to a point where we are grovelling to the customers?

For example, in France one would never argue with the chef. If one likes one's steak well done, the waiter will suggest the idea to the chef, but after muttering something about 'Les sales anglais!' the

©iStock.com/gerenme

chef will produce a steak which looks as if it needs a bandage. Contrast this with America, where the customer tells the chef exactly what to put in and leave out of the food: 'No salt, hold the mayo, just a little tabasco' and so forth. No doubt the American chef is much more customer-centred, but aren't we, as the customers, paying for his expertise? What's the point of going to a restaurant where we have a trained chef with years of experience, and then second-guessing the guy? Can we really trust the customer to know what is best for them? After all, doctors and lawyers don't expect people to know what is best for their health or legal well-being.

So where is customer-centrality really located? In France, or in America?

Marketing strategies should therefore not only seek to influence consumers, they should also be influenced by them. Planning for a consumer-led future means putting consumer behaviour at the centre of the firm's thinking. In the world that we live in today, it is the consumer who holds the power: there is evidence that people consider their spending power to be a form of voting, a way of expressing approval for what the supplier is offering (Shaw et al. 2006). People are aware that they have choice: at first, when choice became widespread, people might have found this confusing and daunting, but as time has gone on people have found it empowering, and they do not hesitate to use their power (Davies and Elliott 2006). This newfound power in the hands of consumers is what has been referred to as 'consumers to business' (C2B) (Urban et al. 2000).

For example, consumer research might show that a specific group of our customers is more profitable than another simply because they are more loyal. This means that we do not need to recruit new customers to replace those who drop out, which is of course substantially cheaper. We might therefore seek (a) to ensure that we continue to retain these customers and (b) try to find more like them. Their loyalty comes from their purchase behaviour – their propensity to repeat purchases on a regular basis – which in itself may be a function of their personalities and the degree of their involvement with the products.

ANTECEDENTS OF CONSUMER BEHAVIOUR

It is really important for the reader to understand that the study of consumer behaviour is, like marketing itself, a combination of other disciplines. As a study, it draws its basic theories and research approaches from sociology, psychology, anthropology, economics and neuroscience. Academics aim to develop a body of specifically consumer-based research, but the influence of the other disciplines will always be at the forefront of the theory that develops, as shown in Figure 1.3.

All of these areas will be discussed in much greater detail throughout the book, but a quick overview of the basic contributions of each discipline should be helpful in understanding how consumer behaviour has developed as an academic study.

C2B

Consumers to business

Loyalty

The degree to which an individual will repeat purchase of a product

Involvement

The degree to which an individual is attracted to, and defined by, a product or brand

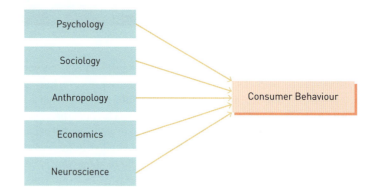

FIGURE 1.3 Antecedents of studying consumer behaviour

PSYCHOLOGY

Psychology is the study of mental processes. Psychologists study the ways people think, which is of course basic to understanding how people think about the products they buy. This includes learning about products, developing an overall perception of products and brands and fitting it into one's overall perception of the world, and the basic drives that encourage people to seek solutions for their needs.

Each of the contributions made by psychologists (as shown in Figure 1.4) will be covered in more detail in Part Two of this book, but for the time being here is a brief overview of the main issues.

DRIVE AND MOTIVATION

Drives are the basic forces that make us want to do things (see Chapter 6). A drive is created when the desired state of the individual is different from the actual state: the greater the difference, the stronger the drive. A drive that has a definite target becomes a **motivation**. Part of the marketer's job is to encourage drives to develop by encouraging shifts in the desired state (it is pretty much impossible to develop shifts in the actual state). The other part of the marketer's job is to direct drives towards a specific target. For example, a marketer might encourage a shift in the desired state by saying, 'Isn't it about time you bought yourself a more luxurious car?' and follow this by saying, 'Why not treat yourself to a new Jaguar XJ?'

GOALS AND INCENTIVES

A **goal** is the rational element of motivation (see Chapter 6). Motives are largely emotional: goals are the rationalisation of a motivation. For example, someone might

Psychology
The scientific study of the human mind and its functions, including behaviour

Drive
The basic force of motivation, which arises when the individual's actual state diverges from the desired state

Motivation
The internal force which encourages people to act in specific ways

Goals
Specific targets towards which consumption behaviour is directed

FIGURE 1.4 Contributions from psychology

decide that they really want to learn to fly (a largely emotional motivation, based on reading adventure stories or on an unspecified emotion). The goals that derive from this might be concerned with finding an appropriate flying school, saving up the money to pay for lessons, and freeing up the time to learn. The **incentive** for achieving these various goals is the satisfaction of the need.

PERSONALITY AND SELF-CONCEPT

Personality is a combination of the various traits that determine who we are (see Chapter 7). The type of person we are dictates what we like and what we dislike, our preferred ways of dealing with our consumption problems, our preferred lifestyles, and so forth. **Self-concept** is about how we see ourselves – this includes how we see ourselves in terms of consumption patterns, branding and other consumption-based aspects. For example, we each have preferred brands, which we feel reflect and express our own personalities. Some of us are Mercedes drivers, for some of us it's Ford; some of us wear Converse footwear while others prefer Nike; and of course there is the perennial argument about which football team should be in the premier league. What we buy and wear (and who we support) expresses who we are.

PERCEPTION

Perception is about the way we make sense of the world (see Chapter 8). Each of us has a particular view of the world, a perceptual map, which enables us to make sense of what is happening around us. We assemble this map by taking in information through our senses and using it to develop an understanding of how the world works and where different things fit into it. Psychologists study the ways in which people sometimes filter out unnecessary information, or conversely group information together into useable 'chunks' and arrange the information to create the perceptual map. Marketers are interested in these processes in order to ensure that their brand is mapped into the most effective place in the consumers' perceptions.

The word perception is often used to mean 'untrue' but in fact this is not the case. The only truth we have is what we hold in our minds, so a person's perceptual map is the truth for that person. Even though we each have different perceptual maps, they are near enough to each other for us to be able to communicate and cooperate.

LEARNING

Learning is the behavioural changes that result from experience (see Chapter 9) and you won't be surprised to learn that this is not a new concept. One of the earliest references to this can be found in the *Nichomachean Ethics* in around 350 BCE, where it is reported that Aristotle wrote, 'for the things we have to learn before we can do them, we learn by doing them'. This has been referred to as 'experiential learning' and defined as 'learning through reflection on doing' (Felicia 2011). How we learn is critical to marketing communications, because marketers want people to remember the messages and act upon them in ways that are favourable to the organisation.

ATTITUDE FORMATION AND CHANGE

Attitudes consist of knowledge, feelings and proposed behaviour (see Chapter 10). An attitude is a tendency to behave in a consistent manner towards a given stimulus: in other words, people tend to react the same way every time towards something about which they have an attitude. For marketers, understanding how attitudes are formed and how they can be changed is useful in creating appropriate attitudes towards brands, products and services: sometimes attitudes need to be demolished and rebuilt if the brand is to continue successfully. An example of this is the negative attitudes held about the car marque Skoda from the Czech Republic. Since the early 1970s, the brand was suffering from a steady decline in attitudes towards its image, largely due to poor workmanship and outdated design. The Volkswagen Group took over in the early 1990s and Skoda became a part of their family of brands. However, the negative image was difficult to change and every time the word Skoda was mentioned in conversation, it would be a subject for humour. Volkswagen naturally considered changing the brand name, but research conducted among the UK public found that the name had a 100% brand recall. Whether this was positive or negative recall was not the point – very few brands enjoy a 100% brand recall. Skoda decided that it wasn't the name, but the attitudes of the people that needed to change. With the launch of their new car, the Fabia, they instigated a campaign that tackled this attitude head on by challenging consumers to sit up, take notice and be impressed by what they saw. So the central message in their marketing communications revolved around 'It's so good that you won't believe it's a Skoda'. This triggered a positive change in sales, considerations, image and above all attitude.

Psychology is not the only behavioural science, however. It is mainly concerned with the individual, but human beings are herd animals: we operate in groups. In prehistoric times, being part of a group meant the difference between surviving and not surviving: even today, people who do not fit in with one or more groups usually lead unhappy lives, and there is medical evidence to suggest that they do not live as long as other people either. The behaviour of people in groups is the province of sociology.

SOCIOLOGY

Group behaviour is crucial to human beings, and therefore is crucial to understanding what motivates people to buy specific brands. Buying the wrong brand can be embarrassing: we are all aware of how, in our early teens, we have to have the right label on clothing, play the right Xbox games, see the right films and stream the right music from Spotify to fit in with the desired group. Even adolescent rebellion is actually just a drive to join a group. The contributions from sociology are shown in Figure 1.5 and described below: the following topics will be covered in much greater detail in Part Three of the book.

REFERENCE GROUPS

People identify groups they would like to join, and also groups they would prefer not to be associated with (see Chapter 11). Almost all such groups involve some type of consumption: clothing to wear, things to use in the group activities, or shared consumption of group-owned items. Most of us define ourselves at least in part by the groups we belong to, whether it is our work group, our group of friends, our family group, our religious group, or our group hobbies.

Attitudes

A propensity to respond in a consistent manner to a given stimulus or object

FIGURE 1.5 Contributions from sociology

FAMILY

Family

A group of people who exhibit shared consumption and who are bound by ties of genetic relationship or adoption

The family is probably the most important reference group because it exerts the most influence on us (see Chapter 12). Families share consumption of many items (food, housing, energy, etc.) and our early upbringing greatly influences our behaviour in later years.

CLASS AND CULTURE

Culture

The set of beliefs, behaviour, customs and attitudes that are common to a large group of people

Culture is the set of beliefs and behaviours that distinguishes one large group of people from another, and it includes such issues as religious beliefs, language, customs, class distinctions and accepted norms of behaviour. For marketers, culture is one of the driving forces of behaviour including consumption behaviour, but perhaps more importantly it is a minefield in which communications and brands can cause offence to people from other cultural backgrounds. In particular, religious beliefs can create problems for marketers since people are often inflexible about religious taboos or restrictions.

SELF-IMAGE AND ROLE

Role

The place one has within a group

Likes

An online widget for expressing positive feeling towards a visual or a statement that someone has uploaded

Selfie

A photograph that one has taken of oneself with a smartphone or webcam and shared via social media

The images we form of ourselves are almost entirely derived from feedback from other people (see Chapter 7). This feedback is derived in turn from the images we project as part of our role in life, both offline and online. In fact, we each perform many roles in our dealings with others: as friends, work colleagues, children, fathers, mothers, professionals, and so forth: we judge ourselves as being good at each of these roles by the feedback of the people we deal with every day. So this begs a question of the current, digitally savvy population – is the only way one can know if one has good friends by the likes one gets on a recently posted selfie?

People often define themselves, at least in part, by the products they consume. Possessions become an extension of the individual – an extended self – and thus project who the person is to others (Mittal 2006). Indeed, many acts of consumption are tribal and role-supporting, even when they do not define the self (Ryan et al. 2006).

ANTHROPOLOGY

Anthropology is a wide-ranging academic discipline, covering everything that makes us human. Anthropology is all about the study of people (human beings) as a whole, from the past and present; and from small, isolated homogenous cultures to large social networks. Of course, the journey of human evolution that has taken place over the past two millennia is an extremely complex one and thus anthropology draws its knowledge from a number of related spheres – socio-cultural, physical and biological sciences, as well as the humanities. The relationship to consumer behaviour thus, accordingly, comes from a variety of anthropological perspectives. First and foremost are the socio-cultural aspects of anthropology. Meaning is derived from how people live and therefore what they consume. Closer scrutiny of the similarities and differences in gender, race, nationality and class, all provide further clues as to the 'meaning of life' for various consumers. These data help organisations to provide consumers with products and services related to a variety of sectors including health, education, environment, agriculture and social change. Secondly, it is the biological and cultural processes which together shape growth, development and behaviour; behaviour that has led humans to adapt to the diverse environments within which they live, work and consume. Cognitive anthropology has been used to study the problem-solving behaviour of green consumers (Wagner-Tsukamoto and Tadajewski, 2006). Interestingly, a natural extension of anthropology is now being examined by some UK universities in the form of 'digital anthropology'; a study of collective lives online or using digital channels.

ECONOMICS

Economics is the study of demand. Economists study demand in the individual transaction, at the level of the firm and its customers (*microeconomics*), and also the overall level of demand in the economy (*macroeconomics*). Although microeconomics appears at first sight to explain consumer behaviour it, in fact, only really explains *rational* behaviour. Economists consider such concepts as utility, value for money and **economic choice**, not such nebulous ideas as whether one's friends will admire one's new outfit.

Economics has provided consumer behaviour theorists with a number of useful concepts that help to explain the rational side of consumer behaviour, and it's worth highlighting a couple of them here in this introduction as their relationship to consumer behaviour is quite insightful.

THE ECONOMIC CHOICE

This simply means that someone cannot spend money on something if he or she has already spent the money somewhere else. So consumers have a choice; a choice on what to spend their money on. This implies that all companies are competing with all other companies for the consumer's money: people have only a certain amount of money they can spend, or commit to borrowing. Of course, economic choice is somewhat blurred by the wide availability of credit. People can be persuaded to borrow the money to buy whatever they want, which means that factors other than money may come into the equation. The theory of *choice* still holds true, though, if we consider the economic choice of how we spend our time, or how we use other

Economics
The study of demand

Economic choice
The choice made when one is unable to afford to buy both alternatives

resources such as our cars or our homes. The theory really talks about use of limited resources in aiming to satisfy one's needs.

Marketers have certainly taken on board the concept of the economic choice, broadening out the spectrum of competitors to include anyone who aims to satisfy similar needs in consumers. Take, for example, cinema owners. They recognise a wide range of other entertainment places as competitors (live theatre, casinos, online films/gaming and bowling-alleys, among others) and in recent years have developed complexes where a variety of leisure activities can take place under one roof. This is not just an example of a deeper understanding of who the competition is; it is also an example of how an organisation can help people make the best use of limited leisure time. With time as the constraining variable, such complexes can make best use of economic choice theory.

ELASTICITY OF DEMAND

This is an economic theory which asks 'how far can an organisation stretch its price-point before the demand for that product or service snaps'? Although a rise in prices generally means a reduction in demand (there are some exceptions), there is a question about the degree to which demand is affected by price. In some cases, a rise in price appears to make very little difference to demand (*inelastic demand*) – salt is the example usually given for this, because it is extremely cheap (and therefore a tiny percentage of a person's income), has no real substitutes and is purchased quite infrequently, so even a doubling of the price would probably go unnoticed. Other products fall into this category: a rise in the cost of water bills doesn't mean that people will disconnect their water supply, and if a commuter relies on a particular train route to get to work, a rise in the fare will usually only result in a very small decrease in demand, as the alternative modes of transport maybe very limited. The opposite of these scenarios is where the price directly affects demands (*elastic demand*). Some fast-moving consumer goods (FMCG) seem to be dramatically affected by even small changes in price: this usually happens if there is a close substitute available, for example if the price of beef rose relative to the price of lamb. In these circumstances, price calculations need to be carried out extremely carefully as a mistake could result in a dramatic loss of business.

There are elasticities other than price. For example, income elasticity of demand tells us that some products are affected by increases in the individual's spending money. In some cases, this will produce an increase in demand – as people become richer, they are likely to buy more clothes and more entertainment products, for example; or if as people become more environmentally conscious, there may be an increase in the number of electric vehicles being sold. In other cases, the demand for an individual product might reduce as people become wealthier: a higher income might lead some-one to buy a more luxurious brand of automobile, say a Mercedes, rather than a Ford. In some cases, a general rise in income reduces demand fairly dramatically, and the humble bread is an example. As people become richer, they tend to buy less bread, and eat more meat and vegetables instead. In recent years, rising standards of living in emerging economies such as China and India have led to steep rises in the cost of many foods, globally, as people in those countries are able to afford more meat and vegetables, and thus do not rely as much on cheap, staple foods such as rice and bread.

Figure 1.6 shows an elastic demand curve. Here the demand for the product is affected greatly by the price – even a small increase in price has a fairly profound effect on the demand for the product.

FMCG

Fast-moving consumer goods

FIGURE 1.6 Elastic demand curve

One point that arises from the **elasticity** concept is that there is no product which has a completely inelastic demand curve. In other words, there is no product which has a demand curve that is entirely unaffected by price. This means that there is no product which is an absolute necessity of life – if this were the case, the producer could charge anything at all for the product and people would have no choice but to pay, since the alternative would be death. This is an important issue for marketers, because it shows us that there is no theoretical basis for considering some products as necessities and other products as luxuries. The difference exists only in the minds of consumers. To some people, a car would be a luxury; to others it is a necessity. Likewise, water might be considered as a necessity of life, yet some people rarely (if ever) drink just plain water: they drink tea, beer, fruit juice, cola, or any one of many different products containing water, all of which are substitutes for the plain and simple tap water.

NEUROSCIENCE

Neuroscience is the study of the ways in which the human brain works. A sub-branch of the discipline, neuro-economics, is the fusion of neuroscience and economics. This field of study analyses the relationship between the internal organisation of the brain and an individual's behaviour (Chavaglia et al. 2015). In other words, it seeks to explain an individual's economic behaviour in terms of the part played by the physiological makeup of the brain in individual decision-making, the social interaction that an individual has (online and offline), and then finally on other external factors like the market within which the individual makes the resulting economic decisions.

Neuroscientists, and especially evolutionary neuroscientists, see the brain as the result of a long series of evolutionary **adaptations** leading to a set of domain-specific computational systems. These systems have evolved to solve recurring problems – originally these problems were characterised by survival problems (finding food, evading predators, cooperating with tribe members, and so forth) and reproduction problems (finding a suitable mate, protection and feeding of children, and so forth). These problem-solving systems act to adapt behaviour in order to improve the individual's chances of surviving, prospering and reproducing (Garcia and Saad 2008). In the modern world, the same systems are applied to apparently new problems – career progression, financial management, learning to operate a smartphone and many other tasks that did not exist when our ancestors evolved on the African savannah.

Elasticity
The degree to which demand is affected by other factors, for example price changes

Neuroscience
The study of the ways in which the human brain works

Adaptation
The process by which goals are influenced by contextual issues

Evolution is, in general, a very slow process, and in the case of human beings it has been further hindered by our dominance of the environment: people are less likely to make fatal mistakes and thus remove themselves from the gene pool.

If neuro-economics can successfully map brain activity onto economic behaviour, then neuroscientists hope to explain consumer behaviour in terms of evolutionary and survival factors. As yet, the discipline is in its infancy, but neuroscientists have already identified some of the mechanisms by which people are affected by packaging (Stoll et al. 2008), and have identified a dedicated response to celebrity-based advertising (Gakhal and Senior 2008). Work on neuro-economics has also recently been extended to looking at the irrationality of the voter during political elections (Chavaglia et al. 2015).

SUMMARY

Consumer decision-making is therefore not isolated from all other human behaviour. People try to behave in ways that enable them to enjoy their lives, to relate to their friends and families, and to contribute to society at large. In almost all cases this behaviour is likely to involve consumption of products and services produced by other people: this is the province of consumer behaviour.

Consumer behaviour studies derive from many different academic disciplines, as well as from direct studies by marketing academics. As a field of study, it has an appeal to most of us because it is, after all, about people. For marketing practitioners, understanding the ways in which people make decisions about their purchasing behaviour is clearly of crucial importance in planning almost every aspect of managing the exchange process.

KEY POINTS

- The study of consumer behaviour is largely derived from other disciplines.
- Consumer behaviour is at the centre of all marketing decision-making.
- Relationships are harder to establish in business-to-consumer situations than in business-to-business situations.
- Psychology is about internal thought processes; sociology is about behaviour within groups.
- Neuroscience is the study of the ways in which the human brain works; anthropology is the study of what makes us human.
- Economics is the study of demand.
- Exchange always makes both parties better off.
- 'Luxury' and 'necessity' are subjective terms: they have no objective reality.

HOW TO IMPRESS YOUR EXAMINER

Relate your answers to the real world. Use examples – this shows that you understand the theory, and can put it into a business context. While you are reading the book, try to think of examples of your own – everybody else will know the examples from the book, the examiner included!

REVIEW QUESTIONS

1. How might marketers use knowledge of indifference curves to affect consumer choices?
2. Would you expect salt to have an inelastic demand curve, or an elastic demand curve? Why?
3. If a product has an inelastic demand curve, what does that imply for marketers?
4. If a product has an elastic demand curve, what are the implications for marketers?
5. How might group behaviour affect purchasing behaviour?
6. Why does exchange always make both parties better off?
7. What is the importance of the concept of perception to marketers?
8. Why is learning important to marketers?
9. Why are customers more important to a firm than, say, employees?

CASE STUDY: TRADE IN EUROPE

Even in prehistoric times, people traded with each other. In the English Lake District a stone axe factory was discovered in the 1930s: the factory, dating from around 4000 BC, produced axes for trade. The axes were sold throughout the UK and Ireland, and some were found as far away as the south of France.

By Phoenician times, trade had increased dramatically. Around 700 BC, Phoenician traders plied the Mediterranean in sophisticated merchant ships, exchanging sandalwood, cedar, pine, fine linen, wine, salt and dried figs in exchange for raw materials such as ivory, papyrus, silk, amber, ostrich eggs and metals. It was the Phoenicians who introduced wine into Egypt, and some successful Phoenician merchants had as many as 50 ships. Naturally, they guarded their trade routes jealously, so they had a military navy to protect their merchant vessels. Phoenician traders also engaged in cross-trade, buying spices and silk from the Far East from Arab caravans and selling them on into Greece and Spain. Some scholars say that the Phoenicians ventured out of the Mediterranean to Britain and even the Americas in search of new trade opportunities. But by far the greatest empire was that developed and conquered by the Persians, from a humble start in what we now know as Southern Iran. From the 6th century BC onwards, the Persians dominated the neighbouring lands from as far east as the Himalayas to the shores of the Aegean sea and Egypt. They had a very welcoming attitude towards new ideas and practices, and were very willing to adapt their own. In fact, Herodotus once wrote, 'The Persians are greatly inclined to adopt foreign customs'. Of course, such a vast empire would need a very slick administrative system, and indeed the Persians had designed one together with a road network which spanned more than 1,600 miles. Nevertheless, the swiftness of their operations meant that they were able to transmit messages across this range (Human Rights Watch 2014). This was also largely due to the fact that the people in charge were highly educated, and meticulously detailed with their recording of data – which we would today refer to as 'big data' – administrative details, payments to workers, information on quality of products, quantity of goods being bought and sold, maintenance and repair schedules, and strategic planning.

In Roman times, the demand for exotic animals for the Coliseum shows meant that traders had to capture and ship wild animals from Africa. Giraffes, hippos, rhinoceroses and lions were all rounded up and shipped across the Mediterranean. The trade grew so much that it led to the extinction if the Libyan lion altogether. (The Romans' environmental record was poor at best – they also created the Sahara Desert by over-farming.)

By the 16th century trade was becoming worldwide. Better ships (mainly being built in India by Persian migrants called Parsees), better navigation and the need to find new markets led to a rapid expansion of exploration – the Far East and the Americas became accessible to European ships in search of precious metals, jewels, spices and exotic foods such as tea, coffee, potatoes and tomatoes. Trade within Europe became taxed and regulated, leading to widespread

Source: whole_world_land_oceans_12000.jpg licensed with PD-US Gov-NASA

smuggling: governments sought to protect their own industries and farmers by imposing heavy taxes on imports, but even this could not prevent trade. In India, the Parsee merchants became a valuable 'conduit' between Britain and the Far East, along the Silk Route. In Britain, wine and brandy were smuggled in from France, while cotton and wool were smuggled into France from Britain. This two-way trade had to exist since there was no way of converting French money into British money, except as gold.

During the late 18th and early 19th century, Britain had a near-monopoly on industrial, mass-produced goods. British factories could produce far more than the domestic market could consume, so the surplus was exported. Since factory-produced goods were vastly cheaper than their hand-made equivalents, there were large profits to be made from international trade. In this case, Britain built an empire on the basis of trading manufactured goods for raw materials. As other European countries industrialised, further tariff barriers were erected, restricting trade: after the First World War, these barriers became extremely onerous, to the point where trade became almost impossible and industry stagnated throughout Europe. The Second World War changed things again, catastrophically: when the war was over, France and Germany agreed the first of the trade agreements which would eventually result in the creation of the European Union.

Currently, trade between the member states of the EU is without barriers (apart from a very few exceptions). Virtually anything which can be sold in one member state can be sold in any other, and there is free movement of people and capital as well. However, following an election promise, the Conservative government gave the British people a referendum in June 2016 and an opportunity to vote for whether they wished to 'Remain' in the EU or 'Leave'. 'Brexit' won by 52% to 48%.

This is not legally binding until the British Parliament ratifies it and invokes 'Article 50 of the Lisbon Treaty' (the formal legal process of withdrawal). But even without

Brexit

Merges the words **Br**itain and **exit** to get Brexit, and used to signify Britain's exit from the EU this happening, there is much political, social and economic unrest both in the UK and in mainland Europe. It centres on Britain losing its place in the world's largest market. Sterling (the British currency) has fallen sharply, trading markets like the FTSE have reacted with steep fluctuations (the Royal Bank of Scotland lost value of £8 billion), racial tensions have increased in various communities up and down the country, the Conservative party is in the middle of a leadership contest, the Labour party has many internal splits and thus it is questionable whether it is currently an effective opposition. In the spirit of preserving both the integrity of the EU and the interests of the remaining countries, Brussels has understandably already sidelined Britain. 'Economies of scale' may no longer apply as Britain will have to negotiate many bilateral trade deals with individual countries. Part of the problem is that prior to the referendum, no one has set out any guiding principles for negotiations with the rest of the EU.

If Britain remains within the single market, it would almost certainly retain free movement rights allowing UK citizens to work in the EU and vice versa. But if the British government opts to impose work permit restrictions, as the UKIP wants, then other countries could reciprocate, meaning that Britons would have to apply for visas to work – thus restricting the free movement of people. The bottom line is that both the collegiality with our EU neighbours and the subsequent trade in Europe has made us wealthy, not just financially but in the broadest sense of the word. However, the referendum has also given all of us a lot more to think about. After nearly 4 millennia of trading with our closest neighbours, our lives may have been richer and we have greater wealth (all through consumer choices and trade), but Britain's future and indeed the future of the EU is now uncertain and insecure.

CASE STUDY QUESTIONS

1. What sociological changes have come about due to trade in Europe?

2. How does trade affect anthropological questions?

3. How did price competition help the rise of the British Empire?

4. Why is trade so important in the European Union?

5. What are the possible effects of Brexit if it was ratified by the British government?

FURTHER READING

Economics by Richard Lipsey and Alec Chrystal (Oxford: Oxford University Press, 2011) is a comprehensive text covering all aspects of economics. It is written in a clear, straightforward style and covers the ground well.

The Silk Roads: A New History of the World by Peter Frankopan (London: Bloomsbury Publishing, 2015) is a book which delves deep into history, religion, economics, international affairs, and investigates the root of some of the societal situations that we find ourselves in today. He concludes by saying that 'Western fashion houses like Prada, Burberry and Lousie Vuitton are building huge stores and seeing spectacular sales figures across the Persian Gulf, Russia, China and the Far East (so that with delicious irony, fine fabrics and silks are being sold back to the place where silk and fine fabrics originated)'.

Anthropology: The Basics by Peter Metcalf (Abingdon: Routledge, 2005) is a fascinating introduction to the subject. There are plenty of examples, some of which you can try yourself, and some excellent in-depth looks at cultural issues.

Sociology by Anthony Giddens (Cambridge: Polity Press, 2009) is now in its 6th edition. The latest version includes a chapter on war and terrorism, and it is jargon-free and comprehensive.

Games People Play: The Psychology of Human Relationships by Eric Berne (Harmondsworth: Penguin Books, 2010) is a humorous way of looking at the ways in which people relate to each other. Berne describes the various interactions in terms of games, with winners and losers and rules. This is not a serious textbook, but it is a fun read and it offers some entertaining insights into human interaction.

Freakonomics: A Rogue Economist Explores the Hidden Side of Everything by Steven D. Levitt and Stephen J. Dubner (Ontario: Harper Perennial, 2005) is another popular-science book. It's very much a light read, and the academic rigour is definitely questionable – but what the authors are looking to do is to shake up some traditional thinking, and examine some economic behaviour from a different angle (for example, they show that New York drug dealers would earn more working in minimum-wage jobs). Not to be taken too seriously, but good fun nonetheless.

REFERENCES

Bennett, P.D. (1995) *Dictionary of Marketing Terms.* Chicago IL: American Marketing Association.

Blackwell, R.D., Miniard, P.W. and Engel, J.F. (2001) *Consumer Behaviour*, 9th edn. Mason, OH: Southwestern.

Booms, B.H. and Bitner, M.J. (1981) Marketing strategies and organisational structures for service firms. In J.H. Donnelly and W.R. George (eds), *Marketing of Services.* Chicago, IL: American Marketing Association, pp. 47–52.

Chavaglia, J.N., Filipe, J.A., Ferreira, M.A.M. and Caleiro, A. (2015) Neuroeconomics: decisions in extreme situations. *EC Business Management*, 1 (1): 14–21.

Christopher, M., Ballantyne, D. and Payne, A. (1991) *Relationship Marketing* (Oxford: Butterworth–Heinemann).

Davies, A. and Elliott, R. (2006) The evolution of the empowered consumer. *European Journal of Marketing*, 40 (9/10): 1106–21.

Felicia, P. (2011) *Handbook of Research on Improving Learning and Motivation* (Hershey: IGI Global).

Gakhal, B. and Senior, C. (2008) Examining the influence of fame in the presence of beauty: an electrodermal neuromarketing study. *Journal of Consumer Behaviour*, 7 (4/5): 331–41.

Garcia, J.R. and Saad, G. (2008) Evolutionary neuromarketing: Darwinizing the neuroimaging paradigm for consumer behaviour. *Journal of Consumer Behaviour*, 7 (4/5): 397–414.

Hewer, P. and Brownlie, D. (2010) On market forces and adjustments: acknowledging customer creativity through the aesthetics of debadging. *Journal of Marketing Management* 26 (5&6): 428–40.

Hui, L. and Subramony, M. (2008) Employee customer orientation in manufacturing organisations: joint influences of customer proximity and the senior leadership team. *Journal of Applied Psychology*, 93 (2): 317–28.

Human Rights Watch (2014) *World Report*. www.hrw.org/world-report/2014 (accessed 24 October 2015).

Mady, T.T. (2011) Sentiment toward marketing: should we care about consumer alienation and readiness to use technology? *Journal of Consumer Behaviour*, 10 (4): 192–204.

Mittal, B. (2006) I, me, and mine: how products become consumers' extended selves. *Journal of Consumer Behaviour*, 5: 550–62.

Richins, M. (2001) Consumer behaviour as a social science. *Advances in Consumer Research*, 28: 1–5.

Ryan, C., McLoughlin, D. and Keating, A. (2006) Tribespotting: a semiotic analysis of the role of consumption in the tribes of *Trainspotting*. *Journal of Consumer Behaviour*, 5 (September–October): 431–41.

Shaw, D., Newholme, T. and Dickinson, R. (2006) Consumption as voting: an exploration of consumer empowerment. *European Journal of Marketing*, 40 (9/10): 1049–67.

Stoll, M., Baecke, S. and Kenning, P. (2008) What they see is what they get? An fMRI-study on neural correlates of attractive packaging. *Journal of Consumer Behaviour*, 7 (4/5): 342–59.

Urban, G.L., Sultan, F. and Qualls, W.J. (2000) Placing trust at the center of your Internet strategy. *MIT Sloan Management Review*, 42 (1): 39–48

Vargo, S.L. and Lusch, R.F. (2004) Evolving to a new dominant logic for marketing. *Journal of Marketing*, 68 (January): 1–17.

Wagner-Tsukamoto, S. and Tadajewski, M. (2006) Cognitive anthropology and the problem-solving behaviour of green consumers. *Journal of Consumer Behaviour*, 5 (May–June): 235–44.

WEBSITES

NASP – National Association of Shoplifting Prevention (2015) *Report on Statistics*, www.shopliftingprevention.org/what-we-do/learning-resource-center/statistics/ (accessed 1 February 2015).

National Customer Satisfaction Index UK, http://ncsiuk.com/ (accessed 1 February 2015).

MORE ONLINE

For additional materials that support this chapter and your learning, please visit:
https://study.sagepub.com/sethnaandblythe

CHAPTER 2

CONSUMER BEHAVIOUR AND THE MARKETING MIX

LEARNING OBJECTIVES

After reading this chapter you should be able to:

* Show how price goes beyond purchase cost.
* Explain how price relates to what people will pay.
* Explain the motivators for shopping behaviour.
* Explain the weak and strong theories of advertising.
* Explain the role of interaction in advertising effectiveness.
* Describe the advantages of radio, cinema and ambient advertising.
* Explain the use and effectiveness of ambient advertising.
* Explain the role of social interaction in evaluating services.
* Describe the importance of getting service levels right.
* Show how physical evidence is used as a surrogate for judging quality of services.

INTRODUCTION

Most of this book is concerned with the theories behind consumer and buyer behaviour, and the influences on their decision-making in purchasing and consumption situations. Thus, marketers need to develop practical marketing programmes with consumers in mind, whether it be for launching new websites/products, expanding existing markets, or raising the profile of brands. The question they must continually ask is, 'do we know how and why our consumers make decisions?'.

The analysis of decision-making from a marketing perspective has, for many years, used the 4P model (product, price, place and promotion). During the 1980s this very *product centric* categorisation was expanded to include a further three factors – people, process and physical evidence (Booms and Bitner 1981) which further took account of services that organisations provided.

Although the *expanded* 7P model is probably far from comprehensive in terms of explaining what marketers do, it does provide a degree of structure and is a convenient 'shorthand' device. There are, of course, other more recent models such as the 'New Marketing DNA' by Harrigan and Hulbert (2011). This model differs from the 7Ps model in that it directly takes into account co-creation of value. This customer-led approach provides prominent and valuable customer insights that enable an organisation to differentiate the marketing strategy by providing real value as opposed to just products or services. This value is often driven by the data that organisations collect from many sources: there is so much of it that it is sometimes referred to as 'big data'. This brings with it its own problems; the gathering, analysing and dissemination of results of such data sets is a big task within many organisations.

SEGMENTATION

Market segmentation is the process of identifying a group of consumers with similar needs and producing an offering that will meet those needs at a profit (financial or otherwise). It has a simple basis in logic: it is that no single product will appeal to all consumers.

Terms such as mass marketing have previously attempted to describe the production and subsequent sale of something that virtually everybody would want and in such large quantities that the production costs could be minimised and thus the price kept low. This approach appealed to production engineers, but is virtually impossible to carry out in the 21st century because people prefer a more individual, tailored product that suits their needs more precisely; what Yasumuro (2015) calls 'adaptable marketing'. A large part of the perspectives that are taken by 'adaptation' are actually embedded in segmentation.

Traditionally, segmentation operates at the following three levels:

1. *Segmented markets*. Here the organisation seeks to find groups of people with similar needs. This is a compromise position for both the producer and the customer: for producers, the production runs will be shorter than would be the case for mass marketing, and for the consumer the product is unlikely to be exactly what is wanted.

2. Niche marketing. Niche marketers focus on one subgroup within the larger segments. Some niche marketers concentrate on a product category rather than on a specific type of consumer – Smiggle and Claire's Accessories are examples. At first sight this appears to be a product-orientated paradigm, but in fact it is consumer-orientated in that it reduces search time for people looking for the specific product category. This type of niche marketing is the direct opposite from the department store or supermarket approach to retailing: instead of stocking a few products in a wide range of categories, niche marketers stock a wide range of products in a single category.

3. Micro marketing. This is the practice of tailoring products and marketing programmes to suit specific individuals and circumstances. Even mass-production operations

---

Big data

Big data is all about managing and maintaining high-volume, high-velocity and high-variety data sets that may, once analysed, uncover associations, patterns and possible trends, especially relating to consumer behaviour and interactions

Mass marketing

A situation in which a standardised product is purchased by a very large number of people

Niche marketing

Targeting a small group of customers

Micro marketing

Those elements of the environment that affect the individual firm such as motor manufacturers can offer new-car buyers a very wide range of options. Offering options is something that Dell Computers is very good at. Each computer is built to an individual customer's specification, using plug-in components. Mass customisation is the ability to produce individual, custom-made products using mass-production techniques, for example producing prescription spectacles on-site, as Vision Express does. Customers are able to have an eye test, choose frames and walk out with the finished spectacles within an hour. In many cases, however, people are not prepared to pay the increased cost of such service (Bardacki and Whitelock 2004). With the advent of 3D printing, customers can achieve the ultimate in personalisation. Retailers such as Asda (a subsidiary of Walmart) in the UK now offer customers the chance to be photographed in a pod where cameras capture between 900 and 1,500 frames which are then stitched together by software to create a 3D image which is then 'printed' into a ceramic figurine; a 'mini me' (www.asda-photo.co.uk/bookings/1-3d-full-body-scan). It would be hard to imagine anything more personalised.

Even though marketers now are able to treat some consumers more as individuals, with individual wants and needs, in most industries we are not yet at the point where we can (or can afford to) provide individual attention for individual consumers. We therefore need to identify groups of people with similar interests and design our approach to fit those groups. In large markets such as the USA (298 million consumers), the European Union (457 million consumers) or Japan (127 million consumers), there are often enough consumers with a specific need in common for manufacturers to be able to obtain the economies of scale enjoyed by British manufacturers in the mid-19th century. For example, Amazon's CEO Jeff Bezos said at the company's annual shareholder meeting in Seattle in 2014 that it had added 30 million new customers bringing its total active user base to 244 million. In 2014 Apple had approximately 800 million iTunes accounts while PayPal were lagging behind in the consumer account stakes with only 110 million accounts. This is what segmentation seeks to achieve.

There are many bases for segmenting markets. Organisations often divide customers into a range of demographic segments. Well known examples of such segmentation categories are: using age profiles (e.g. 18–35s, 40–50, seniors, etc.), gender profiles (e.g. single women, lesbian gay bisexual transgender (LGBT)), societal profiles (e.g. middle class, working class, millennials), income profiles (e.g. high net worth individuals, state benefit seekers), or perhaps a combination of some of these (for example, the estimated purchasing power of China's LGBT community is USD 470 billion). From a consumer behaviour viewpoint, consumers are changing fast, and demographic segmentation as a way of targeting customers is proving to be less reliable than in the past. More effective segmentation approaches are those with a psychological and/or behavioural perspective. Take, for example, Asian consumers who are currently being delighted with the reinvention of *Wayang Kulit*, a fading ancient art of shadow puppetry, but with a modern twist; instead of narrating the story of epic historical battles, modern audiences are shown a version of Star Wars Episode IV, complete with cut-outs of all the characters.

PSYCHOGRAPHIC SEGMENTATION

Personality characteristics appear, at first sight, to be an extremely useful way of segmenting markets because an individual's personality changes relatively slowly. Unfortunately, in the past it has been difficult to measure personality traits on a mass scale, so it is difficult to identify groups of people with similar traits. For example, an insurance company might like to target people who are excessively afraid of burglary (physical or cyber), but who are also wealthy and have many possessions. Such people might be expected to be careful about locking their houses, would have burglar alarms, and would also invest in security locks and cyber security systems. The result would be a group of people who are unlikely to make a claim against their policies – the ideal customers for insurance companies. There is, however, no easy way to target such a group: there is no single advertising medium directed at these people. In practice the only realistic way of approaching these groups is by allowing them to self-select against a mass marketing communications approach, which is expensive and wasteful. Our hypothetical insurance company would need to model the product's use using actors who portray the particular personality traits that are of interest. Conversely, technology (and the data it can generate) has enabled similar scenarios to be acted upon. Insurance companies view all new and 'young drivers' as a very high risk considering their lack of experience and therefore usually charge an extortionate price for car insurance. To combat this blanket attitude towards young drivers, car insurance companies such as ingenie® fit a recording device (a black box) into the vehicle which then treats the driver as an individual, collecting and building up a picture of the individual's driving style (speed, acceleration, braking and cornering). Every ten days the driver is 'scored' out of 100, and feedback messages are communicated by text messages and email. Essentially, the higher the individual's score, the less they pay for insurance.

A potentially very important segmentation variable has emerged in recent years. Segmentation by environmental attitude may be a good predictor of people's purchasing behaviour, and several attempts have been made to categorise people this way. For example, one study found that 30% of Americans are indifferent to environmental issues, whereas the other 70% have pro-environmental attitudes, of varying strengths (Englis and Bamossy 2010). The degree to which people act on these attitudes is, of course, another story; as we will see in Chapter 10, intended behaviour (conation) does not necessarily result in actual behaviour. However, in a study conducted in Mexico, Husted et al. (2014) found support for the idea that as attitudes become more pro-environmental, they more than proportionately boost the consumer's willingness to pay a premium (or marginal WTP) for environmentally certified products.

Marginal willingness to pay (WTP)

A consumer's willingness to pay a premium price for environmentally certified products

Alternatively, people can be divided into groups according to their lifestyles. Lifestyles are both created by products, and dictate which products will be bought and used; someone who owns a penthouse flat along the River Thames in London has a different psychology (and lifestyle) from someone who chooses to buy a smallholding in Oxfordshire and be self-sufficient, but both dwellings are products as well as lifestyle determinants. Incidentally, it is likely that the cost of each type of home will be similar: the choice is about lifestyle, not about financial considerations.

Lifestyle segmentation has the major advantage that it relates directly to purchasing behaviour. It has been said that marketing delivers a lifestyle, so considering consumers on the basis of their chosen lifestyles is certainly logical. It is relevant for marketers in Hong Kong to investigate the effects of a decrease in the proportion of married women from 65% to 55%, as more women are opting to stay single (Census and Statistics Department, Hong Kong, 2015). The VALS model discussed later in Chapter 6 is an example of lifestyle segmentation: consumers are divided into nine lifestyle positions, determined by their attitudes to other people and (to an extent) by their level of wealth.

BEHAVIOURAL SEGMENTATION

According to a Kantar Worldpanel Survey in 2014 (Kantar Report 2014), the growth in sales of male grooming products in Asia is outpacing that of beauty products for women with 62% of men disagreeing with the idea that a groomed appearance is 'just a woman thing'. So behaviour can be a useful and reliable way of segmenting. At its most obvious, if we are marketing to these men who buy male grooming products we are not interested in how old they are, what their views are on strong drink, or where they live. All we care about is that they go shopping (online or offline), and might therefore be customers for a new type of moisturiser. Accessing the segment would be easily undertaken by advertising in marketing communications media which are read by men. At a deeper level we might be interested in such issues as where they buy their products, how much they usually spend on a moisturiser, what kind of look they are after, and so forth, but this information is easily obtained through questionnaire-type surveys.

The main behavioural bases for segmentation, summarised in Figure 2.1, are as follows:

- *Benefits sought.* Different people look for different things in each product purchase. Sampson (1992) divided people into three groups: functionality seekers who look for the simple, practical aspects of ownership; image seekers, who look for products which will enhance their self-image in various ways; and pleasure seekers, who look for the hedonic aspects of owning products. For example, someone who buys a car as simple transportation for themselves, their family and their luggage would be classified as a functionality seeker. Someone who buys an upmarket car for its prestige value, to show off to the neighbours, is an image seeker, while someone who simply enjoys driving or looks for an exceptionally comfortable car is a pleasure seeker.

- *Purchase occasion.* Some products are bought on a regular basis, whereas others are bought as an occasional treat. More importantly, the same product might be a regular purchase for some people, but a treat for others – for example, someone on a strict diet may only buy a chocolate bar very occasionally, whereas someone else might regard a chocolate bar as a normal element in the weekday lunchbox. Likewise, 60 years ago chicken was regarded as an occasional Sunday lunch treat (beef was the usual Sunday lunch roast meal in the UK) but intensive farming has brought the relative price of chicken down to the point where it is one of the cheapest meats available. In the 1950s people ate chicken either because they were wealthy enough to do so or because they considered the extra cost to be worthwhile – as is the case with lamb in the 21st century. Another aspect of purchase occasion relates to gift-giving: the vast majority of sales of aftershave are made to women. Relatively little aftershave is bought by men for their own use. Purchase occasion might also relate to situational factors: buying a new car battery may come about because of a growing awareness that the existing battery is getting old, although it is more likely to be as a result of a sudden failure of the battery far from home. Different versions of the same product might also be purchased at different times – someone travelling for business purposes may decide to stay in a four-star business-class hotel, but when on holiday might prefer an old bed-and-breakfast in a village because such places have more character. Going to a restaurant because one is too tired to cook results in a different choice of restaurant from that chosen when celebrating a wedding anniversary or a birthday. Even the choice between a romantic restaurant with cosy corners (for a wedding anniversary or first date) and a lively restaurant with entertainment (for celebrating a birthday with friends) is an example of purchase occasion differences.

- *Purchase behaviour* relates to time of purchase, place of purchase, quantities bought on each occasion, and degree of willingness to buy innovative products. For example, books might be bought from a variety of outlets: a bookshop, second-hand from a charity shop, online from retailers such as Amazon, or even in a street market. Each type of behaviour relates to the consumer concerned, but may not relate to other characteristics: someone might enjoy shopping online, whereas another person might prefer the bargain-hunting aspects of browsing in a second-hand bookshop. The same person might enjoy both ways of buying books – online for practical, work-related purchases, second-hand for personal books for leisure reading. The individual's motivation may or may not be concerned with saving money; many people shop online because it is more convenient than shopping in retail stores (for example, because the individual lives in a remote area, is housebound or their working life makes it difficult to get to a bricks-and-mortar retailer). Brand loyalty is also an element in purchase behaviour: high involvement with the brand means that the marketer will try to identify and recruit those customers, whereas brand switchers – those customers who are unlikely to stay 'loyal' to a particular brand – can be lured by sales promotions.

- *Usage.* Some customers use the product more frequently and in higher quantities than do others. Users are usually divided into heavy users, medium users, light users, ex-users and non-users. The aim of marketers is to move people from being non-users to being heavy users, if possible. Non-users are not, of course, consumers of the product but they may present an opportunity if the product is appropriate for their needs – clearly there will always be some people who will never buy the product under any circumstances. Light users and medium users can be encouraged to use more of the product, and although this is probably a great deal easier than recruiting new customers most firms still spend the greater part of their effort on recruitment rather than development. A neglected area of marketing has been customer win-back, which is the re-enrolling of former customers. These people represent a good opportunity – they already know the company and its products, and in many cases defected to another company for fairly trivial reasons. In many cases, firms seek to recruit heavy users from their competitors, but this can be a dangerous tactic if it provokes heavy competitive responses.

- *Buyer readiness stage.* Some people may be on the verge of buying the product, whereas others may never have heard of it. Still others may have an interest in the product but do not have any money, others might be aware of the product but are not yet interested, others might be interested but do not at present have a need for the product, and so forth. Marketers need to be aware of these stages and be prepared to act at the appropriate time: for example, a couple who have just bought their first house will not currently be in the market to buy another larger house, but very well might be in five to seven years' time, when perhaps

FIGURE 2.1 Behavioural bases for segmentation

they have started a family or are earning more money. Contacting people at the wrong time (when they are not ready to buy) is irritating for the customer and a waste of resources for the company, whereas contacting people at the right time (when they are considering another purchase) is helpful and productive in terms of generating business.

- *Attitude towards the product.* In some cases, the non-user's attitude towards the product is so hostile that there is really no point in trying to change it. Political parties know that many of their supporters will be loyal no matter what happens, and that the same is true of their opposition. However, politics has changed so much over the past 20 years that now nearly every major political party concentrates their efforts on the 'floating voters' who might be persuaded one way or the other.

- *Media usage.* The types of media the individual consumes are clearly of interest since (as marketers) we need to communicate with our target audience. Additionally, the quantity of media consumed is relevant – an individual who surfs several news portals on a smartphone (e.g. SkyNews, China Daily, News India, Russia Today), or who watches a wide range of TV channels, will be exposed to a great deal more advertising than one who rarely opens a newspaper or watches very little TV.

- *Preferences.* There are a number of drivers which affect consumer preference. The pace of change, fluidity within society, ready access to information, an efficient market place, and of course the democratisation of innovation. Technology brings us the ability to have access to the same information the world over; this means exposure to the same products and the same brands. This has inevitably meant that large swathes of the world are becoming increasingly progressive in their outlook to life and consumption. This is very evident online with people using social media to craft their own identities and leave behind their unique digital footprint.

Segmenting markets according to the behaviour of the customers within them makes perfect sense since our interest in customers lies ultimately in how they behave. What people do is a great deal more important than who they are or what they think, at least in terms of marketing.

Life events can have a profound effect on brand preferences (Mathur et al. 2003). Andreason (1984) first examined the various changes that occur in a person's life and how they affect brand preferences. Adjustments to new life situations brought about by moving to a new place, bereavement, a major conflict with a family member, a change of job or financial status, and so forth may lead to a change of brand. Life events and life status changes might prove better predictors of behaviour and hence be a better base for segmentation, but it is hard to see how such a segmentation base could be quantified or the actual segments identified.

PRODUCTS

A product is a bundle of benefits, but those benefits are likely to go far beyond the physical item itself. The overt features and benefits of a product are based on the individual's cognitive faculties (to do with mental processes), but many aspects of the product will appeal to the individual's affective (to do with emotion) and conative (to do with behaviour) aspects. The following aspects of products go beyond the rational decision-making process:

- *Branding.* The brand may increase the observability of the product and strengthen the individual's self-image. Using the right brand of mobile phone, wearing the right brand of clothing and driving the right brand of car are all ways of telling the world who one is: getting it wrong can lead to at best a social *faux pas* or at worst a social disaster. The brand of the product appears to be more important than the corporate brand, at least on packaging (Laforet 2011): this may be due to the greater immediacy of the product brand, and for the tendency for packaging to become the 'enabler' of people becoming involved with the brand.

- *Styling.* The appearance of many products adds to the hedonic aspects of the product. For example, a sports car may stand out for its styling rather than for its road performance or brand. Even the appearance of the packaging affects people's perception of the product: since people process positive information differently from the way they process negative information, unattractive packages register in the same part of the brain as unfair offers or disgusting pictures (Stoll et al. 2008).

- *Manufacturer's reputation.* Although reputation is often part of the cognitive aspects of ownership, reputation also colours affective aspects. For example, a manufacturer might have a good reputation for socially responsible business practices, or may have been exceptionally helpful on a previous occasion. People will form a view about a company's ethical credentials based on relatively little information (Brunk 2010). This makes control of corporate reputation a rather challenging proposition.

The affective aspects of purchase often outweigh the cognitive. For example, motorcycle manufacturers know that they are largely selling on a stereotypical self-image platform: older men often buy the bikes to re-live a dream of youth. This has virtually nothing to do with the practical need for economical and, compared to the motorcar, often more convenient mode of transportation which was the motorcycle's original reason for existence.

Being the first to own a new product can be a powerful motivation for an individual. Again, this can be an esteem issue: showing off to one's friends can be impressive. Equally there is a degree of pleasure in just owning something that very few other people have – *exclusivity* is a compelling factor not only in buying new products, but inevitably also in buying expensive products. Buying a 'tailor-made' fitted suit has a persuasive appeal: tailors on Savile Row, London offer an exclusive service to the capital's elite. The result has been an explosion in mass customisation in recent years, accompanied by a sharp rise in subjectivity (Addis and Holbrook 2001).

From the viewpoint of a supplier, offering a product that appeals to self-image, self-esteem and aesthetic needs is at least as important as offering one that meets practical needs.

The brand is an important factor in judging products. Bengtsson (2003) has suggested that the personification of brands by consumers is a result of marketing activities, specifically the discourse from marketers about relationship marketing. This may or may not be true, but it raises interesting issues about how marketers may be able to manipulate opinion. Let us remember that brands are often a reflection of what people consider to be social norms. In many parts of the world these social norms are dissipating and giving way to newer non-traditional lifestyles and the brands with which people interact need to reflect these diverse lifestyles. However, people may therefore conceive a dislike of some brands, sometimes because of what the brand symbolises (for example, a global brand might represent cultural imperialism) or because of a dislike of the organisation rather than the actual product characteristics (Dalli et al. 2006). For this reason organisations would be well advised to avoid manipulative behaviour. For instance in many parts of Asia, cultural traditions are being both preserved and reinvented (as we saw early with the *Wayang Kulit*) and (in a similar fashion to the notion of 'shabby chic' furniture), what we may be seeing is 'heritage chic'.

Trust has sometimes been engendered by carrying out socially responsible activities such as sponsoring charities. However, companies that carry out socially responsible initiatives that do not appear to have any connection with the firm are often distrusted – perhaps because people perceive it as a 'tick the box' exercise or an attempt to 'whitewash' the firm (Becker-Olsen and Cudmore 2004). During a brand crisis (for example, a major accident on an airline) the news media can amplify the crisis and destroy trust, even when the consumer has direct experience of using the brand (Yannopolou et al. 2011).

PRICE

The **price** of something is the total cost of adopting the product. This includes the purchase price, the cost of switching from an existing product to the new product and the cost of maintaining and using the product. The balance between these various elements of the total cost will vary from one product to another, of course, but the astute supplier will recognise that (in some cases) prices can be adjusted in one area to take account of costs in another.

Costs to the customer include internal costs (learning to use the product, time spent buying it and getting it to work properly, disposing of the product after use), acquisition costs (purchase price, delivery, installation, etc.) and costs related to risk. The total of these costs will be taken into account when assessing whether the benefits outweigh the price. Note that not all these costs can be expressed in financial terms, and not all of the price asked by the supplier is monetary. For example, a supplier

Price

That which is given in exchange for receiving the benefits of a product

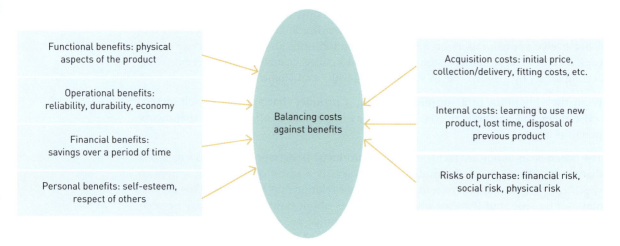

FIGURE 2.2 Cost–benefit trade-offs

might expect a customer to accept a greater part of the risk in exchange for a lower price, as is the case when someone buys a 'standby' theatre ticket. In exchange for a lower price, the customer accepts that the ticket may not be honoured at the desired time – the supplier has traded off the risk of not being able to sell the seat against getting a lower monetary price.

As can be seen in Figure 2.2, customer benefits fall into functional, operational, financial and personal categories. The functional are those that come to mind most readily, related to the physical aspects of the product – these often relate closely to the individual's cognition of the product. In the longer term, operational benefits such as reliability and durability, financial aspects such as savings made over the period of ownership, and personal benefits such as feelings of well-being and of ownership, will assume greater importance.

Consumers need to balance these factors carefully in order to arrive at a final evaluation of the product's worth. Provided the benefits exceed the costs, the consumer will be happy with the outcome; if the costs exceed the benefits, the consumer will not be happy with the outcome. In the long term, marketers should seek to ensure that benefits always outweigh costs, but either side of the equation can be adjusted: if the marketer can offer greater benefits without increasing the cost to the consumer, this is a valid way of achieving value for money. If benefits cannot be improved, then the only way to improve value for money is to reduce the costs – not necessarily the initial acquisition price, but (possibly) the other costs.

PRICE SENSITIVITY

Establishing the needs of each target segment is a precursor to developing appropriate pricing for each segment that the organisation is trying to target. In some cases, a product can be customised to meet the specific needs of a segment and priced at a premium specifically because of the extra cost involved in customisation. In setting prices for specific segments, the Chief Marketing Officer (CMO) must estimate the price sensitivity of that particular market segment. Dolan (1995) listed factors that

TABLE 2.1 Factors affecting customer price sensitivity

Economics
• Percentage of total expense
• Type of consumer
• Level of involvement
Search and usage
• Cost of information search
• Ease of comparing competitive alternatives
• Switching costs
Competition
• Differentiation
• Perception of price

affect customer price sensitivity: see Table 2.1. While communications technology has played a part in the ways consumers interact with each factor, the fundamentals of these are all as true and relevant today as they were in 1995.

The major categories are customer economics, search and usage, and competition. Customers will be more sensitive if the percentage cost of the particular item is large in comparison to the total expense that the customer is making to achieve a particular end. Should the item be of extreme importance to the consumer, price sensitivity will tend to decline because reliability becomes paramount. Of course, some people are simply more frugal than others and therefore sensitive to prices across the board: some students are more frugal in their student lifestyles, for instance drinking habits (Rose et al. 2010). Equally, in times of economic austerity, even the most loyal customers can be swayed by price promotions (Rajagopal 2008).

Reviewing the search and usage category, customers will be more price-sensitive if information search is easy and cheap, and competitive offerings are easily compared. This factor has been exploited successfully by comparison websites. Price sensitivity is also increased substantially where switching costs are low: switching costs are all the costs associated with changing from one particular product or service to another. For example, a consumer might become persuaded that having a business account with one high street bank is better than continuing the relationship with another high street bank, but if the individual has a large number of standing orders and direct debits already set up, change would be difficult because of the extra time needed to switch all the regular payments, learn new systems and develop new relationships. These costs may outweigh the benefits seen from a potential new bank account. Finally, price sensitivity is decreased where the manufacturer's offering is clearly differentiated from its competition and where price perception gives an aura of quality to a particular product. In general, people are less sensitive to a downsizing in pack size than they are to a price increase: this is presumably an error of perception on the part of the individual, but for routine purchases a slight reduction in quantity is apparently less noticeable than an increase in price (Gourville and Koehler 2003). An example of this is the popular chocolate biscuit bar Wagon Wheel. It has noticeably reduced in size over the past 25 years, while the price point has remained more or less the same.

Price sensitivity has also been shown to be affected by changing currencies. Research conducted in Germany following the replacement of the Deutschmark with the euro showed that people perceived the quality of the products to be higher when priced in Deutschmarks because the number of Deutschmarks was higher than the number of euros, although the actual price had not changed (Molz and Gielnik 2006).

Price sensitivity can be affected by marketing, and especially selling, approaches. In some cases customers have an unrealistically low expectation of prices. Salespeople will sometimes therefore suggest (in a subtle manner) that the price might be very high indeed so that the real price comes as a pleasant surprise. This technique is also used by some catalogue and online marketers: by including extremely high-priced articles in the catalogue/website, marketers can 'price-condition' potential customers into believing that other products in the catalogue represent a bargain (Krishna et al. 2002).

Some pricing methods take no account of customers at all. Cost-plus pricing, in which the total costs of manufacturing the product are totalled up and a profit margin added on, is still commonly used by manufacturers even though it takes no account of what the customers are prepared to pay. The result of this exercise will hardly ever be a price that a consumer would recognise as 'correct': it will almost certainly either be too high or too low. If the price is too high, people will not pay it; if it is too low, people may be suspicious of the quality of the product or at the very least the firm will be forgoing a surplus profit.

CUSTOMER-BASED PRICING METHODS

The various approaches to customer-based pricing do not necessarily mean offering products at the lowest possible price, but they do take account of customer needs and wants.

DEMAND PRICING

Demand pricing

Calculating the price of a product according to consumer demand at different price levels

Demand pricing is the most market-orientated method of pricing. Here, the marketer begins by assessing what the demand will be for the product at different price levels. This is usually done by asking customers what they might expect to pay for the product, and seeing how many choose each price level.

As the price rises, fewer customers are prepared to buy the product, as fewer will still see the product as good value for money. The fall-off is not necessarily linear, i.e. the number of units sold might fall dramatically once the price goes above a particular point. This kind of calculation could be used to determine the stages of a skimming policy (see below), or it could be used to calculate the appropriate launch price of a product.

For demand pricing, the next stage is to calculate the costs of producing the product in the above quantities. Usually the cost of producing each item falls as more are made (i.e. if we make 50,000 units, each unit costs less than would be the case if we only make 1,000 units). Given the costs of production it is possible to select the price that will lead to a maximisation of profits. This is because there is a trade-off between quantity produced and quantity sold; as the firm lowers the selling price, the amount sold increases but the income generated decreases.

The calculations can become complex, but the end result is that the product is sold at a price that customers will accept, and that will meet the company's profit targets.

PRODUCT-LINE PRICING

Product-line pricing means setting prices within linked product groups. Often sales of one product will be directly linked to the sales of another, so that it is possible to sell one item at a low price in order to make a greater profit on the other one.

Product-line pricing
Pricing that takes account of the price of related products

CONSUMER BEHAVIOUR IN ACTION: GIVING THE PRODUCTS AWAY

King C. Gillette, the inventor of the safety razor, was faced with something of a problem in marketing the product. He realised very early on that the revolutionary disposable blades in the razor would be expensive to manufacture unless he could produce them in their millions – but without a large, established market to sell to he would not be able to obtain those economies of scale. The razors themselves were a revolutionary idea, and consequently each prospective purchaser needed to be persuaded to try the new system, but this was simply too time-consuming.

©iStock.com/SamiSert

Gillette had, in his youth, been a salesman. He applied his knowledge of customers to the problem and came up with a new idea that is still in use today, over a hundred years later. He simply adjusted the pricing so that the up-front cost of adopting the product was low, and the ongoing maintenance cost relatively higher than it would otherwise have been. He gave away the razors, so that customers could try the new system for free: Gillette knew that hardly any of them would return to using cut-throat razors after using the disposable blades, and he made his money selling the blades.

Safety razors became so well-established in the market that, only a short while later, cut-throat razors are virtually unheard-of. Gillette's company successfully used the same marketing ploy some 80 years later to introduce a multi-blade system.

SKIMMING

Skimming is the practice of starting out with a high price for a product, then reducing it progressively as sales level off. It relies on two main factors: first, that not all

Skimming
Setting price high when a product is launched, then gradually lowering it as competitors enter the market

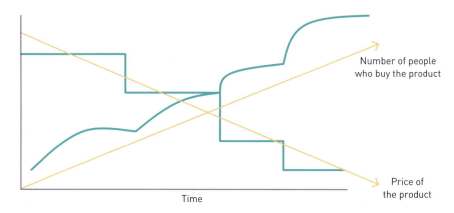

FIGURE 2.3 Skimming

customers have the same perception of value for money, and second that the company has a technological lead over the opposition which can be maintained for long enough to satisfy the market.

Skimming is usually carried out by firms that have developed a technically advanced product. Initially the firm will charge a high price for the product, and at this point only those who are prepared to pay a premium price for it will buy. Profit may not be high, because the number of units sold will be low and therefore the cost of production per unit will be high. Once the most innovative customers have bought, and the competition is beginning to enter the market, the firm can drop the price and 'skim' the next layer of the market, at which point profits will begin to rise. Eventually the product will be sold at a price that allows the firm only a minimum profit, at which point only replacement sales or sales to late adopters will be made.

Figure 2.3 shows how skimming works. At each price level, the product shows a standard product life cycle curve. As the curve tops out and begins to fall back, the company lowers the price and the cycle starts again with a new group of consumers. The process continues until either the market is saturated or the company decides that it cannot make any further price reductions.

The advantage of this method is that the cost of developing the product is returned fairly quickly, so that the product can later be sold near the marginal cost of production. This means that competitors have difficulty entering the market at all, since their own development costs will have to be recovered in some other way.

Skimming relies heavily on consumer perceptions and attitudes. In effect, it takes advantage of basic segmentation – people who are prepared to pay a premium price will do so, whereas the laggards and those prepared to pay less will enter the market later.

PSYCHOLOGICAL PRICING

Psychological pricing

Applying prices to goods based on perceptual issues such as quality

Psychological pricing relies on emotional responses from the consumer. Higher prices are often used as an indicator of quality, so some firms will use prestige pricing. This applies in many service industries, because consumers are often buying a promise;

a service that does not have a high enough quality cannot be exchanged afterwards. Consumers' expectations of high-priced restaurants and hairdressers are clearly higher in terms of the quality of service provision; reducing prices in those industries does not necessarily lead to an increase in business. **Odd–even pricing** is the practice of ending prices with an odd number, for example £3.99 or €5.95 rather than £4 or €6. It appears that consumers tend to categorise these prices as '£3 and a bit' or '€5 and change' and thus perceive the price as being lower. The effect may also be due to an association with discounted or sale prices; researchers have, for some time now, reported that '99' endings on prices increase sales by around 8% (Schindler and Kirby 1997).

In addition, research has also shown that odd–even pricing does not necessarily work in all cultures (Suri et al. 2004). In Poland, for example, the effects are negligible. Odd–even pricing also has effects on perceptions of discounts during sales. For example, rounding the price to £5 from £4.99 leads people to overvalue the size of the discount, which increases the perception of value for money (Gueguen and Legoherel 2004). Thus the positive effect on sales of using a 99-ending can be negated when the product is on offer in a sale. There is also evidence that rounding prices up to an even amount encourages trial of products (Bray and Harris 2006). Other cultural nuances are also applicable here. For instance, there is evidence to suggest that in China prices ending in 8 are more effective than prices ending in 4 because 8 is a lucky number and 4 is unlucky (Simmons and Schindler 2003).

Online retailers have found that 'bundling' the price and including 'free' shipping and handling appears to work effectively as a purchasing incentive, leading to more favourable memories and fewer product returns (Roggeveen et al. 2006). A similar effect may exist in hire-purchase or credit deals: people relate the benefits they gain from the product to the actual payments they are making at the time. This means that, as the product gets older and the benefits reduce the customer perceives the payments as worse value for money (Seigyoung and Chuang-Foh 2006).

SECOND-MARKET DISCOUNTING

Second-market discounting is common in some service industries and in international markets. The brand is sold at one price to one market segment, and at a lower price to another. Often these discounts are offered to even out the loading on the firm; for example, mid-week discounts fill the restaurant on what would otherwise be a quiet night, so making more efficient use of the premises and staff.

Figure 2.4 shows how second-market discounting works. Cinemas are now constantly competing with online downloads and streaming, so may use second-market discounting to attract customers back into the cinema. At the bottom of each column is the amount of full-price business a cinema does on each day. Friday and Saturday are the busiest days, so on the other four days of the week the cinema offers various discounts. On Monday they offer 10% off to all customers, which boosts business that day to a level higher than that of the weekend trade. Tuesday is senior citizen day, and Wednesday and Thursday are student discount days. These days are aimed at people who are able to go to the cinema mid-week.

Obviously these discounts may cannibalise sales on other days: a senior citizen might have been willing to view on a Saturday and pay the full price (or might even have viewed on a Tuesday anyway, simply because the cinema is quieter).

FIGURE 2.4 Second-market discounting

In international markets products might be discounted to meet local competition. For example, Honda motorcycles are up against strong local competition in India from Royal Enfield, so the price of their basic 110cc motorcycle is around Rs41,000 (about £450). A similar Honda motorcycle in the UK costs around £1,849. The specifications of the motorcycles do differ somewhat, and the import duty structures are different – however, it is difficult to see any difference that would account for a £1,400 price differential.

PLACE

Place

The element of the marketing mix concerned with the location where the exchange takes place

Place refers to the location where the exchange takes place. The place element of the marketing mix goes beyond mere convenience: often the place is, in effect, part of the product because it provides hedonic benefits of its own. For example, consider the purchase of antiques. Some antique buyers will scour car boot sales, house clearance sales, auction rooms and travel to far flung places in the hope of picking up a bargain. There is, for instance, currently a trend in the UK of dealers buying French Louis XV style oak armoire wardrobes, which are extremely ornately carved and are being sourced from various French and Belgian chateaux. Others will go to antique shops where most of the searching has already been done, while others will visit upmarket antique galleries where the pieces will be artfully displayed and the customer will be offered a glass of wine and a canapé while browsing.

In the course of the antique item's passage from reclamation yard to gallery, the price may well have risen from a few pounds sterling to many thousands of pounds, yet at each stage of the process the purchaser has bought a bargain. The reason is that the place element has added value in some way or another. The car boot bargain hunter may have spent weeks or months trawling through, and sometimes buying, what can only be described as worthless junk in order to find that one valuable item. However, the hedonic aspects of bargain hunting make the search worthwhile. This is the principle upon which the hit TV series *Storage Wars* has been based. The basis of the show is that people bid on the contents of abandoned lock-up storage spaces which are being sold off by the landlords, and where the buyer has no prior clue as to what they may be getting. Sometimes they win by buying valuable items, sometimes they lose by buying a storage shed full of useless items. At the other end of the chain, the wealthy collector enjoying a glass of wine at the gallery is enjoying having someone explain the history of the item, and is able to invest a substantial amount of money in something he or she knows is of *real* value. The reputation of the gallery ensures that the product is the genuine article – something the average car boot sale bargain hunter cannot be sure of. This said, there is also an argument to be made here about what *real* value actually is. Is it not just what the item is actually worth to the buyer?

Buying goods from a catalogue, online, from a street market or from a retailer each has its hedonic aspects, and marketers need to balance the place utility (cognitive) aspects against the hedonic (affective) aspects of the point of purchase.

SHOPPING BEHAVIOUR

Whether an individual is shopping online by surfing the world wide web, or offline by walking the high streets and shopping malls in major cities around the world he or she has many motives for shopping, which often go beyond a simple need to obtain goods and services. These can be divided into social motives and personal motives, each of which determine the choice of retailer, the time spent shopping and much of the effort which is expended.

Social motives include the following:

- *Social experience outside the home*. Talking to shop assistants, going shopping with a friend or friends or getting out of the house for a while are included here.

- *Communication with others having a similar interest*. Whether shopping for clothes or computers, people enjoy taking a friend along, especially if the friend has a specific expertise that can be used, or being an active part of an online blog.

- *Peer group attraction*. Going to specific shops means mingling with people from a similar social background, or actively contributing to review sites. This is reassuring in terms of self-image.

- *Status and authority*. Being a customer is a pleasant experience – the shop assistants (if they are well trained) are attentive and interested in the customers' needs which means that customers enjoy the warm glow of being looked after.

- *Pleasure of bargaining*. In some situations in every country, bargaining is acceptable, and in some countries it is normal practice almost everywhere. The bargaining process is enjoyable because it has the elements of power, of exercising skill and of getting a bargain.

Personal motives include the following:

- *Role playing*. Playing the part of the customer is a pleasant experience: some people even adopt a new persona when shopping, in order to enhance their own self-esteem.

- *Diversion*. Looking at new products is an entertainment in itself, and browsing both online and offline shops can be a relaxing way of spending some time.

- *Ease of buying and returning*. Given that in an online buying situation it is virtually impossible to 'try for size', many retailers are very happy to accept numerous returns. This means that consumers are tempted into buying a variety of sizes which can be tried on at home, knowing that the return of unwanted items is a painless process.

- *Self-gratification.* Meeting one's own needs by buying goods relieves the tensions set up by lacking something that is regarded as essential.

- *Learning about new trends.* Learning is, in itself, a pleasurable thing. Being the first to know about new products is important for some people's self-esteem, and perhaps as important for some people's jobs (for example, an audio-visual home entertainment systems salesman would need to know what is currently available in the market place, and given the rate of change with which this happens, he would be well-advised to stay abreast of the numerous developments).

- *Physical activity.* Working people tend to have sedentary lives – sitting in front of a laptop or PC for the majority of their day: going for a walk round the shops can relieve this. Often people experience this motivation when on holiday – relaxing on the beach or by the pool quickly becomes boring.

- *Sensory stimulation.* Simply exposing one's senses to new sensations is pleasurable, and shopping fulfils this role admirably.

PROMOTION

Promotion

The element of the marketing mix concerned with communication

Promotion is about creating appropriate perceptions in consumers' minds (see Chapter 8 for more on this). However, people also consume marketing messages through the media – they enjoy watching some advertisements, they enjoy watching films which have brands placed in them and they enjoy reading informative articles about product categories with which they are involved.

How advertising works (and occasionally whether advertising works) has been a topic for debate in marketing academia for a number of years now. Part of the problem is that there is no way of telling whether something works unless one first defines what it is that one is trying to achieve. Since there are many possible objectives for an advertising campaign, ranging from increasing purchases through to reinforcing attitudes, there can be no single explanation for whether advertising works (Wright and Crimp 2000).

Two general theories about advertising have emerged from the debate, summarised in Figure 2.5. The strong theory suggests that advertising is a powerful force that can change attitudes and make a significant contribution to people's knowledge and understanding. The weak theory of advertising suggests that advertising can only 'nudge' people in the direction in which they are already moving; in other words, it reinforces rather than persuades (Ehrenberg 1992).

FIGURE 2.5 Strong and weak theories of advertising

CONSUMER BEHAVIOUR IN ACTION: MEASURING ADVERTISING IN AUSTRALIA

The Australian government, in conjunction with six universities and the state governments of Victoria and Queensland, has established the National Information and Communications Technology of Australia organisation. NICTA, as it is known, has the role of encouraging excellence in research into communications technology.

One of NICTA's inventions is a software system that can recognise faces and determine in which direction they are looking. Linked to a camera, this system allows advertisers to know how many people look at their billboards, and even which area of the billboard has attracted their attention. The software, Targeted Advertising Based on Audience Natural Response or TABANAR, has offered advertisers a golden opportunity to fine-tune their billboard ads and also to have a direct measure of audience response. This is of course much more accurate than traditional methods of measuring response, which involve, for example, coupon returns, calls made to free telephone numbers, returned text messages or auto-returned emails.

In some countries there may be issues of privacy involved with putting secret cameras on billboards and recording people without their consent, but the system itself uses remarkable technology to provide information that has been previously unobtainable.

The main criticisms of the strong theory of advertising are first, that there is little evidence to show that consumers develop a strong desire for the brand before trying it, and second, the model only considers non-buyers who become buyers. In most markets, advertising is intended to affect people who have already tried the product, either with a view to informing them about changes in the product, or to remind them about the product, or to encourage increased purchases of the product. The strong theory tends to be more prevalent in the United States, and it is of course possible that American experience is different from European experience; the weak theory tends to have more adherents in Europe. Research in FMCG (fast-moving consumer goods) markets shows that people are not usually loyal to one brand, and that it is extremely difficult for a new brand to become established in the portfolio of brands people buy. In these circumstances, most advertising is intended to improve brand loyalty and therefore defend the brand: this would tend to support the weak theory, because it implies that the main people to be affected by the advertising are existing customers for the brand.

Level of involvement has a role to play in determining the effects of advertising, and may also have a bearing on when the strong theory applies, and when the weak theory predominates (Jones 1991). In the case of a high-involvement purchase, consumers are more likely to access sought communications (Blythe 2003), and are likely to be more affected by advertising since they will be actively seeking out advertising messages. In the case of low-involvement purchases, consumers are less likely to seek out advertising and are therefore only likely to be moved slightly by the unsought communications around them.

Unsought communications

Messages that have not been looked for by the recipient

CHALLENGING THE STATUS QUO

If advertising is only a weak force, and doesn't persuade anybody, why is so much money spent on it by companies? Surely they wouldn't pay out billions of pounds, dollars, yen and euros every year just on the chance that it might work? Or is it just about providing potential consumers with information about the choices and options available to them?

On the other hand, when was the last time you saw an advert and then went rushing out to buy a product? Have you *ever* been persuaded by an advertisement? Are advertisements like the bumble bee – in theory too aerodynamically unsound to fly, but in practice it still flies? In recent times, advertisers have taken to online and digital platforms such as Facebook which attracts over a million advertisers who spend in excess of $8 billion annually. In fact, Facebook advertising has seen an exponential growth of over 680% since 2010. This is predominantly because Facebook adverts target real people with real interests, hobbies and jobs, and not just a random association with 'keywords', like for instance Google Adwords.

When there are many competing advertisements for similar products (for example, in specialist websites and magazines such as sport or hobby media), varying the context in which the advertisement is seen will increase its memorability (Unnava et al. 2003). In other words, if some method exists for repeating the advertisement in a different context (for example, by integrating it into a multi-channel social media campaign – e.g. via Twitter, Instagram, LinkedIn, YouTube and Pinterest), it is more likely to have an impact on the target audience.

ACTIVE MEDIA: TV, RADIO AND CINEMA

TV, radio and cinema are powerful media because they are active (Figure 2.6) – they actually do something. TV and radio are probably the most pervasive media in most countries – in Western Europe, TV ownership is almost 100% and many homes have several television sets. Radio ownership is at least as widespread. People watch TV while eating, doing housework, relaxing or even while entertaining friends. In some homes the set is rarely switched off. Significantly, the biggest-selling consumer magazines in most Western European countries and in the United States are the TV programme guides.

Because television advertising is an unsought communication (people rarely, if ever, switch on the TV in order to see a favourite advertisement) it works best for activating needs or providing information for the internal search. In most cases, advertisers are aiming to build the image of their product or firm, and to a large extent these aims can be met by television (McKechnie and Leather 1998).

Research at the London Business School shows that people do not necessarily watch the advertisements even if they are still in the room when the advertisement airs (Ritson 2003). The researchers identified a total of six behaviours that occur while the advertisement is on-screen: these are shown in Table 2.2 and Figure 2.7. The first three activities are interesting in that the standard method of measuring advertising on TV, which is the people meter, would have shown that people were in the room and would therefore have assumed that they were watching the advertisement. In

FIGURE 2.6 Active media

fact, in each of these three cases, presence in the room does not mean observation of the advertising.

Interestingly, there is research evidence that advertisements that are **zapped** (i.e. the viewer flicks to another channel or turns the sound off) or **zipped** (fast-forwarded if the viewer is watching a recording) are more likely to have a positive effect on brand purchase than those that are not (Zufryden et al. 1993). This is presumably because the viewer has to watch at least part of the advertisement and process the content before knowing that it is a candidate for zapping. Luckily for some people, we now have technology (in the form of hard-drive recorders) which will cut out the recording of advertisements altogether. This is likely to have a negative effect on advertisers, and consequently programme makers.

The theory behind fast-paced advertisements says that they appear to have a positive effect on involuntary attention, in other words they are more eye-catching, but have little effect on involuntary attention (they are no more likely to be watched actively) (Bolls et al. 2003). Furthermore, fast-paced advertisements tend to focus people on the style of the advertisement, not on its content: people remember the advertisement, but not the brand. Mood affects people's response to advertisements, so placing the advertisement in an appropriate programme may have a critical effect on its success or otherwise (Bakamitsos and Siomkos 2003).

There is a clear relationship between liking the advertisement and subsequent sales, but this is not always a positive relationship. Liking the advertisement seems to be related to whether the product is meaningful and relevant to the person at the time (Biel 1990), and there is evidence that advertisements relating to food, drink and technology are more likely to be liked than are non-food advertisements (Biel and Bridgwater 1990). Liking is usually linked to a positive view of the product, which in turn is likely to lead to sales (Biel 1990; Stapel 1991). This situation is sometimes reversed when dealing with, for example, insurance products and the like, where the advertisement might contain shocking imagery as a 'cautionary tale' to show people what can go wrong if they do not have insurance.

Zapping

Using a remote control device to avoid advertisements by switching to another channel. Also called flicking

Zipping

Using a remote control device to fast-forward through advertisements on a recorded programme

TABLE 2.2 Behaviour in commercial breaks

Behaviour	Explanation
Reading	Many people watch TV with a book or magazine at hand, to read during the breaks. Sometimes the reading will be a TV guide. It is increasingly common now for people to have their smartphone in one hand and the TV remote control in the other
Social interaction	People often talk about their day, discuss household problems or gossip while the commercial break runs. This is not just with the people that they are with physically, but also using social media, e.g. Beamly
Tasking	The commercial break often affords an opportunity to check incoming communications on your phone, load the dishwasher, clean the house, do the ironing, pay bills or send text messages
Flicking (zapping)	Flicking falls into two categories: almost random surfing across a number of other channels while waiting for the programme to restart, or alternatively going to a 'visit channel' such as a news channel for a specific length of time before returning to the programme
Watching the advertisements	In many cases, advertisements are actually watched, and often commented on by the family members. In fact, in the UK there is a reality TV show called *Gogglebox* dedicated to family members providing a constant commenting on the programmes and advertisements
Advertising interaction	The final behaviour involves not only watching the advertisement, but commenting on it, singing along with the jingles and even playing a game in which family members score 'points' by being the first to recognise the brand

It may be difficult to deconstruct all the factors involved, since a truly unpleasant advertisement is likely to be ignored, so that the viewer is less likely to process the information cognitively. Such 'cautionary tale' advertisements are difficult to produce because the affective element is likely to repel the customer, whereas the cognitive element is likely to attract. Products can be placed on an approach–avoidance continuum, with products that are inherently attractive (food and beverages) at one end, and products that are inherently unattractive and are only bought out of dire necessity (pensions, life insurance, and so forth) at the other (Wells 1980).

CHALLENGING THE STATUS QUO

Are advertisers making a conscious effort to make sure that their marketing communications campaigns are truly integrated across a variety of media output? Are the same messages being sent out through all the channels being used? And if people tend to 'switch off' from unpleasant advertisements, why produce them at all? Why show people scenes of crashed cars and devastated homes in order to frighten them into buying insurance? Or maybe people have to be terrorised into buying insurance – otherwise they would just keep putting it off until after they have been burgled or crashed the car! After all, in most countries it is a legal requirement to have car insurance – so doesn't this prove that people won't buy it unless they are threatened with jail?

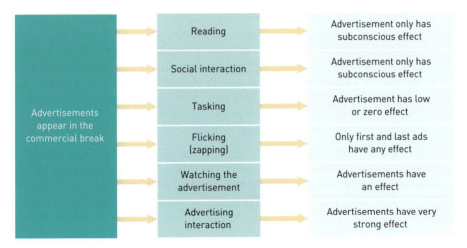

FIGURE 2.7 Activities in commercial breaks

RADIO ADVERTISING

Radio used to be the Cinderella of advertising, often ignored in favour of the higher profile of television. However, with the advent of digital radio, things have changed. According to research conducted for Red Dragon Radio, commercial radio (especially that listened to via a digital signal) has a strong impact on people's lives. According to Red Dragon:

- 44% of radio listeners wake up to a radio alarm.
- 27% of people listen to the radio in the bathroom, and 43% of the 15–24 age group do so.
- 72% of adult listeners listen to the radio in the kitchen.
- 44% of car drivers listen to the radio while driving.
- 44% of employees listen to the radio in the workplace.
- 53% of adults aged 15–24 listen to their radios in the garden.

Radio is a powerful medium because it is intimate: people listen to the radio in private situations, often when on their own. Thus radio acts as a substitute for human company. Radios are cheap and portable, and listening does not require the audience's full attention, so people can do other things (drive, do housework, put on make-up, etc.) while listening. With the digital signal, thousands of radio stations from around the world are now accessible to people wherever they live. Thus waking up in Sydney while listening to San Francisco's 'The Bay' radio is perfectly possible.

CINEMA ADVERTISING

For many years the cinema was the only visual advertising medium. Television meant that cinema audiences declined dramatically in the 1950s and 1960s, but in recent years the trend has reversed. A combination of blockbuster movies that have attracted audiences, and the emergence of comfortable, well-equipped cinemas in entertainment complexes has led to a resurgence of cinema attendance as part of a night out.

From the advertiser's viewpoint, cinema has all the advantages of television plus one other: it is impossible to zip, zap or leave the room while the advertisements are on. Consequently, cinemas provide an unrivalled opportunity to speak to a captive audience. British Film Institute (BFI) statistics show that while cinema attendances were at around the 34 million per annum mark in 1988, by 2014, UK film box office revenues exceeded £1 billion for the third year in succession: no small audience for advertising. This is of course in addition to video on demand (VoD). According to an online report by the British Film Institute (2014):

> *market data on VoD, which enables audiences to access films through a range of devices, anytime, anywhere, is limited but was estimated to be worth £323 million, showing a 37% growth on 2012 and is now 400% higher since 2002. Apple was the highest earning VoD provider in the UK with Netflix the fastest growing provider.*

This makes a significant addition to any advertiser's reach.

Typical cinema audiences are young people in their teens and early twenties: 48% of cinema-goers are aged 7 to 24, although they represent only 22% of the UK population (British Film Institute 2014). The audience in Western countries is also strongly ABC1 in socio-economic profile, while in other less developed countries cinema attendance is widespread because of the relatively low level of terrestrial television ownership.

AMBIENT ADVERTISING

Traditional marketing communications techniques are becoming less effective as markets fragment, costs increase, audiences diminish and clutter worsens (Evans et al. 1996). Therefore, new routes for communicating with customers and consumers are being sought.

Ambient advertising

Commercial messages that are designed to become part of the environment

Ambient advertising is somewhat difficult to define, although plenty of examples of it are around. In general, it is advertising that becomes part of the environment, where the message is built into the medium. For example, for one campaign an underarm deodorant manufacturer arranged to replace the hanging straps in London Underground carriages with empty bottles of the deodorant. Strap-hanging commuters are acutely aware of underarm odours, and holding onto the bottles instead of the usual straps meant that they had already assumed the position one uses when applying the deodorant. Another development is the invention of a device that converts shop windows into loudspeakers so that the window can 'talk' about the products on display (Grapentine 2003).

Ambient advertising offers the following advantages:

- It is often cheaper than sales promotions, and when used near the point of purchase gives a good incentive without the loss of profit associated with sales promotion discounts.
- Well-executed ambient campaigns enhance brand image and cut through clutter.
- Novel ambient campaigns often create press coverage: some ambient campaigns are designed with this in mind.
- Ambient advertising is very effective for activating needs.

TABLE 2.3 Mapping of ambient advertising against the ATRN model

Stage	Explanation	Role of ambient advertising
Awareness	Consciousness of a new brand is followed by interest	Consciousness is developed by a high-impact, innovative campaign, e.g. replacing straps with deodorant bottles
Trial	Trial purchase of the brand may occur, perhaps with the consumer in a sceptical frame of mind	Ambient advertising close to the point of sale may be enough to nudge the consumer towards one brand rather than another
Reinforcement	Satisfactory use of the brand will encourage further purchase, or even establish a habitual propensity to buy the brand	Ambient advertising only has a reminder role to play at this stage, and may be no more effective than other advertising
Nudging	Propensity to buy may be enhanced or decreased by the nudging effect of advertising – either the firm's own or that of competitors	Ambient advertising is thought to be better than other advertising for nudging consumers, since it has greater proximity both to the problem and to the point of purchase

Ambient advertisers need to consider the relationship between the medium being used, the integration of the advertised product or service into a plethora of communications, and the proximity to the point of sale as well as the basic objectives of the campaign. Ambient advertising works best when it is either close to the location of the problem or close to the point of purchase. For example, Swiss watchmaker IWC enabled bus travellers in the vicinity of Berlin airport to use bus straps which had been fashioned from images of IWC's Big Pilot's watch. The thinking was that having seen what an image of the watch looks like on their wrist, they may be tempted to walk into the IWC showroom at the airport; almost a case of try before you buy. Another example comes from an American-Italian food outlet called Eatalica in Chennai, India. In order to promote their burgers, they placed a 'Caution Wet Floor' A-signboard near a poster for the company's burger products. The copy on the board read as follows: 'Oogling at the burger may involuntarily cause drooling which may in turn lead to a wet floor: Issued for your safety by the management of Eatalica restaurant'.

Consumers tend to exhibit little pre-purchase decision-making for low-involvement purchases (Foxall and Goldsmith 1994), and some studies have shown that 70% of all decisions to purchase specific brands are made inside the store (POPAI 1994). Trolley advertising makes around 19% difference to the purchase of specific brands (Shankar 1999a), which demonstrates the power of ambient advertising to nudge consumers. Table 2.3 maps ambient advertising against Ehrenberg's ATRN (Awareness, Trial, Reinforcement, Nudging) model of advertising effects (the weak theory) (Barnard and Ehrenberg 1997; Ehrenberg 1997).

Ambient advertising is, of course, difficult to measure. First, the creativity of some campaigns is such that no advance predictions can be made. Second, research into the effects of ambient advertising has been relatively small as yet, so suitable test instruments have not been devised, although some studies have started to investigate this area, for example Abdul-Razzaq et al. (2009). Third, there is no industry-wide evaluation system: nor is there an estimating system to find out how many people picked up a particular petrol nozzle and therefore saw the advertisement, for example Shankar (1999b).

In the future, it seems likely that ambient advertising will grow. Although greater creativity is needed in developing a campaign, the impact is high and the cost is relatively low, especially considering the potential spin-off in terms of news coverage. Ambient advertising fits well within an integrated marketing communications approach because it both supports, and is supported by, other communication tools.

VIRAL MARKETING

Viral marketing uses electronic communications to trigger brand messages throughout a widespread network of buyers, and of course a small part of this is Internet advertising. This is called a buzz – technology which creates a positive or negative buzz around a brand, product or service. In a study conducted by Dye (2000), McKinsey estimated that 67% of all goods and services in the USA are affected by buzz. But as Huck (2003) notes, 'The instant buzz can be cruel'. An early development in Internet advertising was the use of viral spam programs, by which virus writers were hired by spammers to develop viruses that would propagate spam messages through the address books of infected computers. Back in 2007 such viral spam programs were used to promote 'penny shares'. Infected computers spread the spam around the world, with some users receiving five to ten copies of the advertisement per day. Clearly as consumers have become increasingly 'tech-savvy', such tactics are now seen as unethical, and there are many programs which are available to filter out such communication: the difficulty is that the Internet is largely unregulated, messages can originate anywhere in the world, and therefore legislation would need to be ratified by virtually every nation on earth if unethical practices are to be stamped out entirely. It may be possible in the future for ISPs to be forced to develop ways of filtering spam from unregulated countries, but in the current macro-environmental situation this is still extremely difficult, and many Internet service providers (ISPs) would regard such measures as being counterproductive since the whole point of the Internet is that it offers worldwide access, in a context where marketers have little control. (Some research has been done (see Dobele et al. 2005) to try and identify some strategies which perhaps could be used by marketers to control this chaotic phenomenon: positioning their brand, changing their image and thus helping to increase adoption rates). People frequently feel afraid that they will lose control of their inboxes and will be swamped by unsolicited emails, which leads them to use tactics such as setting up different email accounts with ISPs or giving false details when buying products. The desire to retain control over what is seen as a private medium is strong, and therefore people go to some lengths to avoid becoming victims of clever marketing tactics.

The Internet has empowered consumers to a greater extent than ever before – the ease with which people can research suppliers (by using consumer-led websites such as Epinions.com or aspokesmansaid.com) and are able to switch between them has made suppliers rethink their approach and become much more interactive (Pires et al. 2006). There is evidence that people use various tactics for self-empowerment, as follows (Henry and Caldwell 2006):

- resignation
- confrontation
- withdrawal
- engagement
- concealment
- escapism
- hedonism
- spirituality
- nostalgia
- creativity.

Trust is sometimes difficult to establish online due to the impersonality of the medium. Interpersonal e-trust is important: people respond better if they feel they are dealing with a person rather than a corporation online (Pennanen 2011). This may in part account for the observation that pull channels (those approaches that seek to attract end consumers) work better than push channels (those channels that seek to push products down the distribution chain) because they are seen to be more trustworthy (Spilker-Attig and Brettel 2010).

PEOPLE

The rise of the service industries sector has led to the development of strong customer loyalties. These loyalties are almost always based on loyalty to the **people** working in the industry – whether the business is a hairdressing salon, a website developer or a restaurant, the customer's loyalty is a function of the personal relationship he or she has with the stylist, the designer or the waiter.

Consumers will tend to use the social interaction as a surrogate measure for judging the quality of the service. A friendly waiter, a confident hairdresser or a knowledge-able designer will tend to inspire confidence in the overall outcome of the service provision, although there is really no guarantee that the actual competence of the supplier relates in any way to these subjective social factors.

Company employees may be divided into four groups (Judd 1987):

1. **Contactors**. These are the people who have frequent, daily contact with customers. Usually their jobs are marketing-related: salespeople, customer service employees or telesales operators. They are usually trained in customer relations techniques, and are often motivated to deal with customers in an effective and friendly way. Being able to offer a customised recommendation to a consumer is important – people who believe that their preferences are fairly stable appreciate a customised approach (Shen and Ball 2011).

2. **Modifiers**. These people deal with customers regularly, but have no official marketing role. Receptionists, drivers, telephonists, progress chasers and some warehouse personnel deal with customers on an occasional basis and may need to have some idea of the organisation's marketing policies. It is helpful if modifiers have good people skills, but they may not need special training in this.

People
The element of the marketing mix concerned with employees and other consumers

Contactors
People within an organisation who have daily interaction with customers

Modifiers
People who deal with customers regularly, but who have no specific marketing role

Influencers

People who exert an advisory
role to members of a
decision-making unit

3. **Influencers**. These people have some role within marketing, but have little actual contact with customers. For example, a designer may have the role of styling the product to make it as attractive as possible, without actually ever dealing with consumers.

Isolateds

Employees who have little or
no contact with customers

4. **Isolateds**. These people have no customer contact and little or nothing to do with marketing. Accountants, personnel managers, office cleaners, and so forth have important support roles within the organisation but are unlikely ever to do anything which directly impacts on customers. Their role is to help create the right conditions for everyone else to carry out their roles.

Word of mouse

Using the Internet to
communicate directly with
other consumers and to
create user-generated
content

A major influence that employees have on customers comes through word of mouth (WOM). Employees all go home at the end of the working day, and talk to family and friends about work. This means that each person helps in creating an overall corporate image, which in turn contributes to the customers' perception of the organisation (Maxham and Netemeyer 2003). In addition to this, the profound use of the Internet and in particular the emergence of social media has created a new channel of communication: **word of mouse** (Sethna et al. 2013).

The natural variability among human beings will, of course, mean that companies will not always be able to provide optimal service; firms therefore need to be prepared to work to recover from service mistakes when they do occur (Rasmusson 1997). This is often done by empowering contactors and modifiers to make amends immediately. Because the employee is the company (from the viewpoint of the consumer), this approach strengthens the social bonding which is the cornerstone of service provision. In some cases, however, employees may act unethically on behalf of the company; this is especially likely if the employees feel that the company would reciprocate by rewarding them in future, or if they identify strongly with the company (Umphress et al. 2010).

PROCESS

Process

The element of the
marketing mix concerned
with the overall delivery of
a service

In services markets, consumers can sometimes be seen as a co-producer of the service. For example, live theatre clearly has serious drawbacks over television: it cannot hope to provide the same level of special effects and scenes, and the actors' performances may not always be perfect (whereas on TV an imperfect performance is simply re-shot). Additionally, going to the theatre involves booking seats, going out in the cold and finding one's way to the theatre, sitting in what are sometimes uncomfortable seats, not being able to have a drink or a snack during the performance, and not being able to press the pause, fast-forward or rewind button. The theatre does not allow one to change channels if the play is boring and it does not allow the viewer to turn up the volume if the actors are speaking too quietly. And yet for this experience, people pay for a ticket – so what is the attraction? The main attraction is that there is an atmosphere in the theatre, generated by the presence of an audience – the other consumers. A half-empty theatre seems bleak; a theatre full of people collectively responding to the show helps generate a response from the individual person watching the show.

As with any other question in marketing, the starting point for developing a service process is the customers' needs. In some cases the needs can be presented as a hierarchy – for example, a cargo ship manufacturer may not require new engines to be delivered urgently, but would probably need spare parts for a broken winch to be delivered quickly, as a docked (and therefore unproductive) cargo ship is an expensive item. The marine engine manufacturer would therefore see the supply of engines as being less important than the supply of spare parts, and would therefore seek to ensure that the stock of spares is kept up to an appropriate level even if this delayed the completion of new engines.

Service processes fall into three general categories:

1. *Before-sales service processes.* These might include helpful sales staff, readily-available information, availability of samples and availability of supplies.

2. *During-sales processes.* These might include progress-chasing of orders, prompt and reliable delivery, and helpful delivery staff.

3. *After-sales processes.* Courtesy calls, prompt attention to complaints, and warranties and service agreements would all be after-sales services.

These processes all involve human interaction, so they all provide opportunities to improve customer loyalty. Unfortunately, they are also easy to copy, and not very difficult to exceed, so it may not be easy to maintain competitive advantage. Also, there is a trade-off between service level and cost: some firms have been successful by cutting back dramatically on service and reducing prices accordingly. High street retailers, low-cost airlines and many fast-food restaurants offer minimal service, and have streamlined processes that reduce cost and deliver the core product efficiently. In some cases, the streamlined process might actually be preferable to the more staff-intensive process it replaces – many people find that booking flights on the Internet is a great deal easier than going through a travel agent, and this has now become the norm.

Setting the right level of service can therefore be a source of competitive advantage. The emphasis here is on setting the right level and getting a balance – too high a level of service and the price will have to rise or the profits will have to fall; too low a level and many customers will go elsewhere. Many firms still try to provide a high level of service for a low price – often at the expense of their employees – but this can be done only by shaving profits or otherwise acting in ways that reduce longer-term competitiveness. Note that segmentation, targeting and positioning as key strategies still apply – some people are happy to pay for an enhanced service, while others prefer to buy the cheapest. Indeed, most individuals often shift between the two levels, depending on the occasion that they find themselves in – for instance, a couple going out for their 25th wedding anniversary dinner will probably not eat at the same restaurant they might go to for a quick lunch during the working week.

PHYSICAL EVIDENCE

The intangibility of most of the benefits of a service means that consumers do not have any evidence that the service ever took place. The evidence might be useful to show to other people (a certificate from a training course, a life insurance policy to show to a bank) or it might be simply something to act as a reminder of the pleasure the consumer obtained from the service (a souvenir of a holiday, a menu from a restaurant, etc.). Physical evidence might also be used as a way of assessing the quality

Physical evidence

The element of the marketing mix concerned with the tangible aspects of the products of services of a product before committing to a purchase (the bank branch's decor or the menu in the window of a restaurant).

CHALLENGING THE STATUS QUO

It's commonly said that you can't judge a book by its cover – yet apparently we are expected to believe that we can judge a bank by its decor. Are we really as naive as that? Of course, long gone are the days of bank staff hiding safely behind secure glass screens and serving their customers through a small hatch! This was totally the opposite to the mantra of 'we are open and approachable' that many banks were trying to position themselves with. Have you noticed how many banks now have developed a stance where the staff mingle among the customers? Some people might think that banks would be better spending their money on reducing their charges or improving their service – but the evidence is that having a smart interior really does affect people's decisions about where to bank. So maybe we really *are* judging the book by the cover! This is even more so the case when we investigate the digital environment. Let's think about a situation where you're looking for a courier to deliver some stuff you've just bought on eBay. The courier's website says on the homepage, 'we give a fast and efficient service', but it takes in excess of two minutes for their webpage to load. Did you wait all that time for the page to load, or have you already moved on to the next company after the first 10 seconds? The Internet is awash with blogs and commentators all talking about why we are so impatient when it comes to online interaction. Reasons include autosound instantly being played, popups appearing all over the screen, multiple pagination (i.e. the viewer having to load a number of pages in order to see material which could easily be displayed on one page), giving priority to adverts before content, badly designed navigation around a website, and perhaps the worst offenders are those who demand that one registers immediately before any information about the product is imparted! Consider the example of an education provider's website which has spelling and grammatical errors, or a product which has been delivered using very poor quality packaging from a company which the customer perceives as being a fairly high quality manufacturer – these are both examples of inconsistencies in the physical evidence.

In some cases the physical element of the product itself is sufficient to act as physical evidence. A meal in a celebrity restaurant fulfils this: the food, the surroundings, the quality of the crockery and cutlery all convey evidence about the quality of the experience, even though the greater part of the bill will be absorbed by the chef's time in cooking the food and the waiter's time in delivering it (not to mention the washing up). In other cases, for example life insurance or other financial services, the physical evidence is likely to be much less or lacking altogether, in which case the firm may need to produce something that will provide evidence, for example a glossy brochure or policy document. For practical and legal purposes, most insurance documents could be printed on one or two sheets of paper, but for marketing purposes the document needs to be much more substantial. This said, most insurers now email policy documents as standard (unless customers specifically 'opt-in' to have the documents sent by 'snail-mail', the post). Because of this, the emailed version can be much more elaborate at lower cost, since printing costs are taken out of the equation.

FIGURE 2.8 Adding value through physical evidence

There are four generic ways to add value through physical evidence (Figure 2.8):

1. Create physical evidence that increases loyalty.

2. Use physical evidence to enhance brand image.

3. Use physical evidence that has an intrinsic value of its own, e.g. a free gift.

4. Create physical evidence that leads to further sales.

Airlines use their frequent-flyer programmes to increase loyalty; the physical evidence of the flights taken is the regular newsletter that is emailed, and the plastic card the frequent flyer uses to gain access to the executive lounges at airports en route. Some airlines (BA Executive Club, for example) also issue special plastic baggage tags which let the baggage handlers know that they are dealing with a very important suitcase: what effect this has on the baggage handlers is debatable, but the effect on the customer is a feeling of importance. KLM is another example of this. At each level of membership of KLM's frequent-flyer programme (Blue Wing, Silver Wing and Gold Wing) the colour of the card changes, as do the benefits to which the holder is entitled. These physical elements of the service are intended to encourage the customer to fly more often with KLM: failure to fly a set number of times a year with the airline will result in a downgrade to a lower level. This in itself has its own psychological negatives as far as the customer is concerned. However, an intangible benefit of membership for the customer is the occasional free flight – membership points can be exchanged for free flights at a set rate per distance travelled, or for upgrades into a higher class of travel comfort.

Brand image can be enhanced by using physical evidence that fits in with the brand's essential qualities. For example, an insurance company that wishes to convey a solid, respectable image will produce a glossy policy document full of high-flown legal phrases and reassuring photographs of solid corporate headquarters. An online charity portal aiming to convey a more down-to-earth, welcoming image might produce a policy couched in simple language, with photographs of smiling staff and philanthropic givers. Physical evidence need not always be up-market: most low-cost airlines emphasise the cost-cutting aspects of their business by requiring passengers to print off their own tickets, or by loading e-tickets on their smartphones. This is about as basic as physical evidence can get, but it does emphasise the point that the airline does not waste passengers' money on anything that is not absolutely necessary.

Physical evidence that has an intrinsic value of its own would include free gifts: this is a common ploy in the financial services industry. The popular website comparethemarket.com has this element at the heart of its communications strategy. Their giveaway of 'meerkat' toys is enhanced by the fact that the more financial products you buy, the more meerkats can be 'collected'. Clearly very few people would take out an insurance policy simply to receive a stuffed meerkat toy, but the existence of the meerkat in the policyholder's kids' bedroom is good evidence of the existence of the policy, and may also help groom the next generation of policy holders.

Physical evidence that leads to further business might include emails sent out by garages to let drivers know that their cars are due for a service. Dentists, opticians, hairdressers and some hospitals use reminders like this to tell people they need check-ups: the physical evidence of the previous visit serves to generate more business.

SUMMARY

While the marketing mix is quite traditional in its approach, it still offers us a useful shorthand tool for analysing the activities of marketers. Every activity carried out by marketers can only be carried out in cooperation with consumers and customers – customers can end the relationship simply by choosing to spend their money elsewhere, a point that sometimes eludes marketers.

The interplay between marketers and customers is what generates business, and (in the last hundred years or so) has generated the highest standard of living in human history. People's daily needs, from food and shelter through to entertainment and education, are met by marketers eager to please and who are prepared to go to considerable lengths in serving customers. All the efforts of marketers, and consequently every aspect of the marketing mix, is designed to meet customer needs more effectively, whether those needs are for better information initially or for better products once a decision has been made to buy or for more convenient delivery once a product has been bought.

KEY POINTS

- The hedonic aspects of products are often more important than the practical, utilitarian aspects.
- Digital marketing is not a 'stand-alone' but should be integrated into all aspects of the marketing mix.
- Price has more components than the simple purchase cost.
- Pricing should always take account of what people are prepared to pay.
- Place provides many of the benefits of buying the product; shopping should be a pleasurable experience.

- Advertising is probably only a weak force, nudging people rather than persuading.
- Interaction with advertisements always increases effectiveness, even if the advertisement is 'zapped'.
- Radio is a powerful medium because it is intimate.
- Cinema advertising appeals mainly to younger audiences.
- Ambient advertising works best when it is close to the point of purchase.
- Ambient advertising is particularly good for 'nudging' consumers when they are close to the point of purchase.
- Consumers often use social interactions as a surrogate for judging quality in service situations.
- Service levels should be correct for the target market, not necessarily maximal.
- Physical evidence is often used as a surrogate for judging quality of services.

HOW TO IMPRESS YOUR EXAMINER

Questions around how marketers influence consumers could come from almost any aspect of the subject, but something to bear in mind is that consumers are not mere recipients of marketing influences, but active participants in developing 'mutual value'. You will gain marks if you emphasise that marketing is all about the creation and exchange of mutual value; consumers co-create value.

REVIEW QUESTIONS

1. Why is cost-plus pricing dangerous?
2. Why is shopping pleasurable?
3. Why might someone ignore an advertisement, even though it is about a product of interest?
4. Why might advertisements that are 'zapped' be more effective than ones that are not?
5. What are the main advantages of radio as an advertising medium?
6. Why do ambient advertisements work well when they are close to the point of purchase?
7. What are the advantages of cinema advertising?
8. How might someone judge the quality of a restaurant they have not visited before?
9. How should service level be decided?
10. What is the difference between skimming and demand pricing?

CASE STUDY: *MAKEUPBYEMAN*

For most women, putting on make-up is a necessary chore – for many it's a daily one. Converting one's own face into a work of art is a skill little girls aim to acquire from a very early age – but by teenage years it becomes a skill to be agonised

over, worked at and prized above many others. It isn't something that is taught in schools (except possibly in expensive finishing schools or drama schools): it is often learned by trial and (painful) error, and it is a skill that requires a lot of advice and assistance from friends.

However, help is at hand. One of the great success stories of YouTube has been the proliferation of online make-up tutorials. The professional make-up artist who goes by the online alias of *makeupbyeman* has made some 170 videos of herself putting on make-up. The results are, needless to say, stunning but more to the point this has become a serious money-making venture. YouTube has

©iStock.com/poba

a system for kicking back some revenue to their big hitters, and *makeupbyeman* is currently in line to receive almost $50,000 in royalties for her home-made videos. This may not mirror the kind of royalties Hollywood may pay out, but it's certainly nice spare-time cash! And of course it hasn't done her main business any harm either – she claims that at least one couple arranged their wedding day around her availability. Eman (her real name) herself is only just past her 30th birthday and lives in Vancouver; her business is thriving, and she has become a wealthy young woman simply through having a passion for make-up.

Of course, Eman is a small-time player compared with the big make-up houses. L'Oréal also has a YouTube presence, offering make-up tutorials that promote their own range of cosmetics. Given that applying make-up is a difficult skill to acquire, it is clearly in the company's interests to ensure that customers get it right when they use L'Oréal products. However, the difference between L'Oréal and Eman is that L'Oréal has the resources of a very large company to put behind the production of their YouTube presence. Their videos are professionally shot, with some of L'Oréal's professional make-up artists applying the cosmetics to models. Attached to the site are links to glamorous events showcasing L'Oréal hair and beauty products, and special 'behind the scenes' shots of Cheryl Cole.

Other cosmetics firms with a YouTube presence include Max Factor and Rimmel. There are, of course, many other one-woman tutorial sites: pixiwoo, sojeanbrodie, CrystallyZed and many others, some of whom are themselves sponsored by make-up manufacturers.

The question is, of course, whether the one-woman shows, with someone (often an amateur) putting make-up on her own face and explaining each stage as she does it, are more effective than the glossy, professional shows where someone is made up by someone else in a slick beauty salon situation. Perhaps each video appeals to a different audience – after all, each woman has her own face, skin, eyes and colouring to contend with when choosing and applying make-up, so it seems likely that different models and different make-up artists will appeal to different women.

Whatever the verdict, women will continue to seek help and advice in putting on cosmetics. Creating a work of art takes time, skill, advice – and a little help from your friends.

QUESTIONS

1. Why might someone prefer to watch a woman who is not a make-up professional putting on her make-up and explaining what she's doing, rather than a trained make-up artist working on a model or film star?

2. Why is make-up important?

3. How might a cosmetics company improve the hit rate on a YouTube entry?

4. Why should a major company like L'Oréal invest so much in creating slick videos?

5. What type of influence is being exerted on the YouTube visitors?

FURTHER READING

There are very few academic texts on pricing, but it is a hot topic for practitioners. For a breezy (and very American) book on practical pricing, try *No B.S. Pricing Strategy – The Ultimate No-Holds-Barred, Kick Butt, Take No Prisoners Approach to Profits, Power and Prosperity* by Dan S. Kennedy and Jason Marrs (New York: Entrepreneur Press, 2011). It might give you something to think about.

For a look at what happens when consumers decide to act for themselves, try C. Moraes, I. Szmigin and M. Carrigan (2010) Living production-engaged alternatives: an examination of new consumption communities. *Consumption, Markets and Culture*, 13 (3): 273–98. This paper looks at how consumption communities question the current paradigm based on one group of people who produce, versus another group of people who consume.

Another paper that looks at consumer self-empowerment is M. McCeachern, G. Warnaby, M. Carrigan and I. Szmigin (2010) Thinking locally, acting locally? Conscious consumers and farmers' markets. *Journal of Marketing Management*, 26 (5): 395–412. The authors examine what happens when consumers decide to avoid the big supermarkets and agri-businesses and buy local produce from local producers. It's not quite anti-marketing – but it does show that consumers are not as biddable as some marketers would like to think.

If you want to know more about what motivates people to shop, you might like *The Art of Shopping: How We Shop and Why We Buy* by Seimon Scammel-Katz (London: LID Publishing, 2012). The author aims the book at retailers, explaining what they can do to make shopping easier, more pleasant and more frequent, using insights gained from many years as a consultant.

For a riveting read from a hero in the advertising world, try *Ogilvy on Advertising* by David Ogilvy, founder of Ogilvy and Mather (London: Prion Books, 2007).

Lastly, a topic that has been talked about in the popular press is the rise of the new super-powers China and India. In his book *Chindia Rising* (New Delhi: India Professional, 2008), eminent Professor Jagdish Sheth talks about how China and India could benefit businesses, and provides a very different perspective on consumer behaviour from those countries.

REFERENCES

Abdul-Razzaq, S., Ozanne, L. and Fortin, D. (2009) Cutting through the clutter? A field experiment measuring behavioural responses to an ambient form of advertising. Australian & New Zealand Marketing Academy Conference (ANZMAC), Melbourne, Australia.

Addis, M. and Holbrook, M.B. (2001) On the conceptual link between mass customisation and experiential consumption: an explosion of subjectivity. *Journal of Consumer Behaviour*, 1 (1): 50–6.

Andreason, A.R. (1984) Life status changes and changes in consumer preferences and satisfaction. *Journal of Consumer Research*, 11 (December): 784–94.

Bakamitsos, G. and Siomkos, G.J. (2003) Context effects in marketing practice: the case of mood. *Journal of Consumer Behaviour*, 3 (4): 304–14.

Bardacki, A. and Whitelock, J. (2004) How ready are customers for mass customization? An exploratory investigation. *European Journal of Marketing*, 38 (11/12): 1396–496.

Barnard, N. and Ehrenberg, A. (1997) Advertising: strongly persuasive or nudging? *Journal of Advertising Research*, 37 (1): 21–31.

Becker-Olsen, K. and Cudmore, B.A. (2004) When good deeds dilute your equity. *Advances in Consumer Research*, 31: 78–9.

Bengtsson, A. (2003) Towards a critique of brand relationships. *Advances in Consumer Research*, 30: 154–8.

Biel, A.L. (1990) Love the ad. Buy the product? *ADMAP*, September: 21–5.

Biel, A.L. and Bridgwater, C.A. (1990) Attributes of likeable television commercials. *Journal of Advertising Research*, 30 (3): 38–44.

Blythe, J. (2003) *Essentials of Marketing Communications*, 2nd edn. Hemel Hempstead: FT Prentice–Hall.

Bolls, P.D., Muehling, D.D. and Yoon, K. (2003) The effects of television commercial pacing on viewers' attention and memory. *Journal of Marketing Communications*, 9 (1): 17–28.

Booms, B.H. and Bitner, M.J. (1981) Marketing strategies and organisational structures for service firms. In J.H. Donnelly and W.R. George (eds), *Marketing of Services*. Chicago, IL: American Marketing Association, pp. 47–52.

Bray, J.P. and Harris, C. (2006) The effect of 9-ending prices on retail sales: a quantitative UK based field study. *Journal of Marketing Management*, 22 (5/6): 601–17.

British Film Institute (BFI) (2014) *Statistical Yearbook*. London: British Film Institute. www.bfi.org.uk/news-opinion/news-bfi/announcements/bfi-statistical-yearbook-shows-uk-film-buoyant-2013 (accessed 24 October 2015).

Brunk, K. (2010) Reputation building: beyond our control? Inferences in consumers' ethical perception forming. *Journal of Consumer Behaviour*, 9 (4): 275–92.

Census and Statistics Department (2015) *The Government of Hong Kong*. Available at: www.censtatd.gov.hk/home/ (accessed 10 May 2016).

Dalli, D., Romani, S. and Gistri, G. (2006) Brand dislike: representing the negative side of consumer preferences. *Advances in Consumer Research*, 33: 87–95.

Dobele, A., Toleman, D. and Beverland, M. (2005) Controlled infection! Spreading the brand message through viral marketing, *Business Horizons*, 48: 143–9

Dolan, R.J. (1995) How do you know when the price is right? *Harvard Business Review*, 73 (5): 174–83.

Dye, R. (2000) The buzz on buzz. *Harvard Business Review*, 78 (6): 139–46

Ehrenberg, A. (1997) How do consumers buy a new brand? *ADMAP*, March.

Ehrenberg, A.S.C. (1992) Comments on how advertising works. *Marketing and Research Today*, August: 167–9.

Englis, B.G. and Bamossy, G. (2010) Green dilemma: libertarian values trump communal values. *Advances in Consumer Research*, 37: 32–5.

Evans, M., O'Malley, L. and Patterson, M. (1996) Direct marketing communications in the UK: a study of growth, past, present and future. *Journal of Marketing Communications*, 2 (March): 51–65.

Foxall, G. and Goldsmith, R.E. (1994) *Consumer Psychology for Marketing*. London: Routledge.

Gourville, J. and Koehler, J. (2003) Downsizing price increases: a differential sensitivity to price over quantity. *Advances in Consumer Research*, 30: 106–8.

Grapentine, T. (2003) Window shopping. *Marketing Research*, 15 (4): 5.

Gueguen, N. and Legoherel, P. (2004) Numerical encoding and odd-ending prices: the effect of a contrast in discount perception. *European Journal of Marketing*, 38 (1): 194–208.

Harrigan, P. and Hulbert, B. (2011) How can marketing academics serve marketing practice? The new marketing DNA as a model for marketing education. *Journal of Marketing Education*, 33 (3): 253–72

Henry, P.C. and Caldwell, M.L. (2006) Self-empowerment and consumption: customer remedies for prolonged stigmatisation. *European Journal of Marketing*, 40 (9/10): 1031–48.

Huck, P. (2003) SMS critique: all publicity isn't necessarily good publicity. *Australian Financial Review Magazine*, 15: 2–3.

Husted, B.W., Russo, M.V., Basurto Meza, C.E. and Tilleman, S.G. (2014) An exploratory study of environmental attitudes and the willingness to pay for environmental certification in Mexico. *Journal of Business Research*, 67 (May): 891–99

Jones, J.P. (1991) Over-promise and under-delivery. *Marketing and Research Today*, November: 195–203.

Judd, V.C. (1987) Differentiate with the fifth P. *Industrial Marketing Management*, 16: 241–7.

Kantar Report (2014) *Kantar Worldpanel Survey*. www.kantarworldpanel.com/cn-en/news/CHINA-MEN (accessed 24 October 2015).

Krishna, A., Wagner, M. and Yoon, C. (2002) Effects of extreme-priced products on consumer reservation prices. *Advances in Consumer Research*, 29: 86–8.

Laforet, S. (2011) Brand names on packaging and their impact on purchase performance. *Journal of Consumer Behaviour*, 10 (1): 18–30.

Mathur, A., Moschis, G.P. and Lee, E. (2003) Life events and brand preference changes. *Journal of Consumer Behaviour*, 3 (2): 129–41.

Maxham III, J.G. and Netemeyer, R.G. (2003) Firms reap what they sow: the effect of shared values and perceived organisational justice on customers' evaluation of complaint handling. *Journal of Marketing*, 67 (1): 46–62.

McKechnie, S. and Leather, P. (1998) Likeability as a measure of advertising effectiveness: the case of financial services. *Journal of Marketing Communications*, 4: 63–85.

Molz, G. and Gielnik, M. (2006) Does the introduction of the Euro have an effect on subjective hypotheses about the price–quality relationship? *Journal of Consumer Behaviour*, 5 (May–Jun): 204–10.

Pennanen, K. (2011) Is interpersonal and institutional e-trustworthiness equally important in consumer e-trust development? Implications for consumers' e-trust building behaviours. *Journal of Consumer Behaviour*, 10 (5): 233–44.

Pires, G.D., Stanton, J. and Rita, P. (2006) The Internet, consumers' empowerment, and marketing strategies. *European Journal of Marketing*, 40 (9/10): 1013–30.

POPAI (Point-of-Purchase Advertising Institute) (1994) Point of purchase consumer buying habits study. In T.A. Shimp, *Advertising, Promotion and Supplemental Aspects of Integrated Marketing Communications*, 4th edn. Fort Worth, TX: Dryden Press.

Rajagopal, P. (2008) Point-of-sales promotions and buying simulation in retail stores. *Journal of Database Marketing and Customer Strategy Management*, 15 (4): 249–66.

Rasmusson, E. (1997) Winning back angry customers. *Sales and Marketing Management*, October: 131.

Ritson, M. (2003) *Assessing the Value of Advertising*. London: London Business School.

Roggeveen, A.L., Lan, X. and Monroe, K.B. (2006) How attributions and the product's price impact the effectiveness of price partitioning. *Advances in Consumer Research*, 33: 181.

Rose, P., Smith, S.T. and Segrist, D.J. (2010) Too cheap to chug: frugality as a buffer against college-age drinking. *Journal of Consumer Behaviour*, 9 (3): 228–38.

Sampson, P. (1992) People are people the world over: the case for psychological market segmentation. *Marketing and Research Today*, November: 236–45.

Schindler, R.M. and Kirby, P.N. (1997) Patterns of right-most digits used in advertised prices: implications for nine-ending effects. *Journal of Consumer Research*, 24 (September): 192–201.

Seigyoung, A. and Chuang-Foh, S. (2006) Balancing giving-up vs. taking-in: does the pattern or payments and benefits matter to customers in a financing decision context? *Advances in Consumer Research*, 33: 139–45.

Sethna, Z., Jones, R. and Harrigan, P. (eds) (2013) *Entrepreneurial Marketing: Global Perspectives*. Bingley: Emerald Publishing.

Shankar, A. (1999a) Ambient media: advertising's new opportunity? *International Journal of Advertising*, 18 (3): 305–22.

Shankar, A. (1999b) Advertising's imbroglio. *Journal of Marketing Communications*, 5 (1): 1–17.

Shen, A. and Ball, A.D. (2011) Preference stability belief as a determinant of response to personalised recommendations. *Journal of Consumer Behaviour*, 10 (2): 71–9.

Simmons, C.L. and Schindler, R.M. (2003) Cultural superstitions and the price endings used in Chinese advertising. *Journal of International Marketing*, 11 (2): 101–11.

Spilker-Attig, A. and Brettel, M. (2010) Effectiveness of on-line advertising channels: a price-level-dependent analysis. *Journal of Marketing Management*, 26 (3 & 4): 343–60.

Stapel, J. (1991) Like the advertisement, but does it interest me? *ADMAP*, April.

Stoll, M., Baecke, S. and Kenning, P. (2008) What they see is what they get? An fMRI study on neural correlates of attractive packaging. *Journal of Consumer Behaviour*, 7 (4/5): 342–59.

Suri, R., Anderson, R.E. and Kotlov, V. (2004) The use of 9-ending prices: contrasting the USA with Poland. *European Journal of Marketing*, 38 (1): 56–72.

Umphress, E.E., Bingham, J.B. and Mitchell, M.S. (2010) Unethical behaviour in the name of the company: the moderating effect of organisational identification and positive reciprocity beliefs on unethical pro-organisational behaviour. *Journal of Applied Psychology*, 95 (4): 769–80.

Unnava, H.R., Rajagopal, P. and Raju, S. (2003) Reducing competitive ad interference by varying advertising context: a test of network models of memory. *Advances in Consumer Research*, 30: 45–6.

Wells, W.D. (1980) *Liking and Sales Effectiveness: A Hypothesis*. New York: MSW.

Wright, L.T. and Crimp, M. (2000) *The Marketing Research Process*. London: Prentice-Hall.

Yannopolou, N., Koronis, E. and Elliott, R. (2011) Media amplification of a brand crisis and its effect on brand trust. *Journal of Marketing Management*, 27 (5 & 6): 530–46.

Yasumuro, K. (2015) Conceptualizing an adaptable marketing system: the end of mass marketing. In R.S. Tedlow and G. Jones (eds), *The Rise and Fall of Mass Marketing*. Abingdon and New York: Routledge, pp. 205–35.

Zufryden, F.S., Pedrick, J.H. and Sankaralingam, A. (1993) Zapping and its impact on brand purchase behaviour. *Journal of Advertising Research*, 33 (January/February): 58–66.

MORE ONLINE

For additional materials that support this chapter and your learning, please visit:
https://study.sagepub.com/sethnaandblythe

CHAPTER 3

THE DECISION-MAKING PROCESS, BUYER BEHAVIOUR AND BRAND INTERACTION

LEARNING OBJECTIVES

After reading this chapter you should be able to:

- Describe the role of goals in decision-making.
- Explain the importance of being included in the 'consideration set'.
- Explain some of the limiting factors on information searches.
- Explain how decision rules are established and used.
- Explain the relationship between involvement and information processing.
- Show how involvement relates to end goals and values.
- Describe how dimensions of involvement can be used to segment markets.
- Explain what is meant by unsought goods.
- Describe the significance of loyalty and branding in buyer behaviour.

INTRODUCTION

This chapter is concerned with the ways consumers approach making purchase decisions and what their goals and motivations are. The methods used depend on whether the product is novel or tried and tested; whether the purchase is routine or out of the ordinary; whether the product is a new one, or whether a repeat of a previous purchase.

Any plan of action carries with it a degree of risk, but the lower the risk to consumers, the more likely they are to buy the product and the less likely they are to complain afterwards. If consumers are familiar with the brand, the perceived risk is reduced, and so the chapter also looks at branding as a way of reducing risk for the consumer.

DECISION-MAKING USING GOALS

Sometimes goals will conflict. In these circumstances, the strongly active goal will inhibit competing goals until the stronger goal has been achieved, at which point the weaker or less active goal will re-emerge (Brendl et al. 2002).

Table 3.1 gives some purchase end goals and motivations, with examples. In practice, marketers have little influence over consumers' main goals, since these often derive from basic values. Marketers can try to influence the less abstract end goals, such as the desired functional or psycho-social consequences, through promotional strategies. For example, although it may be difficult to persuade someone that he or she ought to dress well in order to impress other people, we can much more easily influence those who already believe in dressing to impress, perhaps encouraging them to shop at a specific retailer or buy specific clothing brands. Thus these factors act as drivers for end goals, as shown in Figure 3.1.

Optimising satisfaction to achieve such end goals are common with websites competing for business, as the following examples show:

- www.chillihotchocolate.com – With a new attitude to shopping online, this website works with new designers as well as more established names to find interesting new things. Their 'no borders' philosophy might feature fantastic new places to eat, Fairtrade kitchenware, a 'one-off' furnishings week, and a preview of new ceramic and jewellery collections.

- www.net-a-porter.com/gb/en/content/about-us – This is another fashion website, but this time at the top end of the market. It provides an information service as well as selling high-end couture (in 2013, it reportedly bought six Dolce & Gabbana red beaded dresses that were subsequently sold online for £32,000 each).

Consumers' relevant knowledge about the product category (or, if you prefer, the problem category) is obviously important in problem-solving (Crosby and Taylor 1981), so inexperienced purchasers are likely to take a knowledgeable friend with

TABLE 3.1 Examples of purchase end goals

Dominant end goal	Basic purchase motivation	Examples
Optimise satisfaction	Seek maximum positive consequences	Buy dinner at the best restaurant in town rather than risking a cheap diner
Prevention	Avoid potential unpleasant consequences	Buy weatherproofing for a house so as to maintain the good appearance of the house, and protect its value
Resolve conflict	See satisfactory balance of positive and negative consequences	Buy a moderately expensive car of very good quality so as to avoid high maintenance costs and unreliability, while still keeping within a reasonable expenditure
Escape	Reduce or escape from current aversive circumstances	Buy an anti-dandruff shampoo, in order to prevent future bouts of dandruff and embarrassment
Maintenance (satisfy)	Maintain satisfaction of a basic need with minimal effort	Buy bread at a local shop. This satisfies the need for bread without having to go to the out-of-town hypermarket where you do your main weekly shopping

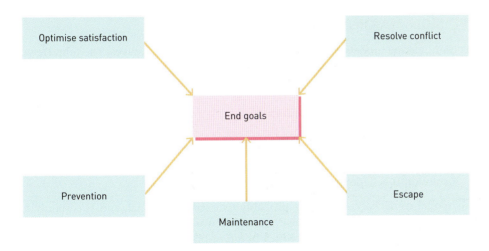

FIGURE 3.1 Drivers for end goals

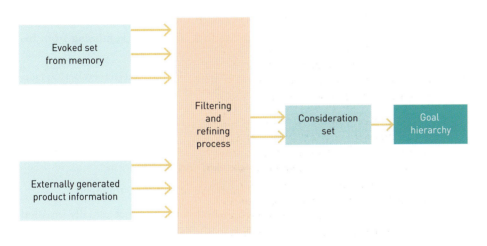

FIGURE 3.2 Developing goals

them when they go to make a major purchase, such as a car. Sometimes relevant knowledge is brought forward from the individual's memory, and some knowledge is acquired during the purchasing process (Biehal and Chakravarty 1983). Any brands that have simply been remembered are part of the **evoked set** and for regular purchases or familiar product categories these may be the only brands that are considered. The result of the information search process is to create choice alternatives, which are further refined into a **consideration set**. The consideration set is the group of products that will be actively considered.

In Figure 3.2, the many brands in the evoked set, and the even more numerous brands that might be brought to the individual's attention, are filtered and refined to create the consideration set, which may only comprise a few brands. The individual will then usually select one or possibly two brands to feed into the goal hierarchy as being the desirable brands for solving the need problem.

Evoked set

The group of brands a consumer can remember spontaneously

Consideration set

The group of brands which a consumer believes will meet his or her need, and which are therefore seriously being considered for purchase

DECISION-MAKING MODELS

Decision-making models are often complex and involve many stages. The John Dewey model (Dewey 1910), outlined more than 100 years ago, gives the following five stages:

1. A difficulty is felt (need identification).

2. The difficulty is located and defined.

3. Possible solutions are suggested.

4. Consequences are considered.

5. A solution is accepted.

This model of decision-making is probably excessively rational, and is certainly far more complex than most purchase situations warrant. Life is simply too busy to spend much time agonising over which brand of biscuit to buy.

Later, Engel, Kollat and Blackwell developed the EKB model of consumer behaviour, which became the CDP (Consumer Decision Process) model (see Figure 3.3), and which follows seven stages (Blackwell et al. 2005). These are:

1. *Need recognition.* The individual recognises that something is missing from his or her life.

2. *Search for information.* This information search may be internal (remembering facts about products, or recalling experiences with them as a result of services) or external (reading about possible products, surfing the Internet or visiting shops, etc.)

3. *Pre-purchase evaluation of alternatives.* The individual considers which of the possible alternatives might be best for fulfilling the need.

4. *Purchase.* The act of making the final selection and paying for it.

5. *Consumption.* Using the product for the purpose of fulfilling the need.

6. *Post-consumption evaluation.* Considering whether the product actually satisfied the need or not and whether there were any problems arising from its purchase and consumption.

7. *Divestment.* Disposing of the product, or its packaging, or any residue left from consuming the product (either as a conscientious consumer or as a result of legislation, for instance 'end of life' for vehicles).

The similarity between Dewey's model and the CDP model is obvious, and similar criticisms apply, but both models offer a basic outline of how people make consumption decisions. People do not buy unless they feel they have a need. A need is felt when there is a divergence between the person's actual state and their desired state. The degree of difference between the two states is what determines the level of motivation the person feels to do something about the problem, and this will in turn depend on a number of external factors.

There are two possible reasons for a divergence between the desired and the actual states: one is that the actual state changes, the other is that the desired state changes. In practice, it is rare for the actual states and the desired states to be the same, since this would imply that the consumer would be perfectly happy and have everything that he or she could possibly want, which is rarely the case in an imperfect world.

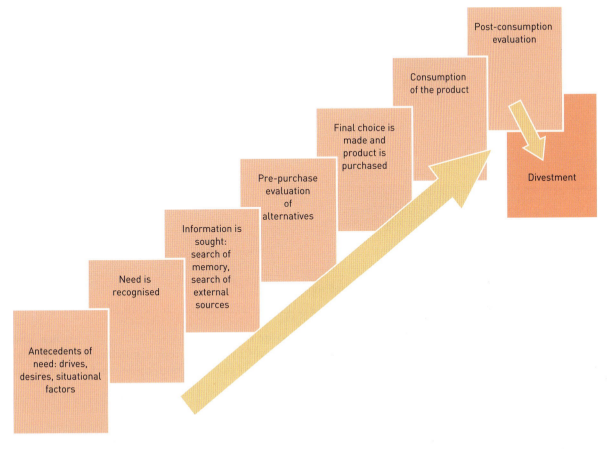

FIGURE 3.3 The decision-making process

Causes of shift of the actual state might be taken from the following list (Onkvisit and Shaw 1994):

- *Assortment depletion*. Consumption, spoilage, or wear and tear on the stock of goods or products within the individual's assortment.

- *Income change*. This can be upwards, through a salary increase or windfall, or downwards through, for example, redundancy.

Assortment depletion
The reduction in one's overall quantity of possessions

Causes of shifts in the desired state are often more to do with marketing activities. This is because new information may change the individual's aspirations. If the individual sees a better car, hears a better digital radio or otherwise becomes aware of a better solution to the problem, there is likely to be a shift in the desired state. From a marketing viewpoint, this approach is most effective when consumers are already dissatisfied with their present products.

Changing desire is often brought on by a change in actual state; a windfall might prompt an individual to start up a social enterprise that they always dreamed of. The relationship between these factors is shown in Figure 3.4.

The psychology of complication says that people complicate their lives deliberately by seeking new products, even though they are fairly satisfied with the old one. The

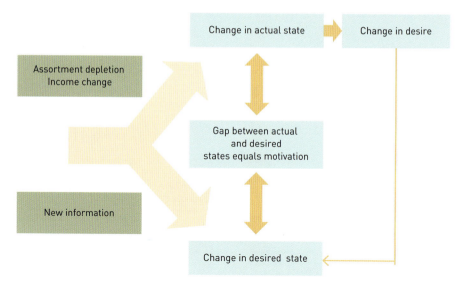

FIGURE 3.4 Actual and desired states

Psychology of complication

The tendency for people to make their lives more complex, and therefore more interesting

Psychology of simplification

The tendency for people to make their lives less complex and therefore less stressful

psychology of complication is the opposite of the psychology of simplification, which says that consumers try to simplify their lives by making repeat purchases of a familiar brand (Hoyer and Ridgway 1984). It is probable that both these mechanisms act on people at different times.

CHALLENGING THE STATUS QUO

Marketers are often accused of creating needs, indeed marketing academics often define marketing as 'satisfying the wants and needs of customers' (Kotler et al. 2013) as a result of meeting the needs of the marketplace by designing products and services and then communicating them (Elliot et al. 2010). There is a view that somehow marketers can persuade people to want things for which they actually have no use – and of course marketers hotly deny this. This of course raises ethical issues (Nantel and Weeks 1996; and for more information on this hot topic see Chapter 14 later in this book). For example how truthful is the advertising that is used to communicate a message? Does it distort reality? Does it create artificial needs? (Takala and Uusitalo 1996).

In practice, of course, marketers have very little influence over the actual state of consumers, but do they have influence over the desired state of consumers? Emphatically yes – otherwise all that advertising is just going to waste. For instance, Harper (2006) noted that marketers are blamed for the obesity epidemic in children in the USA. The intimation was that it is marketers who have negotiated for schools to install vending machines serving unhealthy soft drinks in order to entice children to be desirous of fizzy drinks. So is it all right to seek to change people's desired state? Is it ethical? Or are we simply continuing the process that all people indulge in – advising each other about ways to make our lives more enjoyable and comfortable?

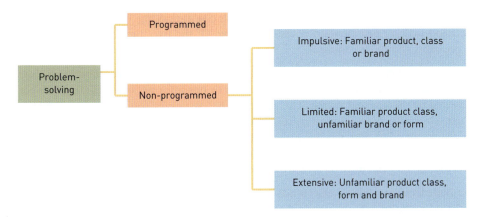

FIGURE 3.5 Programmed and non-programmed problem-solving (from Onkvisit and Shaw 1994) Used by Kind Permission

Since people often make decisions on the basis of immediate gain and emotion, neurological factors often contribute to our understanding of how and why people buy (Foxall 2008).

Assortment adjustment is the act of entering the market to replenish or exchange the assortment of products the consumer owns. Assortment adjustment can be *programmed* (habitual) or *non-programmed* (new purchases) (see Figure 3.5). Non-programmed assortment adjustment divides into three categories. *Impulse purchases* are not based on a plan, and usually just happen as the result of a sudden confrontation with a stimulus – for example, in-store promotions might trigger an impulse purchase. People often buy as a result of lowered stimulation levels; in other words, bored shoppers might buy as a result of a stimulating promotion in-store (Sharma et al. 2010).

Assortment adjustment can take the form of either assortment replenishment, i.e. replacing worn-out or consumed products, or assortment extension, adding to the range of products owned. Assortment replenishment will usually require very little information searching or risk, since the product is already known. Assortment extension is more likely to lead to an extensive problem-solving pattern.

Impulse buying has been further subdivided into four categories (Hawkins 1962): *pure impulse*, based on the novelty of a product; *reminder impulse*, which relates to a product that has been left off the shopping list; *suggestion impulse*, which is about products that fulfil a previously unfelt need; and *planned impulse*, which occurs when the customer has gone out to buy a specific type of product but is prepared to be swayed by special offers.

For example, someone may set out to the supermarket to buy the week's groceries, plus something for lunch today. On the way round, he sees a jar of almond-stuffed olives and decides to buy some to try (pure impulse). Next he notices the green lasagne, which reminds him he's out of pasta (reminder impulse) and also on the shelf near it a recipe book for pasta (suggestion impulse). Finally, he notices that the smoked chicken is on special offer, and decides to buy some for lunch (planned impulse). This type of scenario is familiar to most people who shop in supermarkets, and indeed supermarkets will often capitalise on this in the way the shelves are stocked and in the way the store is laid out.

Assortment adjustment

The process of substituting some possession for others in order to improve one's overall position

Assortment replenishment

Replacing possessions that have been worn out or used up

Assortment extension

Increasing one's overall quantity of possessions

The other two types of non-programmed decision-making involve either limited decision-making or extended decision-making. Of the two, limited decision-making is probably the most common.

Limited decision-making takes place when the customer is already familiar with the product class and merely wants to update his or her information or fill in a few gaps revealed by the internal search. This is typical behaviour for someone who is replacing a car; since this is usually an infrequent activity, consumers often find it necessary to check out what new models are available and renew acquaintance with the price levels being charged, even though (as a driver) the consumer will have considerable knowledge of what a car is and what it can be expected to do.

Limited decision-making also tends to occur when the consumer is not completely satisfied with the existing product and seeks a better alternative. Here the individual is only looking for something that overcomes the perceived problem with the exist-ing product. A trigger for this might be a change of context: someone who moves home will have their usual routines disrupted and may be open to changing his or her purchasing behaviour across a spectrum of goods (Neal et al. 2008).

Extended decision-making occurs when the consumer is unfamiliar with the product class, form and brand. For example, the majority of us are still unaware of consumer drones and the current state of the art in remote-controlled aircraft. This is a new class of product and an interested consumer would have to undertake a fairly exten-sive information search before committing to a particular model. Extended decision-making is caused by unfamiliarity; consumers who know little about the product category, brands, and so forth will tend to shop around more.

INTERRUPTS

Sometimes the buying process cannot be followed exactly because events occur that force the individual to rethink the situation. These events are called interrupts, and they fall into four categories:

Interrupt

Something that diverts an individual away from a goal, usually temporarily

1. *Unexpected information that is inconsistent with established beliefs.* For example, if the shop that the consumer had expected to buy from has changed hands or closed, the individual has to look for a new supplier.

2. *Prominent environmental stimuli.* An in-store display might offer an alternative to the original purchase (perhaps by offering a large price discount on a similar product). This may divert the consumer away from his or her usual brand choice, or at the very least cause the consumer to consider switching.

3. *Affective states.* Hunger, boredom or tiredness during a shopping trip might lead to a change in goal. This may be a change away from looking for a new jacket, and towards looking for the coffee shop.

4. *Conflicts.* These are the motivational conflicts discussed in Chapter 6. If an individual is confronted with an approach–approach conflict, or an approach–avoidance conflict, there will be a temporary cessation of goal attainment while new goals are formulated and the conflict resolved.

The effect of interrupts will depend on how consumers interpret the interrupting event. On the one hand, the interrupt may activate new end goals (as when the shopping trip turns into a search for a cup of coffee). On the other hand, a choice

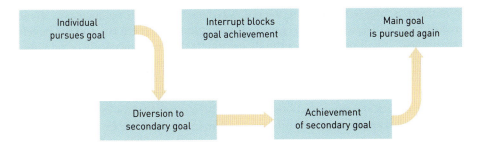

FIGURE 3.6 Temporary effects of an interrupt

TABLE 3.2 Goal and interrupt strengths

	Strong goal	Weak goal
Strong interrupt	Powerful stress set up in the individual	Goal will be ignored or abandoned and a secondary goal will be established
Weak interrupt	Goal will continue to be pursued	Goal may be interrupted or abandoned or interrupt may be ignored

heuristic might be activated – for example, if the unexpected information is a friend recommending a brand, this may activate a heuristic about acting on friends' recommendations. Sometimes the interrupt is severe enough that the individual shelves the problem-solving behaviour indefinitely (for example, if the unexpected information is that the person has lost his or her job, the buying of a new jacket might be postponed indefinitely, or if a prominent environmental stimulus such as a substantial governmental tax increase on diesel fuel is levied, one might think twice about buying a diesel vehicle) (see Figure 3.6).

Heuristic
A decision-making rule; sometimes also seen as a shortcut rule (see Chapter 6 for further detail)

The strength of the interrupt is also important (see Table 3.2). If the goal is a strong one, and the interrupt weak, the individual is unlikely be diverted. A weak goal and a strong interrupt will clearly result in a break in the problem-solving behaviour (for example, the intention to check the prices online for a possible purchase of a holiday following a windfall is unlikely to take precedence over a desperate need for the toilet). A weak goal and a weak interrupt may or may not result in a divergence from the planned behaviour, and a strong interrupt and a strong goal are likely to lead to considerable stress on the individual.

In most cases people tend to resume an interrupted task fairly quickly. Even though a marketer might be able to distract somebody away from their shopping to have a cup of coffee or a snack, the shopping task will be resumed fairly quickly afterwards.

RISK AND UNCERTAINTY

Inexperienced buyers have, by definition, less knowledge of the product category they are trying to buy into. Any action by a consumer could produce unpredictable consequences, some of which might be unpleasant. These consequences form the perceived risk of the transaction. Financial risk is present since the consumer could lose money; for houses, cars and other major purchases the risk is great because the commitment is long-term. Because the risk is reduced as knowledge increases, greater perceived risk will tend to lead to greater information search efforts, and the benefits of such a search will be correspondingly greater. If the consumer feels certain about the decision already, there will be correspondingly less benefit in carrying out a search for information. Between individuals, a further factor is the degree to which the individual is risk-averse – clearly some people are quite happy to take risks in life, where others are more cautious. This can be a crucial factor in some marketing situations: for example, financial advisers in Britain are required by law to assess the individual's degree of risk-aversion before making recommendations for investments or borrowing. People tend to become more risk-averse as they grow older, since it would be more difficult to recover from any loss. In recent years, there have been several scandals concerning the mis-selling of financial products (Gilad 2015), in particular high-risk high-return products sold to people who are in fact risk-averse and did not realise that there was a risk of losing part (or even all) of their investment. A recent study of female dentists found that as age increased, the risk-averse behaviour of women declined (McGrath and Rossomando 2015), perhaps due to dentists wanting (or probably 'needing') to keep up-to-date with technological advancements, in order to remain competitive.

The fear of losing face with friends and associates is the major component of social risk. It is determined in part by product visibility; consumers who buy an inappropriate car can risk ridicule from their friends and colleagues, and might therefore carry out a more extended information search to ensure that the car will not provoke this reaction.

Perceived cost is the extent to which the consumer has to commit resources to the search. People will frequently cut the search down simply because it is taking too much time, money or effort. This is because the potential loss of making a wrong purchase decision is seen as being less than the cost of making a full search.

Risk reduction strategies are shown in Figure 3.7. The main tactic for reducing risk is to increase one's knowledge about the product category. A prospective aircraft purchaser is likely to seek a great deal of advice from a great many sources, and is likely to have the aircraft thoroughly inspected by a qualified and experienced aeronautical engineer. If the risk is still perceived to be high the consumer will simply not make the purchase. This is why most retailers offer money-back guarantees or no-quibble return policies: such guarantees reduce risk for the consumer, so making purchase more likely. Since most purchases work out reasonably well products seldom need to be returned.

People often spend considerable time looking both online and offline, increasing their knowledge of the product categories before buying and in order to reduce risk of making the wrong decision. It used to be the case that the need to inspect products personally as a way of reducing risk had been identified as a barrier to Internet purchase (Dailey 2003). On the other hand, some aspects of Internet purchase appear to reduce people's aversion to risk: especially as *returns* are so easy to process. Sales made by e-tailers (Internet companies such as Amazon, Asos and made.com) which do not have any physical stores surpassed online sales of store-based UK retailers (£21.8 billion versus £21.5 billion) for the first time in 2015, according to a Mintel report.

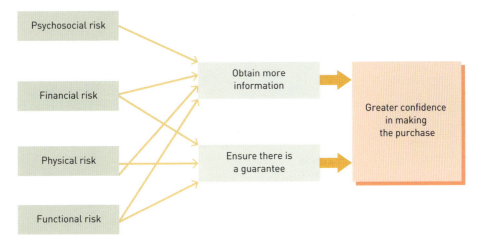

FIGURE 3.7 Reducing risk

People will frequently choose the middle-ranked or mid-priced brand as a compromise between buying the worst alternative on the one hand, and risking spending too much by buying the 'best' brand on the other. In a two-choice situation, a brand's chances of being bought are helped if a third brand is available which places it in the middle range (Sheng et al. 2003). This implies that a company in second place to a major brand should consider introducing a third, cheaper, brand into the market in order to boost sales of its existing brand.

Other tactics for reducing risk might include seeking help from a competent friend, or taking out insurance against the risk, or hedging the risk by setting aside resources (typically money) to cover against anything going wrong.

Mood can have an effect on risk-taking behaviour: people tend to buy more lottery tickets if the weather is bad, but whether this is a way of making life more exciting in dull weather or whether it is a way of cheering oneself up with the prospect of a big win is debatable (Bruyneel et al. 2006).

PRE-PURCHASE ACTIVITIES

Having recognised the need, the consumer will undertake a series of pre-purchase activities.

The information search comes from two sources: an internal search (from memory) and an external search (from outside sources). In both cases most of the information originates from seller-based sources, and is therefore readily available and low-cost. If the internal information search is insufficient, that is to say the individual does not have enough knowledge of the product category to be able to make a choice, an external search will be undertaken.

Sources of information might be marketer-dominated (advertising, blogs, vlogs, brochures, product placements in films and TV shows, websites, salespeople, retail displays, Twitter campaigns, and so forth) or non-marketer dominated (friends, family, influential journalists, opinion leaders, consumer organisations, government and

FIGURE 3.8 Information searching

industry reports, news stories, and so forth) (Figure 3.8). Word of mouth/mouse communications are generally more powerful than any marketer-generated communications, for the following reasons:

- Word of mouth is interactive, because it involves a discussion between two or more parties. This forces those involved to think about the communication.
- It allows for feedback and confirmation of the message in a way that one-way communications like advertising do not.
- Because the source is a friend or family member who has no profit motive (unlike the marketer) the communication is more credible.

'Peer review' as seen in the CityFalcon case study in Chapter 13 is now an important consideration for many companies. People often discuss products and services: they like to talk about their own recent purchases, to advise people about purchases and even to discuss recent controversial marketing communications. It should be noted that non-marketer generated sources are themselves influenced by marketers, and also much of the consumer's memory of the product comes from marketer-generated communications, so that even the internal search is affected by marketers.

From a marketer's viewpoint, the problem is that people will talk about products and companies whether the firm likes it or not, and may very well discuss products in negative terms. A great deal of word of mouth is negative; bad news seems to travel twice as fast as good news, and there is very little marketers can do about this, apart from be seen to be responsive in some shape or form (Kim et al. 2016; Yin et al. forthcoming).

Sometimes an individual will set out with the belief that he or she has sufficient internal information to make the purchase, but is then presented with new information at the point of purchase. In other cases, people experience 'choice paralysis' brought on by having too wide a range of possible products to choose from (Shankar et al. 2006).

Because choosing involves a degree of emotional effort as well as cognitive effort (people often become stressed when faced with a choice between expensive options) the individual may well make a hasty choice (Baumeister 2004). In other words, if the individual is finding it hard to choose, he or she might cut the decision-making process short by just grabbing the nearest product, simply to end the stress of trying to reach a decision.

THE SEARCH EFFORT

It is common for people with limited information to base their decisions on price, simply because they lack the necessary understanding to make a judgement based on other features of the product.

Search efforts are not very extensive under most circumstances, even for major purchases such as houses, because of the amount of time and effort that has to be expended. Usually consumers will continue to search until they find something that is adequate to meet the need, and will then not look any further; with comparison websites carving out a niche for themselves. A Financial Conduct Authority (FCA 2014) report stated that most customers use the option of short-listing upper-most quotes on price comparison websites before making decisions.

Information searches such as those carried out on the Internet and price comparison websites can be time-consuming, but as users become more adept, and as website design improves, searching is becoming much more rapid. It is likely that people will become more price-sensitive as the ease of searching becomes greater – the cost of searching is low in terms of both money and time, so it becomes easier to shop around for bargains (Campo and Breugelmans 2015; Melis et al. 2015). Limits on the search are shown in Figure 3.9.

In some cases, consumers will visit websites that carry complaints about companies, for example www.aspokesmansaid.com. This is a public platform that leverages the power of social media to force a response to a consumer complaint about a company. Online product recommendation agents gather information from consumers, then search the web to find products that match the consumer's needs; there is evidence to show that these agents should offer more than one solution for the consumer to choose from, which of course dilutes the advantage to some extent (Aggarwal and Vaidyanathan 2003). Apart from specialist recommenders like aspokesmansaid.com, there are of course other popular examples such as Twitter and Facebook which both provide a platform for consumer complaints.

FIGURE 3.9 Limits on the information search

FACTORS AFFECTING THE EXTERNAL SEARCH FOR INFORMATION

The extent and nature of the external search for information will depend on a range of factors connected with the consumer's situation, the value and availability of the information, the nature of the decision being contemplated and the nature of the individual. Figure 3.10 illustrates how these factors interrelate.

The type of problem-solving adopted will depend on the task at hand. A programmed decision pattern will lead almost immediately to purchase; these are the regular, always-buy-the-same-brand type decisions. Non-programmed decisions may still lead immediately to a purchase by impulse, but this type of decision pattern will more likely lead to limited or extensive information search patterns.

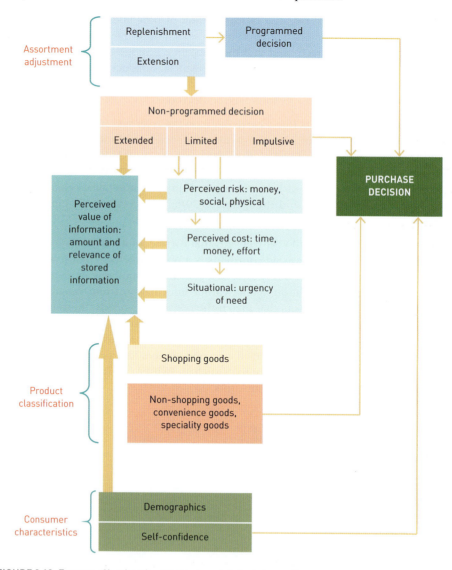

FIGURE 3.10 Factors affecting the external search for information

The perceived value of the information is important in terms of how extensive the information search will be. In other words, the extent of the external search depends on how valuable the information is. If there is plenty of information in the 'internal files' within the consumer's mind, the extent of external information seeking will be correspondingly less; consumers who are highly familiar with the product will search less than those who are only moderately familiar (Bettman and Park 1980).

The relevance of this information is also a factor; if it's a long time since the last purchase, the stored information may not be relevant any longer. New alternatives may have developed or the product may have improved. If the individual was satisfied with the last product (which may by now have been consumed or has worn out) the internal information will probably be regarded as relevant, and the search will be less extensive or non-existent (Kiel and Layton 1981).

Time is a cost relating to search. It is sometimes measured in opportunity cost, or in terms of what the person could be doing instead of spending time searching. For example, highly paid people may value their time highly because they can earn more money at a desk than they save by shopping around, so they are prepared to spend money in order to save time. Poorer consumers may be more prepared to spend time shopping around in order to save money (Urbany 1986).

Money costs are the out-of-pocket expenses of searching. Clearly a consumer who wants to buy organic virgin olive oil might compare different brands in Waitrose but is unlikely to drive to Sainsbury's to compare prices, and would certainly not fly to Italy even though olive oil would almost certainly be cheaper there.

The psychological costs of the information search include frustration, driving, visiting different shops, trawling through websites, avoiding pop-ups and re-targeted online advertising, talking to shop assistants and generally giving a lot of thinking time to the search. Often people become overwhelmed with the quantity of information available, and will be unable to reach a decision because of information overload.

Sometimes the reverse happens and the consumer actually enjoys the shopping experience as an entertainment. Ongoing search is different from external search in that consumers go to look for product information to augment stored product knowledge, often just for the fun of it. This can be a more important motivator than a genuine need to buy something (Bloch et al. 1986).

Situational factors will also affect the product information search. The search will be limited, for example, if there is an urgent need for the product. If one's car has broken down on a motorway, one is unlikely to phone around for the cheapest breakdown service. Other variables might include product scarcity, or lack of available credit.

CHALLENGING THE STATUS QUO

Some people really do seem to enjoy shopping. In fact, most of us do at one time or another – we go to the shops when we are on holiday, we wander round high streets trying on clothes or we wander round car showrooms looking at the cars. Browsing in bookshops, trying out new electronic equipment, even cruising the aisles of the supermarkets all provide entertainment for some people.

So where does that leave Internet shopping? Can consumers enjoy the same tangible thrill while accessing the Internet either from a laptop or a mobile device? How can we try on the dress, or test drive the wheels convincingly when they are only on a screen? Well, our friends in South Korea have a solution. Back in 2011 they created the first successful augmented reality supermarket chains in subways. Called E-Marts, these virtual stores and 'connected shelves' are stocked by supermarkets such as European grocery store giant Tesco – but they sell their goods via glowing pictures on subway platforms. Shoppers waiting for a train can simply look at the walls to view potential groceries, scan the respective QR codes with their smartphone, and then have their groceries delivered by the time they reach their homes. But if you add sensors on smart shelves (Microsoft technology developed this for its Kinect gaming tool) you can track the age and gender of passing shoppers so that offers can be instantly displayed to match the assumed needs, wants and desires of that demographic!

©iStock.com/Prykhodov

And as we're *talking tech* here, let's have a look at some even more recent developments ... very soon we'll see storefront windows becoming interactive and revolutionising the architecture of high streets. Displaying goods will simply become a thing of the past when these screens will enable shoppers to see entire catalogues, forthcoming offers and new ranges by tapping their fingers on the glass – even when the shop is closed.

Did you think that holograms were only something in *Star Wars* films? Well very soon we'll see holograms in changing rooms which will enable shoppers to try on clothes without the need to get undressed using radio-frequency identification technology (having had their body image pre-scanned in 3D).

You may have encountered speed dating, but nothing has really prepared the shopping market for 'speed shopping'. For those people who still need to physically walk around a supermarket, can you picture a world where you walk into the supermarket, having input your shopping list on a mobile app, which will then link to in-store beacons (technology that can pinpoint your location in-store) and within seconds you'll be sent a map of the store and the order in which you can pick up your desired goods in as short a time as possible, knowing where the queues are, which aisles are congested and if any products are close to selling out?

And finally, if that's not personalisation enough, what about personalised pricing? What if stores got rid of public pricing altogether on their products, but used vast in-store data mines which will gather all they can about an individual – where they shop, what they buy, their income and brand loyalty, and then use that profile and purchase history to give the customer a better deal? Safeway supermarket has just begun a trial in the US: the Just For U scheme is an app-based promotion to create individually tailored pricing, making shopping a more meaningful experience.

In terms of product classification, shopping goods are those for which a new solution has to be formulated every time. Non-shopping goods are those for which the person already has a complete preference and specification, and therefore is able to buy the same brand almost all the time (Bucklin 1963). For example, tomato ketchup is usually a non-shopping product, whereas a 55" curved OLED TV is a shopping product.

Consumer characteristics are those features of the consumer that affect the information search. Demographics affect the search in that outshoppers (people who shop outside the area in which they live) have higher incomes, and are mobile. This factor may be product-specific, since outshopping most frequently occurs when buying groceries at an out-of-town shopping centre or buying consumer durables. Outshopping can also occur in the form of a shopping trip to a major city, or even a day trip to another country to take advantage of lower prices there.

People feel varying levels of pain in paying for things. Spendthrifts feel relatively little pain in making purchases, whereas careful savers (tightwads) feel a great deal of pain in making purchases. Tightwads outnumber spendthrifts by a ratio of 3 to 2, so it is important for marketers to understand how and why the pain of paying varies across the population (Rick et al. 2008).

MAKING THE CHOICE

Having gone through the procedures of collecting information, whether by a lengthy search or by simply remembering all the necessary facts, people make a choice based on the collected information. The first procedure is to establish a consideration set, which is the group of products from which the final choice is to be made. Option framing means creating a base model for the decision, then adding or subtracting options from it: in most cases people will limit the number of options under consideration, and will tend to delete more than they add (Biswas 2009).

Consumers construct the consideration set from the knowledge obtained in the information search. They will often use cut-offs, or restrictions on the minimum or maximum acceptable values. Typically consumers will have a clear idea of the price range they are willing to pay, for example, and any product priced outside this zone will not be included. Incidentally, this price range may have a minimum as well as a maximum; price is often used as a surrogate for judging quality. Again, marketers need to know what the consumer's cut-off point is on given specifications; this can be determined by market research.

Signals are important to consumers when judging product quality. A signal could be a brand name, a guarantee and even the retailer the product is bought from. Because it is common for consumers to equate quality with high price, a useful tactic for low-priced manufacturers is to undermine this perception in as many ways as possible. The use of price as a quality signal is somewhat reduced when other signals are present. For example, if the consumer is easily able to judge the quality by inspecting the product, the relationship may not apply.

Finally, consumers will often select a decision rule or heuristic. Consumers develop these rules over a period of time; for example, a rule might be always to buy the best quality one is able to afford at the time. Some consumers have rules about brand names, or shops they know and trust, or people whose preferences they will always respect.

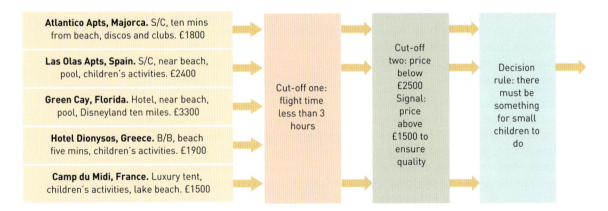

Atlantico Apts, Majorca. S/C, ten mins from beach, discos and clubs. £1800

Las Olas Apts, Spain. S/C, near beach, pool, children's activities. £2400

Green Cay, Florida. Hotel, near beach, pool, Disneyland ten miles. £3300

Hotel Dionysos, Greece. B/B, beach five mins, children's activities. £1900

Camp du Midi, France. Luxury tent, children's activities, lake beach. £1500

Cut-off one: flight time less than 3 hours

Cut-off two: price below £2500 Signal: price above £1500 to ensure quality

Decision rule: there must be something for small children to do

FIGURE 3.11 An example of a decision-making process for a holiday purchase

Figure 3.11 shows an example of a decision-making process for a holiday purchase. The consumer begins with a choice of five different holidays, which form the consideration set. The relevant information about each holiday has been included, and now the decision rules need to be applied. First of all, the consumer decides that a long flight would be difficult with children so he or she sets a limit of three hours. This cuts out Greece and Florida. Then there is a cut-off on cost (not to go above £2,500). This cut-off has no relevance, since none of the remaining holidays costs above £2,500, but the consumer also uses price as a signal by which to judge quality, and cuts out the tent in France because it is too cheap. The remaining decision rule is that there must be something for the children to do, and this leaves only the apartment in Spain as the final choice.

Sometimes the consumer will find that applying all the decision rules cuts out all of the alternatives, so that a revision of the rules needs to take place. This can result in establishing a hierarchy of rules according to their relative importance (Bettman 1979). There is also an effect caused by simply thinking about the product group – people often judge the desirability of the options on the basis of their ability to consider the options in advance. In other words, being able to think through and understand the implications of owning a product tends to make the product more desirable (Morewedge and Wegner 2008).

CATEGORISATION OF DECISION RULES

Non-compensatory decision rule

A heuristic that cannot be offset by other factors

Non-compensatory decision rules are absolute; if a product does not meet the decision rule for one attribute, this cannot be compensated for by its strength in other areas. In the holiday example in Figure 3.11, despite the fact that the Florida location is near to Disneyland, and is therefore a very strong candidate as far as entertaining the children is concerned, the cost and the flight time rule it out. In the lexicographic approach the consumer establishes a hierarchy of attributes, comparing products first against the most important attribute, then against the second most important, and so forth. Decisions can be made by elimination of aspects whereby the product is examined against other brands according to attributes, but then each attribute is checked against a cut-off.

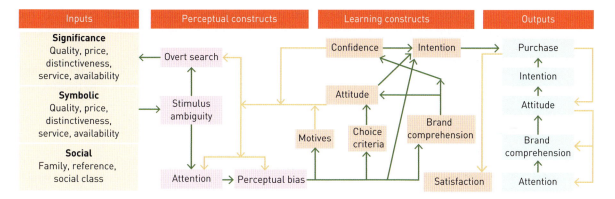

FIGURE 3.12 Howard–Sheth model (adapted from Howard and Sheth 1969)

The conjunctive rule is the last of the non-compensatory rules. Here each brand is compared in turn against all the cut-offs; only those brands that survive this winnowing-out will be compared with each other.

Compensatory decision rules allow for trade-offs, so that a weakness in one area can be compensated for in another. The simple additive rule involves a straight tally of the product's positive aspects, and a comparison of this tally with the tally for other products. The product with the most positive attributes will be the one chosen. A variation of this is the weighted additive approach, which gives greater weight to some attributes than to others. In each case, though, the products do not necessarily have to have all the attributes in common (or, indeed, any of them).

Phased decision strategies may involve using rules in a sequence. For example, the consumer may use a non-compensatory cut-off to eliminate products from the consideration set, then use a weighted additive rule to decide between the remaining products.

Two more special categories of decision rule exist. First, the consumer may need to create a constructive decision rule. This means establishing a rule from scratch when faced with a new situation. If the rule thus created works effectively, the consumer will store it in memory until the next time the situation is encountered, and 'recycle' the rule then. Second, affect referral is the process whereby consumers retrieve a 'standard' attitude from memory. For example, a consumer may strongly disapprove of a company's business practices (ZMEScience 2015), which may prevent the inclusion of its products in the consideration set.

If consumers are using a weighted additive rule, it would be useful to know which attributes are given the greatest weightings. If they are using a conjunctive rule with cut-offs at known levels, the product can be designed to fall within the cut-offs. To become part of the consideration set it must pass the cut-offs and signals employed in the decision process.

Several attempts have been made to bring the factors in consumer decision-making together in one model. Most of these models are complex, since there are many factors which interrelate in a number of ways; an example is the Howard–Sheth model shown in Figure 3.12. This is a somewhat simplified version; the original requires one diagram to be superimposed on another. In the diagram the solid arrows show

Conjunctive rule

A heuristic by which brands are compared to all cut-offs until only a few surviving brands remain the flow of information; the dotted arrows show the feedback effects. Essentially, the diagram deals with the way the inputs are dealt with by perception (see Chapter 8) and by learning (see Chapter 9), and eventually become outputs.

Following on from the purchase, there will be an evaluation of both the product itself and the decision process. The learning process will feed back into the internal search, and new heuristics will be developed.

INVOLVEMENT

Involvement is the perceived relevance of the object based on the person's inherent needs, values and interests (Zaichowsky 1985). It is about the degree to which the individual feels attached to the product or brand, and the loyalty felt towards it. Involvement has both cognitive and affective elements: it acts on both the mind and on the emotions.

CHALLENGING THE STATUS QUO

Do we really become that emotionally attached to products? Surely we are not so shallow that the most important thing in our lives is a brand of cereal? Well perhaps it is when you've three tired and grumpy children sitting at the breakfast table! People are often in the habit of saying, 'I really love my car!' but isn't that just a figure of speech? Saying that we like something a lot is not the same as saying we love it, and saying that we think a product is the best available does not mean that we cannot live effectively without it.

©iStock.com/GregorBister

Well let's take some products that we're familiar with and add some emotion into the equation ...

- iPhone – 'My phone can do anything' (hhhmmm, it may be true, I can remotely shut my curtains from a 1,000 miles away, and using Hive – a British Gas app – my home heating system recognises when I am 3 miles from home and automatically switches the heating on in winter!).

- Bose noise-reducing headphones – 'increases my very personal space' (absolutely, if you put some blinkers on too, you'd be in a world of your own!)

You get the picture ... In the course of a long life we fall in love with many people and products – but are we so blinded by our love of particular products that we cannot be aware, at all, ever, of the possibility of change? (When it comes to people, that's a different textbook!)

Inertia	Willingness to listen	Interest in anything about the product	Active search for information	Total commitment

Regular routine purchases of generic products

Identification with a brand to the point of obsession

FIGURE 3.13 Involvement continuum

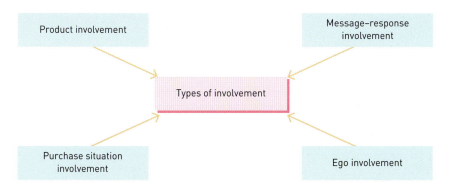

FIGURE 3.14 Categories of involvement

Involvement is sometimes seen as the motivation to process information (Mitchell 1979). At a low level of involvement, individuals only engage in simple processing of information: at high levels of involvement, people will link incoming information to their pre-existing knowledge system, in a process called elaboration (Otker 1990). The degree of involvement will lie somewhere on a continuum from complete inertia through to high involvement where we might expect to find an intensity of feeling that borders on the religious. At the extreme, we would expect to find people who worship celebrities, or are fanatical about religious beliefs or who have a brand tattooed onto their skin (Harley-Davidson owners have been known to do this). Such *extreme* people have often become involved with cult product offerings such as Star Trek memorabilia, Vans shoes or the Volkswagen Beetle.

Inertia

Making decisions out of habit rather than from any conscious loyalty

Figure 3.13 shows the continuum in action. Someone who has no real interest in the product category and makes only routine purchases of generic products (or no purchases at all) exhibits inertia. Someone with a mild interest in the product exhibits a willingness to listen to explanations or advice about the product. Someone who is involved at a medium level would take an interest in anything he or she happens to see concerning the product, and someone who is highly committed would actively seek out information. Finally, someone who is totally committed to the brand identifies with it to the point of obsession.

Figure 3.14 summarises categories of involvement. Involvement is not always confined to products. People can experience message–response involvement or advertising involvement in which they become eager to process information obtained from advertising (Batra and Ray 1983). In some cases the messages are passive (as in the case of TV advertising) whereas in other cases messages involve more effort on the part of the observer (for example print advertisements) and some marketing communications permit a great deal of interaction (some mail shots and some Internet advertising).

Purchase situation involvement is about the different contexts in which purchase takes place. For example, if one were buying a gift for a new girlfriend or boyfriend, one might be extremely involved in the purchase since there is a high social risk involved if a mistake is made. If, on the other hand, the gift-buying is almost obligatory (e.g. buying a birthday gift for a relative one has little liking for and rarely sees) the involvement level will be considerably lower.

Ego involvement is about the importance of the product to the individual's self-concept. Making a mistake in purchase could lead to a high social risk – the individual's self-concept might be damaged, to embarrassing effect. For example, a committed vegan would be horrified to find that a supposedly vegan product contained animal fat. In some cases, the product purchase is linked to a 'tribe': such communities are supported by social networking sites, celebrity affiliations and self-generated communications (Hamilton and Hewer 2010).

High product involvement is driven by the degree to which the individual feels that the product's attributes are linked to end goals or values. Lower levels of involvement occur if the attributes only link to function, and very low levels of involvement occur if the product attributes are irrelevant to consequences.

In other words, high-involvement products are those that figure strongly in the individual's lifestyle. They involve decisions that are important to get right, preferably first time. In most cases these products are ones the consumer knows a lot about, and about which he or she has strong opinions. This means that high-involvement consumers are hard to persuade: they will not easily be swayed by advertising, or even by persuasive sales pitches. For example, a website developer might favour specific software, but if the software is unavailable he or she is unlikely to be persuaded by a salesperson that a different application is just as good. The discrepant information is ignored or disparaged, so the source of the information (the salesperson) will lose esteem in the eyes of the developer.

Intrinsic self-relevance

Sources of involvement derived from means–end knowledge stored in the individual's memory

Levels of involvement are influenced by two sources: personal sources and situational sources. Personal sources (also called **intrinsic self-relevance**) are derived from the means–end knowledge stored in the individual's memory, and are influenced both by the person and by the product. People who believe that the attributes of the product link to important end goals are likely to be more heavily involved with the product because the importance of the end goal means that it is more important to be right first time. Even products such as snacks can have personal involvement issues – pre-teen girls have been shown to have very specific requirements for snacks, based on what friends find acceptable (Dibley and Baker 2001). Involvement does not necessarily depend on the outcome being positive; sometimes involvement might be greater if the possible outcomes are negative, since the consumer will take care to choose products which will avoid negative outcomes.

CONSUMER BEHAVIOUR IN ACTION:
HORMAZD NARIELWALLA

Consumer wants and needs find a way of weaving into all avenues of society, and art is no exception. When wealthy collectors such as Saatchi take an interest in a particular artist, there are many art lovers who are likely to follow suit. Indeed, one such artist has been identified as using his art to develop wants among fashion and design-led consumers by creating collages made out of unwanted tailoring patterns; they are ahead of their time, anthropomorphic in origin and beautifully abstract in isolation.

Hormazd Narielwalla. Image credit: Denis Laner. Reproduced with permission.

Hormazd Narielwalla is a London-based artist who works in collage. Narielwalla uses bespoke Savile Row tailoring patterns, and their antiquarian and contemporary trade counterparts, to create artworks exploring the body in abstract form (www.narielwalla.com). His practice began in the workrooms of the tailoring firm Dege & Skinner in London's Savile Row with an artist's book, *Dead Man's Patterns* (2008), which reflects on the bespoke suit patterns of deceased customers.

In an interview with Hormazd, he indicates how he uses 'intrinsic self-relevance' to entice consumers to his work:

'Tailoring patterns are a means to an end. These technical mathematical drafts have been developed since the late 1500s, drawn on various kinds of paper, and used to create structured clothing. They carry with them the outline of the garment, and also a representation of the body. Every artwork or series begins with a response to the patterns as the fundamental focus bringing to light their qualities as shapes in themselves. Tailors construct them in order to understand the interface between 3D (the body) and flat drawings (the pattern) before returning to 3D forms (the garment). This interaction between the dimensions is considered and articulated whilst creating artworks. The role of the 'body' has played a recurring theme in artworks since *Dead Man's Patterns* (2008) an artist's book inspired by the bespoke suit patterns of a deceased customer, cut by the eminent Savile Row tailors Dege & Skinner. The tailors would ceremoniously shred the patterns of former clients, since there is no value in the parchment without the body. The photographic sequence depicting the making of the garment is charged and ghost-like within the context of the title *Dead Man's Patterns*; where the patterns make the absent figure tangible. Each section of the book suggests different physical states of the 'man' with a sense of formal preparation for burial. The physical man is never there; the book's pages gesture towards intimacy even though they are merely paper. Subsequently I responded to lingerie tailoring patterns sourced from a London designer (c. 1970), by making the series Love Gardens by layering them with coloured paper to create abstract representations of female anatomy refer-encing the work of Georgia O'Keefe. To complement this series I used Savile Row shirt collar tailoring patterns and newspaper clippings, with spray paint mounted on inkjet prints to create phallic collages. Suits are the predominant international uniform of men in positions of power. Does Sir dress left or right? This charming tailoring euphemism has a fascinating equivalent in radiology. The John Thomas sign refers to the orientation of a penis in an anteroposterior x-ray. I take the discarded Savile Row menswear tailoring patterns and make their masculinity shockingly explicit. Does the viewer see them as proud or ridiculous? Perhaps, like the x-ray, John Thomas exposes the vulnerability a suit conceals. In 2013 I was commissioned by Crafts Council, England to exhibit five sculptures at the Saatchi Gallery for Collect. The works were intimate, fragile structures created from quarter-scale military patterns of uniforms from the British Raj (1850–1947). The works epitomised a romantic memory of falling in love with a fictional charac-ter – a handsome English officer from the TV mini-series *The Far Pavilions* (1984). Inspired by the construction of Anthony Caro's work, the structures were created from the negative space around the patterns to narrate the absent body. The body and its story is no more but my memory and patterns live on. My work proposes a new interpretation of tailoring patterns as interesting abstracted drawings of the human form which have an inherent aesthetic quality that can be used innovatively to develop a contemporary art practice. Freed from function they are drawings ahead of their time, anthropomorphic in origin and beautifully abstract in isolation.'

Reprinted by Kind Permission of the artist, Hormazd Narielwalla

DIMENSIONS OF INVOLVEMENT

It is possible to use these dimensions of involvement (see Figure 3.15) to segment the market for a given product. For example, for some people an Apple Watch might have a strong sign value, while for others it has a strong pleasure value: the approach to each of these groups would be different in terms of marketing communication. There are, of course other factors at play here too – a high status sign can give pleasure to an individual, not to mention the possible hedonistic and functional values that could also be derived from owning such products.

Laurent and Kapferer (1985) whose seminal paper initially showcased this five-factor model for assessing the dimensions of involvement, described the factors as follows:

1. The personal interest a person has in the product category, its personal meaning or importance. For example, people often become very involved in art galleries or orchestras (Camic et al. 2015).
2. The perceived importance of the potential negative consequences associated with a poor choice of product (risk importance).
3. The probability of making a bad purchase.
4. The pleasure value of the product category.
5. The sign value of the product category (how closely it relates to the self).

Chocolate scores high in terms of pleasure, but low on sign value and risk value. The evi-dence is, therefore, that different products may be high involvement for different reasons.

FIGURE 3.15 Dimensions of involvement

INVOLVEMENT WITH BRANDS

People often develop relationships with brands. Typical examples might be favourite perfumes, jeans, cars, cigarettes, coffee, and so forth. Research by Brann Consulting showed that people are more likely to think of their brand of coffee as a friend than they are to think of their bank this way: banks are acquaintances at best, enemies at worst. This may seem surprising considering that banks are composed of people, whereas coffee is inanimate, but it is perhaps due to the fact that coffee is consumed at home or with friends whereas bank services are often regarded as an unpleasant necessity.

The relationship that the individual has with both the brand and the product is very closely intertwined. Drivers often develop affectionate relationships with their cars, personalising them with stickers and accessories, and not infrequently giving them a name. Drivers even talk to their cars (sometimes in less than flattering terms). And recently a lot of us have been talking to our voice activated personal assistant, Siri! But how many of us would switch loyalties and employ the services of either Alexa (from Amazon Echo) or Cortana (from Microsoft)? Involvement also has an influence on decision-making styles (Bauer et al. 2006). Even when the product itself might be considered to have few differences, people are prepared to pay more for the branded product – research in the United States showed that people would pay more for branded pork than for unbranded pork (Ubilava et al. 2011).

Involvement can also be considered in terms of attachment theory, specifically avoidance and anxiety factors. Avoidance factors are those that make people shun relationships due to a fear of intimacy while anxiety factors are those that make people fear loss, anxiety or rejection. People who are low or high on both dimensions report high satisfaction with brands, whereas people who are high on one dimension and low on the other report low satisfaction rates (Thompson and Johnson 2002). This means that people with a fear of becoming dependent, and a fear of loss, will be less likely to form relationships with brands and will therefore have no problems with them, whereas people who have no fear of becoming dependent and also no fear of loss

TABLE 3.3 Categorising consumers according to involvement

Brand loyalists	These are people who buy what they think is the "best" brand in the category. This is because they tend to have strong views about the relevance of the brand to their daily lives – the brand itself has personally-relevant consequences for them, and they are highly involved with it.
Routine brand buyers	These people have a favourite brand, but don't necessarily feel involved with it at a personal level. Typically, they will buy the same brand on a regular basis, but would not have a big problem in buying a substitute brand if their usual brand were unavailable. In other words, they have a low level of involvement with the brand.
Information seekers	These people feel strongly about the product category, but do not identify one brand as superior. They have positive means-end information about the category, and spend time and effort choosing the final brand within the category, but have low involvement in the actual brand.
Brand switchers	These people do not have a strong view about the brands on offer, and will choose whichever happens to be the most convenient at the time of purchase. They have low involvement with the brand, even if they have high involvement with the product category.

Source: adapted from Peter and Olson (1994)

will have many favourite brands. There are gender differences in brand relationship formation: when considering the two propositions, 'I understand the brand' and 'The brand understands me', women use both dimensions to judge their closeness to the brand, whereas men judge only by their own actions towards the brand (Monga 2002).

For any given product category, people can be classified according to their level of involvement, as shown in Table 3.3. The relationship between these factors is shown in Figure 3.16. Even when the product has other products associated with it, the involvement may only apply to one of the products: for example, someone might be staunchly loyal to a brand of gin (say Hendrick's) without caring much which brand of tonic water (Fentiman's, Canada Dry or Schweppes) goes in with it. While it is true that some people may be heavily involved in several brands, there is no evidence that high involvement in one brand will lead to high involvement in another brand from a different product category.

Involvement does not always equate to price. A high-involvement product is not necessarily a high-priced one, nor is a low-involvement product always a cheap one. Beer drinkers can be heavily committed to their brand of beer, costing only a few pounds a pint, whereas other people might not care what make of car they drive as long as it gets them from point A to B. High involvement always has a strong affective component, and this does not necessarily mean a high cost commitment – people also fall in love with cheap (or rather more cost-effective) products.

INCREASING INVOLVEMENT LEVELS

From a marketer's viewpoint, increasing consumers' involvement levels is clearly a priority. Marketers will try to increase consumer involvement with the products whenever it is possible to do so, since this will make communications easier and loyalty levels higher. As Figure 3.17 summarises, there are various techniques available to marketers for encouraging consumers to process relevant information, as follows (Stewart and Furse 1984):

FIGURE 3.16 Categorising consumers

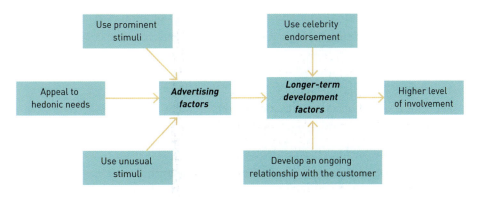

FIGURE 3.17 Increasing involvement

- *Appeal to hedonic needs.* Advertising that appeals to the senses generates higher levels of attention (Holbrook and Hirschman 1982). There is evidence that the pleasure of shopping tends to increase involvement with clothing (Michaelidou and Dibb 2006).

- *Use unusual stimuli to attract attention.* Using 5D technology to further involve the participant and inculcate a real experience, including elements such as rain water, aroma and smoke.

- *Use celebrity endorsement.* The viewer's involvement with the celebrity is likely to transfer to the product, although there are dangers with this approach.

- *Use prominent stimuli,* such as fast action or loud music. This will help to capture the viewer's attention.

- *Develop an ongoing relationship with consumers.* This can often be done by using a well-designed interactive website to generate involvement.

Ultimately, of course, consumers develop their own ideas about involvement, and will only become involved in products which appeal to their innermost selves. Marketers can only facilitate a process which would have happened (at least to some extent) in any case.

LOYALTY IN BUYER BEHAVIOUR

Involvement with a brand should, in the vast majority of cases, lead to feelings of loyalty. In recent years, marketers have taken the view that it is better to generate loyalty and therefore retain customers than it is to keep recruiting new customers. This view has been expressed most clearly by Ehrenberg, who proposed the 'leaky bucket' theory. In the past, most companies have operated on a 'leaky bucket' basis, seeking to refill the bucket with new customers while ignoring the ones leaking away. According to research by Gupta et al. (2004) a 1% improvement in customer retention will lead to a 5% improvement in the firm's value. In other words customer retention is five times as effective as cutting costs, especially as a 1% improvement in customer acquisition cost only generates a 1% increase in firm value. Ehrenberg (2000) noted that loyalty differs far less between brands in a category than does the number of buyers for each brand. Recent work by Dawes et al. (2015) has succinctly encapsulated some of the areas used to measure behavioural loyalty towards brands:

- Repeat-purchase rate (Fader and Schmittlein 1993; Colombo et al. 2000).
- Tenure (Length of time a buyer remains a buyer) (Reichheld and Teal 1996; East et al. 2001).
- Share of category requirements (Bhattacharya et al. 1996; Jung et al. 2010; Pare and Dawes 2011).
- Repertoire size (Uncles and Ehrenberg 1990; Banelis et al. 2013).
- Purchase frequency (Morrison 1966; Sharp and Sharp 1997).
- Proportion of buyers who are solely loyal (Raj 1985).

Satisfaction is not necessarily enough to generate loyalty, however. East et al. (2006) found no evidence that satisfaction breeds loyalty, but have found evidence that satisfaction leads to personal recommendations and therefore to recruitment of new customers. In fact, in many ways people are not loyal, and their loyalty cannot be bought: only a small percentage of loyalty card holders actually are loyal (Allaway et al. 2006), because most people carry several cards (Meyer-Waarden and Benavent 2006). Loyalty to the store tends to be higher in the case of online suppliers, which may be a function of trust (Buttner and Goritz 2008). Trust lends itself to purchase incidence meaning that heavy buyers of a category buy more brands, and are consequently less loyal to any particular brand (Banelis et al. 2013). There are also those who only make one-off purchases and should therefore not count as 100% loyal (Uncles and Lee 2006).

The importance of the purchase has an effect on satisfaction and also on loyalty: the more important the purchase, the more disastrous a failure in performance will be and the greater the effect on satisfaction and loyalty. Perhaps surprisingly, if the purchase importance is low, perceived performance has a stronger influence on satisfaction (Tam 2011).

If loyalty can be generated, though, it does increase profitability (Helgesen 2006). Since companies are often not good at acquiring new customers, loyalty becomes important (Ang and Buttle 2006). It also has the effect of reducing the evaluation of brand extensions – people tend to assume that the extension will be as good as the original brand (Hem and Iversen 2003). When a brand grows, therefore, it is the change in penetration which is generally larger than the change in loyalty (Baldinger et al. 2002; Dawes 2009).

UNSOUGHT GOODS

So far, we have looked at consumer behaviour when seeking out goods to meet a specific, recognised need. While most products fall into the category of being sought out as a way of meeting a need, there is a category of **unsought goods** that consumers do not look for.

Unsought goods are those goods for which consumers will recognise a need, but which they nevertheless tend to avoid buying. Examples are life insurance, wills and funeral plans (because people prefer not to contemplate their own deaths), and some home improvements (because major capital expenditures can always be postponed).

The possible reasons for not seeking out the products, summarised in Figure 3.18, are as follows:

- People do not like to think about the reasons for needing the products. Because people do not like to think about old age and death, they prefer not to think about pensions and insurance.

- Given the vast number of stories in the press (for instance the Payment Protection Insurance or PPI scandal), the consumer has come to perhaps mistrust marketers of such products.

- The products are expensive or require a long-term commitment, and people do not like to risk making a mistake.

- There is no urgency about seeking a solution. Retirement may be a long way off, or the roof may last another year or two.

- The consumer may not see any immediate benefit. In the case of life insurance, the insured person never benefits directly, since the policy only pays out on proof of death.

- Some unsought goods are new on the market, so the level of knowledge about them is low and the individual automatically rejects any marketing approach because the benefits are not obvious. Trust in both the product and the brand needs to be established first before information can be transferred.

Unsought goods

Products that are bought as a result of coercion rather than through desire

FIGURE 3.18 Reasons for postponing purchase of unsought goods

TABLE 3.4 Decision-making model for unsought goods

Stage	Techniques for management
Need recognition	Sales representatives activate the need by asking questions about the individual's current circumstances. For example, a representative from a breakdown insurer (AA or RAC) selling 'peace of mind' to those who recognise that they may have to call upon such services at some stage soon due to the age/condition of their motor vehicle
Information search	The sales representative performs a lengthy presentation, explaining the product's features and benefits. Questions and objections are dealt with as they arise
Evaluation of alternatives	The salesperson 'no-sells' competitors by pointing out ways in which the competitors' products are inferior. This is of course quite culture and country specific; for instance, such practices would not be deemed professional nor tolerated in the UK
Choice decision	The salesperson closes the sale by using a phrase or technique that elicits a yes or no decision
Post-purchase evaluation	The company may follow up on the sale by sending comments forms, the salesperson may call back to elicit feedback, or a sales manager might call back. In the case of buyers' remorse, there will be a return visit by the salesperson or by a sales manager

Marketers can overcome these problems with a series of tactics, but the main one is to use salespeople to explain the benefits of the product and close the sale. These salespeople usually have to overcome an initial resistance to the idea of spending time listening to a presentation, since the consumer of unsought goods is not engaged in an information search and is therefore unlikely to want to spend time and resources on a sales presentation. The salesperson will therefore need to employ a tactical device to gain the customer's attention for long enough to activate the need for the product. Table 3.4 shows how a salesperson can contribute to each stage of decision-making for this type of purchase. Admittedly, not all companies use the high pressure selling techniques illustrated in Table 3.4. Some organisations will seek to highlight the positive aspects of their own service and will draw attention to some of the negatives that are avoided.

The selling techniques used for unsought goods have attracted a great deal of adverse publicity, but it is worth bearing in mind that the vast majority of double-glazing owners are perfectly happy with the product, as are the vast majority of timeshare owners. Generally speaking, while some vulnerable people are often targeted, most people are not naive enough to commit large sums of money to products they do not want and do not see a need for.

SUMMARY

This chapter has been about consumer decision-making processes. The processes often happen largely below the conscious level, and people often fall in love with a product without having much real knowledge of it, but the processes nevertheless occur, even if only at the subconscious level.

Decision-making flows from both needs and from attitudes. People need to be able to justify their decisions, both in terms of cost and of the usefulness of the products they buy; marketers need to be able to influence the decision by influencing attitudes, cost and utility as well as understanding the mental processes people go through both before and after making purchases.

KEY POINTS

- Needs become activated when there is a divergence between the actual and the desired states.
- Any information search is likely to be limited, since there is a cost attached as well as a risk reduction aspect.
- Heuristics are decision rules intended to reduce cognitive effort and risk.
- Interrupts usually only delay problem-solving behaviour, but the delay depends on the strength of the interrupt and the strength of the goal.
- The type of problem-solving undertaken will depend in part on whether the consumer is replenishing the assortment or extending it.
- The consideration set doesn't include every possible solution.
- Most decisions involve decision rules, either pre-programmed or invented on the spot.
- Involvement is the motivation to process information.
- High involvement is linked to end goals and values.
- Dimensions of involvement can be used to segment markets.
- Word of mouth is a strong factor in high-tech purchases.
- Unsought goods are those for which people recognise a need, but still avoid buying.

HOW TO IMPRESS YOUR EXAMINER

You are likely to be asked to compare various decision-making models. If so, remember that they are not necessarily mutually exclusive: some are simpler than others, but the more complex ones still only add extra stages or influences to the basic models. Also bear in mind that decision-making is not necessarily linear, and it certainly isn't necessarily rational: emotions play a large part.

Candidates sometimes forget that goals go in hierarchies, both in terms of which goals are more important than others and in terms of which **sub-goals** need to be achieved if the main goal is to come to fruition. If you can remember Huffman's model, it will certainly help you avoid this error. A further common error is to forget the role of heuristics in enabling people both to set goals and to achieve them – so make it a rule never to forget about heuristics!

Sub-goal

A target that forms part of a greater aim, and needs to be achieved before the main goal can be achieved

REVIEW QUESTIONS

1. What type of information search would you expect someone to undertake when buying a new type of television?
2. How might a marketer seek to make an interrupt more effective?
3. How might a compensatory decision rule operate when buying an expensive item such as a new car?

4.   What factors cause people to become involved in products or brands?

5.   How might a marketer increase involvement?

6.   How can marketers reconcile the sale of unsought goods with the marketing concept?

7.   What causes a product to move from being an unsought good to being a sought good?

8.   Why might someone become involved with a brand, rather than with the benefits of the product itself?

CASE STUDY: UNDER ARMOUR, INC

When decisions are made with a degree of creativity and ingenuity, even small businesses can and have built strong branded businesses going up against much larger competitors with infinitely higher resources. One such example is a company called Under Armour.

Under Armour today is a major American sports clothing and accessory company founded by Kevin Plank in 1996, just after he graduated from college at the age of 23. The company specialises in sportswear and casual apparel. In particular, Under Armour focuses on hi-tech sportswear for professional athletes and thus has come to be known as a brand that specialises in professional sports.

The origins of the brand go back to the time when, as a high school and college level athlete, Plank got tired of the way his sport attire felt as sweat accumulated, as a result of his physical activities. To remedy this problem, he set out to design and manufacture sportswear that would not be weighed down by sweat. He believed that this would be appealing to professional athletes. The vision was there, the product was there and the quality was there. What were still missing were the awareness and the legitimacy of the brand.

Plank knew that he had limited resources and could not compete head on with the marketing power of the major players such as Nike, Adidas and Reebok in the sportswear industry.

©iStock.com/Anna Bryukhanova

Instead of advertising through mainstream channels such as TV, billboards and magazines, as the major players did, Plank turned to his network: he took his brand to his friends in the locker room. By giving the clothing he had designed to his college friends who had now been drafted into professional football, he was able to get his clothing line into the locker rooms of a dozen or more professional football teams, as some of his friends who really liked what Under Armour had to offer started to use his line of clothing in practice sessions and after games.

Other sport celebrities who were introduced to the product by word of mouth in locker rooms also started to wear Under Armour clothing, becoming de facto free endorsers for the brand. As the Under Armour brand awareness and popularity grew among professional players, it also became apparent to the broader consumer market for athletic apparel, establishing the brand firmly in this broader market, both in terms of awareness and credibility. The company has since been invited by Warner Brothers to provide outfits for major films as well as having expanded into numerous other sports (for instance speedskating teams in the 2014 Winter Olympics). If this wasn't enough, they made a strategic decision to buy popular digital apps in the sports market. 'MapMyFitness', 'MyFitnessPal' and 'Endomondo' are now all wholly owned by Under Armour. Thus, aligning a good product with a well-thought-out brand communication strategy can transform a small business into a successful branded business, even in a category dominated by global majors.

QUESTIONS

1. How was the need for the product activated?
2. What is the relevance of the information search process to Under Armour?
3. How does involvement figure in the promotional process for the product?
4. Why would someone recommend Under Armour to a friend?
5. Why is the brand name important?

FURTHER READING

For an indication of some of the surrogates people use when deciding on whether to buy a new product, see Roger Bennett and Helen Gabriel (2000) Charity affiliation as a determinant of product purchase decisions. *Journal of Brand and Product Marketing* 9 (4/5): 255–68. It turns out that people's perception of the value for money aspects of products sold by charities affects their view of other products that may be entirely unrelated to the first products.

For a much deeper account of loyalty programmes and involvement, take a look at Wan Jou-Wen's book *The Effect of the Reward Programme Scheme: The Effect of Timing of Reward, Business Longevity and Involvement on Consumers' Perception and Behavioural Intention Toward the Reward Programme* (Saarbrücken: VDM Verlag, 2009). The title is almost as long as the book, but it does offer a very deep (and academic) insight into the interrelationship between loyalty programmes, involvement and timing.

Many models of consumer behaviour seem to assume that people think about what they are doing when making decisions. Gerd Gigerenzer disagrees – and his book *Gut Feelings: Short Cuts to Better Decision Making* (Harmondsworth: Penguin, 2008) outlines the idea that we make our best decisions based on gut instinct rather than conscious thought. This is a book for people who enjoy some controversy!

Involvement, and especially involvement in luxury brands, is alive and well and lives in Japan. *The Cult of the Luxury Brand: Inside Asia's Love Affair with Luxury* by Radha Chadha and Paul Husband (London: Nicholas Brealey International, 2006) tells the whole story of how Asian countries have discovered consumerism – and gone for it in a big way.

An aspect of decision-making which is often ignored is the decision to say 'enough is enough'. John Naish's book *Enough: Breaking Free from the World of Excess* (London: Hodder Paperbacks, 2009) offers as its main premise the idea that human beings are hard-wired to grab as much as they can of anything they like, when in fact there is a point at which further acquisitions simply become tiresome. It's an interesting read for those who have doubts about the consumerist society in which we live.

Jonathan Fields' *Uncertainty: Turning Fear and Doubt into Fuel for Brilliance* (New York: Portfolio Hardcover, 2011) is a self-help book. The author talks about ways of reducing the fear that arises from uncertainty – and he certainly experienced the downside of uncertainty, having opened a new business in Manhattan the day before the 11 September terrorist attacks.

REFERENCES

Aggarwal, P. and Vaidyanathan, R. (2003) Eliciting online customers' preferences: conjoint vs. self-explicated and attribute-level measurement. *Journal of Marketing Management,* 19 (1/2): 157.

Allaway, A.W., Gooner, R.M., Berkowitz, D. and Davis, L. (2006) Deriving and exploring behaviour segments within a retail loyalty card programme. *European Journal of Marketing*, 40 (11/12): 1317–39.

Ang, L. and Buttle, F. (2006) Managing for successful customer acquisition: an exploration. *Journal of Marketing Management*, 22 (3/4): 295–317.

Baldinger, A.L., Blair, E. and Echambadi, R. (2002) Why brands grow. *Journal of Advertising Research*, 1: 7–14.

Banelis, M., Riebe, E. and Rungie, C.M. (2013) Empirical evidence of repertoire size. *Australasian Marketing Journal*, 21: 59–65.

Batra, R. and Ray, M.L. (1983) Operationalising involvement as depth and quality of cognitive responses. In A. Tybout and R. Bagozzi (eds), *Advances in Consumer Research*. Ann Arbor, MI: Association for Consumer Research, pp. 309–13.

Bauer, H.H., Sauer, N.E. and Becker, C. (2006) Investigating the relationship between product involvement and consumer decision-making styles. *Journal of Consumer Behaviour*, 5 (July–August): 342–54.

Baumeister, R.F. (2004) Self-regulation, conscious choice, and consumer decisions. *Advances in Consumer Research*, 31 (1): 48–9.

Bettman, J.R. (1979) *An Information Processing Theory of Consumer Choice*. Reading, MA: Addison-Wesley.

Bettman, J.R. and Park, C.W. (1980) Effects of prior knowledge and experience and phase of choice processes on consumer decision processes: a protocol analysis. *Journal of Consumer Research*, 7 (August): 234–48.

Bhattacharya, C.B., Fader, P.S., Lodish, L.M. and Desarbo, W.S. (1996) The relationship between the marketing mix and share of category requirements. *Marketing Letters*, 7 (1): 5–18.

Biehal, G. and Chakravarty, D. (1983) Information accessibility as a moderator of consumer choice. *Journal of Consumer Research*, 10 (June): 1–14.

Biswas, D. (2009) The effects of option framing on consumer choices: making decisions in rational versus experiential processing modes. *Journal of Consumer Behaviour* 8 (5): 284–99.

Blackwell, R.D., Miniard, P.W. and Engel, J.F. (2005) *Consumer Behaviour*, 10th edn. Mason, OH: Thomson Southwest.

Bloch, P.H., Sherrell, D.L. and Ridgway, N.M. (1986) Consumer search: an extended framework. *Journal of Consumer Research*, 13 (June): 111–26.

Brendl, M., Markman, A. and Irwin, J.R. (2002) Suppression and activation of competing goals. *Advances in Consumer Research*, 29: 5.

Bruyneel, S., DeWitte, S., Franses, P.H., DeKimpe, M. and Arnik G. (2006) Why consumers buy lottery tickets when the sun goes down on them: the depleted nature of weather-induced bad moods. *Advances in Consumer Research*, 33: 46–50.

Bucklin, L.P. (1963) Retail strategy and the classification of consumer goods. *Journal of Marketing*, 27 (January): 50–5.

Buttner, O.B. and Goritz, A.S. (2008) Perceived trustworthiness of online shops. *Journal of Consumer Behaviour*, 7 (1): 35–60.

Camic, P.M., Baker, E.L. and Tischler, V. (2015) Theorizing how art gallery interventions impact people with dementia and their caregivers. *The Gerontologist*. doi: 10.1093/geront/gnv063.

Campo, K. and Breugelmans, E. (2015) Buying groceries in brick and click stores: category allocation decisions and the moderating effect of online buying experience. *Journal of Interactive Marketing* (accepted).

Colombo, R., Ehrenberg, A. and Sabavala, D. (2000) Diversity in analyzing brand-switching tables: the car challenge. *Canadian Journal of Marketing Research*, 19: 23–36.

Crosby, L.A. and Taylor, J.R. (1981) Effects of consumer information and education in cognition and choice. *Journal of Consumer Research*, 8 (June): 43–56.

Dailey, L. (2003) Understanding consumers' need to personally inspect products prior to purchase. *Advances in Consumer Research*, 30: 146–7.

Dawes, J. (2009) You need more customers: the key is how many you have, not how much they buy. *Marketing Research*, Summer: 30–1.

Dawes, J., Meyer-Waarden, L. and Driesener, C. (2015) Has brand loyalty declined? A longitudinal analysis of repeat purchase behaviour in the UK and USA. *Journal of Business Research*, 68: 425–32.

Dewey, J. (1910) *How We Think*. Boston, MA: DC Heath & Co.

Dibley, A. and Baker, S. (2001) Uncovering the links between brand choice and personal values among young British and Spanish girls. *Journal of Consumer Behaviour*, 1 (1): 77–93.

East, R., Hammond, K. and Gendall, P. (2006) Fact and fallacy in retention marketing. *Journal of Marketing Management*, 22 (1/2): 5–23.

East, R., Lomax, W. and Narain, R. (2001) Customer tenure, recommendation and switching. *Journal of Consumer Satisfaction, Dissatisfaction and Complaining Behaviour*, 14: 46–54.

Ehrenberg, A.S.C. (2000) Repeat-buying: facts, theory and applications. *Journal of Empirical Generalisations in Marketing Science*, 5: 392–770.

Elliot, G., Rundle-Thiele, S. and Waller, D. (2010) *Marketing*. Milton, Queensland: John Wiley and Sons.

Fader, P.S. and Schmittlein, D.C. (1993) Excess behavioral loyalty for high-share brands deviations from the Dirichlet model for repeat purchasing. *Journal of Marketing Research*, 30 (4): 478–93.

FCA (2014) Price comparison website: consumer market research report. www.fca.org.uk/static/documents/research/price-comparison-website-consumer-research.pdf (accessed 22 September 2015).

Foxall, G.R. (2008) Reward, emotion and consumer choice: from neuroeconomics to neurophilosophy. *Journal of Consumer Behaviour*, 7 (4/5): 368–96.

Gilad, S. (2015) Political pressures, organizational identity, and attention to tasks: illustrations from pre-crisis financial regulation. *Public Administration*, 93 (3): 593–608

Gupta, S., Lehmann, D.R. and Stuart, J.A. (2004) Valuing customers. *Journal of Market Research*, 41 (1): 7–18.

Hamilton, K.L. and Hewer, P.A. (2010) Tribal mattering spaces: social networking sites, celebrity affiliations and tribal innovations. *Journal of Marketing Management*, 26 (3/4): 271–89.

Harper, M.G. (2006) Childhood obesity strategies for prevention. *Family Community Health*, 29 (4): 288–98.

Hawkins, S. (1962) The significance of impulse buying today. *Journal of Marketing*, 26 (April): 59–62.

Helgesen, O. (2006) Are loyal customers profitable? Customer satisfaction, customer (action) loyalty and customer profitability at the individual level. *Journal of Marketing Management*, 22 (3/4): 245–66.

Hem, L. and Iversen, N.M. (2003) Transfer of brand equity in brand extensions: the importance of brand loyalty. *Advances in Consumer Research*, 30: 72–9.

Holbrook, M.B. and Hirschman, E.C. (1982) The experiential aspects of consumption: consumer fantasies, feelings and fun. *Journal of Consumer Research*, 9 (September): 132–40.

Howard, J.A. and Sheth, J.N. (1969) *The Theory of Buyer Behaviour*. New York: John Wiley.

Hoyer, W.D. and Ridgway, N.M. (1984) Variety seeking as an explanation for exploratory purchase behaviour: a theoretical model. *Advances in Consumer Research*, 11: 114–19.

Jung, S., Gruca, T. and Lopo, R. (2010) Excess loyalty in CPG markets: a comprehensive examination. *Journal of Empirical Generalisations in Marketing Science*, 13 (1): 1–13.

Kiel, G.C. and Layton, R.A. (1981) Dimensions of consumer information seeking behaviour. *Journal of Marketing Research*, 18 (May): 233–9.

Kim, S.J., Wang, R.J.H., Maslowska, E. and Malthouse, E.C. (2016) Understanding a fury in your words: the effects of posting and viewing electronic negative word-of-mouth on purchase behaviors. *Computers in Human Behavior*, 54: 511–21.

Kotler, P., Burton, S., Deans, K., Brown, L. and Armstrong, G. (2013) *Marketing*, 9th edn. Harlow: Pearson Publishing.

Laurent, G. and Kapferer, J. (1985) Measuring consumer involvement profiles. *Journal of Marketing Research*, 22 (February): 41–53.

McGrath, J.J. and Rossomando, E.F. (2015) Risk-averse purchasing behavior of female dentists and innovation in dental practice. *Dental Hypotheses*, 6 (2): 53–9

Melis, K., Campo, K., Breugelmans, E. and Lamey, L. (2015) The impact of the multi-channel retail mix on online store choice: does online experience matter? *Journal of Retailing*, 91 (2): 272–88.

Meyer-Waarden, L. and Benavent, C. (2006) The impact of loyalty programmes on repeat purchase behaviour. *Journal of Marketing Management*, 22 (1/2): 61–88.

Michaelidou, N. and Dibb, S. (2006) Product involvement: an application in clothing. *Journal of Consumer Behaviour*, 5 (September–October): 442–53.

Mitchell, A. (1979) Involvement: a potentially important mediator of consumer behaviour. In William L. Wilkie (ed.), *Advances in Consumer Research*, Vol. 6. Provo, UT: Association for Consumer Research, pp. 191–6.

Monga, A.B. (2002) Brand as a relationship partner: gender differences in perspectives. *Advances in Consumer Research*, 29 (1): 41.

Morewedge, C. and Wegner, D. (2008) Effects of merely thinking about what one might acquire. *Advances in Consumer Research*, 35: 153.

Morrison, D.G. (1966) Interpurchase time and brand loyalty. *Journal of Marketing Research*, 3 (August): 289–91.

Nantel, J. and Weeks, W.A. (1996) Marketing ethics: is there more to it than the utilitarian approach? *European Journal of Marketing*, 30 (5): 9–16.

Narielwalla, H. (2008) *Dead Man's Patterns*. London: Narielwalla. www.narielwalla.com/dead-mans-patterns/ (accessed 10 February 2016).

Neal, D., Wood, W. and Pascoe, A.M. (2008) Triggers of real-world habits: implications for consumer behavior. *Advances in Consumer Research*, 35: 145.

Onkvisit, S. and Shaw, J.J. (1994) *Consumer Behaviour, Strategy and Analysis*. New York: Macmillan.

Otker, T. (1990) The highly involved consumer: a marketing myth? *Marketing and Research Today*, February: 30–6.

Pare, V. and Dawes, J. (2011) The persistence of excess brand loyalty over multiple years. *Marketing Letters*, 21 (2): 163–75.

Peter, J.P. and Olson, J.C. (1994) *Understanding Consumer Behaviour*. Burr Ridge, IL: Irwin.

Raj, S.P. (1985) Striking a balance between brand 'popularity' and brand loyalty. *Journal of Marketing*, 49 (Winter): 53–9.

Reichheld, F.F. and Teal, T. (1996) *The Loyalty Effect: The Hidden Force Behind Growth, Profits, and Lasting Value*. Boston, MA: Harvard Business School Press.

Rick, S., Knutson, B., Wimmer, E., Prelec, D. and Loewenstein, G. (2008) Neural predictors of purchases. *Advances in Consumer Research*, 35: 139.

Shankar, A., Cherrier, H. and Canniford, R. (2006) Consumer empowerment: a Foucauldian interpretation. *European Journal of Marketing*, 40 (9/10): 1013–30.

Sharma, P., Sivakumaran, B. and Marshall, R. (2010) Exploring impulse buying and variety seeking by retail shoppers: towards a common conceptual framework. *Journal of Marketing Management*, 26 (5&6): 473–94.

Sharp, B. and Sharp, A. (1997) Loyalty programs and their impact on repeat-purchase loyalty patterns. *International Journal of Research in Marketing*, 14 (5): 473–86.

Sheng, S., Parker, A.M. and Nakamoto, K. (2003) Decision uncertainty, expected loss minimisation, and the compromise effect. *Advances in Consumer Behaviour*, 30: 47.

Stewart, D.W. and Furse, D.H. (1984) Analysis of executional factors in advertising performance. *Journal of Advertising Research*, 24: 23–6.

Takala, T. and Uusitalo, O. (1996) An alternative view of relationship marketing: a framework for ethical analysis, *European Journal of Marketing*, 30 (2): 45–60

Tam, J.L.M. (2011) The moderating effect of purchase importance in customer satisfaction process: an empirical investigation. *Journal of Consumer Behaviour*, 10 (4): 205–15.

Thompson, M. and Johnson, A.R. (2002) Investigating the role of attachment dimensions as predictors of satisfaction in consumer–brand relationships. *Advances in Consumer Research*, 29: 42.

Ubilava, D., Foster, K.A., Lusk, J.L. and Nilsson, T. (2011) Differences in consumer preferences when facing branded versus non-branded choices. *Journal of Consumer Behaviour*, 10 (2): 61–70.

Uncles, M.D. and Ehrenberg, A.S.C. (1990) Brand choice among older consumers. *Journal of Advertising Research*, August/September: 19–22.

Uncles, M. and Lee, D. (2006) Brand purchasing by older consumers: an investigation using the Juster scale and the Dirichlet model. *Marketing Letters*, 17 (1): 17–29.

Urbany, J.E. (1986) An experimental investigation of the economics of information. *Journal of Consumer Research*, 13 (September): 257–71.

Yin, D., Mitra, S. and Zhang, H. (forthcoming) When do consumers value positive versus negative reviews? An empirical investigation of confirmation bias in online word of mouth. *Information Systems Research*.

Zaichowsky, J.L. (1985) Measuring the involvement construct in marketing. *Journal of Consumer Research*, 12 (December): 341–52.

ZMEScience (2015) Why Nestle is one of the most hated companies in the world. www.zmescience.com/science/nestle-company-pollution-children/ (accessed 22 September 2015).

MORE ONLINE

For additional materials that support this chapter and your learning, please visit:
https://study.sagepub.com/sethnaandblythe

CHAPTER 4

INNOVATION AND DIGITAL TECHNOLOGIES

LEARNING OBJECTIVES

After reading this chapter you should be able to:

- Explain how the product life cycle drives innovation.
- Describe some of the characteristics of innovators.
- Show how innovators are not necessarily innovators under all circumstances.
- Describe different types of innovation.
- Explain the role of mavens in the adoption of innovation.
- Explain how resistance to innovation can happen, and formulate some ideas for dealing with this problem.

INTRODUCTION

The word innovation itself is quite subjective. There are many synonyms that could be used to describe it: change, upheaval, transformation, alteration, revolution, renovation, variation, restyling, remodelling, reorganising and metamorphosis are among a few. In essence, what we are talking about is the translation of a new idea into a product or service or a new method/way of doing something which creates a value for consumers (or for which consumers will pay money!). And there is of course an element of risk-taking. This is especially true because revolutionary innovations create new markets. Take, for example, the Benz Patent-Motorwagen, built and patented in 1886, which is widely regarded as the world's first automobile and which changed the face of transportation over the following 20 years. This was one of the first modern-era innovations. Other major innovations that have appeared since include telecommunications and its younger sibling the mobile telephone, analogue photography, computers and the world wide web. Evolutionary innovations, however, occur as a

Innovation

The translation of a new idea into a product or service (or a new way of doing something) which creates value for consumers

Revolutionary innovation

These drastic, radical and momentous changes are sometimes also referred to as 'discontinuous innovations' as they are often disruptive and brand new; forcibly overthrowing the 'old'

Evolutionary innovation

Occur as a result of incremental advances in both technology and processes

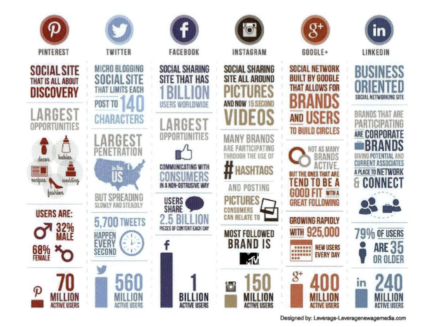

FIGURE 4.1 The influence of social media

©Leverage, LLC. Used with permission. (Source: https://leveragenewagemedia.com/.)

result of incremental advances in both technology and processes (for example, take Henry Ford's mass production vehicle, the Model-T, which within a short space of time destroyed many competitors in the fledgling automobile industry). There are many societal contexts within which innovation can be described. In the world of business, when organisations successfully innovate, they have deliberately applied their imagination, together with real data/information and a little initiative, in order to derive greater or different values from the available resources. Innovation is, therefore, said to be the lifeblood of successful companies. Firms that fail to innovate are thought to become moribund very quickly, and eventually to disappear altogether because competitors introduce new products that supersede the old ones.

However, this constant stream of innovation does create problems from a consumer behaviour viewpoint. Decision-making and information-gathering are both at their most complex when consumers are considering an innovative product. Thousands of new products are launched onto the market every year, with varying success rates; the vast majority never recoup their development costs. (Estimates of new product success rates vary, largely due to the difficulty of defining what constitutes success.)

The influence that social media has on consumers today is undoubtedly a major factor in the decision-making process. Figure 4.1, an infographic by Leverage New Age Media, just shows the kind of power those social media platforms weald on the consumer.

THE PRODUCT LIFE CYCLE

Innovation means that products are constantly being superseded by newer, more effective products. For this reason firms seek to develop new products; those firms

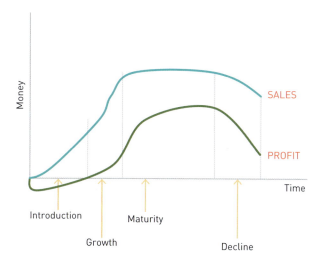

FIGURE 4.2 The product life cycle

that fail to innovate will, eventually, only be producing products that are obsolescent. However, the timescales for such cycles is continually shrinking. The route to market is either shortening, or there are many more people on the road. Tuten and Solomon (2015) highlight some very interesting statistics about the reach of social media. They start by telling us that it took 38 years for the medium of radio to reach 50 million listeners. Television, however, took 13 years to reach 50 million viewers. And if you think that transition was short, think about the fact that the Internet only took 4 years to reach 50 million people. Of course, the most impressive statistic is that Facebook added 100 million users to its platform in less than 9 months! So what exactly is the product life cycle?

The product life cycle illustrates the process of introduction, growth, maturity and obsolescence in products. Products tend to lose money when they are first introduced, because the amount of marketing support they need is not justified (in monetary profit terms) by the initial sales as the product tries to become established in the market. As the product moves into a growth phase, financial profits begin to come in, and when the product becomes well-established (i.e. mature) the profits are also at a peak. Eventually, the product will go into decline as competing products enter the market, or fashions change, or the market becomes saturated.

In fact, the situation is often much more complex than this, so the basic product life cycle (as shown in Figure 4.2) does not always describe what actually happens in practice. The product life cycle is a useful concept for explaining what happens to products, but it suffers from a number of weaknesses. First, the model is no use for making predictions, because there is no good way of knowing what the length of the maturity phase will be: for a fashion item, the maturity phase might only last a few months, whereas for a staple product such as bread (in all its various forms) the maturity phase has already lasted several thousand years and shows no sign of changing. Second, the model ignores the effects of marketing activities. If a product's sales are declining, marketers might decide to reposition the product in another market, or might run a major promotional campaign, or might decide to drop the product

FIGURE 4.3 Product dropped shortly after introduction

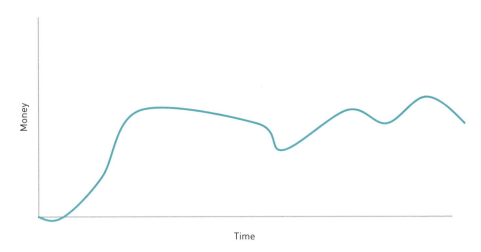

FIGURE 4.4 Effects of marketing activities on the product life cycle

altogether and concentrate resources on another product in the portfolio. These alternatives are shown in Figures 4.3 and 4.4.

Third, the model does not account for those products that come back into fashion after a few years in the doldrums. Recent automotive examples include the Fiat 500, Mini Cooper, the Volkswagen Beetle. Products such as the yo-yo seem to undergo revivals every 10 to 15 years.

Fourth, the model does not take account of the fact that the vast majority of new products fail. This would give a life cycle such as that shown in Figure 4.5, where the product never moves into profit.

Finally, the product life cycle looks at only one product, whereas most marketing managers have to balance the demands of many different products, and decide which of them is likely to yield the best return on investment (or perhaps which one will take the company nearest to achieving its strategic objectives).

FIGURE 4.5 Failed product

CHALLENGING THE STATUS QUO

It is not unusual for products to disappear almost as soon as they are launched: test marketing sometimes shows disappointing results, so the product is taken off the shelves. In recent times we have seen a number of technology products fail. Google Glass was one such product.

Google developed a pair of high-tech glasses that scanned your surroundings and beamed relevant information to your retina. But it needed a very large battery in order for the glasses to download and process the shear amount of data. This made the design of the glasses very bulky and somewhat distracting from its original purpose. In another example, Amazon was left with $83 million dollars'

©iStock.com/eternalcreative

worth of unsold Fire Phones; a product they launched to compete with iPhone/Android smartphones or other smart products. But given that the $199 device did not offer the consumer anything better (e.g. superior technology/features), it only took four weeks for the company to reduce the price to just 99 cents! One would have to question the consumer research that was done during the development phase of the product. Was there a need? Who would buy it and why?

There are also products that appear to be eminently sensible and yet do not find a market, possibly through a lack of professionalism on the part of the marketers. So should there be a marketer's life cycle instead? If the product doesn't perform, should we keep the product and fire the managers?

Smart product

A data processing object which has interactive functions and which combines the physical and software interfaces

The product life cycle can be explained in terms of consumer behaviour. In the introduction and growth stage, innovative consumers are adopting the product. In the maturity phase, more cautious consumers buy the product, until finally another product comes along which has more benefits or which does a better job, and people switch to the new product. The basic problem for marketers lies in knowing how long the maturity phase will last; the product life cycle does tell us, though, that all products eventually fade and die (or at least go into hibernation for some time before re-emerging), and marketers should therefore develop new products to replace the old ones as these products fall out of favour with consumers.

Cultural anchoring

The process by which an innovation becomes part of everyday life

Although we can be reasonably sure that all old products will eventually fail, we cannot by any means be sure that a new product will succeed. The lack of a good predictive system for forecasting product success wastes resources since producers will spend time and effort making things that consumers do not want to buy. The ideal outcome for a producer is to develop products that become **culturally anchored** – that become part of modern life. Recent examples are the mobile telephone, cable television and the personal computer – none of which would have been part of the average household 30 years ago, but which now would be difficult to manage without. In practice such breakthroughs are hard to achieve. Nowadays, each of us interacts with other people using communications technology and that technology places us, the end user, at the centre of every digital experience. Understandably, with so much at stake for firms, there has been a great deal of research interest in innovation, with many researchers trying to determine what the critical factors are in new product success (Cherubini et al. 2015; Tarhini et al. 2015; Urban et al. 2015).

ADOPTION OF INNOVATION

The process of adoption of innovation is as much to do with communication throughout the population as with individual decision-making. Each individual will make decisions by the processes already outlined for existing products; the main difference is that there will be many fewer sources of information about an innovative product, since few people will have any experience of it as yet. But that's where the power of the Internet, world wide web and social media help mitigate this problem, especially in developing economies. Barrett et al. (2015) have listed examples such as South Africa leading developments in mobile health, to countries in East Africa leading mobile financial services. This, they further suggest, 'is why large companies such as IBM, Cisco, GE, Siemens and Microsoft are using emerging economies as labs in which to develop, test, and scale service innovations using digital technologies'.

Everett M. Rogers (1983) postulated that products would be adopted if they possessed most of the attributes shown in Table 4.1 and the seminal work still rings true today.

There have been several models of the adoption process, most of which assume a somewhat complex process of assessing the new product. In the case of radically new products (those that will alter the user's lifestyle) this may well be the case, but since most products that are classified as new are, in fact, adaptations of existing products, it might be safe to assume that consumers do not necessarily carry out a lengthy evaluation of the type assumed by most researchers. Five adoption models are shown in Figure 4.6.

TABLE 4.1 Attributes necessary for adoption

Attribute	Explanation	Examples
Relative advantage	The product must have some advantage over the products already on the market. It must offer the consumer a better range of benefits than the existing solution, in other words	Before the Sony Walkman was launched, the only way to listen to stereo-quality music was to carry a 'ghetto-blaster' on your shoulder. The Walkman replaced this cumbersome and anti-social device within a few years – and iPods have replaced the Walkman equally effectively, with wireless and bluetooth providing the relative advantage now
Compatibility	The product must fit in with the consumer's lifestyle	Video on demand (e.g. Netflix, Amazon Prime, NowTV, Blinkbox, among others) have become extremely popular, allowing people to watch TV shows or movies at times that suit them, rather than the broadcaster
Complexity	The product must not be too complex for the consumer to understand	Amazon's Kindle device was designed around the concept of being so simple to use that people would forget the device and simply enjoy reading the book. In other words, it was designed to be as easy-to-use and intuitive as a paper book. As technology has progressed, even the complexity of the screen makes it 'very easy on the eye' compared to reading a book
Trialability	Products that can be tried out and are easy to use are far more likely to succeed	Whenever a motor manufacturer launches a new vehicle people are invited to test drive it for a short period. The thrill of driving a new car with the alluring aroma of new leather is sometimes too much to resist adoption!
Observability	The more observable the product, the quicker the diffusion process. If other potential consumers are able to see the product in use, this is bound to raise interest in it	Part of the reason for Apple's worldwide success is that it can clearly be observed in use without even being seen; the iconic white ear buds show that the customer has an Apple product

Diffusion

(of innovation) is a theory that seeks to explain how, why and at what rate new ideas and technology spread through cultures and are adopted by consumers/users

The AIDA model is probably among the oldest models in marketing. It is commonly quoted when considering promotions, but it applies equally well to adoption and diffusion of innovation. The model is somewhat too simplistic, however; it implies that the process is mechanical, without any conscious thought on the part of the individual who adopts the product. There is also the view that the model implies something being done *to* consumers (leading them through a process) rather than something that is done *for* them (meeting a need).

The Adoption Process model includes some thought on the part of the customer. In this case, becoming interested in the product leads to some serious evaluation before trial and adoption. This model portrays adoption as a sequence which the individual follows, using conscious thought and interaction with the product to come to the adoption decision.

The Hierarchy of Effects model suggests that each stage of the process leads the customer closer to the decision – as each stage is passed, the individual is further up the hierarchy and therefore becoming more committed. Obviously an individual might drop out of the model at any stage, and thus the sale will not happen, but the model

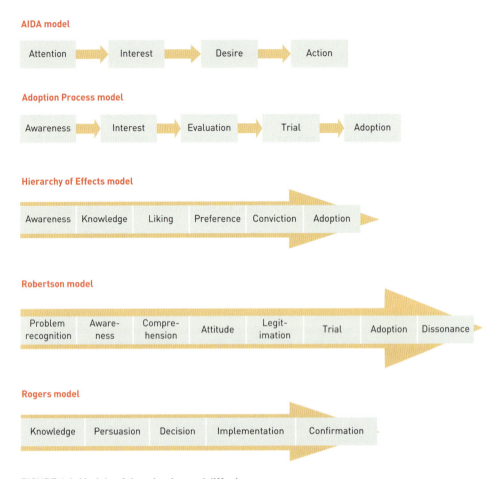

FIGURE 4.6 Models of the adoption and diffusion process

implies that people must normally pass through each stage in the correct order if a sale is to result. This is a suspect proposition, since people are likely to skip stages or even buy the product on impulse without any real evaluation at all.

Robertson's (1967) model is by far the most complex, seeking to break down the process into more stages. Robertson shows how the attitude is formed rather than simply subsuming it into a category of 'liking'. This model provides more of an insight into the internal workings of the adopter's mind, rather than simply describing behaviour.

Rogers (1983) includes the concept of persuasion in his model. Persuasion does not necessarily come from outside, however – it may just as easily come from within the individual. Persuasion is clearly of interest to marketers, whether it is marketing-generated or whether it is produced socially via peer pressure (normative compliance).

The main feature that all these models have in common is that they imply that adoption of innovation is a linear process, following logical steps. This may or may not be true – individuals may follow a straight line, or they may be diverted by circumstances. The models also show that innovations take a period time to be adopted, meaning that it also takes some time before a new product begins to show a return; this is implicit also in the shape of the product life cycle curve, where the introduction phase shows a slow start as consumers get used to the idea of the new and innovative product.

CATEGORIES OF INNOVATION ADOPTERS

A second focus in the research has been on the consumers most likely to buy new products – in other words, the **innovators**. The reason for this is that there is an assumption that innovation is diffused by word of mouth, or that innovators are likely to influence others to buy the products. This is implicit in the product life cycle, and in Rogers' observability criterion (Rogers 1983). Consumers also have access to a new channel of communication called '**word of mouse**'. With the Internet creating opportunities for marketing in all sectors, it has also enabled companies of all sizes to have more direct contact with consumers and to place more emphasis on the recommendations of others, or user-generated content (Stokes and Nelson, 2013).

It is perfectly feasible to classify consumers in terms of their attitude to new products; the problem with identifying innovators is that they are not usually innovative in all their buying habits. That is to say, an innovator for state-of-the-art audio-visual equipment is not necessarily an innovator for breakfast cereals, and although there is some evidence that there may be a kind of super-innovator who likes virtually everything that is new, these people are difficult to find, and it is debatable whether they are likely to influence other buyers anyway.

Everett Rogers classified consumers as innovators (2.5% of the population), early adopters (13.5%), early majority (34%), late majority (34%) and laggards (16%) – see Figure 4.7. These classifications were originally devised from agricultural product adoptions, but have been widely accepted as applying to more general consumer products equally well. The percentages given are arbitrary; everybody is at some point along a continuum, and Rogers decided that those whose scores lay more than two standard deviations from the mean would be classed as innovators, those whose scores lay

Early adopters

Those who, although not the first to buy a new product, do so very shortly after its introduction

Early majority

Those who adopt a new product after it has been on the market for a while, but before most people have adopted it

Late majority

People who only adopt a new product after most people have already done so

Laggards

People who are the last to adopt a new product

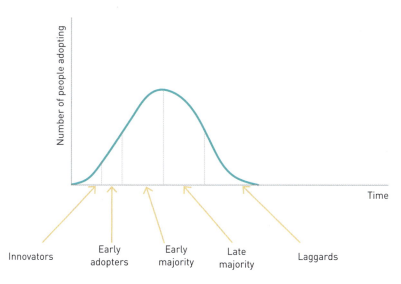

FIGURE 4.7 Classification of innovators

between one and two standard deviations would be early adopters, and those whose scores lay within one standard deviation from the mean would be the early majority. Scores below the mean were classified in the same way: those within one standard deviation of the mean were classified as the late majority, and everyone else as laggards. This means that Rogers' classifications involve circular reasoning: people are innovators because they innovate, and laggards because they are slow to innovate. You should note also that the classification tells us nothing about the characteristics of the people involved.

CONSUMER BEHAVIOUR IN ACTION: IT'S ALL ABOUT ME, ME, ME

We've already seen that the level of interaction that consumers have online with each other and with other organisations is increasing exponentially. There are lots of digital channels that are available to us and which allow others to delve deep into our own lives. Organisations that understand this have already changed their products, services and the way in which they build their new applications so that they can tap into these 'points of access'. In doing so, organisations can supposedly create experiences that are not only interesting and engaging for consumers but, more importantly, are highly personalised for the individual, and therefore seek to build the consumer's trust.

Think about your own life just for one moment and ask yourself the question, is it all about me? My Twitter-feed, my playlist, my pinboard, my blog, my Facebook friends, my new Jawbone Jambox speakers, customised online by me!

How do organisations take advantage of all of these customers' preferences and habits? How do they weave the daily experiences into a context that's relevant to the audience they are trying to target? And how important is it that during each 'moment of truth' the customer is kept informed and delighted? Digital technologies can already enable organisations to imitate 'customer intimacy'; the notion that the organisation knows their customer intimately. We see this manifesting itself online by the advertisements that quickly 'pop-up' and which reflect your latest purchases. The systems are still not perfect: even after people make online purchases, pop-ups continue to promote similar products, which is somewhat irritating since there is clearly no longer a need for the product.

As consumers, we encounter a digital experience every way we turn, from the smart refrigerator in our kitchen, to the adaptive security system in our home (which we can monitor from our smartphone). We can install a smart lighting system (Engineering. com, 2014) in our homes which will react to environmental factors. When we sit in our car, it has already learned the driver's habits (Ask.cars.com, 2013) and can fine tune the car's performance accordingly (let alone the automatic seat configuration depending on whether it's the owner or her husband who opens the car door). Finally let's not forget that big brother is always watching us in big cities with the digitalised 'Automatic Number Plate Recognition' systems, and that's even before we get to the car park which has digital parking meters!

Moment of truth

The moment or instance of contact or interaction between a customer and an organisation that gives the customer an opportunity to form or change an impression about the organisation

There are of course many benefits to having all this digital technology. Sports fans love the fact that stadiums which are accessible 'online' provide shorter lines and can offer a plethora of associated content which really engages the fan from a variety of perspectives. Event-goers also love being notified of flash sales (Bajarin 2014) on nearby food and merchandise. The technology can therefore be a two-edged sword: on the one hand, creating a convenient world in which much of the thinking has been done for us, but on the other creating a world in which we become ruled by the machines which serve us.

Innovativeness is the degree to which a person tends to adopt innovations earlier than other people. It can be measured very simply using the Goldsmith–Hofacker Innovativeness Scale, which uses six questions to determine an individual's innovativeness in respect to a particular product category (Goldsmith and Hofacker 1991). The Goldsmith–Hofacker scale is, in a sense, too simplistic because it merely asks what the individual's behaviour is, without finding out what it is about people that makes them into innovators. In order to try to discover what it is that makes somebody an innovator, studies have been carried out into known innovators to find out what they have in common.

Three main groups of variable have been identified thus far: socio-economic factors, personality factors and communication behaviour (see Figure 4.8). It should be noted, again, that all these studies are based on limited product categories, and are therefore not necessarily generally applicable.

Socio-economic variables that are positively related to innovativeness are as follows:

- education
- literacy
- higher social status
- upward social mobility
- larger-sized units
- commercial rather than subsistence orientation
- more favourable attitude towards credit
- more specialised operations.

Clearly, higher-income people are in a much better position to take the risk of buying new products. Those who are educated and literate are also more likely to hear about new products before other people do.

Personality and attitude variables associated with innovativeness are as follows:

- empathy
- ability to deal with abstractions
- rationality
- intelligence
- favourable attitude towards change
- ability to cope with uncertainty
- favourable attitude towards education
- favourable attitude toward science
- achievement motivation
- high aspirations.

Innovativeness

The degree to which an individual or firm creates or adopts new products

Socio-economic variables

Those factors that derive from an individual's class and income

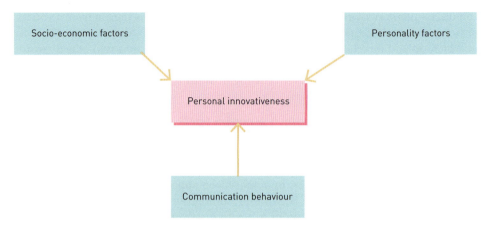

FIGURE 4.8 Variables that affect innovativeness

There are some personality traits that militate against innovativeness, however:

● dogmatism

● fatalism.

One personality trait that appears to have a strong influence is the degree to which someone likes to be different from other people. All of us have a need to be assimilated into the group, and also an opposing need to be distinct from the group, i.e. an individual. Someone's position on that continuum will influence their attitude to innovation (Timmor and Katz-Navon 2008).

M.J. Kirton (1986) showed that consumers can be classified as either adapters or innovators. Adapters tend to take existing solutions and adjust them as necessary to fit the current need problem; innovators tend to look for radical solutions. Kirton's Adaption–Innovation Index has proved to be a very reliable measure of innovativeness.

Cognitive innovators tend to be those who seek out new intellectual experiences, whereas **sensory innovators** are those who seek new sensory experiences. In both cases the innovators are seeking something new for its own sake; and there is ample research to indicate that novelty is an attractive feature of a product in its own right.

The last set of variables that affect innovativeness consists of those associated with communications, as can be seen in Figure 4.9 below:

Although innovators for one product group are not necessarily innovators for other groups, there are some correlations. For example, **technophiles** are people who like technology for its own sake, and who are prepared to take an interest in (and even buy) new audio-visual equipment, laptops/tablets and electronic gadgets, etc. Recent research by Acquity Group (2014) showed that two-thirds of consumers are expected to purchase a connected home device within the next five years and the ownership of consumer wearables is expected to double year on year by 2016. On the other hand, **technophobes** have a loathing for such devices. In general, the level of involvement with the product category will go a long way towards explaining an individual's innovativeness: research has shown that people who are very environmentally aware are also likely to adopt new environment-friendly products. This is due to a favourable configuration of values, beliefs and norms (Jansson et al. 2011).

Cognitive innovators

Those who seek new intellectual experiences

Sensory innovators

Those who seek new sensory experiences

Technophiles

People who like new technology for its own sake

Technophobes

People who are fearful of new technology

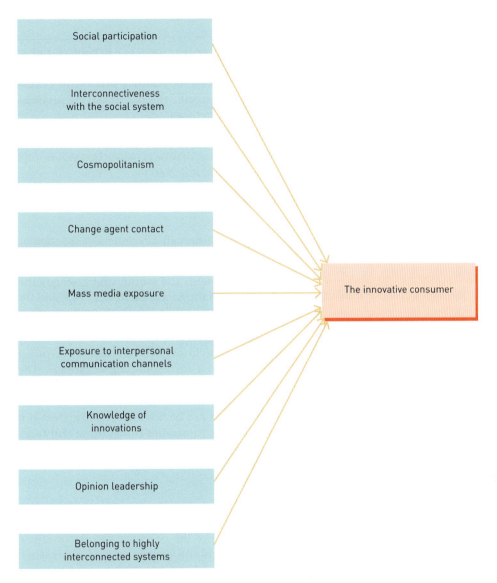

FIGURE 4.9 Communication variables associated with innovativeness

Feick and Price (1987) identified a group of influencers they called *market mavens*. A market maven is someone who has an intense interest in, and a high level of knowledge about, a specific category of product. Mavens are able to provide price and availability information to others, as well as information about the products themselves: in effect, they act as an extension of the gatekeeper role in disseminating information about new products. Mavens are usually motivated by the desire to share information, to show off their knowledge and to help others in reaching the right decisions (Walsh et al. 2004). Mavens are also sometimes known as *infomediaries*, particularly when they operate predominantly online: many forums, blogs and helpdesks are inhabited by such experts, who enjoy helping others with purchasing decisions.

INNOVATIVE PRODUCTS

From the viewpoint of a marketer, it would appear that there is a demand for new-ness *per se*. In other words, as a general rule people like new things and like to feel that the product they buy now is better than the one they bought previously. On the other hand, people are not necessarily prepared to take the risk of buying products that are radically different from their existing purchases.

In terms of the effect on the consumer's lifestyle (and consequently the risk to the consumer), innovations, from a theoretical perspective, may be classified (see Figure 4.10) under three headings (Robertson 1967; Herring and Roy 2007):

Continuous innovation

A new product that follows closely on from a previous product and has a clear relationship to the previous product

1. **Continuous innovation**: a relatively minor change in the product, for example the packaging or the styling.

Dynamically continuous innovation

The development of a new product that differs radically from its predecessors while still retaining some commonality

2. **Dynamically continuous innovation**: changes which materially affect the core functioning of the product. An example might be a coupe version of a family saloon.

Discontinuous innovation

Developing a new product that relates only distantly, or does not relate at all, to previous products

3. **Discontinuous innovation**: a product that is new to the world, and changes the lifestyles of those who adopt it. In recent years the Kindle electronic book and the iPhone have revolutionised people's approach to reading, and to communications respectively.

For someone to take the risk of adopting a technologically advanced product (i.e. a discontinuous innovation) there must be a corresponding advantage. The technology acceptance model (Davis 1989; Bagozzi and Warshaw 1992) states that new technology adoption relies on two factors: ease of use and usefulness. If a product is too difficult to use in practice it will not be adopted readily, even if it is really useful; likewise, a product that is easy to use but fulfils no useful function will not be adopted. It is for this reason that both the Kindle and the iPhone were designed to be simple to use: both are intuitive in use, with little need for an instruction manual.

The technology acceptance model has been criticised on the grounds that it has limited heuristic value, and very little predictive value – in other words, it doesn't help much with decision-making or with predictions of the potential success of a new technology (Chuttur 2009). Having said that, it is still widely used as an explanatory tool for understanding new product success (and failure) when considering discontinuous innovation.

A study by Calentone and Cooper (1981) found that the most successful new products were, in fact, only incremental improvements on existing products, rather than radically new products; this study also emphasised the need for the product to have a marketing synergy rather than be simply a wonderful idea that only the engineering department thought might succeed. For example, all employees at Google Inc can have about 20% of their working time allocated to individually initiated projects. This promotes the notion of everyone (across different units, levels and divisions) having a responsibility towards digital innovation, and maximising creativity (Avital and Te'eni 2009; Yoo et al. 2012). But of course this will only work when the culture in an organisation allows such individualised improvisation to capture successful outcomes and is tolerant of impending failures too!

| Continuous innovation | Dynamically continuous innovation | Discontinuous innovation |

| New model of an existing car | New type of car | Instantaneous transportation booth |

FIGURE 4.10 Degrees of innovation

CHALLENGING THE STATUS QUO

If the most successful products are *me-toos*, and the easiest and cheapest way of refreshing the product range is to copy someone else's designs, why does any firm bother to take the risk to innovate at all? Is it perhaps because we just get carried away with the fun of inventing something new, and then we have to find a market for it? Or is it that being first to market with a radical, life-changing new product could mean making millions, instead of just rubbing along showing a decent profit?

Well let's have a quick history lesson here. When the first online shopping websites were created, what we saw is not much more than a copy of their printed mail order catalogue.

©iStock.com/PetarChernaev

But what we have seen is a channel developing 'in its own right'. Yes it is convenient for consumers to go online, and often there is a financial benefit to be had too with the sourcing of cheaper products, but there is so much more that is offered now. Companies such as Amazon have changed the way that people not only find products online, but also search for information. 'Recommender systems', as they're known, is a technology which has evolved over the past 15 years. It studies the various patterns of online behaviour which are emitted by consumers when surfing the world wide web. From those patterns, the software and tools behind the recommender system will ascertain what a consumer will prefer from among a collection of things he or she has never bought or experienced. In doing so, companies such as Amazon who use these recommenders are providing a really innovative way of presenting online retail goods consumption.

Benchmarking

Measuring the firm's performance against that of other firms across a wide range of factors

In this connection, the trend towards benchmarking is likely to lead to even more 'me-too' or incremental product offerings. Benchmarking is the process by which firms compare their activities with the best in the industry, and try to match the best practice of their competitors in each area. The aim is to become the best of the best. To this end, motor manufacturers buy their competitors' cars and strip them down to see how they are made and what their features are, then try to emulate the best of them in their own product offerings. This is called reverse engineering. Inevitably this will lead to more copying of competitors' products if the philosophy is applied to new product development.

But digital innovation doesn't just end with online consumption. Digitally enhanced components are being embedded into everyday products such as toothbrushes too, which then in turn enable organisations to complement physical goods with online and mobile services that utilise the data generated (Bharadwaj et al. 2013), thus not only engaging with digital innovation but also enhancing the overall consumer experience. However, many organisations also have doubts about the longevity of such experiences. A primary focus, here, has to be one that questions the factors which govern the consumer adoption of digital products and services. Allied to that, and just as important as consumer adoption rates, is the challenge which organisations face in making sure that they scan the digital technology arena to ensure it relates to their business and to identify any gaps which can be seen as opportunities for innovation.

MARKETING APPROACHES TO NEW PRODUCT LAUNCHES

Relative advantage

The degree to which a new product is superior to the one it replaces, altering it in some way

Combining decision-making theory and diffusion theory, it is possible to come up with some broad recommendations for launching new products:

1. *Need recognition.* Marketers should activate needs by mentioning them in advertising. The advertising needs to make people aware of what's new, and how it will have a relative advantage over current competitors.

Compatibility

The degree to which a new product matches the individual's existing lifestyle, attitudes and possessions

2. *Pre-purchase activities* or *search.* Information sources are strongly linked to marketing strategy; brochures, product information adverts, leaflets, PR activities and salespeople all contribute to the process. Marketers should ensure that there is an emphasis on the product's compatibility with the target market's lifestyles and aspirations.

Complexity

The degree to which a new product requires extensive learning before it can be used effectively

3. *Evaluation and purchase decision.* Salespeople have a strong contribution to make to this part of the process; marketers must ensure a high quality of presentation of information materials, and the salesforce must be able to guide consumers through the complexity of the product.

Trialability

The degree to which a product can be tested before the customer needs to commit to its adoption

4. *Act of purchase and consumption.* The product has to be right for the task, and fulfil the manufacturer's claims. Allowing the customer to try the product out is a good means of reducing the risk, so trialability is a key issue in this context.

Observability

The degree to which the purchase of a new product can be seen by others

5. *Post-purchase evaluation.* After-sales service has a strong role to play here, and ideally there should be some observability in the product if there is to be rapid diffusion of the product to the broader market.

Some new products have greater potential than others for consumer acceptance. Sometimes it is difficult to analyse exactly what it is that makes one new product more acceptable than another – if marketers knew this, there would be fewer failures of new products. There is, after all, no point in trying to market a product for which consumer acceptance will be limited.

One route around the acceptance problem is mass **customisation**. Here customers are able to design the product or service themselves from a range of possible options: the application of this concept ranges from NikeiD (where customers can design their own unique trainers) to a number of start-ups who are competing for a share of the 'on-demand services' market by offering platforms and apps to take advantage of the current trend towards providing instant solutions for daily and onerous tasks (take for example the case of Uber transportation which uses an app to link drivers with passengers). It is no surprise that leading the way currently is the evolution of 3D printing. The advantage is that customers are able to design something that meets their own needs very closely indeed, and do not have to accept (or pay for) features which are only present because most people want them. This level of need for digital design has found itself moving into all industry sectors – even clothing (with websites such as www.continuumfashion.com enabling female customers to 3D print their own bikinis from solid Nylon). At first sight, it would seem that a driver for mass customisation would be that customers can save money by paying only for features they actually need, but in fact research shows that such customers are actually prepared to pay a substantial premium in order to design something to their own specification (Schreier 2006). This may be due to a better perceived fit, it may be due to perceived uniqueness of the product or it may be simply pride of authorship – the pleasure of knowing that one has created something unique. In addition, websites such as www.thingiverse.com enable individuals to upload their user-created digital designs, which are then licensed and shared so that they can be physically created using 3D printers, laser cutters or milling machines.

Customisation

Redesigning a product to make it fit a customer's needs more exactly

RESISTANCE TO INNOVATION

Resistance to innovation can come from several sources, as can facilitation of innovation. First, channels of communication might create a barrier: as we'll see in Chapter 12, communications received from respected family members and opinion leaders will be taken seriously and often acted upon, whereas communications from a member of a dissociative group will be ignored or will tend to militate against action. Poorly executed advertising and branding campaigns can create negative attitudes about the product, as can other poorly executed approaches such as insensitive salespeople, over-persuasive email shots, or negative press coverage. On the other hand, some forms of communication have greatly aided the adoption of innovation – the Internet has provided a wide variety of online blogs and forums which have enabled people to exchange information rapidly about new products. Likewise, mobile devices have provided people with rapid interpersonal communication (as opposed to landlines, which provide communication only from one place to another). Text messages, and in particular commercial permission-based text messages, have greatly increased the rate at which information about new products is disseminated. With an estimated 7.5 billion mobile phone users worldwide (GSMA 2015), the net result is that those who are likely to adopt the product hear about it much faster than they might have done a few years ago. Of course this also means that the rate at which bad news travels will also increase. By far the most efficient and effective way of keeping the public informed when disaster strikes, is by using mobile communications. Take, for instance, social media site Facebook's Safety Check button. It is a feature which can be activated by the company during either natural or man-made disasters to determine whether people in the affected geographical area are safe. So for example, within hours of an earthquake in Nepal in May 2015, doctors working in the area were able to click one button on Facebook in order to inform their friends and family that they were ok and not in trouble (Medscape 2015).

However, the social system can also create a barrier. The social system is the physical, cultural and social environment within which decisions are made: for marketers, it usually corresponds to the market segment (or target market). For example, there is a social system that functions in most jobs or professions: lawyers discuss cases, Young Farmers societies organise social events, academics have conferences, and students have Student Unions. Social systems might have traditional values, in which case innovation is likely to be stifled, or they may have modern values, in which case innovation is likely to be stimulated. The characteristics of social systems which were identified by Rogers and Shoemaker (1971) still ring true in today's societal makeup:

- A positive attitude towards change.
- An advanced technology and skilled labour force.
- A general respect for education and science.
- An emphasis on rational and ordered social relationships rather than on emotional ones.
- An outreach perspective, in which members of the system frequently interact with outsiders.
- A system in which members can easily see themselves in different roles.

Social systems can be of any size, up to and including entire countries. The prevailing social climate will be discussed in more detail in Chapter 11 but it clearly has relevance for innovation.

CONSUMER BEHAVIOUR IN ACTION: TECHNOLOGICAL TRENDS

So far we have looked at ways in which consumer behaviour affects adoption of new technology. However, technology also affects consumer behaviour, and indeed over the past 25 years numerous technological changes have affected our lives. They have created new possibilities for social interaction, new possibilities for entertainment and new possibilities for improving one's standard of living. These improvements are, of course, the motivation for adopting new products, but in many cases marketers are taken by surprise by consumer responses. So what are your thoughts and responses to key questions about the technology which affects your life? Do you recognise some of these technological trends?

Undoubtedly the current buzz is about all things 'social'. 'Mobile Social' enables consumers to engage in real-time. When one considers that futurologists are predicting that by 2020 there may be as many as 40 billion devices connected to the Internet, this makes those moments-of-truth so much more relevant, especially for those who have only ever known the 'mobile' way of life, Generation Z (Poggi 2013; Howe 2014).

From searching for information to buying to reviewing, it's all about what other people are saying, what our friends are saying, and it is this which has increased the popularity of messaging apps (for example Whatsapp, Skype, Facebook Messenger, Snapchat and Twitter) in recent years. This, in turn, generates an 'on-demand' culture, and with our mobile apps we can demand, wherever and whenever.

©iStock.com/daboost

All of this online interaction of course means that mobile payments are on the increase. Actually that's an understatement ... the trajectory that mobile payments is taking is on an exponential rise. Tracking loyalty is key here, and nearly 60% of consumers are happy to be tracked as they use their smartphones to make payments in places such as Starbucks and the London Underground, which has now enabled customers to pay using Apple Pay.

But have smartphones come to the end of their natural life cycle? Will 'wearables' take over? This is debatable at the moment. While the Apple watch has stirred the imagination of a few people, such nanotechnology is beyond many people, who fail to understand the possibilities of these devices. Indeed these products as standalone devices may not actually be of much use to us, until we can start to integrate their use in a multitude of ways, and with a plethora of apps which enable seamless usage.

This then triggers another issue – one of 'big data'. By 2020, 40 billion mobile devices will be generating a virtual shedload of data about the way in which consumers are engaging with organisations, and with each other; our geolocation, our brand preferences and affinities through webrooming and showrooming, and attitudes towards customer service quality are just some of the areas which can be investigated using the data generated. Some commentators have talked about the 'Data Lake'; a centralised pool of disparate data sources in one location. But should there be concerns about security and governance of such a place?

Geolocation
The identification of real-world geographic location of an Internet-connected device (e.g. mobile phone)

Just as Google has launched their parent company, alphabet.com, we see that the chief technology officer, Mr Gopichand Katragadda, at Tata Sons Ltd (part of Tata Group of Companies), has recently spoken about upcoming technological trends which will affect the R&D budgets of major international organisations. Here are three key trends he lists:

1. *Digital assistants.* Let your smartphone do the work for you. Applications such as Siri (Apple), Cortana (Microsoft), and Now (Google) have changed the way that we interact with our smartphone by giving it access and letting it take control of our data. Add a layer of an open-source computing platform, such as Sirius (designed by the University of Michigan) to the smartphone and cloud computing, and digital assistants can provide a multitude of opportunities and applications in all sorts of sectors – especially combined with the power of 'wearables'.

Aggregator

A website or software which aggregates a specific type of information from multiple online sources (e.g. data, news, reviews, social networks, blogs, payments)

2. **Aggregator** apps. With the rise of companies such as Uber whose app and company are valued at $50 billion, aggregator apps which connect buyers and sellers are obviously doing something right. This digital technology uses Bluetooth to transmit and receive messages to and from various mobile devices. This, coupled with cloud messaging (a technology which pushes messages and updates to an individual smartphone), means that industry sectors such as transport, retail and social enterprise are set to be revolutionalised. Can you see the possibilities?

3. *Commercial drones.* Also known as an unmanned aerial vehicle (UAV), but more commonly known as a drone, this is an aircraft without a human pilot on board; a flying robot. These devices have come a long way in the past few years. They are made of composite material structures and use nanotechnology batteries which gives them a battery life of up to 30 minutes. And when you combine this with artificial intelligence, chaos theory and cloud computing, the use for such devices is endless and is opening up a myriad of applications: film-making, industrial inspection, security firms, real estate, precision agriculture and medical facilities, to name a few. But how does this translate into a commercial application that could be marketed successfully? Well think about if drones could enable organisations to deliver products. Amazon is already talking about delivering small packages to customers (via its Prime Air service). This future service will deliver packages up to five pounds in weight in 30 minutes or less using small drones. The drones will fly under 400 feet and the total weight will be less than 55 pounds. Amazon wants to take full advantage of sophisticated 'sense and avoid' technology to safely operate beyond the line of sight to distances of 10 miles or more. Can you envisage a day when we'll have UAV-based food delivery and your pizza is delivered via a drone? You may be surprised to learn that a company in California has already launched the 'Burrito Bomber', a UAV that uses GPS navigation to drop burritos by parachute! Commercial photography has an obvious stake here enabling aerial shots of properties, concerts, etc., to be taken by the drone-savvy photographer. Of course security services could also use these images in conjunction with face recognition systems to identify 'wanted' people! And it doesn't just stop at identifying people – wildlife could be surveyed and documented using high flying drones. We could of course also use the very same technology in search and rescue missions using solar-powered UAVs which can reportedly stay airborne for five years. Which then actually triggers a final thought … could these solar-powered drones act as movable wireless access points for remote parts of the world where the infrastructure prohibits such access? Interesting, right?

SUMMARY

In this chapter we have seen a chain of events unfold. Some individuals will have a revolutionary idea, for example the Wright brothers with their invention of an aeroplane. It was other individuals who made the evolutionary advances by implementing the innovation so that it could be used for commercial airlines, military purposes and also to deliver airmail. Adoption of new products is a somewhat hit-and-miss affair. Companies need to engage with some form of innovation regularly in order to avoid being left with an obsolete product portfolio, but on the other hand it is extremely difficult to predict consumers' responses to innovative products. Many firms therefore simply make minor incremental changes to their products rather than making radical innovations. It is our ability to innovate digital technologies which enables organisations to make such small changes in a cost effective way.

On the other hand, most people like some novelty in their lives, and many people like a lot of novelty. The words novelty and personalisation may be interchanged in this context, and a classic example of this 'in action' is www.moonpig.com, a company set up by Nick Jenkins in 2000 which sells personalised greeting cards online. By 2007, it had captured 90% market share of the online greeting card market in the UK. Its unique selling point has now evolved into its ability to personalise a range of products – from gift boxes, food gifts and wall art to t-shirts, alcoholic gifts and phone cases.

The problem for marketers lies in knowing which innovations and which new product categories will be acceptable and to which target market segments.

KEY POINTS

- The product life cycle shows that all products eventually become obsolete and must be replaced.
- Innovators for one product category are not necessarily innovators for any other product category.
- The most successful products are often me-toos or continuous innovations.
- Mavens have a high level of interest in specific product categories, and enjoy airing their knowledge.
- Innovation can be continuous, dynamically continuous or discontinuous.
- Resistance to innovation can come from many sources.

HOW TO IMPRESS YOUR EXAMINER

You may be asked about the influences of social media on both strategic decisions that an organisation takes as well as the specific campaigns it runs. Different platforms are used for different objectives. Short, sharp messages can be transmitted via Twitter to a potentially very large audience, especially if your tweet starts trending. Instagram and Pinterest can be used very creatively to build a brand. A study by Ahalogy (2015 Pinterest Media Consumption Study) showed that active pinners are more likely to see themselves as trend seekers and more than half of them have clicked on the promoted pins, and more than 40% of those have made a purchase! According to the study, 'Pinterest is more "search" than "social". The Pinner experience is more geared towards personal content discovery than outward social expression'. However, consumers belong to a multitude of sites. Their time (and their loyalty) is therefore divided among all their platforms. When Ahalogy (2015) compared the amount of time 'per visit' on some of these sites, Pinterest came top, with an average of 34 minutes (Facebook 33 minutes; Twitter 24 minutes; Instagram 24 minutes). So why does this matter to both the individual and the organisation? How do these digital technologies affect innovation and the adoption of innovative products?

Trending

An 'urban' word for topics which are currently popular on Twitter

Pinners

Name given to people who are active users of Pinterest

Promoted pins

The term given to tags on pictures used as advertising units, and a way to ensure your best images get seen by your target audience

CASE STUDY: CONTINUUM – 3D PRINTING YOUR OWN CLOTHES

Continuum is a New York based company which was founded by Mary Huang, a designer and technologist. The name 'Continuum' refers to continuity of an idea from inspiration, to design and manufacturing.

Part design label, part lab, Continuum has been a pioneer in ideas such as software-based fashion collections and 3D printing. A number of their pieces have been showcased by leading press and museums internationally.

©iStock.com/Riccardo_Mojana

Their online store features products that encapsulate their inspiration and process in ready-to-wear pieces, as well as some concept products that may be more akin to art. All the items are made in NYC.

Their central belief is that fashion should express how we live our digital lives, and that products express the process and story of their creation. They consider that the most beautiful fashion could be created entirely by robots, in an autonomous choreography, without any human labour. That is their prime motivation for their work in 3D printing.

Some Continuum products have revolutionalised the thinking behind the way in which garments are made. Two products in particular exemplify this, the bikini and shoes.

THE N12 BIKINI

The N12 bikini is the world's first ready-to-wear, completely 3D-printed article of clothing. All of the individual pieces that make up the bikini, closures included, are made directly by 3D printing and snap together without any sewing. The N12 represents the beginning of what is possible for the near future.

The N12 is named for the material it's made out of: Nylon 12. This solid nylon is created by the SLS 3D printing process. The material is white, strong and flexible, because its strength allows it to bend without breaking when printed very thin. With a minimum wall thickness of just 0.7 mm, it is possible to make working springs and almost thread-like connections. For a bikini, the nylon is beautifully functional because it is waterproof and remarkably comfortable when wet. The bikini's design fundamentally reflects the beautiful intricacy possible with 3D printing, as well as the technical challenges of creating a flexible surface out of the solid nylon. Thousands of circular plates are connected by thin strings, creating a wholly new material that holds its form as well as being flexible. The layout of the circle pattern was achieved through custom written code that lays out the circles according to the curvature of the surface. In this way, the aesthetic design is completely derived from the structural design.

N12 is significant in being a ready-to-wear design. Not only is it comfortably wearable, it is also immediately buyable at an approachable price point, differing from pre-existing experimentation with 3D-printed fashion that is more avant-garde. And of course as one would expect, the product is offered in a selection of sizes.

MYTH – THE 3D PRINTED SHOES

'Myth' is the first 3D printed shoe collection designed to be ready-to-wear. Each design is 90–100% made from components manufactured on small desktop machines and optimised for scalable 3D printing production. The hand finishing on the shoes is kept to a minimum, in keeping with the goal of making finished consumer products from 3D printers, so that designs manifest directly from digital to physical. According to Mary Huang, 'there is a definite feeling of magic when pulling out a complete shoe from a glowing box' (continuumfashion.com 2014).

The collection contrasts overtly digital geometry with very organic, natural forms. The tree-like designs are inspired by Bernini's statue of Apollo and Daphne – the story of the nymph who turns into a laurel tree. These designs were created to exemplify the beauty of how objects are made on a 3D printer, where the object 'grows' layer by layer. The triangulated design is inspired by Tron, and computer graphics ... avatars in video games that are composed of low resolution polygons. So they are both about the body transformed, and myths old and new.

The first design available for purchase from the collection is the Laurel Tree Sandal, which features the sculptural 3D printed platform with silk ribbon laces that tie around the ankles. The company plans to gradually release the other designs after a pre-order period, so that testing and finishing details can be completed.

In future, there will no doubt be many technical improvements in 3D printing. Costs of both machines and finished products will drop, and consumer acceptance of the technology will increase. Meanwhile, Continuum and Mary Huang are at the cutting edge of fashion in more ways than one.

QUESTIONS

1. What appeals to you about printing your own clothes and shoes?
2. Why might the N12 and Myth product range catch on as a mainstream product?
3. What would be the driving force behind the adoption of such technological products?
4. Is this a quirky and temporary fad or have Continuum really got something here?
5. What other products could the company complement its collection with?

FURTHER READING

3D printing is a hot topic by all accounts. Reeves and Mendis (2015) have written a report (commissioned by the UK Government's Intellectual Property Office), which addresses some of the key issues: *The Current Status and Impact of 3D Printing within the Industrial Sector: An Analysis of Six Case Studies.* The publication is available from the IPO website (www.gov.uk/IPO).

Innovations can easily disrupt industries, and sometimes even very large companies fall victim to someone else's innovation. *The Innovator's Dilemma: When New Products Cause Great Firms to Fail* by Clayton Christensen (Boston, MA: Harvard Business School Press, 1997) shows how new ideas create big problems.

Following on from this book, Christensen co-authored another with Jeff Dyer and Hal Gregerson. This book, *The Innovator's DNA: Mastering the Five Skills of Disruptive Innovators* (Boston, MA: Harvard Business School Press, 2011), outlines the traits and behaviours that innovators exhibit – in particular those who come up with the radical ideas that disrupt business for their competitors.

Websites are notorious for disappearing, but this one is great fun provided it is still around when you buy this book: www.dailyfinance.com/photos/top-25-biggest-product-flops-of-all-time/#photo-1. Although it is mainly concerned with brand extensions, it does highlight some fairly appalling new product launches – and although we shouldn't gloat over someone else's failure, there are certainly lessons to be learned here.

The Art of Innovation: Success Through Innovation the IDEO Way by Tom Kelley (with Jonathan Littman) (London: Profile Books, 2001) describes techniques for becoming more innovative. It is written entirely from a practitioner's viewpoint: Kelley is the co-founder of an innovation and design company, and outlines how the firm brainstorms for ideas (including how *not* to manage a brainstorming session).

The Effect of Negative Ties on the Innovative Consumer's Creativity: An Empirical Study of New Service Idea Generation in a Social Networking Environment by Phillippe Duverger (Cambridge: Proquest/UMI Dissertation Publishing, 2011) is a PhD thesis that explores the relationship between social networking and the empowerment of consumers as innovators for the firms they buy from. Although the thesis is very academic in style, and therefore hard going at times, the author offers some very good insights into ways in which consumer creativity can be fostered, and ways in which it can be damaged.

REFERENCES

Acquity Group (2014) The Internet of things: the future of consumer adoption. www.accenture.com/t20150624T211456__w__/us-en/_acnmedia/Accenture/Conversion-Assets/DotCom/Documents/Global/PDF/Technology_9/Accenture-Internet-Things.pdf (accessed 26 January 2016).

Ahalogy Research (2015) Pinterst media consumption study, www.ahology.com/research

Ask.cars.com (2013) What is an adaptive transmission?, 19 September. http://ask.cars.com/2013/09/what-is-an-adaptive-transmission.html (accessed 28 June 2015).

Avital, M. and Te'eni, D. (2009) From generative fit to generative capacity: exploring an emerging dimension of information systems design and task performance, *Information Systems Journal*, 19 (4): 345–67

Bagozzi, R.P. and Warshaw, P.R. (1992) Development and test of a theory of technological learning and usage. *Human Relations*, 45 (7): 660–86.

Bajarin, T. (2014) Meet Levi's Stadium, the most high-tech sports venue yet. *Time*, 18 August. http://time.com/3136272/levis-stadium-tech/ (accessed 26 January 2016).

Barrett, M., Davidson, E., Prabhu, J. and Vargo, S.L. (2015) Service innovation in the digital age: key contributions and future directions. *MIS Quarterly*, 39 (1): 135–54

Bharadwaj, A., El Sawy, O.A., Pavlou, P.A. and Venkatraman, N. (2013) Digital business strategy: toward a next generation of insights. *MIS Quarterly*, 37 (2): 471–82

Calentone, R.J. and Cooper, R.G. (1981) New product scenarios: prospects for success. *American Journal of Marketing*, 45: 48–60.

Cherubini, S., Iasevoli, G. and Michelini, L. (2015) Product-service systems in the electric car industry: critical success factors in marketing. *Journal of Cleaner Production*, 97: 40–9

Chuttur, M.Y. (2009) Overview of the technology acceptance model: origins, developments and future directions. Indiana University, USA. *Sprouts: Working Papers on Information Systems*, 9 (37). www.globelegislators.org/pdfjs/test/pdfs/TAMReview.pdf (accessed 10 February 2015).

Davis, F.D. (1989) Perceived usefulness, perceived ease of use, and user acceptance of information technology. *MIS Quarterly*, 13 (3): 319–40.

Engineering.com (2014) Smart light bulb saves energy as it learns, September 14, www.engineering.com/ElectronicsDesign/ElectronicsDesignArticles/ArticleID/8489/Smart-Light-Bulb-Saves-Energy-as-It-Learns.aspx (accessed 26 January 2016).

Feick, L.F. and Price, L.L. (1987) The market maven: a diffuser of marketplace information. *Journal of Marketing*, 51: 83–97.

Goldsmith, R.E. and Hofacker, C.F. (1991) Measuring consumer innovativeness. *Journal of the Academy of Marketing Science*, 19 (3): 209–22.

GSMA (2015) Definitive data and analysis for the mobile industry. https://gsmaintelligence.com/ (accessed 1 August 2015).

Herring, H. and Roy, R. (2007) Technological innovation, energy efficient design and the rebound effect. *Technovation*, 27 (4): 194–203.

Howe, N. (2014) Introducing the Homeland Generation (Part 1). *Forbes*, 27 October. www.forbes.com/sites/neilhowe/2014/10/27/introducing-the-homeland-generation-part-1-of-2/#60564ffc4fdc (accessed 26 January 2016).

Jansson, J., Marell, A. and Nordlund, A. (2011) Exploring consumer adoption of a high involvement eco-innovation using value-belief-norm theory. *Journal of Consumer Behaviour*, 10 (1): 51–60.

Kirton, M.J. (1986) Adapters and innovators: a theory of cognitive style. In K. Gronhaugh and M. Kauffman (eds), Innovation: *A Crossdisciplinary Perspective*. New York: John Wiley, pp. 65–85.

Medscape (2015) The emerging role of social media in disasters. www.medscape.com/viewarticle/847183_3 (accessed 11 July 2015).

Poggi, J. (2013) Nickelodeon targets post-millennial's in upfront. *Advertising Age*, 26 February. http://adage.com/article/special-report-tv-upfront/nickelodeon-targets-post-millennials-upfront/240045/ (accessed 26 January 2016).

Robertson, T.S. (1967) The process of innovation and the diffusion of innovation. *Journal of Marketing*, January: 14–19.

Rogers, E.M. (1983) *Diffusion of Innovation*. New York: Free Press.

Rogers, E.M. and Shoemaker, F. (1971) *Communication of Innovation*. New York: Macmillan.

Schreier, M. (2006) The value increment of mass-customised products: an empirical assessment. *Journal of Consumer Behaviour*, 5: 317–27.

Stokes, D. and Nelson, C.H. (2013) Word of mouth to word of mouse. In Z. Sethna, R. Jones and P. Harrigan (eds), *Entrepreneurial Marketing: Global Perspectives*. Bingley: Emerald Publishing, pp. 243–58.

Tarhini, A., Ammar, H. and Tarhini, T. (2015) Analysis of the critical success factors for enterprise resource planning implementation from stakeholders' perspectives: a systematic review. *International Business Research*, 8 (4): 25

Timmor, Y. and Katz-Navon, T. (2008) Being the same and different: a model explaining new product adoption. *Journal of Consumer Behaviour*, 7 (3): 249–62.

Tuten, T.L. and Solomon, M.R. (2015) *Social Media Marketing*, 2nd edn. London: Sage.

Urban, S., Bobek, S. and Polona, T. (2015) Critical factors within organizations influencing effective use of CRM solutions. In S. Chatterjee, N.P. Singh, D.P. Goyal and N. Gupta (eds), *Managing in Recovering Markets: Proceedings in Business and Economics*. New Delhi: Springer India, pp. 223–33.

Walsh, G., Gwinner, K.P. and Swanson, S.R. (2004) What makes mavens tick? Exploring the motives of market mavens' initiation of information diffusion. *Journal of Consumer Marketing*, 21 (2): 109–22.

Yoo, Y., Boland Jr., R.J., Lyytinen, K. and Majchrzak, A. (2012) Organizing for innovation in the digitized world. *Organization Science*, 23 (5): 1398–408.

MORE ONLINE

For additional materials that support this chapter and your learning, please visit:
https://study.sagepub.com/sethnaandblythe

CHAPTER 5

CONSUMPTION IN B2C VS. B2B

LEARNING OBJECTIVES

After reading this chapter you should be able to:

- Describe and explain the main pressures that influence industrial buyers.
- Explain the role of the decision-making unit.
- Explain the role of customers in driving the reseller market.
- Describe approaches to government markets.
- Explain how to approach institutional markets.
- Show how industrial markets can be divided.
- Describe the different types of buying situation, and the factors that are involved for making buying decisions within those situations.
- Understand the role of team selling in industrial markets.

INTRODUCTION

Organisational buyers (B2B) are often supposed to be more rational and less emotional than when they are buying items for consumption by their friends and family. However, it would be wrong to assume that organisational buying is always entirely rational: those responsible for making buying decisions within organisations are still human beings, and do not leave their emotions at the door when they come to work, so it seems unrealistic to suppose that they do not have some emotional or irrational input in their decision-making. Organisational buyers often struggle with the effective management of business-to-business (B2B) services (Hawkins et al. 2015).

B2B

(business-to-business)
Where there is an exchange
of products, services
or information between
businesses

B2C

Business organisations that
sell directly to consumers
for their own use

Businesses, government departments, charities and other organisational purchasers actually represent the bulk of marketing activities, yet much of the attention in marketing is focused on business-to-consumer (B2C) developed markets rather than on business-to-business markets. The reasons for this are obscure, but may have much to do with the fact that we are all consumers and can therefore relate more easily to consumer marketing issues. Interestingly, the results from a comparative analyses study by Reijonen et al. (2013) found that a notable difference exists between emerging and developed markets, as our propensity for buying branded goods and our general brand orientation contributes to growth in the latter.

This chapter looks at the ways organisational buyers make decisions, and also at some of the influences buyers are subject to. It should be noted here that the divide between B2B and B2C becomes somewhat fuzzy when using these terms in an online/Internet context. The exchange here is referred to as e-biz and the subsequent 'exchange' is also known as e-commerce. There are many examples of firms which serve both sectors. Samsung and Daewoo, for example, are more generally known for their B2C products such as mobile phones and kitchen appliances, but are also very big players in the B2B sector as two of the leading shipbuilders in the world. In fact, in 2015 Daewoo designed and built the worlds' biggest ship at nearly 400m long – thus making it a few metres greater than the height of New York's Empire State building … and a far cry from the humble Daewoo mobile phone.

THE DECISION-MAKING UNIT

Decision-making unit

A group of people who
influence, control or carry
out purchasing activities

Buying centre

See Decision-making unit

Initiators

The members of a decision-
making unit who first
identify a need

Gatekeepers

People who control the flow
of information to a decision-
making unit

Buyers

Those with the responsibility
of making the actual
purchase of a product, often
(in the industrial context)
working to a specific brief

It is rare for an organisational purchasing decision to be made by only one person. Even in a small organisation it is likely that several people would have some input into the buying process at some stage or another. Because of this, the decision-making process often becomes formalised, with specific parts of the process being carried out by members of the decision-making unit (DMU), so that roles and responsibilities are shared and quite often based on behavioural issues that affect managerial price setting processes (Iyer et al. 2015). The DMU, also called the buying centre, often cannot be identified on the company organisation chart because it varies in make-up from one buying situation to another. Individuals may participate for only a brief time, for a specific buying decision, or alternatively may be part of the group right through the process from beginning to end.

One of the early proponents of the decision-making unit (Webster and Wind 1972) developed a model which is still quite relevant today and is generally thought to contain the following categories of member:

- **Initiators**. These are the individuals who first recognise the problem.
- **Gatekeepers**. These individuals control the flow of knowledge, either by being proactive in collecting information, or by filtering it. They could be junior staff members who are perhaps given the task to research potential suppliers of a particular component, or a receptionist or personal assistant who sees his or her role as being to prevent salespeople from 'wasting' the decision-makers' time.
- **Buyers**. These individuals are given the task of making the actual purchase. Often this is merely a case of completing the administrative tasks necessary for buying, but it is likely to involve finding suitable suppliers and negotiating the final

deal. Buyers usually work to a specific brief, and may have very little autonomy, even though they may be the only contact a supplier's salespeople have at the purchasing organisation.

- **Deciders**. These are the people who make the final decisions, and may be senior managers or specialists. They may never meet any representatives of the supplying companies. Deciders generally rely on advice from other members of the DMU, so they are influenced strongly by gatekeepers.

- **Users**. These are people who will be using the products that are being purchased: they may be engineers or technicians, or even the maintenance staff who use cleaning products. Their opinions may well be sought by the deciders, and in many cases the users are also the initiators.

- **Influentials**. These people have direct contact with the deciders, and are often asked for advice. They are trusted advisers, but from the supplying company's viewpoint they are extremely difficult to identify. Influentials may be employees of the purchasing firm (for example, engineers, information systems managers or research managers) or they may be consultants (for example, architects, health and safety consultants, or business advisers such as lawyers and accountants). An influential might even be the decider's best friend, tennis partner or favourite uncle.

The relationships are summarised in Figure 5.1.

These categories are not, of course, mutually exclusive. A user might also be an influential, or a gatekeeper might also be an initiator. The categories were originally developed to explain purchasing within families – which may be an example of the apparent similarities between business-to-business marketing and consumer marketing.

Members of the decision-making unit are, of course, human beings so they are affected both by rational and emotional motivations. Buyers are affected by their liking or dislike for the suppliers' sales representatives, and often buyers have their own work agendas, for example seeking a promotion, or feeling threatened in terms of job

Deciders

Members of a decision-making unit who have responsibility for making a final purchase decision

Users

Those members of a buying group who will actually make use of a product (not necessarily consumers)

Influentials

People who are respected for their opinions and lifestyles, and who therefore inform purchase behaviour

FIGURE 5.1 Relationships in the DMU

security, or even conducting a vendetta with a colleague. Any of these influences might affect the buyers' behaviour, but all of them would be difficult or impossible for a supplier's salesperson to identify correctly and act upon.

Members of a decision-making unit are likely to be more risk-averse than consumers because they have more to lose in the event of a wrong decision: for a consumer, the main risk is financial, but even that is limited since most retailers will replace or refund goods purchased in error. For industrial purchasers a serious mistake can result in major negative consequences for the business as well as embarrassment in front of colleagues, loss of possible promotion, or even losing one's job if the mistake is a big enough one. The professional persona of the industrial buyer is liable to be compromised by purchasing errors, which in turn means that the buyer will feel a loss of self-esteem.

Depending on the purchasing situation, the relative power of each member of the DMU will be different. This makes it hard to know what each member's influence will be on any specific decision, within environments which are increasingly more complex and competitive (Besharov and Smith 2014). Some of this more recent work has been built on earlier work by Ronchetto et al. (1989), who identified the following characteristics of individuals who will probably exert the most influence in a DMU:

- important in the corporate and departmental hierarchy
- close to the organisational boundary
- central to the workflow
- active in cross-departmental communications
- directly linked to senior management.

Fairly obviously, buyers within organisations (industrial buyers) are most important in repetitive purchases while the members of the C-Suite (i.e. CEO, managing director and other senior management) will only become involved in buying decisions which are unique, expensive or expose the organisation to significant risk.

It is because industrial buyers are likely to suffer from risk more than would be the case for consumers, they use a variety of risk-reducing tactics (Hawes and Barnhouse 1987). These are as follows, and are presented in order of importance:

- Visit the premises of the potential supplier to observe its viability.
- Talk to existing customers of the supplier about their experience with the supplier.
- Multi-source the order (buy the same component or materials from several suppliers) to ensure a backup source of supply.
- Insert penalty clauses in the supplier's contract.
- Ask colleagues about the potential supplier.
- In choosing a supplier, favour firms that your company has done business with in the past.
- Confirm that senior management are in favour of using the supplier.
- Limit the search for, and ultimate choice of, a potential supplier to well-known firms only.
- Obtain the opinion of a majority of your colleagues that the chosen supplier is satisfactory.

Of course, all of these have various personal characteristics attributed to them. Following on from this work, Veres (2012) also explored the importance which was attributed to the individual competences, such as:

- professional (financial, human resources, innovation, technological, project management)
- trustworthiness (experience, credibility, financial, ethics, authority)
- communication (skill, willingness, language)
- relational (network, relationship management)
- delegational (responsibility, powers, recognition of limits of competence, extension of competence).

So let's turn our attention to how some of these issues manifest when it comes to B2B and B2C consumption.

INFLUENCES ON BUYERS

Buyers are affected by individual, personal factors as well as environmental and organisational factors. On a personal level they are subject to many of the same influences on the buying decision that consumers have: the desire to play a role, for example, may cause a buyer to be difficult to negotiate with as he or she tries to drive a hard bargain. The desire for respect and liking may cause a buyer to want to give the order to a salesperson who is exceptionally pleasant or helpful, and to deny the order to a salesperson who is regarded as being unpleasant or pushy. Business buyers are likely to be affected by some or all of the following environmental influences (Loudon and Della Bitta 1993) which are summarised in Figure 5.2:

- *Physical influences.* The location of the purchasing firm relative to its suppliers may be decisive, since many firms prefer to source supplies locally. This is especially true in global markets, where a purchasing company may wish to support local suppliers, or may prefer to deal with people from the same cultural background. In many cases, buyers seem reluctant to source from outside their own national boundaries, even when cost and quality considerations mean that the foreign supplier would be better.
- *Technological influences.* The level of technological development available among local suppliers will affect what the buyer is able to obtain, but also the technology of the buyer and the seller must be compatible. International technical standards remain very different for most products, which means that cross-border sourcing can be complex. Despite efforts within the European Union to harmonise technical standards, Europe still does not have standardised electrical fittings, plumbing fittings or even computer keyboards. For this reason, European firms often find it easy to trade with former colonies thousands of miles away simply because the technical standards are identical.
- *Economic influences.* These divide into the macro-economic environment (which is concerned with the level of demand in the economy, and with the current taxation regime within the buyer's country) and the micro-economic environment, which is about the firm's current financial health. Obviously the state of the company finances dictates buyers' budgets for good or ill. Macro-economic conditions can

affect buyers' ability to buy goods as well as the firm's need for raw materials: if demand is low, demand for raw materials will also be low. On a more subtle level, the macro-economic climate affects the buyer's confidence in the same way as it affects consumer confidence. For example, a widespread belief that the national economy is booming will encourage buyers to commit to major investments in stock, equipment and machinery. In a global context, the fact that countries enter and leave recessions at different times will affect the timing of marketing efforts on the part of vendors. Of course the converse is true as well. Countries that are in economic trouble send ripples across to other nations who may then believe that hard times are coming their way too.

- *Political influences.* Governments frequently pass laws to regulate businesses, particularly in international trade. Trade sanctions, trade barriers (both tariff and non-tariff), and preferred-nation status all affect the ways in which buyers are permitted or encouraged to buy. In some cases, governments help businesses as part of an economic growth package, but in other cases international agreements prevent them from doing so. The political stability of countries also affects the risk level of doing business with suppliers – a revolution in a supplying country can disrupt business for a long period.

- *Legal influences.* Laws may lay down specific technical standards that affect buyer decisions. Buyers may be compelled to incorporate safety features into products, or may be subject to legal restrictions in buying some raw materials. Often, suppliers can obtain competitive advantage by anticipating changes in the law. For example, in May 2007 a scandal regarding food additives broke when a Chinese company supplied animal feed containing melamine, a compound used in the manufacture of plastics. American pet food manufacturers incorporated the feed in their products, causing thousands of pets to die from kidney failure and other diseases. In fact, adding melamine to food products was banned in China only a few weeks after the supply had been made.

- *Ethical influences.* In general, buyers are expected to act at all times for the benefit of the organisation, not for personal gain. This means that, in most cultures, buyers are not allowed to accept gifts and/or bribes, for example. However, in some cultures the act of giving gifts/money or some other inducement in order to dishonestly persuade someone to act in one's favour – bribery – is built into normal business life, which leaves the vendor with a major ethical problem – refusing to give a bribe is likely to lose the business, but giving a bribe is probably unethical or illegal in the company's home country. The OECD Anti-Bribery Convention has now been widely adopted, so most companies would be breaking the law if they offer or accept bribes. For instance, in the UK, the Bribery Act 2010 makes it an offence if a commercial organisation fails to prevent persons associated with them from bribing another person on their behalf. So, as a general rule, buyers are likely to be highly suspicious of doing business with a salesperson who appears to be acting unethically – after all, if the salesperson is prepared to break the law and cheat his or her employer, he or she might be even more prepared to cheat the buyer.

- *Cultural influences.* When dealing internationally, cultural influences come to the forefront: in the UK it might be customary to offer a visitor a cup of tea or coffee, whereas in China it might be customary to offer food. Dim Sum originated as a

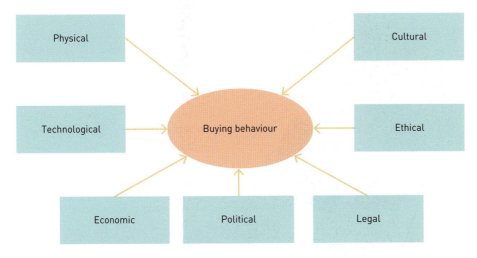

FIGURE 5.2 Environmental influences on buyer behaviour

way for Chinese businessmen to offer their visitors a symbolic meal, as a way of establishing rapport. There is evidence that national culture is less important than it once was, however; other barriers to international trade such as political issues, geographic distance and even time zone differences are often more important (Pressey and Selassie 2003). Within the national culture is the corporate culture, sometimes defined as 'the way we do things round here'. Corporate culture encompasses the strategic vision of the organisation, its ethical stance and its attitudes towards suppliers among other things. In addition, many businesspeople act in accordance with their professional culture. Each of these will affect the way business is done.

Organisational factors derive from corporate culture, as well as from strategic decisions made by senior management within the firm. Organisational policies, procedures, structure, systems of rewards, authority, status and communication systems will all affect the ways buyers relate to salespeople. Figure 5.3 shows the main categories of organisational influence on buyers' behaviour.

CONSUMER BEHAVIOUR IN ACTION: TERRACYCLE

Every time you open a waste bin to throw something away, do you stop to think where your 'waste' is heading? More importantly, do you even care? Well perhaps we would all care more if we knew that globally, solid waste management costs are predicted to be about $375.5 billion a year by 2025, according to Rachel Kyte, VP Sustainable Development, the World Bank.

The story really is a rags to riches tale. When as a freshman at Princeton University, 19-year-old Tom Szaky visited Montreal for the Autumnal break, he learnt that they fed kitchen scraps to red worms and then used the resulting fertiliser to

©iStock.com/tyannar81

feed some of their indoor plants. The results were amazing and the idea for TerraCycle was born: to help eliminate the idea of waste by producing organic fertiliser from organic waste. He initially accumulated this waste from the dining halls and cafeterias of his university. Essentially, he took the waste and had it processed by worms in order to create fertiliser or 'worm poop', and began packaging it in soda bottles and marketing it as bonafide 'worm poop'. Once he was selling through the Home Depot and Walmart in Canada, there really was no stopping him. Today, TerraCycle has grown into a highly successful green organisation, known for producing a variety of consumer products from pre-consumer and post-consumer waste. The organisation differentiates itself in the waste management industry today by recycling traditionally non-recyclable waste, such as toothbrushes, chips bags and drinking pouches. TerraCycle then recycles these waste items in order to produce products such as garden tools, tote bags, cutting boards, water coolers, benches and bike racks, to name just a few. Before TerraCycle the post-consumer and non-recyclable waste ended up in landfill sites. Landfills are one of the oldest forms of waste treatment, and essentially involve dumping waste into the ground. This is a major issue in North America as dumping waste into landfills negatively affects our environment, causing infrastructure disruption and soil contamination to name but two. By recycling traditionally unrecyclable waste into consumer products, TerraCycle addresses a systems gap; a previously unmet need which is minimising the waste that gets dumped into our landfills. This outstanding social innovation ultimately contributes to a cleaner environment. TerraCycle's unique and diverse solution to collecting and re-purposing pre- and post-consumer waste has not only impacted the environment, but society as a whole. TerraCycle is now considered a highly successful and environmentally beneficial business model. It has influenced many other organisations within North America, and around the globe, to begin re-purposing material as well as incorporating this type of strategy into their business models. For example, TerraCycle partners with Kenco to offer customers 100 locations around the UK that will collect coffee packaging waste from local residents. By influencing the members in other organisations and society, TerraCycle has had great scalability, and thus created a movement which will help minimise and maybe in time diminish the amount of waste around the world.

Buying tasks differ greatly between firms, but may also differ significantly within firms. For example, the buying task for a supermarket clearly differs from that for a manufacturing company, since the supermarket intends to sell the vast majority of its purchases unchanged, whereas the manufacturer is largely concerned with sourcing

FIGURE 5.3 Organisational influences on buyer behaviour

components and raw materials. The supermarket has other, internal variations in the buying task: buying canned goods will be totally different from buying fresh produce such as vegetables or fresh fish. Equally, the manufacturer will have a different approach when buying basic raw materials compared with buying components, and yet another set of approaches when buying lubricating oil or business services or new factory premises. The different purchasing tasks affect the buyer's thinking and negotiating approach, so firms will usually have separate buyers for each type of buying task.

Structure of the organisation falls into two categories: the formal structure is what shows on the organisation chart; the informal structure is the network of personal relationships that dictates staff behaviour in most cases. The formal organisation structure determines such issues as the degree of centralisation in purchasing decision-making, the degree to which buying decisions follow a formal procedure (i.e. how constrained by the rules the buyers are) and the degree of specialisation in buying for different purposes or different departments in the organisation.

The informal structure dictates such issues as rivalry between buyers, recognition by management, cooperation between buyers in maintaining each other's status in the eyes of the boss, and so forth. The maze of informal relationships can be extremely complex, especially for a salesperson observing it from the outside, and this complexity is likely to be crucial in the success or failure of key-account selling. In the global context, the informal structure is subject to many cultural influences – the Oriental concern with gaining or losing face, for example, can be a crucial factor in doing business. The informal structure is also the major factor in determining who will be the most important influentials in the decision-making unit; some colleagues' opinions may be regarded as more trustworthy than others, for example.

The organisation's technology base also affects the buyer's level of control over purchasing. For example, computer-controlled stock purchasing, particularly in a just-in-time purchasing environment, can limit the buyer's ability to negotiate deals and in many cases removes the buyer from the process altogether. Models for inventory control and price forecasting are also widely used by buyers, so that in many cases the negotiating process is virtually automated with little room for manoeuvre on the part of the buyer. If this is the case, the selling organisation needs to go beyond the buyer to the other members of the DMU in order to change the rules or find creative ways round them. Technology-minded companies are likely to use electronic communications systems (communications using 'mobile' means being only one example) to a greater extent than other firms; research shows that technology-mediated communications have a positive, direct effect on future intentions to buy, but of course this is still affected considerably by factors of trust and commitment (McDonald and Smith 2004). E-commerce in business-to-business marketing relies on the following factors (Claycomb et al. 2005):

- compatibility with existing systems
- co-operative norms with customers
- lateral integration within the firm
- technocratic specialisation
- decentralisation of information technology.

The characteristics of the people involved in the organisation will determine the organisation culture, but will in any event control the interpretation of the rules under which the purchasing department operates. At senior management level, the character of the organisation is likely to be a function of the senior management, and in many cases the organisation's founder will have set his or her personality firmly on the organisation's culture. Virgin is clearly an offshoot of Richard Branson's personality, as The Body Shop is an offshoot of Anita Roddick's.

CLASSIFYING BUSINESS CUSTOMERS

A business customer is one who is buying on behalf of an organisation rather than buying for personal or family consumption. In everyday speech, we usually talk about organisations as the purchasers of goods, but of course this is not the case: business customers, in practice, are human beings who buy on behalf of organisations.

TABLE 5.1 Classification summary of buying organisations

Type of organisation	Description
Business and commercial organisations	These organisations buy goods that are used to make other goods, and also those items that are consumed in the course of running the organisation's business. These organisations buy foundation goods and services (goods used to make other products), facilitating goods and services (those that help an organisation achieve its objectives) and entering goods and services (those that become part of another product)
Reseller organisations	Resellers buy goods in order to sell them on to other organisations or to final consumers. Typically, resellers will be wholesalers or retailers, but they may also be agents for services, for example travel agents or webmasters who act as facilitators for other firms
Governmental organisations	Governments buy everything from paperclips to submarines through their various departments. Because national and local government departments operate under specific rules that are often rigid, negotiations can be difficult to conduct: buyers are often severely constrained in what they can do. Contracts are often put out to tender, with the lowest bidder being awarded the contract
Institutional organisations	Institutional organisations include charities, educational establishments, hospitals and other organisations that do not fit into the business, reseller or government categories. These organisations may be in the market for almost any kind of product, but they are used to achieve institutional goals that probably do not include profit

Organisations might be classified according to the types of buying and end-use they have for the products. Table 5.1 shows a summary of the commonly accepted classifications, followed by a fuller explanation. It is important to understand the different buying and selling situations which arise here, and how these situations will affect the buyer behaviour (especially as in this B2B context the buyer is not typically the 'consumer').

BUSINESS AND COMMERCIAL ORGANISATIONS

Business and commercial organisations can be segmented as original-equipment manufacturers, users and aftermarket customers. Original-equipment manufacturers (OEMs) buy foundation, entering and facilitating goods including machinery and equipment used to make products, and products that are incorporated directly into the final product. For example, computer manufacturers may buy machine tools to make computer cases and also buy silicon chips from specialist producers: the chips are incorporated into the final product, but the same type of chip might be incorporated in computers from several different OEMs. The Intel Pentium chip is an example.

OEM
Original-equipment manufacturer

For OEM buyers, the key issue will be the quality of the products or services. Such buyers are usually operating to fairly exact specifications laid down by their own production engineers and designers; it is unlikely that the supplying firm will be able to do very much to have the specification changed, except by approaching the designers during the design process. This means that introducing a new product to an OEM will be a lengthy process, since the supplying company will need to establish a long-term relationship with the customer in order to become involved at the design stage for new products.

User customers buy products that are used up within the organisation, either as components in their own equipment or to make the equipment perform properly, for example lubricating oils or cleaning products. These products are not re-sold, but may be bought in considerable quantities. Many of these user products are services – accountancy or legal services, cleaning services, and maintenance or building services are all contained within the firm and not resold.

Aftermarket customers are those involved in the maintaining, repairing and overhauling (MRO) of products after they have been sold. For example, central heating systems are likely to be maintained by independent contractors rather than the original manufacturers or installers. The reason for this is that maintenance requires an investment in expensive testing equipment and different training from that required for installation or manufacture. These contractors buy the components, supplies and services they need from the most convenient supplier.

MRO
A company that carries out maintenance, repair and overhaul

The classification split between OEM, users and aftermarket customers is only relevant to the supplier. OEMs can also be user customers for some suppliers. For example, a plastic moulding company may sell components to an OEM and plastic tools to a user as well as plastic replacement parts to an aftermarket organisation: in some cases these may even be the same organisation. Buying motivations for each type of purchase are clearly very different, and the supplying firm is likely to be dealing with different buyers for each category of product, if the customer company is a large one. In Figure 5.4, the same suppliers sometimes provide goods or services for several firms in the supply chain. In some cases there will be considerable crossover between firms.

RESELLER ORGANISATIONS

The majority of manufactured goods are sold through reseller organisations such as retailers and wholesalers. Intermediaries provide useful services such as bulk breaking, assortment of goods and accumulation of associated product types: due to increased efficiencies resulting from these services, intermediaries tend to reduce overall prices for the final consumer. Cutting out the intermediaries usually reduces efficiency and tends to increase prices; if this were not so, the intermediaries would be unable to justify their existence and firms would simply bypass them.

Reseller organisations are driven almost entirely by their customers. This means that they will buy only those products they believe will sell easily; there is therefore a premium on employing buyers who have a clear understanding of customer needs. Unlike the OEM buyers, there is little need for resellers to understand the technical aspects of the products they buy – they merely need to feel confident that the ultimate consumers will want the products.

Reseller organisations carry out the following basic functions:

- negotiation with suppliers
- promotional activities such as advertising, sales promotion, providing a salesforce, etc.
- warehousing, storage and product handling
- transportation of local and (occasionally) long-distance shipments
- inventory control

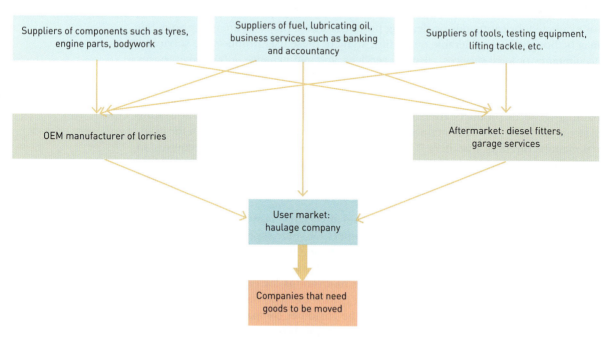

FIGURE 5.4 Types of purchase

- credit checking and credit control
- pricing and collection of price information, particularly about competitors
- collection of market information about consumers and competitors.

For manufacturers, this places a premium on establishing close, long-term relationships with resellers. Shared information, as part of an integrated channel management strategy, becomes crucial to forward planning.

GOVERNMENT ORGANISATIONS

Government and quasi-government organisations are major buyers of almost everything. In some markets, the government is heavily involved in industry. For instance, all insurance in India used to be a government monopoly and the oil industry in Mexico is controlled by PEMEX, a quasi-government entity. Governments are thought to be the largest category of market in the world, if all levels of government are included in the equation. The structure of government varies from one country to another: for example, in Spain there is the national government based in Madrid, the regional governments (e.g. the Junta de Andalucia), the provincial governments (e.g. Provincia de Granada) and the local town halls (e.g. Ayuntamiento de Ugijar). Sometimes these local town halls group together to form an alliance that carries out mutually beneficial activities such as tourism marketing or funding a local swimming pool, but frequently they act independently of one another within the frameworks of their own jurisdictions. Figure 5.5 summarises the types of purchase that might be made by each of the tiers of government.

Because of the strict rules under which most government organisations operate, special measures are often needed to negotiate deals. In particular, government organisations almost always put contracts out for tender, so that firms are asked to bid for contracts. The contract is usually offered to the lowest bidder, unless there are overwhelming reasons to do otherwise. From a supplier's viewpoint, this is likely to be problematic, since the lowest price is likely to be the least profitable price, so selling firms will often try to circumvent the process by ensuring that they become

FIGURE 5.5 Tiers of government and their typical purchases

involved before the tender is finalised. In this way it may be possible to ensure that the tender is drawn up in a way that favours the proactive firm over its competitors (for example, by including features that competitors cannot offer) thus ensuring that competitors either do not bid at all, or bid at too high a price.

In some cases, governments need to purchase items that are not available to the general public or to other businesses. Military and defence hardware is an obvious example; clearly ordinary businesses are not allowed to buy submarines or nuclear bombs. On a more subtle level, there are many other examples of specialist markets. So, goods such as handguns are not permitted for private organisations in the UK, but can be sold to the army or the police force; some types of computer software are only appropriate for use by the tax authorities; and academic research is paid for largely by the government in the UK.

From a marketing viewpoint, these specialist markets present an interesting challenge, since in some cases the products need to be tailored to a specific government or a specific government department. This may mean that there is considerable scope for negotiation, but since the contract will still have to go out to tender (under competitive and fair practice legislation), the bidding company may find that it has spent a lot of time developing a specification for a contract which is then awarded to another firm.

In some circumstances governments may issue a 'cost-plus' contract, in which the organisation is given a specific task to carry out, and charges according to the cost of the contract plus an agreed profit margin. In the early days of space exploration this type of contract was common, since it was impossible to predict what the costs might be when dealing with an unknown set of circumstances. More recently these contracts have fallen into disrepute since they reward inefficiency and waste.

INSTITUTIONAL ORGANISATIONS

Institutions include charities, universities, hospital trusts and non-profit organisations of all types, schools, and so forth. In some cases these are government-owned but independent for the purposes of purchase and supply (for example, secondary schools); in other cases they are totally independent (for example, registered charities). The traditional view of these organisations is that they are chronically under-funded and therefore do not represent a particularly wealthy market, but in practice the organisations actually have a very substantial aggregate spending power. Figure 5.6 summarises the factors that have to be taken into account in marketing to institutions.

The marketing organisation may need to be creative in helping the institution to raise the money to buy its products because budgets are almost always very tight. For example, a firm that produces drilling equipment may find that it has a substantial market at Oxfam, since Oxfam drills wells in many arid regions within developing countries. Oxfam relies on public generosity to raise the money to buy the equipment, so the manufacturer may find it necessary to part-fund or even manage a fundraising campaign in order to make the sale.

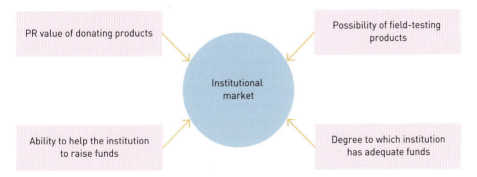

FIGURE 5.6 Factors in institutional marketing

CHALLENGING THE STATUS QUO

We are often told that marketing is about managing the exchange process, yet government departments and many institutions seem to lay down the ground rules from the start. Marketers have to play by the buyer's rules to be in the game at all – so how can they possibly be managing the process? Pushed from one set of constraints to the next, it would seem that the average marketer is just a pawn in the buyers' hands!

Yet maybe that is how it should be if customers are at the centre of everything we do. Not to mention that the management process itself could be construed as a clearing-house for pressures rather than as a directive force – in a sense, no manager is actually in control, so why should marketers be any different?

Suppliers are often asked to contribute to charities, in cash or in products. This may not always be possible, since the supplier's only market might be the charities, but in some cases firms may find it worthwhile to supply free products to charities in order to gain PR value, or sometimes in order to open the door to lucrative deals with other organisations. For example, a charity working in a developing country might be prepared to field-test equipment that could then be sold to a government department in the same country.

BUYERS' TECHNIQUES

Buyers use a wide variety of techniques according to the buying situation they are faced with. Buying situations are generally divided into three types:

1. **Straight rebuy**. Most organisational buying is routine: for example, a car manufacturer needs to buy much the same number of wheel nuts each month. A straight rebuy is a situation where the buyer is buying the same product in very much the same quantities from the same supplier. In these circumstances the buyer needs no new information, and does not need to engage in much negotiation either. Prudent buyers may occasionally look at other possible sources of components in order to ensure that no new technology is available or that other suppliers are not able to supply the same components more cheaply, but in general the order placement is

Straight rebuy

A situation in which a previous order is simply repeated in its entirety automatic. In some cases the whole process is automated through an electronic data interchange (EDI) link with a supplier, or there may be an automatic buying procedure facilitated through the Internet without any human involvement. If the product is of minor importance, or represents a low commitment in terms of finance or risk, the buyer will probably not undertake any information search and will simply order the goods. This is called *causal purchasing*, because it results automatically from a cause such as low stock level. For example, a buyer for a large engineering firm probably spends very little time deciding on brands of paper for the photocopier. On the other hand, buying copper cable might be a routine purchase, but the buyer might monitor the market for alternatives occasionally. Such buying is called *routine low-priority buying* because it has a lower priority than would be the case if an entirely new situation were being faced. The company is unlikely to get into serious trouble if it pays 10% more than it should for cable, for example.

Modified re-buy

A purchase that, although similar to previous purchases, has been changed in a minor way

2. **Modified rebuy.** In this situation, the buyer re-evaluates the habitual buying patterns of the firm with a view to changing them in some way. The quantities ordered, or the specification of the components, may be changed. Even the supplier may be changed. Sometimes these changes come about because the buyer has become aware of a better alternative than the one currently employed (perhaps through environmental scanning), or sometimes the changes come about because competing suppliers succeed in offering something new. Internal forces (increases or decreases in demand for components) might trigger a renegotiation with suppliers or a search for new suppliers. In such circumstances the buyer is faced with a limited problem-solving scenario in which he or she will need to carry out some negotiation with existing or new suppliers, and will probably need to seek out new information as well. The buyer may well require potential suppliers to bid against each other for the business: the drawback of this approach is that it often results in damaging a well-established relationship with existing suppliers.

New task

A type of purchase for which previous experience does not exist

3. **New task.** This type of buying situation comes about when the task is perceived as being entirely new. Past experience is therefore no guide, and present suppliers may not be able to help either. Thus the buyer is faced with a complex decision process. Judgemental new task situations are those in which the buyer must deal with technical complexities of the product, complex evaluation of alternatives and negotiating with new suppliers. Strategic new task situations are those in which the final decision is of strategic importance to the firm – for example, a bank looking for software for online banking will be investing (potentially) hundreds of thousands of pounds in retraining staff, and in transferring existing records, not to mention the risks of buying software which lacks the necessary security features or which fails under high demand. In these circumstances, long-range planning at director level drives the buying process, and the relationship with the suppliers is likely to be both long-term and close.

From the viewpoint of the business marketer, the main chance of winning new customers will come in the new task situation. The risks for buyers involved in switching suppliers are often too great unless there is a very real and clear advantage in doing so; such an advantage is likely to be difficult to prove in practice. In the new task situation, potential suppliers may well find themselves screened out early in the process, and will then find it almost impossible to be reconsidered later.

The various trade-offs in the buying situation are shown in Figure 5.7.

FIGURE 5.7 Trade-offs in type of buying situation

THE BUYGRID FRAMEWORK

Organisational buying can be seen as a series of decisions, each of which leads to a further problem about which a decision must be made (Cardozo, 1983; Iyer et al. 2015). From the viewpoint of the supplying firm, it would certainly be valuable to be able to diagnose problems by examining the sequence of decisions. The difficulty here is that the decision sequence is probably not known to the marketer unless the firms involved already have a close relationship. If the sequence can be known, marketers can identify the stage at which the firm is currently making decisions, and can tailor the approach accordingly.

The industrial buying process can be mapped against a grid, as shown in Figure 5.8. The most complex buying situations occur in the upper left portion of the frame-work and involve the largest number of decision-makers and buying influences. This is because new tasks require the greatest amount of effort in seeking infor-mation and formulating appropriate solutions, but also will require the greatest involvement of individuals at all levels of the organisation. The more people who are involved, the more complex the decision process because each individual will have a personal agenda.

However, the Buygrid framework is not without its criticism. Like most models it tends to over-simplify the case. As in consumer decision-making, the sequence may not be as clear-cut and events may take place in a different order in certain circumstances. For example, a buying firm may not be aware that it has a problem in a particular area until a supplier approaches the firm with a solution, thus cut-ting out several stages of the process: the firm may well recognise the need and the problem, but will probably not need to acquire proposals and select a supplier

Stage	Buying situations		
	New task	Modified rebuy	Straight rebuy
Anticipation or recognition of a problem (need) and a general solution			
Determination of characteristics and quantity of needed item			
Description of characteristics and quantity of needed item			
Search for and qualification of potential sources			
Acquisition and analysis of proposals			
Evaluation of proposals and selection of supplier(s)			
Selection of an order routine			
Performance feedback and evaluation			

FIGURE 5.8 The Buygrid framework

Reproduced with permission of the Marketing Science Institute.

since the supplier is already offering a solution. Second, suppliers go to great lengths to differentiate themselves from competitors as effectively as they can, so that the buyer is unlikely to have any other potential suppliers of the exact product on offer. Third, the model assumes a rational approach to purchasing which is often simply not there. Finally, the boundaries between new task, modified rebuy and straight rebuy are by no means clear-cut.

Buyers are influenced by both rational and emotional considerations. The potential supplier needs to be aware of the personal agendas of each member of the decision-making unit. Even at a rational level, each member of the DMU will apply different criteria for judging which suppliers should be included and which excluded (Kelly and Coaker 1976; Hawkins et al. 2015): the finance director might emphasise low prices, whereas the chief designer might be concerned with product quality, and the production manager with reliable delivery. The buyer might be concerned with the relationship with the supplier's salespeople. In many cases, brand equity is less important than issues of price and delivery (Bendixen et al. 2004; Mourad et al. 2011). At the personal, emotional level, office politics, rivalries, jockeying for promotion, liking or disliking the salesperson and many other factors will affect different members of the DMU in different ways.

In the case of key-account management, this problem of dealing with different members of the DMU is often overcome by taking a team approach to the sale. While the **key-account manager** handles the initial contact and the management of the process, other specialists are brought in to deal with financial and technical aspects. In this way each member of the DMU is speaking to someone with whom he or she has a common language and a common understanding of the conceptual environment within which each specialty operates. In some cases the number of people working on the account can become large: when IBM were dealing with Lloyds Bank (one of the Big Four UK banks) they had more than 100 people working on the account, and set up a special branch office in the Canary Wharf area to be near Lloyds head office.

Key-account manager

A salesperson who has the responsibility of dealing with the most important customers of a firm

Managing the key-account networks means identifying the key network, developing a strategy for managing the individuals who operate within the network and developing methods at the operational level for managing those actors (Ojasalo 2004). The responsibility for managing the actors is often divided between the members of the selling team. The internal culture of the firm (and the external culture, in an international context) affects the nature of each of these network types.

According to Moller and Svahn (2004), there are three types of business net:

1. *Stable*. These are networks that are perhaps still growing, but they are following a predictable course.

2. *Established*. These networks are fixed and relatively unchanging, and the rules are known by the members.

3. *Emerging*. These networks are still growing and changing.

Recent work conducted by La Rocca et al. (2015) provides a powerful case for focusing on the role that interaction behaviours play in business relationships. In their model, there are two perspectives which could be examined; the socio-cognitive perspective and the practice-based approach to both markets and marketing.

VALUE ANALYSIS

Value analysis is a method of evaluating components, raw materials and even manufacturing processes in order to determine ways of cutting costs or improving finished products. Value-in-use is defined as a product's economic value to the user relative to a specific alternative in a particular application (Kijewski and Yoon 1990). Value-in-use is the price that would equate the overall costs and benefits of using one product rather than using another.

Value analysis
The process of calculating the worth of a purchase in terms of the returns made from its use

Proponents of a similar concept, Vargo and Lusch (2004), used their Service Dominant Logic (SD Logic) framework to explain how competencies are used in achieving competitive advantage. Veres (2012) explains that in order for the firm to create competitive advantage (and thus to develop a 'value-creating problem-solving' strategy) it has to leverage the intangible assets of the company. Quite often, when organisations are under pressure to perform, the intangible assets suddenly manifest themselves in technology, products and/or management (Veres 2012). How well the organisation has the ability and capability to 'learn', will determine the final competencies that it has. The final contribution that SD logic makes here is to do with the value-offer (something which is done by the supplier) and value-creation (something which is carried out by the buyer); a concept Vargo and Lusch (2004) call 'co-creation'.

For example, consider LED light bulbs. Even though these bulbs are between five and ten times as expensive to buy as compared to the old tungsten-filament bulbs, they last at least five times as long and use only 20% of the electricity. For a domestic consumer, this represents a considerable saving, more than enough to cover the initial outlay for the bulbs, but for a business customer the saving is even greater, since the cost of paying someone to replace blown light bulbs is significant. The LED lamp market was worth somewhere in the region of $2 billion in 2014 and is predicted to rise to around $25 billion by 2023.

TABLE 5.2 Assessing suppliers

Attribute	Assessment method
Technical capability	Visit the supplier to examine production equipment, inspect quality control procedures and meet the engineering staff
Managerial capability	Discuss systems for controlling processes, meet the managerial staff and become involved in planning and scheduling supplies
Financial stability	Check the accounts filed at Companies House or other public record office, run a credit check, examine annual reports if any
Capacity to deliver	Ascertain the status of other customers of the supplier – would any of these take priority? Assess the production capacity of the supplier, warehouse stocks of the product, reputation in the industry

Some buyers do use the type of calculation seen in Table 5.2 to assess alternative solutions to existing problems. A capable salesperson will be prepared with the full arguments in favour of the new solution, including all the relevant factors that make the product more attractive. On the other side of the coin, astute purchasers will involve potential suppliers in the discussions and in the value analysis process.

EVALUATING SUPPLIER CAPABILITY

Purchasers also need to assess the capability of potential suppliers to continue to supply successfully. This is a combination of assessing financial stability, technical expertise, reliability, quality assurance processes and production capacity. In simple terms, the purchasing company is trying to ensure that the potential supplier will be in a position to keep the promises it makes. Business customers can gain competitive advantage from tracking the performance of suppliers because they are better able to manage the supply chain (Bharadwaj 2004).

TABLE 5.3 Evaluation approaches

Approach	Explanation
Categorical plan	Each department having contact with the supplier is asked to provide a regular rating of suppliers against a list of salient performance factors. This method is extremely subjective, but is easy to administer
Weighted-point plan	Performance factors are graded according to their importance to the organisation: for example, delivery reliability might be more important for some organisations than for others. The supplier's total rating can be calculated and the supplier's offering can be adjusted if necessary to meet the purchasing organisation's needs
Cost-ratio plan	Here the buying organisation evaluates quality, delivery and service in terms of what each one costs. Good performance is assigned a negative score, i.e. the costs of purchase are reduced by good performance; poor performance is assigned a positive score, meaning that the costs are deemed to be greater when dealing with a poor performer

Table 5.3 illustrates some of the ways in which buyers can assess potential suppliers. These methods rely (in most cases) on judgement on the part of the purchaser, who may not in fact have the necessary expertise to understand what the supplier's capability really is.

EVALUATING SUPPLIER PERFORMANCE

Even after the contract is awarded, the purchasing company will probably re-examine the supplier's performance periodically. In some cases, suppliers have been known to relax and reduce their service level once the contract is awarded, and of course the circumstances of the buying organisation are likely to change over time. If the relationship with the supplier is to continue, then (like all other human relationships) it must adapt to changing circumstances. The basic evaluation methods are outlined in Table 5.3. All of these methods involve some degree of subjectivity, in other words each method requires buyers to make judgements about the supplier. Expressing the evaluations numerically makes the method appear more credible, but if the basic assumptions are incorrect, no amount of calculation will generate the right answer. Those involved in evaluation exercises of this nature should be aware that the evaluation exercise itself should be evaluated periodically, and the (usually subjective) criteria used by the various individuals involved need to be checked.

In fact, suppliers tend to adapt more often than do purchasers when there is an ongoing relationship (Brennan et al. 2003). This is due to the relative power each has (buyers being more powerful in most circumstances), and managerial preferences. Suppliers that are market-orientated tend to develop a greater customer intimacy, which may also drive suppliers to change (Tuominen et al. 2004). Buyers that are themselves market-orientated tend to become more loyal to their suppliers (Jose Sanzo et al. 2003). Having said that, suppliers do sometimes end unprofitable relationships; many B2B relationships are unprofitable, and often companies lack the skills to make relationships profitable, so they simply end them (Helm et al. 2006).

Plaster saint

A person who makes a show of being without moral faults or human weakness, especially in a hypocritical way

SUMMARY

Buyers have a large number of influences on their decision-making. At the very least, buyers have their own personal agendas within the companies they work for; in the broader context, a wide range of political, environmental and technological issues will affect their decision-making. The end result is likely to be a combination of experience, careful calculation and gut feeling.

Although industrial buyers are often assumed to be much more rigorous in their buying, and less swayed by emotion, this is only partly true; consequently, they are as susceptible to good marketing as any other person, and can be influenced by good marketing communications and especially by good salespeople.

KEY POINTS

- Buyers are subject to many pressures other than the simple commercial ones; emotions, organisational influence, politics and internal structures are also important factors.
- The decision-making unit (DMU) or buying centre is the group of people who will make the buying decision. The roles and composition of DMUs vary widely.
- Business and commercial organisations are likely to be swayed most by past experience with a vendor, product characteristics and quality.
- Resellers are driven by their customers.
- Government markets are large, and almost always use a tendering system.
- Institutional markets may need special techniques to help them afford to buy the products.

- Markets can be divided into those buyers who buy products designed to make other products or who will incorporate the purchase into their own products (original equipment manufacturers); those who consume the product in the course of running their businesses (user markets); and those who serve the aftermarket.
- A purchase may be a straight rebuy, a modified rebuy or a new task. These are given in order of increasing complexity, and do not have discrete boundaries.
- A team approach to buying usually dictates a team approach to selling.

HOW TO IMPRESS YOUR EXAMINER

Industrial buyer behaviour is not always included in consumer behaviour courses, but there are parallels between the ways consumers meet their needs and the ways buyers make decisions. If you are asked about industrial buying behaviour, it is worth remembering that buyers are also human beings – they are as affected by emotion and 'gut feeling' as anyone else, but need to keep this in control in the working environment. Using parallels from family decision-making will show that you understand the issues.

REVIEW QUESTIONS

1. How would you expect a government department to go about buying a new computer system?
2. How might internal politics affect a buyer's behaviour?
3. What factors might be prominent in the buying decision for cleaning materials?
4. What factors might a supplier take into account when evaluating a purchasing company?
5. How might the directors of a company go about setting standards for evaluating suppliers? What objective criteria are available?
6. What are the main problems with evaluating supplier performance?
7. How should a seller approach a government department?
8. What are the main differences between marketing to commercial organisations and marketing to charities?
9. How might a seller find out who the influentials are in the DMU?
10. How might a seller act to reduce the risk for the buyer?

CASE STUDY: SELL2WALES

©iStock.com/jmci

Wales is a small country. It is characterised by small enterprises and small local authorities, and indeed a small government – the Welsh Assembly Government (WAG). Even the cities are small: Cardiff, the capital and largest city, has a population of around 350,000 people. Despite being small, Wales has a strong sense of patriotism, and has a unique culture distinct from the rest of the UK.

This sense of patriotism, of Welshness, has led to a major initiative by the Welsh Assembly Government. WAG has set up a system whereby Welsh companies and entrepreneurs can register to be informed of upcoming tenders and contracts for all WAG departments, universities, National Health Service trusts and local authorities in the country. The website acts as a one-stop shop for suppliers and buyers, so that buyers can easily register their requirements and obtain access to a large group of suppliers, while at the same time suppliers can register for automatic email alerts when potentially attractive tenders come up. Even in a small country the total spend by the public sector runs into billions of pounds a year, money which can be crucial to firms in Wales.

In addition, the Sell2Wales site publicises help and events for businesses. WAG offers a business advice service, including mentoring for small firms, and also provides workshops and seminars on topics such as tendering for contracts and supply chain management.

Obviously the site has to be open to companies from anywhere in the UK, and even (at the time of writing) the European Union, but the bulk of companies registered on the site are based within Wales, if only because many of the tenders are for services. Thus much of the money remains within Wales, supporting the Welsh economy.

For example, Kelray Building Maintenance Ltd is a company based in Merthyr Tydfil, a notoriously depressed area which suffers from high unemployment levels. Managing Director Carl Raynes registered with Sell2Wales almost at the outset, and has had many contracts from local authorities for the maintenance of social housing stock. A one-year contract for Torfaen County Borough Council involved Kelray in refurbishing empty houses to provide housing for homeless people, a project which not only earned money for the company but which also provided work for the extra people needed to service the contract. Another example is Ocon Fire and Security Ltd. Ocon was established in 2006, and now employs 27 people in two locations: one in West Wales and another in England. Ocon uses Sell2Wales extensively, and has secured contracts with Pembrokeshire County Council, Dyfed Powys Police, and Murco oil refinery. The company website says:

For Ocon, the advantage of using Sell2Wales is that the information for upcoming contracts is e-mailed to us every morning instead of our sales team having to chase procurement departments constantly to get information on upcoming tender opportunities. This allows our sales team the time to grow the business in other areas instead of constantly chasing for information on the larger tenders coming up.

The Sell2Wales website allows suppliers to enter keywords and filters so that they only receive relevant information, rather than being bombarded with every tender that comes up. This saves a great deal of time, which for a small company is important because such firms often do not have sufficient staff to dedicate to trawling through large amounts of information. Some businesses are tiny: even microbusinesses comprising one or two people have successfully used Sell2Wales.

From the buyer's viewpoint, sourcing a suitable supplier could not be easier. All the buyer needs to do is establish the criteria for a tender and post it on the website. Sell2Wales notifies suitable companies, who can then bid. The buyer then simply chooses the company that best fits the specification. Sell2Wales has been a tremendous success, acting as a facilitator for small businesses who may not have the commercial selling expertise that a large firm would have. For a small country with small businesses and small customers, Sell2Wales is the ideal solution.

QUESTIONS

1. Why would a buyer use Sell2Wales?
2. What might be the disadvantages of using Sell2Wales, from a supplier's viewpoint?
3. Why might there be a bias in favour of Welsh companies?
4. Why does WAG offer business advice to small firms?
5. What are the key factors in the success of Sell2Wales?

FURTHER READING

The following is a small selection from the many available books on business-to-business marketing.

The Reputation Playbook: A Winning Formula to Help CEOs Protect Corporate Reputation in the Digital Economy by Jennifer Jenson (Petersfield: Harriman House, 2014). This book provides a detailed look at traditional B2B brands and organisations which understand the value of social media and the transparency it brings to us as customers. Some excellent examples and case studies are used.

To Sell Is Human by Daniel H. Pink (New York: Riverhead Books, 2012). A detailed insight into what actually makes a sale, and what makes people want to buy.

There Is No B2B or B2C: It's Human to Human #H2H by Bryan Kramer (San Jose, CA: Pure Matter, 2014). The author takes a perspective here which focuses on creating a dialogue that helps solve consumer needs, as opposed to separating marketing into B2B and B2C.

The B2B Executive Playbook: The Ultimate Weapon for Achieving Sustainable, Predictable and Profitable Growth by Sean Geehan (Cincinnati, OH: Clerisy Press, 2011). A great text about how to target potential and current clients.

Thinking, Fast and Slow by Daniel Kahneman (New York: Farrar, Straus and Giroux, 2011). Outlines two 'systems' and ways of thinking which enable readers to predict how others will think, make decisions and which strategies could be used to satisfy consumer needs.

REFERENCES

Bendixen, M., Bukasa, K.A. and Abratt, R.A. (2004) Brand equity in the business to business market. *Industrial Marketing Management*, 33 (5): 371–80.

Besharov, M.L. and Smith, W.K. (2014) Multiple institutional logics in organizations: explaining their varied nature and implications. *Academy of Management Review*, 39 (3): 364–81.

Bharadwaj, N. (2004) Investigating the decision criteria used in electronic components procurement. *Industrial Marketing Management*, 33 (4): 317–23.

Brennan, R.D., Turnbull, P.W. and Wilson, D.T. (2003) Dyadic adaptation in business-to-business markets. *European Journal of Marketing*, 37 (11): 1636–65.

Cardozo, R.N. (1983) Modelling organisational buying as a sequence of decisions. *Industrial Marketing Management*, 12 (February): 75.

Claycomb, C., Iyer, K. and Germain, R. (2005) Predicting the level of B2B e-commerce in industrial organisations. *Industrial Marketing Management*, 34 (3): 221–34.

Hawes, J.M and Barnhouse, S.H. (1987) How purchasing agents handle personal risk. *Industrial Marketing Management*, 16 (November): 287–93.

Hawkins, T.G., Gravier, M.J., Berkowitz, D. and Muir, W.A. (2015) Improving services supply management in the defense sector: how the procurement process affects B2B service quality. *Journal of Purchasing and Supply Management*, 21 (2): 81–94.

Helm, S., Rolfes, L. and Gunther, B. (2006) Suppliers' willingness to end unprofitable customer relationships. *European Journal of Marketing*, 40 (3/4): 366–83.

Iyer, G.R., Hong Xiao, S., Sharma, A. and Nicholson, M. (2015) Behavioral issues in price setting in business-to-business marketing: a framework for analysis. *Industrial Marketing Management*, 47: 6–16

Jose Sanzo, M., Leticia Santos, M., Rodolfo, V. and Alvarez, L.I. (2003) The role of market orientation in business dyadic relationships: testing an integrator model. *Journal of Marketing Management*, 19: 73–107.

Kelly, P. and Coaker, J.W. (1976) Can we generalise about choice criteria for industrial purchasing decisions? In K.L. Bernhardt (ed.), *Marketing 1776–1976 and Beyond*. Chicago, IL: American Marketing Association, pp. 330–3.

Kijewski, V. and Yoon, E. (1990) Market-based pricing: beyond price-performance curves. *Industrial Marketing Management*, 19 (February): 11–19.

La Rocca, A., Snehota, I. and Trabattoni, C. (2015) Construction of meanings in business relationships and networks. *The IMP Journal*, 9 (2): 163–76.

Loudon, D.L. and Della Bitta, A.J. (1993) *Consumer Behaviour: Concepts and Application*. New York: McGraw-Hill.

McDonald, J.B. and Smith, K. (2004) The effects of technology-mediated communication on industrial buyer behaviour. *Industrial Marketing Management*, 33 (2): 107–16.

Moller, K. and Svahn, S. (2004) Crossing east–west boundaries: knowledge sharing in intercultural business networks. *Industrial Marketing Management*, 33 (3): 219–28.

Mourad, M., Ennew, C. and Kortam, W. (2011) Brand equity in higher education. *Marketing Intelligence & Planning*, 29 (4): 403–20.

Ojasalo, J. (2004) Key network management. *Industrial Marketing Management*, 33 (3): 195–205.

Pressey, A.D. and Selassie, H.G. (2003) Are cultural differences over-rated? Examining the influence of national culture on international buyer–seller relationships. *Journal of Consumer Behaviour*, 2 (4): 354–68.

Reijonen, H., Hirvonen, S., Nagy, G., Laukkanen, T. and Gabrielsson, M. (2013) The impact of entrepreneurial orientation on B2B branding and business growth in emerging markets. *Industrial Marketing Management*. doi: 10.1016/j.indmarman.2015.04.016.

Ronchetto, J.R., Jr, Hutt, M.D. and Reingen, P.H. (1989) Embedded influence patterns in organizational buying systems. *Journal of Marketing*, 53 (4): 51–62.

Tuominen, M., Rajala, A. and Moller, K. (2004) Market-driving versus market-driven: divergent roles of market orientation in business relationships. *Industrial Marketing Management*, 33 (3): 207–17.

Vargo, S.L. and Lusch, R.F. (2004) Evolving to a new dominant logic for marketing. *Journal of Marketing*, 68 (January): 1–17.

Veres, Z. (2012) Uncertainty-reducing project-competences as organizational capabilities. *The IMP Journal*, 6 (2): 154–66.

Webster, F.E. and Wind, Y. (1972) *Organisational Buying Behaviour*. Englewood Cliffs, NJ: Prentice-Hall.

MORE ONLINE

For additional materials that support this chapter and your learning, please visit:
https://study.sagepub.com/sethnaandblythe

PART TWO

PSYCHOLOGICAL ISSUES IN CONSUMER BEHAVIOUR

Psychology is the study of human thought processes. Psychologists have made a great many contributions to our understanding of how people make consumption decisions, not least in the areas of perception and learning.

Chapter 6 is about the basic urges that make people want to change their circumstances. Many of these urges centre around seeking pleasure, so marketers will usually try to make the buying and consuming processes as pleasurable as possible. This holds true even for such mundane, practical products as commercial vehicles and tools. Chapter 7 is about the self and personality – what it is that makes us who we are. These differences between one person's mental make-up and that of another create the differences in choices and choice behaviour which drive marketing.

For many people, marketing communication is mainly about establishing the brand in consumers' mental map, so an understanding of perception has a clear importance for them. Chapter 8 therefore looks at perception. For others, marketing's main aim should be to ensure that customers have a good experience of the products and come back to buy more – in which case the learning process becomes of great interest. This is the subject matter of Chapter 9.

Finally, Chapter 10 looks at the ways in which attitudes are formed and changed. Understanding how people develop their attitudes to brands, and how marketers might seek to change those attitudes, is an obvious area of interest. Equally important is understanding how people's attitudes towards one's brands might be changed by other forces (such as competitors). Maintaining a positive brand attitude is therefore equally important.

Psychology always centres around the individual, and marketers would do well to remember that each of us is an individual, with our own particular traits, talents and failings. It is all too common for businessmen and women to refer to 'the consumer' as if all people were the same. Psychologists offer the antidote to this type of thinking.

CHAPTER 6

DRIVE, MOTIVATION AND HEDONISM

LEARNING OBJECTIVES

After reading this chapter you should be able to:

- Explain the role of the subconscious in motivation.
- Understand the difference between needs and wants.
- Explain how drives are generated.
- Explain the role of needs and wants in marketing.
- Explain the relationship between motivation and behaviour.
- Critique the concept of hierarchy of need.
- Explain how motivations change with changes in wealth.
- Explain the role of hedonism in purchasing behaviour.

INTRODUCTION

Dissatisfaction is the beginning of all behaviour. If we were not dissatisfied, we would simply stick with what we have – there would be no need to change what we do. The gap between where we are now and where we want to be is what drives us to make changes in our lives, and of course this is what makes us change the products we own and the services we consume.

Understanding what motivates people has clear implications for marketers. If we know what drives people to buy particular products and services we are in a much better position to ensure that our products have the features and benefits that people want. If we understand how the pressure to buy develops, we can communicate better with people to show how we can meet their needs (before the need actually arises, in some cases). If we know how people rank their needs, we know when they are likely to be ready to buy our products. Of course, marketing practitioners do not yet have all the answers, so we are a long way from being able to predict consumption behaviour with anything like real accuracy.

Much of what drives us as individuals is the desire for pleasure. In the wealthier countries of the world, our basic survival needs have long been taken care of. We no longer simply eat to survive, for example: we eat more than enough simply for pleasure, so that few of us have ever experienced real hunger. The same applies to our housing, our clothing and so forth. We therefore look to satisfy our emotional, aesthetic needs – in other words, we look for things that are pleasurable or fun.

This chapter examines the forces that drive behaviour. Beginning with drive (the basis of all motivation) the chapter goes on to look at different studies of motivation, what role goals play in our lives and the role of hedonism (pleasure-seeking) in consumer behaviour.

DRIVE

Actual state

The condition in which the person happens to be at a given time

Desired state

The condition the individual would like to be in

Drive is the force that makes a person respond to a need. It is an internal stimulus caused by a gap between someone's actual state and their desired state. In other words, drive is created when the position someone is in at that moment differs from the position they would like to be in. A typical example would be someone becoming thirsty. The actual state is 'thirsty', the desired state is 'not thirsty', so a drive 'to get something to drink' is created.

As shown in Figure 6.1, the greater the gap between the actual state and the desired state, the greater the drive to do something about it. Once the gap between actual and desired states has closed, the drive disappears: our thirsty person, having had a drink, now no longer feels any pressure to look for a drink. The energy formerly devoted to finding something to drink can now be channelled elsewhere. In some cases, achieving the desired state may lead the individual to raise his or her sights and aim for something even better. For example, someone who has saved for years

FIGURE 6.1 Creating a drive

to buy a BMW may finally buy the car, but immediately start saving for an even more expensive car. These are what we sometimes refer to as goals, and we'll have a look at these in more depth a little later in this chapter.

Marketers cannot usually do very much about the actual state. We cannot make somebody thirsty, or hungry, or remove their possessions: what we can sometimes do is encourage people to revise their desired state, in other words encourage people to aspire to something new. Most of the effort marketers put into generating drives is directed at changing the desired state, in other words encouraging people to feel that they deserve something better than whatever they currently possess. Marketers can also remind people about their actual or desired states in order to encourage them to move a purchasing decision forward.

If the drive state is at a high level (i.e. the gap between the actual and desired states is large) the individual is more open to the idea of trying a new way of satisfying the need. This is fairly obvious: if a thirsty person finds that his or her favourite brand of soft drink is unavailable in the local shop, there are two choices available. Either the person can buy a different brand, or he or she can go to a different shop. If the person is not feeling especially thirsty, he or she might be prepared to make the trip to the next shop, but if the thirst is very strong the individual will be much more likely to buy a different brand. Most of us tend to overbuy when food shopping if we are hungry because our drive level is high, for example.

If the drive state is at a low level, a reminder might stimulate the individual to take action. For example, when driving in Britain, it is common to see signs left by fast food vendors saying 'Teas, Coffees, Sandwiches, Burgers 250 Metres'. These signs are placed at the right distance from the vendor so that passing drivers have time to be reminded that they are getting hungry or thirsty before they pass the vendor.

The fast food vendor is unlikely to have analysed the psychology of drive, but will have found through trial and error that the sign needs to be approximately 250 metres away from the pop-up food stall/van in order to give drivers enough time to think, discuss with a passenger the possible need, and pull over safely. Reminding people that they may have a need is called *activating the need*. Although the motorist is not actively looking for a cup of coffee or a snack, the sign acts as a reminder that a cup of coffee is enjoyable, and helps to strengthen a low-intensity drive by moving the desired state further from the actual state. Motorists whose drive state is at zero (perhaps because they have just had lunch) will simply drive straight past.

CHALLENGING THE STATUS QUO

Marketers are constantly telling us about how customer-orientated they are. To hear most of them talk, you would think they are engaged in some kind of charity work – meeting the customers' needs, listening to the customers, helping consumers achieve a lifestyle and so forth.

So what's all this about 'activating' a need? Either the need is there or it isn't – and if it isn't, should we really be trying our best to put it there? Should we be

© iStock.com/Rawpixel Ltd

messing around with people's drive states, trying to raise them and make them dissatisfied with life? In short, are we in the business of creating a need, then (just by chance) happening to have the solution to hand? Or is this what marketing cynics would call manipulation? Back in 2001, Dame Zarine Kharas started a company called JustGiving and launched the UK's first online fundraising platform (www.justgiving.com) with a simple mission – 'to ensure no great cause goes unfunded'. To date, the platform has helped people in 164 countries raise over $3.3 billion for good causes. If that's not creating a need 'to give', what is?!

Allowing the drive to become stronger can make the consumption experience more enjoyable. Delayed gratification increases the pleasure of satisfying the need – although it is not always the case that this is worth the wait (Nowlis et al. 2003). Most of us enjoy a meal much more if we are really hungry, and even saving up for a special treat increases the pleasure when the goal is finally attained. Each of us has a level at which the drive provides a pleasant stimulus without being uncomfortable or threatening: this is called the optimum stimulation level, or OSL, and was first simultaneously published by both Hebb (1955) and by Leuba (1955) in the psychology literature as a seminal piece. If the drive goes above the OSL, the individual will seek to make an immediate adjustment by satisfying the need. If stimulation falls below the OSL, the individual is likely to allow the drive to strengthen before acting on it. In fact people often enjoy the anticipation more than they do the actual consumption (Raghunathan and Mukherji 2003).

OSL is subjective, that is to say it varies from one individual to another. Research has shown that people with high OSLs like novelty and risk-taking, whereas those with low OSLs prefer the tried and tested. People with high OSLs also tend to be younger (Raju 1980).

Drive acts as the basic component for motivation: motivation is drive directed at a specific objective. If we consider drive as a general feeling that things are not as they should be, we can see that motivation is a drive that has crystallised into a definite decision to do something about the problem. Marketers are able to help people (or direct people) towards specific ways of satisfying the drive by giving them a specific solution which they might be motivated to adopt.

Optimum stimulation level (OSL)

The point at which a need has become strong, but before it has become unpleasantly so

MOTIVATION

Motives can be classified according to the list shown in Table 6.1. Although it is difficult to separate out people's motivations for making a particular purchase, emotional and dormant motives often take precedence over rational and conscious motives.

Motives should be distinguished from instincts, which are automatic responses to external stimuli. A motive is simply a reason for carrying out a particular behaviour; instincts are pre-programmed responses which are inborn in the individual, and are involuntary. Although behaviour may result from an instinctive source (for example,

TABLE 6.1 Classification of consumer motives

Primary motives	The reasons that lead to the purchase of a product class. For example, an individual might look for a new car to replace one that is becoming old and unreliable
Secondary motives	These are the reasons behind buying a particular brand. Our prospective car buyer might have reasons for buying a Toyota rather than a Ford, or a Ford rather than a BMW
Rational motives	These motives are based on reasoning, or a logical assessment of the person's current situation. The car purchaser may need a car that will carry three children and a large amount of camping equipment, for example, or that is a hybrid (thus able to run on petrol and electricity and therefore save money)
Emotional motives	Motives having to do with feelings about the brand. Sometimes emotions get the better of us – our prospective car buyer may end up with a sports car, despite having three children and a tent to accommodate
Conscious motives	These are the motives of which we are aware. Because our car buyer knows he needs a new car, this element of his motivation is conscious
Dormant motives	These motives operate below the conscious level. The car buyer's desire to buy a sports car may be linked to his approaching middle age, but he may not be aware of this!

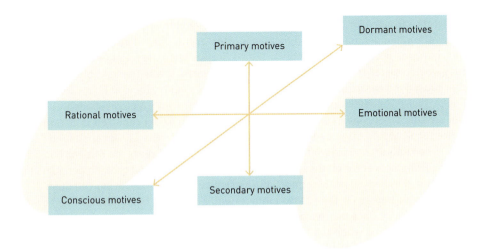

FIGURE 6.2 Dimensions of motives

Volition

(or will) The cognitive process by which an individual decides on and commits to a particular course of action

ducking when a helicopter suddenly appears to fly out of a 3D cinema screen), virtually all consumer behaviour is non-instinctive, or volitional.

Figure 6.2 shows the dimensions of motives. Motives can be classified across three dimensions, with the rational/conscious/primary ends relating to each other, as do the dormant/emotional/secondary ends. Any given motivation can be placed within the three-dimensional space represented by the diagram.

CLASSIFYING NEEDS

Need

A perceived lack of something

Want

A specific satisfier for a need

There have been many psychological studies of motivation, and several that have focused on consumer behaviour issues. Needs are the basis of all motivation, so it may be worth remembering that needs are a perceived lack of something, whereas wants are specific satisfiers. In order for someone to recognise a need, the individual not only should be without something, but should also perceive this as something that would make life more pleasant or convenient. Unless the individual understands how the proposed product will make a positive difference to his or her lifestyle, the product will not be perceived as filling a need and the individual will not want it.

CHALLENGING THE STATUS QUO

There are, of course, many examples of humankind 'perceiving a need', and one such example comes from the Yamana tribe from Tierra del Fuego which lies at the southernmost tip of South America. The region is buffeted by gales from the Antarctic, and is so far south that much of the land is covered in snow throughout the harsh winters. It is inhabited largely by penguins, and by a small number of hardy farmers who use the short summers to grow their crops, and then do whatever it takes to survive the winter.

The Yamana tribe inhabited this harsh country for thousands of years, but lacked something that most cold-country people discovered very early on: clothes. The Yamana never invented nor discovered clothing, apart from tiny loincloths and a few strips of cloth worn for decorative purposes. They spent their days canoeing in the icy waters, hunting penguins (which formed a large part of their diet) and fishing. They had, however, discovered the ability to light a fire, so when the weather got really bad they would cluster round large bonfires to keep warm. It was the light of these fires that caused the early European explorers to call the country Land of Fire – Tierra del Fuego. There is some evidence that the Yamana underwent a biological adaptation to the conditions. European explorers (including Captain Cook) reported that Yamana tribespeople would often be sweating in conditions which the Europeans found cold even when fully dressed in winter clothing. For thousands of years the Yamana had felt no need whatsoever for clothes. Standing around their fires and cooking penguins in the winter, they had perfectly comfortable and happy conditions for living: although this may seem strange to us, their early contacts with Europeans must have seemed even stranger to them. Once the concept of clothing was explained, they suddenly recognised the need for it, and when the last pure-blooded Yamana died in the late 1990s they were certainly fully clothed and indistinguishable from any other Argentinians. Their traditional way of life, however, represented an extreme example of not recognising something as a need until a solution is presented.

There have been many attempts on the part of psychologists to develop lists of needs. It is worth looking at one of the earliest such lists which was developed by Murray (1938) who listed 20 separate need categories. The list included categories such as: succourance, nurturance, sentience, deference, abasement, defendence, infavoidance, harmavoidance, achievement, counteraction, dominance, aggression, affiliation, autonomy, order, rejection, sex, understanding, exhibition and play. Murray developed this list from his extensive clinical experience rather than from a programme of organised research, so much of the evidence for the list is anecdotal. This said, virtually all these needs have consumer behaviour and thus marketing implications. The need for rejection is used by brand owners when they exhort consumers to reject own-label products, and the need for nurturance is emphasised in advertisements for cold cures and soup. The need for sentience is met by documentary cable stations such as the Discovery Channel and the History Channel. Murray's list is long, and by no means definitive, and some needs on the list conflict with each other, for example dominance and deference.

CONSUMER BEHAVIOUR IN ACTION: THE SKY TV EXECUTIVE'S DILEMMA

Sky TV, as the name suggests, had its beginnings in the satellite TV business. In 1989 Sky Television began broadcasting via the Astra satellite direct to homes in the UK and Western Europe: at that time, viewers needed a satellite dish mounted on their houses to receive the signal. The following year, Sky merged with rival British Satellite Broadcasting (BSB) to form BSkyB. Currently there are over 690 channels available on the Sky TV network, of which there are 79 radio channels, 50 time shift channels, and 60 high-definition and 3D channels.

©iStock.com/EduLeite

So if you were a Sky TV executive, one of the questions you'd be asking yourself daily is 'who needs 690 channels?' The answer is quite simple: nobody. There is no conceivable way that anyone is going to watch whole programmes and get through over 690 channels every day. However, a large number of people have common interests in packages selected from the 690 channels. Sky offers a number of 'packs' with a varying number of channels in each. Current packs include Knowledge, Children's, Music, Style and Culture, Movies, Sports, News and Events, Pay-per-view Movies, and Pay-per-view Adult channels.

In addition, subscribers can also pay for premium channels such as movies, kids, adult and major sports channels, and can also get access to various stand-alone channels such as Zee TV or ViewAsia.

Although television stations appear to be meeting a need solely for entertainment, Sky offers solutions for a wide variety of subdivisions of need. If you were an executive working with Sky TV and tasked with coming up with a new 'package', what might this look like and why?

It is because human beings are complex creatures with strong social bonds and we tend to have a broader range of needs than animals, that we also have many needs that go beyond mere survival. Some commentators divide needs into primary needs, which are concerned with biological functions and survival, and secondary needs, which are concerned with everything else. In some cases, researchers have concentrated heavily on the idea that most needs are biologically determined. Internal genetic stimuli are driven by homeostasis, which is the tendency for any living entity to try to maintain a state of equilibrium: in the natural world, change is death. The drives that maintain homeostasis are involuntary, as is the behaviour that results from it. If one becomes too hot, for example, one begins sweating, and if one becomes too cold one develops goose pimples and one may even begin shivering. A sudden shock will result in adrenaline entering the bloodstream, which may be exciting (a positive outcome, which is often generated by white-knuckle rides at theme parks) or may be merely frightening (a negative outcome, which may be generated by a near-accident or a threatening situation such as a street robbery).

Hunger and thirst are obviously biologically generated, but most eating and drinking happens as a result of social or aesthetic demands. Socially motivated eating might include dinner parties, meeting friends for a meal, business lunches and picnics. Curiosity is often supposed to be socially generated, and there is certainly evidence that exploration of the world has a connection with particular countries and cultures, but we also know that some curiosity is biological. Most carnivorous animals display an innate tendency to explore and investigate their environment: cats, dogs and humans all display this behaviour, and bears in zoos are generally happier if their food is hidden from them so that they have to explore and find it.

The best-known biological motivator is, of course, sex. Marketers have used sexual imagery in advertising throughout its history, and at various times there have been advertisements that have over-stepped the boundaries of good taste and have been attacked or withdrawn. There is certainly evidence that Valentine's day gift-giving is associated with power relationships between the genders (Rugimbana et al. 2003).

The arousal theory of motivation (Zuckerman 2000) proposes that people need to be aroused if they are to become motivated (see Figure 6.3). People seek to maintain an optimum level of arousal: too little and they become bored, too much and they become stressed. Zuckerman developed a 'hierarchy' of stimulation, as follows:

1. *Thrill-seeking.* Through extreme sports, or adventure travel – the highest level of arousal.

2. *Experience-seeking.* Through travel, walking, the arts, books – the second highest level.

3. **Disinhibition** (removing the internal inhibitors that control behaviour). Social stimulation, parties, drinking alcohol, etc.

4. *Boredom.* The need to change things around, perhaps to buy new products, try new things, etc.

Disinhibition

Removal of the internal inhibitors which constrain behaviour

At the lowest end of the hierarchy – boredom – the individual has a risk-free but also stimulation-free existence: at the highest level – thrill-seeking – the individual has an

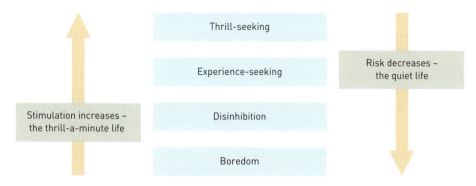

FIGURE 6.3 Zuckerman's hierarchy of stimulation

exciting but dangerous life. Most people establish a balance between the quiet life and the stimulating life, at some point on the continuum which is specific to them.

The best-known motivation theory is probably Maslow's Hierarchy of Need (Maslow 1954) (see Figure 6.4) which sought to show that people are motivated to fulfil different needs in a specific order, beginning with survival needs (as the most pressing needs to satisfy) and ending with **self-actualisation** needs (the need to fulfil a long-held ambition, or to act independently of the pressures and opinions of other people, or to act for action's sake). The reasoning behind the model is that needs cannot always be met all at once. Sometimes one need must be fulfilled at the expense of another, creating motivational conflict.

Self-actualisation

The need to become the ideal self

At the lowest level of the hierarchy – *survival needs* – marketers offer houses, clothes and food. However, in most cases these are not sold as survival items – more commonly the marketing communications emphasise other aspects of the products such

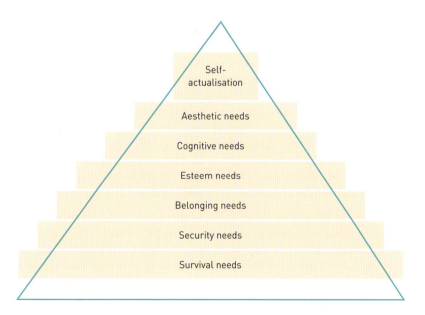

FIGURE 6.4 Maslow's Hierarchy of Need

as their location, style and flavour. Relatively few products are offered purely on the basis of survival, and most of these are in the category of safety equipment for sports such as those that involve either air or water.

At the security level, people buy products such as insurance policies, savings plans, burglar alarms and car breakdown memberships. In recent years, we have developed new safety needs: we need to secure our computers and our data against fraudsters and malicious viruses, and we need to be careful about our personal information on social networking sites. This has led to the development of whole new industries, developing software to combat such dangers. People also spend money safeguarding their health, hence the huge sales of products designed to help people lose weight or give up smoking. The popularity of such products in the period immediately following the New Year celebrations indicates the degree to which people believe they should safeguard their health.

At the belonging level, we know attitudes towards 'belonging' have been changing over the past 60 years since Maslow first introduced his hierarchy. Social identity used to be measured using markers such as social class, religion, geographic location, income, etc., but as society has progressed and the standard of living has risen in most parts of the world (as compared to 60 years previous) people now belong to many offline and online groups and communities. People can thus align themselves to a wide variety of brands and lifestyles which then enables them to indulge in buying a wide range of products: fashion clothing, club memberships, sports equipment, and so forth. In order to be accepted as a member of a professional concierge service (www.innerplace.co.uk) that offers privileged access to the finest nightlife and entertainment in London, members not only need to pay their membership fees, they also need to know about the right venue – the service is aimed at 'like-minded urban socialites, who are well dressed, well heeled, well behaved and who know what they want'. Belonging needs are therefore of considerable interest to marketers.

Esteem needs include anything that someone buys as a status symbol. Products that make a statement about oneself include technological gadgetry, fashion, cars, expensive hobbies such as sailing, and exclusive sports such as polo. Almost any product might have an esteem value in the right quarters, and there are even circumstances in which a lack of consumption generates esteem – backpackers may have more respect for someone who has managed to cross Asia for less money than anyone else, for example. Esteem needs may also play a part in seemingly altruistic behaviour – people who buy *The Big Issue* (the UK magazine devoted to helping homeless people) do so not so much for the actual magazine content, but because there is a dimension of helping others in the purchase (Hibbert et al. 2005). This may be coupled to the fact that the magazine is a visible purchase helping a tangible individual, whereas with a contribution to a charity the individual beneficiary is usually not seen.

Aesthetic needs can be met in many ways. In the main, such needs are traditionally associated with the arts: paintings, sculptures, books, theatre, film and music being the main ways aesthetic needs have been met. However, a hiking holiday in an area of outstanding natural beauty is also a way of meeting aesthetic needs, as is a microlight aircraft or a yacht.

At the self-actualisation level, needs might be fulfilled in a great many ways. This is all about a person's ability to realise their own personal potential and growth, self-fulfilment in life and peak experiences (Maslow 1943). In the 21st century – in the consumerist world that we live in – in some cases, self-actualisation needs are met by actually reducing consumption, for example if the individual decides that a 'green' lifestyle should be adopted. Someone who has worked in a city for many years might, for example, buy a smallholding in the country and grow his or her own food, use solar power for electricity and run a wood-burning stove for heat. In other cases, it may be about pushing oneself to the absolute limit of physical and mental endurance – the peak experiences. Self-actualisation might include the concept of freedom: the ability to make choices as a consumer is an expression of freedom, and is derived in part from having the necessary wealth to buy whatever one wants or needs, and in part from a lack of legal restrictions on purchases (Mick and Humphreys 2008). Of course it could also be said that although famous artists such as Van Gough lived a life of poverty, they had arguably reached a point of self-actualisation through their creative work.

CHALLENGING THE STATUS QUO

Humans are born with a fear of falling, yet we often go to theme parks and fun fairs, and some indulge in 'extreme sports' such as cave diving, ice climbing, cliff jumping and bungee jumping. Falling off a bridge with lengths of elastic round your ankles is certainly thrilling, in that it gives you a huge adrenaline rush. But if we like to be thrilled by such things, why isn't it fun if someone pushes you off a cliff?

Of course the context and situation has a lot to do with your reaction. If your friend playfully pushes you into a swimming pool, the normal response would be to laugh – but if a complete stranger did it, you'd probably not find it funny at all.

So where do we draw the line? How do we decide what is fun, and what is frightening? When do we stop being frightened and 'enjoy' the thrill of jumping off a tower with a bungee strapped to our body? Why do we put our lives in danger (threatening our survival needs) whether it be giving up our jobs in favour of a social enterprise or jumping off a cliff for a thrill – just for esteem or self-actualisation needs?

Maslow's hierarchy has been widely criticised for being too simplistic, and for ignoring the many exceptions that can easily be seen in everyday life. For example, an artist starving in a garret is clearly placing aesthetic or self-actualisation needs ahead of survival needs, and someone who gives up a good career in order to work with poor people in developing countries is giving up security in favour of esteem or self-actualisation needs. Such anomalies are commonplace. Another criticism of the hierarchy is that it is largely irrelevant to the vast majority of people in the wealthy countries of Europe and North America because they already have their survival and security needs taken care of, and indeed many of them are operating at the self-actualisation level already (McNulty 1985).

A further criticism is that an individual may move to different parts of the hierarchy even within a single day: for example, being primarily concerned with esteem needs during the working day, with aesthetic needs when enjoying an evening meal at a good restaurant, and with belonging needs when meeting friends for a drink afterwards.

One final criticism is one that McLeod (2007) highlighted: Maslow had tested the self-actualisation level with a sample of 18 white male subjects whom he believed displayed the characteristic qualities. This would cause considerable bias in the data sample, testing and collection.

These criticisms notwithstanding, Maslow's model is widely taught and widely referred to: there is little doubt that the needs themselves exist and can be categorised in this way, but whether they truly operate as a hierarchy is open to question. There may be evidence that the hierarchy operates for large groups of people, so that there will be a prevailing social paradigm in which some needs are brought to the forefront. Research by McNulty (1985) showed that an increasing number of people in the UK were operating at the self-actualisation level, presumably as a result of rising living standards. In the intervening 30 years, it would appear to the casual observer that this trend has not reversed, and has (if anything) accelerated. A five-year (2005–2010) longitudinal survey was conducted by Tay and Diener (2011) who tested Maslow's theory by analysing the data of 60,865 participants from 123 countries, representing every major region of the world. Their results showed that the existence of universal human needs regardless of cultural differences is very much a fact. However, the results also showed that ordering of the needs within the hierarchy was not necessarily correct in the way that was being displayed by the respondents of the survey. A variation of Maslow's hierarchy has been the VALS (Values, Attitudes and Lifestyles) model (Mitchell 1983), which describes nine different lifestyles and segments consumers accordingly, as shown in Figure 6.5.

The model by Arnold Mitchell was developed using data from a sample of over 1,600 Americans and their partners who were asked about their primary motivation (the horizontal dimension) and the resources available to them (the vertical dimension). Here, we see segmentation based on the degree to which people innovatively use their resources such as previous education, income, self-confidence and leadership skills. They were also asked about how much they were driven by their knowledge, principles, ideals, achievements, and their desire for social and physical activities. The model supposes that people at the lower levels (which correspond with Maslow's survival and security needs) are controlled by their basic needs for food, shelter and a measure of security. After these very basic needs have been met, there is a divergence: some people become inner-directed (driven by internal motives) while others become outer-directed (motivated by the opinions of others). Inner-directed people may become selfish and uncaring of other people's well-being, they may become interested in new experiences, or they may fulfil a burning ambition to change the world for the better despite opposition. Outer-directed people may seek to copy other people whom they regard as successful, or may seek to impress other people by achieving or by conspicuous consumption. Finally, Mitchell postulates that people may adopt an integrated position, where concern and respect for others is combined with knowledge of their own needs and desires.

Mitchell's model has been used for market segmentation purposes, and the lifestyle types have been identified both in the United States and in Europe. As wealth increases, more people operate at the higher levels: we might reasonably expect that, as countries become wealthier, levels of consumption increase but so do levels of social concern, and levels of crime increase as more people become inner-directed.

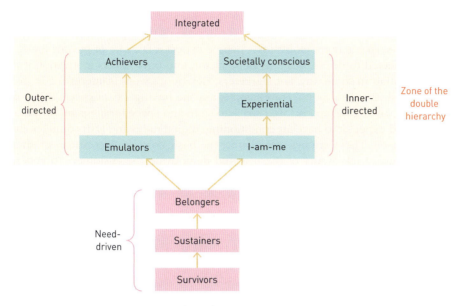

FIGURE 6.5 The Values and Lifestyles (VALS) model

CHALLENGING THE STATUS QUO

Mitchell's categorisations are all very well for segmentation, but what happens when we are dealing with people at the self-actualisation level? By definition, these people might do *anything*! They are professional individualists.

Also, how clear are the boundaries? To say that someone is outer-directed means that they care about the opinions of other people – but do they care about the opinions of everyone else, or just a few people? Are they attracted to or repelled by the opinions of the other people in question? Then of course there is the significant question of how different family structures affect the categorisations. Do different family structures hold differing knowledge, principles and ideals? How does their desire (or lack of) for social and physical activities mould their attitudes towards being either inner- or outer-directed?

Finally, if someone acts rebelliously, is this because they don't care what other people think – or because they care very deeply? Being a rebel is a statement made to impress other people, is it not?

The basic problem here is that people consistently refuse to be categorised!

MOTIVATIONAL FACTORS

An alternative approach to considering motivation was that advanced by Herzberg (1966). Herzberg was a medical researcher who developed the idea that some factors in life are motivational, while others are simply expected as a matter of course: the absence of these factors would be demotivating, but more of the same would not be motivational. Herzberg called the first group of factors motivators, and the second group, hygiene factors (he was a medical researcher, remember). The hygiene factors

Hygiene factors

Those aspects of a product which consumers would expect as a basic feature of any product in the category needed to be present in order to prevent the 'disease' of demotivation. Herzberg's findings were considered revolutionary at the time of their publication because he claimed that salary is not a motivator – people expect a fair rate of pay for the work they are expected to do, so it is a hygiene factor, and only affects motivation if it is seen to be unfair in some way. For marketers, Herzberg's work is interesting in that it explains product **differentiation**. For example, anyone buying a car expects that it will have wheels, an engine, an enclosed space to sit in and space for luggage. Nowadays, people would expect it to have air conditioning, digital radio and USB connections as standard as well. These are hygiene factors, the basic core product features that any car would have. Lack of any of these would demotivate the customer. To generate motivation to buy, though, the vehicle manufacturer would need to add features as motivators: a wifi-hub, smarter upholstery, alloy wheels, parking sensors, etc.

Differentiation

Providing a product with features that distinguish it from competing products

CONSUMER BEHAVIOUR IN ACTION: DIFFERENTIATION

The history of the automobile has been one of continuous adaptation, additional features and added inducements to buy. The basic need is for transportation: ever since the first human being jumped on the back of a horse we have wanted to travel further, faster and more comfortably, and although the earliest cars were less reliable (and sometimes slower) than horses, they at least had the convenience of starting fairly quickly (without the need for saddling and bridling) and of going pretty much where the driver wanted them to go rather than setting off into a field with the other horses.

Starting with Daimler and Benz's first practical automobile in 1885, manufacturers have added optional extras on a regular basis ever since. For example, in 1890 Canadian Thomas Ahearn invented the car heater. In 1901 disc brakes were added (invented by Lanchester). In 1911 Charles Kettering invented the starter motor, which eliminated the need for hand cranking the engine to start it (Kettering also invented Freon, the gas which has been identified as a major cause of holes in the ozone layer). In 1929 Paul Galvin invented the car radio, although it had to be bought as an optional extra: car manufacturers did not fit radios as standard until the 1970s. Galvin called his new radio the Motorola. Daimler introduced electric windows in 1948, and in 1966 British engineers developed electronic fuel injection. Not all the inventors were men, incidentally. Mary Anderson invented windscreen wipers (hand-operated at first), and Helen Blair Bartlett, a geologist, invented alumina ceramic insulators for sparkplugs in 1930.

Why all this **Innovation**? Simple. Any car manufacturer could meet the basic hygiene factor of transportation. In order to motivate people to buy a specific model, manufacturers had to add extras, making the car more comfortable, safer, more reliable, or more fun than the competitors' vehicles.

But have our requirements changed? Do we all crave state-of-the-art satellite navigation, radar-controlled cruise control, intelligent braking systems with ceramic brake pads and nitrogen-filled tyres? Do we in the 21st century now yearn for the flying car? Every so often someone will go back to basics and produce a car with 'no frills' for a low price, but the optional extras soon cease to be optional because price is not a good motivator – it is a hygiene factor! So if you were designing a car for a major motor manufacturer, what would be the standard *must haves* and what would you put on the *optional extras* list?

Innovation

A new product of service: the act of adopting a new product or service

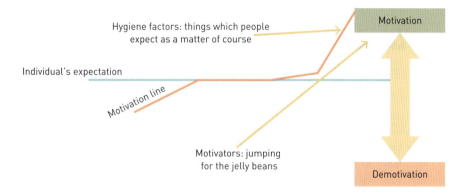

Motivation

Hygiene factors: things which people expect as a matter of course

Individual's expectation

Motivation line

Motivators: jumping for the jelly beans

Demotivation

FIGURE 6.6 Dual-factor theory

As a way of categorising needs, Herzberg's theory is undoubtedly useful, but part of the problem in applying the theory is that people have differing views on what should be a hygiene factor. Once again, it is difficult to make generalisations about people because we all have different priorities. (Herzberg's theories have also been applied to personnel management, but that is outside the scope of this book.)

In Figure 6.6, the motivation line rises as the individual recognises that the hygiene factors are improving, but this is really a reduction in demotivation. Motivation as such does not start until the motivators begin to arrive, but even so there is no sharp rise until the motivators go beyond expectations. At this point, further increases in hygiene factors have no real effect.

INDIVIDUAL FACTORS

A third approach to analysing motivation is Vroom's Expectancy Theory (Vroom 1999). Vroom suggested that motivation is the result of rational calculations made by individuals, taking into account the value of the reward itself, the expected likelihood of being able to obtain the reward, and the effort needed to achieve the reward. The trade-offs between these factors are the subject of the calculation, and if the reward is not adequate compared to the effort needed to win it, the individual will simply not bother to try for it. Equally, if the likelihood of gaining the reward is perceived as being small, the individual will not be motivated to try. Vroom's theory has much to offer – it is more comprehensive in its approach than other theories, and it takes much greater account of individual differences than do either Maslow's or Herzberg's models. As we saw already, individuals may believe that aesthetic needs are more important than survival needs, and (in terms of Herzberg) individuals may have different ideas of what constitute motivators and hygiene factors.

David McClelland suggested that people have three categories of social need in terms of motivation: *achievement* (the need to excel at something), *affiliation* (the need to be part of a group) and *power* (the ability to control outcomes).

Different people place different levels of emphasis on these needs, but people who are achievers need constant feedback and praise, people who have a high need for affiliation will tend to want to fit in with their immediate social group, and people who seek power will try to dominate those around them (McClelland 1955). McClelland's

FIGURE 6.7 Emphases on power, affiliation and achievement

work has mainly been used in human resources management, but there are implications for consumer behaviour as well: a person with a high need for affiliation will buy things that make them popular and respected, a person with a high need for power will want to be in control of spending, and so forth.

An aspect of motivation that is not considered in either of the above models is the idea of pain avoidance. Although needs are the basis of all motivation, there is a difference between the need to avoid bad consequences and the need to acquire a benefit. In most cases, someone who wishes to obtain a positive benefit from a purchase has only one way to obtain the benefits, whereas there are many ways to avoid a negative outcome. This was demonstrated by Skinner in his famous **experiments** with rats, in which rats were taught to push buttons in complex sequences in order to obtain food and avoid electric shocks: the rats became very inventive in the ways they avoided the shocks, but were unable to find any other way to obtain food (Skinner 1953). Human beings are, of course, not rats: we are probably better able to understand the longer-term consequences of our behaviour than a rat would be (although some of us don't always take heed!), so we may be more susceptible to pain-avoidance messages. On the other hand, we may be even more inventive in avoiding the pain.

For example, **cautionary tale** advertising in which the negative consequences of an action are shown may result in someone behaving in the desired manner, or it may (and perhaps is more likely to) result in the individual avoiding the advertisement. This may be part of the reason why government campaigns against smoking or drinking often fail – shocking people by telling them about the diseases their habit might cause simply results in people not reading the warnings, unless of course the government passes legislation against such practices, thus making it illegal (e.g. the UK Parliament has approved regulations which makes smoking in cars carrying children illegal from 1 October 2015, and failure to comply could result in a £50 fixed penalty notice).

One way in which marketers can use pain avoidance in motivating consumers is by **modelling**. This is a process whereby people are shown the negative consequences of a given action through an actor who demonstrates the behaviour, and suffers the consequences. For example, an advertisement might show a commuter who has been prosecuted for fare dodging, complete with a detailed account of the consequences of the action ('It was the embarrassment of having to stand up in court and admit fiddling a £5 fare. And I lost my job, because I now have a criminal conviction'). Another example might be a housewife who 'can't shift those greasy stains'. In each case the consumer is invited to see the potential negative consequences of fiddling the fare, or using the wrong washing powder. Modelling can also be used for positive reinforcement, of course (see Table 6.2), for example the advertisement about the regular man on the street who saved a fortune in car insurance payments by using the online portal 'moneysupermarket.com'.

Experiment

A controlled activity in which a given stimulus is offered to respondents in order to discover their reactions

Cautionary tale

A story intended to illustrate the possible negative outcomes of a particular course of action

Modelling

The act of demonstrating by example behaviour which the marketer would like the target audience to imitate

TABLE 6.2 Using modelling for positive reinforcement

Modelling employed	Desired response
Instructor, expert, salesperson using the product (in an advertisement or at the point of purchase)	Use product in the correct, technically competent way
Models in advertisements asking questions at the point of purchase (whether that is online, e-mobile or in-store)	Ask questions at the point of purchase that highlight product advantages
Models in advertisements receiving positive reinforcement or punishment for performing undesired behaviours	Extinction or decrease of undesired behaviours
Individual (or group) similar to the target audience using the product in a novel, enjoyable way	Use the product in new ways

Source: adapted from Nord and Peter (1980)

Reprinted with permission from Journal of Marketing published by the American Marketing Association, Walter R. Nord and J. Paul Peter, Vol 44, No.2 1980: 36–47.

Models should be as similar as possible to the target audience in order to promote the maximum amount of 'affiliation', but at the same time need to be seen as attractive: this may appear to be a contradiction in some cases, but models show ourselves as we wish we were, rather than as we actually are.

For human beings, and especially human beings living in the developed and wealthier countries of the world, most physical needs have been met long ago. We are therefore driven much more by social, aesthetic or psychological needs than by physical needs. This manifests itself most clearly in our eating habits. We eat for pleasure (the flavour and texture of the food), for social purposes (going for a meal with friends, sharing a snack, going to a dinner party), and even as a means of self-expression (cooking a special meal for friends or family). These needs sometimes override our need to live a healthy lifestyle: we become obese or develop hardening of the arteries, bad teeth and many other diseases caused by eating the wrong things. This is especially the case in some developing economies where childhood obesity is reaching epidemic proportions (Midha et al. 2012).

MOTIVATIONAL CONFLICT

When needs conflict, motivational conflict occurs. This can take one of three basic forms:

1. *Approach–approach conflict.* This happens when the individual is faced with two or more desirable alternatives. For example, the person might have been invited to a party on a weekend when his or her football team is playing a match 300 miles away. Approach–approach conflicts are common, since most people have limited financial resources and often have to choose between spending money on one item, or spending it on a different item.

2. *Avoidance–avoidance conflict.* This occurs when the individual is faced with two or more equally unappealing choices. For example, someone might be faced with the choice of either buying new shoes to replace an old, comfortable pair, or continuing to wear the old pair despite the fact they are now letting in water and coming apart at the seams.

3. *Approach–avoidance conflict.* This occurs when the course of action has both positive and negative consequences. For example, some drugs have dangerous side-effects. Most purchases have an element of approach–avoidance conflict since they involve spending money or giving up something else: many purchases of new products involve a **switching cost**, i.e. the effort and sometimes cash expenditure involved in moving from the old product to the new one.

Switching costs

All the costs associated with changing from one particular product or service to another

The relationship between these motivational conflicts is shown in Figure 6.8.

In many cases, the situation is far more complex than a simple dichotomy. This is because we are usually faced with several possible courses of action, each of which has both positive and negative consequences. If the motivational conflict is to be resolved, the individual needs to prioritise his or her needs. This is largely a matter for the individual concerned: even though Maslow tried to produce a general model for this, we have already seen that the model is far from perfect.

The intensity of the motivation is sometimes strong enough to override all other considerations, whereas at other times it may be much weaker. Sometimes motivational intensity is high due to a high level of drive (a 13-year-old who is being teased at school for wearing the wrong brand of trainers will be highly motivated to obtain the right and more acceptable brand, for example), and sometimes motivational intensity is high due to personal involvement with the product category. Involvement means that the individual places a high importance on having exactly the right product: for example, a pilot would place great importance on obtaining exactly the right spares, fuel and oil for the aircraft, since this affects the safety of the plane (and, of course, the pilot). Similarly, a musician might be very concerned to obtain the right instrument; an academic would be concerned to use the right and relevant resources, etc. Having to put some effort into the consumption experience will often increase the satisfaction the consumer has with the product – this is obviously the case with sports equipment, but may even be the case for such mundane items as self-assembly furniture (Wadhwa and Trudel 2010). Each of us has at least some products with which we are highly involved.

From the viewpoint of marketing, generating involvement is clearly crucial to establishing loyal customers. The greater the involvement, the greater the degree to which

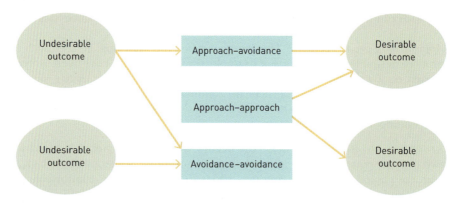

FIGURE 6.8 Motivation conflict

consumers make an effort to satisfy the need, and the greater the propensity to remain loyal in future. In some cases firms are able to run loyalty programmes to keep customers involved: supermarket loyalty cards and airline frequent flyer programmes are the usual examples. In other cases involvement is generated by the way the products are promoted, or by celebrity endorsement.

Motivations can be divided into positive and negative. People may act to obtain a reward, or may act to avoid an unwanted outcome. For example, someone may buy aspirin in order to treat a headache (obtain a positive outcome) or to take one half of an aspirin per day to prevent a heart attack (negative motivation). Other commentators divide motivation into internal motivations, which are those originating inside the individual, and external motivations, which are those resulting from an external stimulus or reward. An internal motivation may arise from a self-actualisation need (such as the desire to learn a new language), whereas an external motivation might arise from social needs or physical needs (such as a need to be accepted by a new group of people, or to move to a larger house).

Alternatively, motives might be divided into rational, emotional and instinctive motives. Rational motives are those resulting from a conscious thought process; emotional motives are those resulting from an irrational source such as anger, love, pride, jealousy, and so forth. Instinctive motives arise from deeper drives, and may result in obsessive behaviour: in most cases, though, instinctive motives simply drive the occasional impulse purchase.

GOALS

As we've seen so far in this chapter, behaviour is driven by needs. Needs develop drives, and drives are focused into motivation, but motivation achieves nothing unless it is backed up by action. The process of converting a motivation into concrete action is one of developing goals. A goal is a concrete objective, one that dictates a specific plan of action, and one that carries with it its own decision-making, risks and rewards.

Any plan of action carries with it a degree of risk. Individuals will usually try to reduce the risks to an acceptable level, sometimes by developing rules of behaviour which have proved to be successful in the past. This type of decision-making is important to marketers because it enables practitioners to put risk-reducing measures in place. The lower the risk to consumers, the more likely they are to buy the product and the less likely they are to complain afterwards.

A goal is an external object towards which a motive is directed (Onkvisit and Shaw 1994). Goals differ from drives in that the goal is external, and pulls the person in a given direction: a drive is internal and pushes the individual. In this way the goal acts as an incentive to take a course of action (or refrain from taking a course of action, as the case may be). Having goals improves task performance: people are more risk-seeking when they have a specific, challenging goal (Larrick et al. 2001). If someone has a drive that needs to be addressed there may be several possible goals that would satisfy the drive. For example, if an individual feels the need for entertainment, this may lead to a drive to find something to do, which in turn causes the person to set some goals that would lead to some kind of entertainment. In these circumstances, several possible alternatives exist, and marketers clearly need to remember that consumers have a choice.

Huffman et al. (2000) produced two models showing how goals relate, and how they are determined. Figure 6.9 shows the first of these.

In Figure 6.9, the individual's goals begin with life themes and values. These are concerned with the kind of person we want to be, or the kind of person we are, and are unlikely to change significantly in the course of our lives. At the doing level, we have immediate concerns, which lead to consumption intentions. Finally, at the having level, we would be concerned with specific benefits from products, which in turn leads to a search for specific features in the products we consume. For example, an individual might have a life theme of being a world traveller. This might translate into a life project to visit every continent in the world. In the process, current concerns (such as earning a living in a profession that allows plenty of time off for travel) might provide a set of goals: the consumption intention might be to have at least one long-haul trip each year. Finally, the individual would be looking for specific benefits from each trip (the possibility to learn about the local culture, for example), which would require specific features when planning each trip.

This model shows a clear sequence from the general needs of the individual through to the final purchase goals for each individual product (in this case, each trip). There are likely to be many products and many sub-goals involved in leading a life that is dedicated to travel: the same would apply to someone whose life is based around

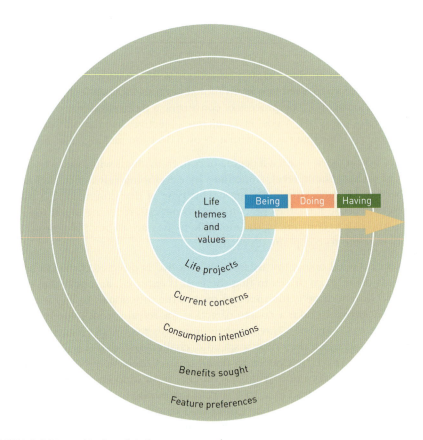

FIGURE 6.9 A hierarchical model of consumer goals

FIGURE 6.10 A model of goal-determination processes

being surrounded by artworks, or around having a large family, or sustaining a highly pressurised working career. The model shows the sequence of events that occurs, and also the relationship between the goals, but it does not illustrate the actual processes involved. These are shown in Figure 6.10.

In Figure 6.10, incorporation refers to the top-down process whereby higher-level goals shape goals at lower levels. Incorporation helps the individual to ensure that all the goals fit together in a logical and sensible way, and also it enables the individual to translate a set of ill-defined and possibly subconscious needs into a coherent set of choice problems.

Abstraction refers to the bottom-up process whereby lower-level goals help to determine what the higher-level goals must be if there is to be consistency between the various goals.

Adaptation is the process by which goals are influenced by contextual issues such as the cultural and social environment, current concerns and consumption intentions. Contextual factors appear to operate in two ways: first, the context may activate a pre-existing set of sub-goals in the individual's memory. Different contexts generate different goals, for example one's goals when planning a visit to one's parents are very different from one's goals when planning a friend's stag night. Second, the context may influence the individual's thinking on what is actually possible. If someone does not believe, for example, that there is any chance whatsoever of being promoted at work, then he or she might not bother to apply for a promotional opportunity. In the case of being-level goals, someone might decide that their circumstances prevent them from ever becoming a particular type of person. At the having level, someone might decide that, much as they would enjoy driving a Tesla Model S, this is unlikely to happen because of financial constraints. Research shows that people with low incomes tend to set very stringent goals prior to their decision-making processes, and thus do not achieve their goals as often – consequently, they often feel less successful in life, and do not enjoy the consumption experiences they do achieve (Scott and Nowlis 2010).

Abstraction

The process whereby lower-level goals help to determine what the higher-level goals must be if there is to be overall goal consistency

HEURISTICS

Another way of simplifying the decision-making process is to establish rules for buying. These are called heuristics, and they consist of simple 'if ... then' decision-making rules, which can be established before any goals are set and the search procedure begins. Heuristics are also subject to alteration in the light of new knowledge, so sometimes they are established as the search procedure continues. Heuristics can be divided into three groups, as follows:

1. *Search heuristics*. These are rules for finding out information. For example, someone might establish a rule to the effect that they will always ask advice from a friend when making a major purchase.

2. *Evaluation heuristics*. These are rules for judging products. For example, someone might have a rule that they never buy products made in a country where child labour is widely used.

3. *Choice heuristics*. These are procedures for comparing evaluations of alternatives. For example, someone might have a rule of never buying the cheapest (or never buying the most expensive). In fact, most people do tend to go for the middle-priced product when offered a choice of three products at different price levels.

Some examples of these heuristics are given in Table 6.3 and can be applied equally well to both offline and online behaviours.

Kahneman and Tversky (1979) went so far as to suggest that people go through a fairly complex process of using heuristics to assess (and probably reduce) risk. They proposed that people will identify possible outcomes and group ones that are seen as being essentially identical: those outcomes that would realise a more favourable result would be considered as gains, while those that would realise a less favourable outcome would be considered as losses. Following on from this, the individual would assess the likelihood of each outcome actually happening, and would be able to calculate which course of action to take in order to balance risk and reward. Kahneman and Tversky took the view that people would vary in their attitude towards risk-taking: some would be risk-averse, and would take the options they considered to be least likely to cause loss, whereas others who are happier to take risks might prefer an option that would lead to the greatest gain. The theory is called *Prospect Theory*, because it purports to explain how people weigh up the prospects of their decisions.

Downside risk is, of course, part of the equation. This might be calculated as the value of the potential loss, calculated against the likelihood of it happening. Someone who buys a Euro Lottery scratchcard for £2 is well aware that the chances of winning anything are slight, and the chance of winning the €75 million jackpot is negligible, but the loss is limited to £2 so the risk is worth taking. Someone buying a second-hand car for £15,000 from a total stranger is taking a much greater risk: on the one hand, there might be a saving of £2,000 over buying from a dealer, but on the other hand there might be a loss of £15,000. Someone who is a risk-taker might reason that the loss is unlikely to be the whole value of the car, but would probably be restricted to a few hundred for repairing something that the buyer has concealed. People use heuristics for this.

TABLE 6.3 Examples of heuristics

Search heuristics	Examples
Store selection	If you are buying meat, always go to the butcher across the street
Source credibility	If a magazine accepts advertising from products it tests and reports on, the tests may be biased in favour of the advertiser
Evaluation heuristics	**Examples**
Key criteria	If comparing processed foods, examine the sugar content
Negative criteria	If a salient consequence is negative (for example, high sugar content) give this choice criterion extra weight in the integration process
Significant differences	If the alternative is similar on a salient consequence (for example, all the alternatives are low sugar) ignore that choice criterion
Choice heuristics for familiar, frequently purchased products	**If choosing among familiar products ...**
Works best	Choose the product that you think works best – the one that provides the best level of performance on the most relevant functional consequences
Affect referral	Choose the alternative you like best (in other words, select the alternative with the most favourable attitude)
Bought last	Select the alternative you bought last time (assuming it proved satisfactory)
Important person	Choose the alternative that an 'important person' such as a spouse, friend or child likes
Price-based rule	Buy the least expensive alternative, or perhaps the most expensive alternative, depending on your beliefs about the relationship between price and quality
Promotion rule	Choose the alternative for which you have a special-offer coupon, or that you can buy at a reduced price (due to a sale or special offer)
Choice heuristics for new, unfamiliar products	**If choosing among unfamiliar products ...**
Wait and see	Do not buy a new product until someone you know has used it for a while and recommends it. In the case of electronic products, wait until the next year or year after its introduction, when the price is likely to have reduced considerably
Expert consultant	Find an expert or more knowledgeable person, have them evaluate the alternatives in terms of your goals, then buy the alternative that the expert suggests

Although Kahneman and Tversky offer a fairly complex formula to explain the calculation process, in fact people rarely calculate the odds. Normally, we use heuristics to simplify the process – the risk-averse don't often buy lottery tickets, and they buy their cars from dealers, and not from private sellers.

Heuristics are used to simplify decision-making. They may be stored in memory, or constructed on the spot based on information received, but in either case they allow the individual to reach rapid decisions without over-stretching their cognitive capacity (or brainpower). In the extreme, the use of heuristics leads to habitual behaviour. For example, someone might go to the same pub every Friday night and order the same drinks and sit at the same table each time. Routinised choice behaviour such as this is comforting and relaxing since it does not involve any decision-making at all. In fact, most people find it uncomfortable if their pleasurable routines cannot be carried out for whatever reason.

HEDONISM

Hedonism
The cult of pleasure

Hedonism is the cult of pleasure. In consumer behaviour, it refers to the pleasurable aspects of consumption: the flavour of food rather than its nutritional value, the comfort of a car rather than its performance, the appearance of clothing rather than its ability to keep out the cold (Holbrook and Hirschmann 1982). Hedonic purchases are sometimes about a need for being cheered up, and can be triggered by feeling unhappy as well as by a normal day-to-day desire for comfort and pleasure. There is even evidence that a near-death experience can encourage greater pleasure-seeking behaviour, as well as encouraging people to change their lifestyles (perhaps by dieting, or sometimes by stopping a diet) (Shiv et al. 2004). Recent research by Chen et al. (2015) has investigated the characteristics of emerging hedonistic consumers in China. They showed that hedonistic consumption value is positively associated with fashion orientation (the trends that society believe to be true among a wider population), responsiveness to commercial stimuli (e.g. belief in advertisements), brand consciousness (an awareness about the existence and meaning of brands) and a preference for foreign brands (Chen et al. 2015).

Marketers put a great deal of effort into designing products that not only work well, but also give pleasure to their owners. This is an important way to differentiate the product from those of competitors, and for some products hedonic content is virtually the entire product: fashion wear, cosmetics, holiday travel, and many service sectors such as food and travel rely heavily on hedonism to sell their products.

When for example, one thinks of hedonism, the last thing one would think of is the light commercial vehicle, or a van. At first sight, a vehicle for delivering groceries, building materials and furniture has to be as utilitarian as it gets – and for 60 or 70 years that was what manufacturers thought as well. Then in 1965 the industry was revolutionised by the Ford Transit. The Transit handled like a car, had comfortable seats, was relatively quiet, and had good heating and ventilation systems. It was easy to load and a real pleasure to drive. Within a few years Ford had captured 30% of the UK light van market. The Transit became known as the People's Van: it was owned by small businesses, by budding rock bands, by hippies who slept in the back, by builders, by couriers and even by private citizens. Camper van versions, minibus versions, open truck versions and high-roof versions were all produced by Ford for the burgeoning market. The comfort and ease of handling made it ideal for drivers who were non-professionals, i.e. drivers who delivered goods as part of their normal business rather than drivers who delivered for a living. Even delivery companies switched to Transits as they found that their drivers performed better when they were comfortable and not tired out by wrestling with heavy steering, or trying to coax some power out of a commercial engine. Drivers of the Transit van have been given a loving accolade and are now commonly referred to as the 'white van man'. Transits were fast

FIGURE 6.11 Hedonism vs. utilitarianism

and manoeuvrable. The police quickly adopted Transits as well, to use as transport for prisoners, as dog-carrying vehicles, or as scene-of-crime vehicles. Throughout its 50-year life the Transit has been the market leader. It still retains its core values: it is the People's Van because it is designed for people, not for companies. The Transit, more than any other van before it, caters to people's hedonic needs.

Hedonism is sometimes regarded as the opposite of utilitarianism, which is the cult of practicality. In marketing, most products have utilitarian aspects, and some are almost entirely utilitarian: most business-to-business products are utilitarian (there is little hedonic value in a bag of cement, although what a builder builds with it might be extremely hedonic). The relationship between hedonism, utilitarianism, needs and products is shown in Figure 6.11. Utilitarian consumer products might include cleaning products, energy (electricity and gas), basic foods and most municipal services such as street cleaning and sewage removal.

In most cases, products have both hedonic and utilitarian features. Even a basic, cheap car has comfortable seats, a radio, a heater, and so forth. This is because such comforts have become regarded as hygiene factors by most people (see above). This means that manufacturers are in a constant race to add even more hedonic features to differentiate their products and in order to stay ahead of the competition. Adding utilitarian features to hedonic products tends to generate negative feelings about the product, however. This may be because the 'pure pleasure' aspect is no longer pure – whereas adding hedonic features to a utilitarian product tends to lead to positive feelings about the product (Saldanha and Williams 2008).

Utilitarianism
The cult of practicality

CHALLENGING THE STATUS QUO

Is it realistic for manufacturers and retailers to make a distinction between a consumer's hedonic needs and utilitarian needs? After all, what is a pleasure to some people is a necessity to others. For example, take sport: for many people, going to the gym is a fun thing to do, a real pleasure, whereas for others it is simply sweaty activity that they don't have to do. But supposing somebody had been told by the doctor to exercise more or risk heart failure? Such a person might take up a gym membership as the 'least worst'

© iStock.com/ferrantraite

alternative, in other words exercise rather than die, but in fact hate every minute of it.

Equally, for a lot of people driving a car is a necessity, purely a means of getting from one place to another conveniently. For others, it might be a real delight – and certainly car manufacturers plug the hedonic aspects of driving far more than they talk about the utilitarian aspects.

Take, for example, BMW with their famous tagline 'The Ultimate Driving Machine', which has been with them since the 1970s. Then as part of their sponsorship of the 2010 Vancouver Winter Olympic Games, they launched a campaign called 'Joy'. Their Vice President of Marketing, Dan Creed, noted that the Joy campaign was specifically moulded in order to attract more women to the brand. The notion of 'joy' would 'warm the brand up and make it approachable' (Henry 2012). Their recent advertisements have made a point of saying, 'We don't make sports cars. We don't make SUVs. We don't make hybrids. We don't make luxury sedans. We only make one thing. The Ultimate Driving Machine'; an approach that reflects more hedonism than utilitarianism.

Maybe the old saying about one man's meat being another man's poison (i.e. things liked or enjoyed by one person may be distasteful to another) has some truth in it! What other examples/scenarios can you conjure up which show either hedonic or utilitarian needs?

Hedonism also includes experiential needs. People need to have stimulating experiences: we have this in common with most other mammals, especially carnivorous ones. The need to learn by trying new things, the need to have something new to think about, and the need for excitement all stem from the need for new experiences. Experiential needs are met by playing sport (especially *extreme* or dangerous sports), by travel and by taking up new hobbies. Often such activities are in conflict with utilitarian and functional needs – there is really no utilitarian value in bungee-jumping or driving from London to Mumbai in a TATA-made Land Rover, but both fulfil an experiential need for someone. A number of commentators have suggested that competitive advantage can be gained by marketers if they concentrate on the consumers' experience of owning the product, and by a greater understanding of customer-perceived value (Slater 2000; McAlexander et al. 2002; Liu and Sun 2015).

Hedonism also accounts for the utopian marketplace. This is the place where people dream (Manuel and Manuel 1979; Galmstrup 2015). Utopia and utopian concepts, which form the divide between what people actually need (Galmstrup 2015) and what they dream of, has been deconstructed as follows (McLaran and Brown 2002):

- *Sensory no-place.* This brings feelings of a world apart from the consumer experience.
- *Creating playspace.* This provides the open-ended playful nature of the utopian text contained within it.
- *Performing art.* This evokes the active life of people in the creation of utopian meanings.

Our dreams and fantasies do not, of course, always turn into reality, and in many cases people prefer to keep a fantasy as just that – remaining within Utopia. This does not prevent marketers from feeding the fantasies – custom car magazines frequently have average readerships aged below the minimum age to have a driving licence, for example.

Interestingly, people sometimes use guilt as a way of controlling their own behaviour. For example, someone who is trying to lose weight might deliberately make themselves feel guilty for eating a chocolate bar, in an attempt to avoid the behaviour in future (Dai et al. 2008). In some cases, people might use 'virtuous' behaviour (such as having salad for lunch rather than sausages and chips) as a guilt-reduction strategy for enjoying a chocolate bar later (Khan et al. 2009). It has even been found that simply having a healthy choice available may lead some people to choose the less healthy (but more attractive) alternative (Wilcox et al. 2010). This is less likely to happen if the individuals use a rejection strategy in decision-making, that is to say they operate by rejecting alternatives until there is only the healthy option left (Machin and Park 2010). Resisting temptation may lead to an angry (or at least irritated/frustrated) mood afterwards – researchers Gal and Liu (2010) found that people who resisted the temptation of a chocolate bar were more likely to choose to see an anger-related film afterwards. In general, hedonic needs account for a large proportion of consumer spending. Over the past two decades, we've seen a trend towards service industries (as opposed to manufacturing industries) which is largely fuelled by hedonic needs, as people travel more, eat out more and enjoy the plethora of services that are provided for us as consumers. Hedonism is a major component in consumerism, which is the cult of consumption: people derive great pleasure from shopping, buying and consuming.

The concept of the consumer society has been around for some time now, and refers to the way in which most human activity in the developed world centres around consumption. We define ourselves by what we consume rather than by what we produce, we spend a large amount of our time consuming things or surfing the Internet in order to learn about things to consume (which is itself a form of consumption) and it is impossible for us to have a social life without at the same time being a consumer. Consider the multitude of social media platforms (for example, Twitter, Facebook, LinkedIn, Xing, Snapchat, Instagram, YouTube, MeetUp) each feeding our innate curiosity and thirst for knowledge, information, ideas and incentives; which collectively enable us to consume even more.

All of this consumption activity is hedonic because it helps us to feel secure in who we are and what we do: it enables us to enjoy our lives more.

UNDERSTANDING MOTIVATION

One of the difficulties with understanding consumer motivation is that people are often unable to explain what has driven them to a specific action. In some cases this is because the motivation operates below the subconscious level, and in other cases it is because the person is not willing to admit to a particular motivation. This is easily observable in everyday life: people often lie about their reasons for taking, or not taking, a particular action since it would involve admitting to something they would prefer to keep to themselves. For example, someone may turn down an invitation to a friend's birthday party on the grounds of being unwell, when in fact the individual is afraid of seeing an ex-husband and his new wife, who may also be at the party. This might be embarrassing to admit to. In some cases, people are motivated by some need that is illegal or immoral, so would be extremely unlikely to admit to being motivated by the need. Equally, someone might be genuinely unaware, at a conscious level, of their real motivation – a reluctance to go to a concert might be a fear of crowds, but the individual might believe that actually he or she is too tired to go and would prefer a quiet night in.

In general, people are not so much rational as rationalising. A middle-aged man who is thinking about buying a sports car might actually want it because he wants to recapture his lost youth, but might rationalise the decision by talking about the car's fuel economy and good looks. 'I need a decent car to impress my clients' (thus invoking feelings of *esteem*) is a common rationalisation.

In the 1950s and early 1960s there was considerable interest in motivational research. Motivational researchers thought that they had discovered underlying reasons for consumer behaviour, and many of their propositions were seized on by marketers. Unfortunately, some of the propositions were so peculiar they could not reasonably be used – the idea that housewives were symbolically washing away their sins when they did the laundry, or were symbolically giving birth when they baked a cake were among the less credible ideas of the motivational researchers.

A further complication is that any given action is likely to be the result of several different motivations, some of which may even conflict with each other. Some actions are the result of a decision to take the 'least worst' alternative, or may be rationalised in some way in order to maintain an attitude. Sometimes people make wrong decisions, and rationalise their motives afterwards rather than admit their mistake.

Overall, then, it is difficult to penetrate the layers of motivations to find the nugget of true motivation within.

RESEARCH INTO MOTIVATION

Identifying consumer motivation is clearly far from simple. Finding out the true motivation for someone's behaviour is similar to finding out a hidden attitude (see Chapter 10). Projective techniques in which respondents are asked to explain the motivation of a fictitious third party will often draw out the individual's real reason for behaving in a specific way: the respondent might be asked to fill in speech bubbles in a cartoon, or be asked what the 'typical' person might think, and so forth. This method was used to research children's motivations for smoking, an activity which (clearly) they would not want to discuss openly (Brucks et al. 2010).

A classic study carried out in the 1950s sought to establish the reasons for poor sales of instant coffee. Housewives were shown two shopping lists which were identical except that one list had instant coffee on it, while the other list had ground coffee. The respondents were asked to describe the type of housewife who would have drawn up each list: the instant coffee list was seen to belong to a woman who is lazy, badly organised and not a good housewife (Haire 1950). The days of a housewife making instant coffee seem like a far cry given our current fascination with the Nespresso brand, and the fact that every Nespresso drinker knows only too well (and is further motivated by) the company's dedication to its sustainability programme. The CEO of Nestlé Nespresso SA, Jean-Marc Duvoisin, was quoted by Kanani (2014) as saying, 'Sustainability is a business imperative for us, as we depend on a natural resource to deliver quality and consistency to consumers. Only 1–2% of the worldwide coffee crop meets our strict quality and aroma requirements. We believe that the best way to protect our supply of these rare coffees is to ensure the protection of the environment where our coffee is grown, as more sustainable farming increases the ability to produce consistent quality far into the future, and to provide a more sustainable and equitable outcome for farmers'.

SUMMARY

This chapter has considered the forces that encourage people to buy. Needs are the basic generators of drive, and consequently of motivation, so it might be true to say that need is the basis of virtually all behaviour. Drives develop when there is a gap between where we are and where we want to be – motivation develops when we can see a possible solution (or solutions) to the need problem. Some motivation relates to our physical, utilitarian needs, but as human beings we also have powerful social, aesthetic and pleasure needs, so much of our buying behaviour relates to drive, motivation and hedonism.

KEY POINTS

- Many motives are irrational or unconscious.
- Need is a perceived lack; want is a specific satisfier.
- Drive is caused by the gap between actual and desired states.
- Most marketing is about activating needs and directing wants.
- Motivation is complex, and cannot always be inferred from behaviour.
- Needs can be ranked, but there is considerable overlap.
- As wealth increases, motivations change.
- Many purchases are motivated at least in part by hedonic needs.

HOW TO IMPRESS YOUR EXAMINER

You are very likely to be asked a question about motivation. Having a clear understanding not only of the models, but also of their weaknesses, will help you to gain extra marks – for example, most motivation models derive from personnel management studies rather than consumer behaviour studies, so something is likely to have been lost in translation. Second, consider whether the models really stack up in practice – is Maslow's hierarchy really a hierarchy? Are people really not motivated by money, as Herzberg suggests? Third, the models usually operate on a 'one size fits all' basis, which clearly does not fit well with reality – people are different from each other, and have different motivations.

REVIEW QUESTIONS

1. Why do some people have higher OSLs than others?
2. What is the difference between primary and secondary motivations?
3. What are the main difficulties in categorising needs?
4. What are the main criticisms of Maslow's Hierarchy of Need?
5. Why is punishment a poorer motivator than reward?
6. What is the purpose of modelling?
7. What is meant by approach–approach conflict?
8. Why is hedonism an important factor for marketers?
9. How might marketers find out which factors are regarded as hygiene factors in a product, and which are motivators?
10. In which areas of marketing would Vroom's Expectancy Theory have most relevance?

CASE STUDY: CRUISE SHIPS

Pleasure cruises are a relatively new phenomenon. The concept was first started in the 19th century, when the Peninsular and Orient Steam Navigation Company advertised trips to Mediterranean ports, starting from Southampton. At that time, long-distance transportation was usually carried out by sea: overland trips were impossibly long and uncomfortable, whereas an ocean liner could carry people between continents in much greater comfort.

However, ships intended for transport across major oceans were generally not suitable for pleasure cruises. The ships were built to withstand ocean storms, and most of the cabins were inside the ship and usually windowless, or with (at most) a small porthole. Since passengers would normally only be on board for a few days, comforts and amenities were limited: a cruise lasting a week or more would require much more in terms of hedonic features.

Eventually companies began to shift away from using transport ships as cruise ships, and purpose-built cruise ships were commissioned. During the 1960s, as long-range passenger jets came into service, ocean liners declined in popularity: for example, only the Cunard line still runs transatlantic liners, and even these have to provide entertainment and superb fine dining in order to attract people away from airlines.

©iStock.com/carterdayne

Modern cruise ships have cabins with private verandas, and stop at interesting ports every couple of days. They have top-class live entertainment, gourmet dining and exceptional personal service – on some ships there are as many crew as there are passengers, in order to provide perfect food, entertainment and personal service. The world's largest cruise liner, *Allure of the Seas,* has a maximum capacity of over 6,000 passengers accommodated in 2,700 cabins. Such town-sized vessels cruise in calm waters such as the Mediterranean and the Caribbean, avoiding hurricane season: they are so stable some even have bowling alleys on board, and it would be hard to know that one was on board a moving vessel if it were not for the view from the private veranda.

Cruise companies compete heavily on price, so they tend to make their profits from selling shore excursions and extras such as alcoholic drinks. Since the alcohol on board a cruise ship is duty-free this can be very profitable: however, food is usually included in the price.

Perhaps not surprisingly, cruising tends to be popular with an older clientele. For an elderly person, a cruise means having a regular change of scenery, plenty of entertainment on tap and good food, all without the need to go out into the streets of a foreign city or indeed go out at all. All the passengers have to do is relax and be pampered – and should anything untoward happen, the medical facilities on board are exemplary. Cruise liners even carry coffins, in case of any deaths among the passengers.

At the other end of the spectrum there are small cruise ships. Some ply the same waters as their larger cousins, but simply have a more intimate feel, while others operate on major river systems such as the Rhine. All try to offer the same level of luxury, but of course a small vessel cannot hope to offer the range of facilities a large vessel has.

One of the major players is, of course, the Peninsular and Orient Steam Navigation Company, although nowadays it is called simply P&O. The company has come a long way since its experiment in offering pleasure trips alongside transport – but the journey has certainly been worthwhile.

QUESTIONS

1. What would be the key factors in choosing a cruise holiday rather than a holiday in a hotel?
2. Why do cruise companies offer excursions?
3. What is the reason for including food in the price?
4. Why might somebody prefer a small ship rather than a large one with more facilities?
5. Why do ocean liners offer entertainment and gourmet food?

FURTHER READING

Classical Motivation Theories: Similarities and Differences Between Them by Stephanie Hoffman is that rare thing, a commercially published undergraduate dissertation. Stephanie is German, and the thesis is published by GRIN Verlag GmbH (Norderstedt, 2006). It provides a very useful and thoughtful set of comparisons between several classical motivation theorists (some of which have not been included in this chapter, for various reasons). Incidentally, the thesis got a B+.

For a psychologist's viewpoint on expectancy models, Henning V., Hennig-Thurau, T. and Feiereisen, S. (2012) Giving the expectancy-value model a heart. *Psychology and Marketing*, 29 (10): 765–81, gives an interesting insight into motivation.

A lot of the time, our attitude towards hedonic behaviour is actually learnt from our family socialisation. Thus communication from within such environments can prove to be an important factor, especially for adolescent children. An excellent article by Hollmann et al. (2015) highlights the motivational antecedents and consequents of the mother–adolescent communication – a fascinating insight into the communication between parents and their children. Hollmann, J., Gorges, J., Wild, E. (2015) Motivational antecedents and consequences of the mother–adolescent communication, *Journal of Child and Family Studies*, July. doi: 10.1007/s10826-015-0258-8.

Christmas is, of course, a time for hedonic behaviour. For a useful overview of how people create meaning for their hedonic consumption, take a look at: C. Tynan and S. McKechnie (2009) Hedonic meaning through Christmas consumption: a review and model. *Journal of Customer Behaviour*, 8 (3): 237–55.

Caroline Tynan and Sally McKechnie also collaborated on a paper about the co-creation of value in hedonic consumption. This takes a somewhat non-traditional view of hedonism. The paper is: C. Tynan, S. McKechnie and C. Chhuon (2010) Co-creating value for luxury brands. *Journal of Business Research*, 63 (11): 1156–263.

There is, of course, a downside to hedonic consumption. Not everything that feels good is good for us – and this applies especially to alcohol. Students are famous for enjoying a drink – but maybe this next paper will provide some food for thought! E.N. Banister and M. Piacentini (2006) Binge drinking – do they mean us? Living life to the full in students' own words. *Advances in Consumer Research*, 33: 390–8.

REFERENCES

Brucks, M., Connell, P.M. and Freeman, D. (2010) Children's ascribed motivations for smoking elicited by projective questioning. *Advances in Consumer Research*, 37: 139, 140.

Chen, Z.X., Wang, C., Chan, A.K.K. and Zheng, Z.C. (2015) The characteristics of emerging hedonistic consumers in China: an empirical investigation. In A.K. Manrai and H.L. Meadow (eds), *Global Perspectives in Marketing for the 21st Century: Proceedings of the 1999 World Marketing Congress*, Developments in Marketing Science: Proceedings of the Academy of Marketing Science. London: Springer International Publishing, p. 63.

Dai, X., Wertenbroch, K. and Brendl, M. (2008) Strategic motivation maintenance: the case of guilt-seeking. *Advances in Consumer Research*, 35: 141.

Gal, D. and Liu, W. (2010) What movie would you watch with your salad? The implicit emotional consequences of exerting self-control. *Advances in Consumer Research*, 37: 123.

Galmstrup, A.M. (2015) Sites of globalization: new cities; reflecting on the dialectics between designer and client. In R. Saliba (ed.), *Urban Design in the Arab World: Reconceptualizing Boundaries*. Farnham: Ashgate Publishing, pp. 167–76.

Haire, M. (1950) Projective techniques in marketing research. *Journal of Marketing*, 14: 649–56.

Hebb, D.O. (1955) Drives and the CNS (Conceptual Nervous System). *Psychological Review*, 62: 243–54.

Henry, J. (2012) BMW: still the ultimate driving machine, not that it ever wasn't. *Forbes*, 31 May. www.forbes.com/sites/jimhenry/2012/05/31/bmw-still-the-ultimate-driving-machine-not-that-it-ever-wasnt/ (accessed 26 July 2015).

Herzberg, F. (1966) *Work and the Nature of Man*. London: Collins.

Hibbert, S.A., Hogg, G. and Quinn, T. (2005) Social entrepreneurship: understanding consumer motives for buying *The Big Issue. Journal of Consumer Behaviour*, 4 (3): 159–72.

Holbrook, M.P. and Hirschmann, E.C. (1982) The experiential aspects of consumption: consumer fantasies, feelings and fun. *Journal of Consumer Research*, 9 (September): 132–40.

Huffman, C., Atneshwar, S. and Mick, D.G. (2000) Consumer goal structures and goal-determining processes: an integrative framework. In S. Ratneshwar, D. Glen Mick and C. Huffman (eds), *The Why of Consumption*. London: Routledge, pp. 9–35.

Kahneman, D. and Tversky, A. (1979) Prospect theory: an analysis of decision under risk. *Econometrica*, 47 (2) (March): 263–92.

Kanani, R. (2014) CEO interview: inside Nespresso's 2020 sustainability strategy. http://news.trust.org//item/20141217011005-2qaye (accessed 26 July 2015).

Khan, U., Dhar, R. and Fishbach, A. (2009) Guilt as motivation: the role of guilt in choice justification. *Advances in Consumer Research*, 36: 27–8.

Larrick, R.P., Heath, C. and Wu, G. (2001) Goal-induced risk taking in strategy choice. In a symposium on goals and decision-making organised by Nathan Novemsky. Association for Consumer Research Conference, Austin, Texas.

Leuba, C. (1955) Toward some integration of learning theories: the concept of optimum stimulation. *Psychological Reports*, 1: 27–33.

Liu, Y. and Sun, Q. (2015) A comparative study of competitive brand based on customer-perceived value: evidences from IAT. *Open Journal of Social Sciences*, 3: 275–82. doi: 10.4236/jss.2015.37040.

Machin, J. and Park, Y.W. (2010) Rejection is good for your health: the influence of decision strategy on food and drink choices. *Advances in Consumer Research*, 37: 75.

Manuel, F.E. and Manuel, F.P. (1979) *Utopian Thought in the Western World*. Oxford: Blackwell.

Maslow, A.H. (1943) A theory of human motivation. *Psychological Review*, 50 (4): 370–96.

Maslow, A.H. (1954) *Motivation and Personality*. New York: Harper and Row.

McAlexander, J.H., Schouten, J.W. and Koenig, H.F. (2002) Building brand community. *Journal of Marketing*, 66 (1): 38–55.

McClelland, D.C. (1955) *Studies in Motivation*. New York: Appleton.

McLaran, P. and Brown, S. (2002) Experiencing the Utopian marketplace. *Advances in Consumer Research*, 29: 1.

McLeod, S.A. (2007) Maslow's Hierarchy of Need. www.simplypsychology.org/maslow.html (accessed 29 July 2015).

McNulty, W.K. (1985) UK social change through a wide-angle lens. *Futures*, August.

Mick, D.G. and Humphreys, A. (2008) Consumer freedom from consumer culture theory perspectives. *Advances in Consumer Research*, 35: 18–19.

Midha, T., Nath, B., Kumari, R., Rao, Y.K. and Pandey, U. (2012) Childhood obesity in India: a meta-analysis. *The Indian Journal of Pediatrics*, 79 (7): 945–48.

Mitchell, A. (1983) *The Nine American Lifestyles*. New York: Macmillan.

Murray, H.A. (1938) *An Exploration in Personality: A Clinical Experimental Study of Fifty Men of College Age*. London: Oxford University Press.

Nord, W.R. and Peter, J.P. (1980) A behaviour modification perspective on marketing. *Journal of Marketing*, 44 (Spring): 36–47

Nowlis, S.M., McCabe, D.B. and Mandel, N. (2003) The effect of a forced delay after choice on consumption enjoyment. *Advances in Consumer Research*, 30: 502–10.

Onkvisit, S. and Shaw, J.J. (1994) *Consumer Behaviour: Strategy and Analysis*. New York: Macmillan.

Raghunathan, R. and Mukherji, A. (2003) Is hope to enjoy more enjoyed than hope enjoyed? *Advances in Consumer Research*, 30: 85–6.

Raju, P.S. (1980) Optimum stimulation level: its relationship to personality, demographics and exploratory behaviour. *Journal of Consumer Research*, 7 (3) (December): 272–82.

Rugimbana, R., Donahay, B., Neal, C. and Polonsky, M.J. (2003) The role of social power relations in gift giving on St. Valentine's Day. *Journal of Consumer Behaviour*, 3 (1): 63–73.

Saldanha, N. and Williams, P. (2008) Mixed indulgences: when removing sin may backfire. *Advances in Consumer Research*, 35: 140.

Scott, M. and Nowlis, S. (2010) The effect of goal-setting on consumption and consumer well-being. *Advances in Consumer Research*, 37: 124.

Shiv, B., Ferraro, R. and Bettman, J.R. (2004) Let us eat and drink for tomorrow we shall die: mortality salience and hedonic choice. *Advances in Consumer Research*, 31: 118–21.

Skinner, B.F. (1953) *Science and Human Behaviour*. New York: Macmillan.

Slater, N. (2000) The positive effect of a market orientation on business profitability: a balanced replication, *Journal of Business Research*, 48: 69–73.

Tay, L. and Diener, E. (2011) Needs and subjective well-being around the world. *Journal of Personality and Social Psychology*, 101 (2): 354–65.

Vroom, V.H. (1999) *Management and Motivation*. Harmondsworth: Penguin Business.

Wadhwa, M. and Trudel, R. (2010) The fruit of labour effect. *Advances in Consumer Research*, 37: 79.

Wilcox, K., Vallen, B., Block, L.G. and Fitzsimons, G. (2010) Vicarious goal fulfilment: when the mere presence of a healthy option leads to an ironically indulgent decision. *Advances in Consumer Research*, 37: 73, 74.

Zuckerman, M. (2000) Are you a risk-taker? *Psychology Today*, November/December: 54–87.

MORE ONLINE

For additional materials that support this chapter and your learning, please visit:
https://study.sagepub.com/sethnaandblythe

CHAPTER 7

THE SELF AND PERSONALITY

LEARNING OBJECTIVES

After reading this chapter you should be able to:

• Explain the role and purpose of self-concept.

• Describe the derivation of self-concept.

• Explain the mechanisms of inner and outer direction.

• Explain the reasons for an increase in inner-directedness.

• Explain self-monitoring.

• Describe the various ways in which personality is studied.

• Define personality.

INTRODUCTION

This chapter is about some of the factors that make up the individual person; the self. As we've already seen from the early chapters in this book, people are complex. Our individual mental make-up affects how we respond to communications, what and how we buy, and thus how we plan for our future lives. Put all of this together and you start to understand the 'personality' behind the individual self. From a marketing viewpoint, understanding the self and his or her personality is useful in segmenting markets and also in planning marketing communications.

SELF-CONCEPT

Of all the personality concepts which have been applied to marketing, self-concept has probably provided the most consistent results and the greatest promise of application to the needs of business firms. (Foxall 1980)

Self-concept is the person's ideas and feelings about him or herself. It has an important role to play in understanding consumer behaviour, since people will buy products that contribute to the self-concept. For example, a woman who thinks of herself as a 'femme fatale' will choose chic clothes to enhance that image; or a man who thinks of himself as a handyman will equip himself with the most sophisticated tools.

Essentially, people project a role and this is confirmed (or denied) by other people. In order for the role to be confirmed, the person will try to develop all the exterior accoutrements appropriate to the role. In this sense, the person becomes a work of art, a sensory stimulus to other people, which is intended to generate affective and appropriate responses. The person may well use all five senses to generate the affective response: sight (by dressing appropriately, wearing make-up, etc.), hearing (by speaking with the right accent, or using the voice well), smell (by wearing perfume or deodorant), touch (by looking after the skin, perhaps by wearing clothes that feel good) and even taste (by using flavoured lipstick, mouthwashes).

Some of these sensory stimuli will, of course, only be available to the individual's closest friends but most people at some time or another will consciously set out to create a work of art of themselves in order to 'make a good impression' on somebody, whether that be employer, friend or lover. The extent to which people do this depends on the following factors:

1. The degree of importance attached to impressing the other person (or people).

2. The degree to which the individual anticipates that the 'target audience' can be impressed.

3. The cost in time and money of creating the desired image.

Clearly, though, the fact that people do create these works of art has led to the invention of whole industries to cater for the need – the cosmetics industry and fashion industry, to name but two. The forces involved can be very strong indeed; even in Nazi concentration camps people were prepared to trade food for clothing and cosmetics, thus placing their survival at risk for the purpose of maintaining their dignity

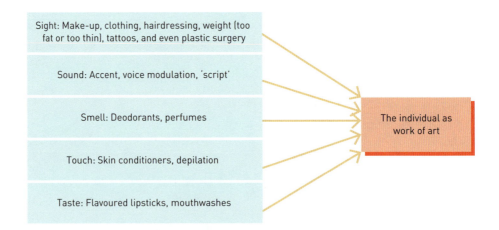

FIGURE 7.1 The person as artwork

(Klein 2003). In some cases fashion items also represent personality determinants and even rite-of-passage symbols. Research by Russell Belk showed that shoes can represent a rite of passage (a girl's first high heels, for example) and that people often define themselves by their footwear (brands of trainer, for example) (Belk 2003). African Americans sometimes wear African clothing as a way of identifying themselves with their roots (deBerry-Spence and Izberk-Bilgin 2006).

Rite of passage

An event or action which marks a change in an individual's life circumstances

CHALLENGING THE STATUS QUO

Re-inventing ourselves is a common event. We change our hair, or our clothes, and effectively become someone slightly different. But are we justified in considering this to be a work of art? Art is supposed to make people rethink the world around them – does this really happen when someone gets a haircut?

Or perhaps the person-as-artwork idea only applies at the extremes, where someone undergoes radical cosmetic (plastic) surgery or an extreme tattoo on a place on the body which is visible most of the time (for instance, tattoos on the face or head).

Also, who is the artist here? The individual consumer, or the cosmetic surgeon, hairdresser, beautician or the tattoo artist who carries out the work? What are the psychological effects on the individual of such reinvention? In some cases, such reinvention is of course necessary in order for the individual to feel 'normal' – for instance, after sex reassignment surgery, or perhaps reconstructive surgery after a mastectomy.

©iStock.com/iconogenic

Self-concept is a learned construct. Children tend to look for role models to imitate; these may not always be the same people, and the child may try several different role models before settling on one that is appropriate. Children can be crushed by a denial of the role being projected, for example if people laugh while the child is copying the behaviour of a favourite auntie or uncle. During the teenage years a further refinement occurs as the individual tries to develop an adult role, and again the role models may shift, typically away from the family members towards a hero (pop star or sporting personality) or sometimes to an individual within a peer group (a school friend, for example). Usually the role model will be an adult a few years older.

Peer group

Those people who are near to being one's equals

Self-esteem is the positive view on the self. People with high self-esteem have a natural expectation that they will be successful at what they aim to achieve. This belief feeds a propensity to take more risks and these people will be very comfortable being the centre of attention. The opposite is true for those with a low self-esteem who believe that they are doomed to fail. And thus they will do whatever it takes to avoid such embarrassing situations.

CONSUMER BEHAVIOUR IN ACTION: THE DIVINE IMAGE

©iStock.com/MikeLaptev

The Divine Image is a consultancy with a strong foothold in a growing market – that of personal image.

Managing director Camelia Fredericks is a former lawyer, now turned image consultant. She is a member of the Federation of Image Consultants, and has built The Divine Image on a foundation of sleek, upmarket chic (to quote the corporate website).

The Divine Image will, under the direction of Camelia and her staff, carry out a personal analysis of what colours the client should wear, what style of clothes, and what hairstyle and cosmetics are appropriate. What the consultancy does goes further than the TV makeover cliché – The Divine Image will advise on correct body language and 'personal branding' to project the right image. The company is quite up front about what they are aiming to do for clients: they aim to develop confidence, develop dress sense and style, improve self-esteem and, overall, improve self-image.

The service does not stop with advice, either. Consultants will go shopping with clients and help them find the right clothes, and will even precede this with a visit to the client's wardrobe to see what is already suitable and (more importantly) what is not. Consultants are available to advise on dating – everything from making the first approach to making a good impression on the night, and making the other person fall head over heels in love. Heaven on earth, for only £50 an hour for a consultation.

The service is not, as one might imagine, confined to women. Exactly the same service is available to men, and The Divine Image has a great many male clients.

Why do people use services like The Divine Image? Simple – most of us know that we would do better in our careers, in our love lives and in our social lives if we could only project the right image. Few of us are experts in this, and we envy people who seem always to wear the right clothes, say the right things and influence the right people. Any money invested in image consultancy will come back tenfold in improved job and personal prospects and less time and money wasted on unsuitable clothing and dating. After all, the investment is in something that can never be lost, repossessed or taken away – yourself.

Self includes gender, and there are many studies on how the individual's perception of gender affects purchasing behaviour (Baker et al. 2015; Bartikowski and Walsh 2015; Oakley 2015; Schmitt and Rasolofoarison 2015). People typically form a view on the gender-appropriateness of brands: there is evidence that men are more concerned about this than women, being less prepared to adopt a brand extension that they perceive as coming from a 'feminine' brand (Jung and Lee 2006). Men also tend to define masculinity in part through advertisements they see (although they may interpret what masculinity means in different ways). Extensions from a 'male' brand are much more likely to be adopted (Tuncay 2006).

Self-concept has four attributes, as follows:

1. It is learned, not innate.

2. It is stable and consistent. Self-perception may change; self-concept does not. This accounts for brand loyalty, since self-concept involves an opinion about which products will 'fit the image'.

3. It is purposeful; in other words, there is a reason and a purpose behind it. Essentially, self-concept is there to protect and enhance a person's ego. It is therefore advisable not to attack a person's beliefs directly; people often become angry or at least defensive when this happens.

4. It is unique to the individual, and promotes individualism.

Self-concept breaks down into different components, or dimensions (Walker 1992). These are shown in Table 7.1.

One other, which was not identified by Walker in Table 7.1, is the **extended self**. There are many objects, items, possessions which we all consider to be an extension of oneself. And the spectrum is wide; from personal possessions to national monuments – there are a variety of items which we use to denote our largesse to oneself.

Extended self
Items which consumers use as an extension of themselves to define their roles in society

There is some overlap, but the differences are quite marked between the dimensions. Each dimension has some relevance for marketers, and the implications are as shown in Table 7.2 below.

For marketers, the differences are useful. The ideal self predicts attempts at upward mobility: purchases of training courses, self-improvement classes, upmarket products, cosmetic surgery, etc. Looking-glass self is relevant for other-directed people.

TABLE 7.1 Components of self-concept

Component	Explanation
Real self	This is the actual, objective self, as others see us. There is a problem with this definition, since other people never know the whole story. This means that the 'real' self may be something other than the face shown to the world
Self-image	This is the subjective self, as we see ourselves. Self-image is likely to differ radically from the real self, but to an extent this is modified over time because of feedback from others. We modify our self-image in the light of the reactions of others
Looking-glass self	The social self, or the way we think other people see us. This does not always coincide with the way people actually see us, since we are not able to read minds. Feedback from others will be constrained by politeness or by a desire to project a self-image on the part of the respondent, so we are not always aware of what other people really think we are like
Ideal self	How we wish we were; this connects to the self-actualisation need that Maslow identified. This self is often the one that provokes the most extravagant spending, as the individual tries to make up the gap between self-image and ideal self
Possible selves	These are the selves we might become, or the selves we wish we could become

TABLE 7.2 Relevance of self-image

Dimension	Relevance to marketers	Examples
Real self	As the face that is shown to the world, this is the one that people most wish to influence	Conspicuous consumption of cars, houses, etc. Cosmetics, fashion and hairdressing
Self-image	Useful in two ways; first, the negative aspects of self-image influence the ideal self, and second the positive aspects influence purchases which reinforce the self-image	Somebody whose self-image is 'cool' will not want to jeopardise that, and will buy appropriate products to match that image. Somebody whose self-image is poor will want to correct discrepancies
Ideal self	The aspect that leads to the greatest purchases of self-improvement products	Correspondence courses, cosmetics, cosmetic surgery, musical instruments and any number of other products that lead to self-development
Looking-glass self	The way we think others see us; this influences us in making changes to those views, or reinforcing views that are perceived as positive	A man who thinks his friends see him as being staid or boring might be prompted to buy something cool and trendy (perhaps a convertible sports car) in order to correct the image. Conversely, somebody more outer-directed might deliberately buy a car to fit in with the image he thinks he has with his friends; perhaps to buy an electric hybrid vehicle because his friends see him as an eco-friendly, down-to-earth person
Possible selves	The selves we might become, or the selves we wish to become, are not necessarily the same. We may fear what we might become (for example, being afraid of becoming overweight, or of contracting a serious disease, or of becoming an alcoholic)	In some cases marketers have a role in helping people to formulate and fulfil their dreams – education and training courses are an example. In other cases marketing techniques are used to enable people to avoid becoming what they fear being: social marketing campaigns encourage people to eat healthily, take exercise, cut down on smoking and over-eating, and control their alcohol intake

In Figure 7.2, self-concept is generated partly by internal factors such as looking-glass self, ideal self and self-image, but these are modified (particularly through looking-glass self) by the real self. This is because those around us give us feedback on how we are coming across, either by showing approval of what we do or by showing disapproval. These forces are so powerful that they even extend to online identities: researchers have found that similar-looking avatars tend to congregate together in virtual reality, and are less friendly and welcoming than are groups of different-looking avatars. This therefore plays a role in web design, influencing both 2D and 3D designs (see for example Visinescu et al. 2015). Even owning the right set of virtual possessions is important in cyberspace (Wood et al. 2009).

Market maven

Someone who is a self-appointed expert about a particular product category or market

In recent years, the concept of the market maven has developed. Market mavens are people who define themselves as knowledgeable about the market for a particular product type: the word 'maven' derives from a Yiddish word for 'wise'. Such people enjoy sharing their knowledge with others, and enjoy the self-concept of being an expert: this improves their self-confidence as well (Clark et al. 2008). Obviously mavens are important to marketers (especially those in high-tech industries), since they influence purchase decisions of others very strongly. Mavens differ from opinion

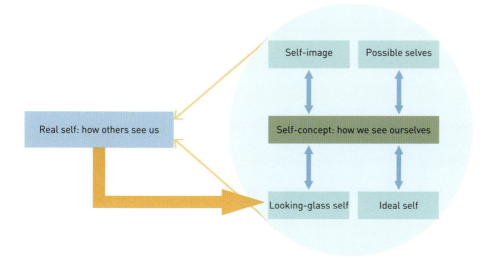

FIGURE 7.2 Relationship between components of self-concept

leaders: opinion leaders tend to have high levels of emotional involvement with product categories, while mavens have a more intellectual, knowledge-based stance. Mavens also show a higher need for variety in their lives than do opinion leaders – in other words, they may well switch brands if they discover information that means the new brand is better (Stokburger-Sauer and Hoyer 2009).

Self can also be categorised as actual self, ideal self and worst self (Banister and Hogg 2003). This is a simpler model, but it includes the concept of the worst self – the self we are ashamed of. For marketers, products can be promoted as being good for avoiding the worst self, or can be promoted as being good for appeasing the worst self.

Self-image is relevant to what we think we deserve; what is the 'right' product for us. Teenagers use music consumption as a way of building social capital, creating boundaries and defining who is excluded or included in the social group (Nuttall 2009). People are swayed by what is promoted as being 'just right for people like you' – children can be told they are having 'the special children's meal'; students can be swayed by a 'special student discount'; elderly people by the special 'senior citizen's service'. Sometimes this type of promotion can backfire – there may be fears about the quality of the service or product, for instance, and (especially in the case of older people) the self-image of the person might differ from the image the marketer has of this particular group. This is why advertising aimed at elderly people often uses actors in their fifties and sixties rather than actors in their seventies or eighties. A related but side-issue is that people tend to relate more strongly to brands that contain letters from their own names: this is probably a subconscious association with the brand (Brendl et al. 2003).

Real self is not known to the consumer, although it is one of the greatest motivators in consumer behaviour. In the words of the Scottish poet Robert Burns, 'To see ourselves as others see us' is not in our gift – and this may be just as well. Achieving the ideal self is very much about getting appropriate applause and critical acclaim, so that we know whether we are getting it right; but perhaps more importantly

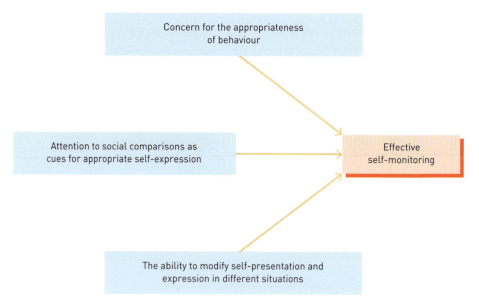

FIGURE 7.3 Self-monitoring

Self-monitoring

The regulatory mechanism which controls behaviour, without outside intercession

there is the element of learning the lines and getting the production right in terms of costume, make-up and script. People therefore modify their behaviour according to the feedback obtained; this is called self-monitoring (Snyder 1974). As shown in Figure 7.3, self-monitoring has three forms of expression: concern for the appropriateness of behaviour, attention to social comparison as cues for appropriate self-expression, and the ability to modify self-presentation and expression across situations (Nantel and Strahle 1986). Another example is people's attitude to credit, especially in these times after the global economic recession: people with strong self-monitoring mechanisms, and people with low price-consciousness, are less likely to rely on credit cards than are people with low self-control or high price sensitivity (Perry 2001; Mokhtar et al. 2015; Wang et al. 2015). Such self-monitoring mechanisms only have a limited amount of mental resources backing them up: often people who normally exhibit great self-control will sometimes 'snap' their self-control and buy something entirely on impulse (Vohs and Faber 2003), where factors and dimensions of extraversion, conscientiousness and neuroticism are found consistently to predict impulse buying (Thompson and Prendergast 2015).

In other words, people ensure that their behaviour is appropriate for the occasion by observing what others are doing and by acting in harmony with that behaviour. Rather like the inexperienced traveller who watches others to see what the local customs are, people take cues from those around them in order to ensure polite behaviour. Low self-monitors are more likely to behave according to some inner drive, and may even prefer to be seen as being different from the rest of humanity; high self-monitors are more likely to conform with those around them, and are therefore more susceptible to appeals to be fashionable.

Some products are transformational, in other words they allow people to change who they are. For example, cosmetic surgery, correspondence courses and self-improvement books all offer people the opportunity to change their self-concept. Identity-related perceptions form the basis for choosing such products and for evaluating their success (or otherwise). People will also decide whether or not their self-concept can accommodate the changes (Kleine et al. 2009). For example, someone who is considering doing a MOOC will evaluate the course on the basis of perceived weaknesses in his or her self-concept, but will also consider whether doing the course will result in a self-concept that is equally less than ideal. Perhaps the individual recognises a need to take a course in computer science and online security (for self-actualising reasons) but does not want to be thought of as a 'nerd'.

People's decisions to undergo drastic transformations (for example, cosmetic surgery) are also influenced in different ways by the people around them and the situations they find themselves in (as we've already seen earlier). For example, in the case of teenage girls contemplating cosmetic surgery, support from family tends to reduce the need for the surgery, whereas support from friends tends to increase it (Pentina et al. 2009).

MOOC
Massive Open Online Course aimed at unlimited participation and open access via the web

PERSONALITY

Personality is the collection of individual characteristics that make a person unique, and which control an individual's responses and relationship with the external environment. It is a composite of subordinate processes, for example attitude, motivation and perception. It is the whole of the person, and is the system that governs behaviour rather than the behaviour itself. However, the concept of personality is actually abstract but can be described in terms of personal traits. Thus, the elements that make up personality are called traits. Considerable research effort has been put towards linking individual personality traits to buying behaviour, but with limited success. This is despite the apparent logic that people would buy products that reflect their personality traits (for example, outgoing flamboyant people might be expected to buy more colourful clothing). In fact, there is some evidence that personality relates to new product (innovation) purchasing behaviour, as we saw earlier in Chapter 4; there is also some evidence that the degree to which someone is influenced by what other people think affects some buying behaviour. Overall, though, it is the total personality that dictates buying behaviour rather than each individual trait.

Trait
A component of personality

Personality has the following features:

1. It is *integrated*. That is to say, all the factors making up the personality act on each other to produce an integrated whole.

2. It is *self-serving*. The characteristics of personality facilitate the attainment of needs and goals. In other words, the personality exists to meet its own needs.

3. Personal characteristics are *individualistic* and unique, in degree and intensity as well as presence. Although many personal characteristics are shared with other people, the possible number of combinations of traits is huge, and therefore each individual is different. This is what makes each person a separate and unique being.

4. Personality is *overt*. External behaviour is affected by personality. In other words, the personality can be observed (albeit indirectly) and deduced from the person's behaviour.

5. Personality is *consistent*. Once a person's basic personality has been established, it will change only slowly and with some difficulty; for practical purposes, an individual consumer's personality will stay constant throughout the buying process.

Because people are individuals it is difficult for marketers to take a standardised approach, yet the exigencies of the business world require standardisation. For this reason, many attempts have been made to establish groupings of personality types, which can be approached with a standardised offering. This is one of the bases of segmentation (the process of dividing the market into target groups of customers with similar needs). For this reason, and of course for the purposes of treating abnormal personalities, there is a long history of studying personality (Davies 2003; Cooper 2015).

APPROACHES TO STUDYING PERSONALITY

There are four basic approaches:

1. *The psychoanalytic approach*. Here the emphasis is on psychoanalysis, or studying the processes and events that have led to the development of personality traits. The focus is on the individual. This approach is typified by Freudian psychiatry, which seeks to help patients to confront the life events that have shaped their personalities.

2. *Typology*. Here the individuals are grouped according to recognised personality types.

3. *Trait and factor theories*. The individual traits of personality can be examined as factors making up the whole person, and each trait can be categorised.

4. *Psychographics*. Consumers are measured using their behavioural tendencies in order to infer personality traits.

The Freudian approach is very much centred on the individual. Here the psychologist asks the patient or subject to talk about anything regardless of logic, courtesy, self-defence, etc.; this is termed as free association. A Freudian would analyse these statements in terms of id, ego and superego.

Id

The unconscious part of the mind responsible for basic desires

Ego

The conscious self

Superego

The component of mind that acts as a restraint on behaviour

According to Freud, the id is the underlying drive of the psyche. It is the source of the most basic, instinctive forces that cause people to behave in particular ways, and operates below the conscious level: it may be responsible for the compulsive behaviour exhibited by some individuals. There is some evidence to show that compulsive behaviour such as buying lottery tickets and scratch cards is linked to other compulsive behaviour such as smoking, and negatively linked to agreeableness and intellectual dimensions of personality (Balabanis 2002). The ego is the conscious self, the part of the mind that makes the day-to-day decisions that lead to the satisfaction of the id; the superego is an internalised parent, the conscience that holds us back from selfish gratification of the id's needs. The superego also operates mostly below the conscious level, and is the 'brake' on behaviour; in a sense, the ego is constantly making compromises between the id's demands and the superego's restraints. This is shown in Figure 7.4.

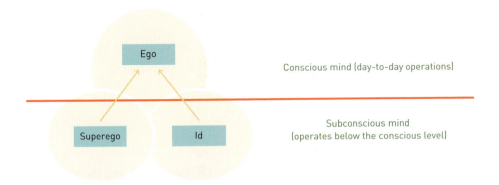

FIGURE 7.4 The id, the ego and the superego

In simple terms, the id acts like a spoilt child, demanding instant gratification regardless of consequences; the superego acts like a stern parent, urging self-restraint and devotion to duty, and the ego acts like a good lawyer, arranging compromises and settlements between the two parties which will not lead to bankruptcy. Hedonic needs (which we studied in the previous chapter) largely derive from the id, so advertising with a hedonic appeal is intended to strengthen the id's demands and encourage the ego to find in favour of the id. Some advertising also weakens the effects of the superego – marketers might suggest that life is too short to listen to your conscience all the time, for example.

The Freudian approach led to motivation research, which purported to explain the underlying reasons for buying. Motivation research was at its most popular in the 1950s and was, for a time, believed to be able to predict consumer behaviour in terms of basic drives that supposedly came from the id. Some of the claims made for motivational research now seem fairly ridiculous to us; for example, it was claimed that crunching cornflakes appealed to the killer instinct because it sounds like crunching animal bones, and that baking a cake is a substitute for giving birth, convertible cars were thought to be a substitute for a girlfriend, and so forth. Motivational research became somewhat discredited because of the extravagant claims made, but still has something to say to marketers. Finding out what people really think, as opposed to what they say they are thinking, enables marketers to address people's underlying needs and wants much more accurately.

Without wishing to turn this chapter into one that investigates research methods, it is worth noting some of the research methods that help uncover 'motivation'. Top of the list here and one which is still quite widely used is the **depth** (or **guided**) **interview**. A small number of respondents (50 or fewer) are interviewed without the use of a formal list of questions. Interviewees are encouraged to express their innermost thoughts and feelings about the object of the research (perhaps a new product). The interviewer needs considerable skill to keep the interview on course without leading the interviewee into expressing beliefs that are not his or her actual beliefs: it is easy to give the interviewee the impression that there is a 'right' answer.

A variation on this is the **focus group**, in which a group of ten or so respondents is invited to discuss their feelings and motivations collectively. The advantage of this

Depth (guided) interview

Open-ended interviews conducted with a small sample of respondents in order to assess their innermost thoughts and feelings

Focus group

A group of people assembled for the purpose of gathering their collective views about a given issue

FIGURE 7.5 Cartoon projective technique

method is that the respondents will tend to stimulate each other, and therefore there is less risk of the interviewer introducing bias into the results: the problem is that people may be reluctant to express attitudes that are embarrassing or might put them in a bad light.

Projective tests are widely used in psychological counselling and psychiatry, and occasionally have applications in market research. They are based on the assumption that the individual may sometimes have difficulty in answering questions directly, either because the answers would be embarrassing or because the answers do not readily come to mind. In effect, a projective technique requires the respondent to say what somebody else might think about a given topic. Sometimes this is done by showing the respondent a cartoon strip of people in a relevant situation: sometimes the respondent is asked to complete a sentence, or perhaps will be asked to draw a picture describing his or her feelings about the attitudinal object. In all cases the intention of the research is to allow the respondents to convey their innermost feelings in a non-personal way.

In Figure 7.5, the person on the left is expressing an opinion that may be controversial: the respondent in the research is asked to fill in what the person on the right might say in response. In theory, the respondent will fill in his or her own opinion, but without the social risk of expressing the opinion openly. This method is particularly useful for uncovering hidden attitudes, perhaps where the individual has an attitude that might be regarded as antisocial or offensive.

Motivational researchers tend to be interested in the id, claiming that this dictates the individual's basic drives. The assumption is that knowledge of the id's demands will enable marketers to shape arguments for the ego to use in overcoming the superego's restraining influence.

From a marketing viewpoint, research of this nature allows firms to determine people's real attitudes to topics such as excessive drinking, cosmetic surgery or sexual imagery in advertising. All these topics have caused people to feel embarrassed and to avoid answering truthfully – but marketers need to get to the truth if they are to address people's real needs without causing offence.

TYPE APPROACH

Freud was the earliest of the scientific psychologists. In subsequent years, additional beliefs to Freud's grew up. The followers of Jung categorise people (in addition to Freudian belief) as introverts (preoccupied with themselves and the internal world) or extroverts (preoccupied with others and the outside world). This was an early attempt to classify people into broad types, and this process has continued ever since, with different researchers discovering different ways of grouping people according to personality types.

Extrovert

Someone who demonstrates his or her personality traits in a strongly overt or obvious manner to other people

Seminal academic texts have defined people across three dimensions (Horney 1945):

1. *Compliant*. Moves towards people, has goodness, sympathy, love, unselfishness and humility. Tends to be over-apologetic, over-sensitive, over-grateful, over-generous and over-considerate in seeking love and affection.

2. *Aggressive*. Usually moves against people. Controls fears and emotions in a quest for success, prestige and admiration. Needs power, exploits others.

3. *Detached*. Moves away from people. Conformity is repugnant to the detached person. Distrustful of others, these people are self-sufficient and independent, and value intelligence and reasoning.

There is empirical evidence to show that these categorisations have some effect on people's buying behaviour. For example, it has been shown that compliant people use more mouthwash and toilet soap, and prefer branded products; aggressive people use more cologne and after-shave. Detached people show low interest in branding (Cohen 1967) and this is reflected in their lack of loyalty towards any particular brands. It seems likely that compliant people will be very eager to please, and reluctant to offend, which is likely to mean that they will be suitable subjects for campaigns emphasising gift-giving or caring behaviour. The problem, as always, lies in identifying these individuals.

Reisman (1953) categorised people against three characteristics, in terms of the sources of their basic drives:

1. *Inner-directed* people are essentially driven from within, and are not too concerned with what other people think.

2. *Other-directed* people get their motivation and take their cues from other people.

3. *Tradition-directed* people get their cues and motivations from the past, from traditional beliefs and sources. These people are nowadays in a very tiny minority.

Reisman's categories (see Figure 7.6) have been used in the past for marketing purposes. Inner-directeds, for example, were shown to be innovators for cars and foodstuffs (Donnelly 1970), whereas outer-directeds have tended to be fashion victims (Zinkhan and Shermohamad 1986). There appears to be a change in the social paradigm, however, which is turning these views in a different direction. Broadly speaking, it would appear that more and more people are becoming inner-directed. This has led to a shift in the prevailing social paradigm away from the basically conformist attitude of the Victorian era towards a more individualistic, free-thinking society. Once again we should assume that most people are on a continuum. To some extent we are all driven by all three factors: Reisman's model is intended to show that some people may lean more towards one type of influence than towards others.

Innovators

People who are the first to try a new product

FIGURE 7.6 Reisman's typologies

The mother and daughter team of Kathryn Briggs and Isabel Myers later developed the Myers-Briggs Type Indicator, shown in Figure 7.7 (Briggs and Myers 1962), with four personality dimensions:

1. Extrovert/introvert

2. Sensing/intuitive

3. Thinking/feeling

4. Judging/perceptive

The combinations can define people into 16 different types; for example, an extrovert-sensing-feeling-judging person is warm-hearted, talkative, popular and likes harmonious relationships. An introvert-intuitive-thinking-judging person is likely to be quiet, intelligent, cerebral and reclusive.

Note yet again that most of us are on a continuum in terms of the Myers-Briggs dimensions. Relatively few people would be at the extremes of any of the dimensions, but the model does provide us with a means of categorising people in broad terms.

This shift in the social paradigm is having several effects: first, the fashion market has fragmented and almost anything goes often with marketers suffering from ethical lapses (Sheth and Sisodia 2015). Second, marketing practice is undergoing a paradigm shift from a transactional to a relationship orientation (Hollensen 2015). Third, there is

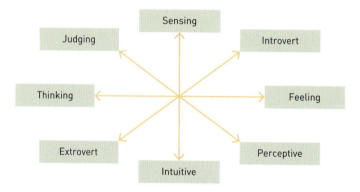

FIGURE 7.7 Myers-Briggs Type Indicator

an increase in the tendency for people to espouse causes and work towards altruistic goals, even in the face of opposition from the Establishment. The shift in the social paradigm is coming about as a result of increased wealth and security in the Western world; as consumers move up Maslow's Hierarchy of Need (see Chapter 6) more of them are operating at the self-actualising level (McNulty 1985). The movement towards a more inner-directed population gave rise to the VALS typology described in Chapter 6.

Overall, the type approach has much to offer marketers. There is little doubt that personality type affects buying behaviour, and since such types are easily identified and are easy to appeal to through marketing communications, it is not difficult to approach these groups, typically by using models.

TRAITS AND FACTORS

Personality is composed of traits, or individual 'atoms' of personality. These individual predispositional attributes exert influences on behaviour, so the traits must be identified before people can be typed or classified.

Traits tend to be enduring facets of personality. In other words, traits tend not to change much over time, and even when they do change they tend to do so rather slowly. Those that might tend to change with age are: anxiety level (which tends to go down as the individual gets older), friendliness (which can change either way) and eagerness for novelty (which tends to go down) (for further information on this you should read Goleman 1987; Roberts and DelVecchio 2000, Roberts et al. 2006). A few traits may vary throughout life, but studies show that adult personalities do not vary significantly as a person ages. This is not to say that behaviour and attitudes never change; merely that the underlying personality tends to stay very much the same. Changing roles, responsibilities and circumstances have much more effect on behavioural changes. For instance, Roberts and Mroczek (2008) show that 'in terms of mean-level change, people show increased self-confidence, warmth, self-control and emotional stability with age'.

The psychologist Raymond Cattell developed a 16-factor trait analysis which has proved useful in defining personality types. Each factor has a high and low range, so that people can be ascribed a position along the continuum between low and high across each factor. Table 7.3 shows the factors and the typical features of someone at either extreme (Cattell 1946; Cattell and Mead 2008).

The study of individual traits as they relate to buying behaviour seems unlikely to produce concrete results. This is probably because personality is interdependent; studying a few traits in isolation gives an insufficiently complete view of the whole person. However, a combination of hierarchically arranged traits has been linked to the propensity to undergo cosmetic surgery or to use tanning studios (Mowen et al. 2009). Traits are clearly interrelated, but given the number of traits that have been identified (several thousand, according to some authors) the interrelationships are likely to be complex, especially as people exhibit the different traits to a greater or lesser degree. One last area to mention here is what Keyes et al. (2015) call positive reciprocity. When one increases self-acceptance (liking most parts of one's personality), and also increases social integration (belonging to a community), 'this may cause improvements in personality as reflected in increased extraversion and less neuroticism' (Keyes et al. 2015).

TABLE 7.3 16 personality factor trait analysis

Low range descriptors	Primary factor	High range descriptors
Impersonal, reserved, detached, distant, cool, formal, aloof	Warmth	Warm, easy-going, participating, likes people, outgoing, attentive to others, kindly
Concrete thinking, less intelligent, lower general mental capacity, unable to handle abstract problems	Reasoning	Abstract-thinking, more intelligent, bright, higher general mental capacity, fast learner
Reactive emotionally, changeable, affected by feelings, emotionally less stable, easily upset	Emotional stability	Emotionally stable, adaptive, mature, faces reality calmly
Deferential, cooperative, avoids conflict, submissive, humble, obedient, easily led, docile, accommodating	Dominance	Dominant, forceful, assertive, aggressive, competitive, stubborn, bossy
Serious, restrained, prudent, taciturn, introspective, silent	Liveliness	Lively, animated, spontaneous, enthusiastic, happy-go-lucky, cheerful, expressive, impulsive
Expedient, nonconforming, disregards rules, self-indulgent	Rule consciousness	Rule-conscious, dutiful, conscientious, conforming, moralistic, staid, rule-bound
Shy, threat-sensitive, timid, hesitant, intimidated	Social boldness	Socially bold, venturesome, thick-skinned, uninhibited
Utilitarian, objective, unsentimental, tough minded, self-reliant, no-nonsense, rough	Sensitivity	Sensitive, aesthetic, sentimental, tender-minded, intuitive, refined
Trusting, unsuspecting, accepting, unconditional, easy	Vigilance	Vigilant, suspicious, skeptical, distrustful, oppositional
Grounded, practical, prosaic, solution-oriented, steady, conventional	Abstractedness	Abstract, imaginative, absent-minded, impractical, absorbed in ideas
Forthright, genuine, artless, open, guileless, naive, unpretentious, involved	Privateness	Private, discreet, nondisclosing, shrewd, polished, worldly, astute, diplomatic
Self-assured, unworried, complacent, secure, free of guilt, confident, self-satisfied	Apprehension	Apprehensive, self-doubting, worried, guilt-prone, insecure, worrying, self-blaming
Traditional, attached to familiar, conservative, respecting traditional ideas	Openness to change	Open to change, experimental, liberal, analytical, critical, free-thinking, flexible
Group-oriented, affiliative, a joiner and follower, dependent on others	Self-reliance	Self-reliant, solitary, resourceful, individualistic, self-sufficient
Tolerates disorder, unexacting, flexible, undisciplined, lax, self-conflict, impulsive, careless of social rules, uncontrolled	Perfectionism	Perfectionistic, organized, compulsive, self-disciplined, socially precise, exacting will power, control, self-sentimental
Relaxed, placid, tranquil, torpid, patient, composed, low drive	Tension	Tense, high energy, impatient, driven, frustrated, over-wrought, time-driven

PSYCHOGRAPHICS

Psychographics is sometimes known as lifestyle studies, since it is concerned with people's values and approaches to life. Essentially, it is a quantitative study of consumer lifestyles for the purpose of relating those lifestyles to the consumers' purchase behaviour. For example, somebody who has a 'green' set of values is likely to have an eco-friendly lifestyle, which in turn means that the individual will be more likely to buy a bicycle than a car, and perhaps lean more towards being a vegetarian than eating red meat, and so forth. These ethical values can be powerful forces in decision-making (Shaw et al. 2005; Fraj and Martinez 2006; Dane and Sonenshein 2015). By knowing what a person's basic lifestyle is we can make a fair prediction as to their purchasing behaviour, and the kind of products and promotions that will most appeal to that individual.

Psychographics
Using behavioural tendencies to infer personality traits

The psychographics approach to personality study combines the strengths of motivation research on the one hand with those of trait and factor theories. The assessment of lifestyle often involves very lengthy and involved studies of large samples of the population; the Target Group Index annual research programme, part of Kantar Media Group, and more recently the Kantar Worldpanel, deals in consumer knowledge and insights based on continuous consumer panels. They ask people (approximately 700,000 people across 60 countries) to respond to a multitude of lifestyle statements. From this survey, market monitoring, advanced analytics and other tailored market research solutions, researchers at Kantar can identify different lifestyles and analyse the attitudes behind what people buy and what they consume, and consequently predict different purchasing patterns.

TABLE 7.4 Lifestyle types

	Lifestyle type	Characteristics	% of population
Sustenance-driven groups; motivated by the need for security	Belonger	People who believe in the Establishment, traditional family values and patriotism. Averse to change	19%
	Survivor	People who are fighting a 'holding action'; accept authority, hard-working, quiet, traditional. Strong class consciousness	16%
	Aimless	There are two main categories: young unemployed whose main motivation is short-term 'kicks', and the very old, whose motivation is simply day-to-day existence	5%
Outer-directed group	Conspicuous consumer	Interested in material possessions, taking cues from reference groups (friends, family). Followers of fashion	18%
Inner-directed groups; motivated by self-actualisation	Social resister	Caring group, motivated by ideals of fairness and a good quality of life at the societal level. Altruistic, concerned with social issues like ecology and nuclear disarmament	11%
	Experimentalist	Materialistic and pro-technology, individualistic and interested in novelty	14%
	Self-explorer	Motivated by self-expression and self-realisation. Tolerant, able to think big and look for global, holistic solutions	16%

Source: adapted from W. Kirk McNulty 'UK Social change through a Wide-Angle Lens', Futures, August 1985. Reproduced by kind permission.

An example of this approach is the VALS breakdown referred to in Chapter 2. A UK equivalent to the VALS breakdown (already shown in Chapter 6) was developed by Taylor Nelson, as shown in Table 7.4. The relative percentages of each group are likely to have changed in the intervening 30 years, of course – as noted earlier, there is a trend towards greater inner-directedness.

Psychographics approaches have in common that they all try to predict behaviour from knowledge of lifestyle and attitudes. The drawback with this approach is that the necessary research is complex, time-consuming and ultimately relies heavily on the judgement of the researchers to decide which factors are appropriate to a particular lifestyle.

CHALLENGING THE STATUS QUO

Trying to infer personality types from behaviour seems to be fraught with risk. Someone who describes themselves as environmentally friendly might still drive a car, for example – running your car on biodiesel might be greener than running it on mineral diesel, but does that make you environmentally friendly? Someone might be a humanitarian, but still join the army because being a soldier might be seen as a way of fighting for the greater good of humanity. The list goes on.

People behave in all sorts of funny ways, so aren't we pushing our necks out by trying to guess why they behave the way they do? Are these 'ethical consumers' that we've just talked about willing to pay more for their ethically produced or sourced products? Are indeed the prices higher because the original costs of production are higher? Maybe we can predict behaviour from knowledge of their personality traits, and maybe we can analyse personality traits by observing behaviour, but isn't it just as likely that personality and behaviour have no connection whatever? Or maybe what we are talking about is not something that is absolute and objective, but rather something that is subjective!

The psychographics approach appears to have strong potential to tell us about what people will buy, since clearly most purchases are related to a chosen lifestyle.

Finally, it would be remiss of us to end a chapter on the self and personality without giving a mention to the **selfie**. People's propensity for photographing themselves and posting the pictures online has become the norm worldwide: the word has recently been included in the Oxford Dictionary Online, showing an acceptance by the Establishment.

Selfie
A photograph that one has taken of oneself, typically taken with a smartphone or webcam and shared via social media

There are mixed views about whether taking a selfie is tantamount to self-objectifying or perhaps even narcissistic. A study by Fox and Rooney (2015) examined the relationship between selfie-posting, photo editing and personality. They looked at this from the perspective that there could be three other traits at work here. The first of these is narcissism, which is the notion that some individuals are extremely self-centred to the point of having a grandiose view of themselves (Raskin and Terry 1988). They also have a need to be admired by others around them in the physical as well as the virtual world. Second, there is psychopathy – an impulsive state with a lack of empathy (Jonason and Krause 2013). Third, there is an element of Machiavellianism: being manipulative with disregard for others' needs (Christie and Geis 1970). Some of the findings from Fox and Rooney (2015) are consistent with other research that says that both narcissism and low self-esteem are related to greater Facebook use (Mehdizadeh 2010). This said, even more recent research (Sorokowski et al. 2015) indicates that there are many motivations for selfie posting other than showing off, so perhaps it is a little early to accuse those who post selfies on Facebook of being narcissistic, self-obsessed psychopaths.

SUMMARY

In this chapter we have looked at what constitutes people's self-concept and personalities. We have also looked at role-playing, and have looked at some of the ways these elements affect consumers' buying behaviour.

KEY POINTS

- Self-concept is concerned with one's feelings about oneself.
- Self-concept is learned, stable, purposeful and unique.
- As wealth increases, more people are becoming inner-directed.
- High self-monitors take their cues from others; low self-monitors take their cues from an inner drive.
- Personality is made up of traits; so far several thousand possible traits have been identified.
- Personality is a self-serving, individualistic, unique, overt and consistent gestalt.

HOW TO IMPRESS YOUR EXAMINER

You may be asked to compare the various type approaches to classifying personalities. Note that these type theories are not necessarily mutually exclusive: it would be perfectly possible to classify people across each of the types, because the typologies are based on combinations of traits, and the same traits might be combined in different ways in order to create a typology.

REVIEW QUESTIONS

1. Why are personality traits an important concept for marketers?
2. Why is self-concept such a useful way of segmenting markets?
3. What might be the impact of increased inner direction on fashion in the future?

4. How might high self-monitors respond to an increase in inner direction in the rest of the population?

5. How might the Myers-Briggs type dimensions be used by marketers for a perfume company?

6. What are the marketing implications of the possible self?

7. What are the marketing implications of the gender perception of brands?

CASE STUDY: THE DECADENCE OF JEAN-PAUL GAULTIER

©iStock.com/TayaCho

Jean-Paul Gaultier was born in Val de Marne, France, but was brought up in Paris. His grandmother introduced him to the world of fashion, but he never had any formal training: he got his start in fashion by sending sketches to leading fashion houses, eventually being hired by Pierre Cardin when he was only 18.

Gaultier has always been a controversial, non-conforming figure in the fashion industry. His playful, irreverent style has caught the attention of film producers and celebrities as well as the general public: he designed the famous (or infamous) cone bra worn by Madonna, and designed the costumes for many films including *The Fifth Element*, *Bad Education*, *Kika* and *The Cook, The Thief, His Wife, and Her Lover*. He pioneered the return of the kilt to fashion, getting his inspiration from the punk era, and has experimented with unisex fashions. His love of the avant-garde has not harmed his career: apart from his own labels, he was artistic and creative director of Hermès from 2003 to 2010, and Hermès now owns a substantial chunk of Gaultier's own company.

He has not confined himself to fashion design, either. From 1993 to 1997 he co-hosted the anarchic, late-night, magazine-style TV show *Eurotrash* (showcasing a comical review of unusual and quite often erotic topics mainly from Western and Central Europe) with Antoine de Caunes, and he released a record in 1988 entitled 'How to Do That'. In recent years he has been at the forefront of the perfume industry, pioneering perfumes for men and even a unisex perfume. Perhaps surprisingly, his perfumes for men have been more successful than those for women: Le Mâle, his flagship male perfume, was the number-one male perfume in Europe in 2008, with strong sales in the USA and Australia as well, while his women's perfume Fragile was discontinued due to poor sales. The distinctive bottles, shaped like human torsos, may have helped a great deal in the success of the products. Some research indicates that the bulk of male perfume and aftershave is actually bought by women, as gifts for their husbands and boyfriends. This may also apply to women's fragrances, of course.

He is also the only fashion designer to have been appointed as a judge for the Cannes Film Festival, and his fashion designs have been exhibited in art galleries worldwide. His talent for self-publicity has led to a documentary about his life.

Gaultier has also been controversial in his use of models. He frequently uses models who do not fit the standard fashion-model image: older men, full-figured women, heavily tattooed or pierced models, and even transgender models have appeared on his catwalks. This has caused him both criticism and acclaim, the former from the fashion industry who see it as a gimmick, the latter from the public who see it as a breakthrough for 'normal' people.

In the world of fashion there are many famous names, yet few famous faces. Pierre Cardin, Christian Dior and Hardy Amies are familiar names yet their faces are largely unknown. Jean Paul Gaultier has one of the best-known faces in fashion, yet people constantly find themselves surprised when they see his designs or film credits. He has had a hugely successful career, mainly from breaking the mould: being the *enfant terrible* of French fashion might have earned him criticism at times, but it has also earned him a great deal of recognition and, of course, money. During the 2015 Spring/ Summer Collection Show, Gaultier announced to the world that he was bringing to an end his ready-to-wear range of labels in order to concentrate on haute couture.

QUESTIONS

1. How might the use of atypical models have helped Gaultier's success?

2. Why might the torso-shaped bottles have been so successful?

3. Why do women buy perfume for men?

4. What needs are served by buying fashion items?

5. What effect might his appearances on *Eurotrash* have had on his customers?

FURTHER READING

For an interesting and wider insight into the issues discussed in the chapter case study, see Cunningham, P. A. (2016) *Fashion in Popular Culture. A Companion to Popular Culture*. Chapter 20.

Concepts of the Self by Anthony Elliott (Cambridge: Polity Press, 2007) gives an overview of the key arguments in self-concept. It's a straightforward, lively account, which gives the counter-arguments as well as the theories, so that the various thinkers are linked together well.

Otto Kroeger and Janet M. Theussen's book *Type Talk: The 16 Personality Types*, 10th edn (New York: Bantam Doubleday Dell, 1989) gives a lot of applied examples of the Myers-Briggs Type Indicator. This is a very useful book in understanding why people behave the way they do.

REFERENCES

Baker, S.L., McCabe, S.D., Swithers, S.E., Payne, C.R. and Kranz, S. (2015). Do healthy, child-friendly fruit and vegetable snacks appeal to consumers? A field study exploring adults' perceptions and purchase intentions. *Food Quality and Preference*, 39: 202–8.

Balabanis, G. (2002) The relationship between lottery ticket and scratchcard buying behaviour, personality and other compulsive behaviours. *Journal of Consumer Behaviour*, 2 (1): 7–22.

Banister, E.N. and Hogg, M.K. (2003) Possible selves? Identifying dimensions for exploring the dialectic between positive and negative selves in consumer behaviour. *Advances in Consumer Research*, 30: 149–50.

Bartikowski, B. and Walsh, G. (2015) Attitude toward cultural diversity: a test of identity-related antecedents and purchasing consequences. *Journal of Business Research*, 68 (3): 526–33.

Belk, R. (2003) Shoes and self. *Advances in Consumer Research*, 30: 27–33.

Brendl, C.M., Chattopadhyay, A., Pelham, B.W., Carvalho, M. and Prichard, E.T. (2003) Are brands containing name letters preferred? *Advances in Consumer Research*, 30 (1): 151–2.

Briggs, K. and Myers, I. (1962) *Manual: The Myers-Briggs Type Indicator*. Princeton, NJ: Educational Testing Service.

Cattell, H.E.P. and Mead, A.D. (2008) The sixteen personality factor questionnaire (16PF). In G. Boyle, G. Matthews and D.H. Saklofske (eds), *The Sage Handbook of Personality Theory and Assessment, Vol. 2. Personality Measurement and Testing*. Los Angeles, CA: Sage, pp. 135–78.

Cattell, R.B. (1946) *The Description and Measurement of Personality*. New York: World Books.

Christie, R. and Geis, F.L. (1970) *Studies in Machiavellianism*. New York: Academic Press.

Clark, R.A., Goldsmith, R.E. and Goldsmith, E.B. (2008) Market mavenism and consumer self-confidence. *Journal of Consumer Behaviour*, 7 (3): 239–48.

Cohen, J.B. (1967) An interpersonal orientation to the study of consumer behaviour. *Journal of Marketing Research*, 6 (August): 270–8.

Conn, S.R. and Rieke, M.L. (1994) *The 16PF Fifth Edition Technical Manual*. Champaign, IL: Institute for Personality and Ability Testing, Inc.

Cooper, C. (2015) *Individual Differences and Personality*, 3rd edn. Abingdon: Routledge.

Dane, E. and Sonenshein, S. (2015) On the role of experience in ethical decision making at work: An ethical expertise perspective. *Organizational Psychology Review*, 5 (1): 74–96.

Davies, M.F. (2003) Confirmatory bias in the evaluation of personality descriptions: positive test strategies and output interference. *Journal of Personality and Social Psychology*, 85 (4): 736–44

deBerry-Spence, B. and Izberk-Bilgin, E. (2006) Wearing identity: the symbolic uses of native African clothing by African Americans. *Advances in Consumer Research*, 33: 193.

Donnelly, J.H. Jr. (1970) Social character and the acceptance of new products. *Journal of Marketing Research*, 7 (February): 111–13.

Fox, J. and Rooney, M.C. (2015) The Dark Triad and trait self-objectification as predictors of men's use and self-presentation behaviors on social networking sites. *Personality & Individual Differences*, 76: 161–5.

Foxall, G. (1980) *Consumer Behaviour: A Practical Guide*. London: Routledge.

Fraj, E. and Martinez, E. (2006) Influence of personality on ecological consumer behaviour. *Journal of Consumer Behaviour*, 5 (May–June): 167–81.

Goleman, D. (1987) Basic personality traits don't change, studies say. *New York Times*, 18 June.

Hollensen, S. (2015) *Marketing Management: A Relationship Approach*. Harlow: Pearson Education.

Horney, K. (1945) *Our Inner Conflict*. New York: W.W. Norton.

Jonason, P.K. and Krause, L. (2013) The emotional deficits associated with the Dark Triad traits: Cognitive empathy, affective empathy, and alexithymia. *Personality & Individual Differences*, 55: 532–7

Jung, K. and Lee, W. (2006) Cross-gender brand extensions: effects of gender of the brand, gender of the consumer, and product type on cross-gender extensions. *Advances in Consumer Research*, 33: 67–74.

Keyes, C.L., Kendler, K.S., Myers, J.M. and Martin, C.C. (2015) The genetic overlap and distinctiveness of flourishing and the big five personality traits. *Journal of Happiness Studies*, 16 (3): 655–66.

Klein, J.G. (2003) Calories for dignity: fashion in the concentration camp. *Advances in Consumer Research*, 30: 34–7.

Kleine, R.E., III, K., Schultz, S. and Brunswick, G.J. (2009) Transformational consumption choices: building an understanding by integrating social identity and multi-attribute attitude theories. *Journal of Consumer Behaviour*, 8 (1): 54–70.

McNulty, W.K. (1985) UK social change through a wide-angle lens. *Futures*, August.

Mehdizadeh, S. (2010) Self-presentation 2.0: narcissism and self-esteem on Facebook. *Cyberpsychology, Behavior, and Social Networking*, 13: 357–64. doi: 10.1089/cyber.2009.0257.

Mokhtar, I., Osman, I., Setapa, F. and Zambahari, S.R. (2015) A qualitative study on the determinants of Islamic credit card ownership and usage. In R. Hashimand Abdul, A.B. Majeed (eds), *Proceedings of the Colloquium on Administrative Science and Technology*. Singapore: Springer, pp. 423–35.

Mowen, J.C., Longoria, A. and Sallee, A. (2009) Burning and cutting: identifying the traits of individuals with an enduring propensity to tan and to undergo cosmetic surgery. *Journal of Consumer Behaviour*, 8 (5): 238–51.

Nantel, J. and Strahle, W. (1986) The self-monitoring concept: a consumer perspective. *Advances in Consumer Research*, 13: 83–7.

Nuttall, P. (2009) Insiders, regulars and tourists: exploring selves and music consumption in adolescence. *Journal of Consumer Behaviour*, 8 (4): 211–24.

Oakley, A. (2015) *Sex, Gender and Society*. Farnham: Ashgate Publishing.

Pentina, I., Taylor, D.G. and Voelker, T.A. (2009) The roles of self-discrepancy and social support in young females' decisions to undergo cosmetic procedures. *Journal of Consumer Behaviour*, 8 (4): 149–65.

Perry, V.G. (2001) Antecedents of consumer financing decisions: a mental accounting model of revolving credit usage. *Advances in Consumer Research*, 28: 13.

Raskin, R. and Terry, H. (1988) A principal-components analysis of the Narcissistic Personality Inventory and further evidence of its construct validity. *Journal of Personality & Social Psychology*, 54: 890–902.

Reisman, D. (1953) *The Lonely Crowd*. New York: Doubleday.

Roberts, B.W. and DelVecchio, W.F. (2000) The rank-order consistency of personality traits from childhood to old age: a quantitative review of longitudinal studies. *Psychological Bulletin*, 126 (1): 3.

Roberts, B.W. and Mroczek, D. (2008) Personality trait change in adulthood. *Current Directions in Psychological Science*, 17 (1): 31–5.

Roberts, B.W., Walton, K.E. and Viechtbauer, W. (2006) Patterns of mean-level change in personality traits across the life course: a meta-analysis of longitudinal studies. *Psychological Bulletin*, 132 (1): 1.

Schmitt, J. and Rasolofoarison, D. (2015) Disentangling individual and contextual shopping motivations. In M. Conway Dato-on (ed.), *The Sustainable Global Marketplace: Proceedings of the 2011 Academy of Marketing Science (AMS) Annual Conference*, Developments in Marketing Science: Proceedings of the Academy of Marketing Science. London: Springer International Publishing, pp. 176–80.

Shaw, D., Grehan, E., Shiu, E., Hassan, L. and Thomson, J. (2005) An exploration of values in ethical consumer decision-making. *Journal of Consumer Behaviour*, 4 (3): 185–200.

Sheth, J.N. and Sisodia, R.S. (2015) *Does Marketing Need Reform? Fresh Perspectives on the Future*. Abington: Routledge.

Snyder, M. (1974) Self-monitoring of expressive behaviour. *Journal of Personality and Social Psychology*, 34: 526–37.

Sorokowski, P., Sorokowska, A., Oleszkiewicz, A., Frackowiak, T., Huk, A. and Pisanski, K. (2015) Selfie posting behaviors are associated with narcissism among men. *Personality and Individual Differences*, 85: 123–7.

Stokburger-Sauer, N.E. and Hoyer, W.D. (2009) Consumer advisors revisited: what drives those with market mavenism and opinion leadership tendencies and why? *Journal of Consumer Behaviour*, 7 (3): 100–15.

Thompson, E.R. and Prendergast, G.P. (2015) The influence of trait affect and the five-factor personality model on impulse buying. *Personality and Individual Differences*, 76: 216–21.

Tuncay, L. (2006) Men's responses to depictions of ideal masculinity in advertising. *Advances in Consumer Research*, 33: 64.

Visinescu, L.L., Sidorova, A., Jones, M.C. and Prybutok, V.R. (2015) The influence of website dimensionality on customer experiences, perceptions and behavioral intentions: an exploration of 2D vs. 3D web design. *Information & Management*, 52 (1): 1–17.

Vohs, K. and Faber, R. (2003) Self-regulation and impulsive spending patterns. *Advances in Consumer Research*, 30: 125–6.

Walker, B.A. (1992) New perspectives for self-research. *Advances in Consumer Research*, 19: 417–23.

Wang, Y.Y., Shanmugam, M., Hajli, N. and Bugshan, H. (2015) Customer attitudes towards Internet banking and social media on Internet banking in the UK. In N. Hajli (ed.), *Handbook of Research on Integrating Social Media into Strategic Marketing*. Hershey, PA: IGI Global, pp. 287–302.

Wood, N., Chaplin, L.N. and Solomon, M. (2009) Virtually me: youth consumers and their online identities. *Advances in Consumer Research*, 36: 23–4.

Zinkhan, G.M. and Shermohamad, A. (1986) Is other-directedness on the increase? An empirical test of Reisman's theory of social character. *Journal of Consumer Research*, 13 (June): 127–30.

MORE ONLINE

For additional materials that support this chapter and your learning, please visit:
https://study.sagepub.com/sethnaandblythe

CHAPTER 8

PERCEPTION

LEARNING OBJECTIVES

After reading this chapter you should be able to:

- Explain the role of analysis and synthesis in perception.
- Explain the role of synergy in creating a perceptual impression.
- Understand the problem created for marketers by selectivity.
- Explain how past experience affects perception.
- Describe Weber's Law.
- Describe the relationship between perception and reality.
- Explain the conscious and unconscious aspects of perception.
- Explain the difference between internal and overt perceptual responses.
- Discuss subliminal advertising.
- Explain the role of colour in perception.

INTRODUCTION

How we analyse the environment around us and develop a picture of the world is of great interest to marketers. Ensuring that the company's brands become part of the world-view of the potential consumers is the main purpose of marketing communications: understanding perception processes is what puts the product there.

Perception is the keystone of building knowledge, not just about products and everything associated with them but also about everything else in the world. Although it is common to refer to perception as if it were somehow different from the truth, this is not the case: perceptions may differ between individuals, but for each person their own perception *is* the whole truth. This is sometimes difficult to remember – but in fact, our whole experience of the world happens inside our heads, filtered by our senses and moderated by our previous experiences within any given environment.

ELEMENTS OF PERCEPTION

Perception is a process of converting sensory input into an understanding of how the world works (Kenyon and Sen 2015). Because the process involves combining many different sensory inputs, the overall result is complex to analyse; for example, people often judge fabrics by touch, but memory and confidence in the evaluation is improved if the 'touch' input is reinforced with verbal information (d'Astous and Kamau 2010). Human beings have considerably more than five senses. Apart from

TABLE 8.1 Conventions about perception

Convention	Explanation
Perception is about more than the substantive part of the message	Messages may be expressed directly in words, but the observer 'reads between the lines' and creates new meanings from what is seen or read
The law of similarity says that we interpret new information in a similar way to information we already hold	If we read a news report in a newspaper we trust to be accurate, we will tend to assume that the news report is also accurate. If we see packaging (for example, a brown coffee jar) we will associate this with similar brown packaging on other brands of coffee
Expectations	If we expect a particular sequence of events, or a particular message, then we tend to see that message and interpret accordingly
'Figure–ground' relationships influence interpretation	An individual will interpret a printed message differently according to which part of the image is interpreted as the message and which part as the background
The Law of Closure	This means that people can only obtain the whole message if they have all the components of the message. This particularly applies in advertisements that are intended to intrigue consumers: an advertisement that contains a puzzle or a visual joke will not be understood by the observers unless they are in possession of enough information to infer the punch line
The Law of Continuity	Gestalt perception is based on the idea that the elements of the overall message form a continuum rather than a set of separate elements. In other words, even when a particular stimulus (for example an advertisement) is composed of music, speech, pictures and moving images the person watching it will still form an overall impression. Of course, someone who is asked to analyse an advertisement will be able to separate out the various elements, but in normal behaviour few people would do this
The whole is greater than the sum of its parts	When the message consists of a number of elements, the elements often combine to create a stronger message
Colour influences perception	Because human beings have a well-developed colour sense, colours are often influential in creating an overall image of a product. This may be due to the need, in prehistoric times, for hunter–gatherers to assess the ripeness or nutritional value of fruit

the basic five (touch, taste, smell, sight, hearing) there are senses of direction, sense of balance, a clear knowledge of which way is down, and so forth. Each sense is feeding information to the brain constantly, and the amount of information being collected would seriously overload the system if one took it all in. The brain therefore selects from the surroundings and cuts out anything that seems or is irrelevant in a given situation.

In effect, the brain makes automatic decisions as to what is relevant and what is not. Even though there may be many things happening around you, you are unaware of most of them; for example, experiments have shown that some information is filtered out by the optic nerve even before it gets to the brain. People quickly learn to ignore extraneous noises; for example, as a visitor to someone else's home you may be sharply aware of the noise from the dishwasher, whereas your host may be entirely used to it and unaware of it except when making a conscious effort to check that the machine is still cycling.

There are eight main conventions regarding perception, as shown in Table 8.1.

Perception is, in part, a process of analysis in which the outside world is filtered and only the most important or interesting (as defined by the individual) items come through. Therefore, the information entering the brain does not provide a complete view of the world.

In Figure 8.1, most of the stimuli surrounding the individual are filtered out. The remaining stimuli are combined and interpreted, then included with memory and imagination to create an overall perception.

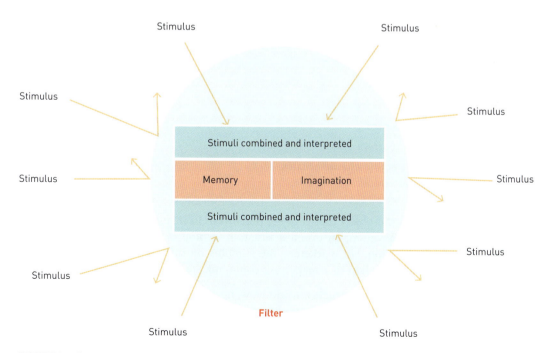

FIGURE 8.1 Selectivity and synthesis

CHALLENGING THE STATUS QUO

If perception is reality, are we imagining most of the world? Over 50 years ago, some research was conducted by Bugelski and Alampay (1961). In their experiment, half of the people were shown pictures of animals in black and white and the other half were shown pictures of humans in black and white. Then they showed every person an ambiguous picture and asked what the people saw. Most of the people that saw the animal pictures before usually said they saw a rat while the people that saw pictures of humans before usually said they saw an old man with glasses. The reason that this happened is because they were used to seeing a human or animal since they had seen so many already and this caused them to have a perceptual set on the ambiguous picture.

Fast-forward 40 years and we still believed what we thought we knew to be true. Research by Professor Patrali Chatterjee of Rutgers University (2001) showed that consumers patronising a familiar retailer, either online or in-store, are less receptive to negative WOM information and seek less information. In short, they will not accept any negativity about a product/brand with which they are very happy. They know what they know, and that's all there is to it!

In both these examples, there is an element of hyper-reality; what was initially simulation or 'hype' suddenly becomes real.

Hyper-reality

An inability of consciousness to distinguish reality from a simulation or reality

CREATING A WORLD-VIEW

The perception process is a social-psychological phenomenon. It involves cue selection and cue interpretation, and combining these cues to create an overall impression. Warr and Knapper (1968) identified six components of perception, as follows:

1. Stimulus
2. Input selector
3. Processing centre
4. Consumer's current state
5. Consumer's stable characteristics
6. Response

The stimulus is the object that is being perceived. In this sense, the object could be a person, an innovation, an event, a situation, a blog or anything that catches the individual's attention. For marketers, the stimulus on offer is likely to be a brand, a product, an e-retail shop or a marketing communication.

When the individual constructs a world-view, he or she assembles information to map what is happening in the outside world. Any gaps (and there will, of course, be plenty of these) will be filled in by using imagination and experience. The cognitive map is therefore not a 'photograph'; it is (at least in part) a construct of the imagination. This mapping will be affected by the following factors:

1. **Subjectivity**. This is the existing world-view within the individual, and is unique to that individual. People have differing views of the world – this is what makes being a human being so much fun, because we argue a lot – and this means that we interpret any incoming stimuli differently according to who we are.

2. **Categorisation**. This is the 'pigeonholing' of information, and the prejudging of events and products. This can happen through a process known as **chunking** whereby the individual organises information into chunks of related items (Miller 1956). For example, a picture seen while a particular piece of music is playing might be chunked as one item in the memory, so that sight of the picture evokes the music and vice versa.

3. **Selectivity**. This is the degree to which the brain is selecting from the environment. It is a function of how much is going on around the individual, and also of how selective (concentrated) the individual is on the current task. Selectivity is also subjective; some people are a great deal more selective than others. Research shows that people judge the authenticity of Irish themed pubs by the behaviour of the employees and the patrons rather than from the decor, showing that people are being selective in the factors they use to judge the pub (Munoz et al. 2006).

4. **Expectations**. These lead individuals to interpret later information in a specific way. For example, look at this series of numbers and letters:

A	13	C	D	E	F	G	H	I
10	**11**	**12**	**13**	**14**	**15**	**16**	**17**	**18**

In fact, the number 13 appears in both series, but in the first series it may well be interpreted as a B because that is what the brain is being led to expect.

5. **Law of Primacy**. Past experience leads us to interpret later experience in the light of what we already know. This is called the Law of Primacy by psychologists. For example, adverts shown early in ad breaks generate greater brand recall than those in later slots (Li 2010). Sometimes sights, smells or sounds from our past will trigger off inappropriate responses; the smell of bread baking may recall a village bakery from 20 years ago, but in fact the smell could have been artificially generated by an aerosol spray near the supermarket bread counter.

An example of cognitive mapping as applied to perception of product quality might run as follows. The individual uses the input selector to select clues and assign values to them. For quality, the cues are typically price, brand name and retailer name. Most of us, rightly or wrongly, assume that a higher-priced product will be better quality, and also that a well-known brand name will be better than a generic product; although the retailer name is less significant, it still carries some weight. For example, many consumers would feel confident that a major London department store such as Fortnum and Mason's would sell higher-quality items than the local corner shop, but might be less able to distinguish between own-label products from rival supermarket chains such as Sainsbury's and Tesco.

The input selector is the mechanism by which the individual selects cues from the stimulus and assigns a meaning to each one. The input selector takes the various environmental factors and processes them one at a time: the processing centre has the task of integrating the cues to generate an overall perception. The input selector

Subjectivity

Judging everything from a personal viewpoint

Categorisation

The pigeonholing of information in order to prejudge events and products

Chunking

The learning process by which items of information are grouped by the brain

Selectivity

The part of perception that deals with rejecting unnecessary stimuli

Expectations

The existing information and attitudes that cause people to interpret later information in a specific way

Law of Primacy

First experiences affect the interpretation of later experiences and the processing centre are not actually separate functions: they almost certainly operate at the same time, because the cues are delivered simultaneously or at least very closely after one another. For example, someone seeing an online advertisement for an e-cigarette might remember the shape but not the make, or might remember the background detail of the advertisement (the environment in which the e-cigarette is being smoked, perhaps) and remember nothing about the product itself. It has been shown that people perceive a task as being more difficult if the instructions on how to do it are written in a hard-to-read font (Song and Schwarz 2009). It becomes even more difficult if the instructions are hidden and impossible to read without first opening the packaging, as is the case sometimes with fresh meat and cooking instructions.

This is a perennial problem in marketing communications. Knowing which cues people most often select is clearly of great interest, especially if we are considering a specific factor such as quality. In some cases people judge quality on the basis of price, in other cases on the physical attributes of the product, but the consensus view is that the use of an extrinsic cue such as price and intrinsic cues such as physical and performance attributes depend on prior knowledge (Rao and Monroe 1988). As consumers become more familiar with the product's intrinsic attributes, price becomes less important as a surrogate for judging quality. In some cases, products are consumed almost entirely for their symbolic value: in some emerging economies, such as China, products are often bought simply because they are Western brands. These brands are sometimes desired even when the consumer has never seen the actual product (Clark et al. 2002).

CONSUMER BEHAVIOUR IN ACTION: E-COMMERCE IN CHINA

©iStock.com/William_Potter

The global press is full of stories about how China is set to become an economic superpower (see for instance *Chindia Rising: How China and India Will Benefit Your Business* by Professor Jagdish Sheth, 2008). However, you really need to have a look at some of the figures and the popular websites to start to understand the impact that Chinese consumers are having on the global economy. According to Alexa (which ranks sites based primarily on tracking a sample of Internet traffic), Taobao (which is similar to eBay and is China's largest consumer to consumer portal) is ranked 8th globally. In 2013, its parent company Alibaba had revenues totalling $250 billion, which is significantly larger than Amazon's $75 billion.

    The number comparisons don't end there. Taobao has over a billion products for sale on its website, and on National Singles Day (celebrated on 11 November 2014)

Taobao sold $9 billion worth of products compared to Cyber Monday in the USA, which only generated $2.65 billion across all its access points.

Then there is the visual perception aspect. The difference between Amazon and Taobao is very easy to see. To consumers who are used to shopping on Amazon, their perception of the Taobao site is that it looks a mess – with products being crammed into every crevice on the screen. Conversely, to Chinese consumers the Amazon site is just too sparse and therefore they cannot make any decent comparisons of products, without wasting time going backwards and forwards between screens.

One final point to consider here is that Chinese consumers are seemingly not attracted by lifestyle, so the wider environment within which we would 'frame' the product using a lifestyle backdrop for advertisements is of little consequence to Chinese consumers. They don't want to see the product being used in situ – they just want to see the product. This said, it is therefore surprising that the Chinese view ecommerce as a leisure activity. Shopping online, receiving super-efficient service and then waiting for that neat package to be delivered is a very important part of the whole ecommerce process which the Chinese consumer relishes.

The processing centre is likely to be influenced by the individual's current state. The current state includes factors such as mood, motivation, goals and the physical state of the individual at the time the cues come along. A mood is transitory: it will pass, no matter how strongly it is felt at the time. When we are in a good mood we tend to feel favourably towards more cues, whereas if we are in a bad mood we tend to be negative about cues. This is partly responsible for the halo effect (or horns effect) in which we tend to think that if one thing is bad about something, everything is bad about it. If people feel a momentary disgust with a company or a product this will carry over into future decisions, changing the status quo (Han and Lerner 2008). Positive moods tend to create less elaboration (i.e. people think less when they are in a good mood) and decisions are often made much more automatically than would normally be the case (Batra and Stayman 1990). There is evidence that marketing messages that express positive outcomes are much more effective than those that

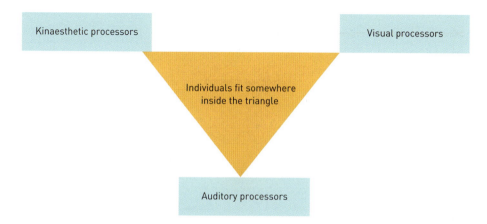

FIGURE 8.2 Information processing types

stress negative outcomes, presumably because the former create good moods whereas the latter create fearful or worried moods (Zhao and Pechmann 2006). On the other hand, sad expressions on the faces of victims generate greater charitable donations, perhaps because donors feel the need to change the unpleasant feelings that arise from seeing the charity's advertisements (Small and Verrochi 2008).

HOW WE PROCESS DATA IN OUR HEAD

Kinaesthetic

A learning style in which learning takes place by the students carrying out physical activities

Individuals process information in individual ways, of course: neuro-linguistic programming theory tells us that some people prefer to process visual information, some prefer auditory information and yet others prefer tactile or kinaesthetic processing. Most of us are on a continuum on which we absorb and process cues from all three areas: it is simply that we prefer one route over another.

Visual processors are likely to respond better to advertising with strong graphics or visual content. Auditory processors prefer the spoken word or music. Kinaesthetic processors prefer to touch or try out products, so would be most likely to respond to advertising that offers a trial or free sample. As shown in Figure 8.2, most people fit somewhere inside a triangle formed by the three processing methods, favouring one or other but still able to process information in all three ways.

Thus we need to start to investigate what influences our choice of the processing methods. There are five main influences on perceptual mapping, as shown in Figure 8.3.

The information is subjective in that people base decisions on the selected information. Each of us selects differently from the environment, and each of us has differing views. In the case of distinguishing between rival supermarket chains, each individual will have a slightly different view of the supermarkets concerned. If this were not so, we would rapidly develop a situation in which only one supermarket chain existed. The individual's previous experience also has a bearing – for example, research shows that adolescents who live in areas where there are high levels of drug use and sexual promiscuity over-estimate their own knowledge of these things (Parker et al. 2006).

FIGURE 8.3 Influences on perceptual mapping

CULTURE AND PERCEPTION

Culture also plays a part in perception – people who come from countries where the architecture is based on circles and cylinders (for example, rural Zambia) rather than squares and boxes sometimes have difficulty interpreting two-dimensional pictures, because they have had less experience in understanding perspective. Equally, culture affects the ways in which people interpret gestures, pictures, tones of voice and many other signals – for example, in many Indian languages a question is indicated by the use of a falling tone at the end of the sentence, whereas in English it is indicated by a rising tone. For an English speaker, someone speaking with a falling tone at the end of a sentence would sound as if they are making a flat statement, which in some contexts may sound strange or even offensive, leading to a false perception of the speaker. This false perception can also be true of many young people who have developed a habit of speaking with an 'upward inflection' – or a rising tone at the end of each sentence they speak; which makes them sound as if they are continually asking questions.

Information about quality will be pigeonholed, or **categorised**, so that products from different categories might be placed next to each other in the cognitive map. For example, an individual may put Jaguar in the same category as BMW, but might also include Pure or Bose in the same grouping. It is common to hear people refer to a product as 'the Rolls Royce of …' whichever product category is under consideration – denoting that Rolls Royce is the comparison point of all brands.

Categorised

Placing products together based on information e.g. quality

Selectivity will depend on how much is going on in the environment, on the individual's interest and motivation regarding the subject area, and on the degree of concentration the individual has on the task in hand. People with a highly developed ability to concentrate select less from the environment, because they are able to 'shut out' the world much more.

Expectations of quality play a huge part: if the individual is expecting a high-quality item, he or she will select evidence that supports that view and tend to ignore evidence that doesn't.

Past experience will also play a part in quality judgement. If the consumer has had bad experiences of Japanese products, this might lead to a general perception that Japanese products are poor quality.

Price has a strong effect on people's assessment of products. Researchers have shown that people's confidence in guessing the 'right' price for an article varies according to how many zeroes there are in the stated price – the more zeroes, the greater the confidence in the guess (Thomas et al. 2010). People tend to think that a bargain is a better bargain if they also think that the marketers have made a mistake, in other words if people think the product has been accidentally marked at the wrong price they will tend to see it as a better bargain than if the marketers are explicit about the offer (Bardhi and Eckhardt 2010).

The downside from a marketer's viewpoint is that price has a negative effect on perceived value and on willingness to buy. The problem therefore lies in knowing how big a price reduction will increase sales without leading to a negative perception of quality. **Weber's Law** states that the size of the least detectable change depends on the size of the stimulus. This means that a very intense stimulus will require a bigger

Weber's Law

The size of the least detectable change will depend on the size of the stimulus change if the change is to be perceived by the consumer. For example, £1 off the price of a bar of Lindt chocolate is a substantial discount of almost 50%, and would attract attention in advertising; £1 off the price of a BMW would go unnoticed. Clearly at this level of intensity (a price of a few pence compared with a price of thousands of pounds) Weber's Law may not work very precisely but in the middle range of prices the Law appears to work well. Incidentally, reducing the price from £10 to £9.99 is very noticeable even though the actual reduction is only 0.01% of the initial price. The important element here is that the reduction should be noticeable.

Weber's Law also applies to product differentiation. The Law can be applied to determine how much better the product has to be for the difference to be noticeable, or conversely to determine how similar the product needs to be to be indistinguishable from the leading brand. Branding is all about perception. The marketer's aim is to develop the most favourable perception possible of the brand through working with its strengths, whether the brand's strength lies in its quality, its price competitiveness, or any other area. Developing a suitable brand personality means encouraging people to imbue the brand with human characteristics – which means assembling a range of stimuli to create an overall image.

USING OUR EARS TO EAT

Since the turn of the 21st century, we have seen a proliferation of studies which emanate from the intersection of neurophysiology, cognitive neuroscience and psychophysics – which according to Charles Spence (2015) 'highlight the multisensory nature of human perception'. Using senses which (at first sight) appear to be unrelated to the primary senses to which the product relates can be extremely powerful: for example, the 'snap, crackle and pop' of Rice Krispies relates sound to the brand, whereas one would normally expect a food product to be primarily concerned with flavour and (perhaps) texture. People are prepared to pay more for food that is well-presented – up to 140% more in some cases (Payne and Wansink 2010).

What essentially we are referring to here is the interaction of audition, aroma, vision, touch and flavour (Spence 2015). Anyone who has eaten crisps will know that it's virtually impossible to do so without making a noise. Some experiments have been conducted in the use of multisensory brands. Sound can most definitely impact on the experience one has with food and drink (Stuckey 2012). Researchers have named this 'eating with our ears' (Spence 2015). Think of the crunch of Walkers Extra Crunchy Crisps (which featured an advertisement with the pop star Lionel Richie) or the bubbles and fizz of the Moët & Chandon champagne campaign with Scarlett Johannsson. In fact, Zampini and Spence (2004) conducted an experiment where respondents graded the sound emanating from individually biting into 180 Pringles. The sounds (both volume and frequency) had been manipulated by a computer, which resulted in participants believing that the crisps had come from different packets and were at different stages of freshness and staleness! A similar experiment was recently carried out with apples too (Demattè et al. 2014). Spence (2015) has also written about the sound of 'carbonation', 'creaminess', 'crunch' and squeaky foods such as halloumi cheese. Conversely, with aroma in mind, Nike found that people who tried out their trainers in a floral-scented room preferred them to the same trainers when they tried them in a non-scented room (Lindstrom 2005). Obviously if the fragrance is an inherent part of the product (for example, soap) any changes in the fragrance will have a profound effect on perception of the brand, even when the primary function of the brand is unaffected (Milotic 2003). So how much does the physical environment affect our perception of a product/service and in turn, our ability to make purchase decisions?

ENVIRONMENTAL INFLUENCES

The environment refers to the physical surroundings in which decision-making takes place. It includes physical objects (the products themselves, the display stands in stores and even the stores themselves), spatial relationships (the location of products in stores, the amount of space available within the stores, the location of the stores) and the behaviour of other people within the environment.

For example, the shopping experience in an upmarket department store such as Harrods in London, El Corte Ingles in Madrid or Bungalow 8 in Mumbai is a great deal different from the shopping experience in markets such as Brick Lane in London, the Rastro market in Madrid or the Chor Bazaar in Mumbai. The actual goods on offer may even be the same in many cases, but the level of service, the behaviour of fellow shoppers and the general atmosphere will be totally different, as of course will be the prices.

Figure 8.4 shows some of the relationships between elements of the environment. The level of service, decor, presence or absence of music, and the other customers in the store all affect the store's brand image, but other factors over which the store management has little or no control will also affect the functional environment, which in turn affects the buying behaviour of the individual shoppers.

FIGURE 8.4 Elements in the environment

PERCEPTION AND STORE ATMOSPHERICS

Class

The social and economic grouping of individuals

At a more subtle level, people may be influenced by factors such as music played within the store, use of colour in the store and the perceived social class of other store users. For a marketer, the difficulty lies in assessing which factors are crucial, and how those factors might affect different people; some people like to have music playing in-store, for example, whereas others are irritated by it. Likewise, some people enjoy the buzz and bustle of shopping in a street market, whereas others might find it distracting or even threatening.

Atmospherics

The factors that create the overall ambience in a retail environment

The concept of store atmospherics was first described by Kotler (1973). Atmospherics are all the factors that go to make up the atmosphere and general 'feel' of a retail store: the decor, the music, the temperature and humidity, and so forth. There are three factors in the information processing of store atmospherics: proxemics, kinesics and paralanguage (see Figure 8.5).

Proxemics

The use of physical space to convey a perceptual stimulus

Proxemics refers to the use of physical space in conveying a perceptual stimulus. In a retail environment, for example, a shop assistant might stand too far away (which might be interpreted as dislike for the customer) or too close (suggesting a threatening invasion of personal space). Kinesics is about body language, eye contact and gesture: greater eye contact between buyers and sellers would indicate positive feelings between them. Paralanguage refers to the way words are used, for example the use of 'here' and 'this' is more positive than using 'there' and 'that'. Some other sound cues such as yawning, speaking too loudly or too softly, or speaking too quickly or too slowly also convey messages about how the individual feels about the product.

Kinesics

The interpretation of non-verbal communications related to body movement

Paralanguage

Communication carried out in a manner other than through words

FIGURE 8.5 Perception and store atmospherics

CHALLENGING THE STATUS QUO

We are all aware that body language makes a great deal of difference to communications. Gestures and subtleties of facial expression can completely change the meaning of words used. Yet most of this happens without us even being aware of it. We operate on gut feeling – we get a sense of when someone is lying, for example, without necessarily being able to say what particular facial expression or gesture gave the game away. Body language coaches will often teach that standing 'openly' is a sign of welcoming – they call this 'open assertion' – a way of both your body and voice talking clearly and assertively but neither dominating nor submitting. Then there is the 'match and move'. Starting off by reflecting the stances – matching body language and employing a similar verbal style. This, coupled with perhaps 'leaning in' a little, helps to create an emotional bond. But beware ... lean in too far and you're in danger of invading 'personal space'!

So how can we possibly expect to train shop assistants to behave in a particular way? Aren't we liable to make poor play-actors out of them, and thus give customers the impression that we are lying to them?

Or maybe we should just hire nice people to begin with? Well, retailers have become adept at training their staff to use tricks of the trade and make subtle moves which use body language to influence their customers. For instance, raising eyebrows or tilting the head slightly to show surprise, smiling to show a liking of the customer and regular soft eye contact that shows a caring attitude are among many others which are designed to engage the consumer on a variety of levels. Companies such as Disney have taken customer service to an even higher level by utilising their very own educational establishment, the Disney Institute. Their 2014 report 'The Secret to Delighting Customers? Put Employees First' makes for very interesting reading (and can be found at https://disneyinstitute.com/blog/2014/01/the-secret-to-delighting-customers-put-employees-first-/233/)

©iStock.com/ÖzgürDonmaz

Another example is the way in which store atmospherics are manipulated to generate perceptions about the products on offer – music played in-store will tend to increase purchases of hedonic products (Lee and Thomas 2010).

Moods can be manipulated to an extent by store atmospherics, which in turn affect purchasing behaviour – moods also affect processing of information from advertising (Bakamitsos and Siomkos 2004). Brand extensions are received more favourably if the individual is in a good mood (Greifeneder et al. 2007), and even the way the message is framed can affect perception: researchers found that smokers who read that almost 1,000 people die of smoking every day found the message more powerful than saying that 440,000 people a year die of smoking. This is apparently because the shorter time-frame means that the message has more immediacy (Chandran and Menon 2003). Time-frames may have other effects – positive cues are often overrated when considering a future event because people broaden the range of factors they take into account when considering the future (Grant and Tybout 2003). Dates are regarded as abstract, whereas time intervals are concrete: in other words, 'six months' interest-free credit' not only sounds a great deal better than 'interest-free credit until 30th November' (LeBoeuf 2006), but also means that the recipient of the message doesn't have to work out the timescales.

Atmospherics go a long way towards determining whether a customer remains in the store longer, spends more (or less) money and returns at a later date. Since Kotler, researchers have taken two basic approaches to researching atmospherics. The first approach concentrates on the factors that make up store atmosphere, whereas the other approach regards atmosphere in a holistic way and concentrates instead on its effects on consumers. Under the first approach, studies have been made of colour and lighting (Bellizzi et al. 1983), social factors (Baker et al. 1992), music and lighting (Kellaris and Kent 1992), crowding (Eroglu and Harrell 1986) and point-of-purchase displays (Philips and Bradshaw 1990). There are two common findings in these studies: first, that manipulating these various elements correctly can result in outcomes favourable to the retailer, i.e. people stay in the store longer and spend more money, and second, that these elements affect people's physical and psychological states, and hence their behaviour.

The second main thrust of research, an examination of the kind of effects atmospherics have on people, has produced some interesting results. Several researchers

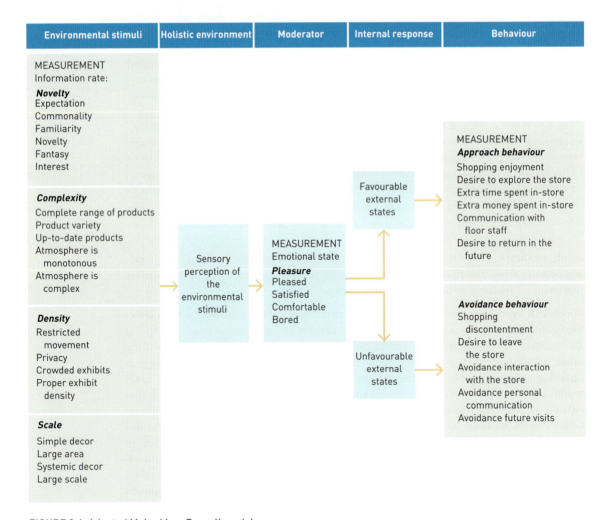

FIGURE 8.6 Adapted Mehrabian–Russell model

have used the Mehrabian–Russell Environmental Psychology Model (M–R Model) to explain some of the features of store atmospherics (Mehrabian and Russell 1974). The M–R Model says that environmental stimuli lead to emotional states (e.g. pleasure or arousal) which then lead to approach or avoidance responses. The opposite is also true, in that the big five factors of personality (openness, conscientiousness, extraversion, agreeableness and neuroticism) themselves can also have a moderating effect on a persons' consumption emotions (Jani and Han 2015). In a study of compact disc shops in Hong Kong, researchers were able to expand and modify the model to provide the example shown in Figure 8.6 (Tai and Fung 1997).

The left-hand box in the model refers to the information rate. This is the degree to which the shopper is exposed to novelty and surprise – the more novel the environment, the greater the information rate. Likewise, the more complex the environment the higher the information rate. Mehrabian and Russell (1974) postulate that an individual's propensity to develop approach or avoidance behaviours is a function of three elements – pleasure (or displeasure), arousal (or boredom) and dominance (or submission). In the study of CD stores, the researchers found that information rates have a marked effect on arousal, but not necessarily on pleasure: in other words customers did not necessarily like having a high information rate, even though they found it stimulating or exciting. The researchers further found that in-store behaviour contributed more to the pleasure of the experience, so from a marketer's viewpoint it would seem sensible to allow people plenty of latitude to examine goods, interact with staff, and so forth.

The environment as perceived by the consumers themselves is called the functional (or perceived) environment (Block and Block 1981). The functional environment will be different for each individual, because individuals differ in their knowledge, beliefs, experience and (of course) preference. Since marketers generally deal with groups of people rather than individuals, subtle differences and idiosyncrasies are likely to be ignored in favour of creating a generally acceptable environment for the target group of customers.

Figure 8.7 shows some of the elements of the functional environment. The macro-environment affects everything else, including the store and its branding: store decor, music, service levels and other customers all affect the store's brand image, but the behaviour and number of other customers also affect the functional environment directly. The current conditions in the store (crowding, cleanliness, availability of assistants) and the current weather (whether it is hot, rainy, cold) have a direct

FIGURE 8.7 The functional environment

bearing on the functional environment. There are of course many other factors that may affect the individual: situational factors such as time pressures, physical interrupts such as hunger or thirst, and so forth. Since the functional environment is subjective, the individual's personality, tastes, moods and behaviour act as moderating factors.

CHALLENGING THE STATUS QUO

It sounds as if the functional environment is really difficult to deal with. It's subjective, it's easily affected by factors over which we have absolutely no control and it changes with every passing minute. So why do we bother? Why not just pile everything up on the counter and hope people buy it?

Maybe that's a bit of an exaggeration, though. Maybe we should influence the bits we can influence, and live with the bits we can't influence. At least we'll be able to make *some* difference to people's perceptions! Take for example the use of digital signage and video screens by the world famous London retailer Harrods of Knightsbridge. They have over 150 screens located in their windows which are undoubtedly adding to the store's atmospherics but will also allow the retailer to generate a substantial media income from companies and brands who are eager to advertise and therefore be 'associated' with the Harrods brand.

The subjective nature of the functional environment can be problematical in an international context, because there are often marked differences between individuals in different countries; even with the European Union this is a problem, despite the relative similarities between member states in terms of wealth, aspirations and product availability (Askegaard and Madsen 1995). Because of this, it is tempting for marketers to treat each country as a separate segment, whereas in fact this can be inappropriate since new transnational segments are appearing as people travel more and the European Union converges (Brunso et al. 1996). Recent research identified four consumer styles which transcend national boundaries (McCarty et al. 2007):

1. *Price-sensitive consumers.* These are people who check prices, shop around for special offers and are not brand-loyal.

2. *Variety-seekers.* These people like to try new things and are the first to buy new products.

3. *Brand-loyal consumers.* These people buy known brands, and are likely to be brand-loyal even when this costs more; they are less likely to check prices or shop around for bargains.

4. *Information-seekers.* These people exchange information with other people, are more receptive to advertising and will try new products but tend to stick to known brands.

Other styles identified in the research differed across cultural boundaries – German consumers are less brand-loyal and more price-sensitive than consumers from some other countries, but they tend to enjoy shopping more than the French do, for example.

In the context of consumer behaviour, the environmental factors can be divided into macro-environmental factors – or the uncontrollables, such as climate, economy, politics, geography, and so forth; and micro-environmental factors – or controllables, such as the shop assistant, the store's cleanliness and decor, the current weather conditions and the other shoppers. Each of these factors is relevant: macro-environmental factors will dictate what people need to buy in terms of clothing, housing, transport, and so forth, as well as what they are able to buy either as a result of their wealth or as a result of legal restrictions or requirements. Micro-environmental factors influence decision-making at the point of purchase: people are unlikely to linger in noisy, crowded or dirty stores, and they become frustrated if there are long queues at checkouts (Park et al. 1989).

Macro-environment
Environmental elements which are common to all firms in a given industry, and are largely uncontrollable

Micro-environment
Those elements of the environment that affect the individual firm, and which could be controlled

PERCEPTION AND CONSUMERS' CHARACTERISTICS AND BEHAVIOUR

A consumer's stable characteristics are the basic factors about an individual that do not change, or change only slowly. Gender, personality, social class, age, educational level and intelligence all affect perception. For example, work by Pfefferbaum et al. (2015) reviewed children's reactions to disasters and the personal and situational factors that influence their reactions. Such differences can and do produce differences in the accuracy of interpretation of cues, and also in the selection of cues. Therefore, wide differences in processing ability (Henry 1980), numeric ability (Callison et al. 2015) and consequently in perception itself, should be expected between different individuals.

Some demographic variables may be responsible for the misunderstanding of cues; however, although the stable characteristics of the consumer might be expected to have a strong effect on perception, the interplay of the various factors is such that researching the effect of each one proves difficult. So far, therefore, research has been somewhat inconclusive on this issue.

Responses are not necessarily overt or external. In terms of perception, a response can just as easily be internal and non-behavioural. The perceptual response has three components: attribution, expectancy and affection (see Figure 8.8 below).

Affection is about emotional responses. In ordinary language, affection implies a positive response, but in psychology affection merely describes any emotional effect, whether positive or negative. Such responses to a given stimulus might

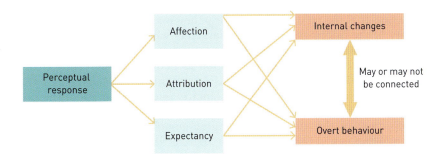

FIGURE 8.8 Perceptual responses

be liking, sympathy, fear, respect, disapproval, disgust, and so forth. An affective response is what we refer to when we talk about gut feeling or instinct: it is not a rational response, but that does not necessarily mean that it is wrong or ill-conceived.

Attribution is about applying a certain characteristic to an object. For example, someone who is scowling might be perceived as being angry. It is possible that the person is actually deep in thought about a problem that has just arisen, but the observer has attributed the characteristic of anger based on the cue of the facial expression. The same process happens when people are confronted with a product or brand: they attribute characteristics to it, based on the cues received.

Expectancy is about what the individual thinks the object will do. In the case of the scowling person, the observer might expect that the person will shout or even become violent. In marketing, expectancy is what leads people to believe that a well-known brand is better than the generic brand, even though the formulation is the same. One of the best-known examples of this is analgesics (pain killers). Branded aspirin actually works better than generic aspirin, even though the active ingredient (acetylsalicylic acid) is identical in each case.

COMBINING FACTORS

The processing centre combines the various cues to create an overall impression. This is likely to include attribution, expectation and affection components, but there are three basic models which seek to explain how this happens in practice. These are as follows:

Inference

Extra detail added to a message by a recipient, based on meta-analysis of the message

1. *The linear additive model* (Figure 8.9). This states that the **inferences** from each cue will build towards an overall perception. This means that the implications that attach to a particular characteristic will become stronger with the addition of each cue, regardless of how intense each cue is. For instance, work by Hu et al. (2015) examined the influence of the physical characteristics of houses on prices at different levels and found that a larger number of rooms, a bigger overall footprint and the fact that a house has been well-maintained and repaired are factors contributing to an increase in the price of a house. A strong cue will not be weakened by a subsequent weak cue, in other words.

2. *The linear averaging model* (Figure 8.10). This is a refinement on the previous model, since it assumes that the implication of a particular characteristic will be strengthened or weakened by subsequent cues, according to their strength. This means that the quality of the information may be more important than the quantity of the information, so that marketers who try to provide people with very large amounts of positive information may find that the effect is weakened if people regard some of the information as being less interesting than other information. Salespeople generally understand this phenomenon well: they are trained to find out first what the customer is interested in about the product, then to talk only about those aspects. While there is some (rather old) research evidence to show that the linear averaging model fits the facts better than the linear additive model (Anderson 1965), there is also some recent evidence that supports the theoretical usage of generalised linear mixed models (Iwasaki and Brinkman 2015).

3. *The configural model* (Figure 8.11). Linear models have the underlying assumption that the meaning of each cue remains the same when other facts are revealed. This is not necessarily the case: as cues are brought together, the meanings of previous cues are likely to be revised in the light of the new information. The configural model is intended to address this issue. The problem with this model is, of course, that it is virtually impossible to calculate what may or may not happen in a particular individual's mind as a result of being presented with a number of cues, and it is even difficult to know what will happen across a target audience of potential customers, which makes advertising difficult. This said, neuroscience is making vast progress towards exactly that.

CONSUMER BEHAVIOUR IN ACTION: HAVE YOU GOT CHIPS ON YOUR MIND?

Your smartphone can already take instructions from you using software such as Siri and Cortana. But could you imagine a world in which your smartphone could read your mind, or is this still confined to science fiction movies? Imagine that you decided to delete a message and just at the moment that you decide to move your finger to delete it, it is already gone!

©iStock.com/Petrovich 9

Well, guess what. Science fiction has become science fact for one human in California. Aflalo et al. (2015) have reported the case of a tetraplegic individual (called 'EGS') who volunteered to have his brain implanted with two small silicon chips that allow researchers to read his intentions directly from his brain activity. The chips, initially developed at the University of Utah, are now commercially available and approved for human use by the US Food and Drug Administration and consist of a matrix of 96 microscopic electrodes that can record the activity of about 100 nerve cells at the same time.

The fantasy is indeed becoming reality.

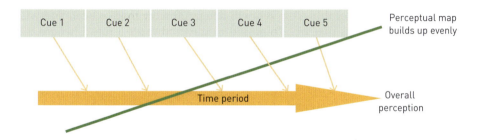

FIGURE 8.9 Linear additive model

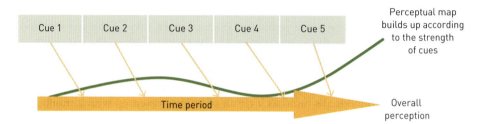

FIGURE 8.10 Linear averaging model

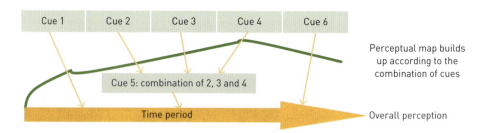

FIGURE 8.11 The configural model

As with any models, all three of the above are simplifications of reality, and therefore do not tell the whole story. It seems likely that people perceive the whole of a given object, rather than breaking it down into individual cues, but this (naturally) varies according to circumstances. Someone choosing to give to a charity will have many questions and be persuaded by many cues. Their own interests or life experiences, whether it's a registered charity or not, an awareness of campaigns, emergency needs following a natural disaster, and the charity's administrative costs will all contribute to an individual's philanthropic choices.

Of course, we rarely have complete information about anything. Our brains are pro-active in filling in the gaps – neuroscience has demonstrated that we continuously generate predictions about what to expect in the environment around us (Bar and Neta 2008). Communications technology and the plethora of data (sensor networks, RFID tags, surveillance cameras, unmanned aerial vehicles and geo-tagged social-media posts) that we can now tap into (sometimes also known as 'big data') means that the environment around us will foresee our every move. Computerised sensing and broadcasting abilities are being incorporated into our physical environment, creating the 'Internet of things' which will telegraph where we've been and where we are going. It seems that we are poised to travel towards a future where these data streams will be integrated into services we receive, platforms and programs that we engage with and will provide a very large window into the lives, and futures, of billions of people.

Equally, the purchase of a brand of biscuits is unlikely to involve the same level of analysis. Few people would trouble to read the list of ingredients and the nutritional information on the packet, or ask a friend's advice, or go online and investigate the company's history and manufacturing methods.

An interesting area of research, therefore, is to try to find out which rules people use at particular times. Sometimes people will use a linear rule, at other times they might use a configural method, and at still other times people might use a combination of rules to form an overall opinion. Research carried out by Meyer in 1987 seemed to indicate that people tend to use configural methods, but later on in the process the decisions move towards additive rules (Meyer 1987).

It may be that the more utilitarian aspects of the product are judged against a linear set of rules, whereas the hedonic or affective aspects are judged against the configural model (Holbrook and Moore 1981).

SUBLIMINAL PERCEPTION

Perception is not necessarily a conscious process. Much of what happens in our minds happens below the conscious level (see Chapter 7), and we know that often people have a 'gut feeling' about something without being able to define why. Some of us have had the experience of falling in love at first sight – with people or with products. This happens without our having any real facts to go on, and without our having any way of analysing the reasons.

Subliminal perception has a controversial history in marketing. During the 1950s it was claimed that subliminal advertising, as it was called, could make people do things they otherwise would not do. The theory was that brief exposure to a message (for example, flashing 'Drink Cola' onto a cinema screen during a film) would cause people to experience a sudden mysterious desire to drink cola. The theory was that the message would appear and disappear much too quickly for the input selector mechanism to operate, so the message would bypass the normal perceptual safeguards and enter the person's consciousness unedited (see Figure 8.12). These claims were so powerful that subliminal advertising was banned in some countries and was regulated in others; in fact, the general air of paranoia in the 1950s may have contributed to the scare, since there is little evidence to support the claims made for subliminal advertising.

Subliminal perception
Perception that occurs below the conscious level

Wilson Key has published several books on the subject of subliminal perception in advertising (Key 1973, 1976, 1980, 1989) in which he claims that advertisers have airbrushed-in words such as 'U Buy' into the shadows around a bottle of rum, and various sexual images in advertisements for cigarettes and even cake mix. In 1957, Vance Packard published a book called *The Hidden Persuaders* in which he analysed

FIGURE 8.12 Subliminal advertising

the various ways in which the media industry manipulates opinion: he included subliminal advertising in his analysis (Packard 1957). However, in both cases the authors have been criticised for failing to produce solid evidence, and for making too many unsupported assumptions.

The evidence for and against subliminal perception, at least as far as marketing goes, is mixed to say the least. There is some evidence that drive and behaviour may be influenced (Hawkins 1970), and there is also some evidence that flashing brand names onto cinema screens has impact when the stimulus is related to right-brain processing (Cuperfain and Clarke 1985). Other studies have failed to find any evidence for subliminal perception (Kelly 1979; Gable et al. 1987; Beatty and Hawkins 1989).

Subliminal perception, and from that subliminal advertising, is supposed to work in the same way as self-hypnosis mpegs or YouTube videos. Such videos are often sold and distributed as a means of losing weight, giving up smoking, and so forth, yet there is no evidence that they have any effect whatsoever (Anon 1991). People's attitudes towards subliminal perception are ambivalent – on the one hand, people tend to fear it, since they are afraid that marketers (and others) might use it to manipulate them unfairly, and on the other hand people often hope that it does work when they buy self-hypnosis recordings (Spencer et al. 2003). In many instances however, it can be seen as just clever design. Take for example the world's most prestigious cycling event, the Tour de France. Its logo has been in existence since 1903, and a closer look shows that the R in 'ouR' and the orange circle make up an image of someone riding a bicycle.

CHALLENGING THE STATUS QUO

©iStock.com/robynmac

Subliminal advertising has been dismissed as a figment of the imagination, a product of Cold War paranoia and people's general mistrust of marketing. But of course marketers would say that, wouldn't they?

We know that a lot of our impressions of the world come from deep below the conscious level, from cues we are not really aware of, so why wouldn't this be true of advertising? If self-help hypnosis podcasts don't work, why do people keep accessing them? Is it simply that there is a widespread belief that they will work (and therefore people subconsciously act on the belief but not on the podcast) or is it more likely that the podcasts do have some effect on the individual's thought processes?

Even worse – are marketers for faceless corporations using subliminal advertising to make us into robots? Take for example the children's story book. A simple, innocent and educational product, which most children dote over and most parents find hours of joy reading from to their little ones. All good so far. Then along comes a book called *The Tale of City Sue*, distributed by *The Guardian* on Saturday (a UK-based national newspaper). The story is all about an Irish farm with a herd of cows.

It starts with:

> This friendly Friesian family were free to roam and browse and eat the freshest, greenest grass which made them happy cows. They belonged to farmer Finn who called them by their names and when it was their birthday he brought party hats and games. He played his violin for them inside the milking shed and sung them soothing lullabies when it was time for bed.

(It's interesting that a lot of children's books and the stories within them are farm-based. Happy animals being bred freely in a happy environment with happy farmers and their happy families. We never seem to read about the darker side of farming: the slaughter house, the castration, the butchery, the battery production or the separation of young animals from their mothers.)

Just before I started reading it to my niece, I turned to the back cover and realised that it wasn't a children's story book at all, but an elongated and extended advertisement disguised as a book – all in aid of selling Kerrygold butter! The subliminal message here of the cows being content and living in some sort of state of ecstasy is indeed one which is quite sinister, from an adult's perspective, of course.

But is it right that young children are exposed to what could be considered as unethical subliminal persuasion?

Even if subliminal advertising were shown to work, it seems probable that it would be ineffective. First, different people have different perception thresholds, so some people might be aware that the message has flashed onto the screen. Second, there is a very high risk of misunderstanding; after all, people frequently misunderstand or misinterpret advertising which is in plain language, so the potential for missing the point in an advertisement which is flashed onto a cinema screen for a fraction of a second must be very much greater. Finally, the selective nature of perception means that most stimuli are ignored or rejected by the input selector, even when the stimulus is strong. The fleeting nature of subliminal messages is likely to mean that they never register with the observer. This view accords with Weber's Law (which we saw earlier in this chapter).

COLOUR

Colours are used to attract attention, but they also convey particular emotions and meanings. These meanings are culturally specific – for example, in Japan white is the colour of funerals, whereas in the United States and most of Europe it is black; in China, bright colours symbolise high quality, whereas in the UK they are often associated with low price, low quality articles. Consumers have a preference for colour and form which varies from one product category to another (Reddy et al. 2015). A study by Madden et al. (2000) found that red is perceived as hot, active and vibrant across all cultures, while black and brown are perceived as sad and stale. Black and brown are also perceived as formal in Brazil, Colombia, China and Taiwan, and as masculine in Austria, Hong Kong and the United States.

Table 8.2 shows some common colour perceptions, particularly as they relate to packaging and advertising.

Colours have a strong effect on perception. Research conducted in the 1960s showed that people believed that coffee from a dark brown container was stronger than coffee from a blue container, and that coffee from a yellow container was weak in both flavour and aroma (Dichter 1964). In fact, the coffee in each container was identical. This research is not generalisable across cultures, and it also suffers from the major weakness that (not unnaturally) respondents will try to find a difference between the

TABLE 8.2 Colour perceptions

Colour	Perceived meaning
Yellow	A strong attention-grabber, yellow often symbolises summer. It works well as a background colour for black print, because it makes the print stand out, but it can sometimes be perceived as 'cheap and cheerful'. Some people associate yellow with warmth, novelty or caution
Orange	Orange is a sociable colour, but in packaging it is mainly used for products (such as orange juice) which actually contain oranges. Some products (and many billboard posters) use Dayglo orange as an attention-grabber; in the UK, this bright orange colour is still successfully used by low-cost airline easyJet
Red	This is a strong attention-grabber because it can stand for most human emotions. It is often regarded as hot, exciting, passionate and strong
Purple	Purple was formerly associated with royalty, and it has retained an upmarket image. Because it is the most expensive colour to reproduce, and has poor resistance to fading, its use in packaging is limited
Blue	Blue is rarely associated with food packaging, because very few foods are blue. It is commonly used to denote coolness or cleanliness, and it is often perceived as having authority and commanding respect. This is why many countries use blue as the colour for police uniforms
Green	The rise of environmentalism has increased the use of green for packaging and advertising. It carries connotations of naturalness, security and calmness
Pink or magenta	Pink has stereotypically been regarded as a feminine colour, so it has been widely used on cosmetics, but in recent years it has been used for baby products and some categories of household goods
White	In most European countries and the United States, white is the colour of purity and cleanliness. In Japan and India it is, however, the colour of mourning
Brown	In food packaging, brown usually denotes strong flavours such as pickles and sauces, or coffee and chocolate. For gardening products, it conveys a rich earthiness
Black	Black is usually associated with death, but combined with gold it can denote exclusivity and premium prices
Grey	Grey can symbolise sadness, transition, compromise, depression, boredom and monotony, but in recent years it has become a fashionable colour for high-tech products and modern design

coffees if they are asked to do so. Having said that, the differences that Dichter found were remarkably consistent between the respondents, with 87% of them agreeing that the coffee from the yellow container was too weak. Fifty years later, a series of experiments conducted by Risso et al. (2015) investigated the association between the colour of a container and the liquid inside: in this case mineral water. In the first experiment respondents perceived the water as more carbonated when contained in a blue or red glass, rather than in a white glass. In another of the experiments, respondents preferred to choose a white glass for still water and blue or red for sparkling water. Had people been inventing differences simply to please the researcher, the differences would have been much less consistent. In packaging colour often has a profound effect on people's perceptions of the actual product: for example, Heinz use turquoise for their baked bean cans (even though most other Heinz cans have different colours) as turquoise makes the beans look brighter orange when the can is opened.

These perceptions may not, of course, translate well into all countries or cultures. In some cases, colour may be a fashion statement – Goths wear black, for example. The naming of colours is a crucial factor in the marketing of products such as paint and fabrics. Names such as midnight blue, dawn pink, apple green or corn yellow have a positive effect on consumer perception because there is an underlying assumption that the information must be useful in some way, which leads people to put a positive 'spin' on the colour name (Miller and Khan 2003). Each year has its 'fashionable' colours – for 2006 it seemed to be white and gold, but in 2015 Pantone reported that the top three colours were Oak Buff, Cadmium Orange and Dried Herb (Pantone 2015). The rainbow flag (commonly the gay pride flag and the LGT pride flag) was designed to reflect the diversity of these communities by assigning a specific meaning to each of the colours (pink/sexuality, red/life, orange/healing, yellow/sunlight, green/nature, turquoise/magic, blue/serenity, violet/spirit).

Rainbow flag
A flag which is a symbol of lesbian, gay, bisexual and transgender (LGBT) social movements

Colour also has a dramatic effect on search times for products (see Figure 8.13). Bright colours and contrasting colours make a product stand out, but people also use colour as a way of identifying brands rapidly (Jansson et al. 2004). Product colour is more important among young adults than older age groups and it is more important to females than males (Akcay et al. 2012). Companies often therefore adopt a corporate colour, or a colour denoting specific brands in the range. Coca-Cola uses red and white, Heinz uses red for its range of soups, and so forth. In the UK, firms have (in recent years) been able to include corporate colours in their trade mark registration, so that, for example, the shade of green used by BP on its forecourts is now protected by law. This does not mean that other people cannot use the same shade of green, but it would mean that other oil companies would not be able to use it as part of their forecourts if the result might be to confuse the public into thinking that they were actually buying from BP. So far, there has been very little litigation based on infringements of corporate colours, although Orange and easyGroup have disputed the use of the colour orange for mobile telephone networks and the low-cost airline respectively. In 2012, Cadbury's Chocolate won a legal case stopping other chocolate firms from using their purple colour and effectively tried to trademark the purple colour (Pantone 2865c) of its Dairy Milk bars. In 2013, Nestlé won an appeal overruling the court decision.

FIGURE 8.13 Colour in marketing

PASSING OFF, BRANDALISM AND SUBVERTISING

Deliberate attempts to confuse consumers are called 'passing off', because one company is trying to *pass off* its products as being from the other company. This is illegal in most countries, since it is obviously against consumer interests as well as against the interests of the brand owner.

Connected concepts are 'brandalism and subvertising' which have been defined as 'a movement with the stated aim of rebelling against the visual assault of media giants and advertising moguls who have a stranglehold over messages and meaning in our public spaces' (Smith-Anthony and Groom 2015). In the article the authors describe subvertising as activists developing spoofs, parodies and other message-changing/obscuring alterations, which they then use through the brand's own marketing channels to make a statement against the brand itself (Smith-Anthony and Groom 2015). It is not uncommon to see artwork which comments on consumerism, cultural values, debt, the environment, body image or specific political messages placed over existing billboards at bus stops and other public spaces. This develops an interesting conflict between the two parties involved, on the one hand the free expression rights of the *subvertisers* and on the other the brand owners and their intellectual property rights.

SUMMARY

From a marketing viewpoint, the fact that perception is so nebulous and individual a thing is probably helpful in the long run. People's views of products and services rely heavily on perceived attributes, some of which have no objective reality; the difficulty for marketers lies in knowing what will be the general perception of the members of the market segments with whom they are attempting to do business.

Perception is, most definitely, an individual thing. The way one person selects and interprets information will be very different from the way someone else selects and interprets the same basic cues. This chapter has dealt with the processes that lead up to the formation of a view of the world: the selection, processing and interpretation of information and the subsequent keying-in of new information to existing knowledge is what enables us to understand our surroundings and deal with problems.

KEY POINTS

- Perception is both synthetic and analytic.
- Stimuli combine synergistically to create the whole impression.
- Selectivity is a key issue in perception, and is a key problem for marketers.
- Past experience contributes to the way new stimuli are interpreted as well as to the overall impression.
- Changes in the stimulus will go undetected if the stimulus is a large one.
- Perception and reality are not intrinsically different.
- Most perception happens below the conscious level.
- Perceptual responses may be internal or overt.
- Subliminal advertising is unlikely to be effective.
- Colour speeds search times, as well as attracting attention.

HOW TO IMPRESS YOUR EXAMINER

You may be asked to explain the process of developing a world-view. You should be very clear about the synthetic aspects of perception as well as the analytic aspects: perception is not about misunderstanding the world, it is about creating a useable working model of the world on which to base decisions. There is a very strong link between perception and learning, and this should also be understood. As always, real-life examples help to show that you understand the theory.

REVIEW QUESTIONS

1. What effect does selectivity have on an integrated marketing communications campaign?
2. How might colour perceptions be complicated in a global market?
3. Why is subjectivity a problem for marketers?
4. How do internal responses create problems for marketers?
5. What is the difference between the linear additive model and the linear averaging model?
6. Explain Weber's Law.
7. What is the difference between kinaesthetic processing and visual processing?
8. What is the Law of Primacy?
9. What is the role of expectancy in branding?
10. What are the arguments for the effectiveness of subliminal advertising? What are the arguments against?

CASE STUDY: POLITICS, SPIN AND THE SCOTTISH REFERENDUM

Between 2014 and 2016, the UK has seen two of the most remarkable referendums in its history. First, in 2014 Scotland held a referendum on whether to remain within the United Kingdom, of which is had been a member (sometimes reluctantly) since 1707. And

©iStock.com/Brian A Jackson

in June 2016, the UK then held a referendum on whether to remain within the European Union, of which it has been a member since 1973. Let's take a look at the Scottish referendum first. Scottish politics have generally tended to be left-wing, with a great deal of support for the UK's Labour party, and very little support for the Conservatives. This of course meant that Labour saw the possibility of a Scottish departure from the Union as a poten-tial major disaster, while at the same time the Conservatives tended to view any break-up of the Union as a negative outcome, since the country as a whole would inevitably weaken – not to mention that the bulk of the UK's oil reserves lie mainly in Scottish waters.

This resulted in an uneasy alliance between the two main British political par-ties, at a time when the country was being run by a coalition between Conservatives and Liberal Democrats – another uneasy alliance. Meanwhile, the left-wing Scottish Nationalist Party, led by Alex Salmond, was making great inroads into people's per-ceptions of Scotland's future. The SNP had been gaining in strength for some time, despite opposition from all major media sources: *The Scottish Sun* newspaper ran a front-page image of a hangman's noose in May 2007 with the headline, 'Vote SNP and you put Scotland's head in the noose' (Macwhirter, 2007). Scots don't take kindly to this type of treatment, and support for the SNP grew rapidly until the party became the controlling group in the Scottish Parliament.

Campaigning on all sides was very determined, and there was a great deal of heated discussion about who should be allowed to vote: some said that Scots living outside Scotland should be able to vote, and it was even suggested that the whole of the UK should be eligible since the outcome would affect the whole country. Eventually it was agreed that anyone living in Scotland over the age of 16 should be able to vote.

The campaigning was organised on the one hand by the Yes campaign (backed by the SNP and the Scottish Socialist Party) and on the other hand by the Better Together campaign, backed by the Conservative and Labour parties from Westminster, and headed by former Chancellor of the Exchequer Alistair Darling. Both groups were funded by public contributions – UK electoral law is very strict on how campaigns are funded, so central government funds could not be used.

Campaigning became complicated by several factors: as a member of the UK, Scotland is also part of the European Union, but would probably have to make a new membership application if it were no longer part of the UK. Second, there was the question of currency. Central government said that Scotland would no longer have the right to use the pound, and would have to establish its own currency or join the Euro. Scottish campaigners countered that they could easily continue to use the pound, and had as much right to it as England – to which Better Together campaigners replied that therefore Scotland would have to take on its share of the national debt. Third, defence was a major issue, since the UK's nuclear submarine base at Faslane is in Scotland, and the major shipbuilding yards in Scotland produce most of Britain's warships. Defence contractors such as Thales said they would be unlikely to invest in an independent Scotland, and BAE said they would resume shipbuilding in Portsmouth in the event of Scotland leaving. The submarines are more of a problem, since there is no alternative location for them at present, and one would have to be built.

The UK treasury issued a report to the effect that the Scottish banking system could not withstand a crisis: some major banks (including, bizarrely, the Royal Bank of Scotland) said that they would have to relocate their headquarters to London, and Weir Group pointed out that 70% of Scottish exports went to the rest of the UK. The Yes campaigners counteracted by pointing out that Scotland has a lower deficit than the rest of the UK, and a higher GDP per capita than France. Also, of course, Scotland has oil. The Yes campaign produced figures showing that Scotland would do better economically if it were not tied to UK central policies.

Meanwhile the emotional campaign built. As opinion polls began to show that there was a very real danger of the Yes camp winning, senior Labour politicians from Westminster went to Scotland in the hopes of bolstering support for Better Together. One humourist followed them round in a rickshaw with loudspeakers playing the Death Star theme from *Star Wars*, while shouting 'These lovely people, they have travelled all the way from England to tell us they are better to rule us than anybody else, our imperial masters' through a megaphone (Nsubuga, 2014). Yes campaigners accused the BBC of bias in its reporting, and protests were held outside the BBC Scotland offices and studios: senior people from BBC Scotland were called to appear before a Scottish Parliament committee to answer questions about apparent bias. As the date of the referendum grew closer, opinion polls began to show a majority Yes outcome by a narrow margin.

Eventually, of course, all the arguments about the economy, and defence, and membership the EU paled into insignificance against the emotive arguments about Scotland being an independent nation again after 300 years. This emotionally-charged atmosphere led to a turnout of over 84%, the largest in UK history: in the event, the No campaign won with 55% of the votes. In the aftermath, there was a palpable sense of relief south of the border, on both sides of the political stage. In Scotland, Alex Salmond resigned from the SNP in favour of his deputy, Nicola Sturgeon. Unfortunately for Labour, Nicola Sturgeon led the SNP to a landslide victory in the 2015 general election, taking 40 seats from Labour and ending up with 56 of the 59 Scottish seats in the Westminster Parliament. Much of this success was attributed to her personality and skill in debate, as well as her obvious patriotism. In the wake of the Leave result Nicola Sturgeon said that it is 'democratically unacceptable' that Scotland faces being taken out of the EU when it voted to Remain (Cooper, 2016). A second independence referendum for the country is now highly likely.

QUESTIONS

1. Why might an emotional argument outweigh the practical discussions about the economy?

2. Why are personalities more important than issues in election campaigns?

3. Why might someone commit funds to an election campaign before hearing all the arguments?

4. Explain voting behaviour in terms of attribute, expectancy and affection.

5. If Scotland had a second referendum to 'remain' in the EU, what effect will that have on the rest of Britain (England, Wales and N. Ireland)?

FURTHER READING

For a paper on brand perceptions, read L. Salciuviene, P. Ghauri, P. Streder and C. De Mattos (2010) Do brand names in a foreign language lead to different brand perceptions? *Journal of Marketing Management*, 26 (11–12): 1037–56.

For more on political marketing and in particular the management of perceptions, see J. Dermody and S. Hanmer-Lloyd (2005) Promoting distrust? A chronicle of the 2005 British General Election advertising campaigns. *Journal of Marketing Management* 21 (9–10): 1021–47 (special edition: The Marketing Campaign: The 2005 British General Election). There are, of course, more papers on political marketing in that special edition: one that provides more insight into the use of emotion to overcome reason is D. Dean (2005) Fear, negative campaigning and loathing: the case of the UK election campaign. *Journal of Marketing Management*, 21: 1067–78.

The perception of the ideal woman in advertising has been a somewhat controversial topic in recent years. The following paper may help to pick out the issues. S. Feiereisen, A.J. Broderick and S.P. Douglas (2009) The effect and moderation of gender identity congruity: utilizing 'real women' advertising images. *Psychology & Marketing*, 26 (9): 813–43.

If you're interested in the perception processes concerned with vision, a very clear and easy-to-read book on the subject is *Basic Vision: An Introduction to Visual Perception* by Robert Snowden, Peter Thompson and Tom Trosciano (Oxford: Oxford University Press, 2012).

For a clear, well-written, basic overview of perception theory you might like *Perception: Theory, Development and Organisation* by Paul Rookes and Jane Willson (London: Routledge, 2000). The book is actually intended for A-level Psychology students, but it covers the major theories well and is very readable.

REFERENCES

Aflalo, T., Kellis, S., Klaes, C., Lee, B., Shi, Y., Pejsa, K., Shanfield, K., Hayes-Jackson, S., Aisen, M., Heck, C., Liu, C. and Andersen, R.A. (2015) Decoding motor imagery from the posterior parietal cortex of a tetraplegic human. *Science*, 906–10.

Akcay, O., Sable, P. and Dalgin, M.H. (2012) The importance of color in product choice among young Hispanic, Caucasian, and African-American Groups in the USA, *International Journal of Business and Social Science*, 3 (6): 1–6.

Anderson, N.H. (1965) Averaging versus adding as a stimulus combination rule in impression formation. *Journal of Experimental Psychology*, 70: 394–400.

Anon (1991) Self-help tapes are worthless, study says. *San Jose Mercury News*, 25 September.

Askegaard, S. and Madsen, T.K. (1995) European food cultures: an exploratory analysis of food related preferences and behaviour in European regions. MAPP Working Paper no. 26. Aarhus: Aarhus School of Business.

Bakamitsos, G. and Siomkos, G. (2004) Context effects in marketing practice: the case of mood. *Journal of Consumer Behaviour*, 3 (4): 304–14.

Baker, J., Levy, M. and Grewal, D. (1992) An experimental approach to making retail store environmental decisions. *Journal of Retailing*, 68: 445–61.

Bar, M. and Neta, M. (2008) The proactive brain: using rudimentary information to make predictive judgements. *Journal of Consumer Behaviour*, 7 (4/5): 319–30.

Bardhi, F. and Eckhardt, G.M. (2010) Market-mediated collaborative consumption in the context of car sharing. *Advances in Consumer Research*, 37: 66–7.

Batra, R. and Stayman, D.M. (1990) The role of mood in advertising effectiveness. *Journal of Consumer Research*, 17 (September): 203–14.

Beatty, S.E. and Hawkins, D. (1989) Subliminal stimulation: some new data and interpretation. *Journal of Advertising*, 18 (3): 4–8.

Bellizzi, J.A., Crowley, A.E. and Hasty, R.W. (1983) The effects of colour in store design. *Journal of Retailing*, 59: 21–45.

Block, J. and Block, J.H. (1981) Studying situational dimensions: a grand perspective and some limited empiricism. In D. Magnusson (ed.), *Toward a Psychology of Situations: An International Perspective*. Hillsdale, NJ: Lawrence Erlbaum, pp. 85–102.

Brunso, K., Grunert, K.G. and Bredahl, L. (1996) An analysis of national and cross-national consumer segments using the food-related lifestyle instrument in Denmark, France, Germany and Great Britain. MAPP Working Paper no. 35. Aarhus: Aarhus School of Business.

Bugelski, B.R. and Alampay, D.A. (1961) The role of frequency in developing perceptual sets. *Canadian Journal of Psychology*, 15: 205–11.

Callison, C., Gibson, R. and Zillmann, D. (2015) Effects of differences in numeric ability on the perception of adversity risk to others and self. *Journal of Media Psychology*, 25 (2): 95–104.

Chandran, S. and Menon, G. (2003) When am I at risk? Now, or now? The effects of temporal framing on perceptions of health risk. *Advances in Consumer Research*, 30: 106–8.

Chatterjee, P. (2001) Online reviews: do consumers use them? In M.C. Gilly and J. Meyers-Levy (eds), *NA – Advances in Consumer Research*, Volume 28. Valdosta, GA: Association for Consumer Research, pp. 129–33.

Clark, I., III, Micken, K.S. and Hart, H.S. (2002) Symbols for sale – at least for now: symbolic consumption in transition economies. *Advances in Consumer Research*, 29: 25–30.

Cooper, C. (2016, June 24) Brexit: Scotland leaving EU is 'democratically unacceptable', says Nicola Sturgeon. *Independent*. Available at: http://www.independent.co.uk/news/uk/politics/brexit-scotland-leaving-eu-is-democratically-unacceptable-says-nicola-sturgeon-a7100691.html (accessed 9 July 2016).

Cuperfain, R. and Clarke, T.K. (1985) A new perspective of subliminal perception. *Journal of Advertising*, 14 (1): 36–41.

d'Astous, A. and Kamau, E. (2010) Consumer product evaluation based on tactile sensory information. *Journal of Consumer Behaviour*, 9 (3): 206–13.

Demattè, M.L., Pojer, N., Endrizzi, I., Corollaro, M.L., Betta, E., Aprea, E., Charles, M., Biasioli, F., Zampini, M. and Gasperi, F. (2014) Effects of the sound of the bite on apple perceived crispness and hardness. *Food Quality and Preference*, 38: 58–64.

Dichter, E. (1964) *Handbook of Consumer Motivations: The Psychology of the World of Objects*. New York: McGraw-Hill.

Eroglu, S. and Harrell, G.D. (1986) Retail crowding: theoretical and strategic implications. *Journal of Retailing*, 62: 346–63.

Gable, M., Wilkens, H.T., Harris, L. and Feinberg, R. (1987) An evaluation of subliminally embedded sexual stimuli in graphics. *Journal of Advertising*, 16 (1): 26–31.

Grant, S.J. and Tybout, A.M. (2003) The effects of temporal framing on new product evaluation. *Advances in Consumer Research*, 30: 1.

Greifeneder, R., Bless, H. and Kuschmann, T. (2007) Extending the brand image on new products: the facilitative effect of happy mood states. *Journal of Consumer Behaviour*, 6 (January–February): 19–31.

Han, S. and Lerner, J. (2008) When the status quo turns sour: robust effects of incidental disgust in economic transactions. *Advances in Consumer Research*, 35: 153.

Hawkins, D. (1970) The effects of subliminal stimulation on drive level and brand preference. *Journal of Market Research*, 7 (August): 322–6.

Henry, W.A. (1980) The effect of information processing ability on processing accuracy. *Journal of Consumer Research*, 7 (June): 42–8.

Holbrook, M.P. and Moore, W.I. (1981) Feature interactions in consumer judgement of verbal versus pictorial presentations. *Journal of Consumer Research*, 8 (June): 103–13.

Hu, Y., Zhao, K. and Lian, H. (2015) Bayesian quantile regression for partially linear additive models. *Statistics and Computing*, 25 (3): 651–68.

Iwasaki, Y. and Brinkman, S.F. (2015) Application of a generalized linear mixed model to analyze mixture toxicity: survival of brown trout affected by copper and zinc. *Environmental Toxicology and Chemistry*, 34 (4): 816–20.

Jani, D. and Han, H. (2015) Influence of environmental stimuli on hotel customer emotional loyalty response: Testing the moderating effect of the big five personality factors. *International Journal of Hospitality Management*, 44: 48–57.

Jansson, C., Marlow, N. and Bristow, M. (2004) The influence of colour on visual search times in cluttered environments. *Journal of Marketing Communications*, 10 (September): 183–93.

Kellaris, J.J. and Kent, R.J. (1992) The influence of music on consumers' temporal perceptions: does time fly when you're having fun? *Journal of Consumer Psychology*, 1: 365–76.

Kelly, J.S. (1979) Subliminal imbeds in printing advertising: a challenge to advertising ethics. *Journal of Advertising*, 8 (Summer): 43–6.

Kenyon, G.N. and Sen, K.C. (2015) The perception process. In G.N. Kenyon and K.C. Sen (eds), *The Perception of Quality*. London: Springer, pp. 41–50.

Key, W.B. (1973) *Subliminal Seduction*. Englewood Cliffs, NJ: Signet.

Key, W.B. (1976) *Media Sexploitation*. Englewood Cliffs, NJ: Prentice-Hall.

Key, W.B. (1980) *The Clam-Plate Orgy and Other Subliminals the Media Use to Manipulate Your Behaviour*. Englewood Cliffs, NJ: Prentice-Hall.

Key, W.B. (1989) *The Age of Manipulation: The Con in Confidence, the Sin in Sincere*. New York: Henry Holt & Co.

Kotler, P. (1973) Atmospherics as a marketing tool. *Journal of Retailing*, 49 (Winter): 48–64.

LeBoeuf, R.A. (2006) Discount rates for time versus dates: the sensitivity of discounting to time-interval description. *Advances in Consumer Research*, 33: 138–9.

Lee, L. and Thomas, M. (2010) Music and consummatory focus: how background music changes preferences. Working paper on www.johnson.cornell.edu/Faculty-And-Research/Profile/id/mkt27 (accessed 25 July 2015).

Li, C. (2010) Primacy effect or recency effect? A long-term memory test of Super Bowl commercials. *Journal of Consumer Behaviour*, 9 (1): 32–44.

Lindstrom, M. (2005) Sensing and opportunity: sensory appeal. *The Marketer*, 10 (February): 6–11.

Nsubuga, J. (2014, September 12) Pro-independence rickshaw rider taunts Labour Party members with Star Wars' Imperial March down Glasgow high street, *Metro*. Available at: http://metro.co.uk/2014/09/12/pro-independence-rickshaw-rider-taunts-labour-party-members-with-star-wars-imperial-march-down-glasgow-high-street-4866053/ (accessed 9 July 2016).

Macwhirter, I. (2007, May 3) The heat of the Scottish sun. *The Guardian*. Available at: https://www.theguardian.com/commentisfree/2007/may/03/theheatofthescottishsun (accessed 9 July 2016).

Madden, T.J., Hewett, K. and Roth, M.S. (2000) Managing images in different cultures: a cross-national study of colour meanings and preferences. *Journal of International Marketing*, 8 (4): 90–107.

McCarty, J.A., Horn, M.I. and Szenasy, M.K. (2007) An exploratory study of consumer style: country differences and international segments. *Journal of Consumer Behaviour*, 6: 48–59.

Mehrabian, A. and Russell, J.A. (1974) *An Approach to Environmental Psychology*. Cambridge, MA: MIT Press.

Meyer, R.J. (1987) The learning of multiattribute judgement policies. *Journal of Consumer Research*, 14 (2): 155–73.

Miller, G.A. (1956) The magical number seven, plus or minus two: some limits in our capacity for processing information. *Psychological Review*, 63: 81–97.

Miller, S.G. and Khan, B. (2003) Shades of meaning: the effects of novel colour names on consumer preferences. *Advances in Consumer Research*, 30: 11–13.

Milotic, D. (2003) The impact of fragrance on consumer choice. *Journal of Consumer Behaviour*, 3 (2): 179–91.

Munoz, C.L., Wood, N.T. and Solomon, M.R. (2006) Real or blarney? A cross-cultural investigation of the perceived authenticity of Irish pubs. *Journal of Consumer Behaviour*, 5 (May–June): 222–34.

Macwhitter, I. (2007, May 3) The heat of the Scottish sun. *The Guardian*. Available at: https://www.theguardian.com/comment is free/2007/may/03/the heat of the scottish sun (accessed 9 July 2016).

Packard, V. (1957) *The Hidden Persuaders*. New York: Pocket Books (reissued Ig Publishing, 2007).

Pantone (2015) The top ten colors for men's and women's fashion for Fall 2015. www.pantone.com/pages/fcr/?season=fall&year=2015&pid=11 (accessed September 2015).

Park, C.W., Iyer, E.S. and Smith, D.C. (1989) The effects of situational factors on in-store grocery shopping behaviour: the role of store environment and time available for shopping. *Journal of Consumer Research*, 15 (March): 422–33.

Parker, A.M., Fischhof, B. and deBruin, W.B. (2006) Who thinks they know more – but actually knows less? Adolescent confidence in their HIV/AIDS and general knowledge. *Advances in Consumer Research*, 33: 12–13.

Payne, C. and Wansink, B. (2010) What is beautiful tastes good: visual cues, taste and willingness to pay. *Advances in Consumer Research*, 37: 49–50.

Pfefferbaum, B., Jacobs, A.K., Griffin, N. and Houston, J.B. (2015) Children's disaster reactions: the influence of exposure and personal characteristics. *Current Psychiatry Reports*, 17 (7): 1–6.

Philips, H. and Bradshaw, R. (1990) How customers actually shop: customer interaction with the point of sale. *Journal of the Market Research Society*, 35: 51–62.

Rao, A.R. and Monroe, K.B. (1988) The moderating effect of price knowledge on cue utilization in product evaluations. *Journal of Consumer Research*, 15 (September): 253–64.

Reddy, S.M., Chowdhury, A., Charkrabarti, D. and Karmakar, S. (2015) Role of colour and form in product choice and variation of preferences across product categories: a review. In ICoRD'15, *Research into Design Across Boundaries Volume 2*. New Delhi: Springer India, pp. 631–40.

Risso, P., Maggioni, E., Olivero, N. and Gallace, A. (2015) The association between the colour of a container and the liquid inside: an experimental study on consumers' perception, expectations and choices regarding mineral water. *Food Quality and Preference*, 44: 17–25.

Sheth, J.N. (2008) *Chindia Rising: How China and India Will Benefit Your Business*. New Delhi: India Professional.

Small, D.A. and Verrochi, N.M. (2008) The face of need: reactions to victims' emotion expressions. *Advances in Consumer Research*, 35: 135.

Smith-Anthony, A. and Groom, J. (2015) Brandalism and subverting: hoisting brands with their own petard? *Journal of Intellectual Property Law & Practice*, 10 (1): 29–34.

Song, H. and Schwarz, N. (2009) Safe and easy or risky and burdensome? Fluency effects on risk perception and effort prediction. *Advances in Consumer Research*, 36: 10–11.

Spence, C. (2015) Eating with our ears: assessing the importance of the sounds of consumption to our perception and enjoyment of multisensory flavour experiences. *Flavour*, 4 (1): 3.

Spencer, S.J., Strahan, E.J. and Zanna, M.P. (2003) Subliminal priming and choice. *Advances in Consumer Research*, 30: 151–3.

Stuckey, B. (2012) *Taste What You're Missing: The Passionate Eater's Guide to Why Good Food Tastes Good*. London: Free Press.

Tai, S.H.C. and Fung, A.M.C. (1997) Application of an environmental psychology model to in-store buying behaviour. *International Review of Retail, Distribution and Consumer Research*, 7 (4): 311–37.

Thomas, M., Morwitz, V. and Pyone, J.S. (2010) The precision effect in numbers: how processing fluency of numbers influences response confidence. *Advances in Consumer Research*, 37: 151–2.

Warr, P.B. and Knapper, C. (1968) *The Perception of People and Events*. London: Wiley.

Zampini, M. and Spence, C. (2004) The role of auditory cues in modulating the perceived crispness and staleness of potato chips. *Journal of Sensory Studies*, 19 (5): 347–63.

Zhao, G. and Pechmann, C. (2006) Regulatory focus, feature positive effect, and message framing. *Advances in Consumer Research*, 33: 100.

MORE ONLINE

For additional materials that support this chapter and your learning, please visit:
https://study.sagepub.com/sethnaandblythe

CHAPTER 9

LEARNING AND KNOWLEDGE

LEARNING OBJECTIVES

After reading this chapter you should be able to:

- Explain what constitutes learning and what does not.
- Explain the role of classical conditioning.
- Describe how operant conditioning works.
- Describe how cognitive learning can be used by marketers.
- Understand the role of motivation in learning.
- Show how experiential learning is more effective than vicarious learning.
- Describe the various components of consumer knowledge and their importance to marketers.

INTRODUCTION

Learning is not only about what happens in a classroom. Most behaviour is learned as a result of external experiences; most of what people know (and almost certainly many of the things they are most proud of knowing) they learned outside school. People learn things partly through a formalised structure of teaching (or of self-teaching, perhaps by correspondence course) and partly through an unconscious process of learning by experience.

Consumption habits particularly are learned. British people were not born with a liking for fish and chips, any more than a Parsee is born with a liking for dhansak or an Australian for Vegemite. Learning is highly relevant to marketing, since consumers are affected by the things they learn, and much consumer behaviour is actually based on the learning process.

Persuading consumers to remember the information they see in advertisements is a major problem for marketers; for example, some years ago a series of humorous advertisements were produced for Cinzano vermouth. The adverts starred Joan Collins and Leonard Rossiter, and were widely screened throughout the UK, yet they were ineffective in increasing sales of the product. The reason for this was made clear when market research discovered that most consumers thought the ads were for Martini vermouth, Cinzano's main competitor. The underlying reason, however, is that humour in advertising appears to impair memory for products but enhance memory for the advertisement itself (Hansen et al. 2009).

This chapter is about the ways in which the brain orders and stores information.

DEFINING LEARNING

Learning is defined as 'the behavioural changes that occur over time relative to an external stimulus condition' (Onkvisit and Shaw 1994). According to this definition, activities are changed or originated through a reaction to an encountered situation. We can therefore say that someone has learned something if, as a result, their behaviour changes in some way. The factors involved in learning are shown diagrammatically in Figure 9.1: existing behaviour is modified by events, information and stimuli, and new behaviour results in future.

The main conditions that arise from the definition are as follows:

1. There must be a change in behaviour (response tendencies).
2. This must result from an external stimulus.

Learning has not taken place under the following circumstances:

1. *Species response tendencies.* These are instincts, or reflexes; for example, the response of ducking out of the way when a stone is thrown at you does not rely on your having learned that stones are hard and can hurt your body.
2. *Maturation.* Behavioural changes often occur in adolescence due to, for example, hormonal changes, but again these are not a result of learning.
3. *Temporary states of the organism.* While behaviour can be, and often is, affected by tiredness, hunger, drunkenness, etc. these factors do not constitute part of a larger learning process (even though learning may result from those states; the drunk may learn to drink less in future).
4. *Damage to the brain.* Changes in behaviour due to surgery, disease or injury are obviously not a result of any learning taking place.

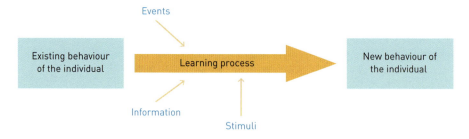

FIGURE 9.1 Learning

STUDYING LEARNING

Regarding the study of learning there are two main schools of thought: first, the stimulus–response approach which further subdivides into classical and operant conditioning, and second, cognitive theories where the conscious thought of the individual enters into the equation.

CLASSICAL LEARNING THEORY

The classical theory of learning was developed by, among others, the Russian researcher Pavlov (1927). Pavlov's famous experiments with dogs demonstrated that automatic responses (reflexes) could be learned. What Pavlov did was present a dog with an *unconditioned stimulus* (in this case, meat powder) knowing that this would lead to an *unconditioned response* (salivation). At the same time Pavlov would ring a bell (the conditioned stimulus). After a while the dog would associate the ringing of the bell with the meat, and would salivate whenever it heard the bell, without actually seeing any meat. This mechanism is shown in Figure 9.2.

Classical conditioning like this occurs with humans: many smokers associate having a cup of coffee with having a cigarette, and find it difficult to give up smoking without also giving up coffee. Likewise, the use of popular music in advertisements is an example of classical conditioning. Repeated exposure to the advertisement leads the individual to associate the music with the product. This leads to two results: first, if the consumer likes the music, that extends to liking the product and second, the consumer will tend to think of the product whenever she or he hears the music. Assuming the song used actually becomes (or is already) a hit, the company will obtain some free exposure whenever the song is played on the radio. Likewise, Christmas music played in retail shops during December tends to create a mood in which consumers are more likely to buy presents and seasonal items.

Unconditioned stimulus

A stimulus that occurs without the intervention of an experimenter

Unconditioned response

A natural response to stimulus

Classical conditioning

The learning process characterised by repeating a stimulus at about the same time as a given behaviour occurs, with the aim of creating a permanent association between the stimulus and the behaviour

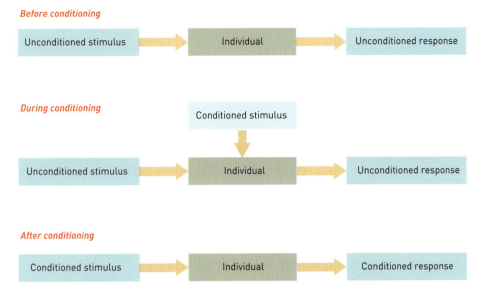

FIGURE 9.2 Classical conditioning

For this to work it is usually necessary to repeat the stimulus a number of times in order for the conditioned response to become established. The number of times the process needs to be repeated will depend on the strength of the stimulus and the receptiveness (motivation) of the individual. Research has shown that, although conditioning has been reported for a single conditioning event (Gorn 1982), perhaps as many as 30 pairings may be required before conditioning is maximised (Kroeber-Riel 1984).

Before conditioning, the unconditioned stimulus feeding into the brain causes the unconditioned response. During the conditioning both the conditioned stimulus and the unconditioned stimulus are presented, so that after conditioning the conditioned stimulus alone will produce the response.

Behaviours influenced by classical conditioning are thought to be involuntary. If the doorbell rings, it is automatic for most people to look up, without consciously thinking about whether somebody is at the door. Most people are familiar with the start of recognition that sometimes occurs if a similar doorbell is rung during a TV drama; or perhaps upon hearing the classic Nokia ringtone. Classical conditioning also operates on the emotions; playing Christmas music will elicit memories of childhood Christmases, and advertisements evoking nostalgic feelings will generate warmth towards the product. For instance, department stores such as John Lewis and Marks and Spencer's have for a few years now been competing every Christmas to see who can produce the most emotionally charged advert.

Another factor in the effectiveness of classical conditioning is the order in which the conditioned stimulus and the unconditioned stimulus are presented (see Figure 9.3). In forward conditioning the conditioned stimulus (CS) comes before the unconditioned stimulus (US). This would mean that the product would be shown before the music is played.

In backward conditioning the US (unconditioned stimulus) comes before the CS (conditioned stimulus). Here the music would be played before the product is shown. Simultaneous conditioning requires both to be presented at the same time.

FIGURE 9.3 Ordering of stimuli

It appears that forward conditioning and simultaneous conditioning work best in advertising (McSweeney and Bierley 1984). This means that it is usually better to present the product before playing the popular tune, or play both together; the responses from this approach are usually stronger and longer-lasting. If classical conditioning is being used, clearly the broadcast media will be better-suited since it is easier to control the order in which the stimuli are presented; with print media this is not necessarily the case. For example, not everybody reads newspapers from front to back. Many people would start with the sports pages (at the back) and work forward, or perhaps read the headlines on the front pages then go straight to the TV pages before coming back to the local news. This behaviour continues today and has been made easier with technology and search functions, with many avid sports fans looking for the 'sports' tab on news websites. Even if the conditioned stimulus and unconditioned stimulus are placed in the same ad on the same page, it is still possible that the reader's eye will be drawn to each stimulus in the wrong order; in other words, people do not necessarily read each page from top to bottom, either.

For these reasons the print media are not as effective for classical conditioning as are the broadcast media such as web, radio and TV, where the order of presentation of the stimuli is controllable.

Extinction occurs when the conditioned stimulus no longer evokes the conditioned response. This occurs in the ways shown in Table 9.1.

Generalisation happens when a stimulus that is close to the existing one evokes the same response. Pavlov found that a sound similar to the bell he used could also stimulate salivation, and it is often the case that a similar brand name can evoke a purchase response. A very common tactic in marketing is to produce similar packaging to that of one's competitor in order to take advantage of the generalisation effect. For an example of this, observe the remarkable similarity in packaging between Tesco Gold instant coffee (£3.98 for 200g) and Nescafé Gold Blend instant coffee (£5.99 for 200g).

Extinction
The process of forgetting a conditioned reflex

Generalisation
The tendency for a conditioned stimulus to lead to a wider than intended set of conditioned reflexes

TABLE 9.1 Extinction

Reason for extinction	Example	Explanation	Techniques to avoid extinction
The conditioned stimulus is encountered without the unconditioned stimulus	The product is shown without the background music	Seeing the product without the music tends to reduce the association of the music with the product; other stimuli will replace the music	Ensure that all the advertising uses the same music, or imagery associated with the music
The unconditioned stimulus is encountered without the conditioned stimulus	The background music is heard without the product being present	In this case, other stimuli may be evoked by the music; it will become associated with something other than the product	Either ensure that the music is not played anywhere other than when the product is being shown, or ensure that the product is available when the music is played. For example, if the product is a drink to be sold in nightclubs, ensure that the clubs have an ample supply of the drink being advertised

Discrimination

The process by which people distinguish between stimuli

Discrimination is the process by which we learn to distinguish between stimuli, and only respond to the appropriate one. Consumers quite quickly learn to distinguish between brands, even when the design of the packaging is similar. Advertisers will often encourage discrimination by pairing a positive unconditioned stimulus with their own product, but not with the competitor's product. For example, the HSBC slogan 'The world's local bank' conveys a clear image of a bank with worldwide experience coupled with familiarity with local customs and banking practice. Other banks are clearly excluded from this slogan. Even greater discrimination occurs when the competitor's product is paired with a negative unconditioned stimulus, for example by using phrases such as 'Unlike our competitors, we do not charge you a service fee'.

Classical conditioning is responsible for many repetitive advertising campaigns, and for many catchphrases which are now in common use. Some advertising fosters this, such as the 'Does exactly what it says on the tin' campaign for Ronseal Woodstain, which has resulted in the slogan entering the language.

Classical conditioning assumes that the individual plays no active role in the learning process. Pavlov's dogs did not have to do anything in order to be 'conditioned', because the process was carried out on their involuntary reflex of salivation. Although classical conditioning does operate in human beings, people are not usually passive in the process; the individual person (like most higher animals) is able to take part in the process and cooperate with it or avoid it. This process of active role-playing is called **operant conditioning**.

Operant conditioning

The learning process in which the learner is rewarded for a correct action, and in which the learner plays an active role

OPERANT CONDITIONING

Here the learner will conduct trial-and-error behaviour to obtain a reward (or avoid a punishment). Burris F. Skinner (1953) developed the concept in order to explain higher-level learning than that identified by Pavlov. The difference between Pavlov's approach and the operant conditioning approach is that the learner has choice in the outcome; the modern view of classical conditioning is that it also involves a cognitive dimension. In other words, Skinner is describing a type of learning that requires the learner to do something rather than be a passive recipient of a stimulus. The modern view is that even Pavlov's dog would have thought 'Here comes dinner' when the bell rang.

The basis of operant conditioning is the concept of reinforcement. If someone buys a product and is pleased with the outcome of using it, then he or she is likely to buy the product again. This means that the activity has had a positive reinforcement, and the consumer has become 'conditioned' to buy the product next time. The greater the positive reinforcement, the greater the likelihood of repeat purchase.

CHALLENGING THE STATUS QUO

How active are people in learning? Do we really seek out knowledge and consider everything that comes our way? Or does most of it go in one ear and out the other? Or is technology perhaps negating the need to learn and thus questioning the relevance of teaching itself? (A calculator exists for those who can't do basic mathematics – audio books for those that can't read – and satnav for those who can't find their way around a map.)

How many times have you been able to answer (say) a quiz question without having any idea where that nugget of information came from? How often do you say, 'Oh, that's common knowledge'.

So were you born knowing this stuff? Games such as Trivial Pursuit are based on this kind of mental fluff – useless facts that just happen to have lodged in your brain, not through repetition (classical conditioning) nor through operant conditioning, but just through some kind of alien implanting process.

Conversely, there are now thousands of people around the world who are actively engaged in

©iStock.com/spectrelabs

playing the Cashflow Board Game, a game developed by Robert Kiyosaki (author of *Rich Dad Poor Dad* (2011) – a book about investing for financial independence). They believe that by actively playing the game, in relatively safe and controlled conditions, they will undergo a process of learning (through both classical and operant conditioning) which they can then replicate in real life. This has become so popular that it is possible to find a group (through www.meetup.com) to play with in most cities around the world.

If the reward works, the consumer will try to think of a way to make it even better: if a little will help, a lot will cure. This can lead to over-indulgence in food or alcohol, or indeed almost any other pleasurable activity. Typically this will happen if the consumer's need cannot be totally met by the product, but will be helped; a person with a serious psychological problem may well find that alcohol helps, but doesn't cure. An increasing intake of alcohol will never result in a complete meeting of the person's psychological needs because eventually sobriety will begin to set in again.

An example of operant conditioning is the growth of loyalty cards in retail stores, for example Tesco's Clubcard. Customers who remain loyal to Tesco are sent extra discounts and offers, and also their purchasing behaviour can be traced through the electronic point-of-sale systems so that offers can be targeted to those Tesco customers who will really be interested in them.

Airline loyalty schemes saw huge growth in the early part of the century, although this growth has levelled off more recently. Most of these are aimed at reinforcing the frequent flyers, whose loyalty is desirable since they are likely to be the most profitable customers. The airlines offer limited free flights to their most regular customers, and for many business travellers these free flights offer an attractive reason for choosing the same airline every time. Loyalty cards are especially attractive to business customers because their flights are often paid for by their firms, so they are less likely to have to shop around for cheap deals.

The problem with this type of loyalty scheme is that it is perfectly feasible for people to carry loyalty cards for several stores (or join the Frequent Flyer clubs of several airlines – AAdvantage, Executive Club, Iberia Plus, Miles and More, Flying Blue, etc.) and thus reap the rewards without actually having to remain loyal to any supplier. In effect, people have been taught to play the system, gaining the benefits without actually having to contribute anything.

CONSUMER BEHAVIOUR IN ACTION: PIZZALAND

©iStock.com/ElNariz

Although pizza appeared on a menu dated 1934, it was virtually unknown in Britain before 1965, when the first Pizza Express restaurant opened in London. Within just a few years, pizzerias were springing up all over the UK, and in the 1970s Pizzaland made its first appearance.

Pizzaland positioned itself as a cheaper version of Pizza Hut (although at first, bizarrely, the restaurants had a Tyrolean-themed decor). The restaurants offered all-you-can-eat promotions, special two-for-one offers and themed evenings. This aggressive approach meant that the chain grew rapidly until there were Pizzalands in every major town in the UK.

On the other hand, an over-use of incentives can lead to negative consequences for the producer. Pizzaland's discount vouchers, which were given away in newspapers, on bus tickets and even on cans of tuna, resulted in a major re-education of customers. Many people would not eat at Pizzaland unless they had a discount voucher. In this way, the positive reinforcement backfired on the company, since there is an implied *negative* reinforcement in *not* going in with a voucher.

Of course, the company was now giving away so many pizzas that profits dropped dramatically: if the two-for-one offer stopped, people simply went elsewhere until the offer was re-instated, so Pizzaland were effectively selling all their pizzas at half price. In these circumstances, the company would hope to make up the difference by selling more desserts, beverages and starters, but since their clientele were mainly bargain hunters (some might say cheapskates) it was not unusual for people to have just the pizza, then go to the pub to buy a beer or a glass of wine afterwards.

Eventually Pizzaland disappeared altogether, a monument to the learning abilities of consumers.

Figure 9.4 charts three forms of operant conditioning. In the first example, positive reinforcement, the individual receives a stimulus and acts upon it. This action works, and the individual gets a good result; this leads to the behaviour being repeated if the same antecedent stimulus is presented at a later date. For example, if you are in a long queue at a retailer such as the DIY store B&Q you might notice that the customer service counter is empty or even the self-service counter, and go there to make your

FIGURE 9.4 Operant conditioning (adapted from Widrick 1986)

Reprinted with permission from Marketing News, published by the American Marketing Association, Vol 20, 1986: 48–49.

purchases instead of the usual tills. This enables you to leave the store quicker, and so if you find yourself in a long queue in B&Q again at some time, you are likely to try the same tactic once more.

The second example in the diagram shows a negative stimulus: this time the operant behaviour relieves the problem, and again the individual has learned how to avoid bad consequences when faced with a difficulty.

The third example shows how punishment fits into the learning process. If the operant behaviour leads to a bad result, for example the customer service counter won't serve you and you lose your original place in the queue, you will not try that tactic again. The problem with punishment as a motivator, in this example, is that it may lead to the individual not shopping at B&Q again. (Revisit Chapter 6 for the discussion on pain avoidance.)

Operant conditioning does not necessarily require a product purchase; marketers will frequently give away free samples in the hope that a positive experience from using the product will encourage consumers to purchase in future (for example, wee drams of malt whisky given out at the airport, or new flavours of coffee outside Starbucks). Likewise, car dealers always offer a test drive; some go even further, and allow the customers and their families to borrow a car for the weekend in order to get a very clear reinforcement of the car's merits (for instance, the new Jaguar XF strap line encouraging a test drive says: 'Don't just drive it. Live it' – www.motoring. co.uk/car-news/jaguar-xf-don-t-just-drive-it-live-it_65933).

Operant conditioning is helpful in explaining how people become conditioned, or form habits of purchase; however, it still does not explain how learning operates when people become active in seeking out information. To understand this aspect of learning, it is necessary to look at the cognitive learning process.

COGNITIVE LEARNING

Not all learning is an automatic response to a stimulus. People analyse purchasing situations taking into account previous experiences, and make evaluative judgements. Learning is part of this, both in terms of informing the process as a result of earlier experiences, and also in terms of the consumer's approach to learning more about the product category or brand.

Cognitive learning

Acquiring and retaining new information through a conscious effort or thought

When considering cognitive learning, the emphasis is not on *what* is learned (as in stimulus–response theories) but on *how* it is learned. Classical learning and operant conditioning theories suppose that learning is automatic; cognitive learning theories assume that there is a conscious process going on. This is true in many cases of consumer behaviour.

The classical and operant theories assume that what goes on inside the consumer's head is a 'black box', in that we know that a given stimulus will prompt a particular response, but for most practical purposes we have no real way of knowing what is happening inside the black box. Within the cognitive learning paradigm, however, we are concerned with what happens inside the box, and we try to infer what is going on by analysing behaviour and responses from the individual. Figure 9.5 illustrates this.

The black box contains the cognitive processes; the stimulus is considered in the light of the individual's memory of what has happened in the past when presented with similar stimuli, his or her assessment of the desirable outcome and an assessment of the likely outcome of any action. Following this processing, the individual produces a response.

Cognitive learning expertise has five aspects, summarised in Figure 9.6.

Cognitive effort

The amount of work needed to consider a course of action or understand a set of issues

Cognitive effort is the degree of effort the consumer is prepared to put into thinking about the product offering. This will depend on such aspects as the complexity of the product, the consumer's involvement with it and the motivation for learning. Making a complex decision can often lead to forgetting not only what the decision was, but in some cases forgetting that a decision has been made (Norton and Chance 2008). Most of us are familiar with making a choice from a packed restaurant menu, then forgetting what it was we had ordered when the food arrives.

Cognitive structure

The way the individual thinks, and the way new information is fitted into existing knowledge

Cognitive structure is about the way the consumer thinks, and the way the information is fitted into the existing knowledge.

Learning diagram

BLACK BOX

STIMULUS → Processing centre

* Memory

* Goals

* Expectations

→ RESPONSE

FIGURE 9.5 Cognitive learning

FIGURE 9.6 Factors in cognitive learning

The *analysis* of information is first concerned with selecting the correct, relevant information from the environment, and second with interpreting the information correctly in order to obtain a clear action plan.

Elaboration is the structuring of the information within the brain, and adding to it from memory in order to form a coherent whole.

Memory is the mechanism by which learned information is stored. In fact, nothing is ever truly forgotten; information will eventually become irrecoverable by the conscious mind (forgotten) but the brain still retains the information and can be stimulated to recall it, either by hypnosis or by association of ideas.

Cognitive learning processes are important to marketers since they are helpful in predicting consumer responses to advertising. Stephen J. Hoch and Young-Won Ha (1986) say that consumers view advertisements as tentative hypotheses about product performance that can be tested through product experience, and this perspective has been added to by Sumpradit et al. (2015) who note that negative attitudes can often interfere with the processing of the message content. Early learning about a product will affect future learning; this is called the Law of Primacy (see Chapter 8). For this reason first impressions count for a great deal.

According to Hoch and Ha (1986), advertising will tend to be ignored if there is unambiguous objective evidence to hand; if you can test the product for yourself, advertising has only a small effect. If the evidence is ambiguous or unobtainable at first hand (as is often the case), advertising might sway you, and in fact advertising appears to have dramatic effects on consumers' perceptions of quality. For example, it is possible for somebody to visit a computer retailer to test a new laptop before making a commitment to buy. Thus, advertising plays a small part in computer purchase, only serving to alert the consumer to what is available within the current technology. Conversely, somebody spending a similar amount on a package holiday has no chance to try out the holiday before buying it, and is therefore more likely to be swayed by the advertising or other communications (brochures, salespeople, etc.). One of the main considerations for a consumer in that position is the reputation of the service provider, since the consumer is, after all, buying a promise.

Learning from experience is a four-stage process, as Table 9.2 shows.

In most cases people prefer to learn by experience, especially for major product purchases; few people would buy a car without having a test drive first, and still fewer

Elaboration
The structuring of information within the brain, relating it to existing memory

TABLE 9.2 Learning from experience

Stage	Explanation	Example	Marketing response
Hypothesising	Developing a rough estimate as to what's happening or what's available	Getting information from a friend, or reading some advertising material; trawling through blogs/websites	Have clearly written and informative blogs and websites, don't use too much jargon, especially if your product is a complex one, or can be 'test-driven'
Exposure	Having a look at the product, trying one out, getting direct experience of it	Visiting a retailer or outlet to try the product and ask questions about it	Ensure that the product is on display, and allow plenty of opportunity for hands-on testing
Encoding	Making sense of the information	Translating the jargon into something comprehensible, perhaps getting some clarification; understanding what the product is and does in terms that fit in with previous experience	Have salespeople who can explain things in lay terms, and who don't frighten off the customer by using too much technical language
Integration	Fitting the new information into the existing knowledge bank	Thinking about the new information gained about the product and discarding previous misconceptions	Ensure that customers feel able to come back for further explanations if they still have problems. Make sure that customers understand everything before leaving the outlet

would buy one online unless they were people with previous direct experience of the car. It is for this reason that online retailers have a no-quibble money-back guarantee; if this were not the case, few people would be prepared to buy online rather than visit a high street shop where they can see and feel the goods. It's interesting to note here that when most people are buying a house – usually the single largest purchase that they will make in their life – there is no chance of 'living in the property' in order to learn from experience, and they will probably only make two or three visits prior to making an offer to purchase.

There are also three moderating factors in the cognitive learning process:

1. *Familiarity* with the domain. This is the degree to which the consumer has pre-existing knowledge of the product category. For example, an IT enthusiast would go through a different, and probably shorter, learning curve for buying a new laptop than would a complete novice. Familiarity with the components of a brand name make it more memorable (Blackston and Lebar 2015).

2. *Motivation* to learn. If the purchase is an important one, or the possible effects of making a mistake would be serious, the consumer is likely to be highly motivated to obtain as much information as possible. People also appear to remember advertising better if they either love or hate the advert; neutral advertising is quickly forgotten (Küster and Eisend 2015).

3. *Ambiguity* of the information environment. If the information is hard to get, contradictory or incomprehensible, this will hinder the learning process. Sometimes consumers give up on the process if this is the case. Researchers at Carnegie Mellon University found that individuals tend to be averse to risk and ambiguity when uncertainty (or other circumstances) makes the information gap unpleasant to think about. Yet when an information gap happens to be pleasant, an individual may seek gambles providing exposure to it (Golman et al. 2015).

Table 9.3 illustrates these moderating factors in terms of classifying readiness to learn from experience.

If someone is highly motivated to learn (for example, a Russian who has committed to studying for an MBA degree in the UK might be highly motivated to learn English) the learning process is most susceptible to management. The individual would probably want to follow a formal course of study (evening classes or a distance learning course) and would welcome help in managing the learning process. If the individual already speaks a little English, but has decided to study in Aberystwyth in Wales, the motivation to learn Welsh might also be strong, but familiarity with the domain (learning a foreign language) might cause the individual to form beliefs that are unrealistic (for example believing that the process will be easier than it actually is).

People who are only weakly motivated to learn are obviously less likely to want their learning managed, or indeed to manage it themselves. If the person is unfamiliar with the domain, he or she is unlikely to be interested in learning at all; if, on the other hand, the domain is all too familiar, complacency sets in and the person is likely to say 'I already know all that stuff' and thus will have no interest in managing learning. Motivation has an effect on the tendency to flick TV advertisements by *channel hopping* – if the advertisement is unpleasant or uninformative, the advert is more likely

Flicking
Also called zapping. Using a remote control device to avoid advertisements by switching to another channel

TABLE 9.3 Managing the learning process

How motivated are people to learn?	What do consumers already know?	How much can experience teach?	
		Little (high ambiguity)	A lot (low ambiguity)
Highly motivated to learn	Unfamiliar with the domain	Learning is most susceptible to management	Learning is spontaneous, rapid and difficult to manage
	Familiar with the domain	Formation of superstitious beliefs is possible. Existing beliefs inhibit suggestibility	
Weakly motivated to learn	Unfamiliar with the domain	Learning is slow to start and difficult to sustain, but is susceptible to management	Learning is difficult to initiate and, once started, is difficult to manage
	Familiar with the domain	Complacency inhibits initiation of learning, so experience is unresponsive to management	

Source: Hoch and Deighton (1989)

Reprinted with permission from Journal of Marketing, published by the American Marketing Association, Hoch, S. J. and Deighton, J., Vol. 53, 1989: 1–20.

to be zapped, but at higher levels informativeness and pleasantness are incompatible because of a reduced motivation and ability to process information (Elpers et al. 2002).

If people are unable to learn much by experience, the situation becomes ambiguous; if learning by experience is the main way of learning, the situation is unambiguous but learning is difficult to manage. From the viewpoint of marketers, encouraging people to learn about products is easiest when the individuals are motivated to learn, and where the situation is ambiguous and therefore needs careful explanation.

Cognitive lock-in occurs when there is a high cognitive cost either in obtaining information, or in switching providers. This happens on the Internet: people tend to stick with the sites they are familiar with rather than going to the trouble of learning how to navigate a new site, especially if the initial setting up or the ongoing usage is difficult (Murray and Haubl 2002; Zauberman 2002; Cheung et al. 2015). It has been found that habit exhibits a significant moderating effect on the relationship between alternative attractiveness and continuous intention (Cheung et al. 2015).

Incidentally, people who respond most favourably to online advertising are those with a high motivation to learn, high social escapism and high Internet ability due to its perceived informativeness (Zhou and Bao 2002). Moreover, the social capital derived from participating in online social networks also contributes to having a positive impact in response to advertising (Pinho and Soares 2015). Evidently a desire to learn affects the ways people learn as well as their capacity for learning.

Cognitive theories recognise that consumers influence the outcome in an active manner, so the learning process is not always easy for an outsider (i.e. a marketing person) to manage. This may be some of the reason why new products fail so frequently; weak motivation to learn about new products leads to difficulty for marketers in starting the learning process.

Cognitive learning can also be viewed as having five elements, as shown in Figure 9.7.

1. **Drive.** As seen in Chapter 6, drive is the stimulus that impels action. It is strong, internal and general. The impulse to learn can be driven by a fear of making an expensive mistake, or by a desire to maximise the benefits of the purchase.

2. **Cue.** This is some external trigger which encourages learning. It is weaker than a drive, is external and is specific. For example, a public service such as the Health and Safety Executive might exhort employers to send for a leaflet on safety in the workplace. Sometimes firms will use advertisement retrieval cues to trigger responses.

3. **Response.** This is the reaction the consumer makes to the interaction between a drive and a cue. With luck, this results in a sale; but humans learn, and will base future purchases on their concrete experience of the product rather than on the marketer's cues.

FIGURE 9.7 Five elements of cognitive learning

4. **Reinforcement**. Purchase response should be rewarded with a positive experience of the product. The object of reinforcement is to get consumers to associate the product with certain benefits.

5. **Retention**. This is the stability of the learned material over time, or in other words how well it is remembered. For example, advertising jingles have very high retention. People can often recall jingles that have not been broadcast for 30 years or more (for example, people often remember the original Nokia ringtone or the theme tune to Sesame Street). This is particularly true for advertisements that were popular when the individual was a child. (The opposite of retention is extinction.)

Cognitive learning usually involves some form of reasoning – people need to think about what they are seeing or hearing in order to remember the information. If the person has a low involvement with the product or brand, it will take a long time for the information to sink in, whereas if the individual has a high involvement with the product the information is processed and absorbed much more effectively, presumably because the person is thinking about the product much more (Krugman 1965). Current examples of such high online and Internet involvement have led to issues of Internet addiction (Wiegman and van Schie 1998). Michelle Wright has recently published some extremely interesting work investigating how adults have learnt about and adopted coping strategies in response to cyber aggression and cyber victimisation (Wright 2015).

Part of the problem for marketers is that they have little or no control over how people think about the messages they are shown. For example, an advertisement may be designed to be as interesting as possible in order to cut through advertising clutter and attract attention, but the people who see the ad may become more interested in the cleverness of the advertising than they are in the brand (Pieters et al. 2002). This is exemplified by the Cinzano adverts mentioned earlier in the chapter – enjoyment of a clever and entertaining advertisement detracted from people's understanding of what was actually being advertised. The reasoning process is shown in Figure 9.8: the stimulus is followed by a reasoning process, which may lead either to retaining the information or forgetting it, according to how interested the individual is in the subject matter.

A further possibility for cognitive learning is vicarious learning, in which we learn from the experiences of others; other consumers or other competitors. This is an extremely useful way of learning, since it requires much less effort and risk than learning directly by trial and error. It requires either direct observation (watching what happens to

Reinforcement
The process of consolidating classical conditioning

Retention
The stability of learned material over time

Advertising clutter
Excessive information, especially applied to advertising; a situation in which the recipient is presented with a large number of stimuli at the same time

FIGURE 9.8 Reasoning and cognitive learning

someone else when they buy a product or behave in a particular way) or effective communication (as when someone describes their learning experiences). Because human beings are excellent communicators compared with most other species, we are particularly good at vicarious learning. In the marketing context, advertisers use models to show how products are used, and to show (or describe) the benefits of using a specific product. Having said that, learning by doing is generally much more effective than vicarious learning – imagine how far you would get in learning to drive a car if all you were ever allowed to do was to observe other drivers and read an instruction book.

CHALLENGING THE STATUS QUO

©iStock.com/skynesher

So learning by doing is more effective than thinking about things. If that's so, why do we still sit in classrooms, read books and (eventually) get a degree or other qualification? Why don't we do all our learning at work? Whatever happened to getting oneself apprenticed at 14 and spending seven to ten years becoming a master craftsman?

Most of us can remember assignments we have written a great deal better than we can remember any lectures we attended – and we can remember how to play cricket, football, netball, hockey, and so forth a great deal better than we can remember Shakespeare's plays (unless we acted in them, of course). So much for schoolroom lessons!

Maybe it's just about motivation to learn, but maybe there is something wrong with the way the education system operates: perhaps sitting through an hour-long monologue delivered by someone in a beige cardigan is not the best way to learn!

Enter the 'flipped classroom'! Many educators are fast running away from the traditional lecture-then-seminar-then-homework model. Instead, they provide the learners with lots of pre-class materials (content-based videos, readings and possibly even assessments). Then in class, the content and learning is reinforced with practical hands-on activities. Thus the students are held responsible for their learning by increasing engagement and therefore by default, attendance as well. The educator has more of a role as a facilitator here rather than a lecturer.

Learned responses are never truly unlearned. The brain remembers (stores) everything, but rather like a computer with a faulty hard-drive it may not always be able to recall (retrieve) everything. Also, the human memory is huge; the *Encyclopedia Britannica* contains around 12,500 million characters, but the brain has approximately 125,000,000 million characters in storage capacity; this is enough storage to hold 10,000 *Encyclopedia Britannica*s.

THE NEED FOR KNOWLEDGE

The purpose of learning about products is mainly to reduce risk. The more one knows about the product and the product category, the lower the level of risk, as shown in Figure 9.9. In many cases, less knowledgeable buyers will ask a more knowledgeable friend to help in making the purchase. In some cases, people will spend considerable time researching information about the product category and individual brands (this is mainly true where there is high involvement with the product or where there is a high risk).

Lack of knowledge may lead to a purchase that is inappropriate: for example, an inexperienced car buyer might miss a sign of potential engine problems, whereas more experienced and knowledgeable buyers would not. Knowledgeable people have a better understanding of what attributes to look for, and how to evaluate the product against those attributes (Alba and Hutchinson 1987).

The key point here, however, is that people understand that they need to know about the products they buy, especially when a major commitment is involved. This means that there is a motivation to learn, arising from a need for knowledge (see Chapter 6). This need is met through the same ways as any other need – goals are set, heuristics are developed and the process is as subject to interrupts and dissonance as the actual purchase itself.

As knowledge
increases, risk reduces

Risk

Knowledge

FIGURE 9.9 Knowledge and risk

CHALLENGING THE STATUS QUO

If we have such a drive to learn, why is it that so many people dislike school? How come truancy rates in school are the highest they have ever been – and later at university, classes are not always as well attended as they might be (especially considering that there has been a significant rise in tuition fees from 2012 to date). And even more to the point, this is in a situation where attendance and learning affect one's capacity to earn money – a project dear to most people's hearts!

Perhaps it isn't so much that we don't want to learn as that we don't want to be told what to learn? So is there a problem with the way that we are taught? Can you see the traditional classroom coming to an end, in favour of new ways of learning, such as, for instance, MOOCs?

This drive to extend knowledge about products accounts for the widespread sale of specialist consumer magazines. For example, a magazine aimed at private pilots will contain flight tests of new light aircraft, information about flying schools and detailed tests of auxiliary equipment such as radios and GPS units. In most cases, the products are supplied to the magazines by the producers in order to gain publicity for the products: this is clearly a marketing communications activity, but the magazine's readers are eager to learn about products that may make their flying easier, safer and more enjoyable.

Each individual has many different types of knowledge, as shown in Figure 9.10. This is far from being a comprehensive list of an individual's knowledge categories, but some knowledge in each category will relate to marketing issues. The main types of knowledge of interest from a marketing point of view are as follows:

1. *Product knowledge.* This subdivides into *product category knowledge* and *brand knowledge.* Product category knowledge is the information an individual remembers about all the possible solutions to the need problem.

2. *Purchase knowledge.* This is about how to buy, what things cost and where to buy from.

3. *Consumption* or *usage knowledge.* This is about how to use the product, how to dispose of whatever is left after use, what the risks are in using the product and what will be done with the product at the end-of-life (EOL).

4. *Persuasion knowledge.* This is an understanding of the goals and tactics of people who might be trying to persuade us to buy – in the main, this is knowledge about marketers, but it includes knowledge about friends, review websites, etc. who might be recommending a product or service to us.

End-of-life (EOL)

A term used to indicate that a product has come to the end of its useful life and where a vendor stops marketing, selling and sustaining it (there may also be a responsibility and requirement for the OEM to dispose of the product in a sustainable way)

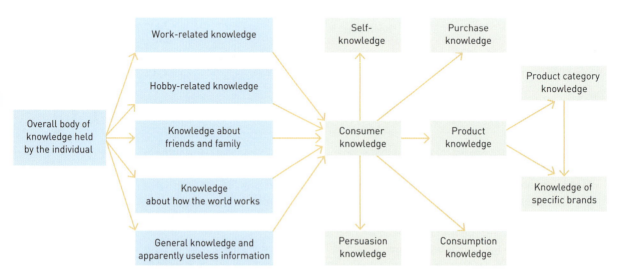

FIGURE 9.10 Categorising knowledge

5. *Self-knowledge.* This is knowledge about one's own needs, including knowledge about one's own failings. For example, an adult deciding to learn how to play the piano will be well aware of his or her lack of knowledge about the instrument, and therefore be more prepared to watch instructional videos on YouTube or www.onlinepianist.com, get piano lessons and extra coaching and, of course, to practise, practise, practise.

PRODUCT CATEGORY KNOWLEDGE

This type of product knowledge is fairly general. For example, we all know what a television set is, and broadly we all know how to operate one, and know what it will do for us in terms of entertainment. Relatively fewer of us would know the difference between a plasma, LCD and LED screen, even if we know that the terms refer to flat screens. Few of us would really understand the technicalities of how digital TV works, even though this is the only available TV system in the UK. If we head into the technical detail of ultra high definition and 4K resolution, almost all of us would be lost. Someone who has basic product knowledge is called a product novice; someone who has a large amount of product knowledge is a product expert. (So, for instance, an enthusiast or expert will know that, technically speaking, the ultra high definition is actually a derivation of the 4K digital cinema standard, but while the local multiplex cinema shows movies in the native 4096 x 2160 4K resolution, the ultra HD consumer format has a slightly lower resolution of 3840 x 2160.) Those who have large amounts of product or market knowledge and enjoy sharing this knowledge with others are called market mavens (see Chapter 7).

Novices

Customers who have purchased the product for the first time within the last 90 days

Knowledge about these different factors would be chunked in the individual's memory under the category of 'TV sets'. For most people, information is frequently cross-referenced, so that information about the microchips might also be contained in the category of 'things I know about electronics' or, in some cases, 'things I deal with in work'.

Product expert knowledge is shown in Figure 9.11. A product expert would also have extensive knowledge of the members of a product category (the brands). A product expert would be able to judge unknown product attributes by reference to known attributes (for example, knowing that the product's components are reliable would

FIGURE 9.11 Product expert knowledge

give an indication of the longevity of the product as well as its reliability), and would influence acceptance of a price for a product since the expert would be aware of the prices of competing products. Knowledge influences responses to salespeople, which places a burden on salespeople to judge quickly and accurately how much the prospective customer already knows.

BRAND KNOWLEDGE

Brand knowledge is concerned with what people know about a specific product within the general product category. From a marketing viewpoint, the starting point of brand knowledge is whether people remember the brand at all. The next level is whether people associate the brand strongly with the product category: further increases in knowledge about the brand may follow, but without knowing that the brand exists and that it relates to a particular product there is no chance whatever that the brand will be included in the consideration set.

To test whether individuals have this level of knowledge, market researchers have two main tools. The first is a *recall test*, which tests top-of-the-mind awareness. Respondents might be asked to list all the breakfast cereals they can think of, for example, and the researcher would be able to tell first whether the brand being tested is included in the list, and second where it stands in relation to the other brands. The second method is a *recognition test*, in which people are shown a list of brand names and are asked to say which ones they recognise. The problem with this test is that people may claim to recognise brands they have never heard of rather than appear to be ignorant: sometimes researchers will include fictitious brands in the list to test for this.

The tests are used for different circumstances. A recall test might be useful for testing advertising effectiveness or to determine the product's position in consumers' perceptual maps. A recognition test might be more useful when testing merchandising success, since it is important that people recognise the brand when they see it in-store.

Symbol

A method of converting thought into something that can be transmitted as a message

Both recall and recognition are enhanced when the brand has a strong **symbol** attached to it. The three stripes of Adidas, the smell of a Zippo lighter or the McDonald's sound tag are all powerful symbols, each in a different way. Each one provokes instant recognition, and a clear image of what the product is and what it does.

Encouraging people to learn about brands is a major part of advertising, and certainly of the more information-based, cognitive approaches to advertising. Many sales promotions are aimed at increasing people's knowledge about brands, encouraging them to learn more: for example, the tourist boards of countries sometimes run informative advertisements about their countries, linked to a competition for which the prize is a holiday in the country. In order to win the prize, participants have to complete a questionnaire about the country, which means that they need to view the website and read the advertisement to find out the answers. For instance, VisitScotland have been running a tourism campaign for several years now, offering 4,000 pairs of foot passenger tickets for a free return trip to one of 23 Scottish islands. In 2014, 63,000 people entered the draw.

Brand associations (see Figure 9.12) are the connections people make between the brand and other concepts (Blackwell et al. 2005). Brand associations include beliefs

FIGURE 9.12 Brand association

and perceptions about what the brand will do, in other words, the consumption benefits. Brand associations are important to marketers because they tend to influence the degree to which consumers will adopt the product, and also the degree to which they will accept brand extensions and recommend the product to others (Belen del Rio et al. 2001). The higher the consumer's perception of brand quality, the more likely he or she is to recommend the brand (no surprises there) and also to buy brand extensions. Some very important work in this area has recently been conducted by Chen et al. (2015), and their paper makes for very interesting reading: the authors were able, through neuro-imaging techniques, to identify the areas of the brain involved in processing brand data and to predict which brand the individual is thinking about based on brand associations and brain activity. This type of work which has focused on 'cataloguing brain regions associated with marketing stimuli' has really advanced the application of neuro-scientific methods to consumer research.

Brand extensions may be in products that have some related production similarities, so that one might assume that a firm which is good at making the first product would also be good at making the other. Saab have played on this assumption in their advertising: since the company manufactures fighter aircraft as well as cars, it might be reasonable to assume that the engineering capabilities within the company would be high. Conversely, there is absolutely no reason to suppose that Virgin would be good at running airlines, commissioning new rock bands, running an insurance company and launching spacecraft. Yet the fact that the Virgin brand appears on the products is apparently seen as a signal of quality, and people who have been happy with one Virgin product seem to accept that other Virgin products will have similar quality values.

Developing appropriate brand associations for new products is an especially challenging task. An almost equally challenging task is that of moving an existing product into a new market, and this is precisely the problem firms have when they move to e-commerce and online trading. A brand that is well known in its home market might be entirely unknown in the rest of the world, so apart from the logistical problems of arranging physical distribution the firm faces the challenge of establishing a consistent brand image across a wide spectrum of foreign media, channels and cultures.

PURCHASE KNOWLEDGE

Purchase knowledge is the information people have about buying products. This includes where the product can be bought (the distribution channel), whether discounts apply at some times or in some places, how much the product should cost, and what the procedure/process is for buying the product.

Price is an important issue, because it is the measure of what the consumer has to give in return for the product benefits. This judgement is made not only on the basis of the cost of the brand from different sources, but also on the cost of products that provide similar benefits (Rao and Sieben 1992). If one has little knowledge of the pricing within the product category, one might assume that a reasonable price is far too high (or be delighted to find that the actual price is lower than expected). In some cases, marketers (and especially salespeople) will try to give an impression that the price will be higher than it actually is, in order to delight the customer with the real price. This is called **price conditioning**. For example, a salesperson selling fitted kitchens might, at an early stage of the presentation, suggest that the new kitchen might cost £20,000 or more. When the actual price turns out to be only £12,000 the customer is delighted, but if the customer had been expecting a price of £6,000 the delight would have been replaced by an entirely different feeling.

Price conditioning

Managing the expectations of a potential customer regarding price

It is useful if marketers have knowledge of what people perceive is a reasonable price for a product (See Chapter 8). This will be a combination of what people believe is reasonable when they see the actual product, and what people already know about the price of competing products (see Figure 9.13). Relative price knowledge is what people know about one price relative to another (Monroe et al. 2015). For example, one American study found that people thought that buying books online was about 3% cheaper than buying them from a bricks-and-mortar retailer, whereas in fact the price difference was an average 10% cheaper online (Tedeschi 2005). The likelihood is that the price difference will be even greater now that people have more search engines available to make price comparisons, that they sometimes buy used books, that occasionally there is an option to 'rent', or that they may just buy an eBook.

Marketers may decide prices (at least in part) on how well informed they believe customers to be about competitors' prices. If the products are rarely purchased, consumers will be unlikely to have very precise knowledge of prices (although this is a major motivator for customers to learn about prices before committing to a purchase). A further factor would be the ease of finding out about prices – in the case of home

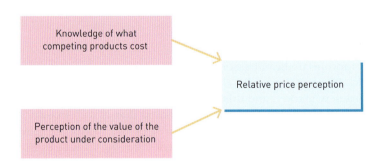

FIGURE 9.13 Relative price information

improvements, for example, it might prove extremely time-consuming to obtain quotes from different contractors, even if the contractors are willing to provide quotes (which they are often unprepared to do, given that this is a time-consuming activity for them and most builders have more than enough work as it is). In this respect, the Internet represents something of a threat to marketers since, as we've seen already with the books example above, price comparisons are relatively easy to make, especially in such areas as booking flights or buying insurance.

Knowing when to buy is also an important part of purchase knowledge. In some cases purchases are seasonal – for example, flights are cheaper at off-peak times, and so also is hotel accommodation. For those with the flexibility to travel at any time, there are considerable savings to be made. Buying in advance may also save money. The advantages of having purchase knowledge are shown in Figure 9.14 – the individual is able to make much better decisions from a basis of knowing about the purchase factors and parameters.

Another example is consumer electronics. Most people are well aware that when a new product is launched the price is high – for example, plasma-screen TV sets started off priced in the thousands of pounds, but prices dropped dramatically as the sets gained in popularity. Partly this is due to reduced manufacturing costs on longer production runs, and partly it is due to the need for manufacturers to recoup development costs, but it is also due to manufacturers knowing that some people are prepared to pay a premium price for the pleasure of being the first to own a new, exciting product.

Knowing where to buy the product is a more complex issue than it once was, due to the increasing number of possible online and offline retail outlets and resellers from which products can be purchased. Fifty years or so ago retailers were much more specific in the range of products they carried: stationers only sold stationery, chemists only sold medicines, and so forth. Items such as soy sauce or spices are often cheaper from specialist Chinese or Indian grocers than they are from supermarkets, for example. In addition, someone may need a specific product and have no knowledge of where to buy it – specialist products for motor or building work might not be available from normal hardware stores, but might instead need to be bought from specialist outlets or ordered from the manufacturers. In these circumstances manufacturers need to be sure that people are aware of where the products can be bought.

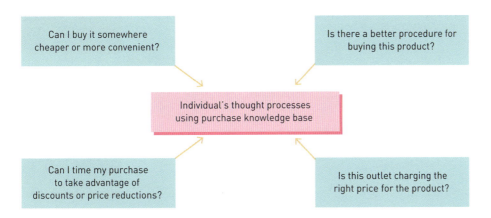

FIGURE 9.14 Advantages of having purchase knowledge

CONSUMPTION KNOWLEDGE

This type of knowledge is the information consumers have about how a product's benefits can be obtained in use. Lack of such knowledge would mean that people would be unlikely to buy the product in the first place: mobile telephones suffered from this problem for some time, since people found the networks, tariffs and choices confusing (many still do). Other high-tech products suffer from similar problems – many people, for instance, don't use all the facilities available on their smart TVs: on-demand video, web browsers, media streamers, networking and coaxial digital connections. A product that is used incorrectly is unlikely to perform to the required standard, which in turn is likely to lead to consumer dissatisfaction or even injury (Staelin 1978).

In Figure 9.15 ignorance about the correct use of the product can lead to two outcomes: either the consumer uses the product incorrectly, which leads to dissatisfaction with the product's performance, or the consumer reads the producer's information about the product (the manual) and learns how to use the product correctly (assuming that the manual is written in a language that the consumer can read!). This should lead to satisfaction. In some cases, consumers effectively re-invent the product, failing to use it according to the manufacturer's instructions, but are still satisfied with the performance. The final possibility is that the consumer knows how to use the product, uses it according to the instructions, and is thus satisfied with the product.

At an obvious level, it is difficult to sell cars to people who do not have driving licences, and difficult to sell computers to people who have no idea how to use one. At a more subtle level, there may be uses for the product which are not obvious to consumers – using baking powder for deodorising fridges is a well-known example, but using bath oil to remove tar spots from cars, or white vinegar as a general household cleaning agent is less obvious. Whether a manufacturer would want to promote this use for bath oil or vinegar is doubtful, but consumers do invent novel ways of using products and this knowledge enters the product experts' minds even when it is not put there by the producers.

FIGURE 9.15 Consumption knowledge

PERSUASION KNOWLEDGE

Persuasion knowledge is what people know about the goals and tactics of those trying to persuade them (Eisend 2015). The seminal model developed by Friestad and Wright (1994) remains one of the most influential theories in this area. People are often sceptical about the motives of marketers, with good reason: marketers are not in business to do consumers a bit of good, they are in business for their own ends, and aim to manage the exchange between consumers and the firm. Consumers who perceive themselves as being immune to 'undesirable persuasion' help to protect and enhance their self-esteem (Eisend 2015). Since most of us resent being managed, we tend to seek out information about marketing tactics in order to strengthen our own negotiating position.

In recent years, people have become more marketing aware, and marketing jargon is commonly heard from people who are not marketers. Understanding how marketers (and perhaps especially salespeople) operate has been shown to affect consumers' opinions of marketer sincerity adversely (Brown and Krishna 2004). A study by Bearden et al. (2001) showed that people were able to make the following statements about their understanding of persuasion:

1. I know when an offer is 'too good to be true'.

2. I can tell when an offer has strings attached.

3. I have no trouble understanding the bargaining tactics used by salespeople.

4. I know when a marketer is pressuring me to buy.

5. I can see through sales gimmicks used to get consumers to buy.

6. I can separate facts from fantasy in advertising.

This clearly has implications for the marketing approach. Marketers cannot naively assume that consumers can be led around on a leash or can be easily persuaded by a glib sales patter: people are suspicious, and are able to see through many marketer-induced ploys.

SELF-KNOWLEDGE

This area of knowledge is about the individual's understanding of his or her own mental processes (Alba and Hutchinson 2000; Vazire and Solomon 2015). People who understand their own strengths and weaknesses, as well as what they like and do not like, are in a better position to make realistic purchasing decisions than people who are not in touch with their own personalities. Self-knowledge and also self-referencing (Turk et al. 2015) are important to market researchers, since much commercial market research is based on self-reports by consumers. For example, Balogh et al. (2015) examined the self-knowledge, attitudes and perceptions of Hungarian car drivers towards biofuels, on the basis that the development of biofuels may provide considerable emission savings and at the same time are socially and environmentally acceptable; therefore support measures need to be based on the sustainable performance of biofuels, in terms which are acceptable to users.

SOURCES OF CONSUMER KNOWLEDGE

People gather information about products from a large number of sources, both personal and impersonal. The sources may be controlled (or at least influenced) by marketers, or may be entirely independent.

Marketer-controlled sources include the following:

- salespeople
- service people
- paid product endorsers (for example, athletes who recommend sports equipment).

Personal sources

Sources of involvement derived from means–end knowledge stored in the individual's memory

These would be classified as personal sources of information, since they are provided by people.

Non-personal sources that are controlled by marketers would include the following:

- the products themselves
- point-of-purchase (PoP) materials
- advertising (online and offline)
- review websites/video logs/blogs
- e-Catalogues/industry forums
- corporate websites
- directories such as www.yell.com.

Non-marketer influences may also be personal or impersonal. Personal sources would include family and friends, work colleagues, other shoppers, market mavens and other influential people, and Internet sources such as forums and bulletin boards. Impersonal sources would include non-corporate websites, TV and radio shows, books, government reports and the press.

In fact, even the non-marketer-controlled sources can be influenced by marketers. Product placement in films and TV programmes is common (in the UK paid product placement in TV shows became legal in February 2011, albeit with many controls).

People are naturally suspicious of marketer-controlled information sources, but will use them and will often base most of their decision-making on the rival claims of different producers. Word of mouth and impartial articles in newspapers and magazines are trusted much more, because people feel that there is no purpose to be served by the source lying to them. It is for this reason that marketers try to influence word of mouth, word of mouse (see Sethna et al. 2013 for more information) and the opinions of journalists (who are, after all, powerful influentials).

The most useful source of information is, of course, consumption of the product itself. Actually using a product and forming a judgement about it is clearly far and away the best route for gaining information.

Sometimes a lack of knowledge can be an advantage. Research shows that giving people a surprise (i.e. providing information for which there are no antecedents) can lead to them evaluating a brand higher than people to whom the information was not a surprise (Vanhamme and Snelders 2003).

SUMMARY

Learning is something that we all do, every day of our lives, and the bulk of what we learn comes from outside the classroom. Learning comes about in many ways: sometimes it happens subconsciously, as in the case of classical conditioning; sometimes it requires conscious effort, as in cognitive learning. We never really forget anything we have learned, however.

From a marketing viewpoint, how people find out about products and brands, and more especially what drives people to do so, is the basis of our thinking when developing communications strategies. How people store the information in memory, and where they store it, is the basis of our communications strategies. Even though some people zap advertisements, we do have a natural desire to learn, and we also have considerable pressures on us to know about the products we buy – the downside of not knowing varies from losing our money, through social embarrassment, to physical injury.

KEY POINTS

- Learning is behavioural change over time relative to an external stimulus.
- Classical conditioning is largely involuntary on the part of the learner.
- Operant conditioning assumes that the learner has choice in the process: 'good' behaviour is reinforced by reward, 'bad' behaviour is reduced by punishment.
- Cognitive learning involves conscious thought and effort.
- Motivation is a key factor in all learning.
- Learning by experience is more powerful than learning vicariously.
- Consumer knowledge breaks down into product knowledge, purchase knowledge, consumption knowledge, persuasion knowledge and self-knowledge.

HOW TO IMPRESS YOUR EXAMINER

You are likely to be asked to compare theories of learning and how they relate to advertising. If you can provide real examples of repetitive advertising (classical learning), interactive websites (operant learning) and viral advertising in which a game is played or something similarly active (cognitive learning), you will show that you understand the theory and can apply it in practice.

REVIEW QUESTIONS

1. How might a marketer use music in classical conditioning?
2. What methods of operant conditioning are available to marketers?
3. What is the role of cognitive learning in major purchases?
4. How might a marketer motivate a consumer to learn about a product?
5. How can learning by experience be used in selling high-value products such as stereo systems?
6. How might mavens be recruited for a word of mouth campaign?
7. What effect does persuasion knowledge have on marketing communications?
8. How can self-knowledge be enhanced by marketers?
9. How can marketers encourage people to improve their purchase knowledge?
10. What should marketers do to ensure that consumers have adequate consumption knowledge?

CASE STUDY: KUMON

Back in 1954, a mathematics teacher by the name of Toru Kumon discovered his son Takeshi was struggling at school. He began to create learning materials so Takeshi could work every day and steadily develop his skills. Toru Kumon knew that if the work was incremental in difficulty, it would allow the learner to master each concept completely before learning a new skill. Each new concept builds on the foundation established by the previous one, and new exercises constantly review and strengthen the previously learned skills. The assignments that were devised are on a 'learn by doing' theory that is intended to motivate students to become independent learners. Just as Toru Kumon had thought, Takeshi's mathematical ability improved and soon word had got out to other parents that there could actually be something interesting in this self-learning method. The Toru Kumon philosophy says that the goal of the programme is to develop a student's confidence so that they will first try to solve a problem on their own before asking for help.

In 1958, Japan saw the opening of its first ever Kumon Centre in Osaka, run by Toru Kumon's wife, Teiko, who became the first Kumon Instructor. Most Kumon centres are franchises. While Kumon encourages students to think for themselves, Kumon Instructors have a crucial role in providing guidance, nurturing and assistance throughout the programme which can last many years.

In 2016, there are approximately 4 million students enrolled on the Kumon pro-gramme (Maths and English) in 49 different countries. That's some achievement. The current Kumon Wembley Central Study Centre has been operating since 2006 and is one of the leading centres in London with 'Elite Instructor' status.

Apart from their core business of providing Maths and native language pro-grammes, the company has also diversified its operations, in some countries.

Learning Therapy – Learning for a Healthy Brain Centres

Books and Educational Toys

Penmanship and Calligraphy (interestingly in an age of technology!)

Education for SEN Children (Special Educational Needs)

English Immersion Camp

Kumon Method at Universities

Child-raising Support.

Image Credit: Kumon Educational (reused by permission)

QUESTIONS

1. Why is this emphasis on extra-curricular education so prolific among parents in this day and age?

2. How does operant conditioning feature in the method?

3. What factors might feature in the choice to enrol in a Kumon programme rather than a one-to-one tutor at home?

4. Who might be most likely to enrol their children into a Kumon programme?

5. Why might penmanship and calligraphy be of interest to educators in an age of technology driven education?

FURTHER READING

A paper by Y.-P. Chen, L. Nelson and M. Hsu (2015) From 'where' to 'what': distributed representations of brand associations in the human brain, *Journal of Marketing Research*, 52 (4): 453–66, is a fascinating read and represents an important advance in the application of neuro-scientific methods to consumer research, moving from work focused on cataloguing brain regions associated with marketing stimuli to testing and refining constructs central to theories of consumer behaviour.

Contemporary Theories of Learning: Learning Theorists … In Their Own Words, edited by Knud Illeris (Abingdon: Routledge, 2009) is a useful book of essays in which leading learning theorists explain their ideas. If you are interested in learning about how people learn, this book provides an excellent overview.

Soap, Sex and Cigarettes: A Cultural History of American Advertising by Juliann Sivulka (Boston, MA: Wadsworth Publishing Inc., 2011) provides an entertaining view of how advertising has both created and been created by American society. The book shows how advertising has helped Americans learn how to be American – and, of course, the same processes have gone on in other countries.

Human Memory: Theory and Practice by Alan Baddeley (Hove: Psychology Press, 1997) is about the mechanisms of memory. It covers the interconnectedness of learning, knowledge and memory, and explores three different types of memory.

Advertising and the Mind of the Consumer: What Works, What Doesn't, and Why by Max Sutherland (London: Kogan Page, 2000) explains how exposure to advertising builds up in people's memories. The author uses a lot of anecdotes and real-life examples, as well as an entertaining writing style to get the point across.

REFERENCES

Alba, J.A. and Hutchinson, J.W. (1987) Dimensions of consumer expertise. *Journal of Consumer Research*, 13 (March): 411–54.

Alba, J.A. and Hutchinson, J.W. (2000) Knowledge calibration: what consumers know and what they think they know. *Journal of Consumer Research*, 27 (September): 123–56.

Balogh, P., Bai, A., Popp, J., Huzsvai, L. and Jobbágy, P. (2015) Internet-orientated Hungarian car drivers' knowledge and attitudes towards biofuels. *Renewable and Sustainable Energy Reviews*, 48 (August): 17–26.

Bearden, W.O., Hardesty, D.M. and Rose, R.L. (2001) Consumers' self-confidence: refinements in conceptualisation and measurement. *Journal of Consumer Research*, 28 (June): 121–34.

Belen del Rio, A., Vacquez, R. and Iglesias, V. (2001) The effects of brand association on consumer response. *Journal of Consumer Marketing*, 18: 410–25.

Blackston, M. and Lebar, E. (2015) Constructing consumer-brand relationships to better market and build businesses. In S. Fournier, M. Breazeale and J. Avery (eds), *Strong Brands, Strong Relationships*. Abingdon: Routledge, pp. 376–392.

Blackwell, R.D., Miniard, P.W. and Engel, J.F. (2005) *Consumer Behaviour*, 10th edn. Mason, OH: Thomson South-Western.

Brown, C.L. and Krishna, A. (2004) The skeptical shopper: a metacognitive account for the effects of default options on choice. *Journal of Consumer Research*, 31 (December): 529–39.

Chen, Y.P., Nelson, L. and Hsu, M. (2015) From 'where' to 'what': distributed representations of brand associations in the human brain. *Journal of Marketing Research*, 52 (4): 453–66.

Cheung, C.M., Zheng, X. and Lee, M.K. (2015) How the conscious and automatic information processing modes influence consumers' continuance decision in an e-commerce website. *Pacific Asia Journal of the Association for Information Systems*, 7 (2): 25–40

Eisend, M. (2015) Persuasion knowledge and third-person perceptions in advertising: the moderating effect of regulatory competence. *International Journal of Advertising*, 34 (1): 54–69.

Elpers, J.W., Wedel, M. and Pieters, R. (2002) The influence of moment-to-moment pleasantness and informativeness on zapping TV commercials: a functional data and survival analysis approach. *Advances in Consumer Research*, 29: 57–8.

Friestad, M. and Wright, P. (1994) The persuasion knowledge model: how people cope with persuasion attempts. *Journal of Consumer Research*, 21 (1): 1–30.

Golman, R., Loewenstein, G. and Gurney, N. (2015) Information gaps for risk and ambiguity. Available at SSRN 2605495, http://ssrn.com/abstract=2605495.

Gorn, G.J. (1982) The effects of music in advertising on choice behaviour: a classical conditioning approach. *Journal of Marketing*, 46 (Winter): 94–101.

Hansen, J., Strick, M., van Baaren, R.B., Hooghuis, M. and Wigboldus, D.H. (2009) Exploring memory for product names advertised with humour. *Journal of Consumer Behaviour*, 8 (2/3): 135–48.

Hoch, S.J. and Deighton, J. (1989) Managing what consumers learn from experience. *Journal of Marketing*, 53 (April): 1–20.

Hoch, S.J. and Ha, Y. (1986) Consumer learning: advertising and the ambiguity of product experience. *Journal of Consumer Research*, 13 (September): 221–33.

Kiyosaki, R.T. (2011) *Rich Dad Poor Dad*. Scottsdale, AZ: Plata Publishing.

Kroeber-Riel, W. (1984) Emotional product differentiation by classical conditioning. *Advances in Consumer Research*, 11: 538–43.

Krugman, H.E. (1965) The impact of television advertising: learning without involvement. *Public Opinion Quarterly*, 29: 349–56.

Küster, F. and Eisend, M. (2015) Time heals many wounds: explaining the immediate and delayed effects of message sidedness. *International Journal of Advertising*. **doi:** 10.1080/02650487.2015.1052616.

McSweeney, F.K. and Bierley, C. (1984) Recent developments in classical conditioning. *Journal of Consumer Research*, 11 (September): 619–37.

Monroe, K.B., Rikala, V.M. and Somervuori, O. (2015) Examining the application of behavioral price research in business-to-business markets. *Industrial Marketing Management*, 47: 17–25.

Murray, K.B. and Haubl, G. (2002) The fiction of no friction: a user skills approach to cognitive lock-in. *Advances in Consumer Research*, 29: 11–18.

Norton, M. and Chance, Z. (2008) Decision amnesia: why taking your time leads to forgetting. *Advances in Consumer Research*, 35: 55–8.

Onkvisit, S. and Shaw, J.J. (1994) *Consumer Behaviour, Strategy and Analysis*. New York: Macmillan.

Pavlov, I.P. (1927) *Conditioned Reflexes*. London: Oxford University Press.

Pieters, R., Warlop, L. and Wedel, M. (2002) Breaking through the clutter: ad originality and familiarity effects on brand attention and memory. *Advances in Consumer Research*, 29: 89–90.

Pinho, J.C. and Soares, A.M. (2015) Response to advertising on online social networks: the role of social capital. *International Journal of Consumer Studies*, 39 (3): 239–48.

Rao, A.R. and Sieben, W.A. (1992) The effect of prior knowledge on price acceptability and the type of information examined. *Journal of Consumer Research*, 19 (September): 256–70.

Sethna, Z., Jones, R. and Harrigan, P. (eds) (2013) *Entrepreneurial Marketing: Global Perspectives*. Bingley: Emerald Publishing.

Skinner, B.F. (1953) *Science and Human Behaviour*. New York: Macmillan.

Staelin, R. (1978) The effects of consumer education on consumer product safety behaviour. *Journal of Consumer Research*, 5 (June): 30–40.

Sumpradit, N., Bagozzi, R.P. and Ascione, F.J. (2015) 'Give Me Happiness' or 'Take Away My Pain': explaining consumer responses to prescription drug advertising. *Cogent Business & Management*, 2 (1): 1–27.

Tedeschi, B. (2005) Cheaper than it seems. *New York Times*, 10 January.

Turk, D.J., Gillespie-Smith, K., Krigolson, O.E., Havard, C., Conway, M.A. and Cunningham, S.J. (2015) Selfish learning: the impact of self-referential encoding on children's literacy attainment. *Learning and Instruction*, 40 (December): 54–60.

Vanhamme, J. and Snelders, D. (2003) What if you surprise your customers – will they be more satisfied? Findings from a pilot experiment. *Advances in Consumer Research*, 30: 48–56.

Vazire, S. and Solomon, B.C. (2015) Self- and other-knowledge of personality. In M. Mikulincer, P. Shaver, M.L. Cooper and R.J. Larsen (eds), *APA Handbook of Personality and Social Psychology, Volume 4: Personality Processes and Individual Differences*. Washington, DC: American Psychological Association, pp. 261–81.

Widrick, Stanley M. (1986) Concept of negative reinforcement has place in classroom. *Marketing News*, 20: 48–9.

Wiegman, O. and van Schie, E.G.M. (1998) Video game playing and its relations with aggressive and prosocial behaviour. *British Journal of Social Psychology*, 37 (3): 367–78.

Wright, M.F. (2015) Emerging adults' coping strategies: longitudinal linkages to their involvement in cyber aggression and cyber victimization. *International Journal of Cyber Behavior, Psychology and Learning* (IJCBPL), 5 (2): 1–14.

Zauberman, G. (2002) Lock-in over time: time preferences, prediction accuracy and the information cost structure. *Advances in Consumer Research*, 29: 8–10.

Zhou, Z. and Bao, Y. (2002) Users' attitudes towards web advertising: effects of Internet motivation and Internet ability. *Advances in Consumer Research*, 29: 71–8.

MORE ONLINE

For additional materials that support this chapter and your learning, please visit:
https://study.sagepub.com/sethnaandblythe

CHAPTER 10

ATTITUDE FORMATION AND CHANGE

LEARNING OBJECTIVES

After reading this chapter you should be able to:

- Describe what is meant by attitude.
- Explain how attitudes can be inferred from behaviour.
- Explain why behaviour cannot be assumed from knowing attitude.
- Describe the components of attitude.
- Explain the role of salient beliefs in forming attitudes.
- Explain the purpose of attitudes.
- Explain the relationship between attitude and behaviour.
- Describe the factors which determine the strength of attitude.
- Explain the difference between public and private attitudes.
- Show the effect of situation on attitude.
- Explain the role of changing beliefs in changing attitudes.
- Explain how emotions are important in changing attitudes.
- Describe the various complaint behaviours that arise from post-purchase dissatisfaction.

INTRODUCTION

Attitudes are what put us in the right position for behaviour. We each have attitudes towards many things – our friends, families, employers, possessions, money, government policies, other people's behaviour, and so forth. Our differing attitudes are (in part) the differentiators between us as human beings, and since attitudes are the precursor to any consumption behaviour they are of great interest to marketers, both in terms of finding out what they are and in seeking to change them.

DEFINING ATTITUDE

Attitude can be defined as 'a learned tendency to respond to an object in a consistently favourable or unfavourable way' (Onkvisit and Shaw 1994). In consumer behaviour terms, it is a customers' thoughts and feelings towards a brand (Pauwels 2015). Whether a product will be bought or not depends to a large extent on the consumer's attitude towards it, and therefore much marketing effort is expended on finding out what consumers' attitudes are to product offerings, and in seeking to change those attitudes where appropriate and achievable.

To break down the definition and make it easier to handle:

- Attitude is learned, not instinctive.
- It is not behaviour; it is a predisposition towards a particular behaviour.
- It implies a relationship between a person and an object. The object of the attitude could be another person, an institution or a physical article; 'object' is used here in the sense of 'an objective'.
- Attitudes are fairly stable; they do not change much with physical states or circumstances. For example, if someone's preferred painkiller is ibuprofen, that attitude remains whether or not the individual has a headache. The behaviour (actually taking the tablets) may not happen, but the attitude remains.
- The relationship between a person and an object is not neutral. It is a vector, having both direction and intensity; if you express an attitude about something, you either like it or you do not. If you are neutral about it, or indifferent, you would say you don't have any attitude towards it.

Attitude has to be inferred from statements or behaviour; it is intangible and not directly observable. In other words, although we can observe and measure behaviour, we have to ask people about their attitudes to various things, and hope that their replies are honest ones. This can cause difficulties if we are researching a sensitive topic.

The formation of attitude is based on experience of the object, normally direct experience; driving a particular make of car, or trying a particular brand of beer, will lead to the formation of an attitude. The individual builds up a mental picture (perception) of the object, and forms an attitude accordingly. First impressions are important, since they colour our later information gathering (see Chapter 8) – this is why people behave in a positive and approving manner on a first date, so that the other person forms a favourable attitude. Both psychology and marketing researchers have highlighted a number of attitudinal metrics (see Table 10.1) over the past few years. We'll be taking a look at attitude measurement a little later in this chapter, but it's important to have some of these in the back of your mind as you read further, so here are nine metrics which have been adapted from Verhoef et al. (2015):

TABLE 10.1 Attitudinal metrics

Trust	Customers' confidence in the quality and reliability of the services provided (Garbarino and Johnson 1999). A more formal definition might be 'a binary relation between two entities: one entity's confidence, belief and expectation that another entity will act or intend to act beneficially' (Xiu and Liu 2005)
Satisfaction	An overall evaluation based on the customers' total purchase and consumption experience within the relationship (Anderson et al. 1994)
Commitment	The extent to which a customer believes that an ongoing relationship with the company is so important as to warrant maximum efforts at maintaining it (Morgan and Hunt 1994), and in conveying those positive experiences to others (Babin et al. 2015)
Payment equity	Customers' perceived fairness of the price paid for their consumed products or services (Bolton and Lemon 1999)
Value equity	The customer's objective assessment of the utility of a brand based on perceptions of what is given up for what is received. Sub-drivers of value equity include quality, price and convenience
Brand equity	The customer's subjective and intangible assessment of the brand, above and beyond its objectively perceived value. Sub drivers of brand equity include brand awareness, customer brand perceptions/associations, and perceptions of brand ethics
Relationship equity	The customer's assessment of interactions with the brand, above and beyond objective and subjective assessments of the brand. Sub-drivers of relationship equity include salesperson and serviceperson relationships, loyalty programmes, customer communities and knowledge of the customer
Net promoter score	The percentage of promoters minus the percentage of detractors
Loyalty intentions	The extent to which customers intend to remain loyal to a firm

CHALLENGING THE STATUS QUO

So attitudes form through experience. And yet we often base our beliefs on very limited experience, do we not? Is this some weakness in the human brain? Or is it, perhaps, a sign of one of our great talents – the ability to develop a working hypothesis based on limited data? Take for instance the rate at which technology continues to advance. This makes some technophobes somewhat nervous, and changing their attitude is a tough call. Unless of course they experience a 'need'. So here's an example. Let's say you're unable to leave home for four days as there is flooding in your village and your nine-month-old baby has a worryingly bad cold and won't stop crying. Or you're walking through a forest and your foot starts to swell up, go red and is severely itching as, evidently, you've been bitten by something. The good news is that, in both of these situations, you'd be able to see a doctor via your smartphone and there is a possibility that the doctor may even be able to prescribe medication, wherever you are. Telehealth and telemedicine are not only more convenient, but are bringing the cost

©iStock.com/AndreyPopov

of healthcare down and thus are less expensive. (Apps such as 'doctorondemand', 'healthtap', 'livehealthonline', will all generally let you see a doctor via a video call.)

If people still need convincing to change their attitudes, enter the world of gamification! There are a number of commentators who have recently written about the economic and societal impact of gaming (see for example Reeves and Reed 2009; Deterding et al. 2011; McGonigal 2011). And the large number of downloads of popular apps such as Foursquare, Facebook and Angry Birds have added to the societal interest in gamification to such an extent that the concept of playing 'games' has been added to other areas of our life. Marketers are now trying to change user attitudes using apps in areas such as health care (see 'fitocracy'), developing loyalty and engagement for TV channels (see 'Beamly'), and environmental awareness (see 'changingice', 'earthnow' and 'offset').

Gamification

The application of typical elements of game playing (e.g. point scoring, competition with others, rules of play) to other areas of activity, typically as an online marketing technique to encourage engagement with a product or service

Some experience is indirect: recommendations and the communicated experiences of friends or relatives are important when forming attitudes towards objects of which we don't have direct experience. This can sometimes lead to superstitious beliefs and prejudices due to the synthetic nature of perception. If your friends and peers have all told you that a particular film is boring, you are likely to maintain that attitude, even if you have not seen the film yourself. Negative attitudes are often formed in this way. Marketing communications generally can help a lot here by providing additional sources of information (think advertising and public relations which both have a particularly important role in this, since they are activities that can form and change attitudes).

Synthetic

That which is constructed from disparate components. In perception, an overall view derived from grouping together a set of stimuli

There is a perceptual component in attitude. The manner in which an object is perceived is affected by the consumer's stable characteristics (personality, intelligence, previous knowledge, culture, gender, etc.) and by current characteristics, such as mood, state of the organism, etc.

DIMENSIONS OF ATTITUDE

Attitude has three dimensions, as shown in Figure 10.1, and Table 10.2 explains the relationship between each of these components.

It is important to note that attitude and behaviour are separate things. Simply because an individual has a particular attitude about something does not mean that the individual will act on the attitude. For example, someone might hear that his

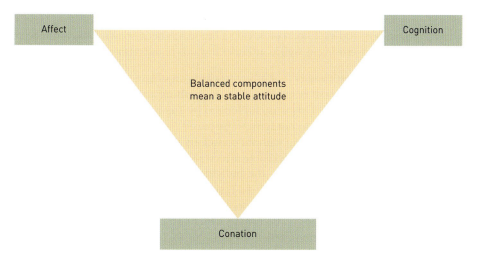

FIGURE 10.1 Dimensions of attitude

TABLE 10.2 Dimensions of attitude

Dimension	Definition	Explanation	Example
Cognition	The perceptual component of attitude	This is the individual's awareness, knowledge, beliefs and images of the attitudinal object. It is the conscious, thinking part of attitude	An individual's attitude towards a car may be composed of comparative information, e.g. the Toyota Prius is cheaper to buy and run than the Volkswagen Golf, but the Golf holds its value better. These are the facts (or beliefs) informing the attitude
Affect	The evaluative component of attitude	These are the emotions, the feelings of like and dislike which do not always have a basis in objective fact	Drivers frequently have affective relationships with their first cars. The car is given a name, and often the driver will speak to it
Conation	Behavioural intention	Conation is about what we intend to do about the attitudinal object; whether to approach it, reject it, buy it, etc. It is not the actual behaviour; merely an intention	Having formed an attitude about a car ('I love the bodywork, it really looks great, and it does 45 to the gallon as well') the consumer forms an intention ('I'm going to take out a loan and buy one'). This intention is the conation

bank is investing in a country with an oppressive regime. This is cognition. He may think that this is unethical; he does not like the bank doing this (affect). He therefore decides to move his account elsewhere (conation). Conation may not always lead to behaviour; our ethical bank customer may have second thoughts later and decide to leave the account where it is, perhaps on the basis that switching to another bank is just too complicated. Other factors often prevent us from taking the course of action we had originally planned.

Cognition
Thought processes: the element of attitude derived from conscious thought or knowledge

Affect
The emotional element of attitude

Conation
The behavioural intentions that arise from attitudes

The three elements are interrelated in a complex way. Purchase intentions relate to beliefs and brand evaluations, and likelihood of buying a brand has been shown to be influenced by attitudes towards advertising as well as attitudes towards brands (Homer and Yoon 1992).

The traditional view of attitude is that affect towards an object is mediated by cognition; in other words, emotional responses about something are controlled to a marked extent by rational evaluation. This was challenged by Zajonc and Markus (1985), who assert that affective responses do not have to be based on prior cognition. People can develop a 'gut feel' about something without conscious evaluation, and even on limited information, then rationalise the decision afterwards. This may sometimes be due to classical conditioning; for example, the individual may form a favourable attitude towards a product because the advert uses a favourite song as background music (see Chapter 9). Affect also influences information processing: there is a 'meddling-in' effect in which cognition is influenced by the way in which information is processed, which is in turn influenced by emotions (Mishra et al. 2006). In fact, forming an attitude about a product might start with any of the three components, with the others coming into play afterwards. Also, if the outcome of any action is expected to be affect-rich (pleasurable, unpleasant, emotionally moving, etc.) the individual will evaluate the action by its effect on feelings. Affect-poor outcomes trigger evaluation by calculation (Hsee and Rottenstreich 2002). In other words, putting a strong emotional bias into marketing communications is likely to lead to emotionally based decision-making.

Although it may seem illogical or dangerous to form an attitude without first finding out a lot about the attitudinal object, most people are familiar with the feeling of having 'fallen in love' with a hopelessly impractical purchase. Likewise, most people are familiar with the feeling of having taken an instant dislike to somebody without first getting to know the person. This is illustrated in Figure 10.2.

Attitude contains components of belief and opinion, but it is neither. Attitude differs from *belief* in that belief is neutral, not implying good or bad. Belief is concerned with the presence or absence of an attribute, and is usually based on a judgement of the available evidence. Attitude contains an element of affect, and evaluates whether the existence of an attribute will result in satisfaction or dissatisfaction. For example, a consumer might believe that a Tesla is an eco-friendly, reliable, and well-engineered car but have no particular feelings about this either way. Conversely, another consumer might feel that the Tesla is an excellent and desirable car, precisely because it is eco-friendly, reliable and well-engineered.

FIGURE 10.2 Starting points for attitude formation

Attitude differs from *opinion* in that opinion is an overt, vocalised expression of an attitude. Attitude can also be expressed non-verbally (facial expressions, body language, etc.), or indeed may not be expressed at all. While opinions may arise from attitudes (i.e. be expressed as the result of an attitude) and attitudes may arise from hearing the opinions of others, the two are in fact separate entities.

ATTITUDE FORMATION

A more complete model of the formation of attitudes about brands shows that it is a somewhat complex process. Figure 10.3 gives an overview of the complete process. The diagram begins with the consumer's needs, both utilitarian (practical) and expressive (emotional). This feeds into the consumer's motivation to process information, as does advertising; motivation and exposure feed into the processing, but the consumer also needs to have the ability and the opportunity to process the information.

Within the processing 'black box' the consumer's level of processing is affected by attention and capacity for processing; in other words, by the degree of interest the consumer has, and his or her ability to process the information. The result of the processing is both cognitive and affective, feeding into the formation of attitudes about the brand.

Situational variables surrounding the brand or product will also affect the attitude formation process. For example, an unpleasant salesperson or an inconveniently located outlet may affect the way we perceive brands. Exposure to advertising stimuli plays a major part in encouraging learning and the formation of attitudes, but the main drive comes (as always) from the consumer's needs (Berger and Mitchell 1989).

FIGURE 10.3 Attitude formation (McInnis and Jaworski 1989)

Reprinted with permission from Journal of Marketing, published by the American Marketing Association, Deborah J. McInnis and Bernard J. Jaworski, Vol. 53, No. 4, 1989: 1–23.

Pre-existing attitudes may colour the formation of attitudes about a particular situation. Researchers have found that people can be categorised according to their attitudes about Christmas, Navroz and Eid, for example; these attitudes are themselves formed by attitudes about religion, about gift-giving and about commercial influences (Gurau and Tinson 2003). Likewise, people who are materialistic will get into debt to fund their purchases even if their incomes are very low (Ponchio and Aranha 2008).

Salient belief

A belief which is key in the formation of an attitude

Consumers acquire salient beliefs about products. Because the cognitive system can only hold a relatively small number of facts in mind at once, the salient beliefs are the ones that are used by the consumer to make a judgement. Usually the salient beliefs will be those that the consumer holds most important, but they may be merely the ones that have been most recently presented (Fishbein and Ajzen 1975).

A consumer's overall attitude towards an object is a function of many attributes of the object. The attitude forms as a result of the consumer's strength of feeling, or the strength of the salient beliefs, about the attributes and also the evaluation of those beliefs. Table 10.3 shows an example of a belief set about a restaurant.

The question marks represent areas where the consumer has no knowledge, or has the knowledge but is not taking it into consideration. In other words, only the salient beliefs are taken into account.

This *multi-attribute attitude model* attempts to explain how the consumer's salient beliefs help to form the final attitude. The attributes listed are integrated to form an overall attitude; in this example, the consumer will form an attitude about the restaurant as to whether it is a good restaurant or a bad one. The attitude may be qualified in some way: the restaurant may be regarded as a good one for lunch, but a bad one for dinner, or perhaps as a good one for a quick meal when one doesn't feel like cooking, but a bad one for special occasions.

Attitude formation is clearly affected by context: conation in particular may be affected by the feasibility of carrying out a particular behaviour, or the need to modify it to take account of what is happening around the individual (Bless et al. 2002).

TABLE 10.3 Example of a belief set

Attribute	Strength of salient belief (out of 10)	Level of importance (out of 10)
Convenient parking	5	7
Good food	6	8
Friendly waiters	?	4
Pleasant décor	7	5
Clean cutlery	3	7
Reasonable prices	?	3
Open on Wednesday	?	5

ATTITUDE MEASUREMENT

Measuring attitudes is clearly a subject of some interest to marketers, since attitudes play such a major role in consumer purchasing behaviour. It is obviously of importance for manufacturers to know what the consumers' attitude is to the product, but it is difficult to quantify. This is because attitude contains elements of both cognition and affect. Here are two contrasting models for attitude measurement: the Rosenberg model and the Fishbein model.

The *Rosenberg model* (Rosenberg 1960) says that an individual's attitude towards an object represents the degree and direction of the attitudinal effect aroused by the object. Put more simply, attitude is composed of a *quantity* of feeling and a *direction*, and has two main components:

1. **Perceived instrumentality**. This is the subjective capacity of the object to attain the value in question, in other words the usefulness of the object.

2. **Value importance**. This is the amount of satisfaction the person derives from the attainment of a particular value. More simply, this is the importance of achieving the result that the consumer is hoping to achieve by buying and using the object of the attitude.

Perceived instrumentality
The degree to which an action or product is thought to be useful in a practical way

Value importance
The level of satisfaction the individual gains from the achievement of a particular value

Perceived instrumentality means the degree to which the person believes that the product will work as it is supposed to. Value importance is the degree to which getting the job done is important to the consumer.

Theoretically, perceived instrumentality and value importance are actually independent, and taken separately they don't predict responses well, but taken together they are good predictors of behaviour that is illustrative of attitude.

The *Fishbein model* (Fishbein 1980) takes a different perspective on the problem by focusing on the consumer rather than on the product. For Fishbein, attitudes can be predicted from beliefs and evaluation. Belief is the probability that the object possesses a particular attribute; evaluation is whether that attribute attracts or repels. This is not compatible with the value importance concept in the Rosenberg model.

In this model, the consumer's belief in the product's capabilities replaces the perceived instrumentality aspect. For example, it may be useful for a car to have a large boot (Rosenberg model) but whether a particular car's boot is large or not is a relative term and relies on the consumer's beliefs (Fishbein model). Furthermore, the belief that a car's boot is large does not necessarily mean that the prospective owner will like that attribute (Fishbein model). This will depend on how important the attribute is to the customer (Rosenberg model).

Combining the two models, there are three distinct aspects of the importance of attitude:

1. Perceived instrumentality.

2. Evaluative aspect (affect).

3. Value importance.

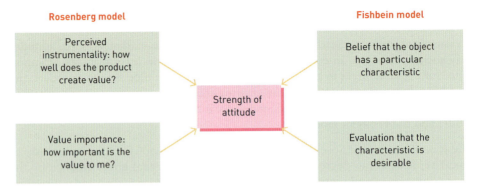

FIGURE 10.4 Strength of attitudes

These are illustrated in Figure 10.4. Examples of these aspects are as follows:

1. I believe the Mercedes ML is the most comfortable car in its class.

2. I like comfort.

3. Comfort is very important to me.

Note that the second two are not identical. Someone can like something without it being very important to him or her.

FUNCTIONS OF ATTITUDES

Attitudes have a function in helping consumers make decisions about their purchasing practices, and also serve other functions according to the individual's circumstances. Four main categories of function have been identified, as shown in Table 10.4 (Locander and Spivey 1978).

TABLE 10.4 Functions of attitudes

Function	Definition	Explanation	Example
Instrumental function	The individual uses the attitude to obtain satisfaction from the object	The individual thus aims to maximise external reward while minimising external punishment	An individual might develop an attitude towards a particular cycling club because his or her friends are members and the facilities are good
Ego-defensive function	Protects against internal conflicts and external dangers	Here the attitude shields the individual from his or her own failings	Someone who is unable to understand how to use the product might have the attitude that manufacturers make products too complex
Value-expressive function	Opposite of ego-defensive; the drive for self-expression	The attitudes expressed often go against the flow of opinion	Most radical political viewpoints are examples of the value-expressive attitude in action
Knowledge function	The drive to seek clarity and order	Related to the need to understand what the object is all about. Comes from the belief that if you know what you like and dislike, decision-making is easy	Somebody who has an interest in audio-visual systems is likely to visit websites about them, to visit exhibitions, engage in online forums and to discuss them with friends so as to know what the latest products are

These functions of attitude may not all be present at the same time: a given attitude may only serve one or two of these functions, while still being valuable. The relationship between them is illustrated in Figure 10.5. In some cases, the **ego-defensive function** and the **value-expressive function** might conflict with each other. If the individual has beliefs that go against the majority, the ego-expressive function may not protect the person from attacks by others. Equally, having attitudes that accord with those of other people may conform well with the ego-defensive function.

Ego-defensive function

The function of attitude which enables the individual to maintain stability of the conscious self

Value-expressive function

The factor in group behaviour that allows the members to display their own beliefs and attitudes

```
Cognition ─┐
           ├─→ Attitude ─┬─→ Instrumental function
Affect ────┤             ├─→ Ego-defensive function
           │             ├─→ Value-expressive function
Conation ──┘             └─→ Knowledge function
```

FIGURE 10.5 Functions of attitudes

CONSUMER BEHAVIOUR IN ACTION: FROM STAGE TO SCREEN

Assume that you're an agent working with pop stars in the UK. Would you be tempted to suggest that your client makes a movie? After all, other agents have suggested it to their clients – One Direction, Katy Perry and Justin Bieber have all had this suggestion made.

This is often a quick way to leverage a star's fame to generate earnings from box-office receipts – and in most cases the stars sing in the movie, which generates record sales. In some cases it works fine – The Beatles made *Hard Day's Night* and *Help*! which were considerable successes, but went on to make *Magical Mystery Tour* and *Yellow Submarine*, both of which virtually disappeared without trace. Later outings by the individual band members were equally poorly received: John Lennon's films (with Yoko Ono) scarcely saw the light of day, and Paul McCartney's *Give My Regards to Broad Street* sank like a stone. The greatest success has probably been Ringo Starr's voice-overs for *Thomas the Tank Engine*. Madonna, The Spice Girls, Britney Spears and Mariah Carey have all made films that have been listed among the Top Ten Worst Films of All Time. *Newsday* said of Madonna's *Swept Away*: 'New ways of describing badness need to be invented to describe exactly how bad this movie is'. The biopic *Amy* (about Amy Winehouse) has, by all accounts, been a sad disappointment.

So why does this happen? No doubt these people are talented individuals, capable of holding an audience's attention and capable of performing a role. They already have a substantial fan base, most of whom are likely to go to see the movie. They have good, capable managers, and they already know the entertainment business.

Is it, perhaps, that we have already developed an attitude towards these stars as singers and musicians, and find it hard to relate to them when they are playing a part? The Beatles' successful movies both showed them purely as a band, to some extent mocking their own success and image, whereas the flops showed them acting a part. Fans want to see their idol, not someone who looks like the idol but is actually supposed to be somebody else! The willing suspension of disbelief is essential for enjoying a night at the cinema, and somehow this is damaged if one is unable to believe in the lead character.

©iStock.com/johnmootz

ATTITUDE AND BEHAVIOUR

The *theory of reasoned action* (Ajzen and Fishbein 1980) says that consumers consciously evaluate the consequences of alternative behaviours, and then choose the one that will lead to the most favourable consequences. Figure 10.6 shows the four main components of the theory – behaviour, intention to behave, attitude towards the behaviour and subjective norm. The subjective norm is the component that reflects the social pressures the individual may feel to perform (or avoid performing) the behaviour being contemplated.

The individual's beliefs about the behaviour and the evaluation of the possible main consequences will combine to produce an attitude about the behaviour. At the same time, the individual's beliefs about what other people might think, and the degree to which he or she cares about what other people think, go towards developing a subjective norm about the contemplated behaviour. The individual will then weight the relative importance of the attitude and the norm, and will form an intention of how to behave. This may, in turn, lead to the behaviour itself.

The theory of reasoned action assumes that consumers perform a logical evaluation procedure for making decisions about behaviour, based on attitude towards the behaviour, which in turn derives from attitudes towards the product or brand.

Logically, attitude should precede behaviour. In other words, we would expect that someone would form an attitude about something, then act on that attitude. In fact, much of the evidence points the other way. It appears in some cases that people behave first, and form attitudes afterwards (Fishbein 1972).

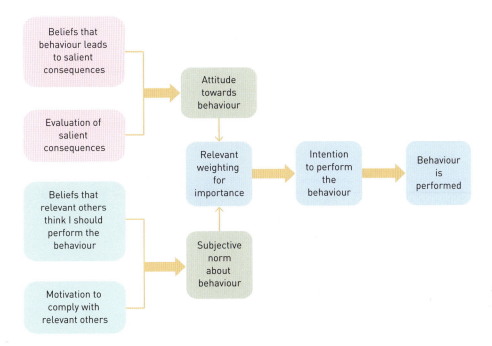

FIGURE 10.6 The theory of reasoned action (Fishbein 1980)

Reprinted with permission from A Look Back, A Look Ahead, published by the American Marketing Association, G.B. Hafer (ed), 1980: 8.

An extension of the theory of reasoned action is the theory of planned behaviour, shown in Figure 10.7. (Ajzen and Madden 1986; Ajzen 1988). Planned behaviour assumes that the individual also takes account of the ease or difficulty of performing the planned behaviour, in other words the degree of control the individual has over the behaviour and its outcomes. This depends in part on past experience, and in part on the anticipation of future obstacles.

Essentially, the model attempts to predict behaviour based on conation (intent to commit the behaviour). The overall attitude towards the behaviour is predicted by the salient beliefs about the behaviour and its possible outcomes, and the subjective norm is determined by the individual's beliefs about what salient others (friends and family) would think about the behaviour, coupled with the level of motivation to comply with the views of others. For example, it appears that women and men have very different attitudes towards genetically modified (GM) foods: women tend to distrust the science (a conative factor) and also tend to have ethical views about GM (an affective factor). In fact, religion, scientific background, education, age and gender all impact upon attitudes towards GM foods (Hudson et al. 2015).

Marketing efforts often encourage people to try products first, then form attitudes; free samples, test drives, demonstrations and coupons are all more powerful in forming attitude and behaviour consistency than are advertisements (Smith and Swinyard 1983). Attitudes formed without trial experience are probably weak and

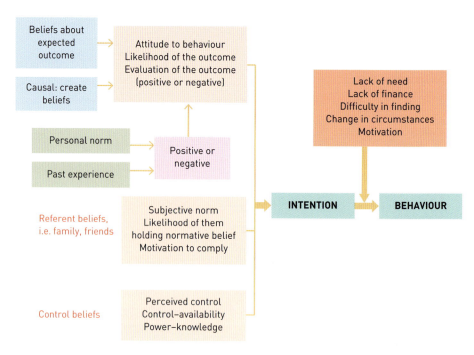

FIGURE 10.7 The theory of planned behaviour

easily changed. In this context, the classic Pepsi Challenge represents a way of persuading people that Pepsi is better than Coca-Cola. Each summer stands are set up
in shopping malls and at seaside resorts and passers-by are offered the chance to
compare Pepsi with Coke in a blind taste test. Part of the reason for this is that the
two drinks do, in fact, taste very similar and without the visual cue of the packaging
the consumers often cannot tell the difference between the two. Since Pepsi has a
smaller market share than Coke, the company only needs half of the respondents to
prefer the Pepsi in order to gain a greater market share than it currently holds. In
fact, there is a slight preference for the Pepsi, since around 65% of people state that
they prefer it in blind taste tests, often to their surprise.

Trial of a product is so much more powerful than advertising in forming favourable
impressions that car manufacturers are prepared to give special deals to car rental
companies and driving schools in the hope that hirers and learners will buy the same
model at a later date.

It may not matter greatly whether attitude precedes behaviour or not. Attitude is
not always followed by the proposed behaviour; most people are familiar with having proposed doing something, then doing something else instead. This may be
because attitude and behaviour are not always consistent. For example, a smoker
may take the attitude that smoking is unhealthy and antisocial, but may still not
give up smoking. Dieting is a similar example: even though an overweight person
may believe that being fat is unhealthy and unattractive, losing weight may not be
the end result. Many other examples abound; in Freudian terms, the attitude may
have come from the superego, but the demands of the id result in a failure to act
(see Chapter 1).

FIGURE 10.8 The cycle of attitude and behaviour

In fact, it seems more likely that, at least regarding fast-moving consumer goods (FMCG), the process of attitude formation and behaviour are interwoven. Figure 10.8 illustrates this. In this model there is a feedback loop that allows the consumer to re-evaluate and reconsider his or her attitudes. The formation of attitude is thus seen as a dynamic process, with the behaviour itself forming part of the process.

THE DUALITY OF PRIVATE VS. PUBLIC ATTITUDES

Often people hold attitudes that they are reluctant to admit to in public. This is particularly true in recent years due to an increase in the requirement to be **politically correct** (PC). This makes attitude measurement difficult because respondents will give a rational or acceptable answer rather than a true one. Few people would be prepared to admit openly that they have racist, sexist or ageist attitudes, for example, yet it is undoubtedly the case that many people harbour such attitudes.

In marketing terms, people are often reluctant to admit to buying products that are embarrassing (or illegal). Many people would be reluctant to admit, for instance, that they like pornography, and therefore it is easier to sell such products over the Internet than it is to sell them through retail outlets. The Internet, at least for the moment, preserves the anonymity of the customer.

Clearly there are implications for market research, since any questions that enquire into these attitudes are likely to meet with evasive answers or just plain lies. Most people will have some private attitudes and some opposing public attitudes, and therefore measurement of these private attitudes can best be carried out by using projective techniques such as sentence completion or cartoon tests. These research techniques were discussed in Chapter 7.

Often people's private attitudes do not have a logical basis and are very subjective; thus the individuals concerned are even more reluctant to admit to holding those views. Sometimes there is a reluctance to express an opinion when it has no logical basis. Attitude, as we have seen, has a strong affective component.

Political correctness

(commonly abbreviated to PC) An ordinarily pejorative term used to criticise language, actions or policies seen as being excessively calculated not to offend or disadvantage any particular group of people in society

ATTITUDE VS. SITUATION

During the 1930s, in a hotel in the South of France, a strange ceremony was acted out daily. One of the Romanoff princes (from the Russian royal family) would ask his chauffeur to mash up a plate of strawberries, and then eat them. This ceremony took place every day, even when the strawberries had to be specially flown in for the purpose. The reason was that the prince loved the smell of strawberries, but was allergic to them and therefore couldn't eat them. His attitude towards the 'product' therefore could not result in his consuming it, due to his situation.

In Figure 10.9, the thwarted conation feeds back information to the cognition element of attitude, which may cause a slight shift in the attitude itself.

Positive attitude towards the product may not equate to positive attitude about the *purchase* of the product. A consumer may have a strong positive attitude towards light-coloured clothes, but not buy them because she works in the city and light-coloured clothes show the dirt.

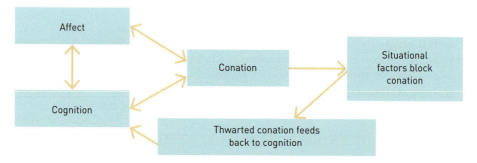

FIGURE 10.9 Effect of situation on attitude

Fishbein suggests that the model be modified to take account of this (Fishbein 1972). The attitude to be measured should, under the extended model, be the attitude towards performing a given act (e.g. purchase or consumption) rather than an attitude towards the object itself. The evidence is that this model is a better predictor of purchasing behaviour than merely measuring attitudes towards the brands themselves, but of course there is greater complexity involved in understanding why a consumer has a particular attitude, since more variables are involved.

CHALLENGING THE STATUS QUO

Presumably if one had an attitude that was permanently thwarted by one's situation, the attitude would have to change. For example, most of us have academic subjects we dislike – many people do not enjoy maths, for example. Yet we often have to study something we dislike in order to be given a particular qualification, or as the precursor to studying something we do like.

Does this ever make us like the actual subject or is it that we simply like the outcome? How can we maintain an attitude in the face of its unpleasant aspects?

Attitudes can be changed due to situational changes. For example, a sudden drop in disposable income following a job loss might lead somebody to think that a subscription to Sky TV is too expensive and thus a luxury, even if it was seen as good value for money previously. Intentions can be checked against later performance by means of garbage analysis or self-report: Cote, McCullough and Reilly found that 'behaviour-intention inconsistency is partly attributable to unexpected situations' (Cote et al. 1985).

ATTITUDE TOWARDS ADVERTS VS. ATTITUDE TOWARDS THE BRAND

An individual may love the ads and hate the product, or vice versa. Although there is an assumption that a positive attitude towards the advertisement will lead to a positive attitude about the product, the two are actually separate hypothetical constructs (Mitchell 1986).

This is because the attitude towards the brand is affected by many more factors than the advertisement, whereas attitude towards the advertisement is only affected by the ad itself. The perception of the brand is much more likely to have a major cognitive element in it, whereas most advertising is intended to produce an affective response.

Early evidence suggested that liking the advertisement relates to whether the product is meaningful and relevant to the consumer at the time (Biel 1990). This has recently been corroborated by Zhu and Chen (2015). They note that even though in 2013 over $5 billion were spent by US companies on social media advertising, a Gallup survey has said that those advertisements had no influence on the majority of consumers' buying decisions. Zhu and Chen (2015) further argue that for social media marketing to be effective it needs to be congruent and aligned with the different needs of social media users. There is also some evidence that food and beverage advertisements are more likeable than non-food advertisements (Biel and Bridgwater 1990). Liking the advertisement will tend to spill over into liking the product, and the combination of the two is also likely to lead to an increase in sales (Biel 1990; Stapel 1991). This situation can be reversed in the case of some financial services products (e.g. insurance) because the advertising is often of the 'cautionary tale' type in which the advertisement shows what can go wrong if the individual does not buy the insurance. This naturally means that the advertisement is unpleasant and worrying. Of course at the other end of the spectrum we see that if there is repeated consumption of both products and experiences, this may well lead to a reduction in enjoyment over time. This is commonly referred to as 'satiation'. Where this happens, we are likely to see a production of dissonance in consumers, especially those with an active identity. This is so because the 'reduced enjoyment with identity-consistent products conflicts with their identity' (Chugani et al. 2015).

Perhaps not surprisingly, people who have a high need to justify their decisions rationally (that is, people with a high need for cognition) are less likely to be swayed by their liking for the advertisement. People with a low need for cognition tend to like products that are advertised in a likeable way (Reinhard and Messner 2009).

Other factors in creating an attitude might include the way the message is framed – emphasising the cost of a better product rather than its higher quality may result in a poorer perception of the product and a lower propensity to buy it (Gamliel 2010). This may be because people experience losses more intensely than they experience gains of the same magnitude (Kahneman and Tversky 1979).

GENERAL VS. SPECIFIC ATTITUDES

It is necessary to look at specific attitudes when attempting to predict behaviour. It is possible to hold one attitude generally, but an opposing attitude in a specific case; for example, it is possible to dislike children while still loving one's own children, or to like wine in general but dislike Pinot Grigio. For marketers, the important attitude to measure is, of course, the attitude to the specific brand rather than the attitude to the product class as a whole.

Having said that, there is an issue regarding brand switching. If a consumer has a generally negative attitude about a product class, but will use a specific brand within that class, it may be possible to switch the consumer towards another brand similar to the one that is already acceptable. Consumers may already be prepared to do this in the event that the desired brand is out of stock; the difficulty lies in knowing why the individual consumer has made the decision to keep to only one brand of a class of products that he or she dislikes.

CHANGING ATTITUDES

Attitudes derive from consumer need, and from beliefs. People select salient beliefs (the beliefs that are most relevant to their individual needs) and build attitudes towards products based around those beliefs. For example, superstitious beliefs have been shown to affect attitudes towards novelty-seeking (Hernandez et al. 2008).

The model is useful to marketers in that it helps when devising strategies for changing consumer attitudes. There are four ways of changing attitudes, as follows:

1. *Add a new salient belief.* For example, a restaurant might point out that it offers music played by a jazz pianist on Saturday nights. This would be a new fact for the consumer to take into account.

2. *Change the strength of a salient belief.* If the belief is a negative one, it can be discounted or played down; if it's a positive one, it can be given greater importance. If a customer has a low level of belief in the cleanliness of the cutlery in a particular restaurant, but a high evaluation of this attribute, then the restaurant needs to address this point specifically in its promotional messages. The restaurant might, for example, make a point of telling customers that the cutlery is specially checked before it reaches the table. In some Chinese restaurants, chopsticks are delivered to the table in paper sleeves: although the chopsticks have been used many times, putting the sleeves on after they have been washed reassures the customers.

3. *Change the evaluation of an existing belief.* A customer may have a low evaluation of the prices in a restaurant, perhaps being more concerned about enjoying a romantic evening than about getting a cheap meal. The restaurant could increase the evaluation of this attribute by pointing out that the low prices mean that the customer can come more often, or treat friends to a meal without breaking the bank.

4. *Make an existing belief more salient.* A restaurant customer might not regard friendliness of the waiters as a salient attribute. The restaurant could therefore emphasise that it makes a big difference to the enjoyment of the evening if the waiters are pleasant.

Using a contrasting example, a Chinese restaurant in Wardour Street, London, called Wong Kei was once famous for the rudeness of its staff, and had acquired the dubious accolade of being London's rudest restaurant. Restaurant-goers would be shouted at ('*Go upstairs!*' or '*Sit down there*') and the general communications were levied with quite some disdain. This, however, was actually seen as a salient attribute, almost an event in itself, since it contrasted so much with other restaurants, and was viewed as characterful. Thirty years later and attitudes (even at Wong Kei's) have changed with a renovation taking place in 2014, and the new owners dismissing the previous forms of 'differentiation' – presumably the joke was wearing thin by then.

If the three components of attitude (cognition, affect and conation) are in balance, it is difficult to change the attitude because the attitude becomes stabilised. For example, if somebody is becoming overweight, believes that this is a bad thing and therefore diets, the attitude is stable and would be difficult to change. If, on the other hand, the same person is overweight, believes that it is bad but just somehow never gets round to dieting, it is relatively easy to tempt the person to a snack or two. In the second case, the attitude is not consistent because the conation does not match with the affect and cognition. Changing a person's beliefs can be an effective route to attitude change (see Figure 10.10).

Inconsistency between the three components of attitude may come about when a new stimulus is presented. New information might affect the cognitive or conative aspects or a bad experience might change the affective aspects. When the degree of inconsistency between the three components exceeds a certain tolerance level, the individual

FIGURE 10.10 Changing beliefs

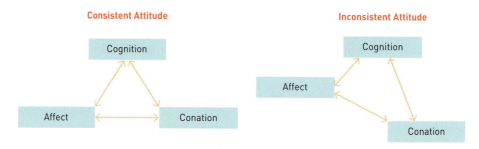

FIGURE 10.11 Consistent vs. inconsistent attitude

will be compelled to undertake some kind of mental re-adjustment to restore stability (see Figure 10.11). This can come about through three main defence mechanisms:

1. Stimulus rejection.

2. Attitude splitting.

3. Accommodation to the new attitude.

Stimulus rejection

The process of protecting an attitude by ignoring information that conflicts with it

Stimulus rejection means that the individual discounts the new information. For example, an overweight person might reject advice that slim people live longer than overweight people, on the grounds that the research does not examine people who used to be fat but are now slim and have kept the weight off. By rejecting the new information, the individual is able to maintain the status quo as regards the cognitive element of attitude. Sometimes stimuli are rejected simply because they come from a marketing source – there is evidence that consumers remember products which have been placed in movies and TV shows, but will often reject them because of a feeling of being manipulated (Bhatnagar and Aksoy 2004). Likewise, teenagers tend to respond better to new media such as the Internet and text messaging rather than to traditional mass media (Brennan et al. 2010). In Thailand for instance, smartphone ownership among teenagers runs at approximately 75% (Harfield et al. 2014) and with an average of 5.3 hours a day being spent on the Internet, Thai teen attitudes are certainly being changed by the Internet superhighway. People are generally much more marketing-literate nowadays, and often know what marketers are trying to do as well as understanding how they intend to do it – marketers would do well to remember this.

Attitude splitting

The process of protecting an attitude by accepting only part of a new piece of information that conflicts with the attitude

Attitude splitting involves only accepting that part of the information that does not cause an inconsistency. Here, the individual might accept that the new information is basically true, but that his or her own circumstances are exceptional. For example, if an individual finds out that the company he or she was planning to sue has gone bankrupt, this will alter the conative element of attitude since it is impossible to sue a bankrupt company. The individual might agree that this is *generally* the case, but decide that the circumstances are such that he or she can sue the directors of the company instead.

Accommodation to the new attitude

Accepting new information and using it to re-form an existing attitude

Accommodation to the new attitude means, in effect, changing the attitude to accommodate the new information. The person with a high body mass index may join a gym and start dieting, the smoker may cut down or give up altogether, the prospective litigant may just put it down to experience, and cut their losses.

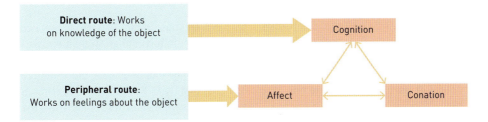

FIGURE 10.12 Peripheral and direct routes to attitude change

The three elements are so closely related to each other that a change in one element will usually cause a change in the others (Rosenberg 1960). New information causing a change in cognition will change the consumer's feelings about the product, which in turn is likely to change the consumer's intentions about the product.

The *elaboration likelihood model* (Petty et al. 1983) describes two routes (see Figure 10.12) by which attitude might be changed. The direct route involves an appeal to the rational, cognitive element; the consumer makes a serious attempt to evaluate the new information in some logical way. The peripheral route, on the other hand, tends to involve the affective element by associating the product with another attitudinal object. For example, if a rock star appears in an ad for a soft drink this might cause the star's fans to change their attitudes towards the drink. This has nothing to do with the attributes of the drink, but everything to do with the attributes of the star. Peripheral cues such as this are not relevant to a reasoned evaluation, but because of the interdependence of the components of attitude, change will occur. In effect, the affect felt towards the star 'rubs off' on the product.

Changing existing attitudes relies heavily on market research, but in particular the teasing-out of the factors that go to make up the attitude can be a demanding task. This is because of the halo effect – the tendency for attitudes about one salient belief to colour attitudes about another. For example, if a diner had a bad meal at a restaurant, this is likely to lead to a view that everything else about the restaurant was bad, too. Likewise, a favourable view of some factors often leads to respondents reporting a favourable view of other factors.

Direct route

A route to attitude change which relies on reasoned argument: an appeal to cognition, in other words

Peripheral route

Using emotional appeals in order to change the affective component of attitude

Halo effect

The tendency for an individual to believe every aspect of something is good, based on a belief that some aspects are good

CHALLENGING THE STATUS QUO

Halo effect is said to be the process by which attitudes about one aspect of a product (or person) tend to colour the whole perception of the product (or person). Apparently, if we think our new car is really comfortable and cosy, we will also think its fuel consumption is good.

How about the reverse case? If we think something is really bad – perhaps the car is unreliable – do we then think its performance is bad as well? Probably so, if the theory is correct. In that case, what happens if something is brought to our attention? If the rock star we loved and admired turns out to be a paedophile, do we stop liking the music? For instance, in 2005, iconic British supermodel Kate Moss lost her modelling contracts with Burberry, Chanel and H&M, following her alleged involvement in a cocaine scandal (Kaulingfreks and Bos, 2007). Where does that leave the organisation that formerly used her in their advertising? (It's of course interesting to note that Burberry's attitude has also since changed, with Kate Moss appearing in their 2015 Eau de Toilette campaigns – maybe organisations can also *suffer* from the halo effect of celebrities?)

Using the peripheral route to attitude change means working on the affective component of attitude. Research has shown that emotional appeals often work a great deal more effectively than do cognitive, logical appeals; emotional appeals (Andreu et al. 2015) also appear to have a greater effect on explicit memory, so people remember the advertisement better. Much depends on the group of individuals being studied. For example, studies have shown that campaigns to discourage smoking among teenagers work best on boys if they use emotional 'cosmetic' appeals (for example, telling boys that the smell of smoke on their clothing is repellent to girls) whereas long-term health appeals (a logical, cognitive approach) work better on teenage girls (Smith and Stutts 2003). In a recent study, it was found that friendship support lowered the level of smoking among men but not women (Alcántara et al. 2015). Mood also has an effect on the interpretation of information: people in a good mood tend to process and remember brands better (Bakamitsos and Siomkos 2004; van Reijmersdal et al. 2015).

COGNITIVE DISSONANCE

Cognitive dissonance theory states that holding two competing cognitions leads to discomfort and an eventual readjustment (Festinger 1957). The readjustment can take two forms: rejecting one or other of the competing cognitions, or introducing a third idea which resolves the conflict between the other two. Studies in neuroscience have used functional magnetic resonance imaging (fMRI) to prove that there is an association between dissonance and increased neural activation in key brain regions (de Vries et al. 2015).

The most interesting aspect of dissonance theory is that attitudes can apparently be changed more easily by offering a low reward than by offering a high reward. In a famous experiment conducted in the 1950s, researchers induced students to lie to other students about a task they were being recruited to undertake. The actual task was to place round pegs into holes, turn the pegs one-quarter turn, then remove the pegs. The students were told that this was a psychological experiment, and were then asked to recruit other students primarily by telling them how interesting and fun the task was. Since it would be difficult to imagine a more tedious task, these students obviously had to lie: the experimenters offered a recruitment reward, but some students were only offered $1 to lie, whereas others were offered $20 (a substantial sum of money in 1959). The students being paid the lower amount were found to actually believe the lie, whereas the higher-paid students simply told the lie as a lie without changing their own attitudes. The theory is that the higher-paid students justified lying on the basis that they were being well-paid for it, whereas the other students could not use this justification and therefore needed to find another reason for lying – in this case, they decided that what they were saying must be at least partly true (Festinger and Carlsmith 1959).

In Figure 10.13, the situation in which lying is linked to only a small reward leads to the attitude that the lie must be at least partly true, since the reward is not in itself sufficient to make lying worthwhile. In the second situation, the individual can justify lying on the basis that the reward is generous enough to justify not telling the truth, and therefore the lie remains a lie.

Cognitive dissonance is a powerful force in attitude change because the individual is, almost by definition, personally involved in the process. Reduction in dissonance always involves some kind of internal debate and (ultimately) some self-justification (Aronson et al. 1974). This happens because the individual tends to believe that the dissonance has arisen through an act or thought that is immoral or stupid. The most common manifestation of cognitive dissonance in consumer behaviour is post-purchase dissonance, in which someone who has just made an important purchase finds out that the product is not quite what was expected (see Figure 10.14).

FIGURE 10.13 Cognitive dissonance

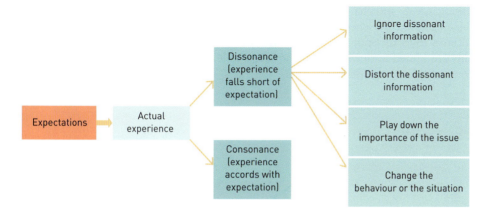

FIGURE 10.14 Post-purchase dissonance

In other words, the individual has been presented with new information that contradicts his or her pre-purchase expectations. In most cases, actual experience with the product conflicts with information obtained in the pre-purchase information search. For example, someone buying a new flat-screen television set might have expected it to be wall-mountable, like a picture. On opening the packing, our new purchaser finds that the wall-mounting bracket makes the TV stand out six inches from the wall, and that this is a necessary factor because of the wiring, controls and air vents at the back of the set. At this point, the buyer has four basic choices:

1. Ignore the dissonant information and look for positive (consonant) information about the product. In the case of the TV, the buyer might just accept that the TV will stick out from the wall a bit and will instead admire the quality of the picture, the excellent sound, the online connectivity, and so forth.

2. Distort the dissonant information. In this case our buyer might convince himself or herself that the TV really does not stand away from the wall too much after all. With some careful lighting, no one will notice.

3. Play down the importance of the issue. Here the buyer simply says that the distance from the wall is really not that important anyway.

4. Change the behaviour or the situation. Our TV buyer might take the TV back to the shop and ask for a refund, or might decide to put the TV on a table instead, and buy a picture for the wall.

For marketers, minimising post-purchase dissonance is key to avoiding complaint behaviour.

SUMMARY

In this chapter we have looked at the dimensions of attitudes and how they are formed and maintained. We have also looked at ways of changing attitudes, and at some of the theories of attitude measurement.

Attitude is the starting point of all behaviour: people's attitudes inform their decision-making, create and change their motivations, and both create and are created by their consumption experiences. Marketers are always concerned with creating favourable attitudes towards both the product and the firm, and most marketing communications are aimed at developing those favourable attitudes so that consumers are not attracted by any competitor brands.

KEY POINTS

- Attitude is a learned construct that shows a person's tendency to respond to an object in a consistently favourable or unfavourable manner.
- Attitude is not neutral.
- Although attitude is not behaviour, it can be inferred from behaviour.

- Likewise, behaviour can be inferred from attitude, but the relationship is not reliable.
- Attitude is multidimensional, comprising affect, cognition and conation.
- Consumers only use salient beliefs when forming attitudes, not all the facts.
- Attitudes serve four useful purposes: instrumental, ego-defensive, value expressive and knowledge.
- Behaviour affects attitude more than attitude affects behaviour.
- The strength of an attitude is determined by perceived instrumentality, evaluative aspect and value importance.
- People may also assess the difficulty of carrying out the behaviour when establishing an attitude.
- Attitudes may be public or private.
- Situations may prevent behaviour without altering attitude.
- Beliefs are the basis of cognitive change: this type of change comes about through the direct route.
- Emotions are the basis of affective change: this type of change comes about through the peripheral route.
- Post-purchase dissonance may evoke several possible complaint behaviours.

HOW TO IMPRESS YOUR EXAMINER

You are likely to be asked how attitudes might be changed. It's very tempting just to dive into the various methods of changing attitudes without first making clear that attitudes actually are quite hard to change from the outside – more typically, attitude change comes from within, as a result of experience. You should also give a brief outline of how attitudes are formed in the first place – this will make the explanation of how to change them much easier.

REVIEW QUESTIONS

1. What is the role of belief in forming attitudes?
2. How might marketers appeal to the cognitive element in attitude formation?
3. What is the difference between the ego-defensive role of attitude and the value-expressive role?
4. How might a marketer increase the strength of an attitude?
5. What is the purpose of measuring private attitudes?
6. How does situation affect attitude?

7. What processes might be important in forming attitudes?

8. What is the relationship between affect and the evaluative aspect of attitude strength?

9. What difficulties might exist when trying to infer attitude from behaviour?

10. How might beliefs be formed?

CASE STUDY: CHANGING COMMUNICATIONS

©iStock.com/mikkelwilliam

Communication is what people do above all else – we talk, we make gestures, we write, we read, we even use Morse code in an effort to inform and persuade other people. In recent years, the communications revolution has created even more opportunities for expressing ourselves, annoying each other and shifting attitudes – but it's easy to forget that the new technology is itself the subject of attitudes.

In the 1980s, the first 'mobile' phones appeared – bigger than a brick and about as attractive, the early mobiles were unreliable, had very short battery life and were extremely expensive – several months' pay for the average earner. These early mobiles were a status symbol for the upwardly-mobile and, for the yuppies (young urban professionals) who bought them, they were the ultimate status symbol. To others, they were a symbol of greed, crass materialism and the worst excesses of the 1980s free-enterprise culture.

However, engineers being what they are, the size and price reduced, reliability and battery life increased, and a competitive war started between the various manufacturers. By the early 1990s the technology was established, but the marketing still lagged behind – put simply, millions or even billions of people had a need for a mobile phone, but the vast majority had no way of paying for such an expensive piece of technology, and without a mass market the price would be unlikely to come down any time soon. Marketers stepped in and created the idea of the phone-inclusive contract, whereby the phone would be (in effect) hire-purchased by the consumer. The mobile phone thus became democratised, and for a while even became a more downmarket product as people who did not have the necessary credit rating to be allocated a landline were able to obtain a pay-as-you-go phone relatively cheaply and easily. By the turn of the century, most people had mobile phones and many people had more than one.

Naturally this led to a hyper-competitive environment in which manufacturers sought to add extra features to the phones, as well as making them ever-smaller and ever-cheaper. At the same time, service providers sought to offer various packages aimed at different market segments: when short message services (texting) appeared, service providers' packages began to include a ration of texts as well as a quota of minutes per month. In recent years, manufacturers have introduced even more refinements – cameras, second cameras for making video calls, apps for everything from a torch to an aeroplane tracker. Coupled with the huge number of packages offered by the service providers, the array of possibilities became almost impossible for the average consumer to weigh up.

As the benefits of fourth-generation (or 4G) technology is embedded in consumer minds, the pressure to upgrade to the latest phone increases: no doubt 5G and 6G will not be far behind. Meanwhile, the concept of wearable technology has come to the fore – the idea that communications devices can be built into clothing or other fashion items, or can be securely attached to the body in some way, has created a whole new range of possibilities. Analysts predict that the global sales of wearable tech will surpass the $50 billion mark by 2019. Of course the idea itself has been around for some time – criminals have been wearing electronic tags since the 1990s, and in Brazil the tags are linked to the GPS (Global Positioning System) so that police know where the criminals are at all times. This allows offenders to hold down jobs, carry out family commitments, and (of course) it saves on the bill for prisons. The commercialisation of this has resulted in the public being able to buy products such as Smart watches and fitness bands.

Some of the applications seem impractical or even nerdy - a cocktail dress which lights up when a call comes in is probably more of an embarrassment than anything else to a woman trying to make the right impression, and the hoody developed by students from the Tisch School of Arts in New York looks like an accident waiting to happen – the hoody sends out text messages in response to gestures by the wearer, which probably makes for entertaining viewing for passers-by but is likely to create all kinds of errors. Similar problems seem likely for the trousers with a built-in keyboard: Wallace and Gromit would be proud. There are, however, some solutions which do make practical sense. Samsung and PayPal may be creating an app to allow payments to be made through a Smart watch which would be very useful for a professional who is constantly on the move. The National Health Service in the UK is also keen to investigate how such wearable technology can help to reduce any unnecessary trips to the doctor's surgery or the hospital – the idea being that both the patient and the doctor would receive warning information in real time.

There are organisational benefits too which can be had by employees using wearable technology. The ability to collect data from the user/customer means that the organisation is able to collect insights into user interaction – a goldmine for marketers wanting to know more about their customers!

New technology and new ways of working bring with them, of course, new privacy and security issues. For instance, if employees bring their own devices into work, the employer's IT department needs to be aware for both support and security reasons, as each device that's connected to an organisation's system creates an access point. But organisations will have to adapt their systems to cater for wearable technology as it becomes even more popular than it is now.

While some people will embrace this new technology, others will ridicule it – history shows that attitudes change as new technology becomes more commonplace or, in effect, becomes old technology. Of course, the changes have been so rapid in recent years that it is difficult to keep up – many people find themselves left behind, unable to understand the new devices which younger people have grown up with.

QUESTIONS

1. What is the role of cognition in forming attitudes to new technology?

2. Why might negative attitudes have formed towards early mobile phone users?

3. How did manufacturers and service providers change public attitudes towards mobile phones?

4. Why do older people sometimes have negative attitudes towards communications technology?

5. How might different people form their attitudes towards wearable technology?

FURTHER READING

As an example of how attitude is formed in an online environment, you might enjoy C.H. Miller, J. Reardon, L. Salciuviene, V. Auruskeviciene, K. Lee and K. Miller (2009) Need for cognition as a moderator of affective and cognitive elements in online attitude toward the brand formation. *Journal of Business and Economics Research*, 7 (12): 65–72.

For an interesting study in how an unpopular or counter-social attitude can affect the way an individual fits into a culture, read M. Piacentini and E.N. Banister (2009) Managing anti-consumption in an excessive drinking culture. *Journal of Business Research*, 62: 279–88. This paper is about the experiences of students who do not like to engage in heavy drinking.

For a good book on attitude and attitude change, try Greg Maio and Geoff Haddock's *The Psychology of Attitudes and Attitude Change* (London: Sage, 2009). In particular, this book explains clearly how attitudes can be used to predict behaviour.

REFERENCES

Ajzen, I. (1988) *Attitudes, Personality and Behaviour*. Milton Keynes: Open University Press.

Ajzen, I. and Fishbein, M. (1980) *Understanding Attitudes and Predicting Social Behaviour*. Englewood Cliffs, NJ: Prentice-Hall.

Ajzen, I. and Madden, T.J. (1986) Prediction of goal-directed behaviour: attitudes, intentions and perceived behaviour control. *Journal of Experimental Social Psychology*, 22 (5): 453–74.

Alcántara, C., Molina, K.M. and Kawachi, I. (2015) Transnational, social, and neighborhood ties and smoking among Latino immigrants: Does gender matter? *American Journal of Public Health*, 105 (4): 741–749.

Anderson, E.W., Fornell, C. and Lehmann, D.R. (1994) Customer satisfaction, market share and profitability: findings from Sweden, *Journal of Marketing*, 58 (3): 53–66.

Andreu, L., Casado-Díaz, A.B. and Mattila, A.S. (2015) Effects of message appeal and service type in CSR communication strategies. *Journal of Business Research*, 68 (7): 1488–95.

Aronson, E., Chase, T., Helmreich, R. and Ruhnke, R. (1974) A two-factor theory of dissonance reduction: the effect of feeling stupid or feeling awful on opinion change. *International Journal of Communication Research*, 3: 340–52.

Babin, B.J., Boles, J.S. and Griffin, M. (2015) The moderating role of service environment on the customer share → customer commitment relationship. In M. Moore and R.S. Moore (eds), *New Meanings for Marketing in a New Millennium*. London: Springer International Publishing, pp. 266–71.

Bakamitsos, G. and Siomkos, G. (2004) Context effects in marketing practice: the case of mood. *Journal of Consumer Behaviour*, 3 (4): 304–14.

Berger, I.E. and Mitchell, A.A. (1989) The effect of advertising on attitude accessibility, attitude confidence, and the attitude–behaviour relationship. *Journal of Consumer Research*, 16 (December): 269–79.

Bhatnagar, N. and Aksoy, L. (2004) Et tu, Brutus? A case for consumer skepticism and backlash against product placements. *Advances in Consumer Research*, 31: 87–8.

Biel, A.L. (1990) Love the ad: buy the product? *ADMAP*, 299 (September): 21–5.

Biel, A.L. and Bridgwater, C.A. (1990) Attributes of likeable television commercials. *Journal of Advertising Research*, 30 (3): 38–44.

Bless, H., Wanke, M. and Schwartz, N. (2002) The inclusion/exclusion model as a framework for predicting the direction and size of context effects in consumer judgments. *Advances in Consumer Research*, 29: 86–7.

Bolton, R.N. and Lemon, K.N. (1999) A dynamic model of customers' usage of services: usage as an antecedent and consequence of satisfaction. *Journal of Marketing Research*, 36 (2): 171–86

Brennan, R., Dahl, S. and Eagle, L. (2010) Persuading young consumers to make healthy nutrition decisions. *Journal of Marketing Management*, 26 (7&8): 635–55.

Chugani, S.K., Irwin, J.R. and Redden, J.P. (2015) Happily ever after: the effect of identity-consistency on product satiation. *Journal of Consumer Research*. doi: 10.1093/jcr/ucv040.

Cote, J.A., McCullough, J. and Reilly, M. (1985) Effects of unexpected situations on behaviour–intention differences: a garbology analysis. *Journal of Consumer Research*, 12 (September): 188–94.

Deterding, S., Sicart, M., Nacke, L., O'Hara, K. and Dixon, D. (2011) Gamification: using game-design elements in non-gaming contexts. In *Proceedings of the 2011 Annual Conference Extended Abstracts on Human Factors in Computing Systems (CHIEA'11)*. Vancouver BC, Canada, pp. 2425–8.

de Vries, J., Byrne, M. and Kehoe, E. (2015) Cognitive dissonance induction in everyday life: an fMRI study. *Social Neuroscience*, 10 (3): 268–81.

Festinger, L. (1957) *A Theory of Cognitive Dissonance*. Stanford, CA: Stanford University Press.

Festinger, L. and Carlsmith, J.M. (1959) Cognitive consequences of forced compliance. *Journal of Abnormal and Social Psychology*, 58: 203–10.

Fishbein, M. (1972) The search for attitudinal–behavioural consistency. In Joel E. Cohen (ed.), *Behavioural Science Foundations of Consumer Behaviour*. New York: Free Press, pp. 245–52.

Fishbein, M. (1980) An overview of the attitude construct. In G.B. Hafer (ed.), *A Look Back, A Look Ahead*. Chicago, IL: American Marketing Association, pp. 1–19.

Fishbein, M. and Ajzen, I. (1975) *Belief, Attitude, Intention and Behaviour: An Introduction to Theory and Research*. Reading, MA: Addison-Wesley.

Gamliel, E. (2010) Message framing of products causes a preference shift in consumers' choices. *Journal of Consumer Behaviour*, 9 (4): 303–15.

Garbarino, E. and Johnson, M.S. (1999) The Different roles of satisfaction, trust, and commitment in customer relationships. *Journal of Marketing*, 63 (2): 70–87.

Gurau, C. and Tinson, J. (2003) Early evangelist or reluctant Rudolph? Attitudes towards the Christmas commercial campaign. *Journal of Consumer Behaviour*, 3 (1): 48–62.

Harfield, A., Viriyapong, R., Nang, H. and Nakrang, J. (2014) A survey of technology usage by primary and secondary schoolchildren in Thailand. In *Proceedings of 11th International Conference on eLearning for Knowledge-Based Society* (eLearningAP 2014), Siam Technology College, Thailand.

Hernandez, M.D., Wang, Y.J., Minor, M.S. and Liu, Q. (2008) Effects of superstitious beliefs on consumer novelty seeking and independent judgement making: evidence from China. *Journal of Consumer Behaviour*, 7 (6): 424–35.

Homer, P.M. and Yoon, S. (1992) Message framing and the interrelationships among ad-based feelings, affect and cognition. *Journal of Advertising*, 21 (March): 19–33.

Hsee, C.K. and Rottenstreich, Y. (2002) Panda, mugger and music: on the affective psychology of value. *Advances in Consumer Research*, 29: 60.

Hudson, J., Caplanova, A. and Novak, M. (2015) Public attitudes to GM foods: the balancing of risks and gains. *Appetite*, 92 (September): 303–13.

Kahneman, D. and Tverksy, A. (1979) Prospect theory: an analysis of decision under risk. *Econometrica*, 47 (2): 263–92.

Kaulingfreks, R., and Bos, R. (2007) On Faces and defacement: the case of Kate Moss. *Business Ethics: A European Review*, 16 (3): 302–312.

Locander, W.B. and Spivey, W.A. (1978) A functional approach to the study of attitude measurement. *Journal of Marketing Research*, 15 (November): 576–87.

McGonigal, J. (2011) *Reality Is Broken: Why Games Make Us Better and How They Can Change the World*. London: Penguin.

McInnis, D.J. and Jaworski, B.J. (1989) Information processing from advertisements; toward an integrative framework. *Journal of Marketing*, 53 (4): 1–23.

Mishra, A., Mishra, H. and Nayakankuppam, D. (2006) Meddling in of affect in information integration. *Advances in Consumer Research*, 33: 48.

Mitchell, A.A. (1986) The effect of verbal and visual components of advertisements on brand attitudes and attitudes towards the advertisements. *Journal of Consumer Research*, 13 (June): 12–24.

Morgan, R.M. and Hunt, S.D. (1994) The commitment–trust theory of relationship marketing, *Journal of Marketing*, 58 (3): 20–38.

Onkvisit, S. and Shaw, J.J. (1994) *Consumer Behaviour, Strategy and Analysis*. New York: Macmillan.

Pauwels, K. (2015) Truly accountable marketing: the right metrics for the right results. *GfK Marketing Intelligence Review*, 7 (1): 8–15.

Petty, R.E., Caccioppo, J. and Schumann, D. (1983) Central and peripheral routes to advertising effectiveness. *Journal of Consumer Research*, 10 (September): 135–46.

Ponchio, M.C. and Aranha, F. (2008) Materialism as a predictor variable of low income consumer behaviour when entering into instalment plan agreements. *Journal of Consumer Behaviour*, 7 (1): 21–34.

Reeves, B. and Read, J.L. (2009) *Total Engagement: Using Games and Virtual Worlds to Change the Way People Work and Businesses Compete*. Boston: Harvard Business School Press.

Reinhard, M. and Messner, M. (2009) The effects of source likeability and need for cognition on advertising effectiveness under explicit persuasion. *Journal of Consumer Behaviour*, 8 (4): 179–91.

Rosenberg, M.J. (1960) An analysis of affective-cognitive consistency. In C.I. Hovland and M.J. Rosenberg (eds), *Attitude Organisation and Change*. New Haven, CT: Yale University Press, pp. 15–64.

Smith, K.H. and Stutts, M.A. (2003) Effects of short-term versus long-term health fear appeals in anti-smoking advertisements on the smoking behaviour of adolescents. *Journal of Consumer Behaviour*, 3 (2): 155–77.

Smith, R.E. and Swinyard, W.R. (1983) Attitude–behaviour consistency: the impact of product trial versus advertising. *Journal of Marketing Research*, 20 (3): 257–67.

Stapel, J. (1991) Like the advertisement but does it interest me? *ADMAP*, April.

van Reijmersdal, E.A., Lammers, N., Rozendaal, E. and Buijzen, M. (2015) Disclosing the persuasive nature of advergames: moderation effects of mood on brand responses via persuasion knowledge. *International Journal of Advertising*, 34 (1): 70–84

Verhoef, P.C., Kooge, E. and Walk, N. (2015) *Creating Value with Big Data Analytics: Making Smarter Marketing Decisions*. Abingdon: Routledge.

Xiu, D. and Liu, Z. (2005) A formal definition for trust in distributed systems. In J. Zhou, R.H. Deng and F. Bao, Feng (eds), *Information Security*. Lecture Notes in Computer Science, Volume 3650. Heidelberg: Springer Berlin, pp. 482–9.

Zajonc, R.B. and Markus, H. (1985) Must all affect be mediated by cognition? *Journal of Consumer Research*, 12 (December): 363–4.

Zhu, Y.Q. and Chen, H.G. (2015) Social media and human need satisfaction: implications for social media marketing. *Business Horizons*, 58 (3): 335–45.

MORE ONLINE

For additional materials that support this chapter and your learning, please visit:
https://study.sagepub.com/sethnaandblythe

PART THREE

SOCIOLOGICAL ISSUES IN CONSUMER BEHAVIOUR

Although people are individuals, they act in groups. Human beings are herd animals, and rely heavily on each other for support, advice, practical help, entertainment and security. Thus this third section in the book takes a look at some of the sociological issues that consumers are subjected to and are influenced by.

Chapter 11 is about the types of group of which we are members. These groups have a great influence on us as sources of information, as 'sanity checks' to ensure that we are behaving appropriately, and as support systems for us in our daily lives. Each group influences us in different ways, but each group has its own role in helping us to function effectively as human beings.

Chapter 12 is devoted to an investigation of age, gender and the most influential group of all – the family. It is through our families that we first learned to behave appropriately, and as we get older and have children of our own we are influenced by their needs (as well as having a role in teaching them to be effective consumers, regardless of which gender they are). However the family is defined, and however humanity might change the structure of what is considered to be the family, the closeness of kinship and shared consumption will always ensure that families are at the heart of what makes us what we are.

Chapter 13 takes a look at how the social environment in which we live and behave is affected by our notions of social class and culture. These are usually derived from the people around us, and form the basis for our social behaviour as well as our understanding of who we are as individuals. This naturally affects our purchase behaviour, since we buy things that tend to validate our status.

Finally, Chapter 14 on ethical consumption is, as a subject matter, still in relative infancy. This is an area which remains to be fully embraced by all societies in all communities. The ethics of consumerism are continuously being influenced by the ever-evolving ways in which we acquire and consume *things*. This chapter takes a brief look at some of the key issues which are facing consumers currently.

CHAPTER 11

REFERENCE GROUPS

LEARNING OBJECTIVES

After reading this chapter you should be able to:

- Explain how reference groups influence individual members.
- Explain what is meant by normative compliance.
- Describe the main drivers for normative compliance.
- Explain the role of word of mouth communication.
- Describe ways of handling complaints.
- Explain the importance of email communication.

INTRODUCTION

Human beings are social animals: we form ourselves into groups, and in fact most of us are members of several different groups, formed for different purposes. In most cases we join groups because we can achieve more as part of a group than we can as an individual, but there are some groups which we belong to without ever having made a voluntary decision to join. Examples are our gender group, our ethnic or racial group and our family group. Because the family, age and gender are such important groups they have a chapter to themselves (see Chapter 12); this chapter deals with other groups that affect consumption.

Groups have considerable influence on our buying behaviour, either because we need to own certain items in order to join the group (there is no point in joining a golf club if one does not own a set of golf clubs, for example, although the loud check trousers are usually optional), or because we have joint consumption within the group for the purposes of saving ourselves time, money or effort. For example, members of a yacht club are able to share facilities such as berthing, a club house, maintenance facilities, and so forth, and many members also share a yacht.

Sociology

The study of human
behaviour in groups

Sociology is the study of human behaviour in groups, so much of the research into groups comes from sociologists rather than from marketing academics. Marketers are, of course, mainly interested in how group behaviour affects attitude formation (Chapter 10), eventual decision-making (Chapter 3) and purchasing behaviour.

FORMATION OF REFERENCE GROUPS

Reference group

A group of people who act
as the yardstick for our
behaviour

A group is two or more persons who share a set of norms and whose relationship makes their behaviour interdependent. A reference group is 'a person or group of people that significantly influences an individual's behaviour' (Bearden and Etzel 1982). The reference groups provide standards or norms by which consumers judge their attitudes and behaviour.

Originally, groups formed for the purpose of cooperating on survival activities. Because human beings could cooperate in such activities as hunting, food-gathering and defence from predators, we were able to increase the chances of survival for the species as a whole. Interestingly, this still appears to hold true; social researchers have reported that social isolation and loneliness are associated with increased mortality (Steptoe et al. 2013) and that socially isolated people have mortality rates between 50% and 300% higher than people who are strongly integrated into groups (Koretz 1990). For all of human history we have cooperated with each other to survive and prosper, and we continue to do so for both practical and social reasons.

Most people prefer to fit in with a group (to a greater or lesser extent). This is either through politeness or through a desire not to be left outside the group. Particularly with groups of friends, people will 'go along with the crowd' on a great many issues, and will tend to adopt the group norms regarding behaviour and attitudes. The process starts from an early age – children as young as eight are aware of the importance of having the right brands of food in their lunch boxes, and this awareness becomes stronger as they grow older (Roper and La Niece 2009). Children in Brazil are able to recognise cigarette logos at an even earlier age (Borzekowski and Cohen 2013).

Experiments conducted by Solomon Asch in 1951 demonstrated this in a graphic manner. In the experiment, subjects were asked to judge the lengths of different lines. The lines were displayed on a large board, and each person was seated with a group of strangers who were also supposed to be making judgements about the line lengths. In fact the strangers were Asch's assistants who had been instructed to agree with each other about the length of each line, but to make errors; the experimental subjects consistently agreed with these errors, even though the errors were sometimes glaringly obvious. Respondents did not make the same mistakes when there were no other people present, however. It appears from this that the fear of seeming foolish or of being the odd one out is enough to make the individual doubt the evidence of his or her eyes, or at the very least to lie about the evidence (Asch 1951).

Responses to group pressures may, in some circumstances, be gender-specific. Fisher and Dube (2003) found that men and women respond differently to emotional advertising depending on whether other people are present. Specifically, women show the same emotional responses to advertisements whether other people are present or not, whereas men are affected by the presence of others, especially if the emotional response is regarded as gender-specific. For example, an advertisement that causes someone to shed tears would cause the same response in a woman whether or not other people are around, whereas a man would be more likely to suppress this response if others are present (even if he were to shed a tear when in private). This said, more recent work by MacArthur and Shields (2015), investigating male athletes and masculinity, has found that even though the populist belief of men compressing their emotional expression and experience is still prevalent, this does not mean that it is either 'typical nor ideal masculinity in contemporary dominant culture'.

Perception of what is fair and what is not also seems to be influenced by social interaction with the group one happens to be in at the time (Carlson and Sally 2002). For example, when associating with a group of middle-class professionals one might perceive welfare payments as unfair, since they are paid for by hard-working taxpayers; in the company of a more left-wing group, one might perceive welfare payments as unfair because they do not provide enough money for a dignified and comfortable lifestyle.

CHALLENGING THE STATUS QUO

Do we really go along with things that easily? Is it so straightforward to lead people around by the nose? If so, how come we get into arguments with our friends? How come we have so many people who are prepared to stand up against the general flow of opinion and disagree?

Asch's experiment might just show that students try to please their lecturers, or that people try to give the 'right' answers in situations that look a lot like exams. Or maybe the results are good, but only when we are in the company of strangers – does our natural politeness (and fear of embarrassment, or worse still public humiliation) make us wary of arguing with someone we know nothing about?

And is this further exemplified if we are in the company of robots? Brandstetter et al. (2014) rightly ask the question of whether we will regard them as mindless machines, as subservient or as peers? The current development of 'human-like' social robots (Breazeal 2004; Kanda et al. 2004; Shaw-Garlock

©iStock.com/iLexx

2009) may well lead to a future where they are actively involved in our lives – from teaching young children basic education to helping with household chores to maybe even working in marketing! In December 2015, scientists at Nanyang Technological University in Singapore introduced the world to 'Nadine', a socially intelligent, human-looking robot who has a personality, possesses moods and displays emotions. The humanoid 'receptionist's' creator, Professor Nadia Thalmann, predicted that 'physical social robots such as Nadine are poised to become more visible in offices and homes in future'. Brandstetter et al. (2014) set out to recreate and expand upon the Asch experiment to see if robots could create conformity by means of group pressure. Their analyses demonstrated that participants behaved significantly different when among robot peers than among human peers and that individuals clearly interpret robot peers differently from human peers.

Will we ever succumb to robotic peer pressure?

Reference groups fall into many possible groupings; the following list is not intended to be exhaustive.

Primary group

The group of people we see daily, and to whom we feel closest

Primary groups are composed of those people we see most often: friends, family and close colleagues. A primary group is small enough to permit face-to-face interaction on a regular basis, and there is cohesiveness and mutual participation which results in similar beliefs and behaviour within the group. Because people tend to choose friends who think in similar ways, and have similar interests, the primary group is often very cohesive and long-lasting. Possibly the strongest primary group is the family, but primary groups might be close friends, colleagues in work or people with whom we share a hobby.

Secondary group

A group of people whom we do not necessarily see every day, and who are not our closest friends, but to which we belong nonetheless

Secondary groups are composed of people we see occasionally, and with whom we have some shared interest. For example, a trade association or a sports club would constitute a secondary group. These groups are correspondingly less influential in shaping attitudes and controlling behaviour, but can exert influence on behaviour within the purview of the subject of mutual interest. For example, if you are a member of a cycling club, you may be persuaded to take part in a sponsored bike ride, or perhaps a protest in favour of creating more cycle lanes. Within a secondary group, primary groups will sometimes form; there will often be groups of special friends whose shared interests go beyond those of the rest of the secondary group. For example, a cycling enthusiast might have a close friend with whom he cycles regularly: the friends might be members of a cycling club and arrange with a few other members of the club to go on an evening out. In this example, the friends are a primary group, but met through a secondary group (the cycling club) and formed a new primary group to enjoy a different shared interest (the evening out).

Aspirational group

A group of individuals which one wishes to join

Aspirational groups are the groups the individual wants to join. These groups can be very powerful in influencing behaviour, because the individual will often adopt the behaviour of the aspirational group in the hope of being accepted as a member. People who feel excluded because of some kind of stigma (perhaps having extremely visible facial tattoos, or being from a seemingly poor background) will modify their consumption patterns (either buying specific products, or reducing their consumption of other products) in order to conceal or reduce the stigma (Crosby and Otnes 2010). Sometimes the aspirational group will be better off financially, or will be more powerful; the desire to join such groups is usually classed as ambition. For example, a humble young office worker, studying part-time for a Chartered Marketer qualification may dream of one day becoming the Chief Marketing Officer (CMO). Advertising commonly uses images of aspirational groups, implying that use of a particular product will move the individual a little closer to being a member of an aspirational group.

Dissociative group

A social group to which one does not wish to belong

Dissociative groups, on the other hand, are those groups that the individual does not want to be associated with. Like a backpacker who does not want to look like a typical tourist, or a Marxist who would not want to be mistaken for a capitalist, the individual tries to avoid dissociative groups. This can have a negative effect on behaviour; the individual avoids certain products or behaviours rather than be taken for somebody from the dissociative group. Like aspirational groups, the definition of a group as dissociative is purely subjective; it varies from one individual to the next.

Formal group

A group of people with a known, recorded membership and a set of (usually written) rules of membership

Formal groups have a known list of members, very often recorded somewhere. An example might be a professional association like, for instance, the Chartered Institute of

Marketing (CIM), or a club. Usually the rules and structure of the group are laid down in writing; there are rules for membership, and members' behaviour is constrained while they remain part of the group. However, the constraints usually only apply to fairly limited areas of behaviour; for example, the CIM lays down a code of practice for marketers in their professional dealings, but has no interest in what its members do as private citizens. Membership of such groups may confer special privileges, such as job advancement or use of club facilities, and may lead to responsibilities in the furtherance of the group's aims.

Informal groups are less structured, and are typically based on friendship. An example would be an individual's circle of friends, which only exists for mutual moral support, company and sharing experiences. Although there can be even greater pressure to conform than would be the case with a formal group, there is no written set of rules. Often informal groups expect a more rigorous standard of behaviour across a wider range of activities than would a formal group; such circles of friends are likely to develop rules of behaviour and traditions that are more binding than written rules.

Automatic groups are those groups to which one belongs by virtue of age, gender, culture or education. These are sometimes also called **category groups**. Although at first sight it would appear that these groups would not exert much influence on members' behaviour, because these are groups that have not been joined voluntarily, it would appear that people are influenced by group pressure to conform. For example, when buying clothes older people are sometimes reluctant to look like 'mutton dressed as lamb' or dressing 'inappropriately as compared to their age'. It would certainly look somewhat odd if an older gentlemen walked into the golf club wearing clothes that made him look like Dr Dre. Also, membership of some racial groups can influence behaviour because of the associated physical characteristics: some cosmetics are specifically designed for skin and hair types that are genetically determined (see for example, www.imancosmetics.com).

Virtual communities (Hiltz and Wellman 1997; Ridings et al. 2002) are a recent phenomenon, brought about as a result of chatrooms on the Internet (Okleshen and Grossbart 1998). The communication is virtual rather than face-to-face, which means that people can (in effect) be whoever they say they are. These virtual groups work together on tasks supported by communications technologies (Lipnack and Stamps 2000). Such Internet communities are based on social interactions that can often be more open and uninhibited than would be the case in a real space rather than a virtual space (Fischer et al. 1996). This allows people to express views that might be controversial, and of course since the chatrooms are not geographically based, people with unusual interests (such as collecting rare whiskies or building light aircraft) are able to share information much more easily, reducing the time and cost of travelling (Baskerville and Nandhakumar 2007) as well as helping to foster a work–life balance (Fonner and Roloff 2010). Satisfaction with virtual communities such as forums, **blogs** and chatrooms comes from interactions with the members: the organisers of chatrooms have little influence over this (Langerak et al. 2004). On the one hand, the platforms allow individuals to discuss issues of common interest, and to share information about whatever topics interest them (however obscure). On the other hand, they open up possibilities for people to misrepresent themselves, perhaps for social purposes (for example to appear more interesting or desirable), or perhaps for sinister purposes such as fraud or paedophilia.

Informal group

A group of people that has no recorded membership and no written rules

Automatic group

A group of people to which an individual belongs by reason of race, gender or other non-changeable factor

Category group

See Automatic group

Virtual community

A group of people with common goals and interests who interact via electronic media

Blog

Short for web log – a publicly accessible personal journal

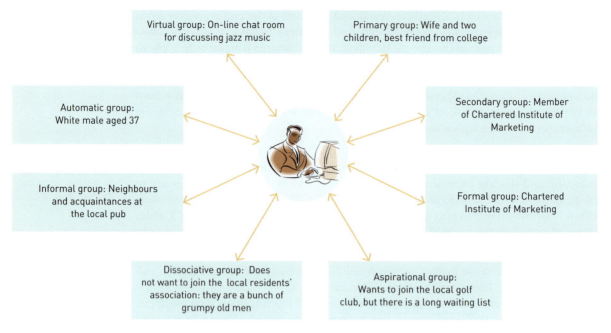

FIGURE 11.1 An individual and his reference groups

There are four types of virtual community, as follows (Muniz and O'Guinn 2001):

- *Brand communities*. These are groups who have a shared interest in a specific brand, for example owners of a particular motorcycle or classic car. These groups share experiences, help each other with obtaining accessories, spare parts etc., and offer each other advice when things go wrong.

- *Communities of interest*. Typically these are hobby sites for people who share an interest such as a sport, or a professional interest.

- *Fantasy communities*. These are based on games, whether fantasy games or ordinary games, such as chess or bridge.

- *Relationship communities*. These are based on common shared problems and experience, for example support groups for people with mental illness, victims of crime, or action groups who campaign for reform.

The above categories of group are not mutually exclusive. A dissociative group could also be an informal one; a formal group can be a secondary group (and often is), and so forth. For example, one may not wish to become friends with a group of drunken hooligans (who see themselves as an informal group of friends having a good time). Likewise, the golf club could be a place of refuge to which one retreats to have a quiet drink with like-minded people, as well as a place where golf is played.

Figure 11.1 shows how an individual might be a member of several groups, each one with different purposes, members and characteristics. Each group develops a set of shared knowledge and behaviours – this is called social constructivism – and therefore the individual will behave (and even think) differently when interacting with each separate group. In some cases the groups will fall into more than one classification: for this person, the Chartered Institute of Marketing is both a formal group (with a known set of members) and a secondary group (one that he relates to occasionally, because he has a professional interest). Social constructivism suggests that we are created as individuals through our social interactions with members of groups to which we belong – this contrasts somewhat with the psychological theories of personality discussed in Chapter 7.

INFLUENCE OF REFERENCE GROUPS

Reference groups affect people in several ways. First, groups tend to modify members' behaviour through a process of socialisation. This is a learning process for the individual, leading to an understanding of which behaviours are acceptable within the group and which are not. For example, there may be a formal set of rules laid down by a golf club regarding care of the greens, dress codes, behaviour in the clubhouse, and so forth, but it is the existing members who will advise new members on which rules are essential and which are often ignored. More importantly, the existing members will advise new members on behaviour that is expected but is not in the written rules – for example, buying a round of drinks when one scores a hole in one. Spending time with friends is an important way of learning what is appropriate and what is not, which may be one of the reasons why adolescent females spend a lot of time shopping with friends (Haytko and Baker 2004). Shopping also provides a shared activity for the adolescent that develops social education, companionship and an understanding of what is safe and what is not in the adult world.

Socialisation

The process of becoming an effective and integrated member of society by attaining and replicating norms, customs and ideologies in order to maintain continuity

CHALLENGING THE STATUS QUO

If shopping has become a hobby, and more particularly an educational experience for young teenage girls, marketers must think they've finally struck gold! But how true is it that young girls behave in this way? Haytko and Baker's research was conducted in the United States, where 'going to the mall' is inbuilt within the culture. But does it apply in Europe, or elsewhere in the world?

Would most European shopping malls be happy for gangs of teenagers to be hanging around anyway? Surely the situation in Europe or the rest of the world is different culturally? For instance, research suggests that young people in Taiwan are certainly taking their reference from their counterparts in the rest of the world. A study by Wu et al. (2015) found that Asian consumers not only consumed large swathes of media commentary, but were also greatly inspired by female celebrities. And when it came to discussing luxury fashion brands with friends, this was an enjoyable yet very serious business. Commentators around the world are noting that 'marketers should be communicating appeals to an aspirational lifestyle in both traditional and social media' (Wu et al. 2015).

Second, people develop a self-concept through their interactions within groups. How we see ourselves is a result of how others see us: feedback from others is the basis of our understanding of who we are. This is particularly apparent when the group has a specific purpose, such as supporting a football team: supporters often wear uniforms to show which team they support, thus identifying with the group and also

FIGURE 11.2 Modifying behaviour through groups

projecting their own identity, not only to the group but to any other observers. This is a way of blending one's personal identity with the culture surrounding the team (Oliver 1999). Marketers use this aspect of group behaviour to sell uniforms; it is also a feature of celebrity endorsement – by using a particular product, the individual associates him- or herself with the celebrity.

Conformity

The social pressure to behave in similar ways to other people

Compliance

Adherence without belief: acquiescence

Third, groups affect people through **conformity**. This is a change in beliefs or actions based on group pressures. There are two types of conformity: compliance and acceptance. **Compliance** happens when an individual goes along with the behaviour of the group without really accepting its beliefs. For example, someone who is not a football supporter might accompany a friend to a match and cheer on the friend's team without actually having any long-term interest in the team's fortunes. Compliance is common in the workplace. Acceptance occurs when the individual not only adapts behaviour, but also adapts his or her beliefs to come into line with the group. This might happen if the non-supporter decides that the experience was so exciting, and the team played so well, that he or she decides to become a supporter. Acceptance also commonly occurs through religious conversions. Overall, conformity can be considered as behaviour one adopts by observing others when confronted with membership of a new group; it is most likely to occur when the costs of conforming are outweighed by the advantages. Advantages might include self-esteem, acceptance by an aspirational group, companionship, practical benefits such as the potential for earning or saving money, and so forth (Homans 1961).

Fourth, people use groups for social comparison. We evaluate ourselves by comparing our performance with others – for example, when we consider our wealth or our social standing we compare ourselves with people whom we consider to be our equals in other respects. Comparisons are not necessarily made with groups with whom we have personal contact: for example, a lawyer might compare his or her salary with what other lawyers earn, or alternatively might make the comparison with other professionals such as doctors or accountants. If the groups are similar, the individual has greater confidence in the comparison (Tesser et al. 1988), but people generally value differing views when they are themselves confident in their own ability and opinions (Wheeler et al. 1969). This may explain why some people opt for cosmetic surgery (breast implants, liposuction, rhinoplasty or a nose job, etc.) whereas other people are apparently quite happy to live with physical 'imperfections'.

In Figure 11.2 the need for social comparison and self-concept drive the socialisation process. These are the reasons why people are prepared to accept socialisation. The result of socialisation is conformity, either by acceptance or by compliance.

TABLE 11.1 Effects of reference groups on consumer choice

Type of influence	Definition	Explanation	Example
Normative compliance	The pressure exerted on an individual to conform and comply	Works best when social acceptance is a strong motive, strong pressures exist from the group and the product or service is conspicuous in its use	Street gangs share common characteristics such as wearing distinct clothing, specific jackets or other uniform. The members want to be accepted, the pressure to wear the jacket is great and the jacket itself is a conspicuous badge of membership. The Los Angeles Police Department have a web page about how gangs are identified: www.lapdonline.org/get_informed/content_basic_view/23468
Value-expressive influence	The pressure that comes from the need for psychological association with a group	The desired outcome is respect from others; this pressure comes from the need for esteem, rather than from the need to belong	The city worker in his pinstripe suit and the lumbersexual hipster in his flannel shirt, well-groomed beard, covered in tattoos and wearing jeans are both seeking respect from others by expressing a set of values in the way they dress
Informational influence	The influence arising from a need to seek information from the reference group about the product category being considered. Small groups tend to exercise more influence (Soll et al. 2010)	People often need to get expert advice and opinion about their product choices. This can often be provided by the appropriate reference group	Many professional organisations and trade bodies offer their members free advice about useful products for their businesses. Clearly a recommendation on, say, computer software for a hairdressing business would be well received if it came from the Hairdressers Federation

FIGURE 11.3 Mechanisms for controlling behaviour

The mechanisms by which reference groups affect consumer behaviour are shown in Table 11.1 and diagrammatically in Figure 11.3.

Of the above three influences, **normative compliance** is probably the most powerful. The source of normative compliance lies in operant conditioning; the individual finds that conforming behaviour results in group approval and esteem, whereas non-conforming behaviour results in group disapproval. Eventually the 'good' behaviour becomes automatic and natural, and it would be difficult to imagine any other way

Normative compliance

The force that compels people towards agreeing with the rest of the group of doing things (see Chapter 9 for more on operant conditioning). For example, materialistic people are often stigmatised by groups, whereas people who enjoy experiential consumption are not. This, in time, results in behaviour modification (Van Boven et al. 2009).

The principles of good moral behaviour are not absolutes; they are the result (in most cases) of normative compliance with a reference group. Normative compliance may be less important now than it used to be for four reasons: first, the influence of the extended family (grandparents, parents, aunts and uncles) may be reducing as people move away from their home towns, and second there is strong evidence that people are becoming more inner-directed (McNulty 1985; Trompenaars and Hampden-Turner 2012). Third, the reduction in face-to-face interaction may be leading to this move away from normative compliance; increasingly people communicate by impersonal means such as text messages and email. Whether this is a cause of the paradigm shift or one of its effects is difficult to decide at present. Fourth, there is a weakening of respect for social norms, generated by a feeling of alienation from society. This is called anomie by sociologists (Durkheim 1951; Hövermann et al. 2015). Some people have little or no respect for rules made by other people, and conform grudgingly or not at all, because they do not feel that they have a position within society as a whole.

Of course, the pressure to conform will only work on someone who has a strong motivation to be accepted. If the pressure is coming from an aspirational group, this is likely to be the case; if, on the other hand, the pressure is coming from a dissociative group, the reverse will be the case and the individual will not feel under any pressure to conform. For example, most law-abiding citizens would comply with instructions from the police, and would usually go out of their way to help the police. Criminals, on the other hand, might avoid helping the police even in circumstances where their own crimes were not at issue.

The conspicuousness of the product or service is also crucial to the operation of normative compliance. For example, if all your friends vote for the Conservative party in the UK general election, you might be under some pressure to do likewise, but since the ballot is secret nobody will know if you vote Labour instead, so there is little pressure for normative compliance. Likewise, if your friends all drink Stella Artois lager you may feel under pressure to do the same, but might be happy with a supermarket own-brand when you're having a beer in the back garden at home. Conspicuous behaviour carries its own downside, though – the more conspicuous the behaviour, the more embarrassing it becomes if the group does not acknowledge the signal (Han and Nunes 2010).

Advertisers often appeal to the need to belong to an aspirational group. Advertising that shows desirable groups having a good time together, all thanks to the product, are so common that they are regarded as clichés. Typically, products with a social element such as beer, entertainment and some food products are advertised in this way.

The reference group will not exert influence over every buying decision. Even in circumstances where group influence does come into play, people will be influenced by other variables such as product characteristics, standards of judgement and conflicting influences from other groups. Table 11.2 shows some of the determinants of reference group influence.

TABLE 11.2 Determinants of reference group influence

Determinant	Definition	Explanation	Example
Judgement standards	The criteria used by the individual to evaluate the need to conform	Judgement standards are *objective* when the group norms are obvious and when the group approach is clearly the sensible course of action. The standards are *subjective* when it is not clear which is the most sensible course of action	Decisions of the ruling party in government are often portrayed as being unanimous; in the UK, the Conservative party is famous for presenting a united front, and individual members of the Cabinet therefore believe it is important to conform. The Labour party, on the other hand, has a tradition of public debate and therefore its shadow Cabinet is more likely to disagree in public, since members do not see a need to conform
Product characteristics	The features of the product that are salient to the group influence	The two main characteristics necessary for group influence to work are that the product should be *visible*, and that it should stand out (*non-universal ownership*)	A member of a judo club will be proud to wear the black belt, since it not only denotes a high level of expertise, but it is not available to other members unless they achieve the same level
Member characteristics	The traits of the group member which make him or her more or less susceptible to group pressures	People vary considerably in the degree to which they are influenced by pressures from the group. Some people remain fairly independent, where others conform habitually. Personality, status and security all seem to play major roles in determining whether an individual will conform	It transpires that university students are much more likely to conform with group norms than are housewives (Manz and Sims 1981). This is possibly because the university students are young, and often away from home, and thus have a greater need to belong
Group characteristics	The features of the group that influence individuals to conform	The power of the group to influence the individual varies according to size, cohesiveness and leadership. Once the group is bigger than three members, the power to influence levels off. This is probably because the group has difficulty reaching a consensus. Likewise, the stronger the leadership the greater the influence, and the greater the cohesiveness the stronger the influence, because the group reaches a clear decision	Many smokers take up the habit as a result of peer group pressure when they are aged around 12 or 13. If a child's friends are strongly anti-smoking, there is likely to be much less of an influence and therefore an uptake
Role model	An individual whose influence is similar to that of a group	A role model is a hero, a star or just somebody the individual respects and admires, and wishes to imitate	Many young women seek to imitate top models by extreme dieting, to the extent that the Madrid fashion week banned all models with a body mass index below 18: Milan threatened to follow suit (BBC News 2006). During the 1930s, when Clark Gable took off his shirt in a movie and showed that he was not wearing a vest, sales of vests plummeted because it became non-macho to wear one

MODELLING

Modelling was briefly discussed in Chapter 6, with regard to motivation and pain avoidance. The effectiveness of the role model in modelling behaviour will depend on the personal characteristics of the role model (see Figure 11.4). *Attractive* models will be imitated more than unattractive ones; *successful-looking* models are given more credence than unsuccessful-looking ones; and a model who is perceived as being *similar* to the observer is also more likely to be emulated (Baker and Churchill 1977). Somewhat

Role model

An individual who acts as a reference point for judging one's own behaviour

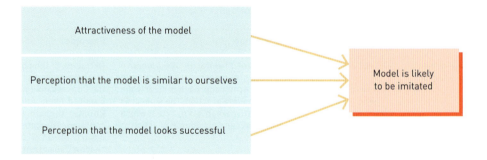

FIGURE 11.4 Factors in modelling

more recent neuro-psychological research has shown that average-looking celebrity models produce high levels of electrodermal response; in other words, they create the strongest physical effect on the observer (Gakhal and Senior 2008; Zuckerman 1988).

There is also some evidence to show that observers are more likely to identify with role models who have some difficulty in completing the modelled task (Manz and Sims 1981). There has, of course, been debate about whether crime shows on TV encourage people to copy the behaviour that is shown in the programmes; according to the theory, modelled behaviour will be copied if the observer feels able to identify with the role model. Presumably, therefore, a programme showing young working-class men making a living from selling hard drugs might encourage other young working-class men to do the same. However, the saving grace of this scenario is that the role model must also be seen to be successful and attractive – and in most TV dramas and movies the criminal is shown as being, ultimately, unsuccessful.

Some recent research has shown that role models can be too good to be true (Contín-Pilart and Larraza-Kintana 2015) – Superman turns out to be too super, so that people who compare themselves to Superman are less likely to volunteer to help others, simply because they feel that they do not measure up to the role model (Nelson and Norton 2005).

MECHANISMS OF PERSONAL INFLUENCE AND WORD OF MOUTH

Personal influence is commonly conducted via word of mouth. The classic definition of WOM was proffered by Arndt (1967): 'Oral person to person communication between a receiver and a communicator whom the person perceives as non-commercial, regarding brand, product or a service'.

Word of mouth communication is informal, and is conducted between individuals, neither of whom is a marketer. Word of mouth is therefore conducted without the ulterior motive of profiting from a sale; the non-commercial perception is dominant. WOM becomes increasingly more influential compared to well-researched sources of product information such as *Which* magazine as a result of consumers being somewhat cynical about the true independence of third party advice (Sethna et al. 2013).

Groups and individuals obviously have a strong influence on people's attitudes and behaviour through word of mouth; there are three main theories regarding the mechanisms whereby this personal influence is exerted. The history of the theory is not so much one of advancing knowledge about the mechanisms involved, but is rather a history of the way society has changed in the period in which the theories were evolving.

Trickle-down theory says that lower-class people often imitate upper-class people (Veblen 1899). Influence is transmitted down from the wealthier classes to the poorer classes, as the poorer groups in society seek to 'better themselves'. In fact, trickle-down is rarely seen in industrialised, wealthy countries like the UK because new ideas are disseminated overnight by the mass media and copied by chain stores within days. This is particularly true of clothing fashions, and the Punk revolution in the mid-1970s was an example of 'trickle-up', where the fashion came up from the poorer classes. What is replacing trickle-down theory is **homophilous influence**, which refers to transmission between those of similar age, education, social class, etc. – in other words, those who already have a lot in common. The 'commonality' (from the perspective of influence) is prolific when one considers the use of Twitter, YouTube and Instagram on which consumers share information about what they've bought and why.

Another area in which trickle-down theory can be observed is in the cult of celebrity: famous people are frequently imitated, and marketers use this to their advantage by obtaining celebrity endorsements of products. Soap operas play an influential role here, because they mimic group life in the real world, so much so that people often associate themselves with the cast of a soap opera in the same way as they would with a real group of people. This has given rise to the popularity of reality television shows, the cast members of which have become 'celebrities' in their own right (see for example *Made in Chelsea*, *The Only Way is Essex* and *Gogglebox*). This can affect people's aspirational consumption patterns (Russell and Stern 2006).

Two-step flow theory says that new ideas flow from the media to 'influentials' who then pass the information on to the rest of society (Lazarsfeld et al. 1948). When this theory was first formulated in the late 1940s and early 1950s it probably had a great deal of truth in it, and there is still evidence for this view; certainly in the **diffusion** of innovative high-tech products there is strong evidence for it. However, there is a weakening of this mechanism due to the preponderance of mass media. In the 1940s most homes did not have TV and there was no commercial radio in the UK; the availability of commercial information was therefore more restricted to the wealthy. Also, two-step flow assumes that the audience is passively waiting for the information to be presented, whereas in fact people actively seek out information about new things by asking friends and relatives and by looking for published information. A comparison of two-step flow theory and trickle-down theory is shown in Figure 11.5.

Trickle-down theory

The belief that innovations are adopted by wealthy, educated people first and eventually 'trickle down' to people in lower socio-economic groups

Homophilous influences

The transmission of ideas between people of similar standing in the community

Diffusion

The process of adoption of an innovation throughout the market

Trickle-down theory	Two-step flow theory
Wealthy classes obtain information and adopt products	Media generates information which reaches the 'influentials'
Poorer classes imitate their 'betters'	'Influentials' adopt the product
	Remainder of the population follows the 'influentials'

FIGURE 11.5 Mechanisms of personal influence

CONSUMER BEHAVIOUR IN ACTION: CONSUMING SPICE

Obviously, in the early 21st century we are well beyond the forelock-tugging attitude of our Victorian forebears, aren't we? Or are we? The plethora of 'I'm a Celebrity' TV shows, where C-list 'celebrities' whom very few have heard of put themselves into embarrassing situations demonstrates that people still have an interest in what the pseudo-famous have to say. Or is it simply that we like to see the once-famous come a cropper? We may

not have much respect for the opinions of the aristocracy, but there are other opinion leaders around – rock stars, TV stars, footballers, and so forth. Even the subtle aristocracy of the TV chef has an influence on what we eat. Take for example a recent BBC Two TV series called *The Incredible Spice Men*.

Cyrus Todiwala and Tony Singh, a couple of Indian-born celebrity chefs have been travelling around the UK and try-

©iStock.com/IDijkinga

ing to convince the great British public that British food needs 'spicing up'. Apparently the British palate has struggled with things such as clove, ginger and cumin. And so we see everything from chilli and cinnamon ice cream to the indelibly staple fish and chips being spiced. Even though the psychology of our taste buds dictates that we have a natural dislike for things that are different, guess what ... we lapped it up! Perhaps first impressions can be wrong ... it turns out that these media influentials have changed our opinions on spice.

The **multistage interaction** model (see Figure 11.6) agrees that some people are more influential than others, but also recognises that the mass media affect both influentials and seekers. The influential doesn't mediate the information flow, as the two-step model suggests, but rather acts as a mechanism for emphasising or facilitating the information flow. Within the model there is a continuous dialogue between marketers, seekers and influentials, with many stages of influence before the new idea is adopted or rejected. If there are several influentials, their influence is very much stronger if they occupy a number of different positions in the network rather than being at the top of the network (Stephen and Berger 2009). This may be because the person being influenced receives the message several times, i.e. there is redundancy in the communication.

Clearly it is important for marketers to identify who the influential people are likely to be, and much research has been carried out into this area. Table 11.2 shows the main characteristics of influentials which have been identified so far. This is probably not an exhaustive list, nor will it be generally applicable to all cases.

Influentials (and market mavens – see Chapter 9) like to pass on their knowledge, and there are several reasons for doing this.

FIGURE 11.6 Multistage interaction model

Involvement is a major force. The influential is usually very interested in the product category, and wants to share the excitement with others; mavens also have a high need for variety (Stokburger-Sauer and Hoyer 2009). An audio-visual entertainment enthusiast who buys a new Bryston-9B amplifier will want to tell friends and colleagues all about it as soon as possible using social media, possibly by even taking a selfie in the store while holding the amp. Telling other people acts as an outlet for the pleasure of owning the equipment.

Self-enhancement is about airing one's superior knowledge. People like to appear to be 'in the know' – perhaps being able to say 'I discovered a wonderful unspoiled place for a holiday'. Appearing to be a connoisseur, whether of fine wines or works of art or classic cars, is something many influentials, and especially mavens, strive for. People often ask a friend or relative to help when choosing a gift for a third party, especially where the gift-giving might be risky (where little is known about the third party, or where a lot of importance is placed on the gift). This usually increases the social bonding between the giver and the adviser (Lowrey et al. 2004).

Self-enhancement

The practice of airing one's superior knowledge in order to create a better image

Concern for others often precipitates influence. The genuine desire to help a friend to reach a good decision often prompts the expert to say, 'OK, I'll come with you when you go to buy that car'. This factor works most strongly when there is a strong link between the individuals concerned, and when the influential has been very satisfied with the product or service concerned. People with high levels of altruism are especially likely to help (Kaikati and Ahluwalia 2010). This can have a very direct effect on consumption: there is evidence that people often feel guilty about buying themselves a treat, but if a free gift for someone else is included, the guilt is very much reduced or even disappears altogether (Lee and Corfman 2004). This implies that firms in the 'treat' or 'luxury' business would do well to offer an extra little something to 'give to a friend'. Laphroaig Whisky Distillers do this: periodically they ask established customers ('Friends of Laphroaig') to pass on the names and addresses of three friends, to whom the distillery sends a small bottle of the whisky. Naturally, people are asked to obtain permission from their friends before passing on their details, but the promotion is successful on two fronts: it rewards the loyalty of the existing customer, and it brings the whisky to the attention of the friends. People generally enjoy giving gifts to their friends and sharing good fortune – people who are given gift vouchers enjoy the vouchers more when it involves sharing with a friend (Norton et al. 2010).

The main practical lesson from this is that 'bring a friend' promotions should reward the friend rather than the original customer: offering someone a free gift for introducing a friend does not work as well as offering a gift to any friends who are introduced.

Message intrigue

The element of a message which arouses the interest of a recipient

Message intrigue is the factor concerned with comments about advertising messages. If an advertisement is particularly humorous or intriguing, people will discuss it; this enhances the message by repetition. Advertisements for Guinness have often used this approach. One such advertisement shows Gareth Thomas (former Wales Rugby captain) talking about how his teammates were there for him when he needed them. In the advert called 'Never Alone', we hear Gareth talk about his life on the rugby field, and the hard times he faced. The viewer assumes that he is talking about the game being gruelling, but half way through the advert we find that Gareth is actually referring to the psychological battle he faced as he harboured the secret of his sexuality. He had not told his fans, or the crowd or his team – the closest people to him, whom he calls his family – about the fact that he is gay, for fear of people rejecting him. The advert subtly intimates that there is a perception associated with men who play rugby, and thus young men take their 'reference' from such portrayals; by implication, it would not be acceptable to have a gay rugby player. The advert ends with the words 'Gareth Thomas. Thought he was alone. Always part of a team. Guinness – made of more'. With music by Ludovico Einaudi playing in the background, it is not only emotionally gripping, but the fact that it was aired just before the start of the rugby world cup meant that people are more likely to watch it, remember it, and continue to make the connections between rugby and Guinness.

Dissonance

A mental state that arises when outcomes do not match with expectations

Dissonance reduction is about reducing doubts after making a major purchase (see Chapter 10). As word of mouth influence this can be good or bad; sometimes the influential will try to reassure him- or herself by telling everybody (the volume relates to the number of people to which the message is relayed) about the good points of the product; more often, though, the disappointed customer will use word of mouth to complain bitterly and explain how the wicked manufacturer has cheated him or her. This is sometimes a way of passing the responsibility over to the supplier rather than admitting that the influential has made a bad decision or a bad choice.

The forces driving influentials are summarised in Figure 11.7.

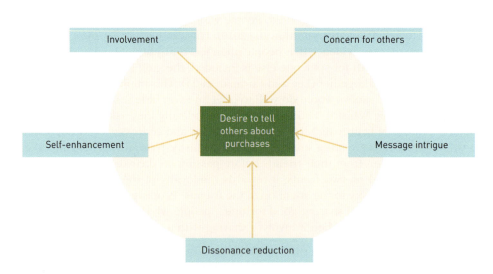

FIGURE 11.7 Forces driving influentials

CHALLENGING THE STATUS QUO

Interestingly, most of the reasons influentials have for passing on what they know are selfish ones. They want to show off their knowledge, pass on an interesting bit of gossip, reassure themselves that they made the right decision by persuading someone else to make the same choice, and so forth.

Only occasionally, apparently, are they motivated by concern for others – passing on a good tip to a friend, in this case. Does this tell us that people are essentially selfish? Or should we give people credit for getting their kicks by being helpful rather than destructive? And what do we actually mean by 'being helpful'?

Take Tinder, for instance. It's a location-based social discovery application that facilitates communication between mutually interested users. The dating app allows users to chat with their matches. It was launched in 2012, and by 2014 it was registering about one billion 'swipes' per day. What makes Tinder different from its competition is that it was among the first 'swiping apps', where the user uses a swiping

©iStock.com/jpgfactory

motion to choose between the photos of other users: swiping right for potentially good matches and swiping left on a photo to move to the next one. In the Fall semester of 2015, the good folks at Tinder posted a blog entitled 'Most Right-Swiped Campuses 2015: Did yours make the list?'. Statistics for the top 50 universities in the USA for right-swipes are shown for both girls and boys, thus passing on 'good tips' about where the rest of the like-minded reference group believes the 'buff tings' are.

Buff ting
A British slang phrase for people who are very attractive, glamorous and good-looking

Overall, word of mouth influence is much stronger than advertising or other marketer-produced communications. For marketers, then, the problem lies in knowing how to use word of mouth to its best advantage. Table 11.3 offers some comparisons and strategies.

It is not usually possible to rely entirely on word of mouth, but marketers should take steps to stimulate it as a promotional tool. Advertising that provokes word of mouth about the advert itself can be very powerful – research shows that a very creative advertisement that prompts people to tell others about it leads to a much greater intention to purchase after the other people see the advertisement for themselves (Moldovan and Lehmann 2010). In other words, someone who is told about a very exciting or entertaining advertisement will be prompted to look out for the advert, and is then much more likely to buy the product. Sometimes marketers are able to encourage word of mouth by giving influential people a product sample and asking them to blog about their experiences with the product. Most people in that position will accept, embrace, ridicule or apologise for accepting the role as a marketing tool, and very few ignore their role by not mentioning in the blog that they were given the product (Kozinets et al. 2008).

TABLE 11.3 Word of mouth

Strong influence	Weak influence	Tactical suggestions
Seeker initiates conversation with source	Source initiates conversation with seeker	Advertising could emphasise the idea of 'Ask the person who owns one'. Network marketers could emphasise a more advisory role for their salespeople rather than a strongly proactive approach
Negative information	Positive information	Because marketers are uniformly positive about the product, the seeker is more alert to any negatives. The essential thing for marketers to do is to ensure that any complaints are dealt with immediately and thoroughly
Verbal communication is stronger for thinking and evaluation	Visual communication is stronger for awareness and stimulation of interest	Where appropriate, marketers could encourage satisfied customers to show their friends the product; this tactic is often used for home improvement sales, where customers are paid a small reward or commission for introducing friends to the product. This is also the basis for party-plan selling, e.g. Tupperware and Ann Summers

If the company is in a position to be able to identify influentials, it is well worthwhile offering to lend them the product (or even give them it, if the cost is low enough) so that they can be stimulated into talking about it to friends. Advertising should be interesting and involving, perhaps even controversial, so that debate ensues. Although it is not true to say that any word of mouth will be good for a company, it is certainly true to say that controversy and debate will always increase brand awareness, even when it does not enhance brand image. For example, Harveytiles (a brand of Harvey Roofing Products Ltd, a South African roofing tile manufacturer) produces advertisements that are extremely controversial. The slogans use religious references ('A roof without Harveytiles is like being burnt in hell without a saviour: Only heaven is covered with Harveytiles') that have proved to be extremely offensive to the committed Christians of Zambia. The result has been that everyone in Zambia has heard of Harveytiles, but of course this does not necessarily mean that people will buy the product. Some people undoubtedly boycott the product because of the religious references.

Another way of stimulating word of mouth is to allow people to try out the product. Car manufacturers usually give exceptionally generous discounts to car hire companies, taking the view that hirers might well be tempted to buy the same model at a later stage, and are also very likely to talk about the vehicle to others.

Marketing theorists have not taken WOM seriously as there is a perception among marketers that one cannot plan, monitor and control WOM. But if one looks at this through an entrepreneurial marketing lens (Sethna et al. 2013), one would assume that marketers would take this activity seriously, as the majority of small and medium sized enterprises (SMEs) use WOM recommendations as their main source of new business (Stokes and Nelson 2013).

CONSUMER BEHAVIOUR IN ACTION: WOM SELLS WORDS

Dan Brown's climb to fame was far from meteoric. He failed at several careers before getting into writing – and even then his earlier books hardly set the world on fire. Yet everyone needs to learn their craft, and eventually Dan hit the jackpot with *The DaVinci Code*, published in 2003.

©iStock.com/DarioRota

The book, which puts forward the theory that Jesus married Mary Magdalene and had children by her, was not exactly a great work of literature, but it caught the public imagination. Initially the publishers planned only a short print run – based on the sales of Dan's other books, it seemed unlikely that the book would be a runaway best-seller. The rest, of course, is history: the book has to date sold in excess of 80 million copies.

So how come this book sold so much better than expected? The publishers certainly didn't hype the book – after all, they weren't expecting to sell it in large enough numbers to justify a big publicity campaign. The answer lies in word of mouth. People told people about the book, and those people told other people, and so the process went on until everybody had heard of it.

Research by Nielsen Bookscan in 2005 showed that a large number of best-selling books have achieved success this way – *Captain Corelli's Mandolin*, *Eats, Shoots and Leaves* and *The Lovely Bones* were all cited as million-plus sellers that had succeeded almost entirely on personal recommendation.

As a result, the World Book Day organisers ran a campaign encouraging people to recommend a book to a friend – another resounding success!

THE EMERGENCE OF WORD OF MOUSE

In recent years word of mouth has been supplemented by the use of the Internet, email communications and of course social media. Collectively, they have contributed to the creation of a new channel of communication which has been referred to as '**word of mouse**' (Sethna et al., 2013).

E-communications are a fast and powerful communications medium, but more importantly they provide a semi-permanent record of what was said, so that communications can contain facts and figures that can be referred to later. Encouraging people to communicate with each other about products has become a growth area for e-marketing, and is a feature of many websites. The decision to forward a message implies that the individual endorses it: the person's involvement in the product is of course important, but the decision to forward a message seems to depend much more on the amount of email traffic between the individuals concerned (Harvey et al. 2011).

The power of word of mouse, however, has grown exponentially with the rapid adoption of all things 'mobile' and m-commerce related (mobile-commerce). This is partly because many consumers are comfortable with the convenience of buying on their mobile devices (iPhones, iPads, tablets, etc.) and it is thought that over a quarter of all e-commerce traffic stems from a mobile device. The prolific use of smartphones has meant that communications using chatrooms, blogs, vlogs, cross-platform mobile messaging apps (for example Whatsapp, WeChat, LINE, Viber, Tango) and virtual gaming are leading the way in the world of m-commerce. From a societal perspective, there are some commentators who believe that fourth-tier cities in emerging economies may not even experience the traditional bricks-and-mortar shopping and retail outlets, mainly due to the convenience and increasing sophistication of mobile shopping. In 2014, nearly 85% of the WeChat revenue came from online gaming (*The Economist*, 2014). Virtual communities are extremely powerful in promoting products – they frequently ask each other for specific recommendations about products (WeChat currently has over 270 million active users). Young consumers have been shown to develop online personalities, which may differ from their real personalities but which act in very similar ways in terms of group behaviour.

Vlog

Short for video log – a blog that includes video clips

CONSUMER BEHAVIOUR IN ACTION: AN INFLUENSTER ECLIPSE

Are we in danger of assuming that it's really only 'young' people who make their opinions count? Are they the only trendsetters? Well, if you were to believe all the media stories about *vloggers*, you'd be forgiven when taking that stance.

The media is awash with names of millennials who transmit their daily dosage of performing prowess on YouTube channels – live and direct from their bedrooms – to millions of adoring fans over whom they have influence – or some might say a stranglehold. Top among this group is Zoella (Zoe Sugg) who reigns supreme with over 10 million subscribers and 542m views of her videos. Her contemporaries are, among others, people such as Danisnotonfire (Dan Howell) who generally makes videos about his own escapades, and Selena Gomez who seems to be the resident fashion and make-up maven. So influential is this group of people that vloggers even have their own physical magazine now called *Oh My Vlog!*. It's similar in style to teen mags about boy bands, but it is aimed at the YouTube generation. Some people have questioned whether such an 'archaic' form of communication is right for the audience – to which the publishers have said, 'Well, you can't print out a vlog and stick it up on your bedroom wall, can you?', which is a fair point.

In reality, it's not all about the millennials. There is a lot to be said about age and experience, and some over fifties are eager to play the YouTube game. Admittedly their view and subscriber scores are not as impressive as those of younger people, but they are still yielding an influence over a substantial number of people. Take for instance, 'Elle is for Living'. She talks about her passions and her life, whether it's product testing, or sharing beauty and style tips – she has an opinion on everything. And with over 1.25 million views and in excess of 15,000 subscribers, it seems that there is an interested audience. Then there's 'Wheaten Beauty' – a 50-something university academic whose vlog is crammed full of beauty tips which she records both in the morning and the night. With thousands of subscribers and nearly 200,000 views, there's a considerable following developing, even more so as her videos talk about her involvement with Influenster. Influenster is a product discovery, testing and reviews platform that uses social media analytics to measure its users' influence on social media. In essence, what the people at Influenster do is to quantify its users' influence via 'social impact' which tracks the number of friends, followers or subscribers a user has. Based on the impact score (the higher the better) and the demographic, the user can then be invited into campaigns that Influenster is running for various consumer branded products. The brands offer complementary products or digital rewards to the Influenster member. Once they've received the shipment and tested the product, all they have to do is create a vlog, share their thoughts with their followers (although there is no obligation to do either) and complete a survey. The more they do, the more chance there is of unlocking a badge of honour – 'expert' or 'lifestyle', part of a gamification type of system to encourage usage and the creation of content. The more content, the more views – and thus the greater the possibility for greater impact. By their own admission, Influenster enables members to compare products and then allows the mavens to guide members on how products can be adopted and integrated into their own life.

It's worth noting that mainly due to the elements of gamification and the way in which Influenster is structured, the response rates to their surveys have regularly achieved over 82% return. This is indeed quite an achievement and has totally eclipsed the research industry average.

Social networking sites that focus around celebrities often generate a very strong sense of togetherness and belonging, amounting to a tribal situation, despite having no reality outside cyberspace (Hamilton and Hewer 2010).

Online communities provide support and help for their members in the same way as offline, face-to-face groups. Online communities on Facebook often 'nudge' each other towards buying particular products (Harris and Dennis 2011), and online communities can be very powerful in raising brand commitment (Kim et al. 2008). A study of a slimming website revealed that there are three main types of participant: Passive Recipients obtain high levels of informational and emotional support, but communicate passively; Active Supporters are much more proactive in communication, and obtain high levels of support; and Casual Browsers communicate passively and receive little support (Ballantine and Stephenson 2011). Sometimes online communities can be damaging for marketers. Counter-brand and alter-brand behaviour is easily facilitated in cyberspace: users can develop dangerous opposition, or even their own products that compete directly with firms, without the need for corporate involvement.

Web forums can be used by companies to attract new customers and to provide an outlet for people's discussions about products. People use such sites as information sources, and as ways of validating their self-concept as being knowledgeable, or as 'insiders'. They can be particularly powerful for arts organisations such as orchestras, art galleries and museums (O'Sullivan 2010).

SUMMARY

There is little doubt that word of mouse will grow as access to the Internet and the world wide web spreads throughout the world. In fact, it could even be the case that the mouse has had its day, and that it's the 'power of the finger' which currently rules our life. That said, we're also seeing a move towards voice command mobile devices which (bizarrely) may bring us back to vocal delivery of messages (word of mouth) but web-enabled viral marketing is likely to be an increasing force for the foreseeable future.

In this chapter we have looked at some of the interpersonal factors that influence purchasing behaviour. In particular, we have looked at the groups and individuals who most influence consumers, and at the ways the influence is exerted. Finally, we have looked at ways marketers can use these interpersonal factors to improve customer relations and customer loyalty.

KEY POINTS

- Most people are members of several reference groups, all of which influence the individual in different ways.
- Normative compliance is probably the most powerful influence on behaviour.
- Conspicuousness is the most crucial product characteristic for normative compliance.
- Word of mouth spreads because the informant (influential) likes to talk about the products concerned.
- Complaints can be turned to the marketer's advantage by generous handling.
- Word of mouse is likely to be a growth area in marketing communications in the 21st century.

HOW TO IMPRESS YOUR EXAMINER

You are likely to be asked to compare different types of reference groups and/or explain their influence on people. You should try to use marketing examples to illustrate your answer – for instance, that peer groups sometimes pressure people into buying the 'right' product, or that dissociative groups will tend to tarnish brand values. This not only shows that you understand the theory, it also shows that you can apply it in a marketing context.

REVIEW QUESTIONS

1. How might companies encourage word of mouth?
2. What is the role of normative compliance in fashion marketing?
3. How might peer pressure encourage people to try new things?
4. Why is word of mouse becoming more popular with companies?

5. How can companies counteract negative word of mouth?

6. How might membership of an automatic group affect buying behaviour?

7. How might membership of an automatic group affect someone's propensity to join a secondary group?

8. How might a secondary group also be a formal group?

9. What are the defining characteristics of a primary group?

10. How might a marketer make use of a virtual group?

CASE STUDY: SOCIAL CARE FOR THE YOUTH – INVOLVING CHILDREN AND YOUNG PEOPLE IN DEVELOPING SOCIAL CARE

Up until 2012, Connexions was the government's support service for all young people aged 13 to 19 in England. It provided advice, guidance and access to personal development opportunities to support a smooth transition to adulthood and working life. 'The Reference Group' was jointly run by Connexions and the youth service in the UK region of Cheshire and Warrington.

The Reference Group was established in 2000 to help meet Connexions' key principle: to involve young people in the organisation's service delivery and planning. The group met once a month and involved two members of Connexions' staff – a youth participation consultant with a practical focus and a director with a strategic focus – and four members from the youth parliament.

At its peak, approximately 30 young people aged 13–19 were involved in The Reference Group. Young people with an interest in youth services were

©iStock.com/SteveDebenport

recruited by personal advisers. The group was a mixed-ability group, including young people with learning disabilities and one young person who was visually impaired.

The Reference Group was involved in organising Connexions' organisational structures, and regularly met with various members of Connexions, including the management board. The Reference Group then became involved in numerous activities including:

• producing job descriptions

• recruiting Connexions' and external organisations' staff

- producing a training video on active involvement

- peer consultancy work on local services

- designing publicity material

- auditing services funded by Connexions

- presenting at conferences

- voting on organisational decisions such as tender bids.

Members also became Connexions staff, through 12 youth link worker roles in the region.

Participation is written in the organisation's mission statement and in the job descriptions of personal advisers, and was in guidance received by staff when they joined Connexions. An 'Active Engagement' working group was established, attended by team leaders for participation. There were also training review days about active involvement that staff at all levels of the organisation had to attend. All staff were given a checklist of 'active involvement' to inform their work. Connexions also had a young person's active involvement plan.

CHANGES OR IMPROVEMENTS AS A RESULT OF CHILDREN AND YOUNG PEOPLE'S PARTICIPATION

The group implemented the following changes:

- Redesigned the previous adult-led participation charter to produce the Young People's Entitlement Charter. This idea came from the group, as they wanted all local organisations to share a common language about involvement. All the local youth services signed up to this.

- Developed questionnaires for young people who access Connexions' service. Personal advisers had to get 50 young people from each school to respond to these each year.

- Evaluated projects with Ofsted, which had been influenced by the value of involving young people.

- Highlighted young person-led issues, such as changing the opening hours of Connexions' services to evenings during the week and Saturday mornings.

- Rebranded Connexions' publication material for young people.

- As a result of feedback from young people, the organisation's annual conference increased opportunities for discussions and debates, leading to an increase of young people attending the conference from 10 to 50.

- Awareness of the needs of care-experienced young people was raised within the local authorities.

- There were increased opportunities for looked-after young people and care leavers to raise issues and present their views to local authority services.

In a quote about The Reference Group one of the young people said:

The young people's panel isn't just talking and answering questions, it has a role. I've got to know the youth services sector, an understanding of all the agencies involved, and the culture of the sector which has played a lot into my career plans and decisions. Now I'm training as a youth worker at university.

EVIDENCE OF OUTCOMES FROM PARTICIPATION

The Reference Group project produced the following documentation to evidence the development of participation:

- Connexions' key objectives, which include the participation of young people.
- Job descriptions.
- Group newsletter and minutes which are circulated to all stakeholders.

EVENTUAL DEMISE

Following the UK election of the Conservative/Lib Dem Coalition, the future of Connexions was called into question. It was no longer clear whether the Connexions brand and the services that it delivered had a long-term future. The government launched a new career service called the National Careers Service which was established on 1 April 2012.

QUESTIONS

1. What is the role of normative compliance in a group such as The Reference Group?
2. What type of group is The Reference Group?
3. Why would the group be composed of people within a specific age group and social status?
4. What is the purpose of the group newsletter?
5. What might be the reason for the increased attendance at the annual conference?

FURTHER READING

For some more on gift-giving, try S. McKechnie and C. Tynan (2006) Social meaning in Christmas consumption: an exploratory study of UK celebrants' consumption rituals, *Journal of Consumer Behaviour*, 5 (2): 130–44. Also, *The Gift of Thanks: The Roots and Rituals of Gratitude* (Boston, MA: Houghton Mifflin Harcourt, 2009) by Margaret Visser explores the other side of gift-giving – gratitude on the part of the recipient.

Ervin Goffman's *Presentation of Self in Everyday* Life is a classic read (Harmondsworth: Penguin, 1990). It explores the ways in which we present ourselves in different group situations, and it explains his 'life as theatre' analogy.

Also by Goffman, *Stigma: Notes on the Management of Spoiled Identity* (Harmondsworth: Penguin, 1990) explores another side of groups – the fate of those who are excluded. His research was carried out among people who were disfigured through birth or accident, people from racial or religious minorities, and people with mental illnesses. Goffman notes that other people tend to focus on the distinguishing feature, not on the whole personality, therefore such people become defined by their differences rather than by their similarities. This is a thought-provoking book, and often a very moving one.

For a humorous look at the fashion industry, and at our obsession with wearing the right clothes, you might like *Fashion Victim: Our Love–Hate Relationship with Dressing, Shopping and the Cost of Style* by Michelle Lee (New York: Broadway Books, 2003). The author takes a wry look at the fashion industry, and pokes fun at some of the 'rules' of fashion ('Thou Shalt Pay More to Look Poor' being one of them). This is a fun read, with some interesting ideas underneath it.

REFERENCES

Arndt, J. (1967) Role of product-related conversations in the diffusion of a new product. *Journal of Marketing Research*, 4: 291–5.

Asch, S.E. (1951) Effects of group pressure on the modification and distortion of judgements. In H. Guetzkow (ed.), *Groups, Leadership and Men*. Pittsburgh, PA: Carnegie Press, pp. 177–90.

Baker, M.J. and Churchill, G.A. Jr. (1977) The impact of physically attractive models on advertising evaluations. *Journal of Marketing Research*, 14 (4): 538–55.

Ballantine, P.W. and Stephenson, R.J. (2011) Help me, I'm fat! Social support in online weight loss networks. *Journal of Consumer Behaviour*, 10 (6): 332–7.

Baskerville, R. and Nandhakumar, J. (2007) Activating and perpetuating virtual teams: now that we're mobile, where do we go? *IEEE Transactions on Professional Communication*, 50: 17–34.

BBC News (2006) Wednesday 13 September.

Bearden, W.O. and Etzel, M.J. (1982) Reference group influence on product and brand purchase decisions. *Journal of Consumer Research*, 9 (September): 184–94.

Borzekowski, L. and Cohen, R. (2013) International reach of tobacco marketing among young children. *Pediatrics*, 132: 26–31. doi: 10.1542/peds.2013-1150.

Brandstetter, J., Racz, P., Beckner, C., Sandoval, E.B., Hay, J. and Bartneck, C. (2014) A peer pressure experiment: recreation of the Asch conformity experiment with robots. In *Intelligent Robots and Systems* (IROS 2014), 2014 IEEE/RSJ International Conference, Chicago, pp. 1335–40.

Breazeal, C.L. (2004) *Designing Sociable Robots*. Cambridge, MA: MIT Press.

Carlson, K.A. and Sally, D. (2002) Thoughts that count: fairness and possibilities, intentions and reactions. *Advances in Consumer Research*, 29: 79–89.

Contín-Pilart, I. and Larraza-Kintana, M. (2015) Do entrepreneurial role models influence the nascent entrepreneurial activity of immigrants? *Journal of Small Business Management*. doi: 10.1111/jsbm.12153.

Crosby, E. and Otnes, C. (2010) Consumption as a strategy for stigma management. *Advances in Consumer Research*, 37: 28–9.

Durkheim, E. (1951) *Suicide: A Study in Sociology*. New York: Free Press.

The Economist (2014) Nice little earner. www.economist.com/news/china/21594312-can-wechat-become-world-beating-app-nice-little-earner (accessed 1 September 2015).

Fischer, E., Bristor, J. and Gaynor, B. (1996) Creating or escaping community? An exploratory study of Internet consumers' behaviours. *Advances in Consumer Research*, 23: 178–82.

Fisher, R.J. and Dube, L. (2003) Gender differences in responses to emotional advertising: the effect of the presence of others. *Advances in Consumer Research*, 30: 15–17.

Fonner, K.L. and Roloff, M.E. (2010) Why teleworkers are more satisfied with their jobs than are office-based workers: when less contact is beneficial. *Journal of Applied Communication Research*, 38: 336–61.

Gakhal, B. and Senior, C. (2008) Examining the influence of fame in the presence of beauty: an electrodermal 'neuromarketing' study. *Journal of Consumer Behaviour*, 7 (4/5): 331–41.

Hamilton, K. and Hewer, P. (2010) Tribal mattering spaces: social networking sites, celebrity affiliations, and tribal innovations. *Journal of Marketing Management*, 26 (3&4): 271–9.

Han, Y.J. and Nunes, J.C. (2010) Read the signal but don't mention it: how conspicuous consumption embarrasses the signaler. *Advances in Consumer Research*, 37: 82.

Harris, L. and Dennis, C. (2011) Engaging customers on Facebook: challenge for e-retailers. *Journal of Consumer Behaviour*, 10 (6): 338–46.

Harvey, C.G., Stewart, D.B. and Ewing, M.T. (2011) Forward or delete: what drives peer-to-peer message propagation across social networks? *Journal of Consumer Behaviour*, 10 (6): 365–72.

Haytko, D.L. and Baker, J. (2004) It's all at the mall: exploring adolescent girls' experiences. *Journal of Retailing*, 80 (1): 67.

Hiltz, S.R. and Wellman, B. (1997) Asynchronous learning networks as a virtual classroom. *Communications of the ACM*, 40: 44–9.

Homans, G.C. (1961) *Social Behavior: Its Elementary Forms*. New York: Harcourt, Brace and World.

Hövermann, A., Messner, S.F. and Zick, A. (2015) Anomie, marketization, and prejudice toward purportedly unprofitable groups: elaborating a theoretical approach on anomie-driven prejudices. *Acta Sociologica*, 58 (3): 215–31.

Huang, L. (2010) Social contagion effects in experiential information exchange on bulletin board systems. *Journal of Marketing Management*, 26 (3&4): 197–212.

Kaikati, A.M. and Ahluwalia, R. (2010) Word of mouth communication as helping behavior. *Advances in Consumer Research*, 37: 127–8.

Kanda, T., Hirano, T., Eaton, D. and Ishiguro, H. (2004) Interactive robots as social partners and peer tutors for children: a field trial. *Human-Computer Interaction*, 19 (1): 61–84.

Kim, J., Choi, J., Qualls, W. and Han, K. (2008) It takes a marketplace community to raise brand commitment: the role of online communities. *Journal of Marketing Management*, 24 (3&4): 409–31.

Koretz, G. (1990) Economic trends. *Business Week*, 5 March.

Kozinets, R.V., de Valck, K., Wilner, S.J.S. and Wojnicki, A.C. (2008) Opening the black box of buzzing bloggers: understanding how consumers deal with the tension between authenticity and commercialism in seeded word-of-mouth campaigns. *Advances in Consumer Research*, 35: 49–51.

Langerak, F., Verhoef, P.C. and Verleigh, P.W.J. (2004) Satisfaction and participation in virtual communities. *Advances in Consumer Research*, 31: 56–7.

Lazarsfeld, P.F., Berelson, B.R. and Gaudet, H. (1948) *The People's Choice*. New York: Columbia University Press.

Lee, S.N. and Corfman, K.P. (2004) A little something for me, and maybe for you too: promotions that relieve guilt. *Advances in Consumer Research*, 31: 28.

Lipnack, J. and Stamps, J. (2000) *Virtual Teams: Working Across Boundaries with Technology*. New York: Wiley.

Lowrey, T.M., Otnes, C.C. and Ruth, J.A. (2004) An exploration of social influence on dyadic gift-giving. *Advances in Consumer Research*, 31: 112.

MacArthur, H.J. and Shields, S.A. (2015) There's no crying in baseball, or is there? Male athletes, tears, and masculinity in North America. *Emotion Review*, 7 (1): 39–46.

Manz, C.C. and Sims, H.P. (1981) Vicarious learning: the influence of modelling on organisational behaviour. *Academy of Management Review*, January.

McNulty, W.K. (1985) UK social change through a wide-angle lens. *Futures*, August.

Moldovan, S. and Lehmann, D. (2010) The effect of advertising on word of mouth. *Advances in Consumer Research*, 37: 119.

Muniz, A. and O'Guinn, T. (2001) Brand community. *Journal of Consumer Research*, 27 (March): 412–32.

Nelson, L.D. and Norton, M.I. (2005) From student to superhero: situational primes shape future helping. *Journal of Experimental Social Psychology*, 41 (4): 423–30.

Norton, M.J., Aknin, L. and Dunn, E. (2010) Putting the 'social' in prosocial spending: interpersonal giving promotes happiness. *Advances in Consumer Research*, 37: 43.

Okleshen, C. and Grossbart, S. (1998) Usenet groups, virtual community and consumer behaviours. *Advances in Consumer Research*, 25 (1): 276–82.

Oliver, R.L. (1999) Whence consumer loyalty? *Journal of Marketing*, 63 (4): 33–44.

O'Sullivan, T. (2010) Dangling conversations: web-forum use by a symphony orchestra's audience members. *Journal of Marketing Management*, 26 (7&8): 656–70.

Ridings, C.M., Gefen, D. and Arinze, B. (2002) Some antecedents and effects of trust in virtual communities, *Journal of Strategic Information Systems*, 11: 271–95.

Roper, S. and La Niece, C. (2009) The importance of brands in the lunch-box choices of low-income British school children. *Journal of Consumer Behaviour*, 8 (2/3): 84–99.

Russell, C. and Stern, B. (2006) Aspirational consumption in US soap operas: the process of parasocial attachment to television soap opera characters. *Advances in Consumer Research*, 33 (1): 36.

Sethna, Z., Jones, R. and Harrigan, P. (eds) (2013) *Entrepreneurial Marketing: Global Perspectives*. Bingley: Emerald Publishing.

Shaw-Garlock, G. (2009) Looking forward to sociable robots. *International Journal of Social Robotics*, 1 (3): 249–60.

Soll, J., Larrick, R. and Mannes, A. (2010) When it comes to wisdom, smaller crowds are wiser. *Advances in Consumer Research*, 37: 95.

Stephen, A. and Berger, J. (2009) Creating contagion: cascades in spatially dispersed social networks. *Advances in Consumer Research*, 36: 37.

Steptoe, A., Shankar, A., Demakakos, P. and Wardle, J. (2013) Social Isolation, loneliness and all-cause mortality in older men and women. In *Proceedings of the National Academy of Sciences of the Unites States of America*, 10 (15): 5797–801.

Stokburger-Sauer, N.E. and Hoyer, W.D. (2009) Consumer advisors revisited: what drives those with market mavenism and opinion leadership tendencies and why? *Journal of Consumer Behaviour*, 7 (3): 100–15.

Stokes, D. and Nelson, C. (2013) Word of mouth to word of mouse. In Z. Sethna, R. Jones and P. Harrigan (eds), *Entrepreneurial Marketing: Global Perspectives*. Bingley: Emerald Publishing, pp. 243–58.

Tesser, A., Miller, M. and Moore, J. (1988) Some affective consequences of social comparison and reflection processes: the pain and pleasure of being close. *Journal of Personality and Social Psychology*, 54 (1): 49–61.

Trompenaars, F. and Hampden-Turner, C. (2012) *Riding the Waves of Culture: Understanding Diversity in Global Business*, 3rd edn. London: Nicholas Brealey.

Van Boven, L., Campbell, M.C. and Gilovich, T. (2009) Stigmatising materialism: on stereotypes and impressions of materialistic versus experiential consumers. *Advances in Consumer Research*, 36: 14–15.

Veblen, T. (1899) *The Theory of the Leisure Class*. New York: Macmillan.

Wheeler, L., Shaver, K.G., Jones, R.A., Goethals, G.R., Cooper, J., Robinson, J.E., Gruder, C.L. and Butzine, K.W. (1969) Factors determining the choice of a comparison other. *Journal of Experimental Social Psychology*, 5 (April): 219–32.

Wu, M.S.S., Chaney, I., Chen, C.H.S., Nguyen, B. and Melewar, T.C. (2015) Luxury fashion brands: factors influencing young female consumers' luxury fashion purchasing in Taiwan. *Qualitative Market Research: An International Journal*, 18 (3): 298–319.

Zuckerman, M. (1988) Behavior and biology: research on sensation seeking and reactions to the media. In L. Donohew, H. Sypher and E.T. Higgins (eds), *Communication, Social Cognition and Affect*. Hillsdale, NJ: Erlbaum, pp. 173–94.

MORE ONLINE

For additional materials that support this chapter and your learning, please visit:
https://study.sagepub.com/sethnaandblythe

CHAPTER 12

AGE, GENDER AND FAMILIAL ROLES

LEARNING OBJECTIVES

After reading this chapter you should be able to:

- Describe the different definitions of family, and explain the influences on creating the definitions.
- Explain the role of culture in creating decision-making styles.
- Explain the roles of family members in decision-making.
- Describe ways in which conflict is generated and resolved.
- Describe the process by which children become effective consumers.
- Explain how brand loyalty is passed down through the generations.
- Critique family lifestyle models and explain the possible alternatives.
- Describe the roles family members take in the purchase and consumption process.

INTRODUCTION

Of all the reference groups we are exposed to, the family is probably the most powerful in influencing consumer decision-making. Almost all of us are members of families: our parents and guardians teach us how to be effective consumers from an early age, and we influence our brothers and sisters, our parents and eventually our own children in their purchasing choices.

The family has gone through many changes in structure, but still remains the most important social grouping. The reasons for this are as follows:

1. In the case of children, the parental influence is the earliest, and therefore colours the child's perception of everything that follows. In fact, the superego (see Chapter 1) is thought to be an internalised parent.

2. In the case of parents, the desire to do the best they can for their children influences their decision-making when making purchases for the family. Clear examples are the purchase of breakfast cereals and disposable nappies, where the appeal is almost invariably to do with the comfort and well-being of the baby.

3. In the case of siblings, the influence comes either as role model (where an older sibling is looked up to by a younger one) or as carer/adviser to younger siblings.

4. Families share a large part of their consumption, and thus joint decision-making often takes place by following formalised rules that control consumption behaviour within the group.

It is precisely because we value the opinions of our family members that we take their advice and often conform to their norms of behaviour. Even though the structure of families has undergone major changes in recent years, it is still true to say that the family is the basic unit of society. We'll discuss the family in more detail a little later. But before we do that, let's turn our attention to the other two constituents listed in the title of this chapter: age and gender.

HOW OLD ARE YOU? (COHORTS AND SUBCULTURES DEVELOPED USING AGE)

When The Who, an English rock band led by Roger Daltrey, formed in 1964 they could not have foreseen that their second single, 'My Generation', would not only become the group's highest charting UK single, but also one of their most memorable. The lyrics from the first two verses emphasise the view that people in each generation go through similar experiences, and can relate to each other, but people from other generations will not share that understanding. This applies equally to events which each generation will remember as being 'my generation'; that is, particular to their 'era' (for instance London's Iranian Embassy siege in 1980, or the 9/11 attacks on New York's World Trade Center in 2001, or the Syrian humanitarian crisis in 2015). This method of categorisation of age and time extends to, among others, food (for example, wartime rationing compared with the 2008 world food price crisis), music (for example The Rat Pack, Queen, The Spice Girls or One Direction), clothing (vintage, new romantic, post-war, anti-modern, designer), and gaming (*Pacman* arcade game in the 1980s in local chip shops compared with the versatility of Sony PSP).

In many cases, this fondness for a past event is closely linked to psychologically comforting experiences (Boym 2001) and is called 'nostalgia'. The *Online Etymology Dictionary* (2015) defines nostalgia is being a 'wistful yearning for the past', and many scholars using qualitative methods have posited that nostalgic memory is usually seen in a positive light (Wildschut et al. 2006, 2010). There are many examples from the world of advertising which use nostalgia as a backdrop (for instance, the Hovis bread advert from 1973, Microsoft's 'Child of the 90s' campaign, and Lego's 55 year anniversary).

AGE SUBCULTURES

Age subcultures exist because the members have differing attitudes and values. This is often called the generation gap. In some cases people retain behaviours and attitudes that were current in their youth – this is typically the case with popular music, for example. In other cases people change their views as they age, for example becoming more politically right-wing as they become wealthier and less inclined towards radical changes.

Let's start with pre-adolescence. This is the stage of development which follows early childhood but precedes adolescence. This age group (10–13) are more commonly known as pre-teenagers, tweenies or sometimes tweenagers. Adolescents or teenagers (13–19) form a distinct, and often international, subculture. Combined, these two groups are important not only because of their own spending power (which can be substantial) but also because they have a strong influence on their parents' spending. Often teenagers have at least some responsibility for the household shopping, and undoubtedly influence family choices about food brands, environmental issues and media consumption. The teen market is notoriously difficult to deal with, since brand preferences change with each year: each group of teenagers wants to have its own favourite brands, so that 14-year-olds are unlikely to be loyal to the same brands as their 16-year-old brothers and sisters. This means that producers need to be at the forefront of what is going on. Teenagers are often very communications-literate in using a combination of both online and offline channels, and understand that they are being 'marketed to'.

Baby boomers are people born between 1946 and 1964. They are sometimes colloquially known as the 'hippie generation'. These years saw an unprecedented number of births, following on from the Second World War as soldiers returned to civilian life and began raising families. This period was also one of rising prosperity and improved health care, so that more people survived into adulthood and had greater expectations from life. These baby boomers are now aged between 50 and 70, and are heading towards (or are already in) retirement: the younger of them are in their peak earning years, and the older of them often have substantial savings and pensions. They have shaped modern society (for instance Bill Clinton and Tony Blair in politics; Sting and Mick Jagger in music). They represent the largest and most affluent market in history, and will continue to have a major economic and social impact for the next 30 years at least. This hippie generation have seen it all: from the swinging sixties (with sex, drugs and rock & roll) to the formation of the civil rights movement, the rise (and fall) of the dot com era and more recently the housing bubble and subsequent global recession. Maybe this is the reason that in 2010 a British politician, David Willets (then Minister of State for Universities and Science), accusingly intimated that the baby boomers had thrown a 50-year long party for which the 'bills are coming in' and it is the younger generation who will pay them. Since baby boomers have tended to have smaller families than did their parents, the spend per child has been much higher, and in the longer term the levels of inheritance that baby boomers' children will receive will also be higher. Baby busters (aka Generation X) is the label given by popular culture to the generation born between approximately 1964 and 1980. They are the children of the Baby boomers.

Millennials (or Generation Y, and sometimes teased as Generation Why?) are generally thought to be those born between 1981–2001 (aged between 15–35 in 2016).

The 21st century saw their coming of age politically, socially, economically and, obviously, technologically. The rise of mass communications and the age of the Internet are both world-changing events that this generation grew up with and witnessed first-hand.

However, when one looks at the population figures a little more closely, we can see that in Europe, Millennials only account for a small percentage of the total population in several countries (for example, Poland 28%, Italy 19%). This, compared to figures for people who are 50 and older, shows a very different picture (for instance, Germany 52% and Italy 51%). This is concrete evidence that we have an ageing population in Europe; a phenomenon of increasing importance within Europe, Japan and the United States. As life expectancies increase, there are progressively more people in the over-50 age group. This is commonly called the grey market, but it should not be assumed that it is homogeneous: it is unlikely that a 55-year-old man would have a lot in common with his 80-year-old mother, at least in terms of consumer behaviour. By 2025 it is estimated that 22% of Europe's population will be aged over 65 (compared with 15.4% in 1995), and this has dramatic implications for pensions, prosperity and of course marketing (Eurostat 2002). In Japan the situation is far more serious – the birth rate is extremely low, to the point where the population is shrinking rapidly. By the end of the century, Japan's population is forecast to shrink from its current 130 million to less than 50 million, most of whom will be very elderly (Dejevsky 2006).

The assumption has always been that these older consumers would be prime candidates for care homes, walking frames, stair-lifts, hearing aids and little else. However, the rising life expectancy has been accompanied by a rise in the level of fitness of older people, due to better nutrition, health care and technological and medical advancements.

The market for the over-fifties is extremely diverse – considering that, in the UK, it currently comprises one-third of all adults, this is not surprising (Office for National Statistics 2012). At the younger end, most of this group are at the peak of their earning power and often have paid off their mortgages and are free of commitments to children. Their discretionary income is therefore higher than it has ever been. As we look at older members of the group, many have retired or are semi-retired and have a great deal more leisure time, while frequently enjoying generous private pensions and savings. Many older people use this time to take holidays, enjoy new hobbies, improve their education, and so forth. These new activities are not necessarily those traditionally associated with elderly people: the holidays on offer in the Saga brochure are just as likely to include windsurfing, skydiving, mountaineering, skiing or motorbike holidays as they are to include bridge playing or coach tours. Some flying schools report that the majority of their students are over 50, and Open University applications from the over-60s run into the thousands. Equally, some other members of the segment fit the more traditional pattern, happy to dig the garden and perhaps do an evening class.

Marketers would be well advised to treat this age group with extreme caution. The 'age appropriateness' of a product is rarely relevant as opposed to the product benefits. The perceived age is an important consideration and can be measured using how old a person feels (feel-age) or how old a person looks (the look-age) (Barak and Schiffman 1981). This is far from being a homogeneous subculture.

DEFINING FAMILIES

The concept of what constitutes a family varies from one culture to another. In the UK and United States, families usually consist of parents and their natural or adopted children: this is called the nuclear family. In some other cultures, families might extend to grandparents, aunts, uncles and cousins all living in the same house and sharing their consumption. These extended families are becoming rare in industrialised countries, partly because of the mobility of workers: someone who finds a job in another part of the country is unlikely to find it convenient to take a large number of extended family members along.

Even in nuclear families there will also be influences from uncles, aunts, grandparents and cousins. While these influences are often less strong in UK households than they might be in some other countries where the extended family is more common, the influences still exist to a greater or lesser extent. For statistical purposes, Eurostat has adopted the United Nations definition of a family, which is as follows:

The persons within a private or institutional household who are related as husband and wife or as parent and never-married child by blood or adoption. (United Nations 2016)

For the purposes of the definition, couples who live together without marrying are still regarded as a family (this applies to both heterosexual and LGBT couples). On the other hand, the European Community Household Panel defines a family household more broadly as a shared residence with common housekeeping arrangements.

From a marketing viewpoint, the level of demand for many products is dictated more by the number of households than by the number of families. For example, most households in affluent countries would have a washing machine, but hardly any would have two washing machines. The relevance of families to marketing is therefore much more about consumer *behaviour* than about consumer *demand levels*.

In terms of its function as a group, the family is defined (see Figure 12.1) by the following characteristics:

1. *Face-to-face contact.* Family members see each other most days, and interact as advisers, information providers and sometimes deciders. Other reference groups rarely have this level of contact.

2. *Shared consumption.* Durables such as fridges, freezers, televisions and furniture are shared, and food is collectively purchased and cooked (although a family eating together is fast becoming uncommon). Purchase of these items is often collective: children even participate in decision-making on such major purchases as cars and houses. Other reference groups may share some consumption (for example, members of a jewellery-making club may hire a workshop and share tools) but families share consumption of most domestic items.

3. *Subordination of individual needs.* Because consumption is shared, some family members will find that the solution chosen is not one that fully meets their needs. Although this happens in other reference groups, the effect is more pronounced in families.

4. *Purchasing agent.* Because of the shared consumption, most families will have one member who does most, or all, of the shopping. Traditionally and historically this

Purchasing agent

Someone who has the task of making purchases on behalf of a group

has been the mother of the family but increasingly the **purchasing agent** is the older children of the family – even pre-teens are sometimes taking over this role. This has major implications for marketers, since pre-teens and young teens are generally better 'connected' online than adults and are therefore more open to marketing communications via a multitude of channels. Other reference groups may well have a purchasing agent, but this is probably only for specific items rather than for all those items the group is interested in – and most informal groups would appoint a purchasing agent for occasional purposes only.

In some cases products are passed on from one generation to another as a way of preserving family identity and values. Whether this means passing on great-grandmother's wedding ring or handing over the family's old car to the newly licensed eldest child, the family link is continued (Curasi 2006). The same behaviour has been found in investments, with parents passing on investments and investment advice to children (Williams 2006). Products passed on in this way can move between 'sacred' and 'profane' values (Hartman and Kiecker 2004). For example, Granny's wedding ring might be worn on a chain round the neck of a teenager: equally, Grandad's old pen-knife might be preserved as a family heirloom. The older generation often pass on these items, complete with their history and an account of their significance, in the hope that the younger generation will continue to cherish them (Curasi 2011).

Family decision-making is not as straightforward as marketers have supposed in the past. There has been an assumption that the purchasing agent (e.g. the mother) is the one who makes the decisions, and while this is often the case, this approach ignores the ways in which the purchasing decisions are arrived at.

Wife-dominant decision-making

Decisions that are left to the female adult of the family

Husband-dominant decision-making

A situation in which the male of the household has the most power in consumption decisions

Syncratic (democratic) decision-making

In group decision-making, the type of decision that is made on the basis of consultation

Democratic decision-making

See Syncratic decision-making

Autonomic decision-making

A type of decision that is made by the individual without recourse to others

Role specialisation is critical in family decision-making because of the sheer number of different products that must be bought each year in order to keep the family supplied. What this means in practice is that, for example, the family member responsible for doing the cooking is also likely to take the main responsibility for shopping for food. The family member who does the most driving is likely to make the main decision about the car and its accessories, servicing, fuelling, and so forth; the family gardener buys the gardening products, and so on.

There is a problem here with terminology. Traditionally, studies of the family have referred to the male partner as the husband, and the female partner as the wife. The increasing number of families in which the parents are not married has rendered this approach obsolete; the research reported in the next section was conducted in the 1970s, when the vast majority of parents were married. The validity and relevance of the research is not in question, since it refers to traditional roles that may or may not actually be adopted by specific families.

Four kinds of marital role specialisation have been identified: **wife dominant** where the wife has most say in the decision, **husband dominant** where the husband plays the major role (Tiwari 2015), **syncratic** or **democratic** where the decision is arrived at jointly, and **autonomic** where the decision is made entirely independently of the partner (Filiatrault and Ritchie 1980). For example, the wife may have the biggest role in deciding on new curtains, the husband may have the lead role in choosing the family car, they may decide together on a home extension, and the husband alone might choose the fertiliser for the garden. Marketers need to identify which role specialisation type is typical of a target market in order to know where to aim the promotional activities. Some more recent research indicates that in the event of disagreement about a joint

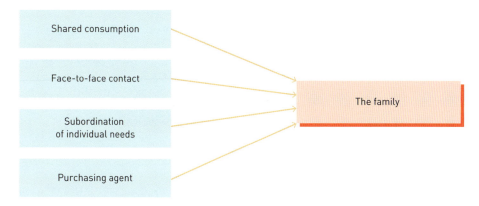

FIGURE 12.1 Defining characteristics of families

decision it is the man's decision which is likely to prevail (Ward 2006). This research was conducted exclusively in Tennessee, however, which may account for at least some of the result.

Product category affects role specialisation and decision-making systems. When an expensive purchase is being considered, it is likely that most of the family will be involved in some way, if only because major purchases affect the family budgeting for other items. At the other end of the scale, day-to-day shopping for toilet rolls and cans of beans entails very little collective decision-making (although it has been known for families to rebel collectively against baked beans which are not Heinz branded). But more generally, where the product has a shared usage (a holiday or a car) the collective decision-making component is likely to increase greatly. Conversely, where the product is used predominantly by one family member, that member will dominate the decision-making even when the purchase is a major one (the chef in the family will have most influence in the decision about the new range cooker, for example).

Culture has a marked effect on family decision-making styles. Religion and nationality will often affect the way decisions are made: followers of the Zoroastrian religion closely abide by their three tenets of 'Good Thoughts, Good Words and Good Deeds' which therefore feed into their decision-making processes on a daily basis (Sethna 2015); African cultures tend to be male-dominated in decision-making, whereas European and North American cultures show a more egalitarian pattern of decision-making (Green et al. 1983). In India, gold carries very strong family significance at weddings. The bride is thought to be purified by gifted and borrowed gold – typically her new husband's family will lend jewellery to her, as a way of binding her to the new family (Fernandez and Veer 2004).

There are two issues here for the marketer: first, what is the effect on the marketing mix of the multi-ethnic society now emerging in Europe, and second what is the effect when dealing internationally? This is a somewhat sensitive area, and one that marketers are still getting to grips with. There is more on general aspects of culture in Chapter 13.

Social class creates patterns of decision-making. Among very wealthy families there appears to be a greater tendency for the husbands to make the decisions, but at the same time the norms of purchase tend to be well-established and therefore discussion is unnecessary (Komarovsky 1961). Lower-class families, with low incomes, have

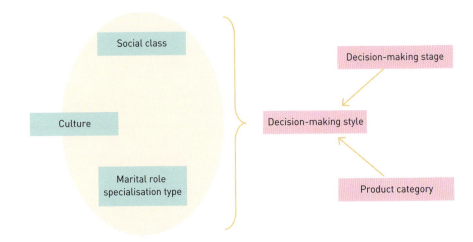

FIGURE 12.2 Determinants of decision-making style in families

traditionally been more matriarchal, with the wives often handling the financial decisions about rent, insurance, food bills and Christmas clubs without reference to the husbands. Poorer families will often divert a large proportion of their limited resources towards ensuring that the children are not stigmatised by poverty: often children of poorer parents will still wear the latest trainers and go on school trips (Hamilton and Catterall 2006). Obviously there is a stronger possibility of conflict when resources are limited, but in most lower-income families there is an emphasis on not allowing conflict to develop in the first place, rather than on conflict resolution after the event (Hamilton 2009). Middle-class families tend to show greater democratic involvement in decision-making. These social class distinctions are gradually breaking down, however, as a result of increasing wealth and mass education.

The family may well adopt different roles according to the *decision-making stage*. At the problem-recognition stage of, for example, the need for new shoes for the children, the children themselves may be the main contributors. The stay-at-home parent (mother or father) may then decide what type of shoes should be bought, and will then be the one to whisk the children off to the shoe shop for a fitting and to buy the shoes. It is reasonable to suppose that the main user of the product might be important in the initial stages, with perhaps joint decision-making at the final purchase.

These determinants of decision-making style are summarised in Figure 12.2.

Other determinants might include such factors as whether both parents are earning. In such families, decision-making is more likely to be joint because each has a financial stake in the outcome. It is now uncommon to find a situation where the family decision-making is more likely to be dominated by the sole earner, and previous research suggests that where couples are both earning, they will make decisions jointly (Filiatrault and Ritchie 1980). Males stereotypically used to dominate highly technical durable products (e.g. computing and audio-visual equipment) but in recent years this imbalance has been redressed with the emergence of the new generation of digital natives; those young people to whom all things digital and technical come as second nature. Interestingly, spendthrifts and careful savers appear to be attracted to each other – a situation that often results in conflict (Rick et al. 2010).

CONSUMER BEHAVIOUR IN ACTION: WOMEN OF THE UNITED NATIONS

In 1995, the United Nations convened the Fourth World Conference on Women in Beijing, China. Delegates had prepared a Platform for Action that aimed at achieving greater equality and opportunity for women.

The Conference was participated in by 189 governments and more than 5,000 representatives from 2,100 non-governmental organisations. The principal themes were the advancement and empowerment of women in relation to women's human rights, women and poverty, women and decision-making, the girl-child, violence against women and other areas of concern. The conference resulted with the Beijing Declaration and Platform for Action documents being published.

©iStock.com/ViktorCap

At its core, it dealt with removing the obstacles to women's public participation in all spheres of public and private lives through a full and equal share in economic, social, cultural and political decision-making. The Platform for Action set out a number of actions that should have led to fundamental changes by the year 2000. It was noted that the implementation of the Beijing Platform for Action was mainly a responsibility of governments, but also of institutions in the public, private and non-governmental sectors at the community, national, sub-regional, regional and international levels. They should have collectively ensured that a gender perspective is reflected in all policies and programmes at the national, regional and international levels.

However, in the 20 years since the Agreement, there has been a significant shift in the role of the state; with both private sector engagement growing and the entry of new development actors into the development policy and practice arena (Cornwall and Edwards 2015). This has meant that while there is a lot of enthusiasm surrounding corporate campaigns promoting women and girls as self-actualising individuals who can lift their communities out of poverty, effective implementation of progressive policies is getting lost.

Enter the HeForShe campaign.

HeForShe is a solidarity campaign for gender equality initiated by UN Women. Its goal is to engage men and boys as agents of change for the achievement of gender equality and women's rights, by encouraging them to take action against inequalities faced by women and girls (McDonald 2014; Suhay 2014). With its ideological roots firmly grounded in the Beijing Declaration, it seeks to actively involve men and boys in a movement that was originally conceived as 'a struggle for women by women'. Some noticed the contradiction of a campaign for gender equality which only takes action against inequalities faced by women and girls, ignoring problems affecting men and boys (Young 2014).

The HeForShe website shows a geo-locater map which then records global engagement in the campaign. Thus it counts the number of men and boys around the world who have taken the HeForShe pledge. The UN Women worked towards its goal of engaging 1 million men and boys by July 2015, which at the time of this book going to press hasn't yet been met (www.heforshe.org 2014). The campaign website also includes implementation plans for UN agencies, individuals and civil society, as well as those on university and college campuses, both through online and sustained engagement.

Gender role orientation is clearly crucial to decision-making. Husbands (and wives) with conservative (many would say traditional and out-dated) views about gender roles will tend towards the assumption that most decisions about expenditure will be made by the husband. Even within this type of decision-making system, however, husbands will usually adjust their own views to take account of their wife's attitudes and needs. A classic example of this is in the 1964 book (and later a musical and screenplay) by Joseph Stein entitled *Fiddler on the Roof* where the father's character believes that he is the dominant party who makes the decisions yet it is the mother who cleverly manipulates him to her way of thinking!

Conflict resolution tends to have an increased importance in family decision-making as opposed to individual purchase behaviour. The reason for this is that, obviously, more people are involved, each with their own needs and their own internal conflicts to resolve. The conflict resolution system is as shown in Table 12.1.

TABLE 12.1 Conflict resolution in families

Resolution method	Explanation
Persuasion through information exchange	When a conflict occurs, each family member seeks to persuade the others of his or her point of view. This leads to discussion, and ultimately some form of compromise
Role expectation	If persuasion fails, a family member may be designated to make the decision. This is usually somebody who has the greatest expertise in the area of conflict being discussed. This method appears to be going out of fashion as greater democracy and negotiation in family decision-making is appearing
Establishment of norms	Families will often adopt rules for decision-making. Sometimes this will involve taking turns over making decisions (perhaps over which restaurant the family will go to this week, or where they will go on holiday)
Power exertion	This is also known as browbeating. One family member will try to exert power to force the other members to comply; this may be a husband who refuses to sign the cheque unless he gets his own way, or a wife who refuses to cook the dinner until the family agree, or a child who throws a tantrum. The person with the most power is called the *least dependent person* because he or she is not as dependent on the other family members. Using the examples above, if the wife has her own income she won't need to ask the husband to sign the direct debit form; if the other family members can cook they can get their own dinner; and if the family can ignore the yelling toddler long enough, eventually the child will give up

Source: adapted from Onkvisit and Shaw (1994) Reprinted with Permission.

Least dependent person
The individual within a buying group who has the highest degree of autonomy

INFLUENCE OF CHILDREN ON BUYING DECISIONS

We live in an era where we expect to live longer. This, coupled with lower fertility rates, means that the share of global population under age 20 has dropped to about 35%. First-born children generate more economic impact than higher-order babies. Around 40% of babies are first-born; they are photographed more, they get all new clothes (no hand-me-downs) and get more attention all round. First-born and only children have a higher achievement rate than those born second, third, etc., and since the birth rate is falling, there are more of them proportionally. More and more couples are choosing to have only one child (or being forced to, for example China's one child policy – Cao et al. 2015), and families larger than two children are becoming uncommon. This is also echoed by service providers such as hotels, restaurants, etc. who are more likely to be able to cater for a family of four than a family of five or more. At the other end of the spectrum, childlessness is also more common now than it was 30 years ago.

Children also have a role in applying pressure on their parents to make particular purchasing decisions. The level of **pester power** generated can be overwhelming, and parents will frequently give in to the child's demands (Ekstrom et al. 1987). It should be noted that this is not a 'first world' problem. Children around the world will utilise pester power to get their way. O'Neill et al. (2013) did some very interesting investigation on whether pester power existed in third world communities which are perceived to have considerably less disposable income. Results showed that over 75% of children admitted to continually making requests until they were granted. And so children rapidly become adept at negotiating with their parents, and are quite able to recognise the various responses parents will make (agreement, refusal, procrastination, negotiation) as well as the parents' reasons for their decisions. This is especially true now that there is an increase in the use of new and social media (Desrochers 2015). Children often see this as a good-natured game between themselves and the parents rather than as a source of conflict as the literature tends to suggest (Lawlor and Protheroe 2011; Shivany 2015).

Pester power

The ability of children to influence their parents by means of repetitive requests

Although the number of children as a percentage of the population has fallen in recent times, their importance as consumers has not. Apart from the direct purchases of things that children need, they influence decision-making to a marked extent. For instance, in recent years, children have become much more aware of where food comes from and what they eat, partly due to in-school health education programmes. Sometimes on-package health claims have a negative effect (perhaps due to a mistrust of marketer-generated information) but education programmes do have an effect in encouraging more healthy choices (Miller et al. 2011). However, children are well aware that 'children's food' often consists of cheap junk food (Elliott 2011). The problem lies in translating this knowledge into action, since children still make unhealthy choices even when they know better (Dias and Agante 2011).

When parents and children are making joint decisions about food purchase, the children will often use subtle techniques to get their own way – offering to help with the shopping reduces conflict and means they are more likely to impose their own choices, for example (Norgaard and Brunso 2011).

Children have to be taught how to be consumers, since they will (eventually) become adults and will need to manage their money and make appropriate choices in their

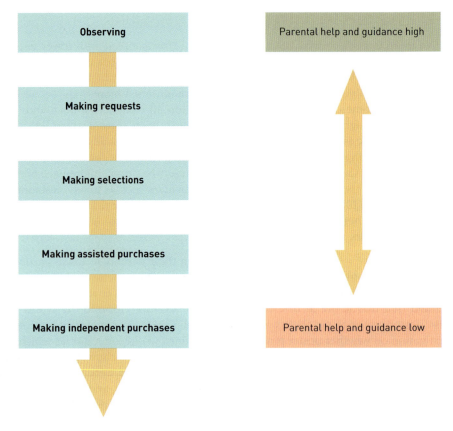

FIGURE 12.3 Children's stages of development as consumers

purchasing behaviour. Children's development as consumers goes through five stages (Figure 12.3):

1. Observing.

2. Making requests.

3. Making selections.

4. Making assisted purchases.

5. Making independent purchases.

In the observing stage, children see how their parents go about obtaining the things they need. At this point, the child will probably not understand that money is a finite resource, but can easily understand the basic system: things that the family needs are available in shops, and they can be bought with money if you know what to do. Observation is actually more important than teaching in children's development, especially when the family has a good quality of relationship between its members (Mittal and Royne 2010). Usually children will begin to consider ways in which they might obtain goods themselves – quite young children can grasp the idea that goods must be paid for, and they will sometimes try using 'money' (perhaps play money or tokens) to pay for things.

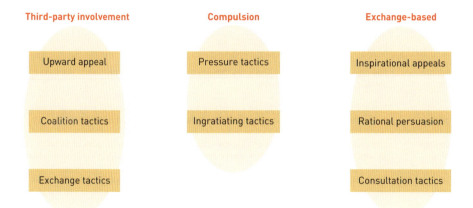

FIGURE 12.4 Children's persuasion tactics

At a very early stage children learn to make requests. Even before being able to talk, children recognise brands and favourite products and are able to reach for them or point to them. As they grow older and more able to articulate requests, they can (and do) develop pester power. This means that they make insistent demands for products, sometimes throwing tantrums or continually wheedling their parents to obtain what they want. At this point parental judgement about the products' suitability and the situation context may vary – some parents will give in fairly quickly and provide the child with what he or she wants, while others will refuse to buy the product. In many cases the request becomes a basis for negotiation – the parent agrees to buy the product on condition that the child behaves in a certain way.

Children use a wide variety of tactics to influence their parents (Wimalasir 2004). These are shown in Table 12.2, and the relationship between them is shown in Figure 12.4.

Parenting style has an obvious effect on the likely response to such requests. Broadly, there are five basic styles of parenting (Carlson and Grossbart 1988):

1. *Authoritarians.* These parents are cold and restrictive.

2. *Authoritative.* These parents are warm and restrictive.

3. *Permissives.* These parents are warm and non-restrictive.

4. *Strict-dependent.* These parents foster dependence in their children, almost to the point of not allowing them to grow up.

5. *Indulgent-dependent.* These parents foster dependence by giving their children everything they want and need, even into adult life.

These parenting styles are not necessarily universal; in fact they happen almost exclusively in collectivist cultures (Rose et al. 2002). It is easy to see that authoritarian and authoritative parents are unlikely to yield easily to pester power, strict-dependents would not allow the child to pester, and permissives and indulgent-dependents are unlikely to need to be pestered – they would simply accede to the request the first time round. Research suggests that authoritative parenting is the most effective style (Milner 2015).

TABLE 12.2 Tactics used by children to influence their parents

Tactic	Explanation
Pressure tactics	The child makes demands and uses threats or intimidation to persuade the parents to comply with his or her request
Upward appeal	The child seeks to persuade the parent by saying that the request was approved or is supported by an older member of the family, a teacher or even a family friend
Exchange tactics	The child makes an implicit or explicit promise to provide some sort of service such as washing the car, cleaning the house or taking care of the baby in return for a favour
Coalition tactics	The child seeks the aid of others to persuade the parents to comply with his or her request, or uses the support of others as an argument for the parents to agree with him or her
Ingratiating tactics	The child seeks to get the parent in a good mood or think favourably of him or her before asking the parent to comply with a request
Rational persuasion	The child uses logical arguments and factual evidence to persuade the parent to agree with his or her request
Inspirational appeals	The child makes an emotional appeal or proposal that arouses enthusiasm by appealing to the parent's values or ideals
Consultation tactics	The child seeks the parent's involvement in making a decision

In most cases, parents will agree to purchases subject to conditions being met. This is an important lesson, because the child needs to know that products are subject to exchange processes. Here, the parent is demonstrating that, in order to obtain benefits, there will need to be concessions in terms of behaviour. So for instance, children who've studied diligently and passed their exams, have been bought holidays to Barcelona or specialised road bikes as a reward for their 'behaviour'. Parents frequently use the promise of supplying (or withholding) products as a way of modifying the child's behaviour. There is evidence to suggest that this is culturally based in some respects: American parents apparently seek to develop autonomy in their children, making them into independent consumers, whereas Japanese parents maintain greater control over their children's consumption, so that the children tend to develop consumer skills at a later age (Rose 1999).

Once children reach an age when they can understand money, parents will typically provide them with pocket money so that they can learn to make their own selections. In most cases pocket money is supplied as a fixed amount: this is so that the child can learn that money is not an infinite resource, and must be spent carefully. In other cases, pocket money might be provided as a reward for specific behaviour (for example, cleaning the car or mowing the lawn) so that the child learns the concept of working for rewards (although some parents might argue that household chores should not warrant any payment and should be done as the price of being part of the family). This is a further reinforcement of the exchange concept. In the early stages of having pocket money, parents will often help the child make choices, applying their own sense of value to the transaction. As time goes on, the child will be able to make choices alone, and will ultimately (perhaps during teenage years) become a fully fledged consumer by spending money earned by doing odd jobs or part-time work.

CHALLENGING THE STATUS QUO

Would you like a cookie?

Should marketers take responsibility for inducing pester power? We hear all the time that wicked marketers are encouraging children to want the latest toys, games, gadgets and even fashions – an industry worth at least £70 million every year: advertising aimed directly at children. So are marketers to blame if the young ones then pester their parents?

Research shows that the average British child has more chance of recognising the Nike swoosh or the Golden Arches (of the M word!) than recognising a picture of Christ, and is familiar with as many as 400 brand names by the time they reach the age of ten.

TV channels are awash with adverts for all sorts of products, from sugar-infused soft drinks to oven-ready fast food to chocolate and sweets. And guess what time they're usually on-air – teatime! The timing, coupled with an inducement – a motivation to buy – means that children are most definitely going to want that product which is linked to the latest film release etc.

©iStock.com/KQconcepts

Of course, advertisers don't have to rely on the timing constraints of watching TV at teatime when they have the Internet at their disposal. And with the Internet, we get 'cookies'. No not the eating kind, but the kind that embed themselves into your web browser to keep track of your visit to a particular website. But here's where things get a little more sinister. Cookies are now retargeting their victim. Companies such as Criteo and Vizury are seeing huge growth in business from e-commerce customers who want to woo back their online visitors. These startups target ads at people who visit e-commerce sites but move on before buying anything. Retargeting means that when they visit other sites, they will continue to see ads for products from those e-commerce sites. Vizury's online ad platform now counts around 500 million monthly users. And digitally native children who have a short attention span are prime candidates to be retargeted.

On the other hand, people do have to buy things, and marketers have been trained to 'repeat' their message a number of times before it's accepted by the consumer. It's the way the world works. Children have to learn to distinguish between advertising and programming – and they have to learn that they can't just demand anything they want in this life. So maybe marketers are carrying out a public service, educating the consumers of tomorrow and teaching children that they can't just have everything!

At this point, the individual is more likely to look to friends or role models for ideas on acceptable consumer behaviour (John 1999). Although younger children respond best to advertising in which the spokesperson is a parental or authority figure, teenagers often buy products simply because their parents disapprove of them (Rummel et al. 2000). For example, triple-earrings, hair dye, army boots and a half-shaven head seem to be the fashion for 15-year-old girls at the time of writing. This is probably part of the process by which people become independent adults, and demonstrates that they are no longer children.

Socialisation continues down the generations even after the child has become a fully independent adult, however. Some research shows that brand loyalties can be passed down from one generation to another, even for three or four generations within the same family (Olsen 1993; Mandrik et al. 2004). The reason for this is that people enjoy using the brands that they remember from their childhood: specific brands of sauces, soups, marmalade or soft drinks commonly remain popular in the family for many years after the child has grown up and left home. In some respects the family identity is carried on through the generations by these means (Epp and Arnould 2006). 'A finger of fudge is just enough to give your kids a treat'; 'Beans means Heinz'; 'Just one Cornetto'; 'webuyanycar.com'. These are all jingles that people of a certain age will vividly remember. This is an important consideration for three reasons: first and foremost is that advertisements really do have an impact on the young brain which soaks up all the communication that it's exposed to. Second, this memory can last for decades. Third, using TV to persuade children to buy things, including sweets, is not new. There is a generation of viewers in the UK who will forever have the 'Go Compare' insurance advert, with the pseudo-opera-singer, emblazoned on to their long-term memory!

CONSUMER BEHAVIOUR IN ACTION: TEENAGERS AND TECHNOLOGY

The communications revolution has certainly made it much harder to monitor the behaviour of teenagers – not that it was ever easy, of course. Each generation of teenagers takes great care to prevent their parents from knowing what they are really doing, but electronic communications have made the situation much easier for teenagers.

In December 2014, when the Christmas holiday season had almost arrived, children around the world were making their lists, and these demands would have a major impact on one of the most expensive purchases a parent makes for their child: a wireless device.

Communicus, a research-based advertising consultancy in Arizona with 25 years of experience in measuring and diagnosing billions of dollars in placed advertising, found that 'child pestering' is one of the top predictors of a parent's purchase intentions to buy a wireless device for their children. Its study, *The Mobile Device Path to Purchase: Parents & Children* found that for Apple, 'child pestering' is the top predictor, being twice as important as social media, while for Samsung, it was the second predictor (first was positive word of mouth, by about 15%) in driving parental purchase intent.

"Tis the season for children to ask for the latest technology and wireless devices', said Ms Jeri Smith, President and CEO of Communicus, Inc. 'We found that "pester power" can even outweigh a parent's beliefs that a device is easy to use or has the best features and functionality'.

So, what influences children to request a particular brand? For the younger generation, Apple's brand success is based on positive word of mouth and fitting in. For Samsung, positive word of mouth and non-traditional tactics such as the 'Samsung Nation' social rewards programme have contributed positively to children requesting the brand.

Further, the study found that for children, the top predictors of requests to parents are people saying good things about Apple and being a brand that a lot of friends have. Similarly, for Samsung, the top predictors of parental requests are Samsung social media efforts and the belief that Samsung is a brand for 'someone like me'.

Advertising can work to build demand for devices, but despite the large advertising budgets involved, success isn't guaranteed. In the case of Apple, children are far more impacted by social influences ('my friends have them') than by advertising. Adults are impacted by Apple

©iStock.com/DougSchneider

brand advertising when it comes to the device they are considering for themselves, but child pestering takes over as the key driver when considering a new device for their child.

Conversely, Samsung's advertising has had a more impactful push on children in boosting awareness, requests and perceptions that the brand is for 'someone like me'. Samsung's advertising is effective across kid age groups, but has shown the strongest persuasive power among younger (6–12) kids.

'When considering advertising, one of the age-old questions brands ask is whether to go negative on competitors', said Smith. 'Our study found that for Samsung and Microsoft, displaying the key attributes of their devices in a positive light was much more impactful than an Apple-bashing strategy among both adults and kids'.

Adapted from communicus.com (2014). More data and insights from *The Mobile Device Path to Purchase: Parents & Children* can be found at www.communicus.com. Courtesy of Communicus, www.communicus.com

CHANGING NATURE OF THE FAMILY

One of the changes currently occurring throughout Western Europe is the increase in the number of single-person households; in the UK, these now represent 28% of all households (Office for National Statistics 2015); there is, of course, a difference

1900:
Typical couple has five children, but
many people do not marry at all

1960:
Typical couple has three
children: most people marry

2013:
Typical couple has one child: many people
either do not marry or do not have children

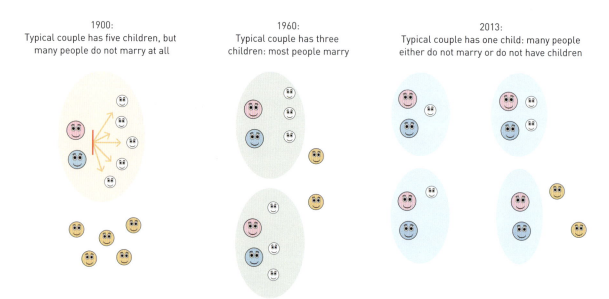

FIGURE 12.5 Effects of falling birth rate

between a household and a family. A further change, coming about through the tremendous increase in the divorce rate, is the growing number of single-parent families. A third major change is the worldwide shift in attitude towards having large families. Since the advent of mass contraception, more and more women say that they would prefer to have fewer children than was the case even ten years ago. Currently, European birth rates are below the replacement rate for the population, meaning that the population would be shrinking if it were not for immigration. One UK study predicted that one in five women born between 1960 and 1990 will never have children, and the birth rate among those women who do have children will be half that of their mothers' generation (European Union 1995).

In Figure 12.5, the 1900 family has more children, but the other five people (those outside the family circle in the figure) remained single, like many other people at that time. From the seven people in the example, only five children are born. In 1960, a more typical family size would be three children, but many more people married and had children (only two people are outside the family circles): that was an expectation of the baby boom years. Nowadays, families are smaller and many people never have children at all, so in our final example the ten people in the diagram only manage four children between them. Two of the family circles contain only one child, the other one contains none, and we have two people who remain single. It should be noted that these are examples only to accentuate the point: the birth rate actually has not fluctuated quite that dramatically over the period.

The family is a flexible concept, and families go through life cycles. There have been various versions of the family life cycle, but most are based on the original work of Wells and Gubar (1966). Table 12.3 shows the stages of the family life cycle.

The main problem with this model is that it was originally developed in the 1960s, when couples rarely lived together without being married, there were very few single-parent

TABLE 12.3 The family life cycle

Stage of life cycle	Explanation
Single stage	Single people tend to have low earnings, but also have low outgoings so have a high discretionary income. They tend to be more fashion- and recreation-orientated, spending on clothes, music, alcohol, eating out, holidays, leisure pursuits and hobbies, and 'mating game' products. Often they buy cars and items for their first residence away from home
Newly married couples	Newlyweds without children are usually dual-income households and therefore usually well-off. They still tend to spend on similar things to the singles, but also have the highest proportion of expenditure on household goods, consumer durables and appliances. They appear to be more susceptible to advertising
Full nest I	When the first child arrives, one parent usually stops working outside the home so family income drops sharply. The baby creates new needs that alter expenditure patterns: furniture and furnishings for the baby, baby food, vitamins, toys, nappies and baby food. Family savings decline, and usually couples are dissatisfied with their financial position
Full nest II	The youngest child is over 6, so often both parents will work outside the home. The employed spouse's income has risen due to career progression, and the family's total income recovers. Consumption patterns are still heavily influenced by children: bicycles, piano lessons, large-size packages of breakfast cereal, cleaning products, etc.
Full nest III	Family income improves as the children get older. Both parents are likely to be working outside the home, and both may have had some career progression; also, the children will be earning some of their own money from paper rounds, part-time jobs, etc. Family purchases might be a second car, replacement furniture, some luxury items and children's education
Empty nest I	Children have grown up and left home. Couple are at the height of their careers and spending power, have low mortgages and very reduced living costs. They often spend on luxury travel, restaurants and theatre – so they need fashionable clothing, jewellery, diets, spas, health clubs, cosmetics and hairdressing
Empty nest II	The main breadwinner has retired, so there is some drop in income. Expenditure is more health-orientated, buying appliances for sleep and over-the-counter remedies for indigestion. The couple often buy a smaller house, or move to an apartment in a retirement area or warmer country
Solitary survivor	If still in the workforce, widows and widowers enjoy a good income. They may spend more money on holidays, as well as the items mentioned in Empty nest II
Retired solitary survivor	These people have the same general consumption pattern as above but on a smaller scale due to reduced income. The individual has special needs for love, affection and security, so may join clubs, etc.

families and the divorce rate was dramatically lower than it is in the 21st century. Towards the end of the life cycle (from Empty nest I onwards) it is likely that the model holds true fairly well, but it is unlikely that the earlier stages will follow the same pattern. This said, it is still important that students of consumer behaviour learn a historical perspective too in order to make sense of what is happening with our current society.

The traditional nuclear family of two parents with their own children has become a minority of households: it is more likely that a household will consist of a mother with her children from her first marriage, a husband or partner who pays maintenance to his ex-wife for the children from his first marriage, and possibly a new child from the new partnership. Even more common is a childless home, either a single-person household (women account for 91% of lone parents with dependent children) or a childless couple living together: these represent more than half of all UK households. Cohabiting couple families have grown by nearly 30% between 2004–14 and are the fastest growing type of family in the UK (Office for National Statistics 2015).

It may be more realistic to consider the life cycle of the individual, and link this to possible family roles and responsibilities rather than consider different possible family structures. Here are some of the life stages an individual might have:

1. *Living alone I.* This is someone who has left home, has a job and is living alone.

2. *Cohabiting, no children I.* This would be a couple who are living together without being married, but have no children.

3. *Cohabiting, with joint children.* This couple have a child or children, but are not married.

4. *Married, no children I.* Similar to 'Cohabiting, no children I' but have a legal relationship as well as a romantic one.

5. *Married, with joint children.* Similar to cohabiting, but with the legal relationship.

6. *Living alone II.* This is someone who is divorced or widowed.

7. *Cohabiting, no children II.* This couple is divorced or separated from earlier partners, and are now living together.

8. *Cohabiting, with children II.* The children may be from a previous relationship, or may not live with the couple at all, but be occasional visitors at weekends or during the week.

9. *Married, no children II.* This couple have been married before, and may or may not intend having children together at some future time.

10. *Married, with children II.* This couple is second-time married, with children from earlier relationships who may or may not live with them.

11. *Married or cohabiting couple with grown-up children still at home.* This situation is becoming more common as single people find it harder to buy a home. These households can be extremely wealthy, since three or more adults are contributing to the overall income.

There are likely to be other, more complex, situations but each of these situations impacts on family decision-making, and (particularly in the case of cohabiting or married couples with children from previous relationships) other people who are not actually part of the family will also need to be considered (in this case, ex-partners). Working out the decision rules between the various players is likely to be difficult in these cases, and in some cases special marketing activities are in place to take account of single parents who have access rights to their children on specific days. The concept of being 'a father for half an hour in McDonald's' has become familiar, and some advertising reflects this.

The divorce–remarry cycle also means dramatic surges in income. Divorce usually means a dramatic fall in disposable income as the economies of scale in shared consumption evaporate and the individuals have to set up their own homes: this can mean a boost for businesses selling furniture, household appliances and homes, of course. Later on, though, the remarry phase often leads to a sudden sharp increase in wealth as the previously single people pool their resources. When people in their forties remarry, having finished paying out for child maintenance and (often) now owning substantial equity in their homes, they will combine their assets and can find themselves suddenly wealthy.

GENDER ROLES

The last census in the UK (2011) showed that there are marginally more women than men in the population (32 million versus 31 million) largely due to two factors: greater infant mortality among boys, and greater life expectancy of women. Women's role has changed greatly over the past 30 years or so; women make more (or most) of the purchasing decisions, earn around a third of the household income and make most of the decisions regarding the home and the children.

The change in gender roles, summarised in Figure 12.6, comes from the following factors:

1. Technology means that most jobs do not require physical strength, so more careers are open to women.

2. Mass contraception has provided women with choices regarding childbearing.

3. A more ordered society has led to greater physical security; there is less need for the defence role of the male.

4. Greater accessibility to education means that women have many more choices and opportunities.

This shift in gender roles and expectations is affecting marketers, who are now changing the appeal of their advertising to meet the new conditions. For example, Flash Wipes are advertised showing a man doing the cleaning: he is portrayed as the average man, doing the cleaning and winning praise for doing so, but revealing to the audience that in fact the cleaning is really no big task. Twenty years ago such advertisements would only have been shown for comic purposes, and even now men are frequently portrayed as being incapable of doing the housework properly. Even as little as 15 years ago if a 'new' father told his dad that he planned to be a stay-at-home dad, his father would have laughed at him because he simply came from a generation where there were very clearly defined roles for men and women. This is why in the film *Meet the Fockers*, the portrayal of a man feeding his grandchild with a rubber boob strapped to his chest (while a little freaky) is actually quite progressive.

Gender roles might also include sexual orientation, which affords another dimension to the definition of family. In the UK, civil partnerships between same-sex couples were introduced towards the end of 2005, and there was consequently a flurry of people in long-term relationships going through the ceremony. Registering a civil partnership in this way gives the couple the same legal status as if they were a heterosexual married couple: giving the relationship a legal status means that such partnerships have the status of being families by the definition. No doubt the people concerned already felt as if they were families, and in many cases they have even had children either from previous heterosexual marriages or by adoption. The Marriage (Same Sex Couples) Act 2013 enabled same sex couples in England and Wales to marry from 29 March 2014. It also has a number of related provisions, including for those in a civil partnership to convert that relationship to a marriage if they choose

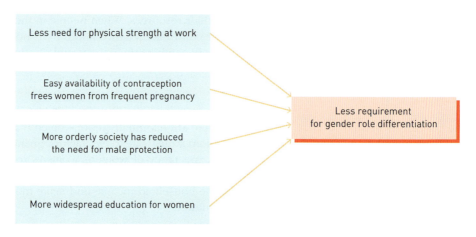

FIGURE 12.6 Drivers for gender role change

to do so and provisions that will enable a person to change their legal gender without ending their existing marriage.

Lesbian, gay, bi, and trans-sexual people tend to be wealthier than heterosexuals: male homosexuals earn on average 23% more than heterosexual men, have twice as many credit cards as the general population, and spend more on entertainment than average (Experian 2012). US research carried out by global information and measurement company Nielsen has concluded that LGBT households make 10% more shopping trips a year than non-LGBT households, and that in 2014 they spent, on average $4,135 at retail stores – 7% more than non-LGBT households. Various market research agencies have conducted surveys to try to show not just affluence, but that disproportionate levels of brand loyalty were a hallmark of gays and lesbians. This in turn meant that gay men were portrayed as being voraciously consumerist, cosmopolitan and thus well-to-do. An Experian report (2012) claimed that the average household income of a married or partnered gay man is 25% more than a straight married or partnered man (£75,000 compared to £60,000). There is no doubt that these research studies view the LGBT community from the perspective of a consumer market; it is worth noting that this is a very different perspective compared with how a social science researcher researching poverty would look at those questions.

In the UK, gay people's disposable income is called the Pink Pound (in the US it is called the Dorothy Dollar) and is worth around £6 billion a year. Of course, marketers like to categorise people for segmentation purposes and some segments are much larger: the 'grey pound' market comprising the older person amounts to nearly £320 billion a year. Nonetheless, £6 billion is a substantial market so gay people have been targeted by some financial institutions and by information services, clubs and even holiday companies, such as Pink Pound Travel. Drinks firm Absolute launched rainbow coloured vodka bottles and publicised recipes for cocktails with names such as Absolute Out and Absolute Proud. The LGBT community is estimated to account for at least 4% of the population (the exact figure is hard to determine as some members of the LGBT community still feel that they would face prejudice or hostility if they were open about their sexuality); they represent a substantial market. No doubt some organisations feel pressure to appear gay-friendly in order to access the pink pound, while not necessarily practising what they preach; this has become known as 'pink-washing'. Recent advertising campaigns give us many examples of this.

American retailer Target in the USA featured a gay couple in their advertising, but unfortunately for Target the press found out that they had some time later donated cash to an anti-gay politician. Heinz ran an advert in 2008 that showed two men kissing but decided to scrap the advert after receiving a backlash from, one presumes, the hetero-sexual community. This of course angered the LGBT community and made a mockery of Heinz's initial pro-gay stance. Timing is everything and it certainly worked for the UK's suit-hire business Moss Bros. They ran an advertising campaign in 2014 entitled 'Mister and Mister' during the same week that gay marriage was legalised in the UK.

Eventually one might expect that gender role will not be an issue in advertising at all, but since advertising (at least in part) reflects society, this may still be some way off.

OTHER FUNCTIONS OF THE FAMILY

Families also provide economic well-being, emotional support and suitable family lifestyles (see Figure 12.7). Because families share consumption, the standard of living of the members is higher than would have been the case had they chosen to live separately. In some families, economic well-being is also generated by employment in the family business. Because the overall tasks within the family are divided between the members, some members might exchange earning their own money for taking on a larger role within the family, for example staying at home to care for small children.

In the majority of UK families both parents work outside the home. There is considerable debate as to whether this has a detrimental or a positive effect on children, but it certainly has a positive effect on the family's finances, increasing spending power and also (on the downside) increasing the need for labour-saving devices and behaviour, for example ready meals, childcare and children's entertainment devices, which leave the parents free to carry out other tasks.

In some societies children are expected to contribute to the family's finances, in particular teenage children are expected to work and contribute. In most Western families, teenagers would expect to retain any earnings, whereas their parents

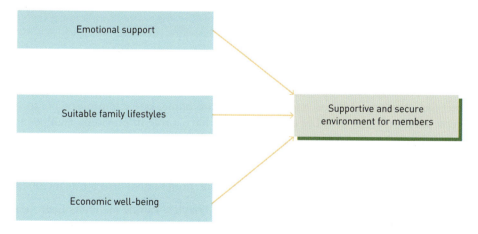

FIGURE 12.7 Other functions of the family

would want them either to save towards their education or adult life in general, or at least to pay something towards their upkeep, e.g. entertainment and perhaps clothing items.

Latchkey kid

A child who returns from school to an empty home because their parent or parents are away at work, or a child who is often left at home with little parental supervision

CONSUMER BEHAVIOUR IN ACTION: THE IMPORTANCE OF FAMILY

Yes parents matter! Yes they are important in shaping the lives of young people. And yes, they leave a negative affect if they get it wrong! Even back in 1966, research which was centred on *Equality of Educational Opportunity* had noted that compared to most other variables, family background has the greatest influence on educational attainment. However, our society is full of examples of both parents working long hours, and where children are latchkey kids, or where the childcare has been sub-contracted to nannies, childminders and childcare centres. At the same time, our politicians are continually extolling the virtues of family values, and suggesting that parents should spend more time with their children. Children can be quite emotionally astute. There are only so many 'gifts' one can bring back following a 'work trip' – sometimes all the children want and value is some quality time with their parents.

It is perhaps this lack or limited 'contact time' which then gives rise to other societal issues – a lack of exercise in young people (Anderson 2006), which is fuelled by a nonchalant approach to eating habits (Savage et al. 2007) and even criminal behaviour and delinquency (Chung et al. 2002). It is also worth noting that the gap which parents sometimes leave in their children's lives is often filled by their friends and peers. Again Milner (2015) points to issues such as use of drugs and smoking, early initiation of sexual behaviour, binge drinking and eating high calorie snacks, but the research notes that it is often difficult to measure the effects of peers precisely.

It is of course easy to fall into a 'blame culture' and lay the responsibility at the door of the parent. What about all the other influences that a family is involved with? Johnson et al. (2009) make a very pertinent point when they assert that 'behaviour in adolescence is a function of multiple interactive influences including experience, parenting, socio-economic status, individual agency and self-efficacy, nutrition, culture, psychological well-being, the physical and built environments and social relationships and interactions'.

So let's go back to basics and ask a very simple question – why is family important?

Economic well-being is also provided when, for example, parents pay for a child's education, or help with the deposit for a house. Sometimes the help goes in the other direction: grown-up children might pay for a care home, or for improvements to an elderly parent's home. In either case, marketers have a role in providing facilities for this to happen. Emotional support is a core function of families. This can comprise love and affection, but also involves moral support and encouragement. When families are unable to provide appropriate emotional support from within the group, it may turn to counselling or even psychiatric services to provide professional help for its members.

Finally, families also help to establish suitable lifestyles. Family members bear more than a physical resemblance to each other; they tend to have similar attitudes about the importance of education, about reading, about environmentalism, about home decoration, about holidays and about appropriate entertainments (sport, dining out, etc.). Even though there is a trend towards family members acting independently rather than sharing activities, we return to the idea of spending 'quality time' with each other as this has recently led to a tendency to seek out activities and experiences that can be shared. Marketers have not been slow to capitalise on this, promoting family leisure activities (for example, the PGL activity holiday), short breaks, and so forth.

ROLES IN FAMILY CONSUMPTION

Within families, a great deal of decision-making is collective. Even such basic decisions as buying underwear might be shared or carried out by one member of the family on behalf of another. The traditional example would be a mother buying underwear for the children of the family, but many women buy underwear for their husbands, and it is far from unknown for husbands to buy lingerie for their wives, often as Valentine or birthday gifts.

Within families, consumption and purchase roles are often divided between family members. There are thought to be eight basic roles in family decision-making, as shown in Table 12.4. Depending on the type of product being considered, family members may adopt different roles for each decision. In other words, deciders are not necessarily deciders for everything – they may be deciders for some categories of product (e.g. holidays) and gatekeepers for another category (e.g. home entertainment systems). Likewise, roles often overlap, or the same person occupies more than one role.

TABLE 12.4 Roles in family decision-making

Role	Explanation
Influencers	These are the family members who perhaps have no direct involvement in the purchase or consumption of the item, but who can offer help and advice
Gatekeepers	These members control the flow of information to the others. A gatekeeper may be the person who scours the websites and reads the e-brochures or watches the advertising on TV
Deciders	These members have the final say on the product being bought or consumed. In most families, the deciders would be the parents, but this is not always the case: it depends on the product being considered
Buyers	Family members who make the actual purchase are the buyers. It may be that a decision is made to book a particular holiday, and the member with the best IT skills is given the task of booking it online
Preparers	These members transform the product into a form suitable for the others to consume it. The obvious example is cooking food, but the concept could equally apply to one of the children of the family setting up the Apple TV box to the new Smart TV
Users	The family members who will consume/use the product
Maintainers	The family members who will ensure that the product is in good condition for the others to use it. This not only applies to someone who mends the kitchen cupboards, it also applies to someone who cleans the house and does the laundry
Disposers	Members who have the job of removing the used products and packaging or arranging for the sale or trade-in of products for which the family has no further use

Preparers
A family member responsible for transforming a product into a condition suitable for other members to use it

FIGURE 12.8 Family roles and decisions

In Figure 12.8 the main arrows show where each individual has a major input. The fine arrows show where the individuals have a lesser input. Obviously the same individual may have more than one role in the purchase decision.

Children appear to have a greater role in family decision-making than in the past. As children (and of course their parents) grow older, parents begin to seek the advice of their children on some aspects, particularly where new technology is concerned or where the child has acquired specialist knowledge. Research shows that parents in lower income groups are more likely to see their children as being 'consumer savvy', especially if the child is female and at the older end of the spectrum (Nancarrow et al. 2011). Parents with a 'warm' approach to parenting are more likely to learn from their children (Grossbart et al. 2002). Children themselves believe that they have considerable influence in many family purchase decisions, even including buying a car among these decisions (Tinson and Nancarrow 2005). The areas in which children believe themselves to be most important as decision-makers are shown in Table 12.5.

Research carried out in Canada indicates that children there have an even greater influence on decisions: 40% of children in one study believed themselves to be the main decision-makers with respect to choice of restaurant when eating out (Labrecque and Ricard 2001). The same study showed that children underestimate their influence on the decision to go to a restaurant in the first place.

There is some evidence to suggest that the family's communication pattern is also related to the child's influence on the decision-making process (see Figure 12.9). Communication patterns usually fall into one or other of the following categories (Shoham et al. 2004):

1. *Pluralistic parents.* These parents encourage their children to express their ideas and preferences. Not surprisingly, these families experience the greatest influence from the children.

2. *Consensual parents.* These parents encourage their children to seek harmony, but they are influenced by the children's ideas.

3. *Protective parents.* These parents believe that 'mother knows best' and in general expect children to agree to the parents' choices.

It seems probable that children with pluralistic parents would be likely to develop consumer skills early, but they might also be the most likely to use pester power to

TABLE 12.5 How children perceive themselves to have influenced the purchase of different products

Product	Percentage influence
Casual clothes for me	91%
Trainers for me	88%
CDs for me	84%
Sweets for me	83%
Computers for me	83%
Soft drinks for me	80%
School shoes for me	80%
A family trip to the cinema	73%
Food for me for lunch at the weekend	73%
A holiday I would go on with the family	63%
Going out for a family meal	52%
A family car	37%

The child's learning to be a consumer reduces

| Pluralistic parents | Consensual parents | Protective parents |

The child's influence on the immediate decision increases

FIGURE 12.9 Communication pattern and children's influence

get their own way. Children with protective parents might take longer to develop consumer skills, but would perhaps be more likely to adopt brands favoured by their parents in later life.

Some teenagers spend a great deal of time on the Internet, and consequently regard themselves as experts at researching information relating to major purchases. These teenage mavens can contribute significantly to family decision-making, especially in the information search phase of the process (Belch et al. 2005).

SUMMARY

Age, gender and the family are important factors in consumer behaviour. Families are often said to be the building-blocks of society. We are influenced more by our families than by anybody else: partly this is because the influence starts at a very early age, partly it is because we spend a large part of our lives living with our families, and partly it is because our family relationships (especially those with our siblings if we have them) are the longest-lasting relationships in our lives. Marketers recognise that children – toddlers, tweenies and teenagers – all yield varying degrees of power and influence. As gender roles are continually defined and re-defined by societies in different cultures, marketing departments continually evolve their notion of what is acceptable, admissible and effective in their campaigns.

Because families share so much of their consumption, the ways in which they interact and make decisions are of great interest to marketers. Families share decision-making in many ways, and the views of family members are still important even when it is the parents who make the final decision.

There are many different patterns of family, but what they have in common is relationships by blood, marriage or adoption; shared consumption; face-to-face contact on a daily basis; emotional, economic and lifestyle support for their members; and finally, shared regard for each other's welfare.

KEY POINTS

- 'Family' has several definitions, each of which is dependent on culture and circumstances.
- Cohorts and subcultures developed using age are affected by differing attitudes and values.
- Culture has a marked effect on decision-making styles.
- All members of a family have some input into decision-making.
- Conflict is common in families because of shared consumption.
- Children (pester power) have to be taught to be effective consumers.
- The fluidity of gender roles is playing an increasingly important part in our lives.
- Brand loyalty can pass down through several generations.
- Family life cycle models are pluralistic in 21st century society.
- Family members often adopt specific roles in the purchase and consumption process.

HOW TO IMPRESS YOUR EXAMINER

You will probably be asked about the effects of age and gender on decision-making patterns in families; and this is especially true for the influence of children. You should be able to differentiate the varying influences between the toddler, tweenie and teenager. It will gain you extra marks if you can provide the downside of decision-making, by outlining the ways in which children are influenced by their peers and by marketers. You should think about the attitudes towards changing gender roles in society. The question also implies that you should understand that decision-making and indeed all consumption behaviour is very much culturally driven.

REVIEW QUESTIONS

1. Why are children powerful in influencing consumption behaviour?
2. Why is the family a culturally based concept?
3. What are the main changes in the family in recent years?
4. How might purchase roles change in the next 20 years?
5. What are the drivers for change in purchase roles?
6. How might the change in the ethnic structure of European society affect family decision-making?
7. To what degree does social class have an influence on consumer behaviour?
8. How does parenting style affect children's consumption behaviour?
9. What are the main criticisms of the family life cycle concept?
10 What are the key functions of a family?

CASE STUDY: LA LECHE LEAGUE GREAT BRITAIN

La Leche League GB (Spanish for 'the Milk') is the British affiliate of La Leche League International: the biggest voluntary breastfeeding support organisation in the world.

Their mission is to help mothers to breastfeed through mother-to-mother support, encouragement, information and education, and to promote a better understanding of breastfeeding as an important element in the healthy development of the baby and mother.

La Leche League (LLL) came from humble beginnings in 1956, founded by seven mothers in Chicago who saw that many of their friends were not being given accurate information about mothering and breastfeeding within their communities, even by some health professionals. Nor were their friends offered wide-ranging ideas and suggestions to try which were compatible with successful breastfeeding. Often challenges were simply met by the firm assertion that the mother should stop breastfeeding. After a picnic in a park the seven women decided to form a group to share their passion for breastfeeding by supporting their friends and offering information.

©iStock.com/ChristopherFutcher

These founding mothers perceived that babies, parents and families were unique, and that a 'one size fits all' approach, with inflexible rules or schedules was rarely appropriate for meeting the needs of babies, which had changed little over tens of thousands of years.

In an age before anyone went to a counsellor and with no wide ranging literature about the art of listening or the importance of acknowledging individual feelings, the founders of LLL understood the need to truly listen to what each woman was saying.

They gave unbiased information and support, empowering each mother to make her own decisions in her individual circumstances.

The founders created a philosophy of core values upon which the global organisation is still based, covering the essential factors of mothering through breastfeeding. They nurtured a network of accredited 'Leaders' who each believed in the values of this philosophy, and who continually keep up to date with breastfeeding and mothering information, as well as communication skills. Each new Leader is asked to undertake the responsibility of starting their own peer support group, take calls from the LLLGB breastfeeding helpline and local calls, and most Leaders offer support through email, Facebook and other social media platforms.

This grassroots organisation now reaches over 60 countries worldwide through a network of thousands of Leaders running 2,500 groups globally.

LLLGB began as part of La Leche League International in 1971. Almost all of their daily work is undertaken by volunteers. Every Leader and every Trustee of the charity is unpaid with only two part-time administrative staff. In Great Britain alone, LLLGB consists of 250 volunteer Leaders, running 70 groups around Great Britain, answering more than 10,000 phone calls, 650 emails and countless social media posts every year.

The original philosophy (which has been slightly altered to ensure inclusion of all), still guides the work of each Leader to this day. Over the decades LLL has influenced government policies in many countries, and maintains a close working relationship with the World Health Organisation (WHO). For example, thanks to the influence of LLL, the WHO now recognises the importance of exclusive breastfeeding for the first six months of the baby's life, which the NHS in the UK also adopted as best practice. Though not a lobbying organisation, LLLGB has representative Leaders sitting on non-partisan, cross-party working groups on child health, providing evidence-based responses to government consultations, providing accurate information to the media, and are often active at a community level to help to ensure the provision of quality breastfeeding support.

The global LLL community continues to work extremely effectively and efficiently as an international organisation, particularly when there is a crisis – natural or man-made. Working together quickly, they raise funds to get Leaders to areas of need as soon as possible, ensuring mothers are supported to continue to breastfeed. In crisis situations feeding artificially could involve contaminated powders, dirty water and unsterilised bottles and therefore in many cases breastfeeding, even re-lactating, can save lives.

An organisation which started as a small local support group in a Chicago mother's house has, over the past 60 years, gone on to positively change the lives of tens of thousands of mothers, babies and families all over the world and to provide invaluable information to those who offer breastfeeding support.

QUESTIONS

1. What role does breastfeeding play in a modern family?
2. How might age feature as a factor in the encouragement and acceptance of breastfeeding?
3. What effects might breastfeeding have on family consumption patterns?
4. What is the role of the male partner in facilitating breastfeeding?
5. What is the role of medical practitioners and support groups in the decision-making process for whether to breastfeed or not (and its effects on the family unit)?

FURTHER READING

For more information about breastfeeding and its benefits to society, please visit www. llli.org/. You could also visit the National Health Service webpage for the health benefits to consumers: www.nhs.uk/conditions/pregnancy-and-baby/pages/why-breastfeed.aspx#close.

If you want to know more about dealing with children who misbehave, you might like *Raising Your Spirited Child: A Guide for Parents Whose Child Is More Intense, Sensitive, Perceptive, Persistent and Energetic* by Mary Sheedy Kurcinka (New York: Harper Perennial, 1992). This American book might seem a bit 'worthy' but it does have some very good advice and techniques for dealing with children who get upset easily, or who challenge their parents.

There are many anthropological texts on childrearing practices in different cultures. An example is the rather scholarly *Turkish Mothers' Attitudes to Child-Rearing Practices* by Gokce Tekin (Cambridge: Proquest/UMI Dissertation Publishing, 2011). It is in fact a PhD thesis, so can be hard going, but it shows how childrearing practices can vary greatly according to cultural differences.

For a look at the other face of marketing to children, Ed Mayo and Agnes Nairn's book *Consumer Kids: How Big Business is Grooming Our Children for Profit* (London: Constable, 2009) reveals some of the alleged tactics used by large corporations to target children. The book is maybe a little one-sided, but it certainly is thought-provoking and raises a number of ethical issues.

Another precautionary tale comes from Juliet Schor. Her book *Born to Buy: The Commercialised Child and the New Consumer Culture* (New York: Simon and Schuster, 2006) outlines some American marketing practices (many of which would be illegal in the UK and indeed in most of Europe). These include an educational TV channel available only in schools in which commercials are embedded in the teaching materials. Scary stuff – and something that certainly goes against the tenets of responsible marketing.

A comprehensive look at the theory of communication within families comes from *Communication in Family Relationships* by Patrick Noller and Mary Ann Fitzpatrick (Englewood Cliffs, NJ: Prentice Hall, 1993). A note of caution, though – although English is a universal language, there are marked differences between American culture and those of other English-speaking countries (not to mention non-English speaking countries). Since family life is very culture-specific, theories developed in the United States may not apply elsewhere – so use your own judgement as well!

REFERENCES

Anderson, S. (2006) How does exercise cause asthma attacks? *Current Opinion in Allergy and Clinical Immunology*, 6 (1): 37–42

Barak, B. and Schiffman, L.G. (1981) Cognitive age: a nonchronological age variable. In K. B. Monroe (ed.), *Advances in Consumer Research*, Vol. 8. Ann Arbor, MI: Association for Consumer Research, pp. 602–6.

BBC (1998) *Business: The Economy. The Pink Pound*. Available at: http://news.bbc.co.uk/1/hi/business/142998.stm (accessed December 2012).

Belch, M.A., Krentler, K.A. and Willis-Flurry, L.A. (2005) Teen Internet mavens: influence in family decision-making. *Journal of Business Research*, 58: 569–75.

Boym, S. (2001) *The Future of Nostalgia*. New York: Basic Books.

Cao, J., Cumming, D. and Wang, X. (2015) One-child policy and family firms in China. *Journal of Corporate Finance*. doi:10.1016/j.jcorpfin.2015.01.005.

Carlson, L. and Grossbart, S. (1988) Parental styles and consumer socialisation of children. *Journal of Consumer Research*, 15 (June): 77–94.

Chung, I.-J., Hill, K.G., Hawkins, J.D., Gilchrist, L. and Nagin, D. (2002) Childhood predictors of offense trajectories. *Journal of Research in Crime and Delinquency*, 39: 60–91.

Communicus.com (2014) Pester power. www.communicus.com/2014/12/17/pester-power-communicus-advertising-study-shows-children-significant-influence-parents-wireless-purchases/ (accessed 10 August 2015).

Cornwall, A. and Edwards, J. (2015) Introduction: Beijing+ 20 – where now for gender equality? *IDS Bulletin*, 46 (4): 1–8.

Curasi, C. (2006) Maybe it IS your father's Oldsmobile: the construction and preservation of family identity through the transfer of possessions. *Advances in Consumer Behaviour*, 33: 83.

Curasi, C. (2011) Intergenerational possession transfers and identity maintenance. *Journal of Consumer Behaviour*, 10 (2): 111–18.

Desrochers, D.M. (2015) Advertising to children in traditional and new media. *Journal of Children and Media*, 9 (2): 272–5.

Dejevsky, M. (2006) Japan: a country in crisis? *The Independent*, 26 August.

Dias, M. and Agante, L. (2011) Can advergames boost children's healthier eating habits? A comparison between healthy and non-healthy food. *Journal of Consumer Behaviour*, 10 (3): 152–60.

Ekstrom, K.M., Tansuhaj, P.S. and Foxman, E. (1987) Children's influence in family decisions and consumer socialization: a reciprocal view. *Advances in Consumer Research*, 14: 283–7.

Elliott, C. (2011) It's junk food and chicken nuggets: children's perspectives on 'kids' food' and the question of food classification. *Journal of Consumer Behaviour*, 10 (3): 133–40.

Epp, A.M. and Arnould, E.J. (2006) Enacting the family legacy: how family themes influence consumption behaviour. *Advances in Consumer Research*, 33: 82–6.

European Union (1995) The population of the EU on 1 January 1995. *Statistics in Focus. Population and Social Conditions No 8*. Luxembourg: Office for Official Publications of the European Communities.

Eurostat (2002) *The Social Situation in the European Union 2002*. Luxembourg: Office for Official Publications of the European Union.

Experian (2012) *A Look at Household Income and Discretionary Spend of Lesbian, Gay and Heterosexual Americans*. www.experian.com/blogs/marketing-forward/2012/07/20/sim-a-look-at-household-income-and-discretionary-spend-of-lesbian-gay-and-heterosexual-americans/ (accessed 14 September 2015).

Fernandez, K.V. and Veer, E. (2004) The gold that binds: the ritualistic use of jewellery in an Indian wedding. *Advances in Consumer Research*, 31: 53.

Filiatrault, P. and Ritchie, J.R.B. (1980) Joint purchasing decisions: a comparison of influence structure in family and couple decision-making units. *Journal of Consumer Research*, 7 (September): 131–40.

Green, R.T., Leonardi, J., Chandon, J., Cunningham, I.C.M., Verhage, B. and Strazzieru, A. (1983) Societal development and family purchasing roles: a cross-national study. *Journal of Consumer Research*, 9 (4): 436–42.

Grossbart, S., Hughes, S., McConnell, P.S. and Yost, A. (2002) Socialisation aspects of parents, children and the Internet. *Advances in Consumer Research*, 29: 66–70.

Hamilton, K. (2009) Consumer decision-making in low-income families: the case of conflict avoidance. *Journal of Consumer Behaviour*, 8 (5): 252–67.

Hamilton, K. and Catterall, M. (2006) Consuming love in poor families: children's influence on consumption decisions. *Journal of Marketing Management*, 22 (9/10): 1031–52.

Hartman, C.L. and Kiecker, P. (2004) Jewellery: passing along the continuum of sacred and profane meanings. *Advances in Consumer Research*, 31: 53–4.

HeForShe website (2014) *Action Kit* (PDF). www.heforshe.org/action-kit (accessed 14 September 2015).

John, D.R. (1999) Consumer socialization of children: a retrospective look at twenty-five years of research. *Journal of Consumer Research*, 26 (December): 183–213.

Johnson, S.B., Blum, R.W. and Giedd, J.N. (2009) Adolescent maturity and the brain: the promise and pitfalls of neuroscience research in adolescent health policy. *Journal of Adolescent Health*, 45 (3): 216–21.

Komarovsky, M. (1961) Class differences in family decision-making. In Nelson N. Foote (ed.), *Household Decision Making*. New York: New York University Press, pp 255–65.

Labrecque, J. and Ricard, L. (2001) Children's influence on family decision-making: a restaurant study. *Journal of Business Research*, 54 (November): 173–6.

Lawlor, M. and Prothero, A. (2011) Pester power: a battle of wills between children and their parents. *Journal of Marketing Management*, 27 (5&6): 561–81.

Mandrik, C.A., Fern, E.F. and Bao, Y. (2004) Intergenerational influence in mothers and young adult daughters. *Advances in Consumer Research*, 31: 697–9.

Marketing News (1983) Teenage daughters of working mothers have a big role in purchase, brand selection decisions. *Marketing News*, 18 (February): 20.

McDonald, S.N. (2014) Emma Watson: feminism too often is seen as 'man-hating'. *Washington Post*. www.washingtonpost.com/news/morning-mix/wp/2014/09/22/emma-watson-recruits-men-to-make-the-world-safer-for-women-with-heforshe-campaign/ (accessed 14 September 2015).

Miller, E.G., Seiders, K., Kenny, M. and Walsh, M.E. (2011) Children's use of on-package nutritional claim information. *Journal of Consumer Behaviour*, 10 (3): 122–32.

Milner, M. (2015) *Freaks, Geeks, and Cool Kids: Teenagers in an Era of Consumerism, Standardized Tests, and Social Media*. London: Routledge.

Mittal, B. and Royne, M.B. (2010) Consuming as a family: modes of intergenerational influence on young adults. *Journal of Consumer Behaviour*, 9 (4): 239–57.

Nancarrow, C., Tinson, J. and Brace, I. (2011) Profiling key purchase influencers: those perceived as consumer savvy. *Journal of Consumer Behaviour*, 10 (2): 102–10.

Norgaard, M.K. and Brunso, K. (2011) Family conflicts and conflict resolution regarding food choices. *Journal of Consumer Behaviour*, 10 (3): 141–51.

Office for National Statistics (2012) Aging in the UK Datasets, 2011 Pensions Act Update (January release). Newport: ONS.

Office for National Statistics (2015) *Families and Households 2015*. www.ons.gov.uk/ons/rel/family-demography/families-and-households/2014/families-and-households-in-the-uk—2014.html (accessed 14 September 2015).

Olsen, B. (1993) Brand loyalty and lineage: exploring new dimensions for research. *Advances in Consumer Research*, 20: 575–9.

Onkvisit, S. and Shaw, J.J. (1994) *Consumer Behaviour: Strategy and Analysis* (New York: John Wiley).

The Online Etymology Dictionary (2015) Definition of nostalgia (n.). www.etymonline.com/index.php?allowed_in_frame=0&search=nostalgia&searchmode=none (accessed 13 September 2015).

O'Neill, T., Vigar-Ellis, D. and Paterson, S. (2013) Pester power in low income families. In K. Kubacki (ed.), *Ideas in Marketing: Finding the New and Polishing the Old. Development in Marketing Science: Proceedings of the Academy of Marketing Science*. London: Springer International Publishing, p. 600.

Rick, S.I., Small, D.A. and Finkel, E.J. (2010) Fatal (fiscal) attraction: tightwads and spendthrifts in marriage. *Advances in Consumer Research*, 37: 36.

Rose, G.M. (1999) Consumer socialization, parental style, and developmental timetables in the United States and Japan. *Journal of Marketing*, 63: 105–19.

Rose, G.M., Dalakis, V., Kropp, F. and Kamineni, R. (2002) Raising young consumers: consumer socialization and parental style across cultures. *Advances in Consumer Behaviour*, 29: 65.

Rummel, A., Howard, J., Swinton, J.M. and Seymour, D.B. (2000) You can't have that! A study of reactance effects and children's consumer behaviour. *Journal of Marketing Theory and Practice*, Winter: 38–45.

Savage, J., Fisher, J.O. and Birch, L. (2007) Parental influence on eating behavior: conception to adolescence. *Journal of Law, Medicine & Ethics*, 35 (1): 22–34.

Sethna, Z. (2015) Entrepreneurial marketing and the Zarathustrian Entrepreneur: thoughts, words and deeds. Academy of Marketing AM2015 Conference Proceedings. Limerick, Ireland.

Shivany, S. (2015) Resolving methods for parent–children conflict engaged by the TV-commercials in the post-war market. *New Media and Mass Communication*, 35: 56-65.

Shoham, A., Rose, G.M. and Bakir, A. (2004) The effect of family communication patterns on mothers' and fathers' perceived influence in family decision making. *Advances in Consumer Behaviour*, 31: 692.

Suhay, L. (2014) Emma Watson and HeForShe: points to flaws in man-hating. *The Christian Science Monitor.* www.csmonitor.com/The-Culture/Family/Modern-Parenthood/2014/0922/Emma-Watson-and-HeForShe-Points-to-flaws-in-man-hating-video (accessed 14 September 2015).

Tinson, J. and Nancarrow, C. (2005) The influence of children on purchases. *International Journal of Marketing*, 47 (1): 5–27.

Tiwari, S. (2015) Exclusion of Madheshi women in decision making. *Academic Voices: A Multidisciplinary Journal*, 4: 68–72.

United Nations (2016) *Households and Families*. http://unstats.un.org/unsd/demographic/sconcerns/fam/fammethods.htm (accessed 14 February 2016).

Ward, C.B. (2006) He wants, she wants: gender, category and disagreement in spouses' joint decisions. *Advances in Consumer Research*, 33: 117–23.

Wells, W.D. and Gubar, G. (1966) The life cycle concept in marketing research. *Journal of Marketing Research*, 3 (November): 353–63.

Wildschut, T., Sedikides, C., Arndt, J. and Routledge, C. (2006) Nostalgia: content, triggers, functions. *Journal of Personality and Social Psychology*, 91: 975–93. doi: 10.1037/0022-3514.91.5.975.

Wildschut, T., Sedikides, C., Routledge, C., Arndt, J. and Cordaro, F. (2010) Nostalgia as a repository of social connectedness: the role of attachment-related avoidance. *Journal of Personality and Social Psychology*, 98: 573–86. doi: 10.1037/a0017597.

Williams, T.P. (2006) Money and meaning: the role of social bonds and capital in inter vivos gifting. *Advances in Consumer Research*, 33: 84–5.

Wimalasir, J.S. (2004) A cross-national study on children's purchasing behaviour and parental response. *Journal of Consumer Marketing*, 21 (4): 274–84.

Young, C. (2014) Editorial as Contributing Editor, *Time Magazine*. http://time.com/3432838/emma-watson-feminism-men-women/ (accessed 14 September 2015).

MORE ONLINE

For additional materials that support this chapter and your learning, please visit:
https://study.sagepub.com/sethnaandblythe

CHAPTER 13

CULTURE AND CLASS

LEARNING OBJECTIVES

After reading this chapter you should be able to:

- Explain what the constituent parts of the social environment are.
- Understand what is meant by culture.
- Explain how subcultural factors colour our purchasing behaviour.
- Describe the difference between high-context cultures and low-context cultures.
- Discuss some approaches to studying culture and consumer culture theory.
- Understand the problems raised for people who move from one culture to another by discussing acculturation.
- Describe how class distinctions have changed in the last 50 years or so.

INTRODUCTION

This chapter is about the contexts within which behaviour takes place. Individual decision-making always occurs within a social, cultural, environmental or class context, since human beings interact and need to consider the responses of others. Also, the physical environment within which decisions are made can affect the outcomes dramatically: some environments are conducive to paying higher prices, or buying more of a specific type of product, whereas others encourage greater thrift.

The social environment includes all the behavioural inputs received from other people. In some cases, these may be direct interactions (a conversation with a salesperson, advice from a friend, an encounter with someone unpleasant) and in other

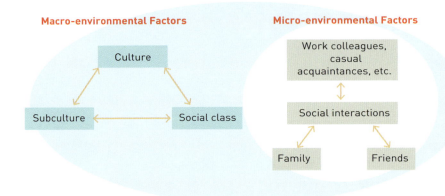

FIGURE 13.1 The social environment

cases they may be indirect (observing how a friend negotiates with a vendor, seeing a banner advert on a website, seeing how other people act in a new social situation either offline or online).

The social environment can also be divided into macro- and micro-environments. The macro-environment has three components: culture, subculture and social class. Each of these has profound influences on behaviour because they have been powerful drivers in the formation of attitudes, beliefs and values. Although people from the same cultural background differ considerably among themselves, there will still be similarities. Each of these elements will be dealt with in more detail later in this chapter.

Subculture

A set of beliefs and attitudes which, while part of a main culture, represents a distinctly separate set

Culture provides the social environment within which people live. This chapter also considers what happens when people change culture, or when their own culture shifts around them; it also considers the variations within a culture that are called subcultures. In the latter part of this chapter, we also take a closer look at 'class'; this is a somewhat ambiguous concept which has been a talking point for sociologists for many years.

As shown in Figure 13.1, the micro social environment comprises the face-to-face social interactions we have with our friends, work colleagues, family and others in the groups of which we are members. These micro-environmental interactions have been dealt with already in Chapters 11 and 12. The macro-environment comprises those factors that are common to everyone living within the same country or region; in other words, those factors that affect us all.

CULTURE

Culture is the set of shared beliefs, attitudes and behaviours associated with a large and distinct group of people. Culture is learned, but it is often so deeply ingrained in people that they imagine that the rules of their particular society or group have the status of natural laws. As a result, culture is one of the main drivers of behaviour and influences almost everything we do, including, of course, our consumption behaviour.

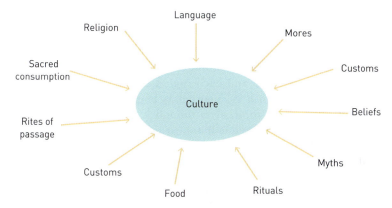

FIGURE 13.2 Elements of culture

The main elements of culture, summarised in Figure 13.2, are as follows:

- *Religion*. Religious beliefs colour people's behaviour in many ways, from laying down rules about which foods are permissible and which are not, through to disposal of the dead. For example, it is frowned upon for a deceased Zoroastrian to be buried. The religious dictate is that if death is the temporary triumph of evil over good, then by using burial as a method of disposal, one is defiling the earth (made by God and thus 'good') for 35 years or more. Zoroastrians (at least in Iran and India) prefer the traditional method of a 'sky burial' using a Tower of Silence.

- *Language*. Language clearly affects purchasing behaviour in many ways. First, the ability to understand and act on marketing communications relies not only on understanding the specific language but also on understanding specific words and sentence constructions within the language. For example, slang terms and puns might not be accessible to all the observers of the communication, and communications written in dialect might not be understood by non-native speakers of the language. Second, some products (such as books and newspapers) are clearly of no use to someone who does not understand the language in which they are written. The market for books in Welsh, for example, is confined to Wales and parts of Argentina, with few (if any) sales elsewhere. The structure and rules of languages can affect consumer perceptions: in languages where brand names acquire gender (Spanish and French, for example) this will affect consumer perception of the product as being either masculine or feminine. In languages that include a neuter gender (English and Greek are examples) this is not an issue unless the marketer deliberately uses a masculine or feminine ending on the brand name (Yorkston and deMello 2004).

- *Customs*. These are norms of behaviour handed down from the past. Some customs grow out of religious beliefs (many of the traditions associated with Christmas have come from Christian belief, although some are pagan or pre-Christian), while others come from traditions associated with climate or shared experiences. For example, throughout most of southern Spain villages and towns celebrate the Fiesta of 'Moros y Cristianos' which refers to the overthrow of the Moorish invaders between 722 and 1492 AD. The date varies in each village, as each village overthrew its Moors on a different date, but for most it is a spectacular celebration

Tower of Silence

This is a circular, raised structure used by Zoroastrians for exposure of the dead, particularly to vultures for the purposes of excarnation involving fireworks (symbolising the fighting and also the traditional destruction of remaining ammunition to show that the shooting really is over) and a great deal of dancing and partying throughout the night.

- *Food*. Food is strongly linked to culture. While cheese is regarded as an essential part of any meal in France, and each region of the country produces several distinct examples, in Japan it is regarded as being as appealing as rotted milk and is a somewhat exotic food, even though it is nowadays available in most supermarkets. In Britain, people will not eat insects but will happily eat prawns, while in Zambia deep-fried caterpillars are a delicacy. In Mexico, the tortilla has a cultural significance that is bound up in what it means to be a Mexican, but (paradoxically) there is an underlying belief that everything emanating from the United States is better than anything Mexican: there is evidence that even American tortillas are considered to be somehow better than Mexican ones (Gabel and Boller 2003). These differences in taste are explained by culture rather than by random differences in taste between individuals: behaviours tend to be shared by people from the same cultural background.

Mores

Elements of a culture

- **Mores**. Mores are customs with a strong moral incentive. In most societies, cannibalism is regarded as immoral and is not part of the cultural mores; in other societies (most of them in the past) cannibalism is not only moral but is regarded as a necessary and respectful way of dealing with dead people. Violation of mores often results in strong reactions from other members of the culture – in some cases these can be abusive or even violent, while in other cases the law becomes involved and the individual receives a formalised punishment. In many countries, the media portrayal of the police treatment of black people is fast becoming a more of sorts. There is certainly deep unrest at the type of cases that are being realised.

- *Conventions*. These are norms regarding the conduct of everyday life. For example, in the UK a dinner guest would normally be expected to bring a bottle of wine, and many dinner guests would also bring flowers; in Hawaii people would bring small snacks called *puu-puus*. From a verbal perspective, some spoken phrases are conventional – for instance when someone who asks you 'How are you?', they are usually expecting the answer, 'Fine, thanks' rather than an actual description of your current circumstances, or detailed health report etc. Table manners, appropriate clothing for formal occasions and rules about when it is permissible to make a noise (for example, play loud music) and when it is not are also examples of conventions. As an exercise to test conventions, try saying 'Hi' to random people on the London Underground, or even trying to strike up a conversation (!) … it's just not the done thing as Brits like to sit in silence!

- *Myths*. A myth is a story that contains symbolic elements expressing the shared emotions and ideals of a culture. The outcome of a myth might illustrate a particular moral pathway, and it thus serves to provide a guideline to the world. An example might be the 'urban myths' that often circulate by email, to warn people of inappropriate behaviour or to provide entertainment. Take for example a truly modern urban myth, Slender Man. It started life in an online competition to Photoshop pictures but to include a supernatural element. One particular entrant to the competition added a suited, faceless, unnaturally tall figure into two black and white photos which were copied and distributed virally over the net. Since then, millions of authors, mostly online, have shared and spread the story on websites such as Creepypasta. The Slender Man's speciality is to abduct people, often children who seem to willingly go with the figure never to be seen again, making him a terrifying version of the Pied Piper.

- *Rituals*. A ritual is a set of symbolic behaviours that occur in a fixed sequence. For example, weddings follow a fairly well-defined path in most cases, and there are many rituals attached to sporting events such as football matches. The singing of specific songs, the consumption of specific foods or beverages (few football fans would watch the match while drinking a glass of Chardonnay wine – beer is the ritual drink) and the wearing of specific clothing are all ritualistic. Many people have grooming rituals (brushing one's hair numerous times each day, showering to a specific pattern, and so forth) which serve to transform the individual from the private persona to the public persona. Gift-giving is another example of a ritual – in most Western cultures, gifts should be wrapped in attractive paper and should contain an element of surprise, the price tag should be removed and the recipient has to look pleased to receive the gift. Deviation from this ritual causes discomfort for one or the other party to the transaction. In China, on the other hand, giving a gift imposes an obligation on the recipient to do the other person a favour at some time or to reciprocate; over-effusive thanks for a gift can be interpreted as an attempt to avoid this obligation.

- *Rites of passage*. A rite of passage is an event or a set of behaviours that moves an individual from one state to another. The Freshers Ball at university is an example, as is the traditional 21st birthday party, which of course relates to the time when 21-year-olds were regarded as full adults. This has been diluted somewhat by changes in legislation, which now confers full responsibilities and rights at different stages during an individual's teenage years. In Japan, where the **age of majority** is 20, there is a special public holiday dedicated to those who will reach age 20 during that year. Some rites of passage are more individual in nature: marriage ceremonies or divorce proceedings are rites of passage between the single and married states, but may occur at almost any stage in the individual's adult life, or may not occur at all. Rites of passage are important to people as statements of status, and new rites are invented periodically to take account of new situations: legislation in the UK now allows marriages between couples of the same sex, and at a more mundane level there are definite rituals that are observed when someone changes job.

Age of majority
The threshold of adulthood as it is conceptualised (and recognised or declared) in law

- *Sacred consumption*. Some places are set apart as special because something of great significance happened there. In some cases these places have mystical or religious significance, for example Stonehenge, Persepolis or Machu Picchu, while in other cases the place might have no religious significance as such but acquires sacred qualities. A prime example is the Millennium Stadium in Cardiff, UK. The actual pitch is often referred to as 'the hallowed turf' and there have been numerous attempts (some successful) to scatter the ashes of deceased Welsh rugby fans on the pitch.

These elements of culture are common to all cultures, but vary in type and importance between cultures. For some cultures, religion is almost the defining factor: Islamic states that operate under Sharia law as laid down in the Koran, and countries such as Spain where fiestas, public holidays and many aspects of daily life are conducted with reference to the Catholic church, are prime examples. For other cultures, other aspects may contribute more.

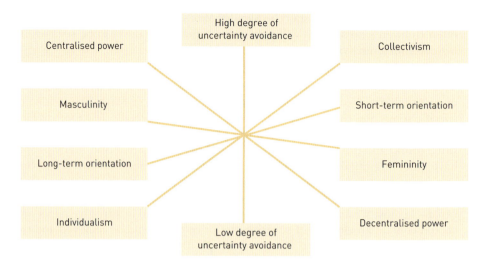

FIGURE 13.3 Dimensions of culture

To an extent, national characteristics can be identified. The most famous (and widely taught) study of national characteristics is that of Hofstede (1980). This research reported on a study of 6,000 respondents in 66 countries, all of whom worked for IBM. Hofstede initially identified four cultural dimensions, as follows:

1. *Individualism vs. collectivism.* This is the degree to which the culture values individualism and individual freedom above that of the group.

2. *Uncertainty avoidance.* This is the degree to which the culture adheres to rules and customs to avoid risk.

3. *Power distance.* This is the degree to which power is centralised in the culture.

4. *Masculinity–femininity.* This is the degree to which the culture exhibits 'masculine' qualities of assertiveness, achievement and wealth acquisition rather than the 'feminine' attributes of nurturing, concern for the environment and concern for the poor.

Hofstede later revisited the data and the problem, and came up with a fifth dimension. This is long-term versus short-term orientation, and is a dimension that is particularly relevant to cultures where perspectives of 'time' are very different (for example China) from that experienced in, say, the UK.

These categorisations, summarised in Figure 13.3, are interesting, and may be useful for planning the overall tone of a communications campaign, but it would be dangerous to make assumptions about individuals based on these broad generalisations. The average Taiwanese may be more collectivist than the average American, but the most individualistic Taiwanese is likely to be a great deal more individualistic than the most collectivist American.

Hofstede's research has been widely criticised for several reasons. First, the research was conducted with IBM employees, and since IBM has a strong corporate culture it seems likely that this will have affected the results. Second, Hofstede was concerned mainly with work-related values rather than with consumer behaviour, yet the research has often been used to justify marketing communication activities. Third, the actual survey was conducted in the late 1960s, around 50 years ago, and the world has become considerably more globalised since then – recent research shows that the opening up of China has resulted in markedly changed attitudes to, for example, cosmetic surgery, formerly the prerogative of Western societies (Lindridge and Wang 2008). Even then, though, the same research showed that participants were encouraged to undergo plastic surgery because of the interplay of traditional Chinese hierarchies of family and society.

CHALLENGING THE STATUS QUO

Hofstede might be getting a critical hammering these days, but there is little doubt that different cultures do generate different behaviours and attitudes – that's sort of the point! So why can't we identify and classify these differences? Is it a fear of being politically incorrect? Or is it just that these differences are notoriously difficult to pin down? And what about our new 'online' cultural presence – has that developed organically or has it also been the subject of manipulation by marketers?

Although we have far greater technical capabilities now than Hofstede did 50 years ago, maybe it's just that we are daunted by the prospect of carrying out a research project on an even bigger scale, for fear of what we may uncover?

APPROACHES TO STUDYING CULTURE

There are three main approaches to studying culture, which are as follows:

1. *Taxonomies of culture*. This involves dividing cultures into different levels and/ or into high-context or low-context cultures (see Figure 13.4).

2. *Lifestyle analysis*. This involves examining the way people live within the culture and looking for commonalities.

3. *Identification of cultural universals*. These are aspects of culture found in all societies. For example, all cultures use some form of bodily adornment (tattooing, cosmetics, jewellery, clothing, etc.). All cultures have sexual taboos (who is 'permissible' for sexual activity and who is not, and even what sexual practices are acceptable), all cultures have gift-giving rituals and all cultures have differences in status between members.

High-context cultures are those in which norms of behaviour and values are deeply embedded in the members of the culture, and thus do not need to be explained in any specific way (Hofstede 1980). Members communicate easily, because they share the same basic beliefs and reference points – there is no need to explain, so people can communicate non-verbally relatively easily. Characteristics of high-context cultures are as follows:

- Communication is rapid and efficient within the group, but rapidly breaks down with outsiders because the group members find it harder to explain matters that they think of as obvious.

- Behaviour within the group is stable and predictable.

FIGURE 13.4 High-context vs. low-context cultures

- The nature of the group is such that outsiders are likely to stereotype the group, as the only way they have of understanding the culture.

- All parties within the group share much the same perceptual field.

High-context cultures are therefore totalitarian, orthodox and conservative. There is little room for personal expression or change, but each member has a clear (and perhaps reassuring) understanding of their role and responsibilities as well as what they can expect from the other members of the culture. Rigidity gives a degree of security in a high-context culture.

Low-context cultures are much less rigid, but require more effort of their members. They have the following features:

- They are individualistic rather than collectivistic.

- Members communicate using clearly coded messages.

- Members' values, attitudes, perceptions and patterns of behaviour are diverse and liable to change quickly.

The United States and most of Western Europe have low-context cultures, because of mass migrations and world travel, which have combined to expose the members of the cultures to many diverse cultural influences. Countries such as Japan, which have relatively few foreigners living in them, tend to have high-context cultures.

Ethnocentrism

The belief that one's own culture is 'correct' and other cultures are derived from it

The degree to which people are ethnocentric affects behaviour as well. **Ethnocentrism** is the belief that one's own culture is the 'right' one, and others are mere copies. It has been shown that ethnocentric people are much more likely to be loyal to products from their own countries; by the same token, people who are culturally sensitive (i.e. understand and respect other cultures) are more open to buying imported products (Lu Hsu and Han-Peng 2008; Nguyen et al. 2008). If the local identity is more accessible than the global one, local products will be preferred (and vice versa). In other words, the easier it is to understand and access local products, the more likely they will be preferred over global ones (Zhang and Khare 2009).

CONSUMER CULTURE

Consumer Culture Theory (CCT) and its proponents cannot be defined easily. There are a number of theoretical perspectives of 'culture' which, when combined as a group, start to investigate how consumers interact with the markets that they find themselves in. Researchers are interested in this heterogeneous set of representations and shared values. However, Zaltman (2003) notes that consumer cultures develop as a result of appeals to our emotions, and are often unaware of the influence that our unconscious has on our thinking. This is so much so that apparently only about 5% of our thinking (cognition) is of a higher-order consciousness and the vast majority happens beneath our levels of awareness (Zaltman 2003). Arnould and Thompson (2005) noted that consumer culture represents a 'social arrangement in which the relations between lived culture and social resources and between meaningful ways of life and the symbolic and material resources on which they depend are mediated through markets'. Thus consumption, apart from being a somewhat central social phenomenon, is very much linked to motivation, and in a wider sense, the consumption of culture itself. So for researchers, there is a very strong element of needing to understand the entire cycle that surrounds consumption, from acquiring an item, through possessing it, to consumption and finally to disposition. We need to understand the dynamics which are driving these consumption cycles in order to be able to theorise about them.

Going back to the seminal article by Arnould and Thompson (2005), which really put CCT on the academic map, we see that they had suggested four distinct areas which could contribute to theory building.

1. *Socio-historic pattern of consumption.* The institutional and structural forces that shape people's consumption patterns. For instance, class (which we'll look at a little later in this chapter), a person's gender, or maybe even the effects of their ethnicity on consumption behaviour.

2. *Consumer identity.* This is all about the individual and how she or he shapes their self-identity using market-related resources, and how these vary from person to person depending on where they are in the world.

3. *Marketplace cultures.* How the relationship between the marketplace itself and the consumers develops networks and cultural communities. In the world with which we are familiar, this manifests itself in what we know as subcultures (for instance, communities of practice, brand communities, etc.).

4. *Consumers' interpretive strategies.* How consumers receive messages (verbal and non-verbal) and then how they are reinterpreted to consume resources in their own lives.

The cult of consumerism identified in Chapter 6 has an effect on the wider culture in which it sits. It can be considered as a subculture: people who consume particular brands can be defined by the brand (for example, people who enjoy the TV series *Star Trek* sometimes define themselves as Trekkies, and people who have been swiped 'right' by others using the dating app Tinder are known as Tinderites, according to the online *Urban Dictionary* (2015).

Problems with consumer culture have been identified, however. First, consumer (marketplace) culture tends to erode national cultures because the culture associated

Ethnicity
The cultural background of the individual

Tinderite
A male or female 'date' which has been swiped right on the Tinder app

with specific brands becomes more important than the 'naturally occurring' cultural identity of the individual. For example, there is strong evidence for a worldwide 'youth' culture based on consumption of music (via MTV and others) and fashion items. This culture means that young people worldwide tend to wear similar clothing and listen to similar music rather than wearing the clothing typical of their countries and listening to traditional music. Second, consumer culture creates superficial social interactions and encourages people to be competitive rather than cooperative. Third, consumerism is regarded as bad for the environment because it encourages excessive use of natural resources (see Chapter 14).

These criticisms do not in fact stand up very well (Miller 1995), since people do still take pleasure in individual narcissistic tendencies (Lambert et al. 2014) and in retaining the traditions of their own region and family background (Sethna 2015). The criticisms do indicate, however, that the consumer society is not necessarily an unmitigated force for good in the world. No doubt debate will continue on this topic.

CONSUMER BEHAVIOUR IN ACTION: GIFT-GIVING BEHAVIOUR

Everybody likes getting a gift – but human beings seem to like giving gifts as well. Every human culture contains some kind of gift-giving behaviour, from small gifts to oil the wheels of our working lives to major gifts to family and friends on special occasions. We give gifts as a way of apologising, as a symbol of respect, as a 'thank you' or because we feel obligated to by social conventions. Gift-giving can also be seen from the perspective of a professional services firm offering *pro bono* services (McColl-Kennedy et al. 2015).

Although gift-giving is common to all cultures, the connotations of some gifts can be different in different cultures. For

©iStock.com/ozgurdonmaz

Pro bono

Latin phrase for professional work undertaken voluntarily and without payment as a public service

example, in China it is common practice for someone to give a small gift to a superior, or someone in power. The gift is not intended to influence the person especially, although it is intended as an ice-breaker; if the superior then makes a decision that goes against the gift-giver, there would not be any special feeling of resentment. However, to a Westerner these gifts look suspiciously like bribes. In the West, one might offer a gift after the business has been concluded, but even this is fraught with social risks: one does not tip one's superiors. In Western cultures, it is more likely that the gifts would come from the superior to the subordinate, not the other way round.

(Bribery is, of course, a horse of a different colour. A bribe is a gift given on the explicit understanding that some advantage will be conferred on the donor as a direct result. This also happens in China, but the rules are different and the outcomes are also different. This is a business transaction rather than a true gift.)

In many Western cultures, the period around Christmas is the main time of year for exchanging gifts. Typically, people aim to spend about the same amount on each other (so as to avoid embarrassment) and sometimes even agree an approximate figure beforehand. For small children, parents maintain that the gifts do not in fact come from the parents at all, but from Santa Claus (also known as Papa Noel, Père Nöel, Kris Kringle, Sinter Klaas, Babbo Natale, Joulupukki, and many other names). The gifts are supposed to be a surprise, although among adults people often ask each other what would be a suitable present. Recipients of the gifts have to look surprised and pleased as they open the gifts on Christmas Day (for the UK and USA, or at Epiphany, or on Christmas Eve, or whatever date is appropriate to the local culture), even if they knew in advance what the gift was, or (worse) if it is something they do not want. All this is regarded as normal, polite behaviour.

A study by Joel Waldfogel (1993) showed that the giving of gifts at Christmas destroyed anything up to 30% of the monetary value of the gift. This was because the recipient of the gift frequently ascribed a cash value to it well below the actual price paid by the donor. What Waldfogel's research did not take into account is all the social aspects of the gift itself – the choosing, the wrapping, the performance rituals attached to the actual exchange of presents. For most people, it seems that these are far more important than the actual gift itself.

SUBCULTURES

Subcultures are distinctive groups of people within a society who share common cultural meanings, behaviours and environmental factors. Although a subculture shares most of the mainstream culture within which it is embedded, its members have a distinct and identifiable set of behavioural norms, customs, scripts, and so forth which distinguish them from the rest of the culture. In some cases, the subculture requires members to buy specific items, and members will often not buy items from outside the subculture (Richardson and Turley 2006; Bush et al. 2015; O'Connor and Portzky 2015).

Subcultures could be based on age or gender type (see Chapter 12), ethnic background or special interests. For example, Goth culture is distinct from mainstream UK culture, but has a distinct set of behaviours and beliefs (O'Connor and Portzky 2015). Likewise, second-generation immigrant populations often develop subcultures that are combinations of the new country's culture and elements from the parents' home country culture. Bicultural consumers often switch between the two cultures and make different judgements depending on which cultural context they happen to be 'switched' to at the time (Chattaraman et al. 2010).

Some subcultures are defined by the ways they interpret messages: these are called interpretive communities (Kates 2002). For example, a subculture of conspiracy theorists would tend to interpret all official statements as evidence of a cover-up. An anti-globalisation interpretive community would respond with deep suspicion or even hostility to any marketing messages, which makes marketing to such communities difficult; however, they are still consumers.

FIGURE 13.5 Culture and subculture

In Figure 13.5 the main culture's beliefs are shared by the subcultures but each subculture has beliefs and behaviours that lie outside the mainstream. Often the behaviours associated with the subculture can create problems for its members as members of the mainstream culture see them as outsiders or rebels, and therefore a threat to the mainstream.

GEOGRAPHIC SUBCULTURES

Geographic subcultures can be very significant for marketers. Most countries have geographic subcultures: Friesland in the Netherlands has a distinct language and traditions, Bavarians regard themselves as culturally different from the neighbouring 'Prussians' (and often feel closer to their Austrian neighbours in Salzburg than they do to their fellow Germans in Stuttgart). In the UK, Wales and Scotland regard themselves as separate countries, and have different food, language and customs from those of England, and Ulster (Northern Ireland) has a different culture from both the UK of which it is legally a part, and Ireland of which it is historically and physically a part. The significance for marketers lies in the possibilities for causing offence – for a Welshman, Wales is not, and never has been, part of England. There is also a positive significance in terms of recognising the differences between the subcultures, perhaps by referring to local events or using local dialects in advertising. For example, some major supermarkets in the UK offer locally sourced products in their stores and have signage in a dual language (for instance stores in Wales show signage in both Welsh and English).

ETHNIC SUBCULTURES

The transient nature of populations mean that cultural identities move with people. Ethnic subcultures are a growing group not just within Europe but globally also. The populist definition of ethnicity is that of Bulmer (1996):

> *An ethnic group is a collectivity within a larger population having real or putative common ancestry, memories of a shared past, and a cultural focus upon one or more symbolic elements which define the group's identity, such as kinship, religion, language, shared territory, nationality or physical appearance. Members of an ethnic group are conscious of belonging to an ethnic group.*

CONSUMER BEHAVIOUR IN ACTION: THE AGE SUBCULTURE

Apparently many older people are not ready for the rocking-chair and daytime TV just yet. We see plenty of people in their fifties, sixties and even seventies joining the gym, taking flying lessons, canoeing up the Amazon and generally behaving like teenagers. Therein lies a clue about the perspective that our societal culture holds about older people; the physical attractiveness might have disappeared, and they are no longer either literally or metaphorically 'sexy'. Yet, over the past 20 years we have seen rising divorce rates resulting in many more older people using dating services and engaging in activity (nightclubs, singles holidays, etc.) which are stereotypically seen as the domain of young people. Our culture (the media, press, general society) is fixated with 'youth culture'. Most adverts, TV shows and films are populated with healthy-looking, fresh-faced young characters, as opposed to older people. Does that mean that our culture values these young people with their sexual attractiveness more than older people? Is old always going to be seen in a negative light; in the same way as one would perceive something useless perhaps?

©iStock.com/Srabin

Who is to say that a 60-year-old cannot or should not be going out dancing, or that a 70-year-old should not be trekking to Machu Pichu, or even that we should not be sky-diving at 80? Perhaps there is no such thing as an age-related product. Perhaps we should ignore age altogether in our planning, yet marketers have only recently started to understand the vast differences that exist in this supposedly homogenous group of people who are all labelled as 'old'. A 55-year-old is very different from an 85-year-old in attitudes and consumption patterns

Of course physically, older people are not going to be as fit as they were when they were young, and mentally things begin to deteriorate as well – greater experience might be a fine thing, but when you can't remember what you came upstairs for, experience may not help a lot. That is a very different life stage from those who are fit, active, financially buoyant and wanting to live life.

So perhaps there will still be a few things we can sell specifically to older people – if only we can get them off the windsurfer.

This said, ethnic marketing is much more advanced in the United States, probably because the US is composed of a wide variety of cultures, whereas within Europe ethnic minorities (or the national minority population as it's known) accounts for less than 15% of the 770 million people who inhabit the continent. These groups are growing as migration continues, and tend to fall into two main groups: those who have emigrated from their country of origin, and are therefore perhaps best considered as members of their home-country culture, and those whose parents came from another country but who were born in the host country. The latter group often develops a distinct culture which is part way between their parents' national culture and the culture of the host country. Ethnicity is measured in the UK Census and other official data sets (for instance the UK's Labour Force Survey) by asking individuals to select among categories that may include nationality (Chinese, Indian, Irish), broader geographic or ancestral categories (African, Asian, Arab), colour (e.g. White, Black), and combinations of these ('White Irish', 'White British'), including explicitly 'mixed' categories ('White and Black Caribbean') (Afkhami 2012). In the UK, the British government includes a question about religious affiliation, since for many people religion is one of the most important defining characteristics of their identity. When such questions are asked in conjunction with those about 'ethnic grouping', they can complement each other and allow for a more distinct picture of a population. Research conducted in Canada, for example, showed that Muslim women used the *hijab* (the face-covering material used by some Muslim women) as a way of indicating that they are traditional and therefore religiously *respectable* when using an online dating service (Zwick and Chelariu 2006). This is a distinct move away from the cultural origins of the *hijab* in the Middle East, showing a willingness to comply with religious norms of conduct rather than a genuine belief in those norms.

The UK's 2011 Census provided some interesting facts about religious effects on culture in the UK. See Table 13.1 below.

TABLE 13.1 Key points about religion in the UK (taken from the UK Census 2011)

1	In 2011, Christianity had the oldest age profile of the main religious groups
2	The number of Christians has fallen and this was largely for people aged under 60
3	The number of people with no religion has increased across all age groups, particularly for those aged 20 to 24 and 40 to 44
4	In England and Wales, over nine in ten Christians (93%) were White and nine in ten (89%) were born in the UK, though the numbers have fallen since 2001
5	Nearly four in ten Muslims (38%) reported their ethnicity as Pakistani, a 371,000 increase (from 658,000 to over a million) since 2001. Nearly half of all Muslims were born in the UK
6	The majority of people with no religion were White (93%) and born in the UK (93%) and these groups have increased since 2001
7	People with no religion had the highest proportion of people who were economically active, Christians and Muslims the lowest. Jewish people had the highest level of employment and Muslim people the highest level of unemployment
8	The main reason for Christians being economically inactive was retirement, for Muslims economic inactivity was mainly because they were students, or because they were looking after the home or family

There is a final point to be made about the religious category in the census. As in 2001, the 2011 census contained a 'write-in' question where respondents had identified themselves as belonging to 'other religions'. Apart from some obviously expected entries such as Zoroastrianism, Spiritualist, Taoist, etc., there were some rather intriguing entries also. Apparently we have among us people who are firm believers of Satanism, Shamanism, Scientology and over 176,000 adherents of the Jedi religion!

Clearly these groups have specific purchasing behaviour: specific foods to meet religious restrictions or personal tastes, non-Christian greetings cards, clothing, cooking utensils, products from the country of origin, and occasionally *Star Wars* memorabilia. In 2013, a do-it-yourself enthusiast even built a working prototype of a Jedi lightsaber and posted various videos on YouTube showing the invention cutting through paper, tape, cardboard and even melting a ping-pong ball. Thankfully, legislation in most countries prevents the sale of such devices.

On the other hand, most immigrants are happy to embrace at least some aspects of the host country culture, and in some cases deliberately seek out local products as a way of expressing a desire to integrate (Bann 1996). Equally, migrant groups sometimes identify themselves around cultural factors from the country of origin – religion is especially powerful in this context. It has been shown that Sikhs in Britain use conspicuous consumption of their religion to establish their identity, while Muslims tend to reject Western cultural values of consumption while embracing British liberalism (Lindridge 2009).

How these groups should be addressed by marketers is a matter for considerable thought. At present, advertising largely ignores ethnic minorities, and attempts to include minorities (or advertise directly to them) have sometimes been interpreted as patronising or even offensive (Sudbury and Wilberforce 2006). Part of the difficulty here is that what some people regard as offensive can be regarded as totally acceptable by others: the UK Advertising Standards Authority, which responds to examples of offensive advertising, will take action even if a relatively small number of people complain. This may cause advertisers to avoid the issue by not including ethnic minorities in their advertising at all.

A SCHEMA FOR CULTURAL CLASSIFICATION OF ETHNIC MINORITIES

Many academic commentators have written about identity (Erikson 1968; Goodson and Cole 1994; McCormick and Pressley 1997). They have all recognised the two defined parts of the person's identity – the personal and the professional – of which the latter's development depends very much upon the entrepreneur's interaction with the wider environment (Weinberger and Shefi 2012), the context within which it takes place (Gee 2001) and also takes into account the period of time over which it takes place (Connelly and Clandinin 1999). This all supports the idea that identities are a complex and ever-changing entity, which Beijaard et al. (2004) noted is in a state of flux, change and evolution through the life cycle.

For instance, understanding ethnic entrepreneurship (Low and MacMillan 1988) and ethno-cultural values is a necessary step to understanding ethnic minority markets and the driving forces behind ethnic entrepreneurial activity in those markets (Chen and Tan 2009; Drori et al. 2009; Down 2010). However, it has recently been noted by Bjorn Bjerke and Claes Hultman (2013) that 'existing ... research ... excludes, for instance, female entrepreneurs and ethnic minorities and what is referred to as the cultural sector'. Consequently, there is a need to provide a schema for identifying ethnic subcultures as a result of ethnic immigration into Britain (Bagwell 2008; McPherson 2008; Panayiotopoulos 2008; Rusinovic 2008) and the 'theory of acculturation' does exactly this (Faber and O'Guinn 1987; Penloza 1989; Cabassa 2003). The degree to which individuals from ethnic minorities differ in their behaviour from the rest of society depends largely on their degree of acculturation. For marketers, consumer acculturation is clearly of more interest: this refers to the process of becoming a skilled consumer in a different culture or subculture (Penloza 1989).

Acculturation

The process of adopting a new culture

Acculturation measures the social, physical and psychological exchanges between individuals from different cultures when there is continuous contact (Ryder et al. 2000). However, the literature poses two versions of this theory. It is described by Khairulla et al. (1996) as 'a process in which ethnic consumers move along a theoretic continuum from low acculturation, where they maintain the cultural values of their ethnic origin, to the other extreme, high acculturation, where they have adopted the cultural values of the dominant culture' (Khairulla et al., 1996). This theory proposes a single continuum which conceptualises a one-dimensional construct (Gordon 1995). This is of great interest to a marketer using this as a segmentation tool because of the depth to which it has the potential to change a person's buying preferences and patterns, and consequently consumption behaviour and attitudes towards the local media (O'Guinn and Faber 1986). However, a number of scholars (Teske and Nelson 1974; Marín and Gamba 1996; Berry 1997; Ryder et al. 2000) have argued that both the adherence to the practices of the host culture as well as maintenance of the original culture should be investigated as independent dimensions, hence bi-directional and reciprocal.

These two perspectives have contributed to the sociological (Brubaker 2001), social psychological (Lambert 1967; Rudmin 2003, 2009; Rudmin and Ahmadzadeh 2001) and anthropological literature (De Vos 1995). Ward (2001) coined the term 'ABCs of acculturation', as it involves 'Affective, Behavioural and Cognitive' changes. As regards ethnic entrepreneurs and the application of the theory of acculturation, De Vos (1995, in Rudmin 2009) argued that 'ethnicity is essentially subjective and symbolic, and that ethnic identity is in competition with other identities depending on the contextual and temporal focus of the individual'. Segal and Sosa (1983) had, 20 years previously, illustrated through their Acculturation Influence Group (AIG) model that ethnic minority groups could be identified and understood much more coherently if the degree of acculturation was ascertained. Based on this work by Segal and Sosa (1983), Nwankwo and Lindridge (1998) devised a framework with four broad classifications for 'identifying levels of acculturation and possible variations even within a subculture' of the ethnic entrepreneur (See Table 13.2 below). They clarified that their framework is based on 'exposure and adaptation to the dominant Caucasian culture', as opposed to age. Furthermore, their hypothesis was that an Indian entrepreneur who 'has lived in Britain all his/her life is likely to display a higher level of acculturation to the Caucasian culture than one who has only recently arrived'.

In sum, even with the tools as described above, there are various limitations of acculturation, not least of all the difficulty with 'defining and operationalizing culture' (Sam and Berry 2006).

TABLE 13.2 Acculturation framework for ethnic entrepreneurs

Cluster 1: least acculturated:

- more at ease with items closely related to their own culture
- tend to live in close-knit family groups and ethnic dwelling areas
- low income and blue collar workers
- very limited knowledge of the host country language
- do not accept the dominant culture as relevant to their lifestyle
- are not motivated to adjust to their new environment
- behaviour heavily influenced by native culture
- poorly educated (based on Western style education systems)
- dress mainly in their ethnic clothes

Cluster 2: moderately acculturated:

- have a working knowledge of the host country language
- prefer to speak in their native language
- behavioural patterns are predominantly influenced by their subculture's values
- combine some characteristics of clusters 1 and 3

Cluster 3: most acculturated:

- fluent in both the host country's language and their native tongue
- at ease in a predominantly host-country environment
- live in areas not predominantly ethnic oriented
- their behavioural patterns are largely driven by the dominant culture
- have some pride in their ethnic background

Cluster 4: totally acculturated:

- fluent only in the host country language
- have little knowledge of their ethnic culture
- likely to be born in the host country
- view themselves as members of the host culture and have patriotic feelings towards the host country only
- ignorant and not motivated to understand their own ethnic background

Source: adapted from Nwankwo and Lindridge (1998)

Adapted from Nwankwo, S., and Lindridge, A., (1998) Marketing to Ethnic Minorities in Britain, Journal of Marketing Practice: Applied Marketing Science, v4 n7 p200–216. Reused by permission.

The degree to which someone can adapt to the new culture will depend on the level of cultural interpenetration he or she experiences. The more the individual interacts socially with members of the host culture, the more he or she is able to adapt. This does not necessarily mean giving up one's original cultural norms and beliefs; it does mean understanding and being sympathetic to the cultural norms and beliefs of the host culture (Andreasen 1990). In some cases, migrant populations use consumption as a way of integrating with the host country – buying a locally made car, eating local food, moving out of immigrant neighbourhoods and buying a house in an area populated by the host society, and so forth (Hughes 2010). This partial **adoption** of the host culture helps migrants to feel part of their new society.

Another way of looking at acculturation is using Oberg's (1960) somewhat sequential four stage model:

1. *Honeymoon stage.* The individual is fascinated by the culture or subculture, but because interpenetration is shallow and superficial, there is very little acculturation.

Adoption

The process of building an innovating product into one's daily life

The honeymoon stage is typical of tourists travelling in another country: on their return from holiday, they may feel a desire to go and live in the country, having only seen the positive aspects of life there.

2. *Rejection stage.* After further cultural interpenetration, the individual realises that previous cultural norms are not adequate for dealing with the new culture, and that new norms and behaviours will need to be adopted. Often people become hostile to the new culture at this point, seeing the drawbacks rather than the advantages. Cultural conflicts are at a maximum in this stage.

3. *Tolerance stage.* Here the interactions have increased to the point where the individual accepts the new culture with all its drawbacks. This stage is reached by a process of cultural interpenetration, learning more about the new culture and reducing the level of cultural conflict.

4. *Integration stage.* At this stage the individual has made the necessary adjustments, valuing the new culture for its good qualities while still retaining important elements of the old culture. The new culture is seen as a perfectly viable way of life, as valid in its own way as the old culture.

In Figure 13.6, the individual's initial degree of happiness with the new culture is high in the honeymoon stage, as is motivation to learn about the culture: actual knowledge of the culture (and therefore ability to function well within it) is low. At the rejection stage, satisfaction with the culture drops dramatically, as does motivation to learn, but ability to function is still rising. With the tolerance stage comes a renewed interest in the culture, and also greater satisfaction with it. Finally, in the integration stage the individual is functioning well, knows about the culture and is consequently much happier within the culture. The initial disappointment at the rejection stage may account in part for the fact that the majority of immigrants return home within a few years. Interestingly, according to Vignola (2015) the migration processes that Europe is learning to handle due to the Syrian conflict are just 'economic liberalization of borders and their security arrangements'.

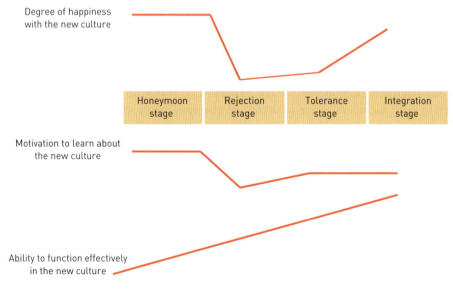

FIGURE 13.6 Stages in acculturation

Recent research by Williams (2015) has indicated the existence of cultural fractures caused by crossing borders (Davies and Fitchett 2004). These are as follows:

- **Emotional fracture**. This can lead to feelings of loneliness and lack of a support infrastructure from friends and family left behind, or could be characterised by a willingness and ability to make new friends in the new country.

- **Symbolic fracture**. This is characterised by running out of things to say in everyday conversation, not knowing what are the appropriate greetings for different people, and a difficulty in 'reading the signs' to understand what people are thinking or feeling. There is also a difficulty in understanding how people socialise in the new country.

- **Functional fracture**. This is about the ease or difficulty of carrying out functional tasks such as opening a bank account, using trains and buses, or buying and preparing food.

- **Culture shock**. This is how life in the new country differs from expectations.

- **Consumer behaviour**. This is the gap between what one would buy at home and what one buys in the new country.

- **Demographic fracture**. This is the disparity between the socio-economic structure one was part of in the old culture, and the socio-economic structure in which one finds oneself in the new culture. Sometimes immigrants move down the social scale, sometimes up, depending on the relationship between the host country and the old country.

CLASS

Some sociologists regard class as being one of the central concepts of the discipline, yet it is an ill-defined and ambiguous concept. For non-sociologists the concept of class is beginning to seem outmoded: at the beginning of the 20th century, around 75% of people in industrialised countries were manual workers of one sort or another, quite clearly distinct in behaviour and wealth from the better-educated white-collar workers and, of course, the aristocracy. As machines have largely taken over from muscle power, education has become universal, the services sector dominates, and differential taxation has eroded differences of wealth – the differences between 'working class' and 'middle class' are almost undetectable. Even aristocrats now work for a living.

According to Nightingale (2012) cited in Marcinczak et al. (2015), using socio-economic status as a tool to sort residents 'is as old as history of urbanisation'. In the 1911 Census in the UK, the government decided to record socio-economic groupings for the first time. The system used is shown in Table 13.3.

This system of classification worked fairly well for several decades, but shifts in social patterns made much of its assumptions irrelevant: Table 13.3 assumes that incomes are lower further down the scale, but in the 21st century plumbers earn more than doctors (at least in much of Western Europe) and changing patterns of working life mean that today's labourer is tomorrow's film star, and film stars become politicians (notable examples include Ronald Reagan, Arnold Schwarzenegger and Glenda Jackson). The basic lifestyles and indeed standards of living do not vary greatly between the groups – Group D individuals probably still own cars and have foreign holidays,

Emotional fracture

The sense of loss of emotional support encountered when moving from one culture to another

Symbolic fracture

The disparity between old and new communication paradigms encountered when moving from one culture to another

Functional fracture

The disparity between old and new systems for daily living encountered when moving from one culture to another

Culture shock

The discomfort that arises from being displaced from one's normal cultural milieu

Consumer behaviour

Activities undertaken by people in the process of obtaining, using and disposing of goods and services for personal use

Demographic fracture

The disparity between old and new socio-economic structures, encountered when moving from one culture to another

Aristocracy

The highest class in certain societies, typically comprising people of noble birth holding hereditary titles and offices

TABLE 13.3 UK socio-economic groupings

Social grade	Social status	Head of household's occupation
A	Upper middle class	Higher managerial, administration or professional
B	Middle class	Intermediate managerial, administrative or professional
C1	Lower middle class	Supervisory or clerical, junior managerial, administrative or professional
C2	Skilled working class	Skilled manual workers
D	Working class	Semi-skilled and unskilled manual workers
E	Lowest level of subsistence	Unemployed, casual or lowest-grade workers, state pensioners

TABLE 13.4 The Socio-Economic Classification System

1	Higher managerial and professional occupations 1.1 Large employers and higher managerial occupations 1.2 Higher professional occupations
2	Lower managerial and professional occupations
3	Intermediate occupations
4	Small employers and own account workers
5	Lower supervisory and technical occupations
6	Semi-routine occupations
7	Routine occupations
8	Never worked and long-term unemployed

even if Group A individuals run bigger cars and go to more exotic destinations. The classification, sometimes known as the ABC classification, is still used in a great deal of published market research. Partly this is because it is familiar to researchers, and partly it is because researchers sometimes need to make comparisons with previous studies, but it is well known that the system is seriously flawed.

In 2001 the UK government introduced an alternative classification method – the Socio-Economic Classification System. This classification system has eight categories, the first of which can be subdivided. There is a ninth category, 'Not classified', which is reserved for students and people whose occupations have not been adequately described. The categories are shown in Table 13.4.

Although this classification system is a better reflection of 21st century society, it still suffers from a number of weaknesses common to all such classification systems. First, it does not take account of the possibility of rapid social movement: someone might change occupations very rapidly, without (presumably) changing lifestyle very much. Equally someone might change lifestyle rapidly without officially changing occupation – a teacher who decides to leave an inner-city school for a less stressful

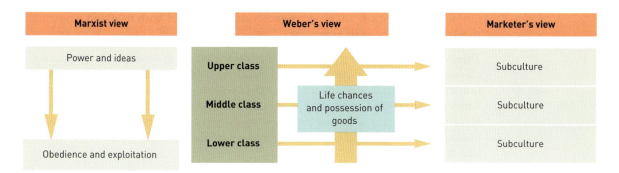

FIGURE 13.7 Studying social class

life in the country would be an example. Third, the classification usually refers to the head of the household, which might have been a reasonable concept in 1911 but which has many possible interpretations now. In 1911, the head of the household would almost certainly have been the father of the family, the main (and probably only) earner. In 2016, several people in the household are likely to be earning, and decision-making is likely to be shared in many different ways.

There is, of course, more to social class than occupation. Class implies a position in the power hierarchy: the further up the class ladder an individual is, the more power and influence he or she will have. This can vary from the small powers and discretions exercised by a warehouse manager up to the hire-and-fire decisions made by a managing director. Early sociologists such as Karl Marx and Max Weber examined social class (see Figure 13.7). Marx saw class as being essentially about the power to set the prevailing intellectual climate. He said that 'The ideas of the ruling class are, in every epoch, the ruling ideas, i.e. the class which is the ruling material force of society, is at the same time its ruling intellectual force' (Marx and Engels 1848). Weber defined class in terms of life chances (Weber 1946). For Weber, a class is a group of people who have in common a specific causal component of their life chances which is represented by possession of goods and opportunities for income, and which operates under the conditions of the commodity or labour markets. In other words, the individual's class is determined by the opportunities presented to that individual in terms of earning opportunities and the level of possession of goods.

More recent studies (Loughnan et al. 2014) about people from working-class backgrounds (or the 'poor' as they were referred to by Jahoda 1999) have shown that there is a tendency for views on social class to perceive people of low socio-economic status (SES) in a very dehumanising way. This is often 'regardless of whether people share the same ethnic or racial categories of their more advantaged peers' (Loughnan et al. 2014). This perspective is not restricted to any one geographic region: examples exist for different parts of the world, from the USA to Australia. For instance, the term 'white trash' is used in the USA and denotes low-SES white people in rural environments as violent, coarse, dirty, stupid and sexually unrestrained (Wray 2006; Spencer and Castano 2007). Jones (2011) describes the UK equivalent of this stereotyped urban group (known as 'chavs') as feckless, crude, unintelligent and criminal. In Australia, a similar grouping of suburban people is called the 'bogans' (Nichols 2011). The commonality, according to Loughnan et al.

(2014) is that they are all 'predominantly white, contain both men and women and they are all stereotyped as bestial'.

This of course gives us a glimpse into the many issues that arise with looking at social class as a measure. For instance, Liu et al. (2016) have found that most of the existing literature on social class and its interaction with say, masculinity, is focused on the heterosexual, be that the single male or those in couples, families and marriages. Having said that, the literature investigating the intersection between the lesbian, gay, bisexual and transsexual communities and social class is indeed growing (Whitcomb and Walinsky 2013).

CHALLENGING THE STATUS QUO

Is the world that we live in obsessed with social class and status? Well social class does seem to be a bit problematic. People move up and down the social scale, they find it hard to define their own social class never mind anybody else's, and changes in the structure of society in general mean that we have trouble now identifying classes anyway. Why is it that the good people of Britain insist on identifying which school a 70-year-old man attended in any news story about him? Arise Sir Snobbery x-public and y-grammar school! Why is it that our friends in the USA are greatly allured by fame and fortune?

Is it still realistic to talk about social class at all? Can we really predict someone's behaviour based on how they earn a living? And if we take more factors into account, are we really looking at social class, or are we defining people in different ways? Well, if you use television programmes as a yard-stick or a measure of the idiosyncratic way in which it feeds culture, one can see an embarrassing overabundance of drivel which is reflective of a population. Take for instance the British fascination with using programmes to poke fun at either end of the spectrum, from using the rich in a rather liberal elite way (*Secret Millionaire*, *Posh People: Inside Tatler*, *Made in Chelsea*, *You Can't Get the Staff*) to using the poor as an endless carnival of the impoverished-on-display (*Benefit Street*, *Britain's Hardest Grafter*, *The Briefcase*). This type of reality TV has been referred to as 'poverty porn'. And it doesn't get any better State-side either. The US TV airways are crammed full of continuous adverts for diets, followed by adverts for an inordinate amount of food, followed by comical contraptions on which to exercise, perhaps to ease the conscience from the earlier over-consumption.

In short, given that people in the 21st century are not only individuals but are also extremely individualistic, is social class a concept that still has any relevance?

It would appear that an individual's consumption pattern is as much a determining factor of social class as it is the result of social class. Those individuals who are able to accumulate possessions and improve their opportunities to earn money can move up the social scale, if they choose to do so. For example, a bricklayer would clearly be classified as working class (skilled manual worker). Yet if that same bricklayer saves some capital and sets up his own business, he could eventually become a wealthy property developer or house builder and thus be redefined as middle class or even upper middle class. His basic attitudes and values might change a little during this process, and he would probably still define himself as working class. This type of social mobility has become more common as class barriers break down, and educational opportunities increase.

From the viewpoint of marketers, social class is more a reflection of the existence of a set of subcultures based on the education level, occupational requirements and economic power of the individual members. In this context, marketers use class-related imagery in advertising in order to involve the consumer. Although the old social class distinctions are disappearing, new social classes are emerging and new ways of categorising people have appeared: the basis is still wealth, societal power, social skills, status aspirations, community participation, family history, cultural level, recreational habits, physical appearance and social acceptance (Kroeber-Riel and Weinberg 1996). Social class represents a set of subcultures because the class distinctions are generally agreed upon within the main culture, and the members of each class share most of their meanings and behaviours. The assumption is that people from one social class are less likely to mix socially with people from other social classes, preferring the company of members of their own class (see for example 'consumption patterns of social class' as depicted in programmes such as *Made in Chelsea* or *The Only Way Is Essex*).

Thus social class is measured in two basic ways. People can be asked which social class they belong to (self-assignment), or their social class can be inferred from objective criteria. In market research, the latter approach is much more common, but in most cases respondents are only asked about their income, occupation and education level, which may not be the only determinants of social class. Certainly there is likely to be some discrepancy between a self-assignment and an objective measure in cases where there has been upward social mobility – an individual who comes from a working-class background but who has become educated, professional and wealthy might still self-assign him- or herself to the working-class category.

More useful measures of social class have emerged in recent years, notably geo-demographic measures such as **ACORN** and MOSAIC. These measures work by classifying people according to the area in which they live and which could, in some instances, be a better indicator of social class than income or occupation data. As we have already seen, due to the diversity of the population and social mobility, even these measures are struggling now to reflect the population with any accuracy.

ACORN
A Classification of Residential Neighbourhoods

Overall, social class still has some very limited relevance to marketing activities, but increasing social mobility and a steady reduction in wealth concentration are eroding the old distinctions between classes.

SUMMARY

Consumer behaviour (and indeed all behaviour) happens against a backdrop of cultural and class factors. These vary from place to place and from time to time, and some of these variations are greater than others, but as consumers we have to learn to operate within the culture we inhabit and the perspectives of class that are held by the people around us.

KEY POINTS

- The social environment can be divided into macro- and micro-environments where the macro-environment has three components: culture, subculture and social class.
- Culture provides the social environment within which people live.
- Cultural factors colour all our behaviour, not just our purchasing behaviour.
- Consumer Culture Theory (CCT) starts to investigate how consumers interact with the markets in which they find themselves.
- Subcultures are distinctive groups of people within a society who share common cultural meanings, behaviours and environmental factors.
- Moving from one culture to another is almost always problematic in terms of learning to be a consumer.
- Class now has a very limited relevance to marketing activities, and social mobility continues to erode the old distinctions between classes which were valid 50 years ago.

HOW TO IMPRESS YOUR EXAMINER

Questions about culture will definitely benefit from giving examples of how culture affects purchasing behaviour. You should be very wary of ethnocentrism – the belief that your own culture is the 'right' one – because this will make you sound patronising. You should be able to critique Hofstede's findings as well.

Class is a shifting concept. Questions about class often assume that people remain in a particular class for their entire lives, so it is worthwhile mentioning social mobility and how it has become a *game-changer*.

REVIEW QUESTIONS

1. What are the core components of the social macro-environment?
2. What might be the problems for someone emigrating from a low-context culture to a high-context culture?
3. What might be the problems for someone emigrating from a high-context culture to a low-context culture?
4. What are some of the main constituent elements of culture?
5. How might social class affect consumption behaviour?
6. What special marketing approaches might be useful at traditional gift-giving times?
7. What are the main problems with the ABC system of social classification?
8. What special difficulties might arise for a firm seeking to export products to a high-context culture?
9. What are the main criticisms of Hofstede's work?
10. How should marketers approach marketing to a subculture?

CASE STUDY: CITYFALCON TAPS CROWD-CURATION CULTURE

All investors are forever thinking about one key question: 'When companies that we have invested in start returning financial performance figures which are somewhat disappointing, or the shares we hold suddenly drop in value, what happens?' Of course, at this stage a novice investor would panic. But by then it's too late. One needs to be ahead of the curve in terms of the information one has before any decisions are made to buy more or to sell now ... But where does that information come from? If investors don't have access to expensive subscription services, they'll struggle to understand why the stock dropped. Of course web searches can be done, but can the data from all the sources be trusted, even if it appears to be relevant? Many small investors and traders have been battling with exactly these issues until one of them, a young guy called Ruzbeh Bacha, decided to do something about it.

©iStock.com/Starcevic

Ruzbeh's business idea was very simple and based on an already existing phenomenon called Twitter. Ruzbeh's interest lay in the fact that Twitter has become a major source of breaking news. This news comes from all sorts of sources – from the crowd, from major financial publications and even influential investors.

Trust is a key issue in any financial information source. In 2000, a large agency in the USA was researching information sources, and discovered that the most trusted source of information was financial analysts. However, in 2003 a new category was identified in the survey and termed 'a person like me'. The 'person like me' is a person the investor feels has similar interests and attitudes to themselves. This could be political interests, financial interests, hobbies, social involvement or any one of a number of factors, but the investor identifies them as someone like themselves. In 2003, the same US agency, through their research, noted that about 23% of people would categorise 'a person like me' as being the most trusted source. By 2004, that figure had gone to 51%, and by 2013 the figure moved to a whopping 65%.

This means, essentially, that peer trust drives business. In the same way that sites such as TripAdvisor generate trust through online reviews by actual hotel guests, investor trust can be generate by peer advice.

In 2013, Ruzbeh Bacha started a new company called CityFalcon which is now firmly on the scene ... it's like a Bloomberg for consumers, and provides the next generation of solutions for both investors and traders. Based in London, CityFalcon offers financial news, with Twitter as its exclusive content source. The app makes use of financial 'big data' from Twitter by leveraging Gnip, and then uses the power of Twitter and crowd curation to provide a comprehensive and timely resource for investors

Crowd curation

Sharing a link to content made available by someone else and thus curating an entire web of interest: followers are pointed to something sign-posters think they should pay attention to and traders. Essentially CityFalcon brings the consumer-investor real-time curated news, views and analysis; helps make sense of this information; and provides it in an easy to consume format. The company takes filtering seriously too, in order to decipher what's right for the client and what's not, and so a large part of the offering is to do with personalisation.

In addition, breaking news is obviously transmitted direct to a smartphone so that the viewer can watch the story as it unfolds. Clients can gain information from what is trending. And what's more, it's nurturing an online culture of enabling clients to follow portfolios and not just people.

The service is provided free to the user – the only thing they have to do is to build a 'watch list' of companies and organisations that they are interested in.

QUESTIONS

1. What are the cultural drivers and major motivations of registering with such an organisation?
2. Why is trust such a huge issue, not just in financial markets, but specifically with crowd curation?
3. How significant is this type of cultural change to online consumer behaviour?
4. How would you analyse the functional environment of CityFalcon?
5. In this type of marketplace, where the consumers are developing networks and cultural communities, what subcultures could you see emerging?

FURTHER READING

Consumer Culture Theory, edited by Russell Belk and John Sherry Jr. (Greenwich, CT: JAI Press, 2007) is the outcome of a major conference on consumer culture theory. It contains papers from a wide range of authors, on a wide range of aspects of consumer culture. For some cutting-edge theory it's hard to beat, although it is somewhat academic in its style.

Consumer Behaviour and Culture: Consequences for Global Marketing and Advertising by Marieke de Mooji (Thousand Oaks, CA: Sage, 2003) gets right to the heart of the problem of culture and marketing. Marieke de Mooji makes the point that the theories which come from the United States do not necessarily apply elsewhere in the world – and ethnocentrism is always hovering in the wings ready to trap the unwary.

Multicultural Perspectives in Consumer Behaviour, edited by Maria G. Piacentini and Charles Cui (London: Routledge, 2012) is another edited collection of papers from a wide variety of authors. The book was originally a special edition of the *Journal of Marketing Management*, so it is a rigorous and academic book, with papers from the UK, Greece, Austria, Germany and China.

Consumer Culture and Postmodernism by Mike Featherstone (London: Sage, 2007) locates consumer culture in the context of global climate change, and further displaces the 'West' from centre-stage.

For something a little more out of the ordinary, you might like *Material Culture and Consumer Society: Dependent Colonies in Colonial Australia* by Mark Staniforth (New York: Kluwer, 2003). This is actually a book about underwater archaeology, but the author examines how material goods served to link early colonists to the home country, to distinguish themselves from the indigenous population, to help establish their own social relationships in terms of wealth and position, and to reassure the colonists about their place in the world.

REFERENCES

Afkhami, R. (2012) *Ethnicity: Introductory User Guide*. ESDS Government, January 2012 update.

Andreasen, A.R. (1990) Cultural interpenetration: a critical consumer research issue for the 1990s. In M. E. Goldberg, G. Gorn and R. W. Pollay (eds), *Advances in Consumer Research*, Vol. 17. Provo, UT: Association for Consumer Research, pp. 847–9.

Arnould, E.J. and Thompson, C.J. (2005) Consumer Culture Theory (CCT): twenty years of research. *Journal of Consumer Research*, 31 (March): 868–82.

Bagwell, S. (2008) Transnational family networks and ethnic minority business development: the case of Vietnamese nail-shops in the UK. *International Journal of Entrepreneurial Behavior and Research*, 14 (6): 377–94.

Bann, G. (1996) Race for opportunity. *New Impact Journal*, December 1996/January 1997: 8–9.

Beijaard, D., Meijer, P.C. and Verloop, N. (2004) Reconsidering research on teachers' professional identity. *Teaching and Teacher Education*, 20: 107–28.

Berry, J.W. (1997) Immigration, acculturation and adaptation. *Applied Psychology: An International Review*, 46 (1): 5–33.

Bjerke, B. and Hultman, C.M. (2013) The role of marketing rationale and natural business start-ups. In Z. Sethna, R. Jones and P. Harrigan (eds), *Entrepreneurial Marketing: Global Perspectives*. Bingley: Emerald Publishing, pp. 63–88.

Brubaker, R. (2001) The return to assimilation? Changing perspectives on immigration and its sequels in France, Germany, and the United States. *Ethnic and Racial Studies*, 24: 531–48.

Bulmer, M. (1996) The ethnic group question in the 1991 Census of Population. In D. Coleman and J. Salt (eds), *Ethnicity in the 1991 Census: Demographic Characteristics of the Ethnic Minority Populations*. HMSO: London, pp. 33–62.

Bush, V., Bush, A.J., Oakley, J. and Cicala, J.E. (2015) The sales profession as a subculture: implications for ethical decision making. *Journal of Business Ethics*, 1–17. DOI 10.1007/s10551-015-2753-7.

Cabassa, L.J. (2003) Measuring acculturation: where we are and where we need to go. *Hispanic Journal of Behavioural Sciences*, 25: 127.

Chattaraman, V., Rudd, N.A. and Lennon, S.J. (2010) The malleable bicultural consumer: effects of cultural contexts on aesthetic judgements. *Journal of Consumer Behaviour*, 9 (1): 18–31.

Chen, W. and Tan, J. (2009) Understanding transnational entrepreneurship through a network lens: the theoretical and methodological considerations. *Entrepreneurship Theory and Practice*, 33 (5): 1079–91.

Connelly, F.M. and Clandinin, J. (1999) *Shaping a Professional Identity: Stories of Educational Practice*. New York: Teachers College Press.

Davies, A. and Fitchett, J. (2004) Crossing culture: a multi-method enquiry into consumer behaviour and the experience of cultural transition. *Journal of Consumer Behaviour*, 3 (4): 315–30.

De Vos, G.A. (1995) Ethnic pluralism: conflict and accommodation. In L. Romanucci-Ross and G.A. De Vos (eds), *Ethnic Identity: Creation, Conflict and Accommodation*, 3rd edn. London: Altamira, pp. 15–47.

Down, S. (2010) *Enterprise, Entrepreneurship, and Small Business*. Thousand Oaks, CA: Sage.

Drori, I., Honig, B. and Wright, M. (2009) Transnational entrepreneurship: an emergent field of study. *Entrepreneurship Theory and Practice*, 33 (5): 1001–22.

Erikson, E.H. (1968) *Identity, Youth and Crisis*. New York: W.W. Norton and Company.

Faber, R. and O'Guinn, T. (1987) Ethnicity, acculturation and the impact of product attributes. *Psychology and Marketing*, 4: 121–34.

Gabel, T.G. and Boller, G.W. (2003) A preliminary look into the globalization of the tortilla in Mexico. *Advances in Consumer Research*, 30: 135–41.

Gee, J.P. (2001) Identity as an analytic lens for research in education. In W.G. Secada (ed.), *Review of Research in Education*, 25. Washington, DC: American Educational Research Association, pp. 99–125.

Goodson, I.F. and Cole, A.L. (1994) Exploring the teachers' professional knowledge: constructing identity and community. *Teacher Education Quarterly*, 21 (1): 85–105.

Gordon, M. (1995) Assimilation in America: theory and reality. In A. Aguirre and E. Baker (eds), *Notable Selections in Race and Ethnicity*. Guilford, CT: Dushkin, pp. 91–101.

Hofstede, G. (1980) *Culture's Consequences*. Beverley Hills, CA: Sage.

Hughes, M.U. (2010) From resistance to integration: changing consumer acculturation practices of immigrants. *Advances in Consumer Research*, 37: 13.

Jahoda, G. (1999) *Images of Savages: Ancient Roots of Modern Prejudice in Western Culture*. London: Routledge.

Jones, O. (2011) *Chavs: The Demonization of the Working Class*. London: Verso.

Kates, S. (2002) Doing brand and subcultural ethnographies: developing the interpretive community concept in consumer research. *Advances in Consumer Research*, 29: 43.

Khairulla, D., Tucker, F. and Tankersley, C. (1996) Acculturation and immigrant consumers' perceptions of advertisements: a study involving Asian-Indians. *International Journal of Commerce and Management*, 6 (34): 81–104.

Kroeber-Riel, W. and Weinberg, P. (1996) *Konsumentenverhalten*, 6th edn. Munich: Vahlen.

Lambert, A., Desmond, J. and O'Donohoe, S. (2014) Narcissism and the consuming self: an exploration of consumer identity projects and narcissistic tendencies. In J.W. Schouten, D.M. Martin and R.W. Belk (eds), *Consumer Culture Theory: Research in Consumer Behaviour*, 16. Bingley: Emerald Publishing, pp. 35–57.

Lambert, W.E. (1967) A social psychology of bilingualism. *Journal of Social Issues*, 13 (2): 91–109.

Lindridge, A. (2009) Acculturation, religion and consumption in normative political ideology. *Advances in Consumer Research*, 36: 16.

Lindridge, A.M. and Wang, C. (2008) Saving 'face' in China: modernization, parental pressure, and plastic surgery. *Journal of Consumer Behaviour*, 7 (6): 496–508.

Liu, W.M, Colbow, A.J. and Rice, A.J. (2016) Social class and masculinity. In Y.J. Wong and S.R. Wester (eds), *APA Handbook of Men and Masculinities*. Washington, DC: American Psychological Association, pp. 413–32.

Loughnan, S., Haslam, N., Sutton, R.M. and Spencer, B. (2014) Dehumanization and social class. *Social Psychology*, 45 (1): 54–61.

Low, M.B. and MacMillan, I.C. (1988) Entrepreneurship: past research and future challenges, *Journal of Management*, 14 (2): 139–61.

Lu Hsu, J. and Han-Peng, N. (2008) Who are ethnocentric? Examining consumer ethnocentrism in Chinese societies. *Journal of Consumer Behaviour*, 7 (6): 436–47.

Marcinczak, S., Musterd, S., Van Ham, M. and Tammaru, T. (2015) Inequality and rising levels of socio-economic segregation: lessons from a pan-European comparative study. In T. Tammaru, S. Marcinczak, M. van Ham and S. Musterd (eds), *Socio-Economic Segregation in European Capital Cities: East Meets West*. Chicago: Routledge, pp. 358–82.

Marín, G.S. and Gamba, R.J. (1996) A new measurement of acculturation for Hispanics: the Bidimensional Acculturation Scale for Hispanics (BAS). *Hispanic Journal of Behavioral Sciences*, 18 (3): 297–316.

Marx, K. and Engels, F. (1848) *The Manifesto of the Communist Party*. London: The Communist League.

McColl-Kennedy, J.R., Patterson, P.G., Brady, M.K., Cheung, L. and Nguyen, D. (2015) To give or not to give professional services to non-paying clients: professionals' giving backstory. *Journal of Service Management*, 26 (3): 426–59.

McCormick, C.B. and Pressley, M. (1997) *Educational Psychology: Learning, Instruction, Assessment*. Longman: New York.

McPherson, M. (2008) HRM practices and systems within South-Asian small businesses. *International Journal of Entrepreneurial Behavior and Research*, 14 (6): 414–39.

Miller, D. (1995) Consumption as the vanguard of history. In D. Miller (ed.), *Acknowledging Consumption*. London: Routledge, pp. 1–57.

Nguyen, T.D., Nguyen, T.T.M. and Barrett, N.J. (2008) Consumer ethnocentrism, cultural sensitivity, and intention to purchase local products: evidence from Vietnam. *Journal of Consumer Behaviour*, 7: 88–100.

Nichols, D. (2011) *The Bogan Delusion: Myths, Mischief and Misconceptions*. Melbourne: Affirm Press.

Nightingale, C.H. (2012) *Segregation: A Global History of Divided Cities*. Chicago, University of Chicago Press.

Nwankwo, S. and Lindridge, A. (1998) Marketing to ethnic minorities in Britain. *Journal of Marketing Practice: Applied Marketing Science*, 4 (7): 200–16.

Oberg, K. (1960) Cultural shock: adjustment to new cultural environments. *Practical Anthropologist*, 7: 177–82.

O'Connor, R.C. and Portzky, G. (2015) The association between goth subculture identification, depression, and self-harm. *The Lancet Psychiatry*, 2 (9): 766–7.

O'Guinn, T. and Faber, R. (1986) Acculturation: the impact of divergent path on buyer behaviour. In R. Lutz (ed.) *Advances in Consumer Research*, Vol. 13. Provo, UT: Association for Consumer Research, pp. 579–83.

Panayiotopoulos, P.I. (2008) Turkish immigrant entrepreneurs in the European union: a political-institutional approach. *International Journal of Entrepreneurial Behavior and Research*, 14 (6): 395–413.

Penloza, L. (1989) Immigrant consumer acculturation. In T.K. Srull (ed.), *Advances in Consumer Research*, Vol. 16. Provo, UT: Association for Consumer Research, pp. 110–18.

Richardson, B. and Turley, D. (2006) Support your local team: resistance, subculture and the desire for distinction. *Advances in Consumer Research*, 33: 175–80.

Rudmin, F.W. (2003) Critical history of the acculturation psychology of assimilation, separation, integration and marginalization, *Review of General Psychology*, 7: 3–37.

Rudmin, F.W. (2009) Catalogue of acculturation constructs: descriptions of 126 taxonomies, 1918–2003. *Online Readings in Psychology and Culture*, 8 (1). http://dx.doi.org/10.9707/2307-0919.1074.

Rudmin, F.W. and Ahmadzadeh, V. (2001) Psychometric critique of acculturation psychology: the case of Iranian migrants in Norway. *Scandinavian Journal of Psychology*, 42: 41–56.

Rusinovic, K. (2008) Moving between markets? Immigrant entrepreneurs in different markets. *International Journal of Entrepreneurial Behavior and Research*, 14 (6): 440–54.

Ryder, A.G., Alden, L.E. and Paulhus, D.L. (2000) Is acculturation unidimensional or bidimensional? A head to head comparison in the prediction of personality, self-identity and adjustment. *Journal of Personality and Social Psychology*, 79 (1): 77–88.

Sam, D.L. and Berry, J.W. (eds) (2006) *The Cambridge Handbook of Acculturation Psychology*. Cambridge: Cambridge University Press.

Segal, M. and Sosa, L. (1983) Marketing to Hispanic community. *California Management Review*, 26 (1): 120–34.

Sethna, Z. (2015) Entrepreneurial marketing and the Zarathustrian entrepreneur: thoughts, words and deeds. Academy of Marketing AM2015 Conference Proceedings, Limerick, Ireland.

Spencer, B. and Castano, E. (2007) Social class is dead, long live social class! Stereotype threat among low socioeconomic status individuals. *Social Justice Research*, 20: 418–32.

Sudbury, L. and Wilberforce, F. (2006) The portrayal of black people in UK television advertising: perception and reality. *Journal of Consumer Behaviour*, 5 (September–October): 465–76.

Teske, R.H.C. and Nelson, B.H. (1974) Acculturation and assimilation: a clarification, *American Ethnologist*, 1: 351–67.

Urban Dictionary (2015) Tinderite, www.urbandictionary.com/define.php?term=tinderite (accessed 16 September 2015).

Vignola, M. (2015) Crossing the border: migration flows in the Mediterranean area. *Nómadas. Revista Crítica de Ciencias Sociales y Jurídicas*, 39 (3): 127–39.

Waldfogel, J. (1993) The deadweight loss of Christmas. *American Economic Review*, 83 (5): 1328–36.

Ward, C. (2001) *The ABCs of Acculturation*. In D. Matsumoto (ed.), *The Handbook of Culture and Psychology*. Oxford: Oxford University Press, pp. 411–45.

Weber, M. (1946) Class, status, party. Published posthumously in Hans H. Gerth and C. Wright Mills (eds), *From Max Weber*. Oxford: Oxford University Press, pp. 180–95.

Weinberger, Y. and Shefi, P. (2012) Professional identity formation through narrative research: how much the personal and the professional are intertwined. *The International Journal of Learning*, 18 (11): 261–76.

Whitcomb, D.H. and Walinsky, D.J. (2013) Lesbian, gay and bisexual issues, social class, and counseling. In W.M. Liu (ed.), *The Oxford Handbook of Social Class in Counseling*. New York: Oxford University Press, pp. 446–65.

Williams, D. (2015) *Leadership for a Fractured World: How to Cross Boundaries, Build Bridges, and Lead Change*. Chicago: Berrett-Koehler Publishers.

Wray, M. (2006) *Not Quite White: White Trash and the Boundaries of Whiteness*. Durham, NC: Duke University Press.

Yorkston, E. and deMello, G. (2004) Sex sells? The effects of gender marking on consumers' evaluations of branded products across languages. *Advances in Consumer Research*, 31: 148–51.

Zaltman, G. (2003) *How Customers Think: Essential Insights into the Mind of the Market*. Boston, MA: Harvard Business School Press.

Zhang, Y. and Khare, A. (2009) Consumers' local–global identity: measurement. *Advances in Consumer Research*, 36: 43, 44.

Zwick, D. and Chelariu, C. (2006) Mobilising the hijab: Islamic identity negotiation in the context of a matchmaking website. *Journal of Consumer Behaviour*, 5 (July–August): 380–95.

MORE ONLINE

For additional materials that support this chapter and your learning, please visit:
https://study.sagepub.com/sethnaandblythe

CHAPTER 14

ETHICAL CONSUMPTION

<table>
<tr><td>

LEARNING OBJECTIVES

After reading this chapter you should be able to:

- Define and categorise ethics.
- Understand the part that morality plays in ethical consumption.
- Explain why consumers sometimes use 'boycott' as a strategy.
- Describe the role of environmental pressure groups.
- Describe and analyse the recycling or disposal choices available to a consumer at the end of a product's life cycle.
- Elaborate on the relationship with ethics and the online environment.

</td></tr>
</table>

INTRODUCTION

This chapter is about the ethics of consumerism.

Yeoman (2012) forecast that by 2050, the population figures for people living on earth will be nearly 10 billion, new consumption patterns will be formed by new middle classes, natural resources such as oil will be scarce, climate change will result in our planet Earth becoming warmer and as regards social mobility, some 5 billion people are forecast to take an international holiday (Yeoman 2012).

We and other consumers around the world, whether from developed or developing societies and economies, are becoming increasingly aware of the part that ethics plays both in the acquisition (through monetary decisions they make) and the consumption of products on an everyday basis. This is because we have ethical values, of some kind or another. For example, some people buy organic food and calculate the 'food miles' their produce has travelled to reach them (thus determining

Sweatshop
A factory or workshop, especially in the clothing industry, where manual workers are employed at very low wages for long hours and under poor conditions

the carbon foot print that those food miles have left) in a bid to satisfy values of environmental friendliness. Others check to see whether or not the clothes they buy have been manufactured in a sweatshop somewhere by 12-year-old girls working 12-hour shifts in an inhumane factory, because human rights as well as working conditions and wage rates are of importance to them. Others are conscious about whether their energy consumption is from renewable sources or not.

DEFINITIONS AND CATEGORIES

Ethics is defined by the *Oxford English Dictionary* as 'the discipline dealing with what is good and bad and with moral duty and obligation'. It adds: 'ethics has been called the science of the ideal of human character'. The second definition reads: 'The principles of conduct governing an individual or group'.

A deeper study takes us to the field of philosophy, and there we see ethics as a branch of normative science as distinguished from the formal sciences. The history of thought in Western civilisation begins with Greece. The earliest consideration of ethics began in the 5th century BCE, and since then the Greek schools of ethics, early Christian ethics, ethics after the Reformation, and ethics since Darwinism have all developed. More recently, since Bertrand Russell, it is seen that ethics should mean complete participation in the life of society with the freedom to express one's nature. As to what is good and what is bad, each school of ethics has its own definition, from cynicism to existentialism. We have lists of prescriptions and proscriptions, do's and don'ts, prepared by each school from the doctrines of Pythagoras through the Bible, and to the Zoroastrian Avesta: in fact we have books that run into several thousand pages each.

For the most part, marketers and consumers do not make a deep study of philosophy, however. Liebe et al. (2014) succinctly summarise our most recent thinking on ethical consumption by saying that it can be defined as:

> *purchase decisions by persons concerned with not only the price of products and services, but also with the political, social and environmental consequences of their purchases.*

The current driver behind businesses adopting ethical business practices in industry has to be, and indeed actually is, the customer: the ethical consumer. Work by Bendell (1998) first mooted an element of 'citizenship' in the consumerist perspective. In a simplistic way, businesses are merely satisfying the consumers' wants and needs, but in fact we've been seeing a growth in the popularity of ethical consumption since the late 1980s, when society started to frown upon the exuberant and indulgent lifestyle of the yuppie with his Golf GTI 16v and weekends away in New York using Concorde.

People started to become a lot more aware of the 'choices' they had through information published in magazines and guidebooks (Brower et al. 1999; Harrison et al. 2005; Jackson 2006). The interests of the early proponents of this movement were firmly centred on areas such as certified timber, and organic and Fairtrade agriculture such as bananas and coffee. Unsurprisingly there was also a significant interest in cosmetics products which instigated the growth of organisations such as The Body Shop (see the Consumer Behaviour in Action example below).

Although some academics (Zadek et al. 1998) had reported early on that ethical consumption would be the norm among the masses, it is not the norm yet. That said, the 'movement' is slowly making its way into society as a way of living. Mainstream retailers are eager to provide us with information about their ethical retailing, and as consumers we have access to material from organisations such as www.good guide.com, an online and app-based tool created by Dara O'Rourke which enables consumers to retrieve evaluations of the health, environmental and social impacts of consumer products such as toys, food and detergents. For instance, apart from just comparing a product to all its competitors on a scale of 1 to 10, one of the features in GoodGuide is the ability for consumers to tell organisations why they made their purchasing decision, using a single click. This allows a customer to tell a company that they have adopted a competitor's product because of information they'd learned on GoodGuide or elsewhere. For example, a consumer might avoid a brand of canned chopped tomatoes because it's lined with BPA-containing plastic whereas the competitor's cans are not. This is clearly something the company would like to know. Wouldn't you like to know?

(Incidentally, Dara O'Rourke is the same industrial ecologist and environmental consultant from the University of California, Berkeley who blew the whistle on Nike's use of sweatshop labour).

One final perspective is that of the distinction between unethical behaviour and selfishness. While this chapter will not go into detail on these aspects, it is worth noting where the boundaries lie. What we already know is that generally speaking, all the research to date on this area tends to investigate situations in which individuals perform unethical actions to benefit themselves (Dubois et al. 2015), hence the aspect of selfishness. This begs the question of how to define ethical behaviours. Jones (1991) took a social psychology perspective on this and noted that ethical behaviour is any action which is illegal or morally unacceptable to the larger community. However, even this is debatable as social norms within different societies vary, and thus what individuals see as moral or immoral could be quite subjective (Monin and Jordan 2009; Ayal and Gino 2011). This approach could encompass a number of variables from lying and cheating (Brass et al. 1998; Treviño et al. 2006; Gino and Bazerman 2009) to general dishonesty (Mazar et al. 2008).

CONSUMER BEHAVIOUR IN ACTION: LUSCIOUSLY LUSH

Founded in 1976 by the late British environmental and human rights campaigner Dame Anita Roddick, The Body Shop started as a small shop in Brighton selling just 25 products. The Body Shop was the first mainstream UK retailer to put a real emphasis on natural ingredients that were ethically sourced and not tested on animals. In its day, The Body Shop was a true pioneer in bringing cruelty free and ethically sourced skincare and body products to the British consumer, and it is hard to imagine how we managed without it. In 2006, it was controversially sold to the cosmetics giant L'Oreal. This is, of course, a subjective view but walk into one of their stores now and you are likely to be affronted with fussy, brash packaging and an array of artificial aromas. So has this particular retailer lost its way?

Lush, on the other hand, is a handmade cosmetics company set up in 1994 by husband and wife team Mark and Mo Constantine. It began in Poole, Dorset (where it still has its headquarters). The company uses fruit and vegetables, essential oils and some synthetic ingredients in its products, and like The Body Shop guarantees no animal testing on any products.

Walk into one of their 600 stores across 43 countries and you are greeted by enthusiastic staff. It has a knack for communicating its ethical messages to consumers in a lively and imaginative way – both in-store and online – such as its recent campaign to encourage shoppers to return plastic bottle tops. Consumers love the approach. Consumers can return the empty black pots from the cosmetics products they'd bought earlier, in exchange for a face mask. These pots are made from a sturdy polypropylene plastic which Lush recycles and thereby works towards a closed loop and, eventually, a self-sustainable plastic supply.

©iStock.com/ChrisGramly

In the beginning, Lush inventors discovered that creating solid products without water meant they could do away with excess packaging and keep products self-preserving. Their soap, shampoo bars, bubble bars and bath bombs have gone on to become global bestsellers; and in 2013 global sales of their solid shampoo prevented 9 million plastic bottles ending up in landfill. The company continually tries to invent ways to reduce packaging and plastics, and makes sure that they recycle and reuse from the factory to the shop floor.

Their black pots have been through a few transformations; at first they were imported from overseas, and in 2010 they found a local supplier close to their Poole factory where they make their cosmetics. This not only reduces freight and transportation costs of the pots, but also allows them to support the local economy. So, when customers return their pots, they already know it's not the end of the road for these robust little guys, who are sent on to be thoroughly cleaned, heated and remoulded, and turned back into new pots for freshly made creams, scrubs, masks and shampoos.

CATEGORIES OF ETHICAL CONSUMER

Over the past 40 years, researchers have used a variety and combination of segmentation variables (behavioural, demographic, environmental and psychographic) to try to categorise consumers in order to chart their position on a continuum of ethical consumption. This has of course been a difficult exercise since quite often it is difficult to identify particular segments in the marketplace (Paco and Raposo 2009). Humphery (2011) and Littler (2008) have also both noted that 'ethical consumption' as a term does not refer to a clearly defined set of practices, but rather has become a convenient

FIGURE 14.1 Variables determining environmental preferences and practices (adapted from Modi and Patel 2013)

umbrella-phrase for a range of tendencies within contemporary consumer economies. Alternative methods for categorisation have been suggested by Straughan and Roberts (1999). As Modi and Patel (2013) rightly surmise (see Figure 14.1), researchers in this area will regularly return to a handful of variables which determine where a consumer sits on the continuum. Let's start with eco-literacy. The concept of eco-literacy is useful in assessing the level of environmental knowledge that a consumer has. The more knowledge one has about the effects of particular types of consumption, the more one can make an informed and conscious choice, leading to environmental consciousness. There is evidence to suggest that environmental consciousness is therefore more closely allied to purchasing behaviour than any socio-demographic measures, which means that people will often change their purchasing behaviour based on their knowledge of, and therefore their attitudes towards, what is more environmentally friendly (Hartmann and Ibanez 2006) or greener (Peattie 2001). This naturally leads to a person's perception about how much their individual behaviour will actually make an impact on the overall environment. Those people who demonstrate a deep, passionate and proactive attitude towards being eco-friendly are said to have a high perceived behavioural control (de Pelsmacker et al. 2002). Unsurprisingly, there is research (Laroche et al. 2001) to suggest that these people will pay more for eco-friendly products.

In the midst of the uptake of ethical consumerism, Roper Starch Worldwide (1997) attempted to categorise the green consumer, as seen in Table 14.1. It is interesting to note that we see here the insertion of the word 'green' to denote an interest in the 'environment'.

At around the same time, the National Consumer Council (which has since been subsumed by the Citizens Advice Bureau) published its own categorisation of 'UK Green Consumers', see Table 14.2, by segmenting the population depending on how green their purchasing, recycling and consumption behaviour was.

It seems that in recent years the individual consumer's perspective has evolved from one which initially assumed that ethical consumption was all about 'less is more' to one which appreciates that there are ways in which their habitual consumption

Eco-literacy

The environmental knowledge that a consumer has

TABLE 14.1 Early categories of ethical consumers

Percentage of population	Segment name	Description
28%	Basic Browns	• People who do not believe that action can make a difference • May have lower educational attainment than other groups
26%	Sprouts	• Middling levels of concern about the environment • Have some green tendencies but not completely translated into behaviour
24%	Grousers	• People who have quite poor environmental behaviour • Often indulge in making excuses for their own lack of ethical consumption and are all too ready to blame others
11%	Greenbacks Greens	• People who are willing to pay higher prices for green goods (often equating a higher price for supposedly greener qualities)
11%	True-Blue Greens	• These people are the most active of green consumers • Will regularly take the lead and will often be seen at the forefront of the movement

Source: adapted from Roper Starch Worldwide (1997)

TABLE 14.2 National Consumer Council's 'UK Green Consumers'

Percentage of population	Segment name	Description
26%	Sceptics	• The sceptics doubt they can influence the environment and think most environment symbols on products are merely a marketing ploy
19%	Affluent Greens	• These are committed buyers of environmentally friendly products even though they think that such products are expensive. They regularly recycle household waste. They are also generally wealthy and mostly female
19%	Recyclers	• These people recycle particular products – paper, glass and cans more than any other group. However, they avoid environmentally friendly products and cannot be described as green shoppers
19%	Careful Spenders	• This group are thrifty with energy use but are the group least likely to recycle. They do not seem to be motivated by any environmental issues
17%	Young Greens	• These people have low incomes, and are recyclers. Their commitment to buying green products is second only to the affluent greens

patterns can be made more eco-friendly. Research carried out by Whan (2010) in 17 countries has confirmed that our individual consumer preferences are only a reflection of the fact that we are increasingly becoming more concerned about the environment.

This 'reflection' can be even further embedded in this context by using the past as a yard-stick. The political and social commentator Professor David Starkey (2015) noted that 'the culture of the past will lay the ground for the future'. There are numerous examples from the past that we can draw upon to learn about the future, not least the English author and philosopher Geoffrey Chaucer, who wrote the following lines in his poem entitled 'Parlement of Foules' (The Parliament of Birds):

> For out of old fields, as the saying goes,
> Comes all the new grain garnered year by year,
> And speaking truly, out of old books flows,
> All the new knowledge men learn to revere.

ETHICS AND THE PERSON

Here we look at the individual and his or her consumption, which is often entwined with morality. We also look at positive and negative ethical purchase behaviour, and finally consumer action in the form of boycotts.

MORAL LIVES – COMPASSION IN CONSUMPTION?

In the years surrounding both the First and Second World Wars, consumers naturally developed ethical and political concerns and were seen very much as 'citizen-consumers' as opposed to 'customer-consumers' (Frank 1985; Bendell 1998; Cohen 2003; Trentmann 2006), and to a certain degree we, in the 21st century, are moving back towards that stance. As consumers in households, our current thinking on issues of, for instance, environmental pollution (Rieuwerts 2015), food scarcity (Findlay and Yeoman 2015) and inequality among consumers (Fernandes and Calamote 2015) is that these areas certainly do impact on our daily lives. Over the past 25 years, there has been an increase of about 25% more 'households' in the UK and thus households account for the majority of energy consumption. It is of no surprise then that these sorts of figures have far-reaching implications for the environment.

Guilt may be a factor in buying and consumption decisions. It is probable that at least some people go through a mental checklist (Table 14.3) each time they buy something.

TABLE 14.3 The guilt checklist of ethical consumption

Tick if the item we're about to buy is:	✓
Free-range	
Fairtrade	
Locally grown	
Environmentally friendly	
Low on food miles	
Non-sweat shop	
Carbon neutral	
Animal-cruelty free	
Recyclable	
Sustainable	
All of the above	

Guilt can be a compelling force when it comes to moderating consumer appetite for products and services. For instance, out-of-season exotic foods that have travelled thousands of miles, or quick-dry clothing, or perhaps even something as mundane as 2-in-1 shampoo/conditioner render consumers partially responsible for some bad things around the world; environmental destruction, animal cruelty and human exploitation. Pre-knowledge of these factors may lead to the individual's self-image being tarnished, to quiet contentment, or perhaps feelings of guilt.

Sometimes these value statements are in conflict with each other. Sometimes the individual is unable to afford the 'ethical' option, or perhaps the 'not-tested-on-animals' moisturiser is based on petrochemicals and packaged in plastic. Research conducted by the School of Oriental and African Studies (SOAS 2014) at the University of London found that Fairtrade certified coffee, tea and flowers do not improve lives of the very poorest rural people in Ethiopia and Uganda. According to the SOAS website, their lead researcher, Professor Cramer, had this to say:

> The British public has been led to believe that by paying extra for Fairtrade certified coffee, tea and flowers they will 'make a difference' to the lives of poor Africans. Careful fieldwork and analysis in this four year project leads to the conclusion that in our research sites Fairtrade has not been an effective mechanism for improving the lives of wage workers, the poorest rural people.

There are of course two sides to every story, and even though the SOAS research is seemingly robust, Fairtrade International (2014) published their own statement about the research:

> While we were given an opportunity to comment at an earlier stage in their report writing process, we are disappointed to see that the final report has not properly taken account of the many issues we raised, particularly regarding what we view as the report's generalised conclusions, unfair representation of data and lack of attention to the specific interventions of the Fairtrade system when attributing their conclusions to Fairtrade or other factors affecting the experiences of waged workers. While we have already taken action on specific issues we have been made aware of, the SOAS data and findings therefore warrant further scrutiny and analysis.

This paradox then also leads us to question whether wealth and social class affect ethical behaviour, or put in another way, 'Are the rich less ethical than the poor?' (Dubois et al. 2015). Their results showed that 'high social class does not inherently lead to unethical behaviour but instead predicts tendencies to behave selfishly. In contrast, low social class can lead to unethical behavior, but more so when it benefits others' (see Chapter 13 for more on culture and class).

Regardless of social class, working out what is most important to the individual should take priority when scrutinising ethical values and consumption. This could then help in making more consistent purchasing decisions and avoiding unconscious hypocrisy (take for instance the fuel hungry 4x4 driven by a city dweller who compensates by filling it with premium petrol, or the same person who uses large quantities of Nespresso coffee pods before going to the supermarket and using jute bags-for-life).

The Ethical Superstore offers consumers a choice so that they can make a decision about value judgements from their own beliefs about what things are important to them. Sometimes there will be conflict, so a vegetarian may not buy a leather purse, but equally someone who doesn't worry about where their raw materials come from will be very happy to have a Fairtrade leather purse.

Ultimately the choices people make in their buying decisions create the coherent moral position within which consumer behaviour operates. Within this, people use 'trade-offs' to pacify their consciences, remembering all the occasions when they have been 'good' (being environmentally friendly) and using these to justify the times when they have not been so environmentally friendly. When rationalising their behaviour, people use a technique called confirmation bias. This enables them to accept information that fits with their current beliefs or decisions, and filter out or simply ignore information that doesn't. The reality is that adjusting behaviour to do what is morally right more often, if not all the time, tends to require some uncomfortable self-appraisal.

Preference is very important. Thirty years ago Fairtrade coffee was usually poor quality, but people drank it because it was politically the right thing to do, not because they enjoyed it. Now there are many good-quality Fairtrade coffees, so that a consumer doesn't have to sacrifice flavour and aroma, and can choose based on the moral argument in favour of Fairtrade. The choices exist because the Fairtrade producers (who want to sell more) have the benefits of improved production methods, wider markets and 'supported entrance' into the market. For each of us there are different things that motivate and excite us, whether it's a leather purse, or vegetarian food, or buying products that support trade in Palestine or Syria, and there will be different reasons for adopting those positions.

Fairtrade is an external benefit to a person many thousands of miles away, and this market has grown, despite the global recession; meanwhile the market for organic produce, which is actually a 'me benefit', i.e. 'I don't want to put anything bad inside me', has fallen since early 2010. Fairtrade has flourished over the past 20 years, benefiting the early pioneers, but big business is now dressing itself up in the same clothes and taking up the standards that ethical organisations were adhering to many years ago.

Fairtrade is a contentious issue in some parts of the developing world where producers are saying that it's of dubious benefit, and has been imposed on them by Western NGOs and charities. What some producers want is to be running big corporates and development themselves. Some research suggests that Colombian coffee producers were making more money selling under the Colombian coffee brand than they were through the Fairtrade coffee brand because they were getting a share of the brand equity. Companies such as Divine Chocolate have come along where the producers own a substantial chunk of the business, so they get to share in the brand, and the brand value, the very thing that capitalism is putting at the centre of it.

PERSONAL ETHICAL CONSUMPTION

One of the early proponents of ethical purchase behaviour and accountability was Smith (1990). Smith asked a very direct and pertinent question that marketers still discuss today: 'Can businesses abandon the axiom that the customer is always right when consumers start questioning the ethics of business practices?'. Much of Smith's early work focused on the negative aspects of disengaging with organisations by boycotting certain products which were deemed to be an unethical purchase due to environmental unfriendliness. However, there are also many positive aspects of

FIGURE 14.2 The ethical consumers' choices (adapted from Tallontire et al. 2001)

So what part does the 'individual' in the household play? What about the 'moral-self'? Do we echo what others in the 'group' are saying, or are we as Bauman (1995) said, 'behaving like a kind of lonely rebel and daring to act morally on behalf of others'? And whatever happened to those other perhaps traditional and institutional moralities as dictated to us by the likes of the church, families and our local community? Have they been eroded?

ethical purchase behaviour (see Figure 14.2). The three broad areas which dominate ethical consumerism are shown in Figure 14.3. Each has both a positive and negative dimension.

There are some commentators who propose that the primary moral consideration for shoppers should not be to consume differently (the positive way of consuming) but to consume less, and that that which is consumed should cause as little harm as possible. Since 2008, many countries have been in economic recession, forcing people to lead more austere lives. Reducing overall consumption seems to suggest making a virtue of austerity – a lot of people will be consuming less, not because they want to be ethical consumers but because they do not have enough money to consume as they would wish.

Global warming is expected to raise temperatures by between 4 and 6 degrees this century, which is potentially catastrophic to the living world and to its people: this may be the greatest moral problem that we face. However, most people do not share any sense of panic about consumption, and still think that economic growth is a good thing, not least in helping raise living standards for more poor people. Environmental arguments are therefore unlikely to get governments elected to pursue non-growth policies.

The Environment

Human Rights and Working Conditions (with Fairtrade)

Animal Welfare

FIGURE 14.3 Ethical consumerism and its constituent areas of interest

CONSUMER ACTION AND THE BIG BOYCOTT

This is nothing new. As a society we have been doing this for many years, and it is even more prevalent before and after times of war when quite often there is a scarcity of product available. The turn of the century saw the rise of the National Consumer Leagues in the USA. These consumer groups wanted to gain social justice by exerting pressure on companies by boycotting the purchase of products and/ or engaging in public protests to bring about wider awareness of ethical issues. One of the by-products of their endeavours was to produce what became known as 'white lists' (Strasser et al. 1998; Glickman 1999).

On the other hand, letting companies know when their behaviour is not acceptable is crucial. Social media is often used to influence companies who are desperate to maintain a good public image, reflecting ethical values. For example, Nestlé used to purchase their palm oil from plantations that were causing the destruction of Orang-utan habitat, but following a Greenpeace campaign, closely followed by widespread support on social media, Nestlé changed its decision and are now purchasing from sustainable sources only. Consumer boycotts seem to work, and money can be a moral agent as well as a means of exchange: consumers might boycott coffee shops who avoid paying their taxes (as happened to Starbucks in the UK), but boycotting may be more about political posturing than about a coherent moral crusade. For instance, the Starbucks political campaign probably did a lot more to shame Starbucks into making an apparent change, than the actual buying decisions.

ETHICS AND THE PUBLIC

In this section we look at the wider impact that ethical consumption has on global societies and therefore, in turn, on organisations. It is certainly true that we as consumers use our buying power to ensure that organisations remain accountable to us as ordinary citizens and to society. Consumers are able to exercise choices, but can exercise very little in the way of 'power of restraint'. An individual might give up driving a car and ride a bicycle instead, but unless that's taking place in a political context in which the government is reducing the road space allocated to cars and increasing the road space for bicycles, all the individual is doing is opening up road space for someone else to occupy. This means that the power of restraint on other

White list

A list containing details of product manufacturers who treat their workers fairly people's actions is limited, because individuals cannot prevent other people from behaving unethically.

PRESSURES ON FIRMS

While companies are coming under increasing consumer pressure, ethical consumers also need to think carefully about the strategies they employ. For example, following the clothing factory fires and subsequent collapses in Bangladesh (reported in www. theglobeandmail.com 2013) which killed 300 workers and injured nearly 1,000 more, there were many calls for boycotts of Bangladesh-made items (for instance from customers of H&M and Nautica), but some commentators pointed out that such a move by Western consumers would devastate the struggling nation's economy and affect mainly women, who make up the bulk of the garment industry's workforce, particularly harshly. Activists were instead persuading consumers to look for brands which had signed up to a new Bangladesh accord, which insisted on safe working conditions.

Websites such as the GoodGuide (www.goodguide.com), Environmental Working Group (www.ewg.com) and Greener Choices (www.greenerchoices.org) aim to make the impacts of consumer consumption transparent for us as consumers, especially those who are time and resource poor. In a similar way, smaller organisations and even many Fortune 500 companies lack the time, money and market drivers to conduct a traditional Life Cycle Assessment (LCA). Without a measurement tool such as LCA, companies that are asked to improve their environmental performance are lost. They may spend extensive resources on an initiative that produces little return while ignoring easier targets. Earthster (sustainablepackaging.org) aims to give life cycle evaluation and publishing power to all companies by helping them obtain a quantitative and visual understanding of the life cycle sustainability impacts of the products they buy and sell; share the results of such an assessment with others using the web; and make use of data shared by actors in their supply chain to obtain a more accurate assessment and to establish a dynamic sustainability reporting and assessment system.

DISPOSAL AND RECYCLING

There is one more element to post-purchase behaviour that is becoming increasingly important – the disposal of unwanted product. After a product has been used up, the consumer has the problem of disposing of whatever remains. In some cases, what is left still has value – the second-hand car market is an obvious example. In other cases, the product has been so totally used up that virtually nothing remains, as is the case with most food products. These issues have become central to the cause of environmentalism in recent years. Recycling, using products to the full and care in disposal into the environment have been near the top of the agenda, and consumer behaviour in these areas has come under considerable scrutiny.

Packrats

Individuals who tend to keep their possessions for a long time

Purgers

People who regularly discard their possessions

People occasionally form strong attachments to products and find it difficult to 'let go'. Favourite clothing, a much-loved car and even now-obsolete vinyl records may be kept until there is really no further possibility of using them any longer. Such possessions are our links with our past, and giving them up removes one of the anchors of our identities (Belk 1989). People who retain possessions have been defined as **packrats**, whereas people who regularly dispose of their possessions have been defined as **purgers** (Coulter and Ligas 2003). Packrats attach more meaning to their possessions, and see themselves as thrifty: they usually do not mind giving possessions away to other people or to charities, but they hate waste. Purgers, on the other hand, think packrats are messy and disorganised, and do not attach much significance to their possessions. Motivations for either of these behaviours are not clear-cut: hoarding in particular is an ambiguous concept (Maycroft 2009). One motivation may be the sentimental value attached to the objects: mothers sometimes keep children's toys as mementos, for example, although they will throw away broken toys (Sego 2010). Certainly if people are temporarily separated from some possessions (for example, leaving a mobile phone in a taxi, or even having to fly economy when one normally flies business class) there is a loss of self-identity (Black 2011). In the last example the opposite is also true – that is, if one always travels in economy, and is suddenly upgraded to business class or even first class, the traveller is likely to encounter some feelings of apprehension at being in an unfamiliar environment with different rules.

No matter how assiduously some of us might try to hoard our possessions, sooner or later everything must go. When the object is no longer of any use the individual has a choice of three options, summarised in Figure 14.4:

1. *Keep the item.* This may mean putting the item away in a safe place – a loft or a garage – or it may mean re-using the product in some way. For example, an old bath might be recycled as a garden pond, or a broken radio might be incorporated into an artwork.

2. *Temporarily dispose of the item.* Christmas decorations might be put away for use the following year, for example. Equally, products might be lent to someone else, or even rented to someone. For example, someone who will be working abroad for a year might rent out his or her house rather than sell it.

3. *Permanently dispose of the item.* This could be achieved by selling the item, giving it away, putting it into the refuse disposal system, or by some other permanent means such as burning it. Trade-in can also be used – exchanging the used product as part-payment for a new one greatly increases the buyer's willingness to buy (Zhu et al. 2008).

The increasing emphasis on recycling items that are no longer of any use results in the recycled article being renovated, cleaned or donated as itself: for example, used spectacles can be collected and sent to developing countries to be worn by people who otherwise could not afford glasses. Since individuals' eyes deteriorate over time, everyone needs new spectacles with a different strength from time to time, so glasses that are still perfectly usable need to be disposed of. Equally, bottles can be cleaned and re-used as bottles rather than being smashed in a bottle bank and re-melted. Before the 1970s virtually all bottles were re-used in this way.

Clothing, books and used household items are often contributed to charity shops where they are sold to new users. Customers of charity shops are not necessarily short of money – some are anti-corporatist, some are looking for vintage clothing, some seek to transform their purchases into new clothing or objects. Charity shops effectively re-commoditise clothing for these buyers (Brace-Govan and Binay 2010). This is a necessary function, because it distances the new owner from the previous wearer of the clothes – most people feel slightly uncomfortable wearing clothes of unknown provenance, but rationalise this by imagining the previous owner as being much like themselves (Roux 2010). Clothing that is completely beyond re-use can be

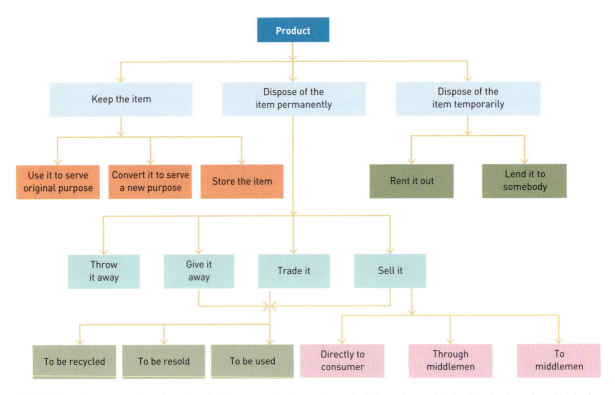

FIGURE 14.4 Disposal options (Reprinted with permission from Journal of Marketing, published by the American Marketing Association, Jacob Jacoby, Carol K. Berning, and Thomas F. Dietvorst, Vol. 41, No. 2 1977: 22–28).

processed for paper-making: high-quality writing paper uses recycled fabric fibres (known in the trade as 'tramp's trousers') to strengthen the paper.

Some countries place a greater emphasis on recycling than do others, and there is also some debate over which recycling options are worthwhile and which are not. In some cases, the cost of collecting and recycling used items (including the energy used) may mean that it is less environmentally damaging to use new materials rather than attempt to recycle. One study showed how specific instrumental goals were linked to abstract terminal values, and thus to recycling behaviour. Lower-order goals that were identified were 'avoid filling up landfills', 'reduce waste', 're-use materials' and 'save the environment'. These were linked to terminal values of 'promote health and avoid sickness', 'achieve life-sustaining ends' and 'provide for future generations'. The perceived effort of recycling turns out to be the best predictor of whether people will actually take the trouble at all. In other words, even when people are sold on the idea of recycling and believe it to be important, difficulty in actually recycling will often outweigh their motivation to do so (Bagozzi and Dabholkar 1994).

There is some evidence that the eagerness to recycle is levelling off somewhat and is certainly far from embedded in people's consciousnesses. Much depends on culture and on the availability of recycling schemes – Germans appear to be far more recycling-conscious than, for example, Spaniards or Britons. There is some evidence that women are more environmentally conscious than men, but this is based on American research and may not be true for other countries (Iyer and Kashyap 2007). These authors conclude that recycling will not succeed unless people are offered incentives

CHALLENGING THE STATUS QUO

In the 1950s everything was recycled. People took bottles back to the shop and were refunded a small deposit, milk bottles were given back to the milkman (and he would get quite upset if he didn't get his bottles back), and in the countryside, food scraps were collected by pig-keepers.

Ashes were spread on gardens or made into building blocks; paper and scrap wood were burned in household boilers to heat water; clothes were repaired, darned and eventually re-cut or unpicked and re-knitted to make new clothes. Newspapers were used to wrap food (notably in the UK, fish and chips), and in some households were used as toilet paper.

©iStock.com/Kali Nine LLC

Do 21st-century consumers really think that recycling is some sort of 21st-century innovation? Sending newspapers away to be re-pulped instead of simply using them as packaging? Breaking bottles and re-melting them instead of re-using them as bottles? Packing milk in one-way, irreplaceable plastic containers instead of in multi-use glass bottles? Since the environmental movement started, we seem to have become *less* environmentally responsible than we were before!

and are reminded regularly about the need to recycle. Interestingly, they also found that recycling attitudes and behaviours correlate weakly with environmental attitudes and behaviours – in other words, having environmentally friendly attitudes in some areas (cycling rather than driving, using eco-friendly products) does not necessarily mean that one also believes in recycling.

As some consumers become more environmentally friendly, they may seek to distance themselves from the materialism of modern life and take a more minimalist approach to consumption. These people experience a transformation as they dispose of their goods, deciding what to keep and what to get rid of, and move away from the profane marketplace and towards a more sacred type of consumption in which they consume only goods that fit into their new lifestyle (Cherrier 2009). Often this disposal process helps develop a sense of community – for example, people who join clothing exchanges participate in the life of the goods by passing them on to friends (Albinsson and Perera 2009).

Lateral recycling is the term given to selling goods on, donating them to others, or exchanging them for other items. Car boot sales (also called flea markets) exist to facilitate this process, as do charity shops. A more recent arrival in the lateral recycling market is eBay and similar websites, on which people can sell almost anything. eBay

Lateral recycling

Donating goods to others, selling them on, or otherwise transferring ownership to someone who will obtain further use of the goods has become an international institution of its own, with people selling and buying in an almost compulsive manner – the website has rules about what can and cannot be sold, but even so some very dubious items have appeared from time to time. The existence of eBay has meant that previously worthless goods have become transformed into valuable stock-in-trade for many people (Denegri-Knott and Molesworth 2009). Online trading of this sort creates a self-sufficient, self-regulating and self-sustaining community (Arsel 2010).

Selling used products has become a lucrative business for some people – clearly antique dealers and the like can make their livings from selling off previously unwanted products, but even dedicated car boot sale attendees and eBayers can make substantial amounts of money from buying and selling. Reclaimed architectural products such as Victorian fireplaces, antique tiles, decorative roofing features, stained glass windows, and so forth are often traded both online and offline. When goods are auctioned off, their previous cultural worth becomes commoditised – in other words, the history of an object becomes eroded by the fact that it is being sold, although some history still travels with the object. For many buyers, it is the history rather than the object that is important (Cheetham 2009).

Given the huge increase in wealth in developed countries over the past 30 years or so, and the correspondingly dramatic increase both in number of possessions per household and in quantities of rubbish produced, disposal is becoming one of the hot issues of the 21st century. People can no longer simply throw things away – in the words of one researcher, there is no longer an 'away' to throw things to (Sherry 1990). Marketers are likely to find that, if they do not address the issue of disposal and find ways to tap the potential of recycling in all its forms, they will be forced to do so by legislation. Already the European Union (largely at the instigation of Germany) is moving towards legislation that will require companies to take cradle-to-grave responsibility for their products.

SUMMARY

The environment of consumer behaviour includes the social environment as well as the physical environment. The social environment is the sum total of the human interactions that surround us, both those we are directly involved with and those we are not. Some of these interactions involve social class as well as personal behavioural preferences. Ethical consumerism has had in the past a number of negative identity connotations, and conversations often revolve around consumer 'denial', 'the cost' and/or 'inconvenience'. These variables nurture a social identity which is distinctly uncomfortable in the present day. This is in contrast to other consumers who receive a 'positive sense of self' following their ethical consumption practices. The individual (or the *person* as seen earlier) who is now far better equipped to make the 'right choice', is far from being gullible, and may well actually be the saviour of consumption. That said, we may suffer from what managers would call 'analysis paralysis' as we're having to deal with complex ethical issues and large quantities of product information before making any buying decisions. This could lead to occasions where we might take the attitude of 'we'll do our bit'. Whether we're motivated by our desires, or whether it's to appease our friends and family (or even the wider society), we'll consume in a manner which somehow brings equilibrium into our lives; our lifestyle and consumer ethics need to be in balance.

One of the earliest examples of organised ethics is in 'religion'. Prophets of the world's religions used ethical dictates in devising plans in order to attract customers to buy in to their products, services, beliefs and brands; even though they won't have consciously called it 'ethical consumerism'. For example, followers of the world's first monotheistic religion, Zoroastrianism, dated approximately 14th century BCE, believe in three core tenets, Humata, Hukhta, Hvarshta (Figure 14.5) which translate to:

Humata, Hukhta, Hvarshta

Three core tenets of Zoroastrianism translating to Good Thoughts, Good Words and Good Deeds

Good Thoughts, Good Words, and Good Deeds
Three core tenets of Zoroastrianism

FIGURE 14.5 Good thoughts, good words, good deeds

These three tenets, this philosophy of pragmatism based on a systematic approach, works very well as a foundation for summarising ethical consumerism.

KEY POINTS

- The driver behind businesses adopting ethical business practices has to be the ethical consumer.
- Ethical consumerism is not new, and has a long history dating back to the 5th century BCE.
- Social media has made it far easier for individuals to connect both with other individuals and with organisations about issues related to ethical consumption.
- Ethical consumption can be categorised using a mix of traditional variables (behavioural, demographic, environmental and psychographic) as well as contemporary variables (eco-literacy, environmental consciousness, etc.).
- Morality and compassion in consumption play a key role in the lives of the individual.
- The 'question mark' gets more of a workout than the full stop in these debates on ethical consumption, as the personal choices we each have in the buying decisions we make are still varied.
- Boycotts seem to work as the pound in your pocket can be a moral agent as well as a means of exchange.
- The disposal of unwanted products as 'ethical post-purchase consumer behaviour' is becoming increasingly important.
- There are three options for disposal: keep and store the article, dispose of it temporarily, or dispose of it permanently.
- Lateral recycling (passing the product on to someone else for re-use) is a growing phenomenon.

HOW TO IMPRESS YOUR EXAMINER

This is currently a very topical discussion, and the media is awash with examples of how companies are either getting it right or not. You should make efforts to collate a file of examples that you can call upon for different scenarios and feel comfortable in applying the categorisation of variables used to measure ethical consumption (behavioural, demographic, environmental, psychographic, eco-literacy) to those examples.

REVIEW QUESTIONS

1. Can ethical consumption always be a rational choice for consumers?
2. Which gaps exist when consumers are faced with a choice of ethical consumption or not?
3. What part does social media play in promoting ethical awareness and behaviour?
4. How can organisations affect the eco-literacy of society for their benefit?
5. Is the moral maze of ethical consumption one that an individual can navigate successfully?
6. In what situations should one boycott a product or an organisation?
7. Landfill or recycle – are the choices always so easy? What does one have to consider?
8. Why might a company encourage environmentally friendly disposal of its products?
9. What are the basic routes for disposal of used products?
10. What are the drivers for lateral recycling?

CASE STUDY: *ETHICAL CONSUMER*

Ethical Consumer (EC) is a website and print magazine which campaigns for a more ethical approach to business, using consumer pressure as a tool to force companies to become more ethically aware. EC is, as one might expect, a co-operative non-profit organisation. Funding comes from magazine subscriptions and advertising from carefully vetted companies, and the organisation also carries out paid research for interested organisations.

EC goes beyond campaigning for the physical environment. The organisation also rates companies against issues such as worker exploitation, tax avoidance, farm welfare and the differential between highest-paid and lowest-paid workers in organisations. EC applies an ethical rating to companies, giving scores out of 20, so that consumers can readily identify companies which are not behaving as ethically as they might. In practice, few companies seem to score higher than around 6 out of 20, so there is some way to go in achieving an ethical paradise on Earth.

EC's manifesto may seem to some to be extreme – but to others it makes perfect sense. The manifesto contains nine essential demands:

1. A Responsible Purchasing Act requiring all public sector institutions to take stated ethical issues into account when making procurement decisions.
2. Compulsory annual social and environmental reporting by all businesses.

3. Socially responsible consumption, and its history and diversity, should be required learning as part of the core curriculum.

4. A 'Tobin Tax' on international currency speculation.

5. A Europe-wide toxics release inventory accessible from an open access website on the US model.

6. Mandatory carbon-footprint labelling and A–E energy consumption labelling on all products.

7. Any company group with subsidiary companies located in specified tax havens should be refused permission to trade.

8. Higher minimum standards for farm animal welfare for both home-produced and imported animal products.

9. Companies should be required to report annually on the ratio between their highest and lowest paid workers.

©iStock.com/Oehoeboeroe

Some of these may even be unenforceable – tax haven status would be difficult – but these are the criteria against which companies are judged. Ethical consumers can check which companies score well, and can boycott those which score least: the organisation even offers explanations as to why companies have scored well or badly, For example, Sainsbury's supermarket scores highly for its widespread stock of Fairtrade products, but lost points for its supply chain management and for selling produce from illegal Israeli settlements on the West Bank.

This ability to break down the ratings into separate issues is useful to ethical consumers because they can decide which issues are most important. For some, workers' rights would be higher on the scale than animal welfare, for example, and there will be those who do not worry too much about environmental reporting provided companies pay their taxes on time.

There is some evidence that campaigns and boycotts by ethical consumers do have some effect – Amazon has announced that it will be revising its tax avoidance schemes, and recent campaigns against Shell Oil appear to have had an effect in reducing oil drilling in the Arctic. Ultimately, though, consumers need to be informed about ethical and unethical practice on the part of companies, and *Ethical Consumer* is well-placed to provide that service.

QUESTIONS

1. What are the main reasons an ethical consumer would want to use *Ethical Consumer*'s ratings system?

2. Why would a company care what *Ethical Consumer* writes about them?

3. What is the purpose of the manifesto?

4. Why do so few companies score well on *Ethical Consumer*'s rating scales?

5. What is the role of *Ethical Consumer* in organising boycotts?

FURTHER READING

For a review of ethical marketing practices, see a *Harvard Business Review* article by Professor Julie Irwin, Ethical consumerism isn't dead, it just needs better marketing. https://hbr.org/2015/01/ethical-consumerism-isnt-dead-it-just-needs-better-marketing (accessed 2 February 2016).

Does the 'conscious consumer' demand transparency as they take an increasing interest in the ethical practices of those they buy from? Jessie Baker in the UK's *Guardian* newspaper takes a stance: www.theguardian.com/women-in-leadership/2015/apr/02/the-rise-of-the-conscious-consumer-why-businesses-need-to-open-up (accessed 2 February 2016).

A Mintel report in July 2015 examines the issue of communicating ethics to different generations, as well as companies needing to improve the visibility of their CSR activity: http://store.mintel.com/the-ethical-consumer-uk-july-2015?cookie_test=true (accessed 2 February 2016).

During the summer of 2014, environmentalists Muna Dajani and Lina Isma'il conducted research for an innovative Palestinian guidebook. The authors visited farmers, artisans and companies throughout Palestine, and wrote 100 profiles introducing their work. The result of their journey is a guidebook (*Conscious Choices: A Guide to Ethical Consumerism in Palestine*) that invites its readers to get to know the people behind the products they buy, and to build and expand their own individual network of producers: https://ps.boell.org/en/2015/05/12/conscious-choices-guide-ethical-consumerism-palestine (accessed 2 February 2016).

REFERENCES

Albinsson, P.A. and Perera, B.Y. (2009) From trash to treasure and beyond: the meaning of voluntary disposition. *Journal of Consumer Behaviour*, 8 (6): 340–53.

Arsel, Z. (2010) Exploring the social dynamics of online bartering. *Advances in Consumer Research*, 37: 67–8.

Ayal, S. and Gino, F. (2011) Honest rationales for dishonest behavior. In M. Mikulincer and P.R. Shaver (eds), *The Social Psychology of Morality: Exploring the Causes of Good and Evil*. Washington, DC: American Psychological Association, pp. 149–66.

Bagozzi, R.P. and Dabholkar, P.A. (1994) Consumer recycling goals and their effect on decisions to recycle: a means–end chain analysis. *Psychology and Marketing*, 11 (July/August): 313–40.

Bauman, Z. (1995) *Life in Fragments: Essays in postmodern morality*. Oxford: Blackwell.

Belk, R.W. (1989) The role of possessions in constructing and maintaining a sense of past. *Advances in Consumer Research*, 17: 669–76.

Bendell, J. (1998) Citizen's Cane? Relations between business and civil society. Paper presented at the International Society for Third-Sector Research (ISTR) 3rd International Conference, Geneva 8–11 July.

Black, I.R. (2011) Sorry not today: self and temporary consumption denial. *Journal of Consumer Behaviour*, 10 (5): 267–78.

Brace-Govan, J. and Binay, I. (2010) Consumption of disposed goods for moral identities: a nexus of organisation, place, things and consumers. *Journal of Consumer Behaviour*, 9 (1): 69–82.

Brass, D.J., Butterfield, K.D. and Skaggs, B.C. (1998) Relationships and unethical behavior: a social network perspective. *The Academy of Management Review*, 23: 14–31.

Brower, M., Leon, W. and Union of Concerned Scientists (1999) *The Consumer's Guide to Effective Environmental Choices: Practical Advice from the Union of Concerned Scientists*. New York: Three Rivers Press.

Cheetham, F. (2009) Out of control? An ethnographic analysis of the disposal of collectable objects through auction. *Journal of Consumer Behaviour*, 8 (6): 316–26.

Cherrier, H. (2009) Disposal and simple living: exploring the circulation of goods and the development of sacred consumption. *Journal of Consumer Behaviour*, 8 (6): 327–39.

Cohen, E. (2003) *A Consumers' Republic. The Politics of Mass Consumption in Post-war America*. New York: Knopf.

Coulter, R.A. and Ligas, M. (2003) To retain or to relinquish: exploring the disposition practices of packrats and purgers. *Advances in Consumer Research*, 30: 38.

Denegri-Knott, J. and Molesworth, M. (2009) I'll sell this and I'll buy them that: eBay and the management of possessions as stock. *Journal of Consumer Behaviour*, 8 (6): 305–15.

de Pelsmacker, P., Janssens, W. and Geuens, M. (2002) Environmentally friendly behaviour with respect to air pollution: the role of environmental knowledge, concern and perceived behavioural control. In M. Farhangmehr (ed.), *Proceedings of the 31st EMAC Conference*, Universidade do Minho, Braga.

Dubois, D., Rucker, D.D. and Galinsky, A.D. (2015) Social class, power, and selfishness: when and why upper and lower class individuals behave unethically. *Journal of Personality and Social Psychology*. http://dx.doi.org/10.1037/pspi0000008.

Fairtrade International (2014) *Statement on SOAS Report*. www.fairtrade.net/single-view+M5a2383b864f.html (accessed 29 September 2015).

Fernandes, T. and Calamote, A. (2015) Unfairness in consumer services: outcomes of differential treatment of new and existing clients. *Journal of Retailing and Consumer Services*, 28: 36–44.

Findlay, K. and Yeoman, I. (2015) Dr Spock's Food Festival. *Journal of Tourism Futures*, 1 (2): 148–51.

Frank, D. (1985) Housewives, socialists and the politics of food: the 1917 New York cost of living protests, *Feminist Studies*, 11: 255–85.

Gino, F. and Bazerman, M.H. (2009) When misconduct goes unnoticed: the acceptability of gradual erosion in others' unethical behavior. *Journal of Experimental Social Psychology*, 45: 708–19.

Glickman, L.B. (1999) Born to shop? Consumer history and American history. In L.B. Glickman (ed.), *Consumer Society in American History. A Reader*. Ithaca, NY: Cornell University Press, pp. 1–14.

Harrison, R., Newholm, T. and Shaw, D. (2005) *The Ethical Consumer*. London: Sage.

Hartmann, P. and Ibanez, V.A. (2006) Green value added. *Marketing Intelligence and Planning*, 24 (7): 673–80.

Humphery, K. (2011) The simple and the good: ethical consumption as anti-consumerism. In T. Lewis and E. Potter (eds), *Ethical Consumption: A Critical Introduction*. London and New York: Routledge, pp. 40–53.

Iyer, E.S. and Kashyap, R.K. (2007) Consumer recycling: role of incentives, information and social class. *Journal of Consumer Behaviour*, 6: 32–47.

Jackson, T.E. (2006) *The Earthscan Reader in Sustainable Consumption*. London: Earthscan.

Jacoby, J., Berning, C.K. and Dietvorst, T.F. (1977) What about disposition? *Journal of Marketing*, 41 (April): 23.

Jones, T.M. (1991) Ethical decision making by individuals in organisations: an issue-contingent model. *The Academy of Management Review*, 16: 366–95.

Laroche, M., Bergeron, J. and Barbaro-Forleo, G. (2001) Targeting consumers who are willing to pay more for environmentally friendly products. *Journal of Consumer Marketing*, 18 (6): 503–20.

Liebe, U. Andorfer, V.A., Gwartney, P.A. and Meyerhoff, J. (2014) *Ethical Consumption and Social Context: Experimental Evidence from Germany and the United States*, University of Bern Social Sciences Working Paper No. 7. ftp://130.92.178.7/files/wp7/liebe-andorfer-gwartney-meyerhoff-2014.pdf (accessed 25 September 2015).

Littler, J. (2008) *Radical Consumption: Shopping for Change in Contemporary Culture*. Berkshire: Open University Press.

Maycroft, N. (2009) Moving things along: hoarding, clutter and other ambiguous matter. *Journal of Consumer Behaviour*, 8 (6): 354–64.

Mazar, N., Amir, O. and Ariely, D. (2008) The dishonesty of honest people: a theory of self-concept maintenance. *Journal of Marketing Research*, 45: 633–44.

Modi, A.G. and Patel, J.D. (2013) Classifying consumers based upon their pro-environmental behaviour: and empirical investigation. *Asian Academy of Management Journal*, 18 (2): 85–104.

Monin, B. and Jordan, A.H. (2009) The dynamic moral self: a social psychological perspective. In D. Navarez and D. Lapsley (eds), *Personality, Identity and Character: Explorations in Moral Psychology*. New York: Cambridge University Press, pp. 341–54.

Paco, A. and Raposo, M. (2009) Green segmentation: an application to the Portuguese consumer market, *Marketing Intelligence and Planning*, 27 (3): 364–79.

Peattie, K. (2001) Golden goose or wild goose? The hunt for the green consumer. *Business Strategy and the Environment*, 10 (4): 187–99.

Rieuwerts, J. (2015) *The Elements of Environmental Pollution*. Abingdon: Routledge.

Roper Starch Worldwide (1997) *Green Gauge Report*. New York: Roper Starch Worldwide Inc.

Roux, D. (2010) Identity and self-territory in second-hand clothing transfers. *Advances in Consumer Research*, 37: 65–6.

Sego, T. (2010) Mothers' experience related to the disposal of children's clothing and gear: keeping Mister Clatters but tossing Broken Barbie. *Journal of Consumer Behaviour*, 9 (1): 57–68.

Sherry, J.F. (1990) A sociocultural analysis of a Midwestern American flea market. *Journal of Consumer Research*, 17 (June): 13–30.

Smith, N.C. (1990) *Morality and the Market: Consumer Pressure for Corporate Accountability*. Abingdon: Routledge.

SOAS (2014) *Fairtrade, Employment and Poverty Reduction in Ethiopia and Uganda*. http://ftepr.org/ (accessed 29 September 2015).

Starkey, D. (2015) An evening of conversation with David Starkey, 21 September, Henrietta Barnet Girls School, Main Hall.

Strasser, S., McGovern, C. and Judd, M. (1998) *Getting and Spending: European and American Consumer Societies in the 20th Century*. Cambridge: Cambridge University Press.

Straughan, R. and Roberts, J. (1999) Environmental segmentation alternatives: a look at green consumer behaviour in the new millennium. *Journal of Consumer Marketing*, 16 (6): 558–75.

Tallontire, A., Rentsendorj, E. and Blowfield, M. (2001) *Ethical Consumers and Ethical Trade: A Review of Current Literature*. Policy Series 12. Chatham, UK: Natural Resources Centre, University of Greenwich.

Trentmann, F. (2006) *The Making of the Consumer: Knowledge, Power and Identity in the Modern World*. Oxford: Berg.

Treviño, L.K., Weaver, G.R. and Reynolds, S.J. (2006) Behavioral ethics in organizations: a review. *Journal of Management*, 32: 951–90.

Whan, E. (2010) *Greendex 2010: Consumer Choice and the Environment – A Worldwide Tracking Survey. National Geographic and GlobeScan*, GSI Publishing, Canada.

Yeoman, I. (2012) *2050: Tomorrow's Tourism*. Bristol: Channelview.

Zadek, S., Lingayah, S., Murphy, S. and New Economics Foundation (1998) *Purchasing Power: Civil Action for Sustainable Consumption*. London: New Economics Foundation.

Zhu, J., Chen, J. and Dasgupta, S. (2008) Exploring the effect of a trade-in on consumers' willingness to pay for a new product. *Advances in Consumer Research*, 35: 157–8.

MORE ONLINE

For additional materials that support this chapter and your learning, please visit:
https://study.sagepub.com/sethnaandblythe

PART FOUR

CONSUMER BEHAVIOUR IN CONCLUSION

The final chapter in the book looks at what happens after purchase. Apart from consuming the product/service, people make assessments of how much they liked (or disliked) it, and also have to consider how to dispose of it when it is no longer useful. In the 21st century, service industries have become far more important than manufacturing industries on almost every measure. Services employ more people, represent a bigger chunk of gross national product, have higher turnovers and are growing more rapidly than any manufacturing industry: this final chapter covers the consumer behaviour aspects of this phenomenon.

CHAPTER 15

POST-PURCHASE BEHAVIOUR

LEARNING OBJECTIVES

After reading this chapter you should be able to:

- Explain how the attributes of a product and the relationship between supplier and consumer contribute to the perception of quality.
- Explain how satisfaction and dissatisfaction are generated.
- Show how complaints develop.
- Explain the advantages and disadvantages of various supplier approaches to complaint handling.
- Show how consumers might reduce dissonance.
- Explain the different routes open to consumers when disposing of used or unwanted products.

INTRODUCTION

For some marketers, the job appears to be finished once the sale is made. For consumers, the purchase is only the beginning of the consumption experience. The post-purchase behaviour of consumers determines (ultimately) whether they will buy again, whether they will come back and complain or (in the worst case) whether they will tell their friends, family and even consumer protection organisations about their bad experience with the product and/or service.

Post-purchase evaluation and behaviour are therefore key issues for marketers, particularly in a relationship marketing context. Organisations need to look carefully at the key components of building relationships with customers and then take strategic action throughout the whole company if they are to pursue customer retention and extract positive behavioural intentions from customers (Hossein and Mohammad 2015). Within this evaluation, expected and actual quality of the products plays a role in leading to a decision as to whether the product represents value for money; a product that falls below the expected quality will create dissatisfaction, but the problem for marketers lies in deciphering and then deciding exactly what consumers believe quality actually is.

QUALITY

Following on from a purchase, people will evaluate whether the purchase has worked out well or not, given the context and the situation. This is a process of comparing the outcome with the previous expectation of the product: the result is an estimate of the quality of the product.

Quality is a complex construct subject to varying definitions. In many cases marketers use the term as a substitute for the word 'good' – very good equates to high quality; bad denotes poor quality. Of course, this is an over-simplification. Here are some definitions of quality in current use:

> *Quality is the standard of something as measured against other things of a similar kind; the degree of excellence of something. (*Oxford English Dictionary*, 2015)*

> *Quality is defined as fully satisfying agreed customer requirements at the lowest internal price. (Bank 1992)*

> *Quality means conforming to requirements. (Crosby 1984)*

> *Quality is about fitness for use. (Juran 1982)*

> *Quality can only be defined by customers and occurs where an organisation supplies goods or services to a specification that satisfies their needs. (Palmer 1998)*

There have been attempts to distinguish between subjective and objective measures of quality. Swan and Combs (1976) defined two elements of service quality. First, they referred to instrumental quality, which describes the physical aspects of the product or service, and second they referred to the expressive dimension, which is about the intangible or psychological aspects. Although the authors were talking about services in particular, there appears to be no reason why the same dimensions should not apply to physical products. Gronroos (1984) identified technical quality and functional quality as the components of overall quality, with technical quality being the quantifiable aspects of the quality construct, and functional quality being those aspects that arise through the interaction between consumer and supplier.

Figure 15.1 shows how the interaction between supplier and customer leads to functional quality, which then combines with technical quality to generate the overall quality.

Because technical quality can be easily measured it is something that both the supplier and the consumer can agree on. For example, the reliability of delivery of a thesis which needs to arrive 'next day' is a technical aspect of the Post Office service: the percentage of parcels that arrive on time can be calculated, and (provided the statistics are honest) both parties can agree that this is, in fact, the technical quality of what is happening. What cannot be agreed is the degree to which individual consumers regard reliable delivery as important. For some who need the thesis delivered next day in order not to miss a university deadline, this becomes crucial. For others this is less important than perhaps a lower (or more competitive) cost of postage.

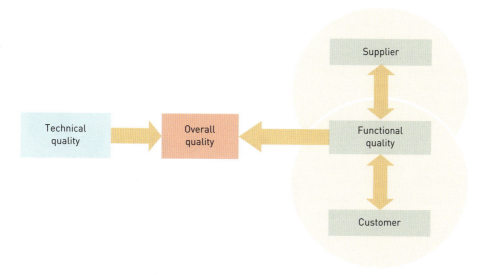

FIGURE 15.1 Components of quality

People are also influenced by how the benefits are delivered to them. This is what Gronroos (1984) calls the functional quality, and it cannot be measured objectively because it is a function of the individual's needs and expectations. This problem of assessing quality is much harder in services markets, because the functional quality forms a much greater proportion of the total product experience. This means that effective communication with consumers becomes more important as we move towards the 'service' end of the product continuum.

In summary, quality seems to relate to the extent to which a product's performance meets customers' expectations and requirements, so it would appear to be a construct between what the marketers provide and what the customer receives. This is, of course, subjective: there is, therefore, no absolute measure of quality.

CHALLENGING THE STATUS QUO

In recent years, especially in the UK, we have heard a great deal about offering people choice. This has been particularly the case in public services such as schools, where formerly people were simply sent to the nearest school whatever their personal preferences or, indeed, needs.

   Now we have league tables for schools and universities, and choices about where and when we receive these services. Yet is that actually improving the situation for consumers? If there is a league table, doesn't that simply place added burdens on already overstretched teachers and administrators? And in reality, what are the actual chances of people further down a list looking to those further up the list to learn best practice?

   The OECD published the biggest ever global school rankings in 2015, based on the 'quality of education'. Andreas Schleicher said that 'The idea is to give more countries, rich and poor, access to comparing themselves against the world's education leaders, to discover their relative strengths and weaknesses, and to see what the long-term economic gains from improved quality in schooling could be for them'. When one looks at the list with countries ranked on achievements in Maths and Science, the top five places are occupied by Asian countries (1 – Singapore, 2 – Hong Kong, 3 – South Korea, 4 – Japan and Taiwan). Closer to home, European countries ranked as follows: 13 – Germany, 15 – Ireland, 20 – UK, 23 – France, 27 – Spain. Others included: 28 – USA, 28 – Italy, 40 – Greece, 45 – UAE, 66 – Saudi Arabia.

©iStock.com/dolgachov

But how does this help individual countries? Wouldn't it be better if we just ensured that all local educational services worked efficiently and effectively for the local market, that is that each country's government should design and implement national educational strategies and plans based on nationally appropriate standards for teaching and curricula? There are of course other 'metrics' that could be used to identify and measure quality in education in each country. For instance, the percentage of teachers trained to nationally adopted standards and who have an awareness of specific academic and gender awareness skills; adequate supply of textbooks, equipment and other learning material; availability of sanitation and toilet facilities for boys and girls; and conflict and violence-free environments for students en route to and within schools. Surely in such a model there has to be an interaction between and engagement with parents, teachers and the local community, otherwise how can we as consumers of education ever hope to improve the learning?

If we get the technical quality right, surely for most people the functional quality will not lag far behind!

POST-PURCHASE EVALUATION

An evaluation of the product's performance against the consumer's pre-purchase expectation will result in several possible outcomes. In most cases, people are satisfied with their purchases to a greater or lesser extent. In some cases, people may be dissatisfied to a greater or lesser extent, and in a few cases they will be extremely dissatisfied. Equally, in a few cases the individual will be more than satisfied, perhaps even delighted, with the product. The process of post-purchase evaluation is shown in Figure 15.2.

Satisfaction has been described as the full meeting of one's expectations (Oliver 1980), but there are probably degrees of satisfaction, i.e. points at which the individual feels less than completely satisfied, but would still feel that reasonable

FIGURE 15.2 Post-purchase evaluation

expectations have been met. From a marketing viewpoint, customer satisfaction is regarded as the most important factor in developing the business and meeting corporate goals: satisfied customers are more likely to generate positive word of mouth, they are more likely to return and buy again and they are more likely to increase the quantities purchased. Satisfaction does not necessarily mean that the customer will always return; dissatisfaction almost certainly means that the customer will not return, however, provided there are other options available. Therefore satisfaction is necessary but not sufficient for developing loyalty in customers.

In choosing between products, customers are likely to anticipate the level of satisfaction they will obtain from making a particular purchase. In anticipating satisfaction, people are more likely to pay attention to product attributes that are 'vivid' in nature (i.e. are easy to visualise, and easy to imagine as experiences) than they are to less vivid attributes (Shiv and Huber 2000). For example, someone who is thinking about buying a new outfit is likely to concentrate more on how it will look when worn, and possibly on how easy it is to keep clean, than on what materials it is made of or even what it costs to buy. After owning the clothes for a while, the individual might find that the material wears out quickly or stretches out of shape. Anticipated satisfaction is therefore related to how the individual thinks the product will function rather than to the actual performance of the product in use.

Measuring satisfaction and dissatisfaction relies on what is called the disconfirmation paradigm. The two variables in this paradigm are pre-purchase expectations and post-purchase disconfirmation. Expectations are matched by either **positive disconfirmation** (the product performs better than expected) or **negative disconfirmation** (the product performs worse than expected). The greater the positive disconfirmation, the greater the satisfaction (Churchill and Surprenant 1982), and if the difference between the two is large enough, then the consumer feels delighted (Oliver 1997). Managing expectations is therefore a key factor in managing overall satisfaction – raising unrealistic expectations will lead to negative disconfirmation, even though low expectations may well mean that the initial purchase is less likely.

Positive disconfirmation

An unexpectedly good outcome of a purchase

Negative disconfirmation

A state of affairs in which the expected outcome is disappointing or fails in some way to satisfy

Santos and Boote (2003) describe four post-purchase affective states, as follows:

1. *Delight.* This occurs when either performance of the product falls between the individual's ideal and desired level of performance (a disconfirmed experience of delight) or when the consumer expected to be delighted (a confirmed experience of delight).

2. *Satisfaction* (or positive indifference). This occurs when product performance falls between desired and predicted level (a disconfirmed experience of satisfaction) or when the person expected to be satisfied (a confirmed experience of satisfaction). This is probably a fairly common experience.

3. *Acceptance* (or negative indifference). Acceptance occurs when product performance falls between the person's predicted and minimum tolerable level of expectation (a disconfirmed experience of acceptance) or when the person expected the performance to be no more than satisfactory (a confirmed experience of acceptance).

4. *Dissatisfaction.* When product performance falls between the minimum tolerable and the worst imaginable levels of expectation, there will be a disconfirmed experience of dissatisfaction. If the consumer expected to be dissatisfied, there will be a confirmed experience of dissatisfaction. For example, if a holidaymaker is setting off on a pre-booked package holiday and the weather forecast is extremely bad, he or she is expecting not to enjoy the holiday – the thunderstorms and gales will come as no surprise, but will still lead to dissatisfaction.

The psychological impact of loss is often greater than the impact of a comparable gain (Hankuk and Agarwal 2003). Interestingly, these researchers found that loss of quality takes precedence over loss of price – in other words, if people feel that they have overpaid for something this is less important than if they feel that they have bought something which is of poor quality. This implies that firms need to make a large reduction in price if people are to be happy with a poor-quality product.

People often evaluate other people's purchases, and often take pleasure from seeing other people's purchases fail (Sundie et al. 2006). Pleasure at the downfall of another is called schadenfreude and may not be the noblest of human emotions, but it does exist. According to Sundie et al., schadenfreude is greater when a high-status product fails than when a low-status product fails: in other words, when your friend's new Porsche breaks down you will feel a certain secret delight, whereas when his new Nespresso machine suddenly stops making espressos, you simply feel sorry for him, and you may even share his pain.

CONSEQUENCES OF POST-PURCHASE EVALUATION

How people act following on from their evaluation of the consequences of their purchases is of course of intense interest for marketers. Typically, post-purchase behaviour falls into the following categories:

- Repurchase
- Complaint
- Word of mouth recommendation
- No change of behaviour at all.

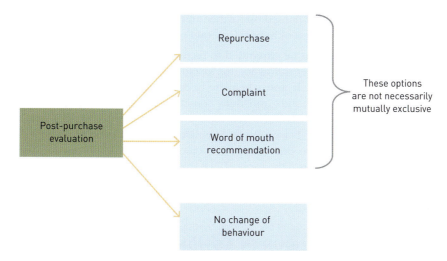

FIGURE 15.3 Consequences of post-purchase evaluation

Repurchase is almost always a clear indicator that the customer was satisfied with the product. Repurchase is perhaps best explained by the operant conditioning model discussed in Chapter 9: an action that has a positive outcome (consuming the product) is likely to be repeated (buying another of the same). Repeat buying behaviour has already been discussed in more detail in Chapter 4.

Figure 15.3 shows the possible consequences of post-purchase evaluation, in other words how evaluation might translate into behaviour. Note that the first three options are not mutually exclusive – it is perfectly possible for someone to complain, but still repurchase (for example, if the complaint is handled to the individual's satisfaction). This might in turn lead to positive word of mouse recommendation on one of the review websites.

Complaining behaviour may take one of three forms (Singh 1988). These are as follows:

1. *Voiced complaints.* These are complaints made directly to the supplier, and are probably the best outcome from the supplier's viewpoint (apart, of course, from complete satisfaction with the product) since they provide an opportunity for the supplier to redress the problem. Such complaints should be dealt with promptly and effectively, since there is some evidence to indicate that customers whose complaints are dealt with to their complete satisfaction may become more loyal than customers who did not have a complaint in the first place. Some people (older people, for example) are often reluctant to voice complaints, so may need extra encouragement (Grougiou and Pettigrew 2009).

2. **Third-party complaints.** In this case, the complainer goes to a lawyer, a consumer rights champion or even the news media to make the complaint. This can create serious problems for the supplier, although to be fair most third parties would check with the supplier first, and give them a chance to make amends, before taking further action.

3. *Private complaints.* Here the complainer tells friends, family, work colleagues and anyone else who will listen about the failure on the part of the supplier. This negative word of mouth can be destructive for the supplier, depending on how far it

Third-party complaint

In complaining, the act of involving someone other than the complainer or the supplier, for example a lawyer or consumer rights campaigner reaches and whether it is passed on further. In recent years, there have been many examples of negative word of mouse (Internet or emailed complaining behaviour).

4. The third category might be expanded to include **social media complaints**. Here the complainer tells his or her followers (for instance on Twitter) about the failure on the part of the supplier. If and when the tweet gets *favourited* and re-tweeted, unless the supplier responds and does something about it very quickly, there is every chance the story could reach thousands (if not millions) of people in a very short space of time. For example, Ellen DeGeneres' picture from the Oscars, flanked by a dozen or so other stars, attracted over 3.3 million re-tweets in the space of about 30 minutes – the same effect, through the ether, might be imagined if there were bad news about a company's products or services.

Social media complaint

The use of any social media platform with which to highlight a complaint about a product or service failure

Shadow websites

Websites that offer an opportunity to post negative stories about specific companies or brands

CONSUMER BEHAVIOUR IN ACTION: SHADOW WEBSITES

The McSpotlight website clearly says on their front page, 'McDonald's spends over $2 billion a year broadcasting their glossy image to the world. This is a small space for alternatives to be heard'. Started in 1996, partly in response to the longest-running libel case in British legal history, this shadow website is the product of a group of anti-McDonald's, anti-globalisation, possibly anti-capitalist activists based in 16 countries. McSpotlight is dedicated to attacking McDonald's on every front – providing information about McDonald's 'exploitation' of meat animals, about the company's low wages, about dubious marketing practices, about the endless stream of litigation which McDonald's has engaged in, and about the health hazards of fast foods. The website owners say that they are not especially against McDonald's, but are rather against what McDonald's represents in terms of globalisation, environmental damage and exploitation of consumers.

The Anti-Nuclear Alliance of Western Australia also runs a website on which it attacks Rio Tinto (the mining corporation) among others. In particular, the site attacks Rio Tinto's Namibian uranium mining operations, attacking exploitation of workers and environmentally damaging mining methods.

In New York, the Killer Coke campaign uses a website to allege that Coca-Cola uses strong-arm tactics to break up union activities in Colombia and elsewhere. The website is detailed in its allegations – and the authors of the website have no problem revealing their address.

McSpotlight also has a website dedicated to Shell Oil, offering similar opportunities for people to attack the company. There is little that Shell can do about this – the website operates from several countries, and therefore it is difficult or even impossible for Shell to locate the perpetrators, let alone sue them (bearing in mind that different countries have different rules about libel and freedom of speech).

Many large companies have attracted the attention of people who are Net-literate enough to create a counter-website. As a way of complaining about a company it certainly puts the customer in charge – if the website is named carefully, and the right keywords are chosen, it should come up within the first ten or so sites and therefore will be seen by anyone accessing the corporation's legitimate site. From the corporation's viewpoint, this is probably not good, but of course most people are aware that the Internet is not a reliable source of information – after all, anyone can say anything on there without much fear of reprisals.

The companies that do respond do so at their peril – being seen as humourless – and perhaps even as using bullying tactics. Either way, it probably does more to damage the corporate image than being pilloried by a small group of people with very limited resources.

The question is, though, if your organisation were targeted, how would you react, given the fact that there is a plethora of social media platforms that are available to you to form an 'integrated' response?

People do not always complain, even when dissatisfied. Complainers are more likely to be involved with the product, and also have impulsive personalities (Sharma et al. 2010). Complaining behaviour will only occur when some or all of the following conditions apply (see Figure 15.4):

1. The consumer blames someone else for the problem. If the individual attributes blame to themselves (perhaps knowing that the purchase decision was a mistake) there is no one to complain to.

2. The experience was particularly negative. A minor problem is likely to be overlooked, for example poor service in a restaurant might not be worth complaining about: the customer simply does not eat at that restaurant again.

3. There is a reasonable chance of some kind of redress being forthcoming. There is no point in complaining if the customer believes that the supplier either will not, or cannot, make amends: if people do not think that their complaint will be taken seriously, they are more likely simply to switch brands than to complain (Richins 1987). For example, if the product was purchased in a closing-down sale and the shop has since gone out of business there is really no point in complaining. Note that this behaviour is not only likely to extend to private complaints as well as voiced or third-party complaints, but is equally applicable to social media complaining. The complaining activity will be possible within the level of the individual's time and money resources. There is no point in complaining about a product bought in a duty-free shop at Istanbul Airport if you're now back at home in Manchester. At a less obvious level, a packet of biscuits that turn out to be almost all broken is unlikely to be worth complaining about, even if the grocery shop is a few hundred yards away.

Customers who are dissatisfied but also powerless (perhaps because the company has high exit barriers) are likely to hold a grudge, avoid further dealings with the company if possible, and will want to retaliate if opportunity presents itself (Bunker and Ball 2009). For example, if someone has a bad experience with their broadband supplier, it may be very difficult to switch providers – having to acquire a new email address, perhaps having a contract to complete, or having to lose favourite TV channels might make it very complex to move. The customer will then avoid taking up any further services, and may well give negative word of mouth to friends and family, and a wider negative word of mouse to a larger online community.

The current thinking is that marketers should actively encourage people to complain: people who are dissatisfied are more likely to spread the bad news to friends and family in private responses than they are to spread good news if they are satisfied (Schibrowsky and Lapidus 1994). Also, it turns out that people whose complaints are

FIGURE 15.4 Factors in complaining behaviour

completely satisfied feel even better about the supplier than they would if nothing had gone wrong in the first place (Speer 1996). This may seem surprising, but actually it makes sense: consumers know that we do not live in a perfect world, and things will occasionally go wrong, so knowing that a supplier will put things right promptly is reassuring and helps build the relationship between supplier and consumer (Alvarez et al. 2011). Another supplier represents an unknown quantity on this dimension. Of course, good complaint handling is no substitute for providing a good service in the first place (Liljander 1999).

The rapid growth in online purchasing has created a further problem in that people often find that what is delivered is not exactly what they wanted. There is an additional risk in making purchases online, because it is much harder to inspect the product: obviously this does not matter if the product in question is something that has been bought before – ordering a printer cartridge or original Nespresso pods online is not very risky – but in other cases the product may well not come up to standard. This means that online retailers need to have a no-quibble return policy in order to reduce the perceived risk. This in turn means that people may abuse the system by using a product once or twice and then returning it. This abuse is not different in kind from someone buying a dinner suit or evening dress, wearing it for one special occasion, and then returning it to the shop: it is part of the risk for the retailer (King and Dennis 2006; King et al. 2007, 2008), but in the online environment it is almost entirely unavoidable if business is to be done at all.

In 2015, the Institute of Customer Service conducted their own comprehensive survey, and the results were supposed to give businesses clear direction on how they could sue social media to improve the levels of customer satisfaction. Interestingly, over an 18-month period, from the beginning of 2014, there has been an eight-fold increase in customer complaints made on social media, probably because complaining in this way is cheap and convenient.

However, there is a downside to encouraging complaint behaviour. First, it can lead people to believe that there are likely to be problems, and consequently the initial purchase becomes less likely. Second, it can lead to a 'complaining culture' in which people complain at the slightest excuse. At the extreme, it can lead to the 'professional complainer' who deliberately searches out something to complain about in order to obtain a price reduction or a free gift of some sort. Professional complainers are known to exist in the package holiday industry, for example.

Obviously the existence of professional complainers creates a problem for suppliers, in that they need to judge whether a complaint is genuine, frivolous or fraudulent. Making a mistake could lead to serious consequences, so (at present at least) most suppliers would rather pay out the occasional fraudulent or frivolous claim rather than risk annoying a genuine customer or being sued for a genuine claim.

CHALLENGING THE STATUS QUO

There was once a cartoon in which a very large man with a cudgel was shown standing underneath a sign saying 'Complaints Department'. Like most jokes, this was funny because it stated a real truth in some companies – complaining will only result in verbal abuse, and being tossed onto the street.

Nowadays we expect our complaints to be taken seriously, because the law is on our side and anyway it's only fair. So if we take a new suit or dress back to the shop, we expect a refund of our money, even if there is nothing wrong with the item except that we changed our minds. Because that's what's right, right?

Well maybe no – maybe it isn't right. People who complain are adding to the cost of products that other people buy. If our complaints department is a large man with a cudgel, our costs will drop – and they would drop even further if we didn't have a complaints department at all, as is the case with some cheap airlines. Those savings can be passed on to customers who do not complain, who accept that the world is not perfect and who accept that life is risky!

©iStock.com/yuoak

So let's then look at the 'cost of complaining'. If you use a 'service' number, as a lot of companies do (you know, those 0844, 0845, 0871 and 0870 numbers), BT will charge anything between 5p per minute (from a landline) to 76p per minute (from a mobile). So this means that by the time you get through, then you're put on hold, and then have the actual conversation itself, you can almost hear the pounds walking out of your bank account. A 45-minute call from a mobile at peak times could cost nearly £35 at the rates shown above. Consumers feel that these blatant *rip-offs* have become a problem to such extent that retaliation is now taking place – type in the expensive telephone number into a website called www.saynoto0870.com and they will actually find you the landline number to which the 08 number is attached – meaning that you can then call that landline number at landline rates!

Finally, research conducted by BBC Watchdog Daily (2015) found that if you're using a mobile, calling Apple to complain can cost up to £1.05 more than when calling them to buy something (and that's before you even speak to someone).

CONSUMER BEHAVIOUR IN ACTION: COMPLAINTS IN ACTION

The British have never been one to complain, for fear of 'making a scene'. Tour operators used to say that Brits were the least likely to complain. If it turned out that the hotel was overbooked, the Swedes and Germans would bang on the counter and demand to be accommodated, while the Brits would shrug their shoulders meekly, sigh a gentle 'Oh never mind' and get back on the tour bus. In recent years, though, consumer protection organisations have been plugging the idea of complaining if things are not entirely satisfactory – with the result that some people seem to think that complaining is compulsory.

©iStock.com/klenger

Not only that, but complaining can be immediate too. Remember, if the company doesn't respond quickly, the complaint may go viral, which means potentially worldwide. This means we're potentially talking about a large number of people viewing negative comments about an organisation. Here are a few examples of how people are using social media to channel their complaints.

A British Airways customer tweeted, 'Don't fly @British Airways. Their customer service is horrendous' and this was seen by 76,000 users. Unfortunately for BA, they didn't respond for eight hours and then wrote, 'Sorry for the delay in responding, our twitter feed is open 0900–1700 GMT. Please DM your baggage ref and we'll look into this'. The response they got was classic … '@British_Airways how does a billion dollar corp only have 9–5 social media support for a business that operates 24/7? DM me yourselves'. The customer makes a valid point here. The nature of social media means that it never sleeps – people are connected 24/7 and will use various media platforms to voice their concerns when it suits them, NOT when the company is available for comment.

Sometimes gentle humour may serve a purpose. A Sainsbury's customer was obviously unhappy with his sandwich and tweeted, 'Dear Sainsbury's. The chicken in my sandwich tastes like it was beaten to death by Hulk Hogan. Was it?'. Sainsbury's were quick to reply back with, 'Really sorry it wasn't up to scratch. We will replace Mr Hogan with Ultimate Warrior on our production line immediately'. And then later, 'Call us on this number xxxx and we're really sorry you had to wrestle your way through the sandwich'. This proves that dialogue between an unhappy customer and an organisation doesn't always have to be antagonistic. A little bit of humour goes a long way in diffusing a situation and reminding everyone involved that ultimately they are communicating with another person.

Of course, celebrities are bound to have many more followers than the average Twitter user. Patrick Stewart tweeted a complaint which then received 1,800 re-tweets and 800 comments. But then it's no surprise as he did play Jean-Luc Picard – the Captain of The Enterprise in *Star Trek*. It would be unlikely that a mere mortal would get that kind of coverage for writing a simple tweet hinting that they have been having difficulty with setting up a new cable account. What this shows is that celebrities wield a lot of power on the basis that their followers are listening to them all the time. The side debate here is whether this diminishes a celebrity's right to say what they feel; for fear of instigating someone into doing something.

Sometimes such complaining behaviour can backfire on the complainant, however. A woman from Florida had apparently not been given a receipt after her last visit to Dunkin' Donuts, and cited a store policy that entitles customers to a free item if they are not given a receipt after a purchase. She then walked into a local Dunkin' Donuts with her smartphone video ready to record. In the video we see her filming herself while being extremely rude and harassing an incredibly patient and polite Dunkin' Donuts employee for her free items. There is a constant hurling of racial epithets and threatening to post the video online. The good news is that as one would expect, the outrageous video did quickly go viral, but not for the reasons that the woman had hoped. People overwhelmingly sided with the Dunkin' Donuts employee and expressed their shock and disgust over the disproportionately aggressive behaviour. The video has received over one million views on YouTube, proving that sometimes even viral complaints aren't valid and don't end up affecting a brand negatively. You can watch the video here (https://www.youtube.com/watch?v=juLHmG76P4Q).

Sometimes the staff in retail stores can feel threatened by customers' complaining behaviour. If the complainant becomes aggressive, staff will sometimes become angry themselves: if they are unable to release the anger, considerable stress may result. In some cases, staff members have organised their own ways of relieving their feelings – there is a website for staff called 'Customers Suck', for example, where staff can post stories about unpleasant, aggressive or even violent customers. The webmasters make it clear that the vast majority of customers present no problems – but the site still provides a valuable safety valve for staff who deal with the problem cases.

Figure 15.5 offers some ideas for dealing with complaints. In the case of a genuine complaint, the supplier should put matters right, but should perhaps also offer some extra compensation as a reward for bringing the problem to the firm's attention. In the case of frivolous complaints, the supplier should explain why the complaint is not going to be addressed, and should reject it. In the case of attempted fraud, the complaint should be rejected and also the firm should consider blacklisting the customer, since this is clearly someone that the firm should not be doing business with in future.

The type of compensation makes a difference to the customer's perceptions. For example, in the event of a service failure a branded form of compensation is better received than a generic form. In other words, if a customer complains about service in a coffee shop, a mug with the coffee shop's name on it is better received than a mug with 'coffee' on it (Mogilner and Aaker 2008).

Complaining behaviour is a way of relieving one's feelings, releasing the anger and frustration that is often felt when a purchase does not go according to plan. This is a way of reducing cognitive dissonance, which will be discussed in the next section.

As we've already seen on a number of occasions in this book, word of mouth/ mouse recommendation often occurs when people are satisfied, either because friends or family ask about the product, or because the individual is sufficiently

Cognitive dissonance
The tension caused by holding two conflicting pieces of information at once

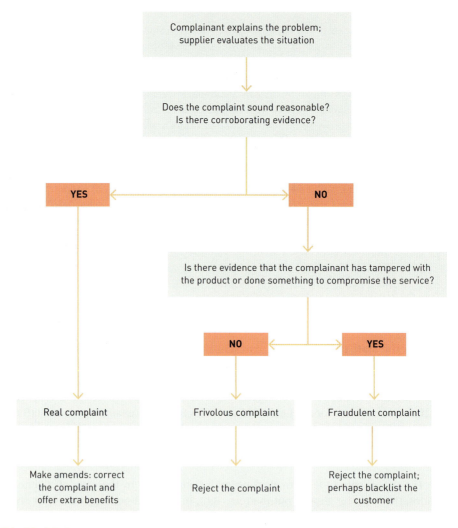

FIGURE 15.5 Dealing with complaints

delighted to want to share the positive experience. Research from Germany indicates that people who have recently switched to a new energy supplier exhibit higher levels of word of mouth activity than people who have been loyal to the energy supplier for a long time, in other words recent 'converts' like to tell people about their new supplier. This is perhaps not surprising – people who have been with the company for a while have probably already told anybody who might be interested all about their experiences. However, people who have switched as the result of a recommendation from someone else (referral switchers) have higher satisfaction levels, are more loyal and give more positive word of mouth than any other group (Wangenheim and Bayon 2004). From this it would seem that, if individuals want to be satisfied with the things they buy, they should be open to friends' and peer recommendations – given that the whole notion of trusting *a person like me* is so prevalent. This of course places an even greater emphasis on word of mouse and word of mouth in promoting products.

COGNITIVE DISSONANCE

Cognitive dissonance is the psychological tension that results from holding two conflicting ideas at the same time. The term came originally from work by Carl Festinger in the late 1950s, in which he experimented on people's motivation to lie. Festinger recruited students to perform a tedious task (specifically, putting pegs into holes, rotating the pegs a quarter-turn, then removing the pegs). He then told the students that he needed more recruits for the tests, and asked them to 'sell' their friends the idea of helping with the tests by telling them that the experiment was really interesting and good fun. He offered some students a dollar for telling this lie, and others $25 (a considerable sum in 1957). Interestingly, the ones who were only paid a dollar actually began to believe the lie themselves: Festinger's explanation for this was that they could not justify their statements on the basis that they were being paid to make them, so therefore the statements had to be true (Festinger 1957).

The mechanism by which dissonance arises is simple. When working through the goal hierarchy, the consumer will form a view of what it will be like to own the product, and will develop a perceptual map of the anticipated benefits. The perceptual map is a mental picture of what life will be like with the product included. The expectancy disconfirmation model (Oliver 1980) says that satisfaction and/or dissatisfaction is the result of comparing pre-purchase expectations and post-purchase outcomes.

In the realm of consumer behaviour, post-purchase dissonance arises when the idea that a product was going to be a good purchase turns out to be wrong. The new information (that the product was not a good purchase) conflicts with the existing information, and the individual needs to resolve the dissonance. Pre-purchase expectations fall into three categories, as follows:

1. **Equitable performance**. This is a judgement regarding the performance one could reasonably expect given the cost and effort of obtaining the product (Woodruff et al. 1983).
2. **Ideal performance**. This is what the individual really hoped the product would do, if the world were a perfect place (Holbrook 1984).
3. **Expected performance**. This is what the product probably will do (Leichty and Churchill 1979).

The level of dissonance depends on the following factors:

- The degree of divergence between the expected outcome and the actual outcome.
- The importance of the discrepancy to the individual.
- The degree to which the discrepancy can be corrected.
- The cost of the purchase (in terms of time, money and risk).

For example, if someone buys an iPhone that turns out to have a scratch on the outer box, this is probably only a minor fault that does not affect the working of the equipment and is, in any case, easily corrected. (This is unless of course the phone is going to be a gift – in which case it would not be seen as a minor issue.) In many cases however, the customer would simply accept the scratch without bothering to seek redress from the supplier: if the scratch is a small one, it probably is not worth the effort of taking box back to the retailer for replacement, especially as the retailer might claim that the customer could have scratched the box while transporting it.

Equitable performance

The level of product quality that the consumer would expect, given the price paid and the other circumstances of purchase and use

Ideal performance

The best possible outcome of buying a given product

Expected performance

The level of product quality that the individual anticipates

CHALLENGING THE STATUS QUO

How upset would you be if you'd bought an expensive iPhone, only to then realise (post-purchase) that actually the 'memory' that you've been charged for comes at an extortionate cost? Apple charges £539 for a 16GB iPhone, £619 for a 64GB iPhone and £699 for a 128GB iPhone.

This means that if you buy your memory in the form of a more expensive iPhone, you pay something on the order of £1.60 for a gigabyte. And remember that this phone doesn't come with an SD slot. A quick look on eBay shows that you can find 128GB Micro SD cards for under £10 and full sized ones for under £5! That equates to 3p per GB, not £1.60.

If later experience shows that the product actually has different attributes, and the expected benefits do not materialise, the purchaser experiences a discord (or dissonance) since there is a clash between anticipation and actuality. Of course, post-purchase consonance is equally important: if the individual is happy with the product, he or she will experience post-purchase consonance, which may lead to recommendations and repeat purchases (see Figure 15.6).

FIGURE 15.6 Dissonance and consonance

Some studies have shown that only one-third of dissatisfied customers will complain or seek redress: the remainder will boycott the products in future or simply complain to others (Day 1984). In the case of minor dissonance, or in cases where there is a high cost of complaint (for instance, returning goods to the duty-free shop at a foreign airport), the reluctance to complain is perfectly understandable.

On the other hand, if the phone has a major fault (turning itself off intermittently being the main one) there is a major discrepancy between the expected outcome and the actual outcome. The biggest problems arise when the product does not live up to expectations but there is no available redress (for example, it breaks down immediately after the warranty has expired). In these circumstances, the dissonance is likely to be considerable since the original goal has been frustrated.

Dissonance reduction is not always straightforward. Cognitive dissonance is a motivator to process information or to act, because the individual is driven to reduce dissonance

FIGURE 15.7 Dissonance reduction strategies

wherever possible. Dissonance can occur at any point in the purchase cycle: when considering a major purchase, pre-purchase dissonance can easily affect the way decisions are arrived at, and in particular can easily delay the final purchase as the individual spends time reducing dissonance. Inevitably some doubt will remain, of course.

In Figure 15.7, the gap between the expected outcome and the actual outcome is what causes the post-purchase dissonance. The actual outcome is used as the benchmark for choosing which route to go down in reducing the dissonance, and the end result of the dissonance-reducing activity is fed back into the dissonance itself to cause the reduction.

From a marketer's point of view, it is important to reduce post-purchase dissonance. The evidence is that people will try to do so themselves, often by complaining about the product. If they do not win redress from the supplier, they will complain about the product to their friends and family. If people experience dissonance, there are four general approaches they take to minimise the problem. These are as follows:

1. *Ignore the dissonant information and look for positive (consonant) information about the product.* For example, a newly purchased car may be slower than expected, but on the plus side it is solidly built and reliable.

2. *Distort the dissonant information.* The car may be slow, but at least it's faster than taking a bus.

3. *Play down the importance of the issue.* The car is slow, but it goes from A to B eventually.

4. *Change one's behaviour.* Perhaps the consumer will sell the car, trade it in for something else, or buy a bicycle.

Marketers are able to back up these general approaches. Some car manufacturers, aware that their cars are reliable rather than exciting, will make use of this in their advertising. For example, Volkswagen used the slogan 'If only everything in life was as reliable as a Volkswagen' for several years. This was ironic given the 2015 scandal in which they were caught using hidden software which would falsify the nitrogen oxide emission levels from thousands of their diesel vehicles worldwide, however.

In general, it is better to avoid the occurrence of post-purchase dissonance by ensuring that the purchaser has accurate information about the product and its performance: in other words, ensuring that the customer's perceptual map conforms as closely as possible with later experiences of using the product.

DISPOSAL

There is one more element to post-purchase behaviour that is becoming increasingly important – the disposal of unwanted products. (Revisit Chapter 14 where we looked at ethical consumption and the natural environment as, of course, the unwanted product will have a profound effect on both these issues.) After a product has been used up, the consumer has the problem of disposing of whatever remains. In some cases, what is left still has value – the second-hand car market is an obvious example. In other cases, the product has been so totally used up that virtually nothing remains, as is the case with most food products.

SUMMARY

Especially in recent years, what happens after the purchase has been made has become increasingly important. First, from the viewpoint of suppliers it is important to know that customers are satisfied with their purchases, and if they are not satisfied it is important to know that they are able to come back and explain the problem so that it can be dealt with at source in future, thus reducing the potential for further dissatisfaction.

Second, the capacity for complaining has been greatly enhanced by social media sites. Opportunities to spread bad news about a company and its products have allowed people to make legitimate complaints with real impact, but have also opened up the possibility of using frivolous or fraudulent complaints to attack legitimate companies.

Third, disposal of used-up products, packaging, accessories, and so forth has become a key issue in the environmental movement. There simply are not enough landfill sites to absorb the quantities of materials being thrown away, and at the same time the world's supply of raw materials cannot keep up with the demands of producers. Recycling has therefore become an essential part of the 21st century consumer behaviour repertoire.

KEY POINTS

- Technical quality refers to quantifiable aspects of the product; functional quality refers to the interaction between consumer and supplier.
- Satisfaction and dissatisfaction are measured by disconfirmation, which may be positive or negative.
- Complaints will only occur if the consumer blames someone else, the experience was particularly negative and there is a good chance of redress.
- Encouraging complaints helps prevent bad word of mouth, but may encourage frivolous complaints.
- Dissatisfied customers will act to reduce dissonance.

HOW TO IMPRESS YOUR EXAMINER

Post-purchase behaviour seems to focus heavily on complaining behaviour – you may be asked to explain the various theories around post-purchase dissonance and complaining. However, post-purchase consonance is equally important and much more common, so you will gain marks if you bring in references to word of mouth/mouse recommendation and mavenism. You should pay particular attention to online behaviour in this regard.

It always helps to think outside the box a little – post-purchase behaviour is also part of the learning process, and will contribute to the information search for pre-purchase behaviour, when it comes to buying a similar product again (repeat purchase). Oh and don't forget the part that ethical consumption plays in the consumer's life. Referring to these other areas (from chapters across this book) will show you understand the whole picture.

REVIEW QUESTIONS

1. How might a company minimise the number of fraudulent or false complaints, without discouraging genuine complaints?
2. What methods exist for customers to reduce dissonance?
3. How does disconfirmation theory affect complaining behaviour?
4. How might a company encourage positive word of mouth from people whose complaints have been satisfactorily dealt with?
5. Why would someone only complain if he or she can blame someone else for the problem?
6. Why is quality not an absolute?
7. How can firms improve the customer's perception of the quality of their products?

CASE STUDY: AIRBNB

Those of us who travel regularly for either work or pleasure know that there are hotels out there which are not always the friendliest or even nicest places to stay in. But how many of us would let those thoughts lead us to thinking about our own post-purchase behaviour following the purchase of our own homes?

One company, founded in 2008, has revolutionalised the hospitality industry and in the process turned itself into a multi-billion dollar company with more than 1.5 million listings in nearly 200 countries. The idea emerged after one of its co-founders, Brian Chesky, rented out air mattresses in the living room of his San Francisco loft apartment.

Airbnb.com, as it's now known, is a website which enables people to list, find and rent accommodation. It has 12 offices around the world, in Barcelona (Spain), Berlin (Germany), Copenhagen (Denmark), Dublin (Ireland), London (UK), Milan (Italy), Moscow (Russia), Paris (France), San Francisco (US), São Paulo (Brazil), Singapore and Sydney (Australia).

Airbnb runs on a marketplace platform model where it connects hosts and travellers and enables transactions without owning any rooms itself. Such platforms disrupt traditional industries by creating new sources of supply and relying on curation for developing quality. Unlike traditional hotels, Airbnb grows not by scaling up its inventory but by increasing the number of hosts and travellers and matching them with each other. Users are categorised as 'Hosts' and 'Guests', both of whom must register with Airbnb using a variety of means. A valid email address and valid telephone number were initially the only requirements to build a unique user profile on the website, but from April 2013 a scan of a government-issued ID (a passport or identity card) is required.

Profiles include details such as user reviews and shared social connections to build a reputation and trust among users of the marketplace. Other elements of the Airbnb profile include user recommendations and a private messaging system. In addition to providing personal information, hosts display listing details including price, amenities, house rules, imagery and detailed information about their neighbourhood. Due to the nature of the business, a merit system is in place to allow guests and hosts to leave references and ratings which are displayed to the public in order to provide an evaluation method.

©iStock.com/Peshkova

Its primary source of revenue comes from service fees from bookings. Fees range between 6% and 12% depending on the price of the booking. Airbnb also charges the host 3% from each guest booking for credit card processing. It has seen exponential growth over the past four years. In February 2011, Airbnb announced its one millionth booking since its inception in August 2008. Then, in January 2012, Airbnb announced its five millionth night booked internationally through the service. In June 2012, the company announced 10 million nights booked, doubling business in five months. Of these bookings, 75% of the business came from markets outside of the continental United States. By October 2013, Airbnb had served 9 million guests and in December 2013 the company reported it had over 6 million new guests in 2013.

In July 2010, the company received more than 300 emails from people who were on the brink of losing their homes through foreclosure due to financial hardship from the economic recession; these people said that they depended on their continued ability to sublet rooms in their residences. Non home-owning users also frequently sublet their homes to renters for prolonged periods (often a breach of tenancy agreements). Yet a July 2014 court in the USA rejected a landlord's eviction plans after his New York City tenant sublet her unit through Airbnb. The judge found that local laws prohibiting short-term sublets only apply to landlords, potentially opening the doors to many more sublets through Airbnb in the coming months and years.

In the aftermath of Hurricane Sandy, Airbnb partnered with New York City Mayor Michael Bloomberg to offer free housing for persons displaced by the storm. Airbnb built a microsite for this effort alone where victims register for housing and meet property owners with free housing. Additionally, Airbnb waived all service fees associated with these listings while maintaining the Host Guarantee for all properties listed.

Airbnb is also appealing to luxury homeowners. While most wealthy homeowners would have never considered renting out their properties over traditional bulletin boards, classified ads, or Internet sites such as Craigslist, Airbnb offers a much more reliable service for affluent users to earn revenue from their second homes. This phenomenon has caused some distress for the American Hotel & Lodging Association as short-term private rentals continue to disrupt the hospitality industry. A further incentive for luxury homeowners occurred in August 2015, when Airbnb partnered with Tesla Motors to provide chargers at certain host houses, firstly in California.

As with many other websites, Airbnb's blog has evolved into a content-rich resource for consumers, written by consumers (all showcasing their post-purchase behaviour). The Local Lens section shares individual narratives in a similar fashion to Stories. One post follows an Instagram photographer who spent a weekend photographing fall foliage in New York, while another taps third-party blogger expertise to explore Moscow's cafe culture. Throughout all of its content channels (neighbourhoods, stories, short films, create) Airbnb makes a point of profiling its more interesting hosts, such as a Stockholm couple who live a vegetarian lifestyle and rent out a converted 1976 school bus for $98 a night. Also included on the blog is a recap of this year's first annual conference for hosts, where over 40 countries were represented.

In order to influence their customers' post-purchase (and even pre-purchase) behaviour, Airbnb's content strategy extends to social media, where it embraces visual marketing to attract fans. On Instagram, the brand posts user-generated photos that it curates from its hosts and guests. Its YouTube channel is home to global content such as the new TV spot, 'Interning at Airbnb' and 'The Making of the Airbnb iPhone App'. 'Wall and Chain' comes with three behind-the-scenes videos that are also posted on YouTube. The company uses Twitter and its Facebook page, which has over a million followers, to promote blog posts and particularly extraordinary listings. Seasonal and timely content collections such as 'Where to Stay for the TCS New York City Marathon' and 'A Host of Haunted Homes' keep the feeds fresh.

Airbnb is a company that has tapped into post-purchase behaviour in a big way. From the post-purchase behaviour of homeowners who use their purchase to earn money, through to the post-purchase behaviour of guests who post about their experiences, the company uses every available tool to create a viable, grassroots led business.

QUESTIONS

1. Why would someone want to post a review on Airbnb?
2. How does post-purchase behaviour of consumers influence a company that doesn't actually own anything and yet is still valued at $10 billion dollars?
3. If a consumer has a complaint, where should it be targeted – the homeowner or Airbnb as the broker?
4. What part do business innovation and technology play in developing post-purchase consonance?
5. How does post-purchase consonance affect the quality of postings?

FURTHER READING

There has been quite a lot published about consumer complaining behaviour, but for some useful ideas on how to handle complaints effectively, see T. Gruber, I. Szmigin and R. Voss (2009) Handling customer complaints effectively: a comparison of the value maps of female and male complainants. *Managing Service Quality*, 19 (6): 636–56.

If you liked that paper, this next one might also be of interest: T. Gruber, I. Abosag, A. Reppel and I. Szmigin (2011) Analysing the preferred characteristics of frontline employees dealing with customer complaints: a cross national Kano study. *The TQM Journal*, 23 (2): 128–44. By some of the same authors, it examines the type of people needed as front-line employees (who are the ones who have to deal with complaints, of course).

For a somewhat academic discourse on complaints and the people who make them, you might like *The Relationship Between Psychological Types, Demographics, and Post-Purchase Buyers' Remorse* by Trevor A. Fried (Charleston, SC: Bibliobazaar, 2011). The author outlines the effects of different demographics and personality types on complaint behaviour, and then goes on to suggest ways of dealing with complainers.

For more on how to handle complaints, and more importantly how to keep your sanity while you do so, read *A Complaint Is a Gift: Using Customer Feedback as a Strategic Tool* by Janelle Barlow (San Francisco: Berrett-Koehler, 1996). It's a book full of ideas, and gives plenty of insight into what makes complainers tick.

Word of mouth is an important post-purchase activity. People like to talk about their purchases: for a brief treatise on how this works in post-purchase scenarios, read *Word of Mouth: Influences on the Choice of Recommendation Sources* by Klaus Schofer (Hamburg: Diplomarbeiten Agentur diplom.de, 1998).

REFERENCES

Alvarez, L.S., Casielles, R.V. and Martin, A.M.D. (2011) Analysis of the role of complaint management in the context of relationship marketing. *Journal of Marketing Management*, 27 (1&2): 143–64.

Bank, J. (1992) *The Essence of Total Quality Management*. Harlow: Prentice Hall.

BBC Watchdog Daily (2015) *Cost of Complaining*. www.bbc.co.uk/programmes/articles/JYsQHlQzNqv3PG5QtZMdfF/cost-of-complaining (accessed 24 September 2015).

Bunker, M. and Ball, A.D. (2009) Consequences of customer powerlessness: secondary control. *Journal of Consumer Behaviour*, 8 (5): 268–83.

Churchill, G.A. and Surprenant, C. (1982) An investigation into the determinants of customer satisfaction. *Journal of Marketing Research*, 19: 491–504.

Crosby P.B. (1984) *Quality Without Tears*. New York: New American Library.

Day, R.L. (1984) Modeling choices among alternative responses to dissatisfaction. In T.C. Kinnear (ed.), *Advances in Consumer Research*, Vol. 11. Duluth, MN: Association for Consumer Research, pp. 496–9.

Festinger, L. (1957) *A Theory of Cognitive Dissonance*. Stanford, CA: Stanford University Press.

Gronroos, C. (1984) A service quality model and its marketing implications. *European Journal of Marketing*, 18 (4): 36–43.

Grougiou, V. and Pettigrew, S. (2009) Seniors' attitudes to voicing complaints: a qualitative study. *Journal of Marketing Management*, 25 (9&10): 987–1001.

Hankuk, T.C. and Agarwal, P. (2003) When gains exceed losses: attribute trade-offs and prospect theory. *Advances in Consumer Research*, 30: 118–24.

Holbrook, M.P. (1984) Situation-specific ideal points and usage of multiple dissimilar brands. In J. N. Sheth, *Research and Marketing*, Vol. 7. Greenwich, CT: JAI Press. pp. 93–131.

Hossein, M.S. and Mohammad, P.M. (2015) Investigation of the effect of brand image and service quality on trust, commitment and behavioural intentions. *Asian Journal of Research in Marketing*, 4 (1): 87–99.

Juran, J.M. (1982) *Upper Management and Quality*. New York: Juran Institute.

King, T. and Dennis, C. (2006) Unethical consumers: deshopping behaviour using the qualitative analysis of theory of planned behaviour and accompanied (de) shopping. *Qualitative Market Research: An International Journal*, 9 (3): 282–96.

King, T., Dennis, C. and McHendry, J. (2007) The management of deshopping and its effects on service: a mass market case study. *International Journal of Retail & Distribution Management*, 35 (9): 720–33.

King, T., Dennis, C. and Wright, L.T. (2008) Myopia, customer returns and the theory of planned behaviour. *Journal of Marketing Management*, 24 (1–2): 185–203.

Leichty, M. and Churchill, G.A. Jr (1979) Conceptual insights into consumer satisfaction and services. In N. Beck (ed.), *Educators' Conference Proceedings*. Chicago, IL: American Marketing Association, pp. 509–15.

Liljander, V. (1999) Consumer satisfaction with complaint handling following a dissatisfactory experience with car repair. *European Advances in Consumer Research*, 4: 270–5.

Mogilner, C. and Aaker, J. (2008) Forgiving by not forgetting: the effect of compensations following brand transgressions. *Advances in Consumer Research*, 35: 149.

Oliver, R.L. (1997) *Satisfaction: A Behavioural Perspective on the Consumer*. New York: McGraw-Hill.

Oliver, R.L. (1980) A cognitive model of the antecedents and consequences of satisfaction decisions. *Journal of Marketing Research*, 17: 460–9.

Oxford English Dictionary (2015) Quality: a definition. www.oxforddictionaries.com/definition/english/quality (accessed 24 September 2015).

Palmer, A. (1998) *Principles of Services Marketing*, 2nd edn. Maidenhead: McGraw–Hill.

Richins, M.L. (1987) A multivariate analysis of responses to dissatisfaction. *Journal of the Academy of Marketing Science*, 15 (Fall): 24–31.

Santos, J. and Boote, J. (2003) A theoretical exploration and model of consumer affective expectations, post-purchase affective states, and affective behaviour. *Journal of Consumer Behaviour*, 3 (2): 142–56.

Schibrowsky, J.A. and Lapidus, R.S. (1994) Gaining a competitive advantage by analyzing aggregate complaints. *Journal of Consumer Marketing*, 11 (1): 15–26.

Sharma, P., Marshall, R., Reday, P.A. and Na, W. (2010) Complainers vs non-complainers: a multinational investigation of individual and situational influences on customer complaint behaviour. *Journal of Marketing Management*, 26 (1&2): 163–80.

Shiv, B. and Huber, J. (2000) The impact of anticipating satisfaction on consumer choice. *Journal of Consumer Research*, 27 (September): 202–17.

Singh, J. (1988) Consumer complaint intentions and behavior: definitions and taxonomical issues. *Journal of Marketing*, 52 (January): 93–107.

Speer, T.L. (1996) They complain because they care. *American Demographics*, May: 13–14.

Sundie, J.M., Ward, J., Chin, W.W. and Geiger-Oneto, S. (2006) Schadenfreude as a consumption-related emotion: feeling happiness at the downfall of another's product. *Advances in Consumer Research*, 33: 96–7.

Swan, J.E. and Combs L.J. (1976) Product performance and consumer satisfaction: a new concept. *Journal of Marketing*, 40 (April): 25–33.

Wangenheim, F. and Bayon, T. (2004) Satisfaction, loyalty and word of mouth within the customer base of a utility provider: differences between stayers, switchers, and referral switchers. *Journal of Consumer Behaviour*, 3 (3): 211–20.

Woodruff, R.B., Cadotte, E.R. and Jenkins, R.L. (1983) Modelling consumer satisfaction using experience-based norms. *Journal of Marketing Research*, 20: 296–304.

MORE ONLINE

For additional materials that support this chapter and your learning, please visit:
https://study.sagepub.com/sethnaandblythe

INDEX